BANKING IN ASIA

The End of Entitlement

Wiley Frontiers in Finance

SERIES EDITOR: EDWARD I. ALTMAN
                  NEW YORK UNIVERSITY

BANKING IN ASIA

The End of Entitlement

Dominic Casserley
Greg Gibb
and the
Financial Institutions Team:
Dominic Barton
Tab Bowers
Milt Gillespie
Leo Puri
Julie Silberger

John Wiley & Sons (Asia) Pte Ltd

Singapore • New York • Chichester • Brisbane • Toronto • Weinheim

Copyright © 1999 by McKinsey & Company, Inc.
Published in 1999 by John Wiley & Sons (Asia) Pte Ltd
2 Clementi Loop, #02-01, Singapore 129809, Singapore.

This publication is designed to provide accurate and authoritative information in regard to the subject matter covered. It is sold with the understanding that the publisher is not engaged in rendering professional services. If professional advice or other expert assistance is required, the services of a competent professional person should be sought.

Other Wiley Editorial Offices

John Wiley & Sons, Inc., 605 Third Avenue, New York, NY 10158-0012, USA
John Wiley & Sons Ltd, Baffins Lane, Chichester, West Sussex PO19 1UD, England
John Wiley & Sons (Canada) Ltd, 22 Worcester Road, Rexdale, Ontario M9W 1L1, Canada
Jacaranda Wiley Ltd, 33 Park Road (PO Box 1226), Milton, Queensland 4064, Australia
Wiley-VCH, Pappelallee 3, 69469 Weinheim, Germany

Library of Congress Cataloging-in-Publication Data
Casserley, Dominic, 1957-
    Banking in Asia: the end of entitlement / Dominic Casserley, Gregg Gibb, and the Financial Institutions Team.
        p. cm. — (Wiley frontiers in finance)
    Includes index.
    ISBN 0-471-83192-1
    1. Banks and banking – Asia – Case studies.   I. Gibb, Greg.
    II. Title.   III. Series.
    HG 3252.C37   1999
    332.1'095—dc21   99-12956
                                                                          CIP

ISBN 0-471-83192-1

Typeset in 10/11.5 points, Times by Linographic Services Pte Ltd
Printed in Singapore by Saik Wah Press Pte Ltd
10 9 8 7 6 5 4 3 2 1

Contents

Foreword

At the end of the 1990s, the population of Asia was about 3.2 billion. Probably less than half of these people had a bank account of any meaningful size, and only about 100 million Asian households had financial balances that met the minimum size to interest the leading multinational banks. Yet in 1997–1998, the Asian financial crisis impoverished the whole region; both those with and those without bank accounts. So, the banking industry permeated every Asian's life.

Banking in Asia: The End of Entitlement is about the long-term changes that will reshape what it takes to win in Asian banking, well into the first decade of the 21st century, changes that will alter the lives of all Asians.

This book was conceived in 1996. At that time, we wanted to cover the large changes we saw gradually remodeling the banking industries across Asia. But soon after, the 1997–1998 crisis struck. The Asian banking industry faced huge losses and the competitive changes that we thought would take perhaps up to a decade to work through, were compressed into just a few years. At the same time, other factors were remodeling the financial markets. This was the period of the demise of Long Term Capital Management in the U.S., the Hong Kong government's direct purchases of close to 10 percent of many leading stocks in order to squeeze speculators against the Hong Kong dollar, the liberalization of many banking and trading markets across the region, and the imposition of capital controls in Malaysia. It was also a period of dramatic negative real economic growth in Asia, with an uncertain future for the first decade of the 21st century. So, as we wrote the book, we had to balance the long-term perspective we had first envisioned with the need to deal with immediate challenges facing banks across the region, and we had to project potential long-term growth of balances, volumes and profits in a period of a great uncertainty. If some of our projections err a little, or some of the specific firms we refer to have lost their way, please excuse us as we were writing in very uncertain times.

Our definition of banking in Asia for this book is specific. By banking, we mean both commercial banking for corporations and consumers, and investment banking and brokerage for corporations, institutions, and consumers. We have excluded Australia and New Zealand from our review of Asia, and have also not spent time looking at the smaller markets of Pakistan, Bangladesh, and Indochina. So, the book focuses on commercial and investment banking in Japan, South Korea, China, Taiwan, Hong Kong, Thailand, Malaysia, Singapore, Indonesia, the Philippines, and India.

The 21st century is often positioned as "the Pacific Century." However, without an effective and efficient banking industry in Asia, it will be no such thing. This book offers a perspective on what it will take to create the banking industry required to give Asia the future it deserves.

Acknowledgments

This book is a team effort. During 1997 and 1998, we led a team to create this book. The team operated at many levels.

Five colleagues at McKinsey & Company led the writing of six chapters: Dominic Barton, the Korea chapter; Tab Bowers, Japan; Milt Gillespie, China; Leo Puri, India; and Julie Silberger, the Retail Banking and No Asia, Just Asian Markets chapters. While we ensured that the messages and styles across the chapters are consistent, these five colleagues were critical to the book.

Julie Pierce led the editing of the book at McKinsey. Julie's constant questioning of our logic, challenging of the flow of each chapter, and then detailed editing of the text were central to the book's creation. We cannot thank her enough for her professionalism, dedication, and good humor. She was keenly assisted by Francine Martin on a number of chapters, and by Davina Stanley. We also thank Julie and Francine for giving up many weekends and long days for the earlier, intense chapter restructuring sessions.

Three colleagues provided leadership of the in-depth factual research that underpins every chapter. Douglas Lam, Jenny Yeh, and Ken Lo, all of McKinsey's Hong Kong office, worked tirelessly to develop, and then continually update, the data and case examples throughout the book. A great thank you to all three for their hard work and long nights at the office. Additional research was provided by Ping Ping in McKinsey's Beijing office on the China chapter, Myunghee Kim from the Seoul office on the Korea chapter, and Anu Madgavkar from the Mumbai office on the India chapter.

All the authors and researchers depended further upon the research and information services provided by Helen Beattie, Meilee Chan, Cherry Hui, Candy Kwong, Cheryl Lee, Lesley Nichols, Darren Tan, Alison Tsai, and Carlo Yu. Compilation of the charts called upon the talents of many visual aids professionals in McKinsey offices across Asia.

We received helpful comments and additions from colleagues inside McKinsey and friends at other firms. Our McKinsey colleagues in Asia, Daniel Adamec, Melissa Ma, Emmanuel Pitsilis, Jean-Marc Poullet, Eric Rajendra, and Mathew Welch reviewed or provided critical input to chapters. Philippe Desgranges of Credit Agricole Indosuez gave us helpful input on margins and trends in the post-crisis environment. Regis Monfront, also of Credit Agricole Indosuez, provided facts and input on Asian equity trading. Adam Howard of JP Morgan reviewed and provided helpful comments on the trading chapter. Finally, Milton Friedman kindly provided the correct facts about his visit to Hong Kong, referred to in the chapter on Hong Kong and Singapore.

We also owe a great debt to our editor at John Wiley & Sons (Asia) Pte Ltd, Gael Lee, and to Nick Wallwork, also at Wiley, who supported the initial conception of the book and gave us great encouragement throughout its birth.

The true reward for patience and consistency must go to Erica Law, for the constant administrative support needed to coordinate all these inputs and the endless updates and changes to the text and charts.

Finally, this book could not have been written without the love and support of Nancy Casserley and Veronica Gibb, and the patience of the three Casserley children, Edward, Henry, and Isabel, who had to put up with their father typing on weekends instead of spending time with them.

Acknowledging this enormous amount of help and all that we have overlooked, it is still true that none of the individuals is responsible for what follows. They provided excellent input, advice and counsel; all the flaws that may be contained herein are ours alone. Specifically, although McKinsey & Company sponsored the research upon which this book is based, the opinions expressed are our own and do not necessarily reflect those of McKinsey as a whole, our colleagues, or our clients. Of course, the examples used in the text are either drawn from public information, or, if drawn from our professional experiences, have been disguised to protect client confidentiality.

Dominic Casserley and Greg Gibb

PART I
NEW CHALLENGES IN ASIA

1
THE END OF ENTITLEMENT

The 1997–1998 Asian financial crisis marked a watershed in Asian banking and finance. This was not just because many banks, securities firms, and finance companies closed, merged, or effectively withdrew from the market, or because many people employed in the financial sector in Hong Kong, Singapore, Tokyo, Bangkok, Kuala Lumpur, Jakarta, and other Asian cities lost their jobs. Neither was it because individual investors and institutions lost huge amounts of money in the declining Asian equity, bond, and currency markets. The crisis was a watershed because banks, securities companies, and finance companies will never earn profits in Asia in the same way again.

However, many of the trends that seemed to be triggered by the financial crisis were under way in most Asian markets even before the crisis struck. What the crisis did was to quicken the pace of regulatory and competitive changes, compressing what most financial industry observers thought would take as long as 10 years into just two or three. Moreover, this increased pressure to change came at a time when most Asian financial industries and banks were very weak. Thus, many players that might have managed a less ferocious transformation would not survive, or be unable to survive alone.

In the 1980s and most of the 1990s, immense fortunes were made as commercial and investment banks funded "the Asian miracle." In most Asian markets then, a banking or securities license gave access to easy profits. So, even though the Asian markets outside Japan were very small when compared to those of the U.S. or Europe, many international bankers felt they had to be part of banking in Asia. But the 1997–1998 crisis brought those days of making easy money in Asia to an abrupt end. What was effectively the age of entitlement in Asian banking is over. In its place will emerge a revamped financial industry, requiring fresh formulas for success and resulting in a new competitive balance among domestic and global players.

No More Easy Money

Banks and investment banks compete in a series of loosely linked markets. They try to earn banking profits from lending to and taking deposits from retail customers, large corporations, and middle-market companies, from trading securities and investing for corporations, institutions, and individuals, and from providing private banking services to the rich.

In each of these market segments in Asia, the first decade of the 21st century will see more sophisticated customers enjoying greater choice in more open markets than existed ever before. As a result, the competitive environment will be more difficult for both local and multinational competitors.

Serving Retail Customers

Many Asian banking markets during the 1980s and most of the 1990s used the retail customer as a cheap source of funding for corporate loans. In the government-directed economies — most notably those of Japan, Korea, China, India, and most of Southeast Asia — the government had formal or informal targets and priorities for corporate growth, and encouraged banks to fund specific entities, for instance, the large industrial groups in Japan, the *chaebol* in Korea, and the state-owned enterprises in China. Consumer savings were encouraged and then funneled through the banking system to these corporate priorities. To ensure their money went into banks, consumers were offered very few savings options. Domestic banks enjoyed reasonably unfettered access to retail deposits, and competition was controlled. For example, foreign competition was constrained by limits on new banking licenses and branches.

Given this controlled environment, retail banking in Asia was mostly of very poor quality compared with typical 1990s offerings in the U.S. and many European markets, where customers could choose from a range of quality payment, deposit, investment, and credit products designed to meet their needs. For instance, an average individual customer of one of China's big four state banks could not rely upon inter-provincial payments systems, had to wait a long time for transfers to clear, was unlikely to have access to consumer lending products or a real credit card, and had few deposit product options. Moreover, this limited service was provided through very unattractive and inefficient branches. As the average Chinese individual had few choices, the banks collected significant deposits to turn into corporate loans.

In summary, many banking systems in Asia were set up to transfer funds and wealth from consumers to the corporate sector. Services were meager, deposit rates uncompetitive, and retail lending products limited so as not to crowd out the all-important corporate loans.

This will change in the first decade of the 21st century. During much of the 1990s, consumers in many markets were demanding more and better service. Surveys showed that many consumers were willing to switch banks if they had the opportunity, and those opportunities are increasing. Aggressive banks targeted consumers as a source of profits by themselves. Cherry-picking of the most attractive consumer accounts by leading players, such as Citibank, Standard Chartered Bank, and the Hongkong and Shanghai Banking Corporation (HSBC), forced all banks to view the retail market differently if they wished to retain their share of deposits. So, from the 1990s local banks in advanced markets, like Hong Kong, Singapore, Taiwan, and Malaysia, sought to strengthen their consumer banking efforts. The 1997–1998 financial crisis illustrates the importance of retaining a strong and stable base of retail deposits in turbulent times. But to attract and keep retail customers in the future, banks must offer real customer service. This will entail providing a broad range of products through diverse distribution channels (upgraded branches, ATMs, telephone, Internet) with service packages that meet the needs of different types of customers. At the same time, banks will need to fend off the incursions of nonbank competitors like utilities and technology firms that will try to gain new financial revenues.

The opportunities for banks that are able to respond to consumer needs will be enormous. In 1997, total retail balances (including deposits, loans, and mortgages) in Asia totaled US$10.6 trillion, of which Japan accounted for 85 percent. By 2010, these balances should total about US$15 trillion, of which two-thirds will be in Japan.

Building Stable Profits from Large Corporations

During most of the 1990s, providing investment banking or commercial loans to large corporations in Asia was tough going. This was partly because profit margins from these businesses were declining around the world, and market share and profits were consolidating with fewer and fewer leading banks. In Japan, the potential volumes were enormous but the margins were very thin. Loans to leading Japanese corporations were often priced with spreads of less than 50 basis points. Outside Japan, there was intense competition for what was really a small opportunity. For example, in 1997, the combined securities underwriting volume in Asia ex-Japan was 22 percent of that in the U.S., but nearly as many banks competed in that market.

Faced with barriers to entry and/or expansion in the retail markets, nearly every major Western bank attempted to compete in Asia's more open, large corporate markets. Driven by strategic plans developed in London, Frankfurt, Zurich, and New York, global commercial and investment banks focused on the Asian growth miracle as justification for pouring resources into the region and for extending significant loans to, and creating derivative products for, well-known local corporations. At the same time, local banks hoped to retain their positions with these companies and tried to build their own investment banking capabilities to supplement lending. Everyone wanted to build volume and market share.

As a result of this intense competition, many commercial lenders and investment banks earned unattractive returns on capital from the large corporate market during most of the 1990s. Only those with significant market share or leading underwriting and linked trading businesses really prospered. Many second-tier firms survived only as long as loan losses remained very low and trading profits remained strong. Then the crisis struck. Many commercial banks had to absorb significant write-offs on their loan portfolios. Meanwhile, investment banks faced problems getting payment on their derivative products, experienced large losses on their capital market products, and saw underlying underwriting and trading volumes shrink. The risk-adjusted returns in the business looked very bad.

The immediate aftermath of the collapse in currency and stock markets in 1997 was the collapse of weaker or less well-managed competitors (most notably Peregrine in Hong Kong) and the withdrawal or downsizing of many firms. For those which survived margins on currency transactions, capital market product trades, and lending improved enormously (although volumes were small). But this phenomenon cannot be permanent.

As competition slowly returns to all the Asian corporate markets and the very large margins of 1997 and 1998 disappear, a new equilibrium will be required. The volume-at-any-cost approach is unlikely to work any further. Instead, each competitor will need to identify those parts of the market in which it has an edge — for example, advantaged access in selected countries, or special expertise in providing certain types of products or in serving certain groups of customers.

At the same time, old drivers of growth, such as trade financing and traditional lending, will return, and new opportunities will emerge. Infrastructure spending will be revived across much of Asia, and will require financing. Debt-laden corporations will need to be recapitalized. Asian corporations will seek new investment options for both corporate cash and their rapidly growing pension funds. Old cultural barriers to mergers and acquisitions will break down.

What will emerge, therefore, will be a more segmented market, with a few competitors targeting a broad array of countries, clients, and products, but with many more focusing on particular areas where they believe they can be particularly successful. In other words, we will see more stable and focused commercial lenders and investment banks serving the large corporate arena, and firms driven by the need to achieve attractive risk-adjusted returns on capital, not just higher volumes of deals or loans. Those that survive the shakeout will benefit from larger opportunities. In 1997, corporate loan assets in Asia totaled US$5 trillion; by 2010, these should reach US$12–15 trillion. Over the same period, securities underwriting volumes will likely increase from US$269 billion to about US$700 billion.

Growing Carefully in Middle-Market Banking

For most of the 1990s, competition among banks for middle-market companies was somewhere between the intense rivalry for large corporates and the highly protected retail arena. First, middle-market companies were rarely clients of the investment banks; this turf was largely restricted to commercial banks vying for loan, deposit, and trade finance business. In theory, middle-market lending was open to all banks. But in reality, cultural and information barriers to competition were significant. The owners of local middle-market companies preferred dealing with local bankers whom they knew socially; at the same time, local bankers had better access to information about these borrowers. In most cases, Asia's smaller private companies provided inadequate accounts, and the only way to judge a borrower's creditworthiness was through careful discussions and close tracking of activities. Foreign or even distant provincial banks could neither build the social links nor develop the risk insights required to play this game profitably, so local banks tended to dominate.

The downside to enjoying such a competitive advantage was that the local banks were completely exposed to the middle market. When the crisis hit in 1997, local players suddenly faced significant loan losses. Middle-market growth companies that had leveraged themselves to take advantage of business opportunities (or in some unfortunate cases to speculate on the stock market) were no longer able to service or repay their debts.

As most Asian markets become increasingly open in the first decade of the 21st century, more banks will gain access to the local business communities and thus, to middle-market banking opportunities. This will increase competition, and most likely reduce margins. So the challenge will be to design middle-market strategies that can earn handsome returns.

The failure of local banks to earn attractive risk-adjusted returns shows that the old ways of doing business with middle-market customers do not make sense. Even the information that these banks had about their middle-market customers was not good enough, and the lack of diversified exposure sank many banks. As long as real economic growth was strong, banks could survive without proper credit analysis and with highly concentrated portfolios. But these times are gone. The new approach to middle-market lending will need to rely upon better corporate information, and diversification of exposures will be critical. The best banks are likely to manage their exposures as an investment portfolio, carefully controlling currency mismatches and country or industry concentrations. Middle-market banking will not be as easy as before.

Generating Sustainable Returns in Investment and Trading Markets

Investor confidence in Asia's capital markets was decimated by the 1997–1998 crisis, and for good reason. Exhibit 1.1 illustrates the scale of the decline in stock market values in local currency and U.S. dollar terms between July 1, 1997 and June 30, 1998. Faced with such steep declines, both international and local retail and institutional investors had every reason to view the markets as poison. The traders who served them had similar feelings. Many had long positions in the markets in order to serve their customers, and so suffered large losses on these portfolios. But the traders' problems were not just short-term. In the years leading up to the crisis, while many had made large profits, they had also seen margins on trades shrink. As long as volumes were good, shrinking margins did not matter. After the crisis, however, volumes plunged and low margins began to matter.

The collapse of both investor and trader interest reflected the fact that here, too, approaches to the markets were immature. Too many investors in Asia's capital markets were "punters" rather than long-term seekers of value. Their hot money inflated these markets, and even more quickly deflated them. Similarly, many traders were not providers of quality research and opinions, but mere stock churners in search of a quick commission or spread.

These approaches to trading and investing in Asia must change. If investors and traders are to make attractive long-term returns, they must adopt disciplined investment and trading strategies based on long-term investment horizons and fundamental research. Participants with shorter horizons will require deep understanding of the trading relationships between different securities and currencies. Investors, be they institutions or retail traders, and buyers of mutual funds, will expect much higher professionalism from their trading advisors. The first decade of the 21st century, thus, should usher in a new professional era of investing and trading in Asia.

Those that adopt more disciplined approaches will be rewarded as the markets grow. The combination of an aging population seeking retirement security and

Exhibit 1.1

Decline in Stock Market Values in Asia: 1997–1998
Stock index price on June 30, 1997 = 100

☐ June 30, 1997 = 100
▨ June 30, 1998, in local currency
■ June 30, 1998, in US$

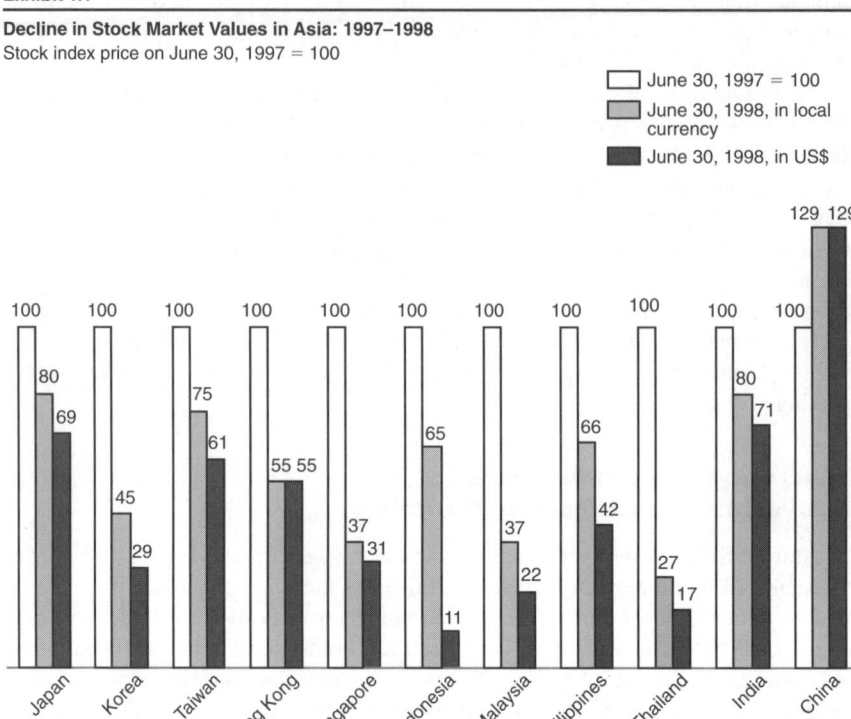

Source: Datastream

increased investment professionalism will spur the rise of larger local Asian institutional investors (pension funds, insurance companies) and mutual fund companies. At the end of 1997, the total capitalization of Asia's capital markets represented 76 percent of those of the U.S., and just 22 percent if Japan is excluded. By 2010, with higher investment from the West, the emergence of local pension funds, and increased listings of equity and debt securities by Asian companies, these markets may more than triple in size and should represent a higher percentage of total securities traded around the world.

Private Banking for Fewer than Before

The tremendous wealth creation in Asia throughout the 1980s and much of the 1990s resulted in some very large and very well-publicized personal fortunes. As a result, many banks favored the private banking market as a means to grow in Asia. International banks led the way here, for they offered confidentiality, offshore accounts, and better investment track records and credentials than their local counterparts.

The private banking market, however, was not simply a market serving the super-wealthy. It contained many sub-segments, in terms of levels of wealth and degrees of sophistication among private clients. Few banks, however, had well-defined strategies that tailored services or focused resources on particular segments. Again, rapid economic growth and wealth creation during this period allowed too many private banks to prosper without having to articulate clear strategies or distinctive value propositions to potential clients.

By the mid-1990s, the sheer number of banks competing for private client business was creating profit problems for many. Major securities firms such as Goldman Sachs and Morgan Stanley, along with banks such as JP Morgan, were attacking the high end of the market (those with over US$5 million to invest). More than 100 international banks were offering services to the middle segment of the private banking market (customers with wealth of between US$1 million and US$5 million). And many of the same global players plus some local banks and securities firms were interested in the "executive" market (clients with US$250,000 to US$1 million in wealth). As a result, while the leaders achieved good returns, too many firms were operating at break-even levels or worse.

The 1997–1998 crisis took its toll on the size of the assets these firms managed, and, hence, the fees they earned. It also caused some firms to incur losses on stock-margin and other loans. The market was unsustainable before the crisis; the dramatic declines in market values merely hastened changes that had been under way.

The new keys to profitability in private banking will include a rigorous definition of target clients and the specific value proposition the bank offers these target clients. These must be accompanied by an organization built to match this strategic intent. Gone are the days of planting a flag in Hong Kong and Singapore, hiring a few former staff of the big Swiss banks, and giving them an expense account and some asset targets.

As in all the other financial markets, the new age of private banking in Asia will be a more disciplined and professional one. But it will also be filled with greater opportunity, as total private banking balances rise from about US$250 billion in 1997 to US$1.3 trillion in 2010.

New Winning Formulas

Throughout Asia's markets, old ways of banking will progressively give way to more rigorous approaches. The easy money is gone.

While each of these product and geographic markets is different, future winning formulas will exhibit some common themes. These will be underpinned by generally more open regulatory environments, and by more educated and demanding customers and clients. Successful firms will adopt new *strategies* involving greater use of segmentation, more geographical diversification, and differentiated product capabilities. They will also employ new *tools*, such as more rigorous risk management, new capital market instruments, stronger management information systems, and increased investment in staff and infrastructure.

Finer Segmentation

An integral part of determining how to make profits will be to segment the markets. This will be true in the corporate, institutional, and retail markets.

The successful corporate bank or investment bank in Asia will, in future, have a clearer idea of the needs and potential risk-adjusted profitability of each customer segment. Accordingly, these banks will invest in working out where they can earn attractive returns, and will sculpt their whole organization to target particular industries, family groups, or geographic areas. They will build special areas of expertise and distinctiveness tailored to the needs of their chosen segments.

In the institutional markets, the best investment and trading houses will also focus on the profitability of different types of institutions, and will tailor their products and services to the needs and expectations of these different groups. Thus, when serving the most sophisticated international institutions, which move money among different equities, bonds, and cash based on both mathematical and fundamental research, the trading firms will tailor their research to these institutions' broad needs. In contrast, when serving central banks, traders will focus their research and sales support very differently because these customers' focus primary on bonds.

In the retail markets, segmentation will be even more important. Banks will need to decide who to target in a potential market of 3.2 billion people. One way to segment this market is by income level, but even this poses complications. Should they focus on hard-dollar income cuts using the same segmentation that they might use in the U.S. or Europe? Or should they use purchasing-power-parity-adjusted income cuts to reflect the lower cost of living in many Asian countries? The latter technique is often used to describe the growth of Asia's middle class, and is certainly relevant in explaining the rapid rise in consumer goods purchases in many countries. However, for bank products, a dollar is a dollar is a dollar. In many cases, hard-dollar cuts can be more relevant.

Beyond income segmentation, the best banks will want to identify behavioral groups that they can target. They will need to work out how they can win customers early in the life cycle of study, marriage, house purchase, parenthood, upbringing of children, empty-nesting, and retirement. They then must tailor their products and services to each segment appropriately.

Banks will also face the issue of how to regard the traditionally "unbankable" markets. By excluding the majority of China's and India's population and the poor everywhere else in Asia, most international banks, in the 1990s, arrived at just 5 percent of Asia's 3.2 billion people as the group they could actually target. They then assumed that profits would come mainly from the top 20 percent or so of this 5 percent of potential retail customers. But banking the "unbankable" will represent a major opportunity. Those local or international banks that can successfully work out the package of products and services, deliverable in volumes that enable them to earn profits from this "unbankable" market, will really prosper.

Wider Geographical Diversification

Given the high margins available in the protected local markets during the 1980s and most of the 1990s, domestic competitors typically did not worry about diversifying their portfolios. Of course, given the regulatory structures, few banks had any options.

Once the regulatory barriers recede, however, and banks face more intense competition in their home markets, they will need to diversify geographically to strike the right balance between portfolio risk and potential returns. Yet few medium-sized banks will be able to achieve diversification across different country markets. The challenges will be easier to overcome for larger banks with the capital and staff needed to run businesses across multiple countries.

Differentiated Product Portfolios

During the 1980s and most of the 1990s, the major banks in each Asian country had very similar product portfolios and limited incentive (and in some places limited freedom) to innovate. In a more competitive environment with more demanding customers, margins on basic products will decline and banks will need to differentiate their product offerings.

Banks basically face a choice between specializing in a narrow range of products or offering a broad portfolio. Specialists will focus on those products in which they can be true experts and low-cost producers. For example, they might stick to credit cards in the retail arena, or equity derivatives in the wholesale markets. The alternative is to meet a broad range of customer needs by offering a broad range of products delivered conveniently. This could involve a universal financial account with an integrated statement and multiple branches, ATMs, and Internet banking support in the retail markets, or a relationship manager system in the wholesale markets. Broad-product providers in retail will argue that a narrow range cannot fulfill all customers' needs or generate enough revenue to cover the fixed costs of systems and branches. In the wholesale markets, where product demand waxes and wanes, the relationship firms will argue that competitors with narrow ranges will suffer volatile earnings in a deregulated environment.

Managing a wider range of products will create new challenges: different systems support will be required, each new product will add new risks, and sales and risk management across the product portfolio must be coordinated. A bank that used to offer mortgages and credit cards to its retail customers, and now adds auto loans, second mortgages, asset management, and stock loans, will have new revenue opportunities with every customer. But this bank will need to strengthen its credit underwriting and coordination to ensure it knows exactly what its exposure is to each customer across the portfolio of products. Banks that cannot invest in the staff and systems required to sell and manage a broadened range of products will lose market share.

Whether they adopt the specialist or broad-product approach, banks will need to differentiate their product portfolios to win enough market share in more competitive times.

More Rigorous Risk Management

The shattered banking industries of Korea, Japan, Thailand, Indonesia, and Malaysia in 1998 offers obvious testimony to the need for more rational and rigorous risk management approaches in Asia. What is needed in these markets, however, is not simply tighter risk control, nor more defensive measures, but entirely new approaches to *making profits from risk*. Financial institutions are unique among companies because they seek to earn profits from risk, rather than earn profits in some other manner and manage risk along the way. So, successful commercial and investment banks in Asia will see improved risk management not just as a means to avoid losses, but as the critical underpinning of sustainable profits in the future.

In practice, this approach is likely to lead to better balance of risk and return. The actual steps involved will, in many cases, be very basic, for example, putting in place the data capture and review processes required to reach rational conclusions. In other cases, firms will need to transfer state-of-the-art approaches from the West. Thus, in some markets (e.g., Korea) the new age will entail introducing the basics of credit analysis. In others (e.g., Malaysia) it will mean moving beyond a simple "lend/do not lend" analysis to pricing differently for different levels of risk, and understanding a bank's overall exposure to a borrower, rather than treating each subsidiary as a separate entity. In the trading markets, investors and traders will adopt approaches based either on high-quality fundamental research or on rigorous quantitative analysis, again trying to weigh risk and reward properly.

Losses on loans secured by property and losses on illiquid investment portfolios were the primary reasons that banks and securities companies suffered in 1997–1998. In the credit markets, therefore, lenders will be especially wary of the boom-and-bust cycle in real estate, and so limit their exposure (either direct or as collateral for working capital loans) to the property markets. In the trading markets, the lack of liquidity, which destroyed so many portfolios and investment firms, will stand as a warning for everyone, and investors and traders will need to manage their positions carefully.

Risk management skills will, thus, be key tools in the first decade of the 21st century in Asia. They will be the basis from which new profits will emerge.

New Capital Market Instruments

Another means to manage risk will be through the use of the latest risk management techniques — from basic interest rate and currency swaps, to more advanced credit derivatives, through to securitization of pieces of a portfolio. These techniques will not only let banks modify their risk profiles but also free up valuable capital, thus enabling banks to continue serving the market with the need for more capital.

New capital market products will also offer new revenue opportunities. As institutional investors in Asia become larger, they will have a growing appetite for securities and derivative products. Corporations will look to the capital markets for recapitalization after the ravages of 1997–1998. Governments will turn to banks to help them privatize major state-owned corporations.

However, the larger better-capitalized banks will have advantages here, too. They will be able to get the best terms from other leading banks that provide derivatives and will have staff to manage these products properly. Their larger capital bases will give them stronger credit ratings, and so enable them to win more business as counter-parties and on better terms than the smaller banks.

Stronger Management Information Systems

Finer segmentation, more rigorous risk management, and more complex products such as derivatives, will require commercial and investment banks in Asia to strengthen their management information systems (MIS).

During the boom times of the 1980s and 1990s, many banks made strong profits despite inadequate information. But, as the need for tighter risk management and segmentation increases each year, so will the need for quality data to underpin these risk and segmentation decisions.

Unfortunately, like many banks around the world, banks in Asia are saddled with old legacy systems that do not offer easy access to really useful data. The task facing most banks is to work out whether they need to restart and rebuild their systems in a more flexible format, or whether they can build such flexibility through improved front-end systems attached to these legacy systems. Such front-end systems draw data from the legacy systems, and allow manipulation of the data for more flexible analyses. Either approach will be expensive, and will raise the fixed costs of competing in all markets. By the end of the 1990s, major international banks had systems budgets of well over US$1 billion a year. Competitors that have unstable or narrow profit streams will not be able to sustain even one-quarter of this level of investment, and will eventually be absorbed by those that can.

The late 1990s struggle to solve the Y2K problem — the risk that many banks' old information systems would interpret the double zero at the turn of the century almost randomly — exemplified the impact of MIS on bank profitability and autonomy. Many companies faced a huge cost of ensuring that systems would perform properly; a major multi-product, multi-country bank would spend at least US$200 million fixing systems for the new century. Smaller banks faced only slightly smaller bills, and charges like this may well force them to seek mergers or alliances with banks that can absorb these types of expenses.

Increased Investment in Staff and Infrastructure

A similar challenge confronts banks in two other areas: building staff skills and putting in place the support infrastructure and technology (e.g., processing systems, branches, and call centers) required by modern financial players.

As competition in all market segments increases, particularly as the World Trade Organization (WTO) forces open many local markets and multinational banks begin to compete openly for customers, local banks will need world-class quality staff and infrastructure. Many local banks had not invested to anything close to world-class levels during the 1980s and 1990s, having been under little pressure to do so. In the next decade, however, customers of all types will be wooed with much higher service levels, and will soon develop new expectations. The leading global investment and commercial banks will offer large corporate customers in Asia the same standards of service they provide elsewhere. The new international owners of local banks will upgrade staff, attracting more middle-market customers. Such banks will bring to Asia approaches to branch and product design that have served them well in their home markets. Small-business and retail customers will also benefit from these upgraded physical facilities, as well as from the advanced telephone, Internet, and direct salesforce distribution approaches that these banks, and some new nonbank entrants, will introduce. The best competitors will train their front-line retail staff to provide true customer service, again differentiating themselves from the pack.

During much of the 1990s, banks in many Asian markets operated with very low cost-to-income ratios. For instance, in 1997 the leading Malaysian and Hong Kong banks had cost-to-income ratios of 34 and 44 percent respectively, compared with 60 percent for leading U.S. banks. As banks in Asia start raising staff skills to those of the best high-performing organizations, and also investing in infrastructure, their cost-to-income ratios will rise closer to Western levels.

New Competitive Balance

The commercial and investment banking industries in Asia will face new pressures in the first decade of the 21st century. There will be visible symptoms of the end of entitlement. Regulatory changes will make markets more open, rapidly changing pricing and cost structures. Increased competition will hasten customers' education and boost their expectations. A number of new technologies, such as Internet-based services, will change the competitive balance. Combined, these pressures will raise the performance bar for earning attractive returns.

Yet the local banking industries of many Asian countries will enter this new environment severely weakened by the 1997–1998 crisis. Given all these pressures, something must give. Specifically, financial market shares and the number of competitors will change dramatically across the region. During the U.S. banking deregulation in the 1980s and 1990s, some leading banks declined or were taken over (e.g., Chase Manhattan Bank) and new leaders emerged through aggressive acquisitions (e.g., NationsBank). Likewise, in Europe, the removal of old regulations and the introduction of the single currency (the Euro) ushered in market consolidation. Similar changes will occur in Asia.

We will see four main structural trends in banking markets across Asia: increasing bank consolidation, growing competition from global players, advancing nonbank competitors, and declining state-owned banks.

Increasing Bank Consolidation

Between 1987 and 1997, bank mergers in Asia totaled just 22, on a base of 1,700 banks. In the first half of 1998 alone, there were more than 25 mergers or acquisitions in the banking sector. Between 1998 and 2008, it is reasonable to assume that there will be several hundreds of major financial sector mergers.

The logic of consolidation is that small banks will be unable to manage the pressures of tougher competition, the increased need for investment in people and systems, and the requirement for diversification. As a result, they will find themselves falling behind, losing clients and good staff to competitors, and unable to earn attractive returns. Yet their remaining customer franchise will be of value to the larger banks, which can retain it but remove a large part of the costs of the acquired smaller bank. Once regulatory (and some cultural) barriers to mergers and acquisitions in the industry are removed, we will see significant consolidation.

Growing Global Competition

Large multinational banks will become more important than they were in the 1990s. As regulatory barriers recede, international commercial and investment banks will enter more and more market segments, and will come armed with higher aspirations. Some of the largest global competitors (such as the 1998 combination of Citibank and Travelers) may well seek to earn at least US$1 billion in profits from the region ex-Japan, and potentially another US$1 billion from Japan. Anything less than that, and Asia will not warrant the management attention it gets. So these firms will be looking to make major capital investments in the region, in order to produce profits at least that high.

The result will be that in every arena, international competitors will hold more market share than they did before. In investment banking, the major Western investment banks will either absorb the smaller local firms or force their retreat to tiny niches. In 1997 and 1998, firms like Merrill Lynch and Salomon Smith Barney were making acquisitions and winning stakes in the local underwriting and trading markets, having finally won access to these previously off-limits areas. In corporate banking, the largest borrowers will want the stability and expertise that only international firms can bring, and so will have them play a larger role in their syndications. As regulations ease, international banks will be able to enter the middle-market and retail segments in ways they could not during the 1980s and much of the 1990s. They will do so either through their existing operations in Asia or through acquisitions of other banks that have the branches and staff required to penetrate these markets. In every segment, international banks will win market share.

Encroaching Nonbank Competitors

During the 1980s and 1990s, a number of nonbanks entered the banking market, especially retail banking, and particularly in the U.S. and Europe. Utilities and telephone companies with extensive customer lists (e.g., British Gas in the U.K. and AT&T in the U.S.) introduced credit card products; supermarkets like Tesco and Sainsbury, and the Virgin Group offered a broad range of banking products to U.K. customers; and new technology entrants like Intuit and Microsoft offered integrated financial management tools to consumers. At the same time, the Internet offered consumers and corporations new ways to search for and purchase financial services. Meanwhile, insurance companies like Prudential of the U.K. entered banking markets through direct banking propositions.

These trends will affect Asia too, and in the first decade of the 21st century we will see similar attempts by nonbank competitors to grab banking industry profits. In nearly all cases, technology will play a key role in these competitors' strategies.

Declining State-Owned Banks

State banks will need to undergo sweeping reforms in this new competitive environment, and so will lose significant market share. In Korea, Taiwan, China, Malaysia, Singapore, Indonesia, and India, state-owned banks played a major role in the banking sector in the 1980s and 1990s. In 1997, for instance, China's Big Four state banks controlled 85 percent of total deposits, and Indonesia's five leading state banks had 41 percent of deposits. But the combination of more aggressive international competitors, more demanding customers, and poorer governments will force these often-unprofitable banks to change.

Few will be able to undertake the fundamental redesign of their products, service philosophy, and staff skills required to compete in this environment. But even for the majority that cannot reform themselves, the realities of their installed base of relationships and branches, and some attempts to modernize, point to a slow decline, not a rapid descent. Nevertheless, with each year, the influence of all but a very few state banks in every market segment will lessen.

Emerging from these forces of change in Asian banking will be a redesigned and reskilled financial industry, and markets offering more opportunities. The Asian financial markets will provide approximately twice as much revenues in 2010 than in 1997. Customers will want new products. Regulations will allow more open competition. Among the winners in the first decade of the 21st century will be new entrants as well as existing players that have undertaken major change programs to upgrade products, skills, infrastructure, and management processes. Those betting on a return to the old world of entitlement — when just having a license was enough to generate good returns — will likely wither, go bust, or be acquired.

This book charts the new world of Asian banking. Chapter 2 examines the nature of Asia and explores how banks can compete across this vast and diverse territory. Part II describes the new competitive environment in the six key banking businesses: corporate banking, investment banking, trading, asset management, private banking, and retail banking. Part III projects the future competitive situation in each of Asia's major markets. Finally, the closing chapter reviews the implications of all the changes for different types of competitors: the global investment banks, multinational commercial banks, state-owned banks, and local privately owned banks.

First, to Asia. Asia covers a vast geographic area and includes economies of very different levels of wealth and development, with different regulatory and legal systems. So we will begin by looking at these questions: What does Asia present to commercial and investment banks? Does it really exist? Can we talk about pan-Asian trends at all?

2
NO ASIA,
JUST ASIAN MARKETS

Is Asia a single region or a Western invention? The answer is — both.

A corporate finance vice president recently transferred to Hong Kong from New York sits in his high-rise office at Exchange Square. Getting ready to call it quits for the day, he contemplates the stunning view of Victoria Harbor from his office window. In Hong Kong it is 8 p.m., Monday, and in New York the working day is just beginning. The phone rings; it is head office. The head of the global debt department is on the line, and excitedly tells the VP that the firm is finally moving forward on an Indian debt syndication, long in the development stage. The New York head says he has just spoken with the client CFO who is in Bangalore and wants to meet with the VP as soon as possible to discuss structuring the syndication. "Can you get there by tomorrow afternoon?" he enquires.

The Hong Kong-based VP considers: he'll have to apply for an express visa at the Indian consulate the next morning before he can even get on a plane. There is an overnight flight he can get on the next day, and it transfers through Singapore and gets into Bangalore at 4 a.m., Wednesday. The earliest he can see the CFO would be 36 hours from the time he received the phone call — minimum. And for that one meeting, he would need to cancel all other commitments through Thursday, spend two working days on the road, and over 20 hours' travel time!

Asia is a vast and highly diverse region — it is home to a variety of cultures, politics, and economies. Asian countries include some of the world's wealthiest and poorest, and range from the most dedicated capitalist enclaves to some of the largest, and last, communist holdouts. Financial institutions trying to establish a regional presence find that they must adapt their strategies significantly to each set of local circumstances: no single strategy applies uniformly.

Despite these differences, however, there are important similarities and ties across the region. Economic and demographic trends are moving in a similar direction in Asia, and linkages in trade and capital flows are increasing. These changes will make it easier for financial institutions to develop product expertise that they can apply across multiple markets, capture new business opportunities in trade and investment banking, and manage interlinked geographic risk.

A Vast Region Marked by Diversity

Asia, as defined by this book, stretches from northeast China to approximately 6,000 kilometers south (below the equator) to Indonesia, and 8,000 kilometers west, to the far edge of the Indian subcontinent. Some companies consider Australasia part of the region. But for the purposes of this book we have not included Australia or New Zealand. We have also excluded the smaller economies in Asia.[1]

---

[1] Bangladesh, Bhutan, Cambodia, Laos, Myanmar, Nepal, Pakistan, and Vietnam.

By comparison, the geographic area of Europe from Scandinavia down to Greece and from Ireland to Moscow is less than half the size of Asia. Equivalent ground in the Americas would span from the northern United States to central Brazil and across most of Canada. Asia encompasses a wider range of economies than Europe, and far more countries and languages than the North American Free Trade Association. The Asian region is home to over 20 countries, 18 major linguistic groups (plus hundreds of local dialects), and economies ranging from the world's wealthiest to those generating less than US$1,000 in GDP per capita.

Home to the Haves and Have-Nots

As recently as the mid-1980s, all Asian economies excluding Japan were viewed as emerging markets. (Japan, long considered part of the developed world, ranked second globally in 1997 with GDP per capita at US$33,200.) By the late 1990s, however, the emerging-market label no longer applied across the board. A number of Asian Tigers had surpassed many Western countries in GDP per capita. For example, the trading ports cum financial centers of Singapore and Hong Kong ranked sixth and eighth respectively in 1997, at US$31,600 and US$26,300 per capita — both ahead of established Western economies like Germany, France, and the U.K. Taiwan ranked 25th at US$12,900, just ahead of Greece. Meanwhile, the heavily agricultural and subsistence-based economies of Indonesia, China, and India remained in the bottom half, at US$1,040, US$750, and US$380 respectively in 1997. (By 1998, Indonesia had dropped to below US$500.) To view the Asian economic spectrum from another perspective, consider the difference in telephone availability in 1996 between Singapore, which boasted 484 phone lines per 1,000 people, and the Philippines, which had only 30 lines per 1,000 people. This type of economic diversity presents very real challenges to a bank or corporation trying to set up or expand its regional presence.

A Bazaar's Worth of Politics, Historic Tensions

In political terms, Asia is similarly diverse and fragmented. Virtually no history of military alliances exists. Loyalties have always been grounded in national or ethnic affiliations, and only in the last few years has any sense emerged of a pan-Asian identity, based on a generalized notion of Asian values separate from Western cultural influence. While a number of regional economic blocs have formed, there have been no concrete moves toward anything resembling the economic and monetary union in Europe.

Asian countries have fought wars with each other, and although the region was at peace in the 1990s, historical enmities and grievances remain fresh for many. On his official visits to Southeast Asia, the Japanese prime minister expressed "regret" for his country's aggression in World War II. Korea has been divided between a hostile North and South since 1948, and in 1994, North Korea triggered off alarms when it launched a build-up of its nuclear capacity. India and Pakistan have remained enemies since they were partitioned in 1947, and still dispute the northern state of Kashmir. In 1998, when India set off a nuclear test blast, Pakistan followed in kind a few weeks later. A long-standing rivalry persists between the once-unified states of Singapore and Malaysia. In 1997, Lee Kuan Yew, Singapore's senior minister, created a diplomatic incident when he made disparaging remarks about a neighboring Malaysian state.

Beyond national conflicts, domestic ethnic rivalries figure prominently in the complex demographic mix of Southeast Asia. Malaysia's government has been able to suppress conflicts among its Malay, Chinese, and Indian population partly by establishing an affirmative action program that guarantees ethnic Malays important government positions, seats on corporate boards, and funding for businesses. Indonesia has been less successful at managing its ethnic diversity. Half a million people were executed or massacred in Indonesia following the 1965 coup; many were ethnic Chinese. During the political and economic upheaval in 1998, Indonesians torched and looted Chinese neighborhoods in many large cities.

Cultural Stew: From Buddhism to the Queen's English

Behind the economic and political landscape in Asia is a complex set of cultures and ethnic and linguistic groups (Exhibit 2.1) that are still very different despite linkages and cross-border influences from centuries of trade and migration. Still, the historical influence of China — its philosophy, religion, language, and script — is probably the single most important link among the disparate societies of Japan, Korea, Taiwan, China, Hong Kong, and Singapore. These countries share aspects of Chinese language and culture, as well as a tradition of loyalty, familial ties, and social hierarchy.

Local custom and modern history, however, have contrived to shape these societies very differently. Japan has taken dedication and hard work to such an extreme that *karoshi* (death from overwork) has become a household word. China, on the other hand, shaped by half a century of communist economic policy, now struggles with a legacy of massive public debt, worker apathy in the state sector, and bankrupt state-owned companies. Some workers in China are actually paid to stay home.

In Southeast Asia, the Indian subcontinent, and parts of China, Islam is a major influence. Islam has an estimated 600 million Asian followers, most of whom are in India, Pakistan, northwest China, and Indonesia. With its population of over 200 million, Indonesia is the largest Moslem country in the world. Among Malaysia's 22 million, the majority Malay ethnic group is largely Moslem. However, Malaysia is compelled to make allowances for its sizable Chinese minority, who are exempt from the women's dress code and from many of the strictures against alcohol, gambling, and other activities unacceptable to Moslems.

Asian Islam has given rise to special banking products (also popular in the Middle East), such as non-interest-bearing Islamic banking accounts. Religious obligations affect business, particularly during the holy month of Ramadan when the population fasts from dawn to sunset, and on Fridays when it is not uncommon for office workers to spend some hours around midday at the mosque. Many companies in Malaysia and Indonesia are also obliged to keep a special prayer room so staff can pray daily at prescribed times.

Exhibit 2.1

Asia's Highly Diverse Cultural Mix

	Country/ Territory	Major Ethnic Group(s)	Language(s)	Dominant Religions/ Philosophies
North Asia	Japan	Japanese	Japanese	Shintoism Buddhism
	China	Chinese	Mandarin More than 50 regional Chinese dialects	Confucianism Buddhism Taoism
	Korea	Korean	Korean	Confucianism Buddhism Christianity
	Taiwan	Chinese	Chinese (Mandarin and Taiwanese dialect)	Confucianism Buddhism Taoism
	Hong Kong	Chinese	Chinese (Cantonese dialect) English	Confucianism Buddhism Christianity
Southeast Asia	Singapore	Chinese Malay Indian	Chinese (Mandarin and various dialects) English Bahasa Malaysia Tamil	Buddhism Islam Hinduism Christianity Taoism
	Malaysia	Malay Chinese Indian	Bahasa Malaysia Chinese (various dialects) English	Islam Buddhism Hinduism
	Thailand	Thai Chinese	Thai	Buddhism Christianity
	Philippines	Filipino	Tagalog English	Catholicism
	Indonesia	Indonesian Chinese	Bahasa Indonesia Numerous local dialects	Islam
	India	Numerous	Hindi plus 7 other major languages English	Hinduism Islam

Buddhism is another major factor in Asia, with followers in all the North Asian countries, as well as in Thailand, Malaysia, and Burma. Buddhism plays much less of a role in the countries' economies and business than Islam. Rather, its influence is more personal and spiritual. Although Buddhism's significance has declined in some countries, its historical dominance in Asia has shaped some of the common features observed across Asian cultures.

Western colonial presence has had an important lingering influence in many Asian countries, including India, Hong Kong, and all of Southeast Asia except Thailand. Here, the Philippines is the best example. Ruled by Spain for over 300 years, the country is still deeply Catholic. It incorporates a system of Latin

American-style oligopoly and land ownership dominated by a small number of families with Spanish surnames. Unlike most other Asian economies driven by new entrepreneurial wealth, the Philippine economy has a sizable upper class supported by old money.

Another colonial imprint is on the language of business. The British and American presence made English the *lingua franca* of business in India, Hong Kong, Singapore, Malaysia, and the Philippines. However, visit China, Taiwan, Japan, Korea, Thailand, or Indonesia, and outside a small Western-educated elite, it is very difficult to conduct business without knowing the local language. Fortunately for the wholesale financial industry, English speakers tend to gravitate toward investment banking and securities. Still, some of the largest and most promising small-business retail financial markets in Asia make language skills or an interpreter indispensable.

This ethnic and political diversity has implications for a bank staffing its operations across the Asian region. Companies have had difficulty staffing mainland Chinese on projects outside China, due to (among other reasons) other Asians' negative perception of mainlanders. Amid the 1998 unrest in Indonesia, Hong Kong Chinese were understandably reluctant to visit Jakarta. Banks operating in Malaysia must consider the ethnic mix in their hiring policies. Offshore, Japanese banks staff operations with local Asians, but the top management is almost always Japanese.

Asian Financial Markets Reflect Region's Diversity

The wide range of cultural, economic, and political influences in the Asian region has generated a set of financial markets at different stages of development. Each has a singular structure, customer needs, regulations, and other entry barriers. The differences between these countries' financial systems often outweigh the similarities, making it difficult for a financial institution to implement a regional strategy. In many markets, it is necessary to build unique approaches, market knowledge, and local products. Success as a regional player will require a strong institutional culture that combines quality execution with the flexibility to adapt to local conditions.

A Whale Among the Minnows

Japan is the most developed financial market in the region, and is usually viewed separately from the rest of Asia for good reason (Exhibit 2.2). As of end-1997, the GDP of Japan alone was larger than that of the rest of Asia combined. At that time, Japan's stock market, the third largest in the world, was capitalized at over US$2 trillion; Hong Kong's stock market, the second largest in Asia, was capitalized at US$414 billion. In 1997, Japan was home to one of the five largest banks and eight of the ten largest insurance companies in the world. Its pension industry totaled US$1.2 trillion, versus just over US$180 billion for the rest of Asia.

Exhibit 2.2

Overview of Financial Markets in Asia: End-1997

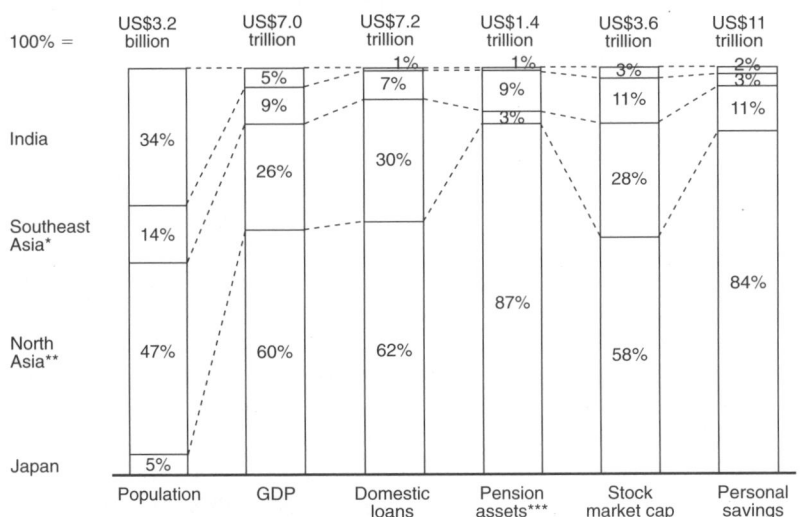

100% =	US$3.2 billion	US$7.0 trillion	US$7.2 trillion	US$1.4 trillion	US$3.6 trillion	US$11 trillion
India	34%	5% / 9%	1% / 7%	1% / 9% / 3%	3% / 11%	2% / 3% / 11%
		26%	30%		28%	
Southeast Asia*	14%					
				87%		84%
North Asia**	47%	60%	62%		58%	
Japan	5%					
	Population	GDP	Domestic loans	Pension assets***	Stock market cap	Personal savings

* Includes Indonesia, Malaysia, Philippines, Singapore, and Thailand.
** Includes China, Hong Kong, Korea, and Taiwan.
*** Includes all public and most private pension assets.

Source: World Bank; Economist Intelligence Unit; 1996 *Asiaweek 500*; Pension Assets: Intersec; Federation Internationale des Bourses de Valeurs; McKinsey analysis

The sheer size and depth of Japan's financial industry is a reminder that Japan in the 1990s generated the majority of industry profits in Asia. Historically, these profits have been available to few outsiders. They have been distributed primarily among local financial institutions, plus a small group of foreign firms that have been able to establish a dominant position in sectors like derivatives, equity, and debt trading, and (to a growing extent) asset management. The degree to which Japan will be a major source of new growth opportunities will depend largely on the speed of financial deregulation and the extent to which new entrants can overcome structural barriers and become insiders.

Regulations Shelter Many Markets

Regulation is perhaps the single most critical factor differentiating and shaping financial systems across Asia. Most Asian countries have maintained relatively closed systems to protect local financial institutions and markets from the shocks of foreign capital flows. Today, however, liberalization is a generally accepted trend. Although the timetable and pace of reform differ from country to country, the Asian financial crisis has accelerated the process.

Hong Kong has the most open financial system in Asia: the Hong Kong dollar is fully convertible; capital flows are unrestricted; a full range of financial products and mechanisms are available; foreign companies may engage freely in wholesale and retail business, though a few branching restrictions remain; and there are virtually no restriction on acquiring local financial firms. Hong Kong's position as the most open system in the region has helped the territory evolve into the leading financial center after Tokyo.

Although Singapore has established itself as the financial hub of Southeast Asia, and Malaysia envisions challenging Singapore as its economy and markets modernize, as of 1998, both countries still protected their domestic markets and restricted the convertibility of their currencies. Foreign banks in Singapore were not allowed to join the local ATM network, and were limited in the businesses they could conduct. Domestic banks had to obtain permission to enter new product areas and acquire other banks. The few foreign stockbrokers that were able to acquire international membership status on the stock exchange were limited in their dealings with Singapore residents to transactions of over S$5 million (about US$3.5 million), which effectively barred them from the retail market. In 1998, as the authorities began to realize that these restrictions limited the market's ability to fully internationalize, they started reviewing regulations. Liberalization should evolve in the early years of the 21st century.

Malaysia's regulations are even more stringent than Singapore's. Although the Malaysian government has made great efforts to develop the equity and derivatives markets, launch new financial products, and promote Kuala Lumpur as a financial center, restrictions on capital flows and foreign participation limit progress. Mutual funds may invest only in Malaysian instruments. Foreign brokers must either trade through a local member firm or establish a joint venture with less than 50 percent foreign ownership. As of 1998, new foreign bank entrants were allowed to own, in most cases, only up to 30 percent of a local subsidiary. The few foreign banks active in Malaysia were tightly restricted with regard to expanding branches, offering new products, and hiring expatriate staff.

Not surprisingly, the Asian economies hit hardest by the financial crisis became the most willing to speed up financial reform and accept foreign capital. Thailand, Indonesia, and Korea had previously imposed strict limitations on foreign ownership. Post-crisis, these economies were desperate for capital. They, therefore, rapidly opened their markets and regulatory systems to foreign acquisition, and (in the case of Korea) gave foreign investors full access to the stock market. Thai financial institutions began selling majority stakes to Western and solvent Asian buyers in 1998.

Products: No Single Solution

Product features, usage, and profitability vary considerably across Asia, partly because of different regulatory frameworks and consumer practices. Credit cards offer one example. In Hong Kong and Taiwan, revolving balances are up to 30 percent of card spend, and hence a major source of profitability. In other Asian markets, revolving balances are low, and issuing banks are forced to rely on annual fees or exorbitant interest rates. In China, debit rather than credit cards predominate — cardholders deposit an amount upfront in their banking account to cover future expenses. Local card-issuing banks make a profit on the float balances. India has a more developed credit card market, where revolving balances reach as high as 20 percent of spend. However, because consumer spend is very low, banks resort to making money from annual fees, and often charge high start-up fees to first-time users.

Consumer financial needs across the region are often similar: to fund purchasing needs and to provide for education, housing, and retirement. But the ways that the industry has developed to meet these needs and channel savings are quite different. In Taiwan, the mutual fund industry grew from nearly nothing to over US$20 billion in just 8 years, following a market downturn in 1990 that drove consumers to professional intermediaries to diversify their investments. In the Philippines, on the other hand, the government restricted the development of a mutual fund industry due to a series of scandals in the 1960s. As a result, an entire guaranteed-savings industry with an estimated 70 firms and over US$10 billion in assets serves the needs of consumers saving for funerals, education, and retirement. Labeled "Pre-Needs," these investment funds guarantee customers fixed-rate returns, and keep the remaining profits for themselves.

At the upper end of consumer financial services, private banking has evolved very differently throughout the region. In much of Southeast Asia, wealthy families have long sought offshore safe havens in nearby Singapore, or in Switzerland. International private banks are effectively barred from many of these countries due to flight-capital controls. Hence, offshore bankers have discreetly provided "suitcase banking" services in hotel rooms or other unofficial locations. Hong Kong, by contrast, allows complete freedom of capital movement: private bankers can offer local clients a complete range of onshore and offshore services. Japan, despite its large pool of wealth, is surprisingly among the smallest established private banking markets. Moneyed Japanese have tended to invest in traditional deposit products, and the private banking industry was stunted until 1998 by regulations limiting offshore investments.

Few Regional Banks

Because each Asian financial market is unique, financial institutions are required by circumstances to consider each market separately and to devise a strategy that fits those specifics. A regional approach to Asia, therefore, must also fit each local situation.

Indicative of the degree of localization in Asia is the fact that few domestic financial institutions have become regional players. For both structural and regulatory reasons, the vast majority of Asian banks have stayed within their own borders, at most setting up small branch offices in Hong Kong or Singapore to serve their nationals abroad. The main exceptions, as of 1998, were Bangkok Bank, which taps into regional overseas Chinese networks, the top Singaporean banks, which have operations in neighboring Malaysia, and two colonial banks, the Hongkong and Shanghai Banking Corporation (HSBC) and Standard Chartered Bank, whose significant operations in Hong Kong, Singapore, and Malaysia predate many regulatory restrictions. The only other notable regional comprehensive retail and corporate bank player in the late 1990s was Citibank (see sidebar), while ABN Amro and Development Bank of Singapore (DBS) were starting to pursue regional strategies.

Similarly, in the securities markets except for the top two Japanese brokers, Nomura and Daiwa, and Hong Kong-based Peregrine Securities (which met its demise in 1997), few Asian brokers have been able to establish themselves beyond their home countries. Regulatory barriers around licensing, exchange memberships, and issuance have prevented many firms from expanding in the region. In addition, local securities firms possess limited distribution capabilities compared with what the large international players can offer. This situation began to change in the late 1990s with the growing number of regional acquisitions and alliances.

Market Similarities and Linkages

While Asian markets clearly differ in many ways, there are, nonetheless, important similarities and linkages across the region. Indeed, similarities in macroeconomic and demographic trends, wealth creation and concentration, and sophistication enable financial institutions to build common approaches and products that can be fine-tuned for each market. Linkages in regional trade and investment enable well-positioned banks to capture cross-border capital flows. A good understanding of the ties between markets is essential to manage market and geographic risk effectively.

Similar Macroeconomic and Demographic Trends

Economic and demographic trends common to virtually every country in Asia include: growing middle classes with an increasing need for investment vehicles; wealth creation and high savings rates that create growing pools of investable money; aging populations that will demand retirement programs; and significant needs for infrastructure development.

Developing middle classes are perhaps the most important common feature in Asia. The middle class is broadly defined as the group that, at a minimum, has the capacity to save money and invest in basic retail financial products like savings accounts, insurance, credit cards, and investment products. The middle and upper-middle classes combined range from 10 to 80 percent of all households per Asian country, and total an estimated 100 million households across the region. The vast majority of these consumers reside in the 25 largest Asian cities. The retail financial market has been an urban phenomenon, though in some developing markets, like Thailand and Malaysia, a growing base of "up-country" consumers constitutes a future market opportunity.

While the middle class is a very significant factor in Asia, there is also a small but powerful group of the super-rich, whose investable funds are greater than US$10 million and who comprise less than 0.005 percent of the region's population. Members of this group have been able to profit hugely by capitalizing on Asia's rapid economic development. The wealthiest individuals and families are naturally quite private and tend to invest through relationships, but significant opportunity exists for banks able to tap into this network.

Citibank: Building from the Bottom Up

Throughout much of the 1990s, Citibank maintained a consistent global corporate identity, and at the same time penetrated Asia's disparate retail markets. In 1996, Citibank earned US$866 million from Asia, much of it from retail banking. Citibank's success in developing a deep knowledge of regional markets, establishing relationships with local governments, and building infrastructure where none existed, demonstrates its ability to respond to local circumstances while leveraging its strengths across the region.

For example, in the early 1990s Citibank decided to make the development of Taiwan's retail banking market a priority. The bank set about building close relationships with the local government and regulators. As proof of its long-term commitment to Taiwan, Citibank located its North Asia headquarters in Taipei.

In Indonesia, Citibank found its retail business hindered by poor postal service. It then worked in partnership with the central post office to develop a better infrastructure.

In India, Citibank discovered that cardholder default was the biggest challenge, so the bank hired people to check on the background of card applicants. Professional checkers questioned neighbors to verify an applicant's address or income level, and paid intimidating visits to cardholders who were delinquent on payments. (The latter practice stopped after a wave of bad publicity.)

Citibank's experience illustrates several ways in which a regional or multinational player can leverage strengths across Asian markets. A key to its regional success lies in tapping the growing pool of talented middle and senior managers in Asia who have regional experience in financial services, in-depth knowledge of specific regulatory and business environments, and the flexibility to adapt to developing market conditions. Another factor is a strong corporate culture and an approach to banking that incorporates world-class products and delivery systems. A successful regional institution must be able to combine excellence in banking with the flexibility to let country managers tailor approaches to implementing corporate strategy.

Asia's high savings rate is well known. According to 1997 estimates, corporate as well as personal savings in Singapore were 51 percent of GDP; in Malaysia, it was 41 percent; in China, 40 percent; in Korea, 37 percent; in Thailand, 36 percent; in Hong Kong, 35 percent; in Japan, 31 percent; and in Taiwan, 25 percent. While the availability of savings allows a high degree of liquidity for bank lending and infrastructure investment, it also constitutes a growing pool that can be tapped for a range of personal financial products.

Common to nearly all Asian countries are aging populations and the need for comprehensive pension systems. Singapore and Malaysia instituted public pension schemes in the 1970s, while Hong Kong has set the year 2000 to start its Mandatory Provident Fund. Other countries are expected to follow suit early in the 21st century. The growth of the pension industry over the next few decades will provide a huge opportunity for fund managers who can capture a share of these assets. As deregulation permits an increasing amount of public money to be directed across borders, fund managers with regional and global expertise will be particularly successful.

Just as demographic trends point to opportunities for retail services, similarities in the pace and scale of economic development provide opportunities in the wholesale financial market. Given the rapid growth of economies and companies in the 1980s and most of the 1990s, the overriding need across all of Asia has been capital to fund expansion, in particular, infrastructure. Asian Development Bank estimates put infrastructure capital needs at up to US$250 billion annually, reaching US$7 trillion by 2023. Institutions that can find innovative ways of structuring long-term financing by combining traditional lending with capital market solutions will be able to leverage their talents regionally.

Growing Cross-Border Financial Flows

The similarities among Asian markets make it possible for financial firms to develop regional products and expertise. Cross-border trade and investment flows and business linkages will provide opportunities in, for example, trade finance, lending, capital markets, venture capital, and acquisition finance. The 1980s and much of the 1990s saw steady growth in the volume of regional trade, particularly among the natural economic grouping of China, Taiwan, and Hong Kong, and the Association of Southeast Asian Nations (ASEAN) bloc. Overseas Chinese business networks, which often tap into private capital sources to finance trade, investment, and other activities, provide another important linkage. Regional direct investment and acquisitions are becoming increasingly common, led by more developed countries like Japan and Taiwan.

Figures from 1996 show just how important intraregional trade has become (Exhibit 2.3). Forty percent of Asian exports were destined for other Asian countries, and 36 percent of all Asian imports were from the region. Prior to the slowdown caused by the 1997–1998 crisis, the total volume of intra-Asian trade was US$766 billion, up from only US$294 billion in 1990.

Regional direct investment flows are also significant and are expanding rapidly as Asian economies develop and companies seek lower-cost manufacturing

Exhibit 2.3

Intraregional Asian Trade as a Percentage of Each Country's Trade: 1996

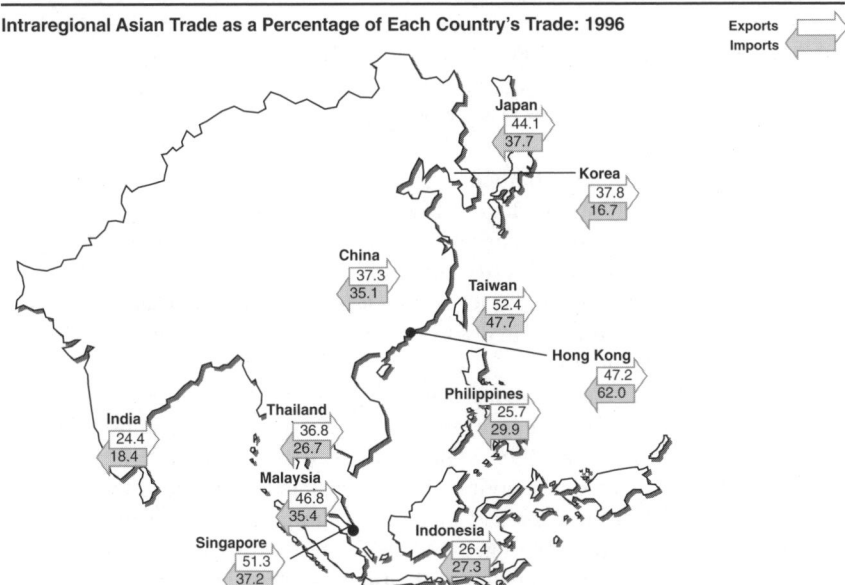

Exports
Imports

Source: Direction of Trade Statistics Yearbook 1997

centers. Japan is the most geographically diversified direct investor in Asia, with an estimated US$13 billion investment in 1997. This includes Japanese companies setting up low-cost production and assembly facilities in China and Southeast Asia, and Japanese construction firms engaged in projects around the region. Before the 1997–1998 crisis, Korean construction firms had also become important players in large infrastructure projects in Southeast Asia.

Japanese and Korean investment is trumped, however, by the large volume of money flowing from Hong Kong into China. In 1996, estimates placed the volume of direct investment outflow from Hong Kong at US$27 billion. Of this, up to 80 percent was targeted at the Chinese mainland and represented Hong Kong firms investing in factories and real estate across the border. This number includes investment into China from Taiwanese and other companies booked through Hong Kong.

In the early 1990s, Taiwan, too, quietly became a major source of regional direct investment. Taiwanese companies poured an estimated US$35 billion in mainland China alone, funding thousands of small and medium-sized factories, and changing the face of entire townships. With the ever-present political tensions between the island and the mainland, Taiwan's government encouraged its manufacturers to diversify into Southeast Asia. Indeed, after the Asian financial crisis, Taiwan continued to advance its position as a leader in regional cross-border direct investments.

Regional mergers and acquisitions are growing through the activities of multinational investment banks, private equity and venture capital firms, and increasingly via some Asian financial institutions themselves. Before the Asian meltdown, several Thai financial holding companies entertained wider regional ambitions, but they were capped by the collapse of the domestic economy. In 1996, leading Thai brokerage house Securities One acquired the Thai parent of regional boutique Asia Equity Securities. That same year, Nava Finance & Securities, also of Thailand, purchased Hong Kong-based Standard Chartered Securities. (Both firms were obliged to sell off their regional holdings in 1997.) Post-crisis, a number of Asian institutions acquired assets in Thailand. Vickers Ballas of Singapore bought into Nava Securities in 1997. In 1998, Development Bank of Singapore (DBS) raised its minority stake in Thai Danu Bank to 50.1 percent, becoming the first foreign firm to acquire majority control of a Thai commercial bank. Later that year, DBS acquired Kwong On Bank in Hong Kong in a new bid to bolster its regional ambitions.

Taiwanese firms are also playing a growing role in regional acquisitions. In 1997, Core Pacific Holdings of Taiwan acquired the Hong Kong unit of Japan's failed Yamaichi Securities. In 1998, KGI Securities, founded by the influential Koo Group in Taiwan, acquired a majority stake in Thailand's Securities One. A pan-Asian start-up, KGI Securities was funded by a group of pre-eminent corporate shareholders from Taiwan, Thailand, Indonesia, the Philippines, Korea, Japan, Singapore, and — an interesting sign of the times — mainland China.

Interwoven Markets

Turning from business opportunities to the critical area of risk management, Asian financial markets are underpinned by linkages that cannot be overlooked. The 1997–1998 Asian financial shakeout illustrated how closely the region's markets are tied, despite their diverse economies. Understanding exactly how markets correlate and differ is critical to managing market and geographic risk.

The crisis that started in June 1997 in Thailand was triggered in part by the downfall of Finance One Securities, which was followed by sharp declines in the baht and market values. The speed at which the turmoil spread through the rest of Asia stunned observers. Analysts at first emphasized the strength of neighboring Southeast Asian economies, citing larger foreign exchange reserves, healthier economies, and stronger bank balance sheets. But the rapid spread of devaluation indicated that market linkages, created in part by Western institutional investors' herd-like investment strategy, were stronger than many had thought.

Beyond investor sentiment, Asian currency and stock markets remain tied by regional trade flows and investment patterns. The crisis also revealed fundamental structural weaknesses from similar patterns of development in many Asian countries: favored companies and sectors, crony lending, weak banking supervision, over-investment, and unhedged short-term borrowing in foreign currencies.

Not all Asian markets were affected in the same way. As Taiwan's financial system had already gone through restructuring its stock market rose 12 percent in local currency terms over the course of 1997. (The New Taiwan dollar fell 20 percent during that period, less than the drop by the currencies of most Southeast Asian countries.) Hong Kong maintained its peg to the U.S. dollar, though the resulting high interest rates and economic slowdown put pressure on the stock market. China maintained strict capital controls, and was able to shield its markets from devaluation in 1997 and 1998.

While every country in Asia was deeply affected by the crisis, the differences in how individual markets and economies reacted indicate the value of diversification across the region. Financial institutions that clearly understand the linkages as well as the fundamental differences between markets, will be in a better position to anticipate and manage risk.

As we have seen, Asia is a geographically fragmented region, with a diverse set of cultural, economic, and financial systems. However, economic and demographic trends are moving in a similar direction across the region, creating demand for more sophisticated financial products. Financial institutions face significant opportunities, but must remain flexible and adopt a set of local strategies that tailor world-class products and systems to specific market conditions and tastes.

Asia is also becoming increasingly linked by regional and global trade and investment flows that will continue to gain strength into the next century. These linkages will offer major opportunities for wholesale financial businesses that can anticipate and manage cross-border correlation in risk. Given these trends, Hong Kong-based corporate finance vice presidents' long trips to India should help instill the common practices that will make Asia, from a banking perspective, more of a region in the decade ahead.

PART II
WINNING IN KEY BUSINESSES

This section examines how the changing dynamics of banking in Asia will play out in the key banking business lines.

We review six businesses, beginning with three corporate and wholesale businesses in the corporate banking, investment banking, and trading chapters. Next comes asset management, which spans both wholesale or institutional investors and retail investors. The final two businesses focus on retail markets: private banking for wealthy individuals, and retail banking for the mass of consumers.

These six businesses not only differ from one other, they also differ from country to country. We, therefore, analyze the factors that will differentiate winners from losers across the region and in the major countries.

3
CORPORATE BANKING:
BIG PROFITS AMONG THE RISKS

Recruiting time at Harvard Business School during much of the 1990s saw the investment banking industry — led by firms such as Goldman Sachs, Morgan Stanley, and Merrill Lynch — seek the best performers and offer them large signing bonuses, good salaries, and stories of huge total pay-out of 2 or 3 years. Interviewees heard about the mergers and acquisitions the firms had managed, the huge capital-raising issues they had underwritten, and the amazingly complicated derivative products they had developed for clients. Meanwhile, the commercial banks found it increasingly difficult to compete with the investment banks for talent. These recruiting trends followed the business trends of the 1980s and 1990s, particularly the inexorable decline of commercial banks' influence in wholesale markets in the face of disintermediation and the rise of the investment banks.

It is fashionable, therefore, to describe the intricacies of corporate banking in the context of how the old world of commercial banks making loans to corporations has given way to a new world. Borrowers with the best credit ratings use investment banks to place securities for them, and are as unimpressed as the recruits with what commercial banks have to offer. Commercial banks are left with offering back-up lines of credit at very narrow margins for the securities that investment banks place. Further, commercial banks' relationships with corporations are pushed out of the chief financial officer's domain to that of the treasurer and deputy treasurer, where "plain vanilla" products belong. Denied access to the most senior decision-makers, commercial bankers find themselves unable to compete in important events like mergers and acquisitions, or to be at the forefront of new product ideas.

Even less creditworthy corporations have found that the public securities markets have a greater capacity than previously for weaker credits, in both bonds and equities. The high-yield junk bond market in the U.S., which grew so dramatically in the 1980s (although it had long been in existence), spawned new thinking around the world about how to structure issues of weaker credits. Again, commercial banks found that clients whom they thought were their monopoly were also being won over by investment banks. In the venture capital world, the enormous fund-raising efforts of the 1980s and 1990s for investment in high-technology or other high-growth opportunities meant that it was no longer just banks that were funding new growth companies.

This Story Does Not Ring Completely True

All in all, the emergence of global institutional investors (pension funds and mutual funds) and talented intermediaries (investment banks and venture firms) has, in this new-world story, fundamentally weakened commercial banks' competitiveness to serve corporations of all stripes. Like so many summaries of strong forces at work, this new-world story is right — and yet wrong. During the

1980s and much of the 1990s, commercial banks funded substantial Asian growth. These banks retain powerful positions in many segments of the market, positions that they can use successfully in the future — if they abide by some basic banking rules. In fact, the story for many commercial banks will not be one of inexorable decline in the face of investment banking competition, but rather, of lost opportunity through slack management. The trends of the new world in finance have been clear to all, seeing the rise of investment banks in the U.S. and Europe during the 1980s and much of the 1990s. In Asia, commercial banks had time to prepare themselves to sustain strong positions into the next century, but many squandered that opportunity.

The reality is that traditional commercial or corporate banking was the core of both local and multinational bank profits in Asia in the 1980s and 1990s. The Asian boom, the Asian miracle, was a banking boom, a banking miracle. Owners of the local banks that financed the boom made huge fortunes. In many countries, these owners reached positions of considerable status and influence. But success bred complacency, and efforts to play the same game continued, even though conditions were clearly changing. Speculative bubbles started to appear, and many borrowers stretched too far or took on unhedged positions, but the banks kept going. The results are well documented. The susceptibility of so many banks to the 1997–1998 financial crisis means that fewer banks will be able to profit from the renewed growth of the next decade — and this is a great lost opportunity.

Fundamentals of a Large Attractive Business

Why was corporate banking fundamentally attractive in Asia during most of the 1990s? Because it had that great business mixture: size, competitive protection, growth, and high margins. By the mid-1990s, however, it could be argued that on a risk-adjusted basis, the margins in many markets were not that attractive. And as became clear in 1997, some margins were illusory: loans had created unsound growth and significant credit risk.

Large Protected Business

In 1996 alone, corporate banking across Asia generated approximately US$56 billion in revenues, of which about 40 percent came from Japan and about 30 percent from Greater China (Exhibit 3.1). Total domestic corporate banking assets in the region were over US$5 trillion, of which Japan accounted for nearly 61 percent. As a percentage of GDP, these assets ranged from 17 to 117 percent (Exhibit 3.2), against 37 percent for the U.S. and 22 percent for the U.K., suggesting that in some countries trouble might have been brewing. As we know now, it was. Yet these worrying figures excluded significant cross-border borrowing in countries like Korea and Indonesia.

Banking markets across the region were largely protected in most of the 1990s: regulators granted few licenses to new foreign banks, and allowed only limited additional branching by already established foreign banks. Except in Indonesia and Taiwan, few new local banks were established during this period either. Banking

Exhibit 3.1

Corporate Banking Revenues* and Loan Assets by Country: 1996 *Estimates*
US$ billions; percent

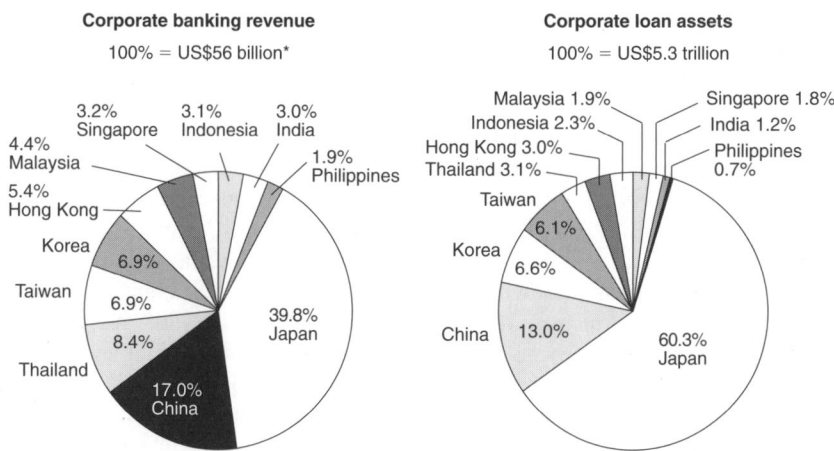

Corporate banking revenue
100% = US$56 billion*

3.2% Singapore
3.1% Indonesia
3.0% India
4.4% Malaysia
1.9% Philippines
5.4% Hong Kong
Korea
6.9%
Taiwan
6.9%
8.4%
Thailand
39.8% Japan
17.0% China

Corporate loan assets
100% = US$5.3 trillion

Malaysia 1.9%
Singapore 1.8%
Indonesia 2.3%
India 1.2%
Hong Kong 3.0%
Philippines 0.7%
Thailand 3.1%
Taiwan
6.1%
Korea
6.6%
China 13.0%
60.3% Japan

*   Based on data for the top 500 banks in Asia, which do not include cooperatives or finance and leasing
    companies, and excluding offshore loan books. Total revenues may be understated by up to 15 percent.
    Revenue figures are pre-loan loss provisions.

Source: Asiaweek; Bank for International Settlements; Standard & Poor's DRI; International Monetary Fund;
    government statistics; McKinsey analysis

Exhibit 3.2

Corporate Domestic Loans as Percentage of GDP: 1996

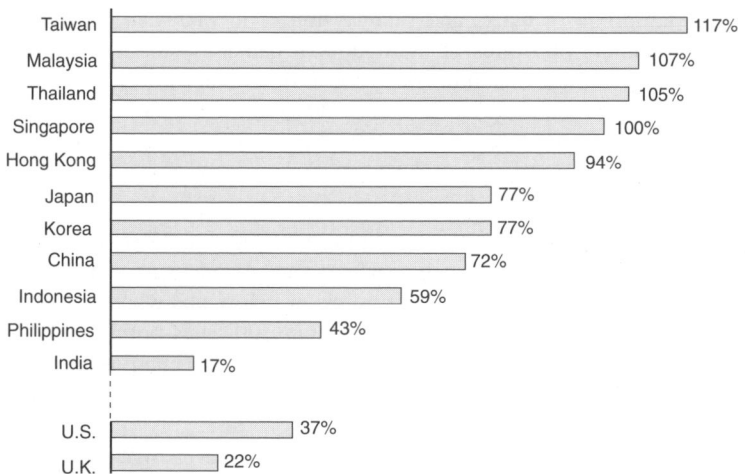

Taiwan	117%
Malaysia	107%
Thailand	105%
Singapore	100%
Hong Kong	94%
Japan	77%
Korea	77%
China	72%
Indonesia	59%
Philippines	43%
India	17%
U.S.	37%
U.K.	22%

Source: Asiaweek; International Monetary Fund; McKinsey analysis

for large corporations was the easiest market to enter for foreign banks which had no existing branches in a country, and so many competed aggressively. But local banks still won large shares in the high-margin middle markets and small-business markets, where branches were critical. As a result, many Western bankers competed at a disadvantage.

The corollary of Western banks' dearth of licenses and branches was that few cross-country, Asian regional banks existed either. For example, Bangkok Bank had difficulty establishing a foothold in Malaysia, and Maybank had similar problems in Thailand. The only regional banks were grandfathered British colonial banks such as the Hongkong and Shanghai Banking Corporation (HSBC) and Standard Chartered Bank (in fact, these two banks were only grandfathered from a regulatory perspective in Hong Kong, Singapore, and Malaysia, and had to compete like other banks elsewhere in Asia), aggressive U.S. competitors like Citibank and Bank of America, and large European competitors like ABN Amro, Deutsche Bank, and some Swiss banks. With their significant capital and human resource commitments to the region, these banks made competition in the large corporate market very intense. Many other foreign banks tried to follow in their footsteps for much of the 1990s, and competition increased significantly during that decade.

Nevertheless, there were opportunities for local banks. Competition in numerous customer segments was limited, and many customer groups remained loyal to local banks (especially in Japan, Korea, and China — where foreign banks could not provide local currency loans). In addition, there was growth.

Growth

Growth during most of the 1990s was spectacular. Exhibit 3.3 illustrates the degree to which Asian corporate lending expanded. The growth of domestic banks across Asia, like Hong Kong and Singapore banks, Bangkok Bank in Thailand, and the Arab-Malaysian group of banks and finance houses in Malaysia, as well as the growth of the lending portfolios of multinational banks in Asia like ABN Amro and Bank of America, was underpinned by the extraordinary increase in corporate lending across these countries.

Margins

Not only was there amazing expansion between 1990 and 1997, margins were good, too. From a Western perspective, where spreads on loans to Fortune 500-equivalent corporations are often 25 basis points or below, and where even middle-market companies can access loans at less than 100-basis-point spreads over matched funding costs, here were markets where all these margins were shifted upward. We know that in many cases they were still not high enough to justify the risks, but they were impressive.

The story of high margins was not uniformly true, however. Where corporations were able to argue that they were the equivalent of a Western risk, they could use intense competition to drive down pricing. With the option of going to the capital

Exhibit 3.3

Growth in Domestic Corporate Lending in Asia: 1990–1997
Percent, based on domestic currencies

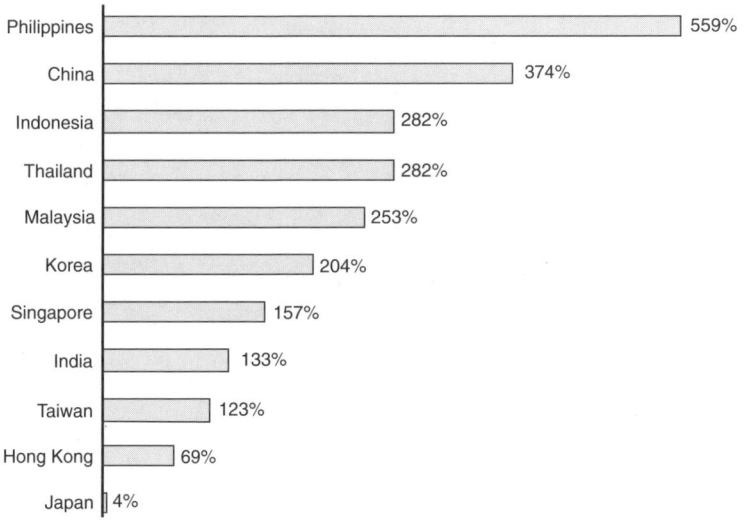

Philippines	559%
China	374%
Indonesia	282%
Thailand	282%
Malaysia	253%
Korea	204%
Singapore	157%
India	133%
Taiwan	123%
Hong Kong	69%
Japan	4%

Source: International Monetary Fund

markets or facing a list of eager international banks, such as Citibank and ABN Amro, as well as local banks in Japan, Hong Kong, and Singapore, the best risks were able to command pricing of about 25 basis points or less on their short-term lending, as well as very competitive commitment fees. Outside Japan, Hong Kong, and Singapore, blue chips paid spreads of around 50 basis points on short-term lending. In higher-risk countries, that number moved to 100 basis points (Indonesia), or much more (200 basis points in India).

Middle-market companies, of course, paid even higher margins. Again, those in the strongest local economies and subject to the most banking competition were able to find the best pricing, often because international banks like Citibank were trying to develop indigenous business in that market. Consequently, while middle-market companies in Japan, Hong Kong, and Singapore paid margins of between 100 and 150 basis points on their short-term revolving credits, in India these spreads could be as high as 400 basis points, and in Malaysia, about 200 basis points.

Corporate banking margins are not just a matter of lending spreads. They are in fact the sum of all product revenues (Exhibit 3.4), minus operating expenses. These profits are then expressed as a return on the capital used, and adjusted for the risks that are taken to generate the revenues. A skilled banker looks at total relationship returns in terms of profit and not just revenue, then expresses it as a return on the accounting capital employed or the risk capital used. The focus on the return on risk assumed reflects the fact that some of the business a client generates is risky (for instance, extending a long-term loan), while other components are much less so (trading foreign exchange with the client or providing cash management services).

Exhibit 3.4

Corporate Banking Revenues by Product: 1996 *Estimates*
US$ billions, percent

100% = US$56 billion*

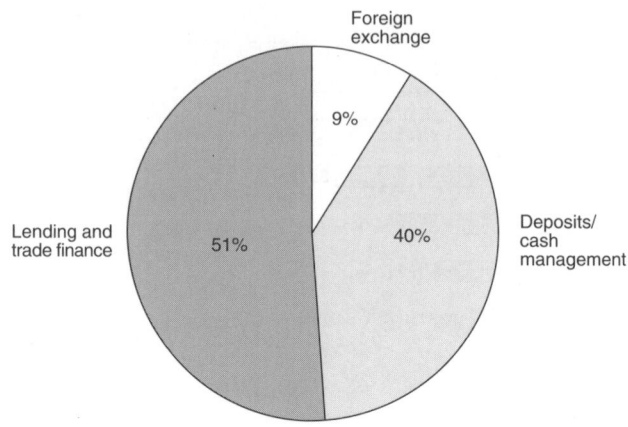

*   Based on data for the top 500 banks in Asia, which do not include cooperatives or finance and leasing companies, and excluding offshore loan books. Total revenues may be understated by up to 15 percent. Revenues are pre-loan loss provisions.

Source: Standard & Poor's DRI; Bank for International Settlements; International Monetary Fund; government statistics; McKinsey analysis

Over the years, the Bank for International Settlements, the nearest thing to a global regulator, has developed increasingly sophisticated capital allocation systems that apply different capital weightings to different types of assets. For instance, the regulations perceive government debt in a home currency as the least risky asset, while cross-border, cross-currency loans to corporations are given the highest capital allocation.

Syndications and Commitment Fees

Besides loan-interest margins that dominate overall relationship income, banks earn fees from syndicating large transactions among a range of banks, and commitment fees for loans that might never or only partially be drawn down. The latter fees were competed away aggressively during much of the 1990s, such that by 1997, they had declined to just 12.5 basis points for a standard U.S. dollar revolving credit facility for blue-chip borrowers. Syndications of very large loans in the mid-1990s (some of the largest banks committed up to US$1.5 billion to the best names in Asia, and then syndicated the exposure to other banks) brought upfront arrangement fees of about 45 basis points. On a US$1 billion facility, that was attractive income. If the lead bank retained 30 percent of such a loan, earning perhaps 45 basis points in spread, then the additional syndication fee income of

US\$4.5 million increased its overall spread on the US\$300 million to an average of 75 basis points over 5 years. Major international banks, such as Citibank, Chase, HSBC, and ABN Amro, tended to dominate major syndications. If a local institution was the lead bank, it was often co-lead, and the international bank would end up with most of the syndication.

Profits from Deposits

Deposit income (i.e., the difference between the interest the banks were paying the corporate customers and what they had to pay on the interbank market to raise deposits or funding of similar maturity) was a surprisingly important source of revenues for banks in Asia during much of the 1990s. In the West, cash management services offered by banks, and the increased sophistication of even middle-market customers, meant that the old world of compensating balances for corporate loans and customers regularly leaving large amounts in non-interest-paying accounts, had long disappeared. But in Asia, customers' relative lack of sophistication, and the fact that many could not be bothered with day-to-day cash management issues due to the phenomenal business opportunities in the region, meant that banks still earned a significant proportion of corporate banking profits from deposits. For instance, even in relatively sophisticated Singapore, big local banks such as United Overseas Bank (UOB) were earning about 10–15 percent of corporate banking revenues from deposits.

The typical corporate customer might have learned to move most deposits into efficient sweep accounts, but many had problems making these approaches work well simultaneously in multiple countries and currencies. The middle-market and small-business customers, on the other hand, were far from this level of sophistication, and simply might have neither the appreciation of the opportunity nor the skills to move the balances regularly into interest-bearing accounts. These customers' cash accumulated and sat relatively idle in banks.

In Indonesia, the Philippines, and Korea, bank deposit earnings were even greater, and accounted for as much as 20–30 percent of total revenues earned from a given corporate relationship. In these countries, both the customers' relative sophistication and the banks' sweep and cash management products were less well-developed, which afforded the banks attractive profits from corporate deposits.

Cash Management and Trade Finance Opportunities

Profits from deposits were very large during much of the 1990s, but cash management opportunities were available for just a few commercial banks. As businesses learned about managing cash, they understood the risks of mismatched foreign exchange exposures on their activities across the region. They sought out banks that could not only improve their in-country cash productivity, but also help them navigate the maze of regulatory issues around cross-border cash movement. These banks allowed them to sweep cash into the most efficient deposits as rapidly as possible. Banks able to provide these services attracted deposits and earned fees on cash management activities.

Loans and deposits may have been the mainstay of corporate banking in Asia, but trade finance was not to be left behind. From 1990 to 1996, the volume of total trade to or from Asian countries rose from US$1.3 trillion to US$2.6 trillion, a 12 percent annual increase. In 1996, about 40 percent of this trade was within Asia. Every banker talked about the importance of trade finance, although few banks' products consistently performed well.

At the simplest level, trade finance was divided into structured and traditional trade finance. In structured trade finance, banks arranged customized transactions to finance large trade contracts, such as for exporting US$100 million of agricultural machinery from the U.S. to an Asian market. In traditional trade finance, banks arranged for the financing of regular trade flows, such as U.S. trading houses importing textile products from Asia, as well as collection services for importers and exporters. In the structured market, only a few banks competed aggressively for the transactions. As a result, the returns were solid, but not spectacular. Traditional trade finance returns could be attractive: once concerns about country risk emerged in 1997, returns dramatically increased. Trade with Indonesia or Thailand, for instance, offered in excess of 250 basis points, for spreads that had averaged 100 basis points pre-crisis. Spreads of 10–40 basis points on collections increased significantly, and letter of credit fees increased too, generally doubling throughout Southeast Asia.

The systems-intensive businesses of trade finance and cash management demanded strict credit and process discipline. Although local banks were developing their capabilities, both areas were dominated by major international banks like Citibank, Chase, ABN Amro, HSBC, and Standard Chartered.

Foreign Exchange Profits

On top of lending, deposit, cash management, and trade finance services, corporate banks saw opportunities to make money from foreign exchange trading for corporate customers. During much of the 1990s, companies in Asia increased investments in factories or subsidiaries outside their base country (for instance, Hong Kong manufacturers expanded into China, or Taiwanese manufacturers expanded across Southeast Asia and mainland China). As trading increased across the region, so did the demand for basic forex services (distinct from the outright speculation that many mid-sized corporations engaged in). After the forex volatility of mid-1997, these clients needed progressively more forex services related to hedging advice and products. Prior to mid-1997, the spreads on this forex activity, especially for large corporate clients, had been under significant pressure. After the crisis, margins increased by as much as 3.5 times in countries such as Thailand.

Although local banks earned solid profits from forex services to local corporations, it was the international banks that had the best networks and staff, and could offer the most innovative products, such as derivatives. Local banks were constrained by domestic regulators' concerns about defending the local currency, which they could most easily do by ordering local banks to limit their forex trading. One local bank, Arab-Malaysian Merchant Bank, recognized the relative weakness of its skills and entered into a joint venture in foreign exchange (and equity) derivatives with Macquarie Bank of Australia.

Operating Expenses and Loan Losses

To generate these various revenues, banks incur operating costs and potential credit or trading losses. Operating expenses are reasonably straightforward, and fall into three broad types: those directly associated with the business; those shared with perhaps one other business (for instance, private banking's use of credit control staff); and those spread across numerous businesses of which a percentage is essentially allocated to corporate banking. Direct costs involve staff and their benefits, telecommunications, office space, report production, and travel and entertainment.

During much of the 1990s, local banks had very low cost-to-income ratios. Compared with the average 60 percent of revenues for major banks in the U.S. and the U.K., leading local banks had 45 percent cost-to-income ratios, or nearer 40 percent in Hong Kong. These very efficient numbers masked a real problem for local banks — a major underinvestment in systems and skilled staff.

Another issue in Asia during the 1990s was that many key unit operating costs were unusually high due to a combination of cartel real estate markets in some locations (Hong Kong and Singapore) and heavily regulated high-cost telecommunications and airline services. At the same time, as the markets were growing so quickly, skilled staff was in amazing demand. Compensation and benefit costs increased dramatically during much of the 1990s, increasing as much as twofold in some countries for senior relationship management positions. Government efforts failed to control staff poaching between domestic banks. The story echoed across the markets: expenses were high, and climbing. The fact that many local banks retained low cost-to-income ratios in this environment illustrates their lack of investment.

Loan losses during the years before the 1997–1998 crisis varied widely among the countries. In countries where government had either been directly channeling funds through state-controlled banks (most obviously Indonesia and China) or encouraging such lending (Japan, Korea, and India) to preferred industries or companies, nonperforming loans had been significant long before the crisis. Although some of these countries did not officially acknowledge the existence of bad debts, nonperforming loans were estimated to be in the range of 10 to 20 percent of loan assets. In the other economies (Taiwan, Hong Kong, Singapore, Malaysia, Philippines, and Thailand), banks were generally too easily lulled into a sense of calm by periods of growth and low loan losses. From 1992 to 1996, banks in these economies provisioned on average only 0.6 percent of assets for bad debts.

Banks whose perspective predated 1990, however, knew that Asia could certainly deliver nasty shocks. In the mid-1980s, Southeast Asia experienced a serious recession and overbuilding crisis; nonperforming loans ran up to 31 percent in Malaysia, 24 percent in the Philippines, and 15 percent in Thailand. Countries such as Indonesia and China, which did not publish nonperforming loan figures at the time, were certainly experiencing problems at least as severe as those of their neighbors. Comparing these peaks from the 1980s with the 1998 levels (Exhibit 3.5) puts them in perspective. Clearly, the 1997–1998 turmoil was not a one-off incident, but part of a pattern of the cost of growth led by lending.

Despite this pattern of credit concerns and the burgeoning costs of doing business in many Asian markets, corporate banking in the high-growth early-to-mid-1990s was a mainstay for the entire banking industry. Why was the business so attractive? Basically, it was a question of supply and demand. Customers urgently needed financing, and supply was often limited. In most markets, growth in corporate lending outstripped growth in demand and savings deposits (Exhibit 3.6). The result: margins rose. Corporate lending was all too often funded with "hot money," that is, high-priced time deposits or interbank deposits. However, when the credit crunch hit in 1997, deposits dried up and banks were faced with liquidity problems. Corporate lines of credit were withdrawn, pushing many companies against the wall.

But other factors raised returns. We have already seen that many countries wanted to restrain foreign entry into their domestic banking systems and build strong local banks. To that end, only blue-chip clients that could access global capital markets or were potential clients of multinational commercial banks could tap alternative banks. The rest had to turn to local banks, which charged them relatively large spreads on loans or paid limited interest on deposits. In addition, in nearly all the markets (Indonesia was the significant exception), regulations during much of the 1990s supported a cozy oligopoly. In 1996, the top five corporate banks held large shares of local currency markets: China, 90 percent;

Exhibit 3.5

Nonperforming Loans in Asia: 1998   *Estimates*
Percent of total loans

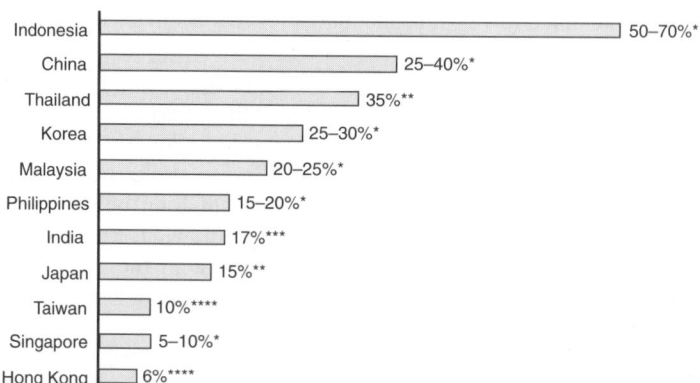

Indonesia	50–70%*
China	25–40%*
Thailand	35%**
Korea	25–30%*
Malaysia	20–25%*
Philippines	15–20%*
India	17%***
Japan	15%**
Taiwan	10%****
Singapore	5–10%*
Hong Kong	6%****

   * Range of estimates from various sources; actual amounts not publicly available.
  ** Actual at June 1998.
 *** Actual at December 1997.
**** Actual at November 1998.

Source: Bank for International Settlements; Standard & Poor's DRI; Jardine Fleming; Goldman Sachs; Morgan Stanley; Fitch IBCA

Exhibit 3.6

Domestic Deposit and Loan Growth: 1990–1996
Compound annual growth rate based on domestic currencie; percent

☐ Deposits
■ Loans

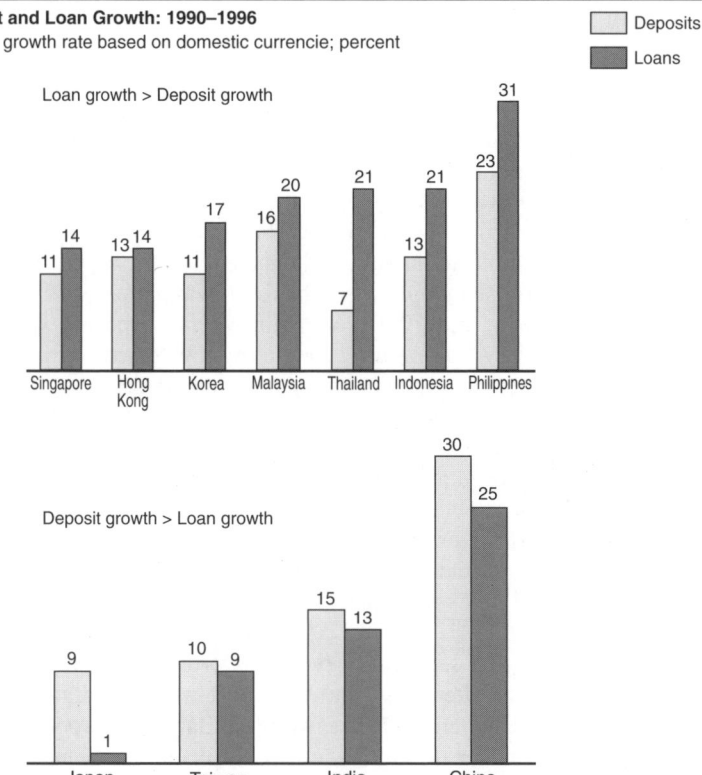

Source: International Monetary Fund

Singapore, 88 percent; Hong Kong, 77 percent; Thailand, 69 percent; the Philippines, 53 percent; Malaysia and India, 51 percent each; Taiwan, 46 percent; Indonesia, 44 percent; Korea, 41 percent; and Japan, 35 percent. These market shares compare with 36 percent for the top five corporate banks in the U.S., but 66 percent in Germany, and 43 percent in France. Asia was heading for the continental European model of market division, with the added advantage for the banks that few corporate customers could easily tap the capital markets directly. For the handful of dominant domestic players, intermediation ruled.

How These Pressures Played Out in Two Markets

We can see how these pressures resolved themselves in two very different markets: Malaysia and Japan. The story in Japan portended what was to befall Malaysia, and other markets in the region. Japan's great bubble economy of the late 1980s burst in the early 1990s with the collapse of real estate and share values. As a result, loan losses and concerns about borrowers' future creditworthiness seriously wounded Japanese banks. Much of the lending of the 1980s had been on the strength of relationships and interlocking shareholdings, rather than on fundamental credit reviews.

Instead of dealing quickly with these issues, banks in Japan endured a prolonged period of low growth. From 1990 to 1996, the top six Japanese banks' loan books grew by 2.5 percent on average each year. Despite repeated government attempts to prime the economic pump through major infrastructure projects, Japanese banks' lending appetite was gone — and they were not developing new skills to differentiate strong from weak credits. The old tradition of relationship- or name-based lending continued. But now, without credibility, it impeded progress. No new, more transparent system replaced it; the result was a prolonged decline.

During much of the 1990s, the Malaysian corporate sector boomed. A combination of the Asian miracle, long-term government infrastructure spending and project sponsorship (culminating in the Multimedia Super Corridor), a vibrant local Chinese business community, and racial laws favoring bumiputra (ethnic Malay) businesses meant that the demand for loans was consistently strong. From 1990 through 1996, total lending rose from US\$30 billion to US\$95 billion, a 20 percent annual growth rate. The corporate customers for these loans included small Chinese businesses, mid-sized high-tech growth companies, and bumiputra-owned property and trading companies. At the very top end, major corporations like Petronas and Telekom Malaysia were courted by all the multinational and investment banks.

The local banking scene, however, was protected. Foreign banks were not issued new licenses after 1981, and those that were grandfathered (for example, HSBC, Standard Chartered, Oversea-Chinese Banking Corporation of Singapore, and Citibank) discovered that they could not open new branches, or even move old branches. Some found that when the buildings in which they had branches became so dilapidated that they were condemned, Bank Negara Malaysia (the central bank and key regulator) insisted the branches could not be relocated.

Within this environment of growth and constrained competition, local banks prospered. Led by Maybank, local banks grew their branch networks and led deposits and lending activity to local corporates. Cash management services were rudimentary, so overall margins were attractive. From 1990 to 1996, Maybank's corporate loans grew 18 percent a year and corporate lending activities of the various entities within the Arab-Malaysian Banking Group increased by an amazing 41 percent a year. Spreads remained attractive during this time; each bank had a return on assets before loan losses of more than 150 basis points.

This growth, often collateralized with property or shares which were subject to rapid price declines if the growth merry-go-round ever stopped, created major credit and liquidity problems for these banks in 1997–1998. If credit policies had been tighter during the bull market, these banks could have fared better later. To some degree, they were victims of their own protection; the *quid pro quo* of government support was a willingness to sign on to and fund government initiatives and the corporations within them. As it was, the foreign banks were well positioned by 1998 to gain deposit and loan share from the weakened locals. Despite the regulators' best efforts, foreign banks began to win market share.

The Malaysian and Japanese examples illustrate a common factor in the corporate lending markets in Asia during much of the 1990s: they were not fully transparent or driven by fundamental economics. The crony capitalism of these markets was sustainable while growth was very strong. Distortions ranged from China's support of loss-making state-owned enterprises, essentially by using the Big Four commercial banks as funding arms of the state, to Korea's leveraging the *chaebol* with huge amounts of short-term debt to support low-return diversification, to Malaysia's bumiputra policies, to Indonesia's cartelized economy. In these environments, corporate bankers were navigating where many of the most interesting opportunities had economics that depended on the continuation of unsound economic policies or political favoritism. Refusing to take part at all in any of these markets limited some foreign banks to bit parts in the story. The local banks, however, had little choice.

As its evolution in the more open Western economies and in Hong Kong and Singapore had shown, fundamental forces were making corporate banking more challenging. In fact, corporate banking was terminally threatened by investment banking and corporations' direct access to capital markets in many creditworthy segments of the Western market. Successful corporate banks in these more open markets had been forced to upgrade their services, introduce new products, select customers carefully, and strengthen credit processes. Crony capitalism and protected banking markets delayed the day of reckoning for local banks in many Asian markets, but it was coming. The 1997–1998 financial crisis was the catalyst for change.

A Segmented Business

The signs that the Asian markets were becoming tougher were in place in the early 1990s: investment banks were much more active; lower-quality credits were gaining access to capital markets through the investment banks' enlarged equity research teams and the opening up of local debt markets; and multinational commercial banks were expanding very aggressively. Between 1990 and 1995, competitors for corporate lending mandates expanded from 30 to about 100 in China (for foreign currency lending), from 14 to 55 in Thailand, and from 10 to 40 in Indonesia. The major international banks increased their presence in Asia enormously during this period, and largely targeted the corporate market. Union Bank of Switzerland (UBS prior to its merger with Swiss Bank Corporation) increased its headcount by about 100 percent during this five-year period, Societe Generale by 95 percent, ABN Amro by 48 percent, Citibank by 41 percent, Deutsche Bank by 40 percent, Banque Nationale de Paris (BNP) by 33 percent, and HSBC by 25 percent.

As a result of these pressures, the stronger competitors recognized that they had to focus their efforts and establish a niche in the market they would be known for serving especially well. That process began by understanding customer segments. The corporate segments that existed during most of the 1990s remain relevant today. Although country markets differ, customers generally fall into six categories: Western multinationals, emerging Asian global companies, large locals, middle-market companies, small businesses, and property-related companies. Because corporate managers have very disparate experiences, objectives, and pressures placed upon them, each segment behaves and chooses corporate bankers differently.

Western Multinationals

The first segment is subsidiaries of Western multinationals operating across the region. Companies like Ford, Procter & Gamble, Unilever, and Disney have many different business units. Each may have a business in an Asian country that may or may not be grouped under a country manager, who in turn may or may not report to a head of Asia. These businesses have long-term capital needs (setting up factories, making local acquisitions), short-term working capital needs, and trade finance, cash management, and risk management requirements, such as hedging foreign exchange exposures. Given the scale and complexity of these requirements, headquarters often selects a fairly senior employee as Asia chief financial officer, and backs the position with a staff of local treasurers to manage local needs and collections. This large segment of the market comprises an estimated 100–200 multinationals, and generates revenues that exceed US$1 billion.

Although this market represents a sizable target, it is a frustrating one for banks operating in the region. These subsidiary businesses often take banking orders from headquarters, so key credit lines may have been assigned in the U.S. or Europe. Available lines are often very finely priced. For instance, in the mid-1990s they ranged from 10 to 15 basis points for leading U.S. multinationals for U.S. dollar revolving credits out of Hong Kong. Although local currency funding may have better margins (for instance, about 20 basis points for the Malaysian ringgit for the same U.S. multinational), lending does not provide a sustainable base for overall relationship profitability. Banks must try to add on risk management, cash management, or trade finance products. The good news is that the local regional financial team will be sophisticated enough to recognize the need for these products. The bad news is that the team's level of sophistication will drive it to place out most requests for proposals to broad bidding by banks, which drives down pricing and raises required service levels. The net impact of the demanding nature of these multinationals is that they typically account for less than 10 percent of corporate domestic bank revenues.

An indication of Western multinationals' demanding approach is the process that a top firm goes through to select the bank that will provide its regional cash management services. Typically, the company puts together a Request for Proposal (RFP), or Invitation to Tender (ITT), that presents the background of the company, its regional cash management objectives, and its key needs and constraints (e.g., the amount of business activity that the company has in countries with tight exchange controls). Then the RFP describes the company's main selection criteria for choosing a bank (breadth of country coverage, type of IT system, reporting methodology and timeliness, credit rating, track record for providing the requested services, and pricing of bid), how the response to the RFP must be structured, required references and appendices that provide detailed data on the past and likely cash flows and liquidity needs of the regional businesses, and key questions and answers about the company. A well-prepared RFP is a large document that requires a serious response from bidding banks. Based on their written responses, two or three banks are likely to be short-listed. Both the coverage officers in the cash management business and the operating staff are asked to make formal presentations. Once a bank has been selected, it usually has to enter into service-level agreements with the new client, who will require that the bank have the MIS in place to report its performance against these benchmarks.

Given these demands, for much of the 1990s multinationals offered lean pickings to inefficient local banks that were used to making returns from very different types of customers. Western multinationals were often funded by bank branches from their home country and perhaps one or two leading local banks, but the spreads on this business were seldom attractive. The more interesting risk management business usually went to leading trading and derivative banks, such as Bankers Trust (acquired by Deutsche Bank in November 1998) and JP Morgan, while most of the trade finance and cash management opportunity was covered by leading multinational providers like Citibank, HSBC, ABN Amro, and Standard Chartered.

Emerging Asian Global Companies

The next group is also a considerable customer segment: emerging Asia-based global companies, which typically account for 10–30 percent of local banks' corporate banking revenue. Both the majority and the largest of these conglomerates are headquartered in Japan. In 1997, based on sales, 85 of the top 100 Asian corporations were located there.

In 1997, the revenues of about 400 listed Japanese companies exceeded US$2 billion, and about 600 had revenues of US$0.5–2 billion. These companies are very active in Asia, and virtually form their own sub-segment. In some Asian countries, a few local banks serve the subsidiaries of these companies, but the local branches or offices of the large Japanese banks cover the bulk of their needs. Sanwa Bank and Fuji Bank, for example, have built up substantial branch networks in countries like Thailand, Malaysia, and Indonesia; these primarily serve the credit and service needs of Japanese subsidiaries.

Emerging global leaders from the rest of Asia include companies such as Acer and Evergreen of Taiwan and Singapore Telecom. In 1997, around 150 Asian companies outside Japan had revenues of more than US$2 billion, and another 550 had revenues of US$0.5–2 billion. Exhibit 3.7 provides a country-by-country breakdown.

While these companies may have a very strong local, country, and regional focus, and may only be taking their first steps globally, the sheer size of their operations and the complexity of their future needs force them to develop sophisticated financial strategies. These conglomerates can access capital markets locally and globally. As such, global investment banks and multinational banks court them aggressively. Again, the margins on this banking business were often unattractive during much of the 1990s, partly because the relatively low levels of perceived risk, compared with many other local opportunities, encouraged ferocious competition for the business.

Exhibit 3.7

Estimated Number of Companies in Asia: 1996
Thousands of companies, percent

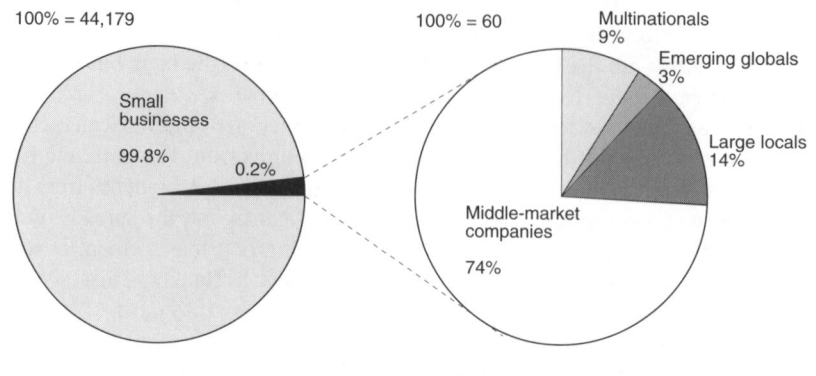

	Japan	Korea	Taiwan	Hong Kong	Singapore	Indonesia
Multinationals	380	60	278	296	898	172
Emerging globals	1,000	194	36	50	90	32
Large locals	5,000	642	403	350	288	100
Middle-market companies	15,000	4,160	2,000	10,000	1,712	500
Small businesses (thousands)	2,428	2,802	947	250	34	2,060
Total (thousands)	2,449	2,807	950	261	37	2,060

	Malaysia	Philippines	Thailand	India	China
Multinationals	462	62	1,066	276	1,273
Emerging globals	84	11	122	42	30
Large locals	500	51	97	227	450
Middle-market companies	3,000	844	704	1,741	5,000
Small businesses (thousands)	363	741	299	2,854	31,342
Total (thousands)	367	742	301	2,856	31,349

Source: Government statistics; McKinsey estimates

Many emerging Asian global companies hire sophisticated managers from Western companies to run their financial affairs. Since these companies usually draw on the practices of multinationals in selecting banks and banking product pricing, many local banks found, during much of the 1990s, that the relationship returns they could achieve from these customers mirrored those from major

Western corporations: the returns tended to be below the cost of capital of the banks, and the relationships were often uninspiring. In markets like Singapore, many local banks found that the leading local companies were not very attractive customers; they tried to maintain business with these conglomerates at a level that saved face — but no more.

Large Locals

This group of customers consists of large local companies. Their needs and capabilities fall short of those of emerging global companies, and as a group, they are far more attractive to bankers. These companies generate revenues of about US$100–500 million, and typically account for 20–40 percent of local banks' corporate banking revenues.

Around 5,000 companies — again, the bulk of the market — are in Japan, and local Japanese banks dominate servicing them. In the rest of Asia, there are around 3,000 of them (Exhibit 3.7). Although these companies may be able to access local capital markets, they have a harder time plugging into global markets. They cannot attract or retain sophisticated financial staff, and have weaker credit ratings and shorter track records — all of which add up to less attention from leading investment banks.

As a group, therefore, these companies are most important to the local banks in each country. They need funds, yet lack the options to force margins down to truly uneconomic levels. They place excess cash in bank deposits, but may not manage their cash as efficiently as possible, so banks earn returns on the "free float" of these balances. As these companies' cash management, trade finance, and risk management needs grow, local banks are well placed to build on their credit relationships and broaden revenue streams. When these companies finally tap local capital markets, local banks' corporate finance departments are well positioned to win at least part of the underwriting opportunity.

An exception to this segment's profile are high-technology companies. Because they are growing so fast, and operating in truly global markets, their risk management and financial knowledge often exceeds what their size suggests. These companies' managers know how to attract a broad range of banks to bid for their business. Computer component manufacturers in Taiwan like Siliconware Precision Industries may have annual sales of only US$250 million, but in many ways their financial behavior closely resembles that of the emerging global segment. This should not be surprising, as in many cases the managers of these companies come from emerging global companies or Western multinationals.

Middle-Market Companies

The middle-market client group is composed largely of local companies that may be involved in significant export activity. In the West, the middle market often includes companies with sales of US$25–250 million. Again, an exception is made for sectors that attract managers from larger companies, and therefore behave like larger companies. In Asia ex-Japan, however, this market is classified differently:

middle-market companies generate sales from US$5 million to US$10 million, up to US$100 million; over US$100 million moves a company into the large local segment in the eyes of many bankers.

Numerous companies make up the middle market. In 1997, in Japan alone, about 15,000 companies fell into this bracket. Hong Kong had approximately 10,000 such companies, and there were over 19,000 in the rest of Asia (see Exhibit 3.7). As a group, they account for 20–50 percent of local corporate banking revenues. Middle-market companies represent a significant share of the corporate banking market in the flexible and entrepreneurial economies like those of Taiwan and Hong Kong. The corporate banking departments of local banks often serve middle-market companies alongside multinationals and emerging Asian global companies. In fact their needs are different enough to warrant focused expertise and organizations within the bank. Middle-market companies rarely have access to capital markets, and depend on their bankers for growth — and even survival. In this context, client loyalty is much higher than in the larger sectors, but at the same time, local knowledge of the companies' true financial condition is critical to extending credit.

These companies' financial statements may be somewhat rudimentary or misleading. The old adage that Asian companies keep one set of books for the public, another for the tax man, and the real set for themselves, really applies to middle-market companies. Given these variables, it is not surprising that local banks dominate this market — and local can mean *very* local. With the best local contacts and knowledge, the smaller banks in Indonesia, Taiwan, and even China can beat the large city-based banks in Jakarta, Taipei, and Beijing. Multinational banks fear to tread in this sector, beyond providing well-documented and secured trade finance to some businesses, although during the 1997–1998 crisis, they discovered that the local banking systems offered significant deposits.

Small Businesses

Companies in this segment generate less than US$5–10 million in annual sales. The relationship between these companies and local branches is symbiotic: most companies depend on local branches for service and products, and most branch systems depend on small businesses' deposits to subsidize the unprofitable revenues of the majority of their retail customers. Given that during much of the 1990s foreign banks generally had very limited branch networks in Asia, they were not positioned well to serve these customers, except on an exceptional basis. Local banks dominated this group, which typically accounted for 10–20 percent of total corporate banking revenues.

The leading local banks justify extensive branch networks in each market going by the large number of companies that fall below the US$10 million sales mark (Exhibit 3.7). They range from start-up manufacturers to small traders, local retailers, and grocery stores. They are expensive to serve through branches, but banks are able to command good spreads on loans to them and on the deposits they leave in the branches. In fact, these deposits often account for as much two-thirds of total revenue. Basic operational services (such as depositing coins and currency at the branch) are very lucrative, as are basic payment and foreign exchange services. In many cases, the owners' personal banking activities are completely intertwined with those of the business. This complicates credit analysis, but creates further revenue opportunities from cross-selling corporate and personal services.

Property-Related Companies

There is arguably a sub-segment that cuts across all five of the previous segments. Many Asian companies are completely dependent on property-related revenues (construction companies, real estate developers, leasing companies). Many others rely on property as an important component of net worth, and use it extensively to collateralize loans for nonproperty purposes. Property-related issues are obviously at the forefront of bankers' minds when serving companies like Sun Hung Kai in Hong Kong. The same issues resurfaced when regarding how to bank the embattled retailer Theme, also of Hong Kong. In the middle of its crisis of declining store sales in 1997 and early 1998, it was Theme's valuable leases in Singapore that underpinned any (eventually false) hope for new financing for the group.

All over Asia, the value of real estate has oscillated wildly as economies developed. Huge bull markets have been followed by crashes when property revaluations became driven by speculation rather than by solid cash flows. Significant corporate customers have been built from real estate developers in each country. At the same time, major manufacturing and service businesses have used real estate holdings to back loans to expand their operating businesses. Corporate banking in Asia, therefore, has been enormously dependent on the understanding of real estate values and the factors that drive them. The crisis in Japan in the early 1990s, and the problems in Southeast Asia in 1997–1998 were partly due to banks funding real estate projects that were simply not viable.

Each corporate banking segment is important in its own right. Exhibit 3.8 estimates the distribution of corporate banking revenues in the five main segments, and provides a sense of relative priority by country. Ascribing an average assumed gross (before losses) return on loans, trade finance, deposits, and foreign exchange to each segment offers a very rough estimate of relative revenue distribution.

The range of customer behavior-types drives different banking skills and product requirements, and the various economics of the businesses. Across all segments, a consistent theme during much of the 1990s was that customers became more educated about new products and about finding opportunities for playing one bank off against another to obtain the best terms and conditions. Customer sophistication created openings in certain markets (enabling some multinational trading banks to find new markets for their derivative products), but also generated fresh threats for domestic banks that had long protected market share and margins — and survived on customer inertia.

This cozy pattern came under pressure in all segments during the 1990s. The crisis in Japan early in the decade, and in Korea and Southeast Asia in 1997 and 1998, further educated corporate customers on the importance of diversifying their funding sources and seeking alternative channels for advice and products.

Exhibit 3.8

Estimated Corporate Banking Revenues by Segment and Country: 1996
US$ billions, percent

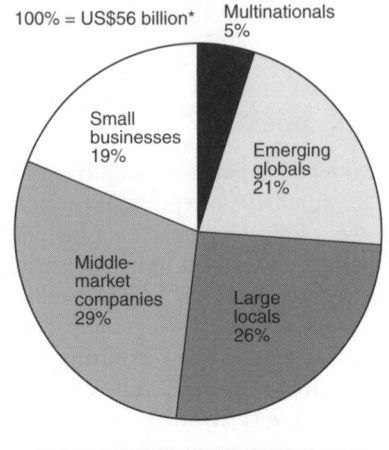

	Japan	Korea	Taiwan	Hong Kong	Singapore	Indonesia
Multinationals	1%	1%	4%	2%	3%	6%
Emerging globals	27%	35%	4%	6%	29%	19%
Large locals	22%	41%	25%	20%	39%	17%
Middle-market companies	24%	11%	49%	60%	21%	30%
Small businesses	26%	12%	18%	12%	8%	28%
100% =	$18.1	4.7	4.2	2.9	1.9	2.0

	Malaysia	Philippines	Thailand	India	China
Multinationals	4%	6%	9%	6%	13%
Emerging globals	20%	37%	20%	31%	11%
Large locals	23%	24%	34%	28%	23%
Middle-market companies	32%	21%	23%	18%	34%
Small businesses	21%	12%	14%	17%	19%
100% =	$3.0	1.3	5.0	2.0	10.6

* Based on data for the top 500 banks in Asia, which do not include cooperatives or finance and leasing companies, and excluding offshore loan books. Total revenues may be understated by up to 15 percent. Revenues are pre-loan loss provisions.

Source: Standard & Poor's DRI; Bank for International Settlements; International Monetary Fund; government statistics; McKinsey analysis

Although blessed by strong growth and good margins, corporate banking in Asia had become tougher by the end of the 1990s.

Clouds on the Horizon: Competition and Risk

As we have seen, corporate banking across its many customer segments in Asia was a fundamentally attractive business in the 1980s and early 1990s. But two clouds on the horizon threatened returns. The first was increasing competition.

Heightened Competition

The returns and growth during this period had encouraged most international banks to put Asia firmly on the agenda for growth. As a result, practically any bank that considered itself a major force had multiple offices across the region, and as we have seen, many substantially increased their regional resources. At the same time, local banks were expanding and new banks were being set up — specifically in Indonesia and Taiwan. The increase in multinational bank capacity focused on multinational subsidiaries and the more creditworthy locals, that is, generally the larger companies. As a result, returns in many of these segments declined during the period. For instance, in Taiwan the influx of foreign competitors, combined with the growth strategies of the 16 new banks established in 1991, meant that corporate loan margins declined dramatically in the middle of the decade and the market became fundamentally unattractive. This activity had a knock-on effect across all segments as local banks exited the large corporates and focused resources on the middle market and small businesses. Competition increased there too, and returns came under pressure.

During this period, regulators in many markets focused on providing maximum protection for their banks. They wanted the banks to be as strong as possible when the WTO force open the markets, which they expected would happen early in the 21st century. The reality was that in corporate banking, international competition was already affecting the returns of local banks. The trend was for markets to become more competitive.

Intensified Risk

The second threat on the horizon was that in their eagerness to retain market share and build revenues, banks extended credit to companies or situations that did not warrant it. In many countries, the whole economy was becoming overleveraged — in some cases to both short-term and foreign currency debt. In Korea, for example, an amazing 46 percent, or US$160 billion of total corporate debt in 1997 was short-term. Thus exposed, these economies were very vulnerable to spikes in interest rates or declines in the values of local currencies, particularly relative to the U.S. dollar or the yen.

The banks faced systemic risk from devaluation and economic slowdown, but in the face of day-to-day competition were inclined to book loans now and hope "all would be well on the night." Some of the leading competitors saw enormous growth in their loan portfolios in the middle of the decade. In Malaysia, for instance, Maybank and the Arab-Malaysian Banking Group grew their portfolios by 70 and 185 percent respectively, between 1994 and 1997. Others were even more rash. In the last half of 1997, Sime Bank grew its portfolio by 54 percent.

Another group of competitors fueling the problem were those on the edge of the corporate lending markets. They included family-owned banks in many markets that were providing insider loans to related group companies without undertaking any real credit analysis, new commercial banks in Indonesia, finance companies in Thailand, and merchant banks in Korea. None had real competitive advantages; with higher funding costs and weaker staff skills than the leading local and international commercial banks, they could compete only by extending credit on terms and conditions that the others would not consider. By 1997, these banks held not insignificant percentages of corporate loans in Indonesia (8 percent to banks owned by relatives of the former President Suharto), Thailand (40 percent to finance companies), and Korea (13 percent to merchant banks). By 1998, these institutions were at the heart of the IMF-sponsored efforts to clean up the financial imbroglio in each country.

When the bubble burst, first, local banks in Japan had to write off about US$475 billion in bad loans, most of them corporate, between 1990 and 1996. They represented 150 basis points in 1996 write-offs in a business where average returns before losses were below 1 percent. In Korea, nonperforming loans in 1997 and 1998 were estimated at 25–50 percent. In Southeast Asia, the story was no better, with nonperforming loans ranging from 25 percent in Malaysia to 30 percent in Thailand, and 50–70 percent in Indonesia. Assuming that in most cases approximately 60 percent of these nonperforming loans will not be recoverable, loan losses could exceed US$800 billion when fully accounted for in the first decade of the next century. At a potential write-off of more than 10 percent of loan books across Asia, this effectively wiped out the capitalization of many domestic banks at the end of the 1990s.

Winning in the New Environment

The banking crises in Japan, Korea, and Southeast Asia created new corporate banking environments in those markets, and reinforced trends in the other Asian markets. Corporate banking must change if it is to become a sustainable business. But, the market will remain one of great opportunity for those who remember the basic rules of sound banking.

Continuing and New Opportunities

Most economists agree that Asia will resume fast growth in the first decade of the next century. Looking forward to 2005, consensus economic forecasts are for average real GDP growth rates of 7.7 percent in China, 6.4 percent in Malaysia, 5.5 percent in Thailand, 5.4 percent in both Korea and Taiwan, 5.4 percent in Singapore, 4.8 percent in Indonesia, 4.8 percent in the Philippines, 4.7 percent in India, 4.6 percent in Hong Kong, and 2.5 percent in Japan. These figures compare with consensus forecasts of 4.7 percent for Latin America, 2.3 percent for Western

Europe, and 2.2 percent for the U.S. Growth in Asia will continue to underpin attractive banking opportunities.

As a result of this growth, and assuming a reasonable loan-growth-to-GDP-growth multiplier, it is likely that in real terms, the overall corporate loan market will probably expand from about US$7 trillion in 1997 to US$12–15 trillion by 2010. By 2010, corporate banking is likely to generate in excess of US$150 billion in annual revenues across Asia.

More Companies Will Seek Financial Advice

Significant infrastructure needs across the region, as well as demand from emerging global corporates, leading Western firms, and the myriad of middle-market and small businesses, will continue to drive loan demand. The good news is that as many of these companies or their managers were humbled in 1997 and 1998, they will look more to bankers for financial advice and balance sheet guidance. This will create opportunities for more interesting product sales, such as a range of risk-management products and longer-term debt products. New securitization opportunities will emerge as banks work hard to manage their balance sheets more aggressively and structure loans for sale to interested investors. Corporate banking promises to be a fundamentally more innovative business in Asia in the next decade.

Margins will trend towards the example of the West. The major creditworthy blue chips will be able to command very fine spreads, having proved during the 1997–1998 crisis that they really are strong players. On the other hand, formerly attractive names that relied on the implicit guarantee of the government (Korean *chaebol* and major Thai corporates) and that performed poorly during the crisis, will find much wider margins on loans.

At the same time, the whole market is likely to remain cyclical. For instance, in 1998 Hong Kong experienced a precipitous decline in bank lending and liquidity for corporates. With the general wariness of all lenders, and local bank weakness, competition will decrease from 1998 to 2000. Loan and foreign exchange spreads will widen in most markets, increasing loan-related fees available to stronger long-term players like Standard Chartered and HSBC. However, by the first few years of the next millennium, bankers will perceive that the worst of the bad credits in many markets have been dealt with, that corporate managers have learned to be prudent, and that growth in many countries is resuming. Margins are likely to decline — until the next credit crisis. It is possible to visualize great opportunities for growth and profits, but they will be earned by those who are prepared to abide by the new rules.

Standard Chartered: Creating its Recipe for Success

The crisis in Korea and Southeast Asia in 1997–1998 produced many corporate banking casualties. But it also showed up those that had adjusted to the new environment. An interesting example is Standard Chartered.

Standard Chartered had suffered enormously in the late 1980s and early 1990s from bad loans and declining investment banking competitiveness. As a result, in 1992 it suffered write-offs of US$650 million. Its attractive, grandfathered network in Hong Kong, Singapore, and Malaysia (as well as Africa and the Middle East), and respected brand name made Standard Chartered look ripe for takeover. Yet, by 1997, prior to the crisis, the management team had engineered such dramatic improvements that the company reported profits exceeding US$900 million, and the share price had risen dramatically, from as low as US$1 in 1991, to around US$15. The crisis shook investor confidence for a while in 1997, but by early 1998, as the resilience of the business became clear and the quality of risk management held firm, the shares bounced back to close to US$13. Additional general worries about Asia and concerns about global financial markets that lowered all bank share prices dramatically drove the price down to about US$6.15 in September 1998, but by January 1999 it rebound again to US$13.

What had Standard Chartered done to bolster the bank? On one side, the management team had cleaned up the bank's overall portfolio, selling off distractions from the core business and refocusing capital and human resources on the best opportunities. This resulted in tremendous growth in retail revenues. On the corporate side, the improvements were no less dramatic — and brave. Against the prevailing fashion, Standard Chartered recognized in the mid-1990s that it could not be a leader in investment banking, and largely exited that business and securities trading in 1995. At the same time, Group chief executive Malcolm Williamson laid down a clear policy that Standard Chartered would not be involved in Asian corporate property lending. This excluded the bank from vast areas of the market, but Williamson had recognized the risks, and that Standard Chartered had no special insights to protect it from any future bursting of the bubble.

Denied access to the "hot" areas of the early 1990s — investment banking and property lending — Standard Chartered's corporate bankers had to look elsewhere. The bank became a leader in cash management and trade finance products during this period. Its Global Trade Redesign project became a benchmark in the industry for how to improve service and productivity in trade business. Before the 1997 crisis hit, the bank's loan losses were relatively light — loan losses increased from approximately US$100 million to US$150 million between 1996 and 1997, and shot up to US$300 million for the first half of 1998 after the crisis hit. The bank benefited from a wave of deposits from concerned customers of weaker local banks, and saw margins widen rapidly on lending, foreign exchange, and trade finance as other banks withdrew from the market. Focusing on the basics and on areas where the bank had competitive advantages served Standard Chartered well.

New Rules for Winners

The new corporate banking rules will naturally follow the fundamental dynamics of the business. That is, competitors will need to recognize that the market is inherently full of risk, and that the incursion of investment banks into the market will only increase risk by removing some of the most attractive credits from bank portfolios. Focusing on markets where a bank can have a credible, sustainable advantage because it has unique insights into credit risk will be critical in the future. "Me-too banking", based on relationships and crony capitalism, will be increasingly hard to justify. So, too, will plain-vanilla lending to the best credits once competition returns, as it is likely to produce very low returns and destroy shareholder value.

Effective Organization Is the Key

Given this more transparent and competitive world, each bank will have to seek a special customer base or product strength. In its chosen market, a bank must access the best information on the risks it is taking, consider how it will evaluate those risks with regard to completing a transaction, and determine at what price it will close transactions. Superior risk and reward management, based on skillfully accessing and analyzing information about corporate credits, will be a critical element of success.

Future winners will recognize the importance of effective organization to support these more focused strategies. To win the business they target, manage credit effectively, and (optionally) have the ability to securitize loans and place them in the market, the best banks will concentrate on designing and managing their organizations professionally. Winning banks will align their organizational approaches to their chosen markets and products. They will recruit and train relationship bankers to cover target client groups and cross-sell the range of products required to generate attractive relationship returns. Successful banks will almost certainly set up focused business units with skills, training, and evaluation and compensation processes that will target discrete segments of the market.

As is already true for the strongest banks, large corporate and probably middle-market banking will be pulled out of branches and organized centrally, with a few outposts to cover far-flung clients. Centralized credit departments organizationally separated from the marketing teams will be set up to drive credit policies and monitor adherence to them. Common product and credit processes will be applied to all clients in each business unit, wherever they are served. As far as possible, banks will try to create centers of excellence in marketing and credit. For large corporations, this may mean organizing coverage by industry group. Even in serving small-business customers, where local branch coverage is essential, the best banks will consider introducing statistically driven credit-scoring systems that help branches make credit decisions much more rationally than in the past.

Finally, improved MIS will be required across all segments of the market. Bankers will need to know where they are lending (many banks in the midst of the 1997–1998 crises discovered that they did not know their total exposure to some distressed conglomerates because their MIS had not identified the many subsidiaries to which they had lent), and what the total returns will be on risk-adjusted assets. Relationships will need to be coded by industry and collateral type, and loans by maturity and repricing structure, so that credit units can undertake simple tests of portfolio sensitivity to new economic conditions. Some important considerations are: how will the portfolio behave if the local currency declines by 15 percent? What if oil prices increase (or fall) by 25 percent? What will happen to the portfolio if 3-month interest rates spike by 100 basis points?

To many bankers in successful corporate banks in the West, these considerations for winning in corporate banking in the new environment may sound simple and old hat. But that is the point. There will be no magic among the winners in this environment, just rigorous execution of the best practices.

Opportunities for Local and Multinational Banks

Focusing on the basics, tailored to the unique situation and opportunities of each bank, will serve commercial banks well in the new corporate banking environment. After the 1997–1998 crisis has worked its way through the system, the remaining banks will face more open markets and foreign competition, but also renewed growth and opportunities. Those that have the discipline to build for the long term, and to align their organizations to produce long-term profits, will prosper. Those that go for the quick kill and never build winning corporate organizations, will be the stories of the next crisis.

These basic lessons apply equally to local banks and multinationals, even though each will have very different customer and product opportunities. Locals will be naturally advantaged in the middle-market and small-business segments, and through regional alliances can build attractive trade finance business. Big multinational banks will have a natural advantage in the large corporate segments, where their sizable lending limits, sophisticated products, and highly skilled staff will win most of the business. These banks will be very strong contenders in the systems-dependent cash management and trade finance businesses. They will also have leading positions in any capital market-related funding or foreign exchange businesses, but will face serious competition from investment banks.

Because corporate banking covers so many customer and product segments, there is plenty of room for both local and multinational banks to find unique, defensible franchises or positions in the market. Parallel to the creation through mergers and acquisitions of very large corporate banks around the world, some of the eventual local winners may be the result of regional mergers. Other leading local Asian banks may eventually be folded into large global banks, leading the Asian corporate banking arm of these global players. This will be a way for these large global banks to access the middle-market and small-business segments in Asia. Whatever the final combinations, corporate banking in Asia in the first decade of the 21st century will see winning and losing banks — local and multinational.

4

INVESTMENT BANKING:
NO ESCAPE FROM GLOBAL TRENDS

Sometimes the smallest things bring the big picture to light.

In the early 1990s, Jardine Fleming, the financial services joint venture between the Jardine Group and Robert Fleming, was looking for senior management housing in Hong Kong. A highly desirable location, and indeed one of the most expensive, was The Peak, offering views of the city and Victoria Harbour below. The Peak was commonly the domain of local tycoons, regional heads of multinational corporations and banks, and senior British civil servants. Jardine Fleming initiated a housing search expecting to recognize the names of the would-be neighbors to its senior management. It came as a surprise, therefore, that many of the homes recently on the market had been taken by unfamiliar employees of U.S. investment banks.

Further checks revealed that these unknowns were often personnel who were one or two layers down in organizations such as Merrill Lynch, Goldman Sachs, and Morgan Stanley. Peak perks for personnel outside top management ranks were unheard of in British institutions, which long had reasonably unfettered access to Asia's emerging investment banking markets.[1] Jardine Fleming and other British institutions grumbled over the unorthodox practices of the U.S. investment banks, which were spoiling costs in the labor market and not so subtly shifting the way investment banking was played and won in Asia.

The acrimony between the incumbent British and the newly arrived U.S. investment banks flourished throughout much of the 1990s, as the battle to lock up corporate relationships, skilled staff, and underwriting transactions played out. The British brokerages and banks, which drew a number of their stock analysts from journalist ranks, leveraged press connections to portray the U.S. firms as "fair weather friends," remaining in Asia only as long as the times were good. In 1991, Morgan Stanley scaled back its Hong Kong operations from 170 to 135 personnel. In 1994, Goldman Sachs executed a temporary retrenchment. The local press heralded these moves as signs that the Americans were closing shop. To the consternation of the British incumbents, the U.S. investment banks stayed put through the 1990s and became the single largest force in arranging cross-border capital flows to Asia. In late 1998, Jardine sold its 50 percent holding in Jardine Fleming to Robert Fleming in exchange for a 15 percent stake in Robert Fleming. For Jardine, investment banking was clearly becoming a business that required connections beyond Asia to succeed.

The forces that propelled global U.S. investment banks to the top in the 1990s will extend into Asia's domestic markets in the first decade of the 21st century. By 2010, domestic investment banks will have lost regulatory protection against foreign competition for entirely domestic investment banking activities. Victory in

---

[1] Investment banking, as described in this chapter, includes all debt and equity underwriting and financial advisory activities (such as mergers and acquisitions), but excludes proprietary trading and stockbroking, which are covered in Chapter 5.

cross-border and domestic transactions will go to those institutions that consistently offer the best problem-solving skills and cost of funding to corporate clients, develop the deepest relationships with institutional investors, and construct sufficient organizational breadth and flexibility to capture the lion's share of volume and profits as clients' needs shift.

Intense competition, along with the challenges of building truly superior skills, will shrink the number of investment banking aspirants in Asia. Prior to the 1997–1998 crisis, there were over 100 global and domestic firms — including investment banks, commercial banks, and securities houses — attempting to garner a slice of the US$5 billion in annual Asian investment banking revenues. By the end of 1998, with underwriting volumes near decade lows, up to a third of international and domestic competitors had either exited Asian investment banking or significantly reduced their resources. By 2010, only five to ten global banks, a few new intraregional players, and a handful of domestic competitors in each local market will likely capture sufficient transaction volumes to generate attractive investment banking returns.

Market leaders will benefit from the substantial restructuring of economies in the wake of the Asian crisis and the continued disintermediation of corporate funding through the capital markets. By 2010, annual investment banking revenues in Asia will likely approach US$15 billion, enabling top competitors to continue to afford The Peak address for their high-performing employees.

Asia's Capital Flows: Too Good an Opportunity to Miss?

Throughout most of the 1990s, investment banking tended to capture more headlines than any other banking business in Asia. Investment banking lends itself to good journalistic drama as it involves the high-profile business elite, large salaries and bonuses, transactions in the hundreds of millions of dollars, and the intrigue of entire teams jumping from one institution to the next. But the drama is ultimately part of a larger story: the desire of financial institutions, both global and domestic, to lock up profits in the funding and investment channels that have been — and will continue to be — a core component of Asia's long-term economic growth. To understand why so many financial institutions poured resources into investment banking in the 1990s, one must understand the fundamental forces that gave so many hopes for large long-term profits in both cross-border and domestic investment banking.

Cross-Border Investment Banking: Filling the Funding Gap

Growth and development were two priorities on the agenda of virtually every CEO and government official throughout Asia, barring Japan, in the 1990s. With Asia's relatively low cost of labor and increasingly easy access to the largest Western export markets, Asian corporations had the opportunity to build substantial businesses within the course of a decade. The fastest track to seemingly ever-increasing profits was to secure business licenses and line up the required funding for investments. The Asian governments' best means to consolidate their own power and legitimacy was to support the emerging growth miracle by ensuring there was sufficient infrastructure to advance industrialization and to attract foreign investment.

The West, and the capital it could willingly provide, was an essential component of Asia's growth agenda. Throughout the 1990s, Asian demand for capital, outside Japan, exceeded the supply of funds available locally. Infrastructure investment requirements alone ran into hundreds of billions of dollars. In 1997, economists estimated that investments in infrastructure, from highways to power plants, would require US$250 billion annually to 2010. This meant that, even with Asia's high savings rates, more than 25 percent of annual savings would have to be channeled into infrastructure to meet local funding needs. In the 1990s, domestic savings (held mostly in bank deposits) were strained as it kept up with demand from just private-sector borrowing. Most of Asia's domestic economies could not generate sufficient new capital to finance their own growth.

Moreover, many Asian countries lacked the mechanisms to provide the blocks of long-term funding required by infrastructure projects and large corporations. Local banks lacked the credit and pricing skills, for example, to lend 10- or 15-year money. The region's emerging bond markets were underdeveloped, with yield curves rarely extending beyond 5 years. Local stock markets in the early 1990s were often too small to handle large public listings. This was particularly true in the case of the privatization of the largest state-owned enterprises, through which governments sought to raise funding for immediate infrastructure needs. When China, for example, launched the listing of 20 large enterprises in the early 1990s — when its stock market capitalization was less than US$40 billion — it was forced to look to New York, London, and Hong Kong for market depth.

Lack of capital market depth was not a problem limited to emerging markets. Singapore had to go abroad when it increased public holdings in Singapore Telecom in the mid-1990s, as did Taiwan when it privatized China Steel and other big government-owned entities. Asian governments had few immediate options for deepening their domestic equity markets. Outside Japan, Singapore, and Malaysia, Asian markets lacked a fundamental component of stable long-term market development: domestic institutional investors. Unlike markets in the West where institutional investors managed large sums of pension and insurance money, most of Asia in the 1990s was in the initial stages of forming such institutionalized capital. The dearth of institutional capital made it difficult to place equities or debt securities with investors that took a long-term perspective and would not necessarily dump new listings at the first sign of trouble. So governments allowed foreign institutional investors into domestic markets, but they limited foreign ownership of domestic shares to 10–40 percent.

Thus, there was a fundamental demand for Western capital, sourced directly in Western debt and equity markets. Such demand was welcomed by many Western institutional investors, who preferred to invest in companies that issued on U.S. and European exchanges and hence, had to comply with more rigorous disclosure requirements. Towards the mid-1990s, the demand for Western capital remained strong, though for equities, direct sourcing in Western markets became less important. This was because many of the largest Western institutional investors set up operations in Asia to buy shares directly, increasing the availability of cross-border capital in the local markets. Global investment banks that served Western institutional investors, at home and in Asia, took advantage of their access to these investors in forging relationships with Asian corporations and governments. The growing sophistication of Asian public and private issuers facilitated the capital intermediation role undertaken by global investment banks.

A number of Asian governments and corporations pursued cross-border debt and equity issues in the 1990s, ahead of actual demand for capital. Governments such as Thailand's worked extensively with JP Morgan in the early 1990s to build a reputation with global institutional investors in the international debt markets. By securing a sovereign rating and liquidity in the global markets, the Thai government cleared a path for Thai corporations to receptive investors and fair pricing for future corporate debentures.

Domestic corporations similarly undertook strategic cross-border equity and debt issuance. Asia's best blue-chip corporations and financial institutions often had access to competitively priced domestic loans to meet most of their short- and medium-term funding needs. But both as a hedge and as a matter of personal pride, large privately owned institutions sought listings on international capital markets. Family-owned groups from Taiwan to Indonesia labored to meet foreign listing requirements, which often involved changes in accounting practices and an unprecedented degree of performance disclosure, in order to win access to new investors in the U.S., Europe, and Japan. The logic in doing so was to build funding channels that over the long term could provide more alternatives to raise capital efficiently as and when needed. In fact, many of these showcase transactions cost the corporate issuers more than if they had simply turned to traditional bank loans. Whereas a Thai blue-chip corporation may have paid 25–50 basis points over the London Interbank Offered Rate (LIBOR) for a bank loan, it was willing to pay in excess of 100 basis points over LIBOR for issuing a corporate debenture in New York. Many, however, were willing to pay the price to create greater funding flexibility, as well as to satisfy a craving for global recognition.

The fundamental demand for cross-border capital, coupled with issuers' desire to create new funding channels, were needs that global investment banks were pleased to meet. Senior vice presidents in investment banking divisions from Tokyo to New York to London salivated at the prospects offered by Asia's funding gap. Cover stories in major periodicals about the rise of China and the growth miracle throughout Asia in the early 1990s spawned intense interest among global institutions to build an Asian presence. For those sitting more than 5,000 miles away, the prospect of one day serving the thousands of state-owned enterprises in China alone prompted calls for a major effort in Asia. In 1993, cross-border debt and equity issuance in Asia ex-Japan topped US$26 billion, a threefold increase in volume over all preceding years (Exhibit 4.1). The emergence of activity in Greater China and Southeast Asia in the early 1990s could not have come at a better time for Western investment bankers in Asia. Many had built a significant presence in Japan only to be disappointed when the bubble burst and no immediate recovery was in sight. With the rest of Asia heating up, literally hundreds of investment

Exhibit 4.1

Asian Cross-Border Underwriting Volumes: 1992–1997
US$ billions

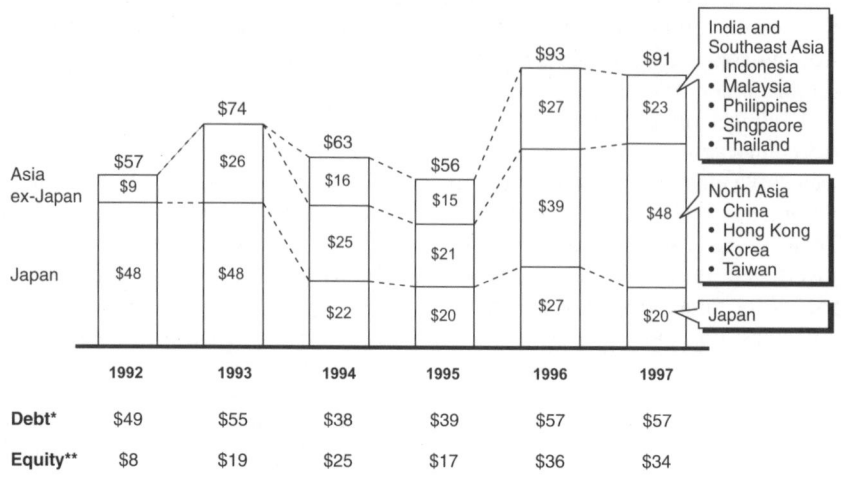

	1992	1993	1994	1995	1996	1997
Debt*	$49	$55	$38	$39	$57	$57
Equity**	$8	$19	$25	$17	$36	$34

* Fixed and floating with maturity >1 year.
** Includes IPOs, right issues, and convertible bonds; does not include private placements.

Source: IFR Omnibase; Japan's Ministry of Finance; McKinsey analysis

bankers were redeployed from Tokyo, mostly to Hong Kong, to develop business throughout the region. The supply to meet Asian demand was quickly mobilized.

This early 1990s excitement among bankers over Asia was in fact part of larger aspirations taking shape in the world's largest financial institutions. A broad range of firms, including ABN Amro, BZW, Credit Suisse First Boston (CSFB), Deutsche Bank, Goldman Sachs, Hongkong and Shanghai Banking Corporation (HSBC), ING, JP Morgan, Merrill Lynch, Morgan Stanley, Natwest, Nomura, Salomon, and UBS, were looking to create truly global investment banking businesses. They had a vision of businesses that were able to originate and structure transactions anywhere in the world and subsequently distribute new issues to investors around the globe. The logic for doing so was that global origination capabilities would allow investment banks to build the strongest relationships with the largest institutional investors, who were beginning to invest globally. By building strong relationships with the world's largest investors, investment banks would be able to offer private and public issuers the broadest placement capabilities and, by correlation, the lowest cost of funds.

These global aspirations were launched by leading competitors from their home markets in the U.S., Europe, and Japan, and extended to the newly opening economies of Eastern Europe, Latin America, and Asia. Such aspirations were realizable only if Japan and the West could supply readily available capital for investment in the world's emerging markets — as was the case in the early 1990s. In the U.S., the post-war baby boom generation was reaching its peak saving years and rapidly expanding the investment pool. In Europe, the long tradition of investing offshore continued, with a growing cache of funds accumulating in pension schemes. In Japan, large institutional investors, such as insurance companies, began to experiment with offshore investing. However, the burst economic bubble, limited international experience, and tight regulations restricting investment risk muted direct Japanese participation in cross-border capital flows to emerging markets. Japanese capital was an important part of the Asia growth story in the 1990s, but it came largely in the form of corporate loans from Japanese commercial banks.

In the case of the U.S., not only was capital readily available but investors actively sought the higher returns that emerging markets could provide. Common wisdom at the beginning of the 1990s dictated that the U.S. stock market was unlikely to generate double-digit returns in the decade ahead. Slowing growth and moderate corporate profits led pundits to believe that the U.S. economy was maturing to a stage where equity investors could expect returns in the region of 8–10 percent. For the baby boomers approaching retirement, lower returns presented a real problem. A history of relatively low savings rates meant that Americans required returns of consistently above 12 percent to finance their golden years. International investment became the trumpeted solution. In theory, it offered higher returns and a means to diversify investments across markets that were not correlated to U.S. performance. For Asia, growing U.S. interest in international investments marked a significant opportunity. A one percentage point change in the allocation of U.S. retail mutual fund investments, for example, represented as much as US$30 billion in capital in the early 1990s.

Of course, as hindsight would prove, the U.S. stock market would offer more than single-digit returns, thanks to one of the longest bull runs in modern history. At the start of the 1990s, however, the alignment of macroeconomic forces fueled the ambitions of international investment bankers: Asia needed the capital, the West had it, and the investment banks themselves were committed to the region. For many international financial institutions, the prospect of intermediating Asia's long-term funding gap was viewed as important virgin territory in an emerging battle for global investment banking profits that was too good to be missed.

Domestic Investment Banking: Spreading the Wealth

From the 1960s and 1970s, Asian governments systematically established corporate banking systems to channel national savings to emerging corporate interests. The governments of each country gave certain banks specific lending mandates to promote certain segments of the economy, ranging from large-scale industrial development to small-business entrepreneurs. By the late 1980s, however, government-directed lending became increasingly complex as economies advanced and diversified. Governments looking to the West for development models appreciated the importance of establishing domestic capital markets to improve efficiency in capital allocation and to provide individuals with an opportunity to share in national wealth creation. Their efforts unleashed a wave of domestic equity and debt issues that outpaced cross-border investment banking volumes throughout the 1990s in all Asian countries, with the periodic exceptions of Indonesia and China.

In the 1980s and 1990s, governments across Asia tried to set up efficient and robust equity and debt capital markets. While understanding that the creation of local capital markets would not entirely alleviate their countries' funding gaps, they hoped to unlock some of the value of the corporate economy and create greater liquidity for further capital investments. In places like China, for example, domestic equity markets were viewed as an important means to build new funding channels for private- and state-owned corporations that were starved of capital as the dominant government banking system choked on years of accumulated bad debt. The establishment of debt markets also gave high-growth countries, such as China, new tools to control inflation and manage economic development. Family businesses that had come to dominate the corporate landscape of Taiwan, Hong Kong, India, and Southeast Asia were enthusiastic about tapping local stock markets to cash out on a portion of their accumulated assets. Indeed, for all but the best blue-chip corporations, which had the financial credentials to tap international capital markets, domestic markets offered an important alternative source of equity and debt financing.

The shared desire of governments and corporations to develop domestic capital markets resulted in an explosion of activity in the 1990s. At the start of that decade, there were 9,700 listed corporations throughout Asia. By the end of 1997, that figure had increased to 16,600. In China, the number of listed corporations grew from less than ten to 720 during this period. New listings combined with capital appreciation rocketed the total capitalization of Asia's stock markets from US$3.4 trillion in 1990 to US$4.9 trillion in 1996. Without Japan, Asia's dramatic growth becomes even more apparent: market capitalization grew threefold to reach US$1.9 trillion in 1996.

By mid-decade, Asian governments had established market mechanisms that could handle the 1996 peak issuance of over US$600 billion in the domestic debt and equity markets (Exhibit 4.2). Though Japan accounted for two-thirds of this 1996 total, the other markets were coming on strong. While the large internationally placed transactions handled by global investment banks captured the headlines, the domestic capital markets represented the largest underwriting volumes in the 1990s. In 1996, domestic equity issuance in Asia ex-Japan — including initial public offerings (IPOs) and rights issues — totaled US$36 billion, compared with US$27 billion in cross-border issues. In debt markets, local issues' dominance was far greater. Issuance of cross-border bonds in Asia ex-Japan totaled US$39 billion in 1996, which paled next to the US$190 billion raised domestically. That year is largely representative of the entire 1990s, when local equity raising outpaced cross-border issues in Asia ex-Japan by two to one, and domestic debt issues outpaced cross-border transactions by at least four to one. In Japan, the domestic investment banking market exceeded cross-border transaction volumes by even greater multiples.

The investor demand that both enabled and fueled new domestic issues in Asia throughout the 1990s differed in many ways from its cross-border cousin. The buyers of cross-border debt and equity issues were largely institutions — insurance

Exhibit 4.2

Asian Domestic Underwriting Volumes: 1992–1997
US$ billions

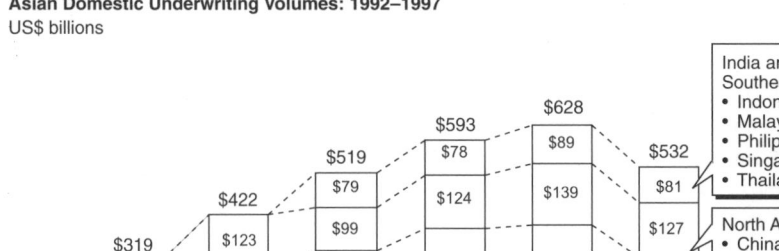

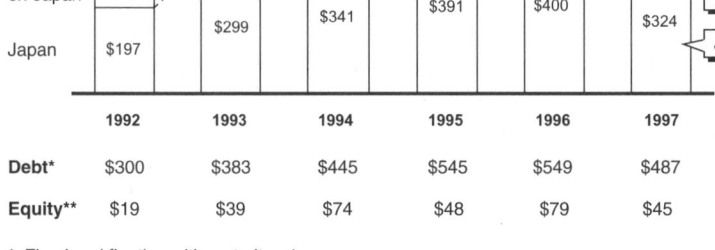

	1992	1993	1994	1995	1996	1997
Debt*	$300	$383	$445	$545	$549	$487
Equity**	$19	$39	$74	$48	$79	$45

* Fixed and floating with maturity >1 year.
** Includes IPOs, right issues, and convertible bonds; does not include private placements.

Source: IFR Omnibase; Japan's Ministry of Finance; McKinsey analysis

companies, asset managers, and hedge fund operators. The key enabler in Asia's domestic equity markets was the person on the street. Domestic IPOs created a public feeding frenzy in markets from Kuala Lumpur to Shanghai in the years leading up to the 1997–1998 financial crisis. Lotteries were often used to allocate new listings to the public. Thousands of people lined up at dawn — in queues extending several city blocks — to get lottery forms that would enable them to get a piece of the action.

Why did individuals want to buy into a new IPO? Did they like the company's fundamentals? Were they impressed with the company's management? More often than not, they had no view on the company or its management. They were there to make money, and for the better part of the 1990s they were not disappointed. In many countries across Asia, new equity issues were listed at a discount to ensure successful placement. In Malaysia, companies actually had to list at pre-determined earnings multiples set by the government. As such, individuals did not need to worry about the company's fundamentals to stand a good chance of making quick profits. Indeed, the combination of discounted listings and a lottery allocation system ensured almost immediate profits. New listings throughout Asia were often over-subscribed by several hundred times, creating strong buying power in the first weeks of a new issue. A case in point was the 1997 listing of Beijing Enterprises in Hong Kong. This new issue was oversubscribed by 1,276 times. The demand was so great that banks and the Hong Kong Monetary Authority had to cooperate closely to ensure that there was adequate liquidity in the financial system to provide the US$28 billion required to fund the lottery subscriptions backed by cash. Not surprisingly, investment banks often made more money on the interest rate float from the underlying cash subscriptions than they made in actual underwriting fees.

In the absence of large domestic institutional investors, the person on the street often accounted for more than 70 percent of new equity issue purchases throughout Asia. Japan was the exception, given its reasonably developed institutional investor base. In China, where equity markets had barely taken shape in 1990, an estimated 30 million individuals owned and traded stocks by 1997. For governments across Asia, the experiment in developing domestic stock markets was an effective means of spreading corporate success and wealth across the broader population. In rapidly growing economies, the fact that individual investors were not buying on fundamentals posed little concern for governments overseeing their capital markets' development, at least prior to the onset of the financial crisis.

The relative success of developing domestic equity markets was harder to repeat in the debt markets. Individual investors in Asia were less interested in buying bonds. Marginally higher interest rates than those paid by local banks were not enough to attract individuals to the bond market. The possibility of earning capital gains as a result of changes in interest rate policy was lost on most. Only in a few markets, such as in China, did retail investors take up substantial portions of bond offerings due to a lack of investment alternatives. Hence, Asian governments relied largely on official policies and highly effective moral suasion to spearhead the development of domestic debt markets in the 1990s. They often required local banks, insurance companies, and other financial intermediaries to buy bonds to fulfill capital adequacy requirements. While in pure volume terms the domestic debt markets dwarfed the domestic equity markets, in terms of total capital raised, they lacked comparable vibrancy and liquidity.

Given strong growth in domestic underwriting volumes, the pre-crisis 1990s was clearly a good time to be a leading domestic investment bank. With many issues oversubscribed, underwriting risk was quite limited. The competitive hurdle was set by other domestic competitors. Everywhere but Japan and Hong Kong, regulatory barriers limited foreign competitors to cross-border transactions. The largest challenge for domestic intermediaries was to install adequate procedures and relationships to stay on the right side of the regulators, who carefully monitored their capital market experiments. There were, of course, bumps along the way. In India, during 1994–1995, fraudulent share certificates flooded the market and undermined investor confidence. In Southeast Asia, allocations of new issues occasionally fell victim to manipulation by insiders. But for the domestic stock brokerages, banks, and bills companies that acted as investment banking intermediaries for debt and equity issues, the strong wave of underwriting momentum and correspondingly strong local investor demand created a battle for market share.

Elusive Profits in the Fight for Cross-Border Dominance

Throughout the 1990s, most international competitors in Asian investment banking had their eyes trained on the future. Armed with projections that supported the long-term growth of Asia and underlined the insatiable demand for global capital, investment banks built research units, relationship management teams, execution groups, and salesforces to position themselves to originate and place debt and equity transactions. In the back pocket of many bankers were "hockey stick" profit projections: invest now, profit later. The problem was that for all but the top five global competitors, profits were elusive. And even for the top five, profits were both volatile and modest. The simple fact was that unless an investment bank captured sufficient volume and ranked high in the league tables, it lost money. The competition for relationships and transactions was simply too great, the costs too high, and the margins and markets too small to support all the investment banks that expanded in the region.

Bulge-Bracket or Bust in the 1990s

Investment banks with aspirations for long-term success could not escape the need to build operations aggressively. Long-term success hinged — and will continue to hinge — on establishing credibility and long-term relationships with key government and corporate decision-makers in Asia. And credibility requires having a proven track record.

In Asia, as elsewhere, there is a virtuous circle in investment banking: the more deals you have done, the better positioned you are to do more. In the U.S. in the 1970s, this virtuous circle gave rise to the term "bulge-bracket firms." Firms that consistently appear at the top of deal "tombstones" are recognized as having a strong track record and so are invited to bid for transaction mandates. The more times a bank is invited to bid, the greater its chances of winning. More invitations and wins enable investment banks to make better use of their costly resources and hence, capture a disproportionately large amount of underwriting volumes and profits. Being a bulge-bracket firm has additional benefits, such as being better-positioned to gauge underwriting risk, transaction pricing, and investor appetite, simply as a result of having done a greater number of transactions.

From the early 1990s, investment banks raced to achieve bulge-bracket status within Asian markets. The tombstones that counted in this race were those heralding Asian transactions. It was not enough for an international investment bank to parade its past success in the U.S. or Europe. Asian governments and corporate issuers new to cross-border capital raising required to see that their chosen intermediaries had adequate placement power (i.e., breadth of investor relationships in order to sell an issue) for Asian names. As the race for cross-border issues played out, the benefits of being among the top five underwriters became starkly apparent. By 1993, for Asia ex-Japan, the top five competitors were capturing 40 and 50 percent of all cross-border debt and equity issues respectively. Over 60 competitors in debt and equity underwriting were left to carve up the remaining half of the markets.

The split between the have and have-nots in cross-border investment banking persisted throughout the 1990s, although the names changed as some climbed into the winners' circle and others exited under growing competitive pressures. But it was the examples of those that won — like Merrill Lynch and Peregrine (albeit temporarily) — that gave hope to many aspirants that if they kept building the right teams and developing the right relationships fast enough, they too could claim profits. Until 1997 when the crisis cast its shadow over the region, underwriting volumes continued to grow, providing aspirants yet further hope of success. But the bulge-bracket split was maintained, forcing many investment banks to push back their profit projections. Taking the cross-border underwriting of equity (rights issues and IPOs) between 1994 and 1997 in Asia ex-Japan as a proxy, the top five underwriters earned, on average, US$36 million in annual underwriting fees; the next five, US$17 million each; and the remaining 81, US$2.3 million each. Similarly skewed revenues occurred in convertible bonds and in fixed- and floating-rate debt, with many of the same names dominating these products outside Japan (Exhibit 4.3). In Japan, the top five securities firms achieved similar domination of cross-border volumes, with the distinction that the top five were entirely Japanese firms that possessed their own global distribution for cross-border placements.

Privately placed transactions, often unrecorded, increased investment banks' revenue by as much as an estimated 50 percent over the above figures and those shown in Exhibit 4.3. But even then, a majority of investment banking teams failed to generate sufficient revenues to cover their costs, especially when their risks were accounted for. The long-term cross-border investment banking opportunities that appeared to carry so much promise, proved elusive for all but a few.

The reality in investment banking is that building sustainable market share and making money is tough anywhere in the world. But in Asia, it is even more difficult, particularly for foreign competitors looking to break into the top ranks for cross-border mandates. Building relationships requires extensive efforts and infrastructure; transactions are difficult, and margins are thin.

Long-term Relationships
Contingent on Real Commitments

Several hundred blue-chip Asian corporations and government-owned entities accounted for more than 80 percent of the US$434 billion in cross-border issuance volume between 1992 and 1997.[2] Prior to the 1997–1998 crisis, most of these corporations could easily command the attention of up to 20 international investment banks if they hinted at the possibility of, say, a US$100 million transaction. Many issuers, however, were only interested in working with banks committed to forming long-term relationships with them — both personal and professional.

Issuers expected their bankers to make numerous calls and to become familiar with their organizations and their multiple echelons of senior management involved in capital market funding decisions. In many cases, they expected bankers to sponsor international trips, golf outings, and extensive evening entertainment to build trust and friendships. It was not unusual for international investment banks operating in Korea, for example, to budget US$300,000 annually to entertain personnel from the conglomerates they were courting.

---

[2] Not including private placements.

Exhibit 4.3

Average Annual Cross-Border Underwriting Revenues in Asia Ex-Japan: 1994–1997 Average
US$ millions

Average annual revenue per underwriter

Product	Average annual revenue available	Top 5	Top 5	Next 5	The rest
Equity					
• Rights issues/IPOs	$453	• Goldman Sachs • Merrill Lynch • Morgan Stanley • Peregrine • ING Barings	$36	$17	$2.3
• Convertible bonds	$118	• Morgan Stanley • Union Bank of Switzerland • Jardine Fleming • Goldman Sachs • CS First Boston	$12	$5	$1.4
Debt					
• Fixed income*	$100	• Daiwa • Nomura • Merrill Lynch • Morgan Stanley • Goldman Sachs	$10	$6	$0.9
• Floating-rate notes	$34	• Merrill Lynch • Chase Manhattan • Deutsche Bank • Standard Chartered • Union Bank of Switzerland	$1.8	$0.9	$0.3

Note: Based on market listings executed by the lead book runner.

* Includes Eurobonds, Samurai bonds, and Yankee bonds; does not include private placements.

Source: Bondware

A strong relationship that could take months, if not years, to build was often just the entry price to the investment banking beauty pageant. Issuers in Asia typically selected five or six investment banks from the initial 20 to compete formally for underwriting mandates. In addition to building relationships, the winners had to demonstrate expertise in the client's industry, agree to bear most of the underwriting risk, provide liquidity and support for listed stocks or bonds in the secondary markets, and be able to approve transactions quickly — sometimes within 24 hours. In markets where long-term relationships were particularly highly valued, as in Korea, Taiwan, and Thailand, corporations would also take into consideration whether or not a bank had supported their needs in the past, for example, through competitively priced corporate loans. In the more sophisticated and demanding markets, like Hong Kong, issuers would consider a bank's ability to provide multi-product solutions integrating lending, equity, debt, and derivative capabilities.

Meeting the criteria for a long-term relationship and subsequent mandates required significant regional infrastructures, decision-making autonomy, and experienced relationship managers respected by senior clients. Often these relationship managers had to be well connected in the local business community and proficient in the native language. To prove their expertise, banks needed star industry analysts, had to be ranked in publications such as *Institutional Investor*, and often commanding anywhere from US$400,000 to US$1 million a year in compensation, based in the region. Additional research analysts and stockbrokers, located in the financial centers of New York, London, Hong Kong, or Tokyo, were required to support placement and trading of new issues in the secondary markets. Senior trusted bank executives had to be located within the region and granted underwriting authority in excess of US$100 million so they could commit quickly to new issues.

Building an effective Asia-wide operation that could effectively meet issuers' demands for winning cross-border mandates required at least 100 personnel and cost (including salaries, bonuses, and rent) upwards of US$45 million a year in the 1990s.

Difficult Time-Consuming Transactions

While building up such an operation quickly and profitably would pose challenges in any market, Asia proved to be difficult ground in ways that no bank could have fully anticipated. The most poignant examples of some of these difficulties arose in China, a market that many international banks targeted because of its scale and projected heavy reliance on foreign capital.

In the early 1990s, after investment banks had invested in identifying opportunities and in developing relationships, the central government decided it would allocate the major underwriting mandates for state-owned enterprises, in part, by nationality. Deals were to be parceled out to the U.S., continental European, British, and Japanese banks with some degree of balance to help China solidify its relationships with the world's economic powers. While that came as a disappointment to those that had hoped to dominate the market but missed out, the winners of China's early 1990s mandates were also in for a surprise. The state-owned enterprises up for listing were often more than just businesses. Their assets included schools, hospitals, and housing estates that provided for workers' families. Investment banks toiled to determine not only how to carve out these assets in preparation for listing, but also how to determine these assets' rightful owners in a communist economy.

Equally challenging was putting these enterprises' accounts in order, to comply with disclosure requirements for Western stock markets. The 1993 listing of Brilliance China Automotive Holding Company was a landmark transaction in this regard. Underwritten principally by CSFB, Merrill Lynch, and Salomon Brothers, the US$80 million equity listing was carried out on the New York Stock Exchange (NYSE). To get Brilliance's books ready for the issue, the investment banks oversaw an 8-month process that required the help of 30 accountants for 11,000 man-hours. All this for about US$5.6 million in fees that were split among the underwriters. Another 1993 transaction on the NYSE for Shanghai Vacuum Electronic Device Company was comparatively easy, requiring only 6,000 man-hours from a 20-person accounting team.

Of course, not all the transactions across Asia were as difficult as these, and even the China transactions became easier as accounting practices improved and as precedents were established. But many of Asia's transactions take more time and resources to complete than similar transactions in the West. Investment banks have to contend with regulations that vary across more than ten countries, compensate for the lack of transparency, work harder to help potential issuers secure investment ratings, and simply spend more time traveling to stay on top of emerging opportunities. All of these factors tie up resources and add to the real costs of operating in Asia.

Intense Competition, Global Costs, Thin Margins

If a bank were to take on these challenges isolated from competition, the task would already be daunting. But each bank was racing to build its organization at the same time, creating substantial competition. Goldman Sachs' trading and investment banking personnel grew from 50 in 1991 to 500 by 1995 to serve Asia ex-Japan. Salomon grew from 100 in 1992 to 350 by 1995, with aspirations to reach 1,000 by the end of 1998. Morgan Stanley expanded from 150 in 1991 to more than 500 by 1995. Merrill Lynch's investment banking and trading operations began the 1990s with less than 300 people in Asia, including Japan. By 1997, after its acquisition of Smith New Court Securities, Merrill's Asian investment banking and trading businesses employed more than 1,000 personnel. Meanwhile, there were more than 50 other firms (including brokerages, and commercial and universal banks) gearing up, with anywhere from ten- to 50-person investment banking teams mining regional opportunities.

With a real battle being fought over a limited supply of talent and experience in the region, investment banks were soon paying Wall Street wages. Indeed, personnel costs sometimes topped Wall Street norms as banks bid to poach entire research, relationship management, or execution teams in the hopes of speeding development of their Asian operations. Headhunters in Hong Kong started to discuss salaries in Wall Street terms. Two years' guaranteed compensation of US$2 million was referred to as a "2 by 2." Option schemes proliferated among banks and brokerages alike as they attempted to anchor their expensively acquired human assets. But more often than not, such schemes only added to overall costs without reducing the fixed costs built up through bonus guarantees and high base salaries. While compensation in investment banks boomed around the world in the mid-1990s, Asia was distinguished by the younger age and comparatively limited experience of those who commanded unprecedented salaries.

The cross-border investment banking game in Asia would have been easier to play if higher fees compensated for the more difficult transactions and higher costs. But the rapid build-up of global competition and the need to establish new relationships in what were essentially small markets quickly squeezed fees across Asia (Exhibit 4.4). By 1997, the average fees charged for cross-border IPOs dropped to 300 basis points. This was about 60 percent of what U.S. banks garnered at home, but in line with what European investment banks charged in their domestic markets. The convergence of U.S. and European competition resulted in the lower European fees setting the pricing benchmark in Asia. Similarly, fees charged for cross-border fixed- and floating-rate bonds were on par with global levels prior to the 1997–1998 financial crisis.

Poor Returns for All but Winners in Cross-Border Issuance

If one combines the relatively small cross-border underwriting volumes that are available in Asia with the higher costs and competitive fees, it quickly becomes clear why the economics of Asian investment banking were and are unattractive for most investment banks. Take for a moment a hypothetical investment bank that ranked tenth in the Asian league tables for all cross-border equity and debt products for an average year, based on underwriting volumes and fees that occurred between 1995 and 1997. Assume also that this bank captured private placement transactions across these products that were proportional to its tenth place ranking.

In an average year, this hypothetical bank would generate US$25 million in underwriting revenues and up to an additional US$3–5 million from advisory services. With a cost base of around US$45 million, it would incur annual losses from underwriting and advisory services of approximately US$15 million. One could argue that US$15 million is not too much to invest annually to build a long-term platform in Asian cross-border investment banking. The question, however, is: what are the chances that this hypothetical bank could capture sufficient volume so as to generate even modest future profits? The answer: it would have to be ranked sixth across all products, consistently beating names such as JP Morgan and Lehman Brothers to get there. Not an easy task, particularly for newer international entrants who are just beginning the relationship development process. For the many that faced this unprofitable picture in the 1990s, taking positions in transactions underwritten and engaging in proprietary trading was viewed as a

Exhibit 4.4

Asian Cross-Border Underwriting Fees: 1989–1997
Basis points

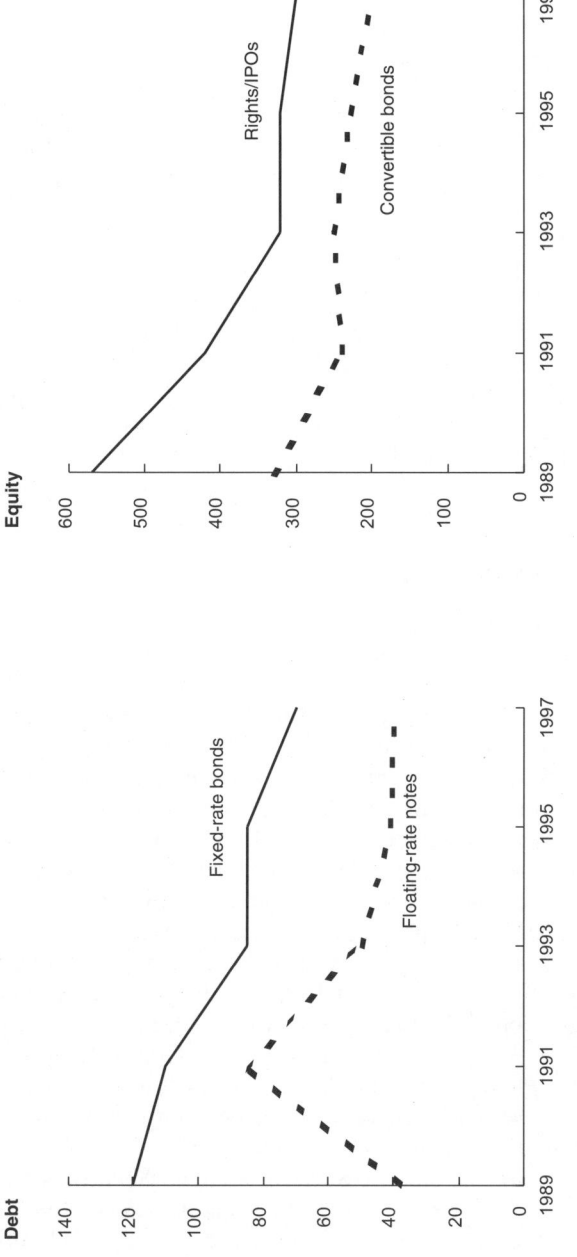

Debt

Equity

Note: Does not include private placements.

Source: Bondware

supplemental path to profits. But, as Chapter 5 highlights, this strategy came with significant and often unjustified risks.

Profits Under Protection
in Domestic Investment Banking

Whereas the fight for Asian cross-border dominance was waged largely by firms with decades of experience, domestic competitors outside Japan were born on the back of the new equity and debt markets. A combination of established industrial family groups and new entrepreneurs formed hundreds of brokerage firms throughout Asia that became the dominant investment banking channels in the local markets. Protected from foreign competition, these domestic players established competitive advantages by leveraging personal relationships with issuers, and not by building deep product, research, and execution skills. As Asia's markets open to foreign competition in the first decade of the 21st century and issuers' needs become more complex, domestic investment banking operations will have to undergo substantial change to survive. The gradually evolving competitive landscape of Japan during the 1990s provides an example of the challenges that domestic investment banks across Asia will face in the years ahead.

The Pluses of Protection

Domestic investment bankers had it easier in the 1990s (up till the crisis) than their global counterparts. A combination of rising volumes, low underwriting risk, protection from foreign competition, and regulated fees created a favorable environment in which leading local banks could generate attractive underwriting returns. Issuers demanded less expertise from their bankers as there was less perceived risk in local listings. Disclosure requirements were less stringent, lessening the difficulty of due diligence and the need for detailed analytical valuations. Investors were less sophisticated, reducing the need for extensive research and road shows in order to place and trade issues successfully in the primary and secondary markets. And product ranges were narrower, requiring fewer specialized, costly personnel to execute transactions.

If there was a challenge particular to domestic investment bankers, it was the relatively small size of individual underwriting mandates outside Japan. The median transaction size for equity issues from 1993 to 1997 was US$6 million in Malaysia, US$13 million in Taiwan, US$15 million in Hong Kong, and US$27 million in the Philippines. But, despite the small transactions and underwriting fees ranging from 1 to 3 percent, lower operating costs (mainly due to lower salaries) allowed leading intermediaries to profit.

A case in point is China's Shenyin Wanguo Securities, which employed approximately 3,000 staff in 1996 to carry out its domestic broking, trading, and investment banking activities. From the inception of China's local debt and equity markets in the early 1990s to 1996, Shenyin Wanguo underwrote 23 percent of all "A-shares" (for local investors only), 37 percent of all "B-shares" (for foreign investors), and 15 percent of all government-issued debt. It also brokered 25 percent of all trades on the domestic stock markets. In 1996, Shenyin Wanguo's profits totaled US$63 million, more than what most international investment banks made from their investment banking and trading businesses across the whole of Asia.

But not all domestic investment banking operations profited. In each of Asia's markets, the top five to ten underwriters typically captured more than 80 percent of underwriting volumes, leaving the remaining 10–30 contenders with insufficient revenues to cover their underwriting cost base. The leading domestic firms typically maintained their bulge-bracket status, thanks to their large stockbroking networks which gave them deeper reach among retail investors.

These firms' large retail networks will likely become their greatest challenge as global competitors gain access to the domestic markets. When a leading global investment bank underwrites a transaction, clear organizational processes allow it to muster the support of its internal research and retail and institutional distribution salesforce to market and place a transaction. The networks of Asia's leading brokers lacked such cohesion in the late 1990s. Most of these networks were staffed by commissioned brokers who had become accustomed to running their own businesses serving their individual base of clients. They were under no obligation to champion the firm's investment recommendations nor to sell the firm's new issues. This was not a problem pre-crisis, when booming markets created excess demand for new issues, with little need for research support or proactive marketing by the salesforce.

Going forward, however, as markets mature, the domestic brokerage firms must fully leverage their distribution networks to ensure successful placement of new mandates. This will require brokerages to revamp their salesforce management and upgrade research quality and coordination so that investment banking teams can legitimately market their placement power to potential issuers. The hurdle for success in deregulated markets will be set by competitors like Merrill Lynch, which has built robust coordination processes harnessing its huge global sales network to market equity and debt products to retail customers.

Japan After Foreign Entry

The experience of Japan illustrates the extent to which domestic investment banking markets can change when foreign competition enters. In the booming 1980s, Japan's Big Four investment banks (Nomura, Daiwa, Nikko, and Yamaichi) seemed untouchable in their home market. In 1989, before Japan's economic bubble burst, the Big Four reported cumulative profits of more than US$4 billion from their broking, trading, and investment banking businesses. By the end of 1997 however, Yamaichi had admitted bankruptcy and the other three lost US$632 million.

This change in fate was, of course, largely linked to declining trading and broking volumes in the wake of Japan's downturn. The Big Four hastened their downfall with a series of internal scandals in which large customers were compensated for trading losses at the expense of retail customers. But inroads by foreign investment banks once they gained easier market access in the 1990s, also eroded the Japanese firms' dominance. The foreign players scored initial wins in cross-border flows that Japanese firms had previously dominated through their own global distribution. By 1996, Morgan Stanley, Merrill Lynch, and CSFB made it to the top ten for underwriting cross-border debt. By 1998, foreign firms grabbed 12 of the top 15 spots in research rankings based on polls of leading domestic and global institutional investors. This provided foreign firms with a strong base on which to build increasing placement power in the domestic primary and secondary markets. The most noteworthy change, of course, was that two of Japan's Big Four came under either direct or heavy foreign control. Upon its demise, Yamaichi sold its retail distribution network to Merrill Lynch. And separately in 1998, Salomon Smith Barney acquired management control of Nikko Securities' investment banking operations.

Foreign firms were able to make such striking gains because of their better research, greater transparency, and track record of acting in clients' best interests. Their ability to attract Japanese talent also facilitated their advance. Until the early 1990s, few top graduates would select a foreign firm over Japan's Big Four. By 1998, a head of research from a foreign investment bank commented that poaching the best research analysts from the leading Japanese firms "was like shooting fish in a barrel." Japan's hierarchy-based compensation and career advancement were no match for global firms' meritocracy-based organizations.

Thus, domestic investment banks in Asia have no cause to be complacent about impending global competition. Superior skills and human resource policies will gradually win over even the deepest issuer relationships. The 1997–1998 crisis heightened the threat to domestic banks' long-term leadership and returns, as it hindered their ability to invest and strengthen capabilities.

Critical Factors for Future Success

The Asian financial crisis demonstrated that investment banking returns, for global and domestic banks alike, are fragile in the face of a wide-scale economic decline. Even the largest global investment banks did not escape the impact. As Thailand's meltdown spread across the region in 1997 and shook up other emerging markets in early 1998, the global bulge-bracket firms such as Merrill Lynch, Goldman Sachs, and Morgan Stanley could not stave off the negative effects of falling broking and underwriting volumes. In late 1998, Merrill Lynch acted first by reducing its global workforce of 63,000 by 3,400 personnel. For the smaller international and domestic competitors in Asian investment banking, the collapse in volumes simply pushed them out of the markets.

From regional and global competitors as large as Peregrine, Schroders, Wheelock Natwest, and Deutsche Morgan Grenfell (which was merged with Bankers Trust in 1998 with Deutsche Bank's acquisition of Bankers Trust) to dozens of smaller local intermediaries in Thailand, Indonesia, Malaysia, and Korea, the combination of risk exposures gone bad, lack of market liquidity, and shrinking issuance volumes made exiting out of or shrinking stakes in Asia inevitable. The "invest now, profit later" approach no longer made sense.

So what investment banking approach will make sense — and profits — in the first decade of the 21st century? To answer this, we must address three questions. First, how will investment banking markets likely evolve in the years leading up to 2010? Second, what types of opportunities will the markets provide, and how large will these be? And third, what skills and processes will be essential to capture these opportunities?

How Will Asian Investment Banking Evolve to 2010?

Asia's investment banking markets are likely to undergo a striking transformation in the first decade of the 21st century. This transformation will not take place overnight. Though the early years of the new millennium will likely be marked by economic inertia and limited investment banking activity, we will also see extensive restructuring of the public and private sectors, further breaking down of barriers to foreign competition, and the emergence of new Asian capital flows and formation. These events will derive their momentum from underlying macroeconomic forces and will result in tangible new opportunities and challenges for investment banks.

Restructuring

Corporations from Jakarta to Seoul are burdened with local and foreign currency bank loans that they are unable to repay. Conglomerates in Japan, Korea, Indonesia, Malaysia, Thailand, and India operate a diverse range of businesses in which they have limited expertise, and across which are limited synergies. Governments in Southeast Asia, India, and China have substantial assets tied up in inefficient state-owned enterprises, many of which are poorly managed, overstaffed, and fitted with outmoded machinery and processes. Recovery of domestic growth depends in part upon resumption of extensive infrastructure projects not only to spur spending, but to resolve bottlenecks in power generation, transportation, and communications. Domestic commercial banks, burdened by bad loans and desperate for equity injections, are part of the problem, not the solution.

Investment banks can play a critical role in the long-term restructuring of public and private sectors that will unfold in the first decade of the 21st century. In the wake of the crisis, investment banks began to help entities address their immediate cash-flow issues by restructuring and rescheduling debt in the international and domestic bond markets. Longer term, conglomerates will require investment bankers to recapitalize and refocus their core businesses through sales of noncore assets. Governments will need the help of investment banks in privatizing state-owned enterprises so that they free up capital. Investment banks will also likely be called upon to bring their capital market expertise to the world of project finance to help kick-start infrastructure programs through new funding channels. Indeed, investment banks can be a linchpin in helping banks themselves to recapitalize their equity base. In essence, investment banks can be an integral part of solutions that unlock assets and mobilize capital in Asia's log-jammed economies. In the short term, they can add value by providing staggered long-term refinancing solutions to alleviate debt obligations in a widespread liquidity crunch. Longer term, they will be at the center of Asia's corporate restructuring.

Deregulation

In the early years of the 21st century, just as investment banks are knee-deep in restructuring challenges, the domestic financial markets are likely to become increasingly open in response to WTO pressures and government attempts to attract foreign capital. International investment banks, traditionally barred from domestic underwriting and financial advisory, could well have the opportunity to dive fully into local markets. Similarly, leading domestic investment banks will be able to diversify their businesses and compete in other Asian markets. In 1998, the crisis forced countries such as Korea, Thailand, and Indonesia to open their financial markets to foreign participants. By 2010, one can reasonably expect that global forces such as the WTO will have led to the further deregulation of markets in China, Taiwan, Singapore, and Malaysia.

New capital flows and formations

Deregulation will open the doors to greater intraregional capital flows. As countries admit foreign competitors into their financial markets, they are also likely to free outbound capital flows, enabling individuals, corporations, and institutions to invest in foreign concerns. By 2010, it may well be possible for a mainland Chinese company to raise capital in the cash-rich "renegade province" of Taiwan. The relaxation of capital flows may also greatly enhance the role that Japan's wealth plays in the region. If Japanese investors leverage their country's "Big Bang" deregulation to diversify holdings, Japan could become a critical market in which Asian investment banks expand their underwriting placement power.

While capital flows broaden across Asia, capital formation in each country is also likely to change. The growth of public pension plans, insurance penetration, and mutual fund holdings that is apt to accompany economic development will increase capital managed by institutional investors. The traditional market dominance of retail investors in the capital markets of Asia ex-Japan will be reduced gradually. Investment banks that can develop the skills to serve emerging institutional investors will have access to deeper, concentrated placement power within the domestic markets.

In the first decade of the 21st century, investment bankers are likely to see a market characterized by broader access to issuers and investors, increasing complexity in issuer and investor needs, growing intraregional flows, and convergence of local and global competition. The transformed markets of 2010 will be larger and deeper, and will provide greater opportunities for highly skilled investment banks to differentiate their services and solidify client relationships.

What Types of Opportunities Will There Be?

Within this transformation there is bound to be a proliferation of investment banking products to meet issuers' new and more complex needs. Pure equity and equity-linked convertible bonds are sure to remain an investment banking staple, with the latter growing in breadth as domestic markets adopt this product to provide the certainty of interest income to investors in the post-crisis period, when earnings are likely to be anything but certain. Privatization of state-owned enterprises and the need for huge equity injections by the region's banks will result in sizable new opportunities.

But the big news is likely to be in debt. After years of false starts in the 1990s, Asia debt issuance, particularly by corporations, is likely to find firm footing. Poor cash flows in the early years of the new millennium will force corporations to explore medium- and long-term debentures. IMF reforms calling for greater disclosure and the emergence of domestic institutional investors will help both corporations and governments source rational long-term capital. Moves taken by the likes of the Monetary Authority of Singapore, which established the basis for a regional debt market in 1998 by enabling foreign and domestic issuers to raise Singapore dollar bonds for offshore use, will expand regional funding sources. As the bond markets gradually gain maturity and depth, new forms of debt such as securitization of loans and receivables will be able to develop. Indeed, the securization of bank loans, credit card payments, and other receivables will likely become a desired way for financial institutions and corporations to free up capital and displace risks. In an early example, the Hong Kong Mortgage Corporation (HKMC) was established in 1997 to enable banks and corporations to offload their mortgages through securitization. As of 1998, up to 15 investment banks had established securitization teams to pioneer this new frontier across Asia.

In 1997, on the eve of the financial crisis, Asia's emerging bond markets scored a number of firsts: the first Hong Kong dollar global bond offering, the first Indian century bond, and the first securitization of retail mortgage loans in Hong Kong. And while the crisis exposed the weaknesses that underpinned these and other firsts, Asia's fundamental demand for long-term capital in the first decade of the 21st century will support the development of vibrant debt markets.

Mergers and acquisitions (M&A), the poor step-child of Asian investment banking in the 1990s, will witness a substantial increase in importance in the years leading up 2010. From India to Japan, Asia's conglomerates will need to substantially restructure their holdings to bolster competitiveness and performance. For the better part of the 1990s, with annual transaction volumes averaging US$15–20 billion across Asia, M&A was a sideshow, something done with a handshake between gentlemen that occasionally required the services of an investment banker. And, if an investment bank was involved, extracting fees for such services was difficult. Many corporations intimated to their bankers that such advisory services were a good way to build a long-term relationship. In the wake of the crisis, the balance of power has shifted. Asia's governments and corporations need investment bankers to pinpoint the opportunities and bring potential buyers to the table. While slow to develop, M&A and corporate finance will likely become an investment banking mainstay in Asia.

In the aftermath of the crisis, with volumes substantially reduced, it may be counter-intuitive to imagine Asian investment banking as source of significant revenues, and even profits. However, by 2010, the investment banking markets of

Asia, including all underwriting and financial advisory services for domestic and cross-border transactions, could generate at least US$14 billion in annual revenues, almost triple pre-crisis levels. This projection rests on a number of simplifying assumptions. First, we have assumed that Asia's economies, currencies, and underwriting volumes will recover to an average of their pre-crisis levels by 2005. Second, we have assumed that annually between 2005 and 2010, underwriting volumes will grow proportionally to their underlying economies, as they did in the early 1990s. And third, to project financial advisory revenues generated from mergers and acquisitions, we have assumed that annual M&A volumes in Asia will range between 2 and 4 percent of the value of each country's underlying 2010 GDP.[3] These were the average ranges experienced in the U.S. and European markets in the 1990s. Implicit in our last assumption is that Asia's legal frameworks and business practices evolve to a point in 2010 where M&A is a common occurrence.

One could easily take issue with these assumptions. However, the projected revenue derived from them is a good ballpark figure that is conservative, if anything. Asian investment banking revenues in 2010 will surely top their 1996 peak and are likely to be founded upon a more diverse range of products and more vibrant markets.

What Skills and Processes Will Be Essential?

Investment banks, particularly those that have operated in protected domestic markets, will have to significantly upgrade their skills and processes to meet the challenges of the new century. Chief among these challenges will be satisfying new issuer needs, broadening while integrating product capabilities, capturing new capital flows, and catering to a new breed of domestic institutional investors. The requisite skills and processes are largely organizational in nature, leading some to comment that organization *is* strategy in investment banking. That is, the volatility and uncertainty of investment banking markets places a premium on building flexible organizations that can both pursue opportunities cost-effectively and attract and retain the top talent needed to profit from uncertainty. However, while there is truth to this generalization, it is possible to analyze the skill and process requirements for success. These skills and processes can be divided into the three key parts of the investment banking business: origination, execution, and distribution.

Origination

In the years leading up to 2010, global and domestic investment banks must be prepared to source (i.e., originate) issuer mandates across multiple geographies and products. Focusing on only one geography can be risky. Providing a narrow product range may result in volatile profits if issuers' needs change, and can

---

[3] 1–2 percent for the less-developed markets of China, India, Indonesia, and the Philippines.

hamper an institution's ability to build sustainable client relationships if issuers' needs require multi-product solutions. Winning investment banks will have to develop effective processes that enable customer relationship managers, product specialists, and research analysts to work in unison, across multiple countries, to cultivate relationships, identify needs, and provide innovative solutions. Investment banks that can maximize the flexibility of their relationship management, research, and product personnel without sacrificing the responsiveness or quality of service stand to optimize costs and minimize earnings volatility by being able to reallocate resources quickly against shifts in product or country demand.

To build cost-effective origination capabilities, investment banks will need to leverage IT and develop compensation schemes that both support information sharing and foster teamwork. As issuer sophistication increases, leading investment banks are also likely to grapple with whether their relationship managers, research analysts, and product specialists should be organized along country or industry lines to maximize their access to and credibility with issuers. For domestic investment banks — most of which are capable of providing only a few products in a single market — the challenges of building new product skills and organizational links will be great, particularly as they face foreign competitors that have dealt with similar IT and human resources challenges for more than a decade.

Execution

Execution is the heart of any investment bank. Execution teams typically work first with origination teams to structure and provide pricing guidelines for a transaction. They then work with distribution teams to assess investors' appetite for a particular transaction structure. Execution teams are responsible for coordinating much of the legal and accounting work that accompanies most investment banking transactions. They are also responsible for assessing the likely underwriting risk associated with a transaction by taking into account prevailing market conditions such as volatility and liquidity. If execution groups, which are typically organized by major product categories (i.e., equity and debt), fumble the structure or pricing of a transaction, investment banks can lose substantial amounts of money.

The work of execution teams in Asia will become more complex in the years leading up to 2010. With global investment banks potentially originating and distributing transactions within and across multiple Asian markets, execution teams will have to master a broad range of new regulations and develop risk management skills to simultaneously evaluate underwriting risks across many markets. Local investment banks, which have traditionally been weak in execution, will have to develop new structuring and risk management skills to provide competitive product structures and pricing to issuers and investors. For all competitors, designing and implementing IT systems that support execution groups will be critical. Competitors that can effectively harness technology to centralize execution skills across markets, probably within a couple of hubs, will be more cost-competitive and in a better position to monitor the increasing correlation of market risks that will accompany growing intraregional capital flows.

Distribution

Distribution is, of course, the sales end of the investment banking pipeline — the part of the organization that develops and maintains a bank's placement power. This is discussed in detail in Chapter 5. It is up to the distribution salesforce, the brokers and traders, to find the best investors for a transaction. They must consider the different risk/return tolerances of different investors, including retail customers, asset management firms, insurance companies, and pension funds. Throughout the 1990s, global and domestic investment banks in Asia typically drew placement power from their own home markets. Indeed, a critical factor of success for the bulge-bracket U.S. investment banks was their ability to leverage their deep penetration of the large U.S. institutional investor base to place Asian issues.

In the first decade of the 21st century, as new capital flows develop, competitors in Asia will have to consider broadening their placement reach. Global investment banks will face the challenge of serving new Asian institutional investors and potentially developing retail distribution within Asian markets. Merrill Lynch did so in 1998 with its acquisition of Yamaichi's 2,000-strong retail brokerage salesforce. Domestic investment banks will have to cope with serving new and more demanding local institutional investors. Adding further to the complexity, distribution salesforces will increasingly need to coordinate internally to accommodate the broadening geographic presence of the world's largest institutional investors. For example, global investment banks must ensure a unified approach by their salesforces in Asia, Europe, and the U.S. to clients buying from multiple locations — for instance, large asset management companies. This is critical to creating pricing consistency and adequate diversification of equity and debt placements. To effectively manage and deploy their placement power, investment banks will have to employ IT and sales tools such as account planning in coordinating, targeting, and differentiating sales efforts.

At the end of the day, the best investment bank is the one that provides the best problem solving and placement power to sellers and the most suitable issues to buyers. It is that simple and that hard. As Asian investment banking becomes more complex, winning investment banks will be those that can build the key skills and processes in origination, execution, and distribution. Investment banks that successfully build these skills while simultaneously leveraging IT and preserving organizational flexibility will be best positioned to pounce on emerging opportunities and control risks, while keeping their costs in check.

Strategic Options for the 21st Century

Around the world, successful investment banks will rely upon the integrated returns from investment banking and trading to generate sustainable profits. To maximize the contribution of investment banking businesses, however, all players in Asia must clearly identify which investment flows they are going to focus upon — which pipelines they are going to build — and establish a distinctive presence in their chosen areas. The separate worlds of global and domestic investment banking in Asia will broaden to offer banks four distinct strategies:

niche local — sourcing and distributing transactions locally within a single Asian market; regional local — sourcing transactions in a single Asian market and placing in several regional markets; regional expert — sourcing and placing transactions in several Asian markets; and global intermediary — sourcing transactions throughout Asia and placing regionally and globally.

After selecting a strategy, the next step is to decide whether to build critical mass in origination, execution, and distribution organically, through joint ventures, or via acquisitions. Finally, investment banks must choose whether to develop their business with or without commercial lending capabilities. A look at several examples of investment banks that failed or succeeded in the 1990s provides a better sense of the available strategic options, as well as their potential challenges and pitfalls.

Core Pacific: A Niche Local
with Regional Expert Ambitions

Core Pacific Securities hails from Taiwan and is a classic example of the niche local investment banks that prospered in the 1990s. By establishing strong local retail distribution, Core Pacific consistently ranked in Taiwan's top ten for local equity underwriting between 1992 and 1997. Flush with its own success, it treated the 1997–1998 crisis as an opportunity to raise its aspirations to the regional level. As the crisis took hold, wounding larger players with established regional operations, Core Pacific tried to step in and pick up the pieces. It attempted to purchase BZW's Asian stockbroking operations and later, the Hong Kong/China equity operations of bankrupt Peregrine. Brushed off by both these firms, Core Pacific was finally able to acquire Yamaichi's Hong Kong investment banking and stockbroking operations for US$80 million in early 1998.

The vision outlined in 1998 by CEO Tony Sheen, once known as Taiwan's "textile king," was to build a Greater China investment bank that could partially fill the void created by the failure of Peregrine. He envisaged a bank that could leverage ethnic ties, and emerging regional investment flows to underwrite transactions in Taiwan and mainland China for distribution within, and eventually across, these markets, with the added help of distribution in Hong Kong and Japan. Of course, in the late 1990s it was not possible for foreign investment banks to participate in China's local markets. Through Yamaichi, however, Sheen hoped to build an initial investment banking presence in China's "B-share" markets, in which foreign investors can buy equity in Chinese companies.

Sheen's strategy is essentially one of purchasing a high-risk option. If China deregulates its "A-share" domestic market, or if Taiwan allows mainland issues in its local markets, Core Pacific could be among the first to develop this new investment banking pipeline in the 21st century. Its long-term sustainability will, however, depend on building superior core investment banking skills that can stand up to global competition. Questions were already being raised in late 1998 amid grumbling among the 120 acquired Yamaichi staff that Core Pacific's "Taiwan approach" to investment banking lacked the rigor and sophistication of other international aspirants.

As Asia recovers, local investment banks from Singapore, Malaysia, Thailand, and Hong Kong are likely to pursue a similar strategy, starting first within their own sub-regions of Southeast Asia and Greater China. This strategy requires both careful development of new markets and effective leveraging of an investment bank's placement power in its home market.

CICC: A Local Joint Venture with Global Ambitions

Mainland Chinese bankers have never been shy in setting their aspirations. China International Capital Corporation (CICC), an offshoot of the China Construction Bank, has intentions to play in the global investment banking markets. The China Construction Bank took the interesting step of setting up the CICC joint venture with Morgan Stanley in 1995. For the Chinese, it was a venture to learn the ropes from one of the world's best. For Morgan Stanley, it was viewed as a platform to tie into Construction Bank's corporate relationships and ultimately into China's domestic investment banking markets.

For both, it proved to be a substantial challenge. In the early years, lack of clear direction spurred internal tensions that found their expression in disputes over large disparities in pay. Morgan Stanley personnel assigned to the joint venture got standard expatriate investment banking packages, which were multiples of the compensation received by the local partner's employees. Differences in working and communication styles created further friction within transaction teams. And differences in strategic priorities brought senior management from both sides into head-to-head confrontations. Morgan Stanley had to change its top manager twice in as many years before finding a leader who could build consensus within the joint venture. But even then, hairs were raised when CICC partnered with Goldman over Morgan Stanley in 1997 to underwrite the US$4 billion global equity offering for China Telecom. China Telecom's choice may have been spurred by the fact that Barton Biggs, Morgan Stanley's chief investment strategist, had warned investors off China as the deal was taking shape. In 1997, CICC established a subsidiary in Hong Kong to compete directly with Morgan Stanley and others for local and global mandates.

By 1998, although the CICC joint venture was profitable, generating close to US$30 million in profits in 1997 from successful underwriting, Morgan Stanley was cited in the press as hinting that the venture had outlived its useful life. Morgan Stanley had not won the access to China's local markets it had hoped for through CICC and increasingly faced the prospect of competing with itself. By late 1998, the joint venture remained intact, but there were growing signs that China may be looking to create its own global investment bank without going through the joint venture channel. Lesson: a joint venture strategy can offer a path to profits for local and global investment banks in Asia, but mutually shared aspirations are essential to long-term success.

Merrill Lynch: A True Global Intermediary
Locking in with Acquisitions

Merrill Lynch's early Asia strategy was similar to those of other bulge-bracket U.S. investment banks such as Goldman Sachs, Morgan Stanley, Lehman, and Salomon, all of which descended upon the region in the early 1990s. Wielding its strong U.S. placement power, Merrill concentrated on hiring key relationship managers and star analysts to build access to, and credibility with, Asian governments and corporations. But as competition intensified, and it became clear that broader participation in secondary distribution and trading would be essential to the underwriting business, Merrill broadened its approach.

In 1995, Merrill paid US$842 million to purchase Smith New Court Securities, a firm with operations in Europe and Asia. In Asia, it picked up a 250-person strong organization with established stockbroking and research staff based within the local markets and a nascent equity underwriting capability. Merrill integrated its purchase into its regional operations, and restructured Smith New Court's Asian investment banking operations, keeping only those bankers who could help it pursue the region's largest transactions. Merrill's 1995 acquisition helped it earn the title "Investment Banker of the Year" in the *Asiamoney* polls of 1995 and 1996 as it continued to push to the top of the cross-border equity and debt league tables. The acquisition was intended to help Merrill achieve in equity what it believed to be key to underwriting profitably: capturing secondary broking volumes of at least 2.5 times the size of the original issue.

As the fallout from the crisis ravaged the smaller investment banks, Merrill used its global profits to bolster its regional presence. It took a majority stake in one of Thailand's leading brokers, Phatra Thanakit, and acquired Yamaichi's 30 retail stockbroking offices and 2,000 staff in Japan as that firm declared bankruptcy. In 1998, Merrill was prepared to tolerate losses of US$125 million from its Yamaichi takeover with hopes that restructuring and a new approach to business in Japan would yield as much as US$30 million in profits by 1999.

Merrill's acquisitions in the late 1990s moved it one step closer to becoming a true global investment bank. In the first decade of the new century, it will be well positioned to both source and place transactions locally in several Asian markets. As it rebuilds Yamaichi's operations, it will enhance its distribution power in Japan, placing it far ahead of other global competitors in this key market. For those that have the deep pockets and the skills to integrate acquisitions, Merrill's aggressive strategy may be well worth emulating.

Credit Agricole Indosuez W.I. Carr Securities:
An Integrated Commercial and Investment Bank

In 1987, French bank Indosuez, with roots in Asia extending back to the 19th century, purchased British broker W.I. Carr. A decade later, Indosuez was in turn purchased by Credit Agricole.

Through the 1980s and into the 1990s, W.I. Carr held rank with other leading British brokers, such as Jardine Fleming and Barings, that dominated cross-border stockbroking in Asia. Indosuez's ambition in purchasing Carr was like that of many other commercial banks (e.g., Barclays BZW, Credit Lyonnais, HSBC/Wardley, Societe General Crosby, UBS Warburg, and Wheelock Natwest) that sought to leverage corporate relationships and a broker's placement power to build an integrated investment bank.

At first glimpse, this strategy seems quite straightforward. Commercial banks, possessing strong corporate relationships but facing thinning margins in Asian lending, can improve returns by using a broker's placement power to also underwrite corporate equity mandates. A stockbroker with strong investor relationships can enhance its returns by capturing underwriting fees facilitated by a corporate bank's issuer relationships. A perfect marriage of capabilities? Yes. A perfect marriage of cultures? No. Indosuez W.I. Carr saw false starts throughout the 1990s as it attempted to merge its banking and broking operations to build an investment bank. Like the many commercial banks that pursued this strategy, integration was frustrated by differences in operating styles, personalities, client handling methods, and compensation. Traditional banks are steeped in standard procedures and tend to be staffed by conservative people who value long-term client relationships and frequently accept seniority-based pay. By contrast, brokers, whose pulse is driven by the daily movement of markets, are accustomed to last-minute, case-by-case decisions and are dominated by young risk-takers who are driven by immediate gains and demand performance-based pay. Placing these two groups together to build an integrated organization that shares the same views on origination, execution, and distribution strategy is incredibly trying.

For Indosuez W.I. Carr, its attempts at integration yielded a secondary position in Asia's investment banking league tables. For some of the larger international banks, such as UBS Warburg, the results were more positive. Others, such as Barclays BZW and Wheelock Natwest, gave up on this approach. For Asia's domestic brokers and banks looking to gear up in the face of 21st century global competition, building an integrated investment bank is an option, but one that requires very strong leadership and unswerving commitment to forging a unified culture. Many will try, but few are likely to succeed.

The Winners' Circle

As organizations build their pipelines and tailor their investment banking strategies in Asia for the 21st century, they may take comfort from knowing that there will be larger markets and ultimately fewer competitors than roamed the region during the late 1990s. Those that survive the coming decade will also likely be significantly stronger.

By 2010, the market will be separated into three distinct groups. The top five to ten global investment banks will continue to dominate service to the largest corporate and government interests. But unlike in the 1990s, their influence will extend deep into domestic and intraregional markets. They will be joined by three to five sub-regional experts, most likely comprising some of today's domestic competitors that manage to expand beyond their home borders to originate and place in several Asian markets. These regional experts will concentrate on building relationships with mid-sized corporations and investors interested in non-blue-chip Asian names. Finally, there will be a handful of entirely domestic investment banks within each market generating sustainable returns. They will focus on the smaller corporations or develop niches in certain industry sectors. They may merge with large local corporations or align closely with important corporate family groups. They will survive for a while behind protective walls, but their share will decline as the markets open to true global competition.

As market conditions wax and wane in the first decade of the 21st century, Asia's investment banking landscape will be dotted with new entrants and subsequent failures. But for those that are able to be consistently placed in the bulge-bracket of their chosen local, regional, or global game, maintain flexibility, manage risks, and control costs, there will be, on average, attractive profits. Enough so that the employees of the winners in 2010 will continue to be able to live in The Peak in Hong Kong, or its equivalent in Tokyo, Singapore, Shanghai, Mumbai, and Asia's other major cities.

5
TRADING:
BACK TO THE BASICS

The late 1980s and the early 1990s were not kind to British merchant banks. As recently as the early 1980s, proud names like S.G. Warburg, Morgan Grenfell, Hambros, Rothschild, Samuel Montagu, Lazard Brothers, Hill Samuel, and Schroders were major competitors in raising long-term finance and managing mergers, acquisitions, and alliances between major corporations. The firms had also built enviable reputations in asset management, leading the charge into global asset management in the 1980s. This competitive position changed in the mid-1980s with the two pressures of the "Big Bang" in the U.K. and the growing importance of U.S.-based investors. Collapsing margins in the U.K. and increasing global capital requirements resulted in European universal banks and U.S. investment banks ascending as the kings of the now global business.

The two leaders of the early 1980s, Morgan Grenfell and Warburg, for very different reasons, effectively ended up as subsidiaries of European universal banks. In 1998, the Morgan Grenfell name effectively disappeared forever. Hambros and Hill Samuel declined into insignificance. Samuel Montagu became the subsidiary of a weakened British clearing bank, Midland, which itself succumbed to acquisition by the Hongkong and Shanghai Banking Corporation (HSBC). Rothschild and Lazards survived as boutiques specializing in mergers, but not as industry leaders in the broad investment banking field.

And yet, in the early 1990s, at least one British merchant bank was expanding alone, building new businesses, and earning respect as a fierce competitor. Considered as being rather sleepy during the go-go 1980s, Baring Brothers had avoided the temptation of expanding into the cut-throat U.K. securities markets, and instead had staked its claim for long-term survival on a stable U.K. advisory business, strong asset management skills, and an emerging Asian franchise in brokerage, advice, and trading. By the early 1990s, the firm's equity research and brokerage services in Asia had placed it among the top brokers used by major institutions worldwide as they moved assets into Asian equities.

The Asian franchise and years of building contacts in the region had also formed the basis for a strong regional corporate finance business. Asian earnings were solid — and growing. Opportunity beckoned it to build on this franchise. One step Barings took was to expand its trading activities beyond the traditional scope of agency equity brokerage, to include more complex instruments and strategies. One of the Singapore-based teams, for example, focused on trading Tokyo Stock Exchange Index (Nikkei) futures that were traded both in Tokyo and in Singapore on its futures exchange, the Singapore International Monetary Exchange (SIMEX). This team was led by a young Englishman who had been with the company for 6 years. His name — Nick Leeson.

The rest, of course, is well-documented history. Leeson, through control of his back-office operations, used dummy trading accounts to hide large losses on proprietary trades in his markets, losses that eventually crippled Barings and, within a few days, saw Barings' proud history of independence end with its sale — for £1 — to ING of the Netherlands. Trading in Japanese equities futures in Singapore had brought the old-line British firm to its knees. The hard work invested in building the franchise meant that most of the businesses survived and grew under ING, but the rapid collapse of the independent entity, Baring Brothers, underlined the opportunities and risks of trading. Leeson, who had earned Barings large trading profits (US$43.8 million in 1994), also single-handedly undermined the firm. Trading can be a boom-and-bust business globally — and Asia is no exception.

Balancing Opportunities and Challenges

The Barings story of trading in Asian markets illustrates many of the truths of these markets: the opportunities are perceived as significant, but so are the challenges. The reality, of course, lies in balancing the two, and in knowing where an institution has the skills to make sustainable returns.

Many trading choices exist in Asia. The securities trading markets are divided by instrument (equities, corporate bonds, mortgages, foreign exchange, and equity, fixed-income and foreign exchange derivatives), by nationality of the issuer of the security, and by the currency of the security (e.g., local currency versus U.S. dollar-denominated bonds issued by Southeast Asian corporations). At the same time, some of these markets are stand-alone trading markets (e.g., forex trading), while others are intimately linked to investment banking markets. In stand-alone markets, traders and brokers have to earn profits from buying, selling, and holding securities. In linked markets, the returns from the entire market (e.g., equity underwriting and trading) must be attractive, while the returns of just the secondary or trading section, can be more or less attractive, depending on the volume in the primary or underwriting portion.

The multifaceted, complex trading markets in Asia are potential sources of very large profits for financial institutions. For instance, in the most mature Western banking markets, trading revenue can be three to four times that of classic investment banking (M&A and securities underwriting). In Asia, the multiple during most of the 1990s might have been slightly smaller than in the West, but the trend to the relative balance of revenues in the West made pure trading businesses a priority for any wholesale-market-oriented firm. First, we will examine the *opportunities*.

Growth Markets

The underlying trading markets in Asia grew faster during most of the 1990s than even high-growth real economies. Market capitalization and turnover volumes in both equity and debt markets rose remarkably (Exhibit 5.1). Over the same period, we saw the same impressive growth trends in the foreign exchange markets, even though many Asian countries maintained *de facto* currency trading controls (Exhibit 5.2). Obviously, the US$:¥ exchange rate was a crucial component of trading volume, although turnover in other local currencies against the U.S. dollar also increased in the mid-1990s (Exhibit 5.3). Finally, the new derivative markets grew quickly in Asia. For instance, the volume of Hang Seng index futures traded on the Hong Kong Futures Exchange swelled from 4,356 to 18,624 lots a day — a 328 percent increase — between 1992 and 1996. In Singapore, futures traded on

SIMEX increased by an impressive 138 percent over the same period. Meanwhile, the less visible over-the-counter (OTC) derivative markets also saw strong growth. For example, turnover in foreign exchange contracts increased by 95 percent between 1992 and 1995 in Hong Kong, reaching US$56 billion a day. In terms of relative size, Singapore's OTC interest rate derivative market ranked fourth in the world in 1995, with more than US$16 billion in daily turnover.

Attractive Margins

Not only did Asian markets grow dramatically through the mid-1990s, they provided attractive margins. For instance, while in London, the equities spread on market-making in major U.K. equities had declined to 15 basis points by 1996, and the commission on New York Stock Exchange institutional trades was 13 basis points, equity trading spreads in Asia were generally far wider. Despite the average 20 percent decline from 1990, institutional equity commissions in 1996 were 25 basis points in Japan, 25 basis points in Hong Kong, 70 basis points in Singapore, and in less efficient markets like Thailand, 75 basis points.

Meanwhile, spreads in the debt markets were very high by global standards. In the Euromarkets, 10-year corporate A-rated Eurobonds might be traded with a 25-basis-point spread in the mid-1990s, while a U.S. corporate bond of similar credit and tenure would be traded with a spread as low as 5 basis points. In the emerging Asian debt markets, secondary trading spreads were much higher. Although very few pieces of 10-year Asian corporate debt existed outside Japan, a 5-year local currency bond issued by a Southeast Asian corporate issuer traded between

Exhibit 5.1

Asia's Financial Markets Growth: 1992–1996
US$ billions; percent

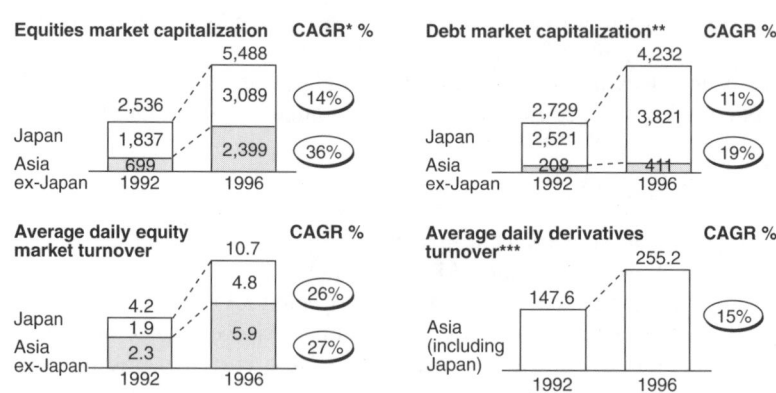

* Compound annual growth rate.
** Public- and private-sector bonds.
*** Financial derivative instruments traded on Asia's organized exchanges, including Australia and New Zealand.

Source: FIBV; World Bank; Bank for International Settlements

Exhibit 5.2

Growth in Asian Foreign Exchange Markets: 1992–1995
Average daily turnover in Hong Kong, Tokyo, Singapore, US$ billions

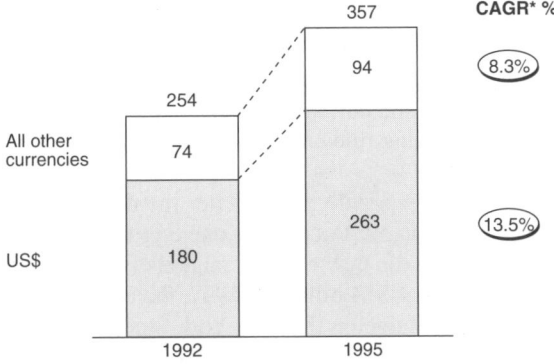

* Compound annual growth rate.

Source: Bank for International Settlements

Exhibit 5.3

Foreign Exchange Trading Volume: 1994–1996
Average daily domestic currency turnover, US$ billions

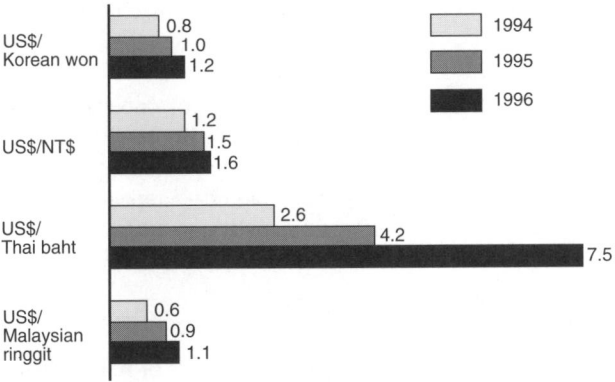

Source: Central banks; McKinsey analysis

institutions with an average 60–70 basis point spread in 1996. These high spreads existed because there was, in fact, very little liquidity in the local debt markets at all; local Asian trading was extremely limited, and only when the London market was open was it often possible to move positions. During the 1997 and 1998 crisis the situation worsened further. Due to a complete lack of liquidity, the same bonds might have traded (sporadically) with an amazing 10 percent spread.

New Markets

Not only did the secondary trading markets in Asia grow rapidly with relatively attractive spreads through the mid-1990s, they experienced swift product and geographic proliferation, similar to that of the traded markets in Europe and the U.S. in the 1980s and early 1990s. New debt and equity derivative markets emerged during this period, most notably the Hong Kong equity options market (1995) and the interest rate and currency options market in Taiwan (1994). Hong Kong loosened its short-selling rules in 1994, and India lifted the ban on options trading in 1995.

New geographic markets started up, too. After the devastation of the Vietnam War, who would have expected it to consider opening a stock exchange in 1998? In China, trading volume in the new equities markets (that only began to emerge in the 1980s) was as high as US$4 billion in 1997, the equivalent of 18 percent of the average daily trading volume on the New York Stock Exchange.

Perhaps the largest market to emerge during the 1990s was for corporate debt outside Japan. Historically, corporations in Asia have been funded by a mixture of equity and bank lending. Lack of corporate account transparency, few corporate ratings, and the paucity of Asia-based large-debt-purchasing institutional investors meant that the corporate debt securities market did not develop in Asia as it had in the U.S. and Europe. Of course, major corporate issuers could tap the Euromarkets or place U.S. dollar Yankee bonds in the U.S. But the average corporation in Hong Kong, Singapore, Indonesia, Malaysia, or Thailand was unable to access long-term fixed-income debt until the early 1990s. The debt market in Asian corporate paper that started appearing then, represented a completely new trading opportunity for trading houses and investors in the region. Of this new market, we shall read more later.

Asian trading markets appeared vibrant and full of opportunity in the early to mid-1990s. Trading and brokerage volumes grew impressively, trading margins were high by global standards, and new products emerged rapidly, with one major cash market — the fixed-income corporate market — appearing for the first time. Opportunities for houses like Barings seemed very attractive. But with these opportunities came harsh realities and *risks*.

Small Markets

Despite their remarkable growth, the securities markets of Asia, other than Japan's, were small by global standards. At the end of 1996, the total market capitalization of the stock markets of Korea, Hong Kong, Singapore, Malaysia, China, Taiwan, Indonesia, Thailand, the Philippines, and India represented only 22 percent of the market capitalization of the U.S. stock markets (New York Stock Exchange, NASDAQ, and the American Stock Exchange). And this was before declining equity values and devalued currencies made the percentage so much lower — by the end of 1997, it had shrunk to 14 percent. (That is, the market capitalization of the stock markets of some 48 percent of the world's population represented 14 percent of the market capitalization of the markets of the United States, a country with 4.5 percent of the world's population.)

Of course, some of these relatively small markets were traded quite heavily, as we saw earlier; in 1996, their combined daily average trading volume represented 23 percent of the three U.S. markets' trading volumes; in 1997, it was 27 percent. Adding in Japan's daily equity trading volume of US$4.5 billion in 1997, the Asian markets represented 38 percent of U.S. trading. Much of this was retail and was not open to professional trading firms or international brokers. True institutional volumes were about 50 percent of this total, but they varied significantly across markets: in 1996, they represented 7 percent of total volume in Taiwan, and in Indonesia, 92 percent.

The pattern of relatively small market size was also visible in the debt markets. Inclusive of Japan, the total market capitalization of Asian fixed-income securities was about US$4 trillion at the end of 1994, compared to the combined Treasury and corporate debt market in the U.S. of US$7.5 trillion. But excluding Japan reduced the Asian total to about US$300 billion, only 4 percent of the U.S. total.

Not only were the combined equity, debt, and foreign exchange markets small by global standards, they were tiny in each country except Japan. The distances between the countries (which had to be covered by using pricey Asian airlines or very costly Asian telecommunications) and the individuality of each market, requiring brokers and traders to develop specialized research, trading, and operations staff, made covering them expensive. Even relatively small markets needed a large staff in addition to the inherently expensive infrastructure and communications costs. A leading pan-Asian ex-Japan equity broker might have had 700 staff and an expense base of close to US$100 million in 1997. This base was acceptable as long as volumes were high and linked corporate finance fees strong. In a downturn, however, the absolute size of available commissions and the collapse of linked underwriting fees made this expense base far too high.

Volatile Markets

If the immediate glamour of the Asian trading markets was dimmed by their relatively small size and the cost of covering them, further concerns lurked. Despite rising trading volumes, these markets were often illiquid and volatile. In the mid-1990s this problem was less obvious or infamous; the volatility seemed to be all on the upside. The 1997–1998 meltdown illustrated how thin and volatile these markets could be. In fact, at one point in January 1998, daily moves of 7–9 percent in the equity markets of Hong Kong, Korea, and Southeast Asia were so common that they no longer justified the screaming front-page headlines that they had commanded in 1997, and certainly would have brought in an OECD market. From August 1997 to February 1998, most Asian exchanges recorded greater volatility than the U.S. or U.K. had experienced during the stock market crash in October 1987. The Kuala Lumpur Stock Exchange, for example, racked up a volatility reading of 0.2 (the standard deviation from the six-month moving average; see Exhibit 5.4). In layperson's terms, the differences between the market's high and low swung as much as 33 percent from the market's mean in the later months of 1997, substantially up from the 4 to 8 percent range in the months before the crisis.

Exhibit 5.4

Volatility in Asian Equity Markets
6-month historical volatilities* (Aug 1997–Feb 1998) of market indices

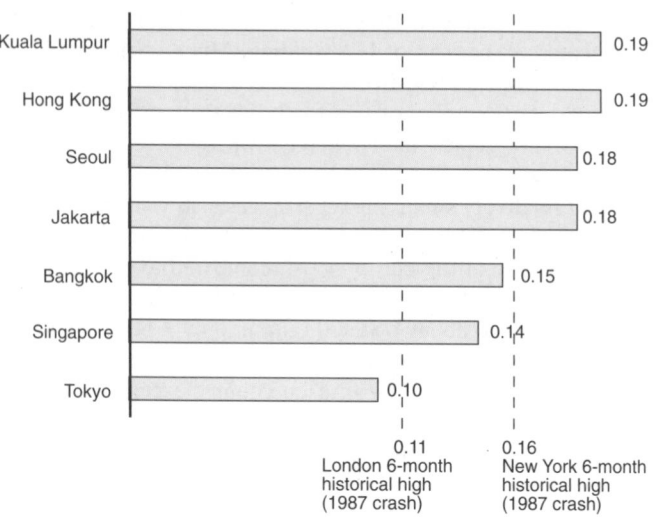

* Standard deviation of consecutive daily closing prices over 6 months.

Source: Datastream; McKinsey analysis

Asia's currencies were similarly volatile. From 1980 to 1996, volatility of the Malaysian ringgit, the Indonesian rupiah, and the Thai baht was extremely low, since these currencies were effectively pegged to the U.S. dollar. However, when the links broke and free market forces were allowed to play, the resulting volatility was astounding. In the same 6-month period, from August 1997 through February 1998, the average daily volatility of these currencies against the U.S. dollar literally shot through the roof. The most extreme example was the rupiah. From July 1, 1997, to June 30, 1998, it depreciated by approximately 80 percent against the U.S. dollar. In early January 1998, it plunged by more than 11 percent against the U.S. dollar, and then shot back up by 10 percent — all within a week. Compare this to only a year earlier, when the rupiah's exchange rate rarely budged by more than a percentage point for months at a time. These swings generated volatility readings of 0.5, or high-low swings from the market mean of as much as 112 percent in the early months of 1998 (Exhibit 5.5).

These extremes of volatility represented great opportunities for those who could remain on the right side of the trades. For instance, Standard Chartered Bank was able to record large earnings on trading the baht during 1997: results showed significant above-the-norm trading profits, which the bank attributed primarily to these opportunities. On the other hand, some European banks reported losses of up to US$240 million on Asian equity derivative trading in 1997.

The truly dark side of the volatility was not just the risk of being on the wrong side of the movements, but that it was symptomatic of very low liquidity levels in these markets. That is, in times of crisis, trading volumes shrink alarmingly, and

Exhibit 5.5

Volatility in Asian Foreign Currency Markets
Average volatility* vs. US$ over a 6-month period

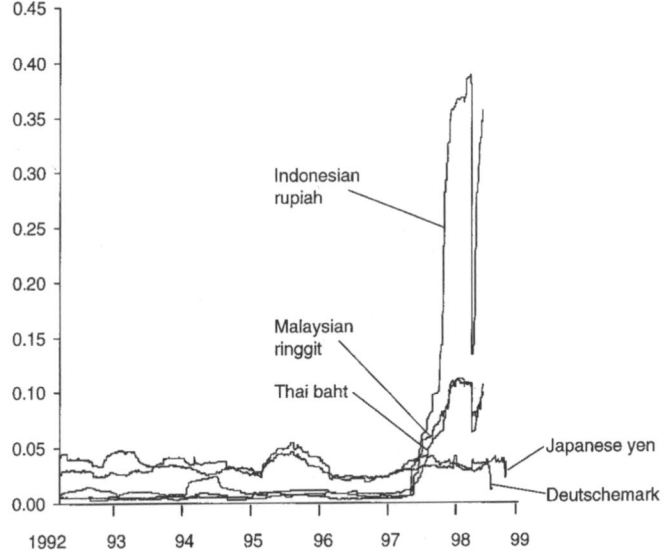

* Calculated by taking the standard deviation of consecutive daily closing prices over a 6-month period.

Source: Datastream; McKinsey analysis

as a result, relatively small trades move market prices by very large amounts. These are dangerous markets to trade in because it is difficult to hedge large positions with any confidence. In addition, the shocks that trading partners might be exposed to can be so large that assessing their potential creditworthiness in a crisis is difficult.

These risk management concerns, of course, feed on themselves. As soon as market participants sense that volatility is increasing and general price trends may drop, they re-evaluate all their trading relationships, implement tougher credit standards, and start to "pull lines" to their trading-counterparties. In turn, the smaller trading capacity reduces volumes and can force trading firms to sell positions they have developed, creating a further dangerous mix of forced sales and reduced trading capacity. After a bout of panic selling and high trading volumes, the long-term decline in trading capacity makes the markets fundamentally more volatile because they are susceptible to even small volumes of sell or buy orders.

Demanding Clients

As the equity, bond, foreign exchange, and derivative markets in Asia grew during the 1980s and 1990s, they attracted more and more institutional investors from the

U.S., Europe, and Asia. While these investors created sources of revenue for traders and brokers, they also produced new challenges.

A number of Western-based investment management firms established offices in Tokyo, Hong Kong, and Singapore in the early 1990s to become more knowledgeable about the markets. To satisfy these more sophisticated clients, brokerage firms in the equity markets, for instance, discovered that the products and services they needed to offer were becoming more complex and expensive each year. These firms needed to provide customers with not only individual stock research and country reports, but industry sector analysis across countries as well. By the late 1980s and early 1990s, traders and brokers in both the equity and debt markets faced increasingly savvy investors who were more costly to serve and who demanded that the intermediaries take more risk. For instance, brokers needed to be able to undertake "basket trades" for clients who requested partially "blind" sales of whole portfolios of stocks in order to quickly rebalance or restructure their portfolios. These trades required significant capital and risk-taking capacity.

Inadequate Skills

The final weakness of the trading markets for major trading firms in the region was that the markets grew so fast during the 1980s and 1990s, that it initially seemed to represent such great opportunities. In this context, many firms were eager to hire any MBA graduate with native language skills. Men and women in their late 20s and with the right profile suddenly found themselves writing credit research reports on companies they had not heard of 3 months earlier, and about which the long-term family proprietor was not about to give out too much information.

Alternatively, these new staff found themselves trading equity, debt, or foreign exchange in these markets, and saw values rise rapidly as global capital flows to the region increased. They came to expect that these markets would always trend upwards. They applied Western textbook trading and hedging techniques, believing that a hedge in Asia was as good as one in the liquid markets of the U.S. or Europe. Finally, along with building their research, trading, and sales capabilities in multiple markets, these firms needed back-office systems and operations to settle, clear, and handle accounting, and, again, relied heavily on new staff.

The Barings catastrophe was a harbinger of events a few years later. The underlying weaknesses of many of the trading businesses in the region were similar to those that allowed Nick Leeson to get himself, and his firm, into so much trouble. Many trading operations were overseen by relatively inexperienced managers and traders who, on the basis of 1 year or 2 years of strong performance, had been given increasingly larger trading limits by headquarters. Staffing of the credit review, risk management, and operations departments was similarly new or lean. Although Nick Leeson was trading in the relatively developed and liquid Japanese equity derivative markets, others with far less experience were dabbling in markets that, in times of stress, would show much less liquidity.

Local Currency Debt: A Sign of the Times

Perhaps no Asian market exhibited all these structural weaknesses more than the market for local currency corporate debt securities, which emerged in the late 1980s and early 1990s. Japan aside, compared with both the U.S. and Europe, there had never been a real corporate fixed-income securities market in Asia beyond some commercial paper or bill markets. Equity and bank lending had financed the "Asian miracle." This gap began to close as enterprising investment banks started identifying potential borrowers who wanted the certainty of (high) fixed-rate debt, and investors who were ravenous for high yield denominated in currencies that appeared then to be effectively pegged to the U.S. dollar.

Unfortunately, not all investors were as worried as they should have been about the lack of full disclosure of some borrowers' financial position or fundamental weaknesses, for example, the mismatch between the currencies of their earnings and the debt they were taking on. With this time-bomb ticking away, the market grew during the early to mid-1990s. Corporate debt instruments issued in Asia outside Japan totaled US$35 billion in 1990; by 1994, this figure had increased to US$78 billion. Although still tiny compared to the nearly US$2 trillion of corporate debt outstanding in the U.S. in 1994, the average 22 percent annual growth and the financing needs that these companies anticipated augured well for Asia to at last develop an indigenous market for local currency corporate debt.

These trends masked the market's fundamental weakness: the trading side of the market never developed properly. The primary investors in the debt market were weak institutions, like merchant banks in Korea and Thailand. These firms did not have the ability to originate attractive transactions themselves, and relished the opportunity of acquiring high-yielding paper to cover their relatively high funding costs (and they also did not always manage the interest rate mismatch between their floating rate deposits and these fixed rate assets). The investor market did not diversify properly to include a range of strong investors, and so did not build a regular trading market with some depth. In fact, as was to become clear in 1997, in many cases the investor market was so weak that the investment banks originating the transactions ended up holding the paper themselves. Quality fixed-income investors in the region, central banks, parastatal institutions, and very wealthy individuals were not major investors in this risky paper. When they wanted to invest in fixed-income securities, they focused on G-7 sovereign debt or high-quality Western corporate debt.

Why was Asia ex-Japan unable to develop a quality fixed-income corporate debt market during this period? Two factors stand out. First, as noted earlier, the local investor base never developed properly, so in times of crisis, there were too few investors considering buying severely discounted securities as part of a long-term commitment to the market. Second, quality institutional interest in this paper was lacking because it was very risky, but in a different way from the risk of another famous, high-yielding fixed-income market, the U.S. junk bond market. At least in that market, although the risks investors took were very real, they were reasonably transparent. The problem in the Asian market was that it did not consistently allow for the level of disclosure that investors need to be able to judge the risks they were taking. For example, Indonesian paper was often sold to investors on the basis of the close ties of the corporate entity issuing it to the ruling Suharto family, rather than on the quality of the cash flows coming from the entity. Investors were supposed to take on trust that the issuer's ties to the ruling family meant that the paper would be serviced. In good times this assumption held up, but in a difficult economic situation, it was unwise to rely upon it.

Further to this credit problem, major corporate debt rating agencies such as Standard & Poor's, Moody's, and Duff & Phelps were relatively new in the region. These firms only really stoked up their Asian operations in the late 1980s. In some cases, they had not yet covered many issuers in the market; in others, they were unused to reading the tea leaves to determine the real quality of the issuers and their debt.

Quality investors — the major insurance companies, pension funds, and mutual funds in Asia and around the world — had real concerns about the reliability of many of the debt issuers due to the lack of transparency in their accounts and business relationships, and the paucity or weakness of their credit ratings. Consequently, many of these investors steered clear of the market.

Yet, not all Asian corporate debt issues were too risky for quality investors. Whereas the local Asian debt market, despite the objections of some U.S. investment banks, used the disclosure requirements based on Euromarket standards (which were originally designed for only the very strongest Western corporations), the U.S. dollar corporate debt market for major Asian corporations was very different; this market demanded much tougher underwriting standards and higher quality work from the rating agencies. However, the risk perceived by some U.S. investors of an Asian meltdown caused the market value of even these issues to plunge as a result of the Asian financial crisis. For example, a 7-year U.S. dollar Yankee bond issued by PT Polysindo Eka Perkasa, a member of the large Indonesian Polysindo group, traded at around US$57 on May 12, 1998, compared with US$114 only 10 months earlier. Certainly, the fact that some Asian issuers, including Polysindo, decided that it was "too expensive" for them to make payments during the crisis did not improve investor confidence.

Resulting Trading Economics in Asia

The results of these opportunities and challenges on traders' and brokers' fortunes were played out somewhat differently, both within and outside the major market of Japan. In both cases, however, great fortunes were made and lost in trading in the 1980s and 1990s.

Outside Japan

Outside Japan, the equity markets dominated the securities markets during the 1980s and 1990s. In the late 1980s, these markets began appreciating, and trading volumes increased as they recovered from the October 1987 debacle (during which the Hong Kong equity market closed for 4 days due to its inability to clear trades). A major driver of this recovery was overseas investor money, as U.S. and European investors focused on opportunities in emerging markets, the Asian miracle, and how international diversification could improve risk-adjusted portfolio returns. In addition, a number of investors chose to invest in the region in line with the market value of all major indices, that required flows to all markets in line with their percentage of the region's market capitalization. In this phase, securities houses rapidly expanded their Asian research capability and staff. In 1990, about 250 research analysts covered Asian ex-Japan equities at the top ten firms. By 1996, that number had tripled to 750. Although overall market trading volumes were rising and more investors were interested in the markets, this increase in capacity could not easily be absorbed.

In the mid-1990s, the trading markets entered a competitive phase: the equity markets, the traditional bedrock of trading in Asia ex-Japan, saw declining commission rates. In 1994, the average commission on an equity trade in the major Asian markets was 60 basis points; in 1996 the same trade was done for 45 basis points. As equity market margins shrank, trading firms sought new opportunities. The most notable was the emergence of the corporate debt market, with all its flaws. Trading firms also expanded their foreign exchange trading businesses, endeavored to develop new markets such as Indonesia and Thailand, and built derivative trading businesses linked to their equity and debt businesses. As commission rates in equities declined, market share became more important. For instance, Merrill Lynch poached Jardine Fleming's nine-person Philippines team to build its business quickly in that country. All this expansion, of course, required more front-office and support staff, and office space. Compensation demands increased, and office rents in prime locations climbed. The rising market prices and increasing trading volumes of the mid-1990s allowed many firms to either temporarily cover these costs, or argue that they were needed to cope with the "inevitable" market growth that was still to come.

Of course, few firms predicted fully what happened next. Instead of markets continuously rising, there was the 1997–1998 crisis, which exposed the fundamental weaknesses of trading businesses in Asia ex-Japan. Equity markets were suddenly seen as not really that big (especially when the currencies in which many of them were traded had shrunk in value by about half or more) and became very volatile. Real hedges were no longer available. All at once counterparties were less reliable than their Western peers, and the lack of disclosure of positions and the opaque nature of corporate accounts became a real problem, not simply "local" practice. In the local currency debt markets, trading collapsed in line with the demise of Korean and Thai merchant banks that held too much of this paper. Foreign exchange was no better; volatility was again a major problem as liquidity disappeared from the markets. For some firms, the wider margins available in the foreign exchange and derivative markets allowed for very good profits for a while, but for many, the decline in volumes was a major problem.

At this point, all the costs and infrastructure that many firms had built up in the hope of breaking into these markets looked very problematic. In equities, the leading institutional brokerage firms had, as noted earlier, annual cost bases of about US$100 million dedicated to research and trading ex-Japanese equities. The best firms, including Jardine Fleming (which became wholly owned by Robert Fleming in 1998) and Barings, had earned commissions well above that figure each year during the mid-1990s, despite declining margins. Suddenly, though, their revenues plummeted. Weaker firms, which perhaps had been spending only US$50–60 million a year but had seen commissions at about break-even levels or slightly worse, found they could get revenues of only about US$20–30 million. There was only one solution: reduce costs. Some firms exited the market (JP Morgan of the U.S., Schroders Securities and BZW of the U.K.); others (W.I. Carr) cut staff back.

Peregrine: Living and Dying by the Sword

The story of Peregrine Securities encapsulates the 1990s development of the ex-Japan trading markets. This company was born when two Citibankers saw that only one way existed from the disasters of the market crash of 1987: upwards. Philip Tose and Francis Leung founded Peregrine with significant help from influential Hong Kong businessmen. They quickly built a strong track record in underwriting China and Hong Kong equity issues (initially for firms linked to their key shareholders). On that foundation, they broadened their Asia ex-Japan equity research, trading, and underwriting business. By the early 1990s, Peregrine was established as a leading Asian equity house, and began to expand into a broad-based investment bank focused on Asia. This meant diversifying its product range beyond equities.

Peregrine moved to the forefront of trying to turn into reality the 1995 World Bank estimate that the potential existed for a US$1 trillion corporate bond market in the region by 2004. Peregrine's bond team was led by the charismatic (but only 33 years old) Andre Lee, hired from Lehman

Brothers. At the same time, Peregrine expanded investment banking activities to include project finance. The firm opened offices as far away as Myanmar (temporarily), and entered the direct investment (principal investing) business. The firm continued its expansion in the first half of the decade, and by the end of 1996 it had over 1,700 staff worldwide.

While Peregrine often led general market trends, it also went beyond this, publicly reveling in the nature of the Asian markets. Philip Tose took sides with authoritarian government leaders, and argued publicly that this type of rule was better for economic growth than democracy. Peregrine worked hard to maintain close ties with the leaders in China and Thailand, and the Suharto family in Indonesia. The company had few complaints about lack of transparency in the markets; it believed that in such markets its special insights and contacts would bring superior returns.

Peregrine, then, was not just a major participant in these markets. In a very real sense it represented the fundamental rationale of traders who believed in the Asian miracle and disliked those who tried to impose Western standards. Through its superior relationships, Peregrine counted on winning in fundamentally inefficient and nontransparent markets.

As the saying goes: those who live by the sword, die by the sword. Just as Peregrine had led so many elements of the trading boom in Asia ex-Japan, so too was it at the forefront of the 1997–1998 collapse. In 1997, to fuel its developing debt business, Peregrine had not only underwritten some weak issues, it had provided loans to potential issuers on the basis that these bridge loans would be paid off by the ensuing debt issue. One such loan, to Steady Safe, a taxi company in Indonesia, was for US$270 million. This rather large sum would surely have bought a lot of taxis (although meant for investment in transport companies, where the money actually went was never clear). This loan was the most conspicuous of an estimated US$400 million of loans and underwritings that were never placed.

Then, in mid-1997 the crisis set in. The value of the rupiah disintegrated, making it impossible for most issuers to service their U.S. dollar debt; the collapse of Korean and Thai merchant banks removed the major buyers of potential issues. The weakness of the market was exposed very crudely, and Peregrine was caught in the middle. Within a few months of the crisis hitting, the firm was seeking outside investors to shore it up. Peregrine found Zurich Insurance, but when that firm took a closer look at the company's books, and further problems developed in Indonesia, the option evaporated. On January 12, 1998, Peregrine was handed over to the liquidators, and by the end of that month its crown jewel, the China equity business, led by Francis Leung, was purchased by Banque Nationale de Paris, an international firm trying to build a position in Asia.

Japan and the Yamaichi Example

If Peregrine epitomized positive and negative trends in the ex-Japanese trading markets, then Yamaichi Securities symbolized much at work in Japan, at the same time. Yamaichi was the fourth largest of the "Big Four" Japanese securities firms, after Nomura, Daiwa, and Nikko. During the 1980s, the Big Four benefited from three trends: the run-up in the Japanese equity market index from 6,768 in 1980 to 38,915 in 1989, which meant booming revenues for these firms' large retail brokerage business; the increased interest of international institutions in the Japanese market, which brought new institutional trading volumes to these firms; and the rise of Japanese corporations and their need for finance, for which they naturally turned to their home country financial firms first. As a result of these trends, in 1987, Nomura became the most profitable company in Japan.

Yamaichi's profits rose from ¥1,837 million in 1980 to ¥98,047 million in 1989, but unfortunately, they were not sustainable. The Japanese bull market was built upon what became known as the bubble economy of artificially low interest rates and overleveraged real estate values (at one point, the land on which the Imperial Palace in Tokyo stands was valued at more than the whole of Canada). When the bubble burst in mid-1991, the Nikkei Index — already depressed since its downturn in 1989 — fell from around 26,000 to under 20,000 by early 1992. With few exceptions, it did not trade above 20,000 from 1992 to 1998. Trading volumes declined from an average ¥1.6 trillion per day in 1989 to ¥500 billion per day during 1990–1997. The dual collapse in real estate and share values brought with it immediate credit problems and long-term economic stagnation. The Japanese economy averaged 1.5 percent in real growth from 1987 to 1997, compared with average growth rates of 2.5 percent for the U.S. and 7 percent for Asia ex-Japan during the same decade. Faced with declining core equity volumes and diminishing domestic economic strength, Japanese securities firms experienced immediate credit losses from margin loans that were not repaid, and then overall declines in income. Nomura's profits fell from a peak of ¥233 billion in 1987 to a ¥271 billion loss in 1996.

Unfortunately, also during the mid-1990s, some financial firms became victims of criminal elements in the Japanese economy. The reputation of the Big Four suffered a considerable blow when some senior executives were arrested in 1997 for illegally funneling funds to corporate racketeers. At the same time, a number of international expansion projects undertaken in the trading boom became liabilities due to weak internal controls. In 1995, U.S. regulators ordered Daiwa Bank (which is separate from Daiwa Securities) to pay fines of US$340 million and shut down its U.S. operations, when it was caught attempting to conceal US$1.1 billion in losses, incurred in unauthorized bond trading at its New York branch.

Finally, Japanese securities firms became subject to increased competition at home as aggressive U.S. firms, such as Morgan Stanley, began invading their core equity trading franchise. Specializing in index arbitrage trading, and trading for international institutions, foreign firms began building important positions in the markets. By 1997, foreign firms represented about 33 percent of all First Section stock trading in Tokyo.

Of the Big Four, Yamaichi was the most vulnerable to the risks and pressures just described. Profits from its core equity business slumped from a peak of ¥243 billion in 1989 to an average of ¥79 billion from 1990 to 1996. Worse, Yamaichi lost control of its internal processes. According to securities regulators, the firm committed more than 92 violations between 1988 and 1991 in connection with *tobashi*, whereby loss-making portfolios were shifted from client to client to cover paper losses.

Yamaichi also ran up huge unhedged trading positions in attempts to bolster profits. These positions, held in secret accounts, were under water for many years. If these accounts had been properly consolidated, technically, the firm would probably have been insolvent years before its eventual collapse. As the firm's published performance deteriorated, senior management resigned, and the head of the firm's core retail equity business — the real franchise of all four of the leaders — was asked to lead the firm. This honor became a nightmare for Shohei Nozawa as he discovered the hidden accounts and realized that Yamaichi was completely bankrupt. In November 1997, just 3 months after taking over, Nozawa announced that Yamaichi was going into voluntary liquidation. He had the humiliating job of disclosing the situation to the Japanese public and apologizing on television. The Finance Ministry of Japan estimated that Yamaichi's off-balance-sheet losses exceeded US$2 billion.

Yamaichi's dramatic demise symbolized the underlying trading mood in Japan during the 1990s: volumes were depressed, credit conditions were uncertain, and the major Japanese firms were not building the new skills required to diversify safely from their core retail franchise. International firms were encroaching on key aspects of the equity markets and leading international debt and equity issues for major corporations. Foreign firms took the lead in devising structured OTC swaps and other hedges and investment products for Japanese clients, even though the markets were not fully open for them.

Faced with the parlous state of trading firms (and big banks) at home, Japanese authorities debated, at length, opening up their markets to more foreign competition — which they knew would serve clients better and would force Japanese financial firms to build new skills. In late 1996, the government announced plans for its Big Bang — the revamp of the financial sector. Old barriers between markets were removed: for instance, securities firms were allowed to trade foreign exchange for the first time; foreign firms were granted the right to manage Japanese funds in Japan; and the government planned to ease access to trading markets by degrees. The major Japanese securities firms' weak performance, the scandals surrounding the industry, and the collapse of firms like Yamaichi and Sanyo Securities signaled that change, however slow, must come — and with it new opportunities and risks for domestic and foreign competitors.

Winning Trading Formulas also Apply in Asia

With the Asian trading markets' history of great opportunities but real limitations and risks, how can trading firms and brokers think about building winning businesses? The answer lies in applying the same principles that have worked around the world. At its simplest, wholesale trading is composed of three types of businesses, within each of which are basically three generic ways of making sustainable returns. This is true in the U.S. and Europe, and it is true in Asia, too.

Three Types of Trading Businesses...

Trading falls into three categories: making a commission or margin on a trade, that is, *agency trading*; making a spread on *market-making;* and *proprietary trading,* either in fine arbitrage or in outright bets on a stock's or market's direction.

Agency trading is where the intermediary does not take any risk on the trade, but receives a commission for providing information or research about the market or a particular stock, and for providing access to the trading floor and executing, clearing, and settling the trade. Commission-paid business is most notable in the equity markets. For instance, the Stock Exchange of Hong Kong has historically set minimum commission levels that investors pay brokers for trading. The New York Stock Exchange still operates on an agency and commission system for most trades, although through deregulation since 1975, commission rates have become far finer than under the fixed-commission system.

Market-making is where the intermediary takes the risk of market fluctuations by offering to make a two-way market in a stock or bond at a particular price. The broker or trader makes money on both the spread between the bid and the asked prices on a trade, and on the carry returns on the inventory if the market is rising.

Proprietary trading contains some elements of market-making. Here, an intermediary takes positions in the market, that is, places outright bets on the direction of a stock, of the whole market, of an industry sector, or of narrower hedged positions. In these hedged trades, for example, the trader might believe that two stocks that normally trade in a certain price relationship to each other have momentarily strayed, and simply takes a position that is neutral to the movement of the overall market. In this case, the trader only makes or loses money based on the price relationship between these two stocks. Whatever the intermediary's position, proprietary trading occurs when the intermediary's return depends on the way prices in the market move, rather than on the basis of customer trading volumes.

Obviously, these three types of trading merge very easily. We have already seen the difficulty of separating the market-making returns of, say, a bond trader from the returns from being long the bonds in which the firm makes markets. As interest rates fall in a particular market, it is probable that more clients will trade the bonds, creating profits from the bid-to-asked spread for the trader. At the same time, however, the value of the constantly evolving positions on the trader's books will inflate as interest rates fall and bond prices rise. The total returns from being a market-maker appear very attractive, but the best firms are able to analyze the trading to account for four factors:

(1) The amount of these profits that are actually dependent upon overall market moves and are therefore really proprietary trading profits;

(2) The amount of capital that is needed to support these positions so that the

return on capital of this trading can be measured;

(3) The potential for loss on these positions, given the historic, (hopefully) statistically reliable volatility of the bonds being traded; and

(4) The risk of loss from credit losses if the trading counterparties are operating in a difficult environment.

In the best of times, that is, rising markets, the most successful trading firms are able to analyze their market-making results to see how profits were made, what risks were taken to produce them, and what return on risk and accounting capital was achieved. From this base they can determine how sustainable the returns really are, and set risk limits (in terms of counterparty limits and overall position limits) that will serve them well in less buoyant times. These disciplines can also be applied to pure proprietary trading desks, which specifically aim to make money from proprietary positions. Here again, the best trading firms carefully measure how returns are being achieved, and set careful limits on positions to control their risk of loss in weak markets, or if the trader gets the direction wrong. In Asia, however, it was often very difficult to "short" a market, or take a position that would be profitable if the market declined. In many Asian markets, market-making and proprietary trading effectively meant being long the market.

...and Three Winning Strategies

Across these three types of trading, there are basically three ways of making sustainable returns. The first is to *segment the trading market* so finely that the intermediary finds hidden opportunities to make returns that others may not see. This can mean that the firm finds particular groups of customers that are prepared to trade at higher commission levels or wider market-making spreads. Even in the most mature and efficient markets, such as the global foreign exchange or U.S. Treasury markets, these anomalies constantly appear. For example, certain customers are less price-sensitive than others, or certain securities get slightly mispriced against a totally efficient pricing level. Major securities trading houses invest significant time and effort identifying these customers or finding small pricing opportunities.

The second trading technique is to *identify statistically valid patterns in markets*, and trade on the probabilities that these trends will hold in the future. As we saw earlier, a trader might be tracking the pricing relationship between two stocks (pursuing pairs trading) — for example, Hong Kong Telecom and Singapore Telecom — and discover that, historically, these two companies have traded within a certain percentage of each other, adjusted for the relative levels of the overall stock markets. Using basic statistical techniques, the trader measures the probability that when the prices of the two stocks diverge by a particularly wide amount, they will converge back to the normal price relationship between them. Applying similar analyses across a range of price relationships of individual stocks, or indices, the trader might construct a portfolio of positions.

The final way of making sustainable returns from trading is *to build a virtuous circle of investor and issuer relationships to dominate a market*. This applies when investment banks use their large base of investor relationships to prove to corporate issuers that they should use them for underwriting their new securities issues. Alternatively, the banks may offer unique research on the markets to investors. The strategy makes the investment bank more attractive as a broker and trading partner to investors, since it is able to offer a stream of attractive new issues (or superior research) in addition to trading already listed secondary issues. The major risk in this strategy is that the bank is forced to be a market-maker in its new underwritten products, and in a bear market, it means being a forced buyer from investors. This inevitably leads to losses. But this virtuous circle of scale may be supplemented by opportunities to cross-sell other traded products to the same investors, so breadth of product range can support depth of investor relationships in a particular market. These ancillary products range from being directly related to trading, such as custody services, to one step removed, such as foreign exchange, to the truly distant, such as commercial lending.

This virtuous circle of scale can sometimes be jump-started by using a firm's capital base to facilitate particularly difficult or large trades for a client or to buy whole new issues from an issuer without having to rely on a syndicate of underwriters. These two methods are not without significant risk, of course. They have led to real problems for many firms when the proprietary positions that are effectively involved in this strategy had gone sour.

Of course, these three trading strategies can be combined. For instance, by building trading volumes through the virtuous circle, a trading firm can both segment its customers to maximize service levels and profits, and undertake proprietary trading based on its increased understanding of trends in the market. As the trading markets in Asia mature in the first decade of the 21st century, careful application of the three trading strategies will be required by the winners.

Building Blocks of Success

All winning trading firms in Asia, like those around the world, need basic processes and infrastructure. This is true across whatever trading strategies they pursue, and whatever products, countries, and currencies in which they trade.

We have seen that all trading involve some risk, so efficient and timely systems to collect and analyze information about a security or market are critical. Superior information, and the means of analyzing it, are at the heart of all good trading strategies. In the mid-1990s, in order to gather up-to-date, advantageous information, local equity brokerage firms, like Credit Lyonnais Securities, depended on local analysts in each country in which it traded. Simultaneously, these trading firms implemented position-taking limit systems to avoid their versions of Nick Leeson or Yamaichi tragedies. The firms were able to measure the volatility of their positions based on historic patterns and limit their positions, such that 99 percent of the time they were only exposed to a maximum loss of a given percentage of shareholders' capital. These firms needed to be able to track counterparties' peak loan equivalent positions on derivative trades and monitor their creditworthiness continuously. We will see in our discussion of Lehman Brothers, however, that these systems are only as good as the history on which they are based, on the ability of the firm to follow their guidance to the fullest, and on the counterparty's acceptance of its obligations.

Obviously, implementing risk management systems requires strong, flexible information technology. In fact, as product opportunities come and go, or as traders require access to new sources of information, these trading firms need information technology that can be restructured quickly. Modular information systems that build on a common low-cost base, which can be cheaply replicated in a new country or which can expand a trading desk, but that also allows for increasing sophistication of traders' needs, is critical for these firms.

During much of the 1990s, firms trading in Asia debated whether a distributed business model, with salespeople and traders located in a number of markets so as to be close to the action, or a centralized model, with staff located in just a few cities so as to control risk and costs, made sense. While conceptually attractive, the distributed model suffered from the fact that many of the markets in Asia were just too small to justify the expense of a local presence. The 1997–1998 crisis sealed the fate of the distributed model in the minds of most managers. Given their superior legal and regulatory environments, and the higher quality of their information technology infrastructure and local staff, most firms had to be in Hong Kong, Singapore, and Tokyo. The decline in trading volumes across the region as a result of the crisis, and increased concerns about risk management and regulatory risk that emerged during the crisis, reinforced the attractiveness of the centralized model for many firms. These firms pulled back from many cities, consequently, except from the three.

Successful trading firms, however, are not just a mix of mathematical systems and limits. The mechanisms are there to help the salespeople and traders who call the clients or make the ultimate trading decisions. Further, they enable winning firms to attract, develop, and motivate salespeople and traders to seek new opportunities — be they clients or new trading strategies — and limit the exposure of the firm to too much risk. Doing this successfully is not as easy as it sounds, as it involves solving the agent principal problem (agent — the trader; principal — the firm the trader works for). The consequence to a trader of losing US$30 million on a series of high-risk trades might be getting fired, but the consequence to the firm — especially a small one — might be complete failure. During much of the 1990s, the mismatch between agent and principal was a problem in Asia, as around the world.

Finally, the best firms need clients. Unfortunately, during much of the 1990s, the pool of sophisticated institutional clients was not large in Japan or the rest of Asia. Sometimes firms pressed the edges of client sophistication on willingness to abide by contracts as they expanded their trading businesses. From 1994 to 1996, Lehman Brothers was involved in a spate of legal battles in U.S. courts with mainland Chinese entities. Among others, state-owned giants China International United Petroleum & Chemicals (Unipec) and China National Metals & Minerals Import & Export Corporation (Minmetals) sued over losses incurred in derivatives trading totaling more than US$100 million. Lehman had advised these companies to take billions of dollars worth of exposure, and in each case the Chinese company refused to meet obligations resulting from losses in derivatives trades that Lehman executed on its behalf. Minmetals countersued Lehman for unfairly misleading it into "engaging in incredibly complicated transactions that were impossible for [it] to understand." In the end, most of the cases were settled out of court.

The question of whether Lehman properly disclosed the risks of derivative instruments to its clients is probably academic, as the firm's relationship with mainland authorities will inevitably be strained for years to come. Lehman's experience illustrates that excellent counterparty credit assessment in Asia goes beyond understanding a counterparty's financial situation: one must also be able to assess a counterparty's understanding and acceptance of standard international financial practice.

Winning Profiles — Most of the Time

As we have seen, these "best" trading practices had to be applied in an environment where the potential for problems was much larger than in the U.S. or Europe. Corporate headquarters in New York, London, Zurich, Hong Kong, or Tokyo demanded forever-rising profits from these markets, and expected Asia to represent a growing percentage of total profits. Yet the regional equity markets outside Japan were relatively small, and Japan's market had been depressed since the beginning of the 1990s. The debt markets outside Japan were also small, and inherently unstable. Information about securities issuers was scanty. Staff at the trading firms was often recently hired, or had little experience in dealing with declining markets. And yet, everyone had to be in Asia. A number of firms did build winning trading businesses in Asia during the 1990s. Although their approaches combined the three trading strategies mentioned earlier, some still suffered during the 1997–1998 trading crisis.

Merrill Lynch

This firm built a virtuous circle strategy based on high-quality broking and research. During the late 1980s and through the mid-1990s, Merrill emerged as a leading underwriter and trader worldwide of both equity and debt securities. Its success reflected very strong placement capabilities in the critical U.S. investor market, and strengthened investment banking groups. Starting in the mid-1990s, Merrill replicated this strategy in Asia by simultaneously building up its secondary trading capabilities and its investment banking team. Its most dramatic action was the 1995 purchase of Smith New Court, a leading London brokerage firm that also had depth in a number of Asian markets outside Japan. The combination of Smith New Court's local strength and Merrill's reputation for easily placing paper in the U.S., generated a truly credible position for Merrill with Asian issuers as a firm that could place their securities with Asian investors — or globally.

The new position naturally produced a virtuous circle with the same investors: they now saw Merrill as a firm that not only provided excellent research and trading, but one that would bring a continuous string of new issues. At the end of 1997, Merrill started the long process of replicating this strategy in Japan. Like numerous U.S. firms, Merrill had been active there for many years, but had been limited to selective issues for large Japanese corporates needing placement in the U.S., and to trading in U.S. equities and Treasuries for large Japanese institutional investors, such as the major life insurance companies. Merrill made a significant move into the indigenous business by purchasing large parts of the defunct Yamaichi retail brokerage force in 1997. Suddenly Merrill's future offered close relationships with investors in the United States and Japan, and a global virtuous circle of providing issuers around the world with the best placement power possible and investors with a broad range of secondary and primary issues.

Merrill was, of course, not immune to trading risks, and in October 1998 announced global cutbacks of over 3,000 staff as a result of declining volumes and increased volatility. Nevertheless, it still had in place a strong base in Asia.

Jardine Fleming

The joint venture investment bank between Robert Fleming of the U.K. and the Jardine Group based in Hong Kong (quoted on the Singapore stock exchange since 1995) pursued a regional Asian version of Merrill's strategy. Jardine Fleming built an enviable position in ex-Japanese markets in the late 1980s and much of the 1990s by combining scale in institutional brokerage and the investment management businesses. Along with Barings, W.I. Carr, and Credit Lyonnais Securities, Jardine Fleming was consistently one of the leaders in the institutional secondary brokerage of ex-Japanese equities, and won a disproportionate share of commissions from institutional investors in the U.S., Europe, and Asia, relative to the number of analysts and salespeople it had and the total cost base it needed.

At the same time, Jardine Fleming was the leading mutual fund company in Hong Kong, and its institutional investment management business was also sizable. A significant percentage (too high, in some cases, as Hong Kong regulators discovered in 1995) of its trades in the mutual fund business were sent through its brokerage business. The high shares in both businesses generated significant economies of scale and ancillary revenues in the 1990s.

The group also tried to build its corporate finance business in the region to reach the same virtuous circle of business between its investment banking and brokerage businesses that Merrill had achieved. Between 1992 and 1996, Jardine Fleming grew its investment banking department to more than 170 strong, and frequently ranked among the top few in underwriting league tables. Significantly, during this period Jardine Fleming was able to sustain its leadership in the core equity brokerage business. By 1998, however, Jardine sold out of the joint venture in exchange for a holding in Robert Fleming. The reason: Jardine realized one had to approach the trading and broking businesses through a globally integrated platform in order to serve institutional investors successfully.

Vickers Ballas

A Singapore stockbroker, Vickers Ballas achieved attractive returns in the mid-1990s through its knowledge of local investors and their needs. At the same time, it built its position in institutional brokerage of Singapore stocks to a respectable level, so that its combined retail and wholesale business gave it a good margin on its costs — as long as the markets were reasonably buoyant. The Vickers Ballas story was repeated in Thailand, the Philippines, Malaysia, Indonesia, and Taiwan: high spreads available to retail brokers in each market allowed a number of local firms to survive on retail business, and from that base, build institutional research and clients. In these markets, foreign brokers were not allowed free entry, and often had to broke trades through local brokers. Furthermore, regulators upheld minimum commission levels. Winners, therefore, relied on gaining good market share and controlling costs, and hoped for strong market volumes.

The Vickers Ballas story unraveled, however, as a result of the 1997–1998 crisis. The firm incurred large margin and position losses, and produced much lower trading revenues as regional stock volumes declined. As a result, it reported losses of nearly US$30 million for the first 6 months of 1998, against profits of about US$25 million in the same period in 1997. The outlook for the rest of 1998 and 1999 for the firm was very weak, and faced with poor markets and an upcoming deregulation of local brokerage commissions, action had to be taken. In September 1998, Vickers announced it would merge with a Singapore government-controlled finance company, ST Capital, becoming part of a broader government strategy to consolidate and strengthen the financial services industry on the island. Now with this larger government influence and broader product range, Vickers could continue its strategy of regional expansion.

JP Morgan

While Merrill Lynch, Jardine Fleming, and Vickers Ballas achieved their profits by winning and sustaining significant market share positions in equities, and then leveraging ancillary revenues from them, the basis for JP Morgan's success in regional trading was fundamentally different. Unlike Merrill or Jardine Fleming, Morgan's historic strength was in bonds — not equities. Its investor strength was most notable with central banks and major fixed-income institutions, rather than equity investors. From this base, Morgan built a fixed-income, foreign exchange, and related derivative business that relied much more on market-making spreads and proprietary trading profits than the commission-driven equity trading businesses of Vickers Ballas and Jardine Fleming.

Morgan made money by trading a wide range of foreign exchange and fixed-income products with its major institutional and corporate clients. Morgan provided these clients with superb service and tailored, structured products on which it made especially attractive spreads. In Japan in the late 1980s and early 1990s, Morgan was a leader in the interest rate and currency swap markets. Through close management of proprietary risk exposure for its carefully segmented and screened clients, Morgan earned attractive market-making spreads.

In the mid-1990s, Morgan extended this approach by providing the same range of tailored products to its key customers in Asia ex-Japan. In those years, perhaps as much as two-thirds of Morgan's Asian profits came from these trading activities. Morgan made markets in traditional foreign exchange and G-7 debt products with these customers, and achieved reasonable bid-to-asked spreads. Morgan earned the right to its profits by providing these same customers with specially tailored hedging instruments or structured investment products that met their individual needs. These clients relied on Morgan's sophisticated, statistically based risk-management techniques to hedge exposures. The intricate products built hedge upon hedge to structure exactly the right exposure for the customer. Within these structures were significant opportunities for Morgan to build small spread upon small spread to make the whole product very profitable. These tailored product businesses, supplemented by the more traditional trading that came with them, earned Morgan attractive returns — until problems arose in 1997.

Risk management is not without risk. As we saw earlier with Lehman Brothers, the risk of default by counterparties when things go wrong is very real in Asia. Unfortunately, JP Morgan also had its share of problems in this area. A lawsuit filed in 1998 with a U.S. federal district court alleged SK Securities of Korea failed to pay Morgan substantial debts due under several currency swap transactions. Once again, industry players were anxious to see the outcome of the court case and its implications on the enforceability of their own contracts.

Morgan's difficulties with SK Securities was perhaps a harbinger of more trouble. Even its renowned risk management techniques and conservative approach were insufficient to shield it from the full brunt of the Asian financial turmoil. On February 27, 1998, JP Morgan announced that it was cutting back 6 percent of its Asia-Pacific staff of 1,700 employees following a 35 percent drop in fourth-quarter worldwide earnings. The poor results were partly attributable to huge losses from its Asian swap contracts, of which US$587 million worth, mostly in Korea, were judged nonperforming. In October 1998, Morgan made further cutbacks in Asia.

Although the layoffs formed part of a worldwide initiative to cut costs, the timing and the lines of business most severely affected in Asia suggest that some of Morgan's operations were no longer as profitable as they had been. The fact that most of Morgan's February 1998 cutbacks in Asia were directed at its Asian equity team was further evidence of the difficulties in the Asian brokerage business, with its high cost base and fluctuating volumes. Previous ambitions to become a dominant player in every field in Asia were replaced by a sober refocusing on core strengths in advisory, debt financing, and derivatives. But the October 1998 cuts reflected the low volumes in Asian foreign exchange and debt trading. Morgan's restructuring was a lesson to others with similar ambitions, of the challenges of pursuing the coveted virtuous circle of scale.

Trading Winners in Asia

As the trading markets of Asia enter the 21st century, which firms will win sustainable returns? After the 1997–1998 meltdown is put into perspective, the surviving firms will have interesting opportunities. The realities of still-growing markets, new product opportunities, foreign exchange and capital market deregulation, the ongoing need for capital, and the newfound realization of the importance of hedging exposures will provide great opportunities for trading and brokerage businesses. Yet we have seen that firms that stray from the three core trading strategies, and that do not build strong customer franchises, unique sources of information and ways of analyzing it, or significant market share, will be unable to survive. In the equity markets, as expenses exceed the commissions or spreads they can earn, and the battle for market share intensifies, middle-sized competitors will suffer unattractive returns. In the debt markets, traders without strong placement capabilities and regular clients of stature will constantly be exposed to the risk of large position losses from illiquid securities in times of crisis or rising interest rates. Finally, those unable to monitor and manage their exposures will be at great risk from markets that will often display high volatility, and from errant staff in distant operations centers.

Four Key Groups of Winners

The winning traders in Asia, therefore, are likely to be firms that focus on the key strategies of successful traders worldwide: they will develop unique or advantaged sources of information in their chosen markets; understand the mathematical or statistical relationships between markets; build market share in their selected arenas; manage their trading businesses with firm risk-management information systems and procedures; and control costs through a centralized business model. These winning businesses will probably fall into four groups, some of which will occur simultaneously in the same corporate entity. That is, it will be possible for a large firm like ING Barings to pursue more than one winning trading strategy concurrently.

Global trading firms

These firms will have the capacity to invest to win market share, to introduce new products, and to research the statistical relationships between securities. Just as the securities trading markets of G-7 securities have become dominated by major global trading firms like Goldman Sachs, Morgan Stanley, Salomon Smith Barney, Merrill Lynch, JP Morgan, Chase Manhattan, Citibank, Deutsche Bank, UBS, Credit Suisse First Boston, ING Barings, ABN Amro, and Barclays Capital, so the Asian markets will be susceptible to their skills, investor relationships, and scale. These firms already have strong positions in many of the Asian markets, and have built attractive businesses in both exchange-traded products and in the large OTC markets for swaps, foreign exchange, and structured products. They will, in the future, consistently be able to attract the best staff: faced with a choice, most Chinese, Thai, or even Japanese young men and women seeking a career in trading will regard these global firms as more attractive than smaller, less well-capitalized local firms (unless they are offered equity positions in such firms). Global firms will also have the financial clout to invest in the newest technology and approaches, further increasing their attractiveness to clients and potential staff.

Regional competitors

This group of likely winners in the Asian equity markets will include the leading brokers in Japan, and Jardine Fleming, Credit Lyonnais Securities, and W.I. Carr outside Japan. Although they face assaults from global firms, these regional entities can survive if they remain focused on their strengths and create barriers to entry or attack. Dedication to the highest quality, on-the-ground analysis, and close coverage of the key institutional investors in their products around the world will enable these firms to remain the best environment for research analysts, salespeople, and traders of their products. These competitors know that only about 100 institutions provide close to 60 percent of all commissions in ex-Japanese equities, and they will work hard to retain their in-depth understanding of these investors' needs.

While the global firms will definitely attack these franchises, the evidence in other equity markets is that focused local or regional entities (PaineWebber in the U.S., Chevreux de Virieu in France, Cazenove in the U.K.) can continue to maintain their positions. Another strength some of these firms have to build on is their retail revenues in the region. Just as in the U.S. where Merrill Lynch and PaineWebber have been able to use the asset and trading base of their local retail markets as a secure keel from which to develop and support their wholesale activities, so too Nomura in Japan, Jardine Fleming in Hong Kong, and even Vickers Ballas in Singapore have the opportunity to build strong foundations in their markets. Despite these opportunities for local and regional firms, the constant increase of costs and the decline in both institutional and retail commissions means that the list of winners among this group will shrink. Just a few local or regional firms will be able to make money consistently from these equity markets.

Proprietary trading businesses

Likely winners in this category of Asian trading markets will be in the tradition of Long Term Capital Management and Salomon Brothers. These proprietary traders will invest significant amounts to understand trends and statistical patterns in trading. They will construct portfolios that are hedged against risks they do not understand, and will only expose themselves to risks they believe they can predict most of the time. In times of crisis, they will keep shifting up to the most liquid instrument in which to take their positions, always trying to remain as liquid as possible (although as Long Term Capital found out in August 1998 when it incurred major losses, even the firms with the best track records can be caught out by low liquidity markets). They will take both short-term (a few days) and long-term (a few years) positions. Their long-term positions will be designed to take advantage of long-term mis-pricing of illiquid Asian markets. Firms such as Tudor Investment Management are likely to invest further in Asia, and local hedge funds may move into more quantitative trading techniques. Many of the leading global firms mentioned above will also implement proprietary trading businesses. Again, those with the best analytical capability and the capacity to hone their portfolios to focus on the risks they understand are likely to earn superior returns. But they will have to remember the lessons of the hedge fund crisis of 1998, that even the best statistical models can fail to predict some periods of volatility, and so portfolio leverage must be controlled.

Firms with protected or practically impenetrable positions

These likely winners trade in national markets where international competition is excluded by regulation or by investor practice. An example is the corporate bond traders in Taiwan. Bonds gained huge popularity there in the late 1990s, and daily trading volumes averaged US$3.6 billion in 1996 — surpassing daily turnover in the Taiwan Stock Exchange by nearly US$2 billion that year. This boom was partly the result of the emergence of a group of firms known as bills finance companies. These entities specialize in guaranteeing and underwriting short-term debt for local corporates as well as market-making in these securities for investors. Companies like International Bills Finance Company and China Bills Finance were among the ten or so major players that actively traded in this market in the late 1990s. The combination of a largely domestic investor base, strong relationships with local issuers, and regulatory barriers allowed these firms to flourish without threat of foreign competition in the late 1990s.

However, competition does not always come from the outside. After 1996, the Taiwan bond market shifted markedly away from short-term debt, or bills, to corporate and government bonds with longer maturities. This development can be attributed principally to the rapid proliferation of bond funds in Taiwan. Previously, investors would have had problems absorbing the large tranches of corporate debt, but with bond funds as an intermediary investment tool, corporate bonds found a niche that led to rapid expansion. The reason for the popularity of bond funds, which traded primarily in the repo market, was the tax advantage over bill trading under Taiwanese tax law. As a result, some bills finance companies lost around 70 percent of their customers in just one year to the bond funds. This example illustrates the extent to which financial markets in Asia are regulation-driven. Regulation not only keeps foreign competitors off the playing field, but determines the rules of the game. To win, firms cannot rely solely on regulatory protection from the outside world; they need the flexibility to adapt quickly to new competitive environments within.

The position of mainland Chinese firms trading in corporate debt and equity will be similar to that of Taiwanese bills traders. Although in the mid-1990s both the debt and equity markets in China suffered from high volatility and corruption scandals, the opportunities in these markets are obviously based on their potential size. Chinese authorities are likely to continue to be able to control international competition in these markets and pursue a policy of seeking the emergence of their own world-class major securities firms. Those that survive intact and scandal-free in the first decade of the next century will have the opportunity of building a strong base at home as a result of protected margins and rising volumes.

Other protected markets will offer similar opportunities if the local firms can grow fast enough and avoid the corruption that comes with protected, high margins. Domestic securities houses, such as Kotak Mahindra and ICICI Securities in India, trading firms such as Asian Securities Ltd in Pakistan, and fledgling traders in the protected markets of Indochina will have opportunities to develop attractive businesses. However, as soon as these businesses grow in scale, the combination of WTO pressure for market opening and global firms' interest in pursuing new opportunities of size will put these margins under pressure.

All eventual trading winners — the global firms, the regional or local firms, the proprietary traders, and those operating in protected markets — will have to ensure their basic businesses are soundly designed and managed. The balance between revenues, costs, and capital usage will need to be modeled and stress-tested in good and bad market conditions; all opportunities for ancillary revenues will need to be taken advantage of; and all will have to remember the lessons of Nick Leeson and his trading in what seemed to Barings a distant corner of the world.

Besides those of Japan, the trading markets of Asia will remain small for a long time compared to those of the U.S. and Europe. As a result, they will be susceptible to bouts of enthusiasm, rising values, skepticism, and declining values. Volatility is likely to be high, which will bring opportunities for many and problems for others, and will continue the cycle of boom and bust in these markets for some time to come.

6

ASSET MANAGEMENT:
POSITIONING FOR PROFITS

Jardine Fleming has long been the fund manager to beat in Asia. Outside Japan, it has been among the largest managers of Asia-bound investments serving institutions and individuals. At its height in 1996, prior to the 1997 stock market and currency crisis, it managed funds totaling approximately US$22 billion. By 2010, however, 1996 will probably be remembered as the year when Jardine Fleming Investment Management started to face the challenges of a new era.

By the mid-1980s, Jardine had established itself as a consistent leader in identifying and capturing investment opportunities throughout the region. Its funds often topped performance league tables on investments extending from India to Japan. Jardine's managers believed the secret of its success was combining good research and fast decision-making. The internal culture thrived on autonomy, yet maintained cohesiveness through strong and often personal relationships among senior management. Jardine management defended this free environment; after all, Jardine was making money for itself and its clients by being able to respond quickly to the inefficiencies and dynamism that characterize emerging markets. To supporters, Jardine's investment management structure was "entrepreneurial"; to those less impressed, it was viewed as an operation of "cowboys."

By the mid-1990s, Colin Armstrong was one of Jardine's top fund managers. Among his responsibilities was overseeing Jardine's highly successful Ninja fund, which focused on equities, derivatives, and, particularly, Japanese warrants. A 1996 probe into Armstrong's trading, however, revealed Jardine's internal compliance had been unable to keep pace with the firm's success and growth. Armstrong had been booking profitable trades into the Ninja fund and his own account, and less favorable trades into other Jardine funds. The impact on Jardine was significant. Important pension funds, including those of the Hong Kong Jockey Club, the Post Office of Britain, and the U.K.-based corporate pensions for IBM and Avon, initiated an immediate review of their asset management mandates with Jardine. Press estimates at the time of the Armstrong scandal suggested that up to US$3 billion of Jardine's funds under management were vulnerable to withdrawals. Authorities in Hong Kong and the U.K. fined Jardine US$1 million, and ordered it to compensate clients disadvantaged by Armstrong's actions a total of US$19 million.

Jardine Fleming's then joint venture owners, Jardine Matheson and Robert Fleming, subsequently demanded far-reaching changes in the way the firm was run. A ten-man supervisory board was established to oversee local Jardine Fleming directors in the region. The number of compliance officers tripled to approximately 20 to institute and monitor stricter procedures. Alan Smith, chairman of Jardine Fleming, who had been with the firm for 24 years, resigned. Initially, Jardine tried to separate Smith's departure from the fallout of the scandal. In the aftermath of his resignation, Smith indicated that he left because he felt the new changes had gone too far and were making the firm too bureaucratic and too inflexible to capture the opportunities that had driven previous growth and investment successes. At Jardine Fleming, 1996 is likely to be remembered as the year the informal organization died.

Asset Management Is Evolving Rapidly

Jardine Fleming had little choice but to introduce stringent internal reform. The asset management industry in Asia is coming of age, and consumers, corporations, and governments in Asia are poised to make greater use of professional investment advice to manage savings, improve returns, and prepare for the retirement of aging societies. In 1998, funds from Asia placed with asset managers totaled roughly US$2 trillion. By 2010, due to increasing demand, this figure is likely to grow to as much as US$10–12 trillion, supporting an industry in Asia with annual revenues of US$50–60 billion. This growth will be spurred and served by an increasing number of asset managers from all over the world, although many will be from the U.S. and Europe.

Hand in hand with asset managers will be the increased presence of industry consultants, such as Watson Wyatt Worldwide, Frank Russell Co., RCP and Partners, Micropal, and Lipper Analytical Services. These firms keep individual and institutional customers abreast of asset managers' performance and operational soundness, and assess risks associated with managers' investment styles and strategies. In short, numerous demands from growth and for performance will be placed on asset managers, particularly those who wish to be more than niche players. Even if Jardine Fleming had not suffered a scandal, would have had to significantly upgrade structures and systems within its organization to cope with increasing business complexity and demands for greater transparency. Not reforming would have left too much opportunity at risk.

A market that grows from US$2 trillion to US$12 trillion in assets under management in just over a decade implies significant opportunity. Indeed, an industry that can potentially generate up to US$60 billion in annual revenues will make asset management one of the larger business line opportunities in Asia. But it is misleading to view this prospect from an all-Asia perspective. Asian asset management opportunities are heavily weighted in Japan. That country has the second largest pool of savings in the world, and in the late 1990s, was in the midst of a deregulation program that should make it one of the largest open asset management markets worldwide. By 2010, Japan should have approximately US$8 trillion in assets under management — approximately 10 percent of the globe's future total. The rest of Asia will remain a small market by comparison, and despite anticipated rapid growth, by 2010 it will represent only 3–4 percent of projected global assets under management.

Despite the differences in size, Japan and the rest of Asia share similar market characteristics. Government regulation in both is the single-largest determinant of how quickly the market for private asset managers will evolve, and how large it will become. In all markets, given the currently low level of investor sophistication, converting curiosity and needs into business opportunities will require significant customer education. Finally, competition in Japan and the rest of Asia is made up of many aspirants, but few have established leadership positions.

Given these market characteristics, competitors that are capable of anticipating and responding to government deregulation, that excel at introducing investment concepts to individuals and institutions, and that aggressively pursue customer relationships through cost-effective distribution will be well positioned to succeed.

As markets develop in the years leading up to 2010, many competitors throughout Asia are likely to establish small but profitable businesses. Several, potentially the likes of Jardine Fleming, will put together medium- to large-sized businesses in Asia ex-Japan. And a small number of firms that successfully penetrate opportunities in Japan may be able to build businesses comparable in size to those of today's market leaders in the U.S. and Europe.

Two Distinct Asset Management Businesses

Opportunities for competitors in Japan and the rest of Asia will come from the two distinct asset management businesses: *retail* and *institutional*. Retail asset management encompasses selling mutual funds and units trusts to individual investors, while institutional asset management entails managing money for pension funds, life insurers, and corporations.

Retail asset management in Asia mirrors the business elsewhere in the world, that is, a professional manages individuals' investments. For a given fund, assets are accumulated from individuals and managed as a single pool. Individuals effectively own a portion of the given fund, and share in gains and losses proportional to the amount of the fund they own. Thousands of retail funds are on offer in Asia by dozens of banks and insurance companies, and by about 100 fund management companies. These funds provide individuals with opportunities to invest in stocks, bonds, money markets, commodities, currencies, and derivatives. At the end of 1997, the retail asset management business in Asia totaled US$547 billion in assets — US$419 billion in Japan and US$128 billion in the rest of Asia. These retail funds were pooled from individuals around the region who had invested the equivalent of as little as several hundred U.S. dollars, to several hundred thousand U.S. dollars' worth.

Institutional asset management in Asia, as elsewhere in the world, caters primarily to government pension funds, private pension funds, insurance companies, banks, and corporations. Prior to the financial crisis, *Institutional Investor* magazine estimated that Asian institutional investors had approximately US$6.8 trillion of assets — US$6 trillion in Japan, and US$750 billion in the rest of Asia. As of 1997, approximately 20 percent, or US$1.4 trillion, of institutional investor funds was actually managed by external asset managers. The remainder was either invested directly in capital markets by the investors, or held locally, more often than not in local real estate, bank time deposits, and government bonds.

About 100 institutional asset managers across the region serve Asian institutional investors. In contrast to the retail asset management business, institutional asset managers provide funds tailored to the specific needs of investors, who typically invest several hundred thousand to several hundred million U.S. dollars. Asset managers attempt to meet the investment objectives of their institutional clients by utilizing a full range of investment instruments (stocks, bonds, currencies, commodities, and derivatives), as well as occasional holdings in unlisted private placements, real estate, and participation in venture capital investments.

Asia: Still a Regulators' World

In much of the developed world, the potential to succeed in the retail and institutional asset management business is largely defined by fundamental market growth and the degree of competition. In Asia, however, market size and the opportunities available to retail and institutional asset managers will be closely tied to domestic regulations for much of the first decade of the 21st century. Shaped by governments in Asia, these regulations will attempt to balance national development objectives with the long-term investment needs of their populations. Government efforts to address both objectives will create barriers and opportunities for asset managers in Asia.

Asian governments' first objective will be to increase the pool of national savings to facilitate restructuring and modernizing of their local economies. Pooled savings are considered a useful stimulus for developing local capital markets. Pooling is particularly important for many Asian governments seeking to expand market liquidity to support extensive privatization programs. These programs, in turn, are seen as a prerequisite for increasing corporate productivity.

Many governments in Asia promote retail mutual funds and pension funds to direct savings into capital markets. Governments view pension funds, which typically are not cashed out in the short term, as particularly useful for heavy investments in long-term domestic infrastructure projects. Governments in Asia also support insurance development to pool assets. If insurance premiums are, for example, invested in local stock markets or placed in local bank time deposits, they effectively help fund domestic growth while providing important coverage for individuals and corporations.

Because local investment needs are so great across Asia, governments have traditionally promoted pooled savings — an opportunity for fund managers to intermediate investment flows — but have often limited offshore investment, which has stymied foreign fund managers in particular. Pooling national savings to fund national growth can generate value for an entire society. However, governments in Asia are increasingly aware, as a result of the 1997–1998 crisis, that a nationally focused pooling and investment strategy is high risk. Should the economy falter with all its eggs in one basket, personal, corporate, and national wealth are simultaneously destroyed.

The destruction of personal wealth impinges on governments' second objective: ensuring adequate savings and investment returns to provide for its aging populations. All of Asia's societies are graying: in 1998, 6 percent of the region's population was over 65 years old. By 2010, that figure will have grown to 8 percent, and will reach 14 percent in 2030.

To prepare for the change in demographics, governments are trying to shape how much people save and how they invest. Singapore has led Asia in regulating savings. Its defined contribution plan, the Central Provident Fund (CPF), draws 20 percent of individuals' annual compensation and required employers to match that amount, until late 1998 when the government reduced the employers' contribution rate (to 10 percent) in a bid to lower the costs of doing business in Singapore. The money gathered is placed in a blocked investment account that provides a guaranteed return to holders. A series of investment rules ensure that pooled savings are placed with experienced managers and invested in instruments that carry acceptable levels of risk and return. The CPF systematically reviews its portfolio to identify where investment returns can be improved. In early 1998, it placed 10 percent of its funds with private asset managers to enhance investment performance and reduce its administrative costs. By the late 1990s, it permitted up to 20 percent of its portfolio to be invested abroad to increase diversification, thereby minimizing destruction of national savings in the event of a domestic crisis. Other Asian governments' programs are not as developed as Singapore's, but many are considering instituting pension reforms to plan for their populations' future. Pension plans that attempt to maximize returns for a populace's savings create significant opportunities for private fund managers.

The same regulators guiding pooling and investing national savings frequently specify which asset managers can mediate investments. In the late 1990s, regulators in many Asian countries preferred that local financial institutions profit from mediation. Regulators curbed foreign asset management competition by limiting market access in the hopes that local financial institutions would develop the skills for investing national savings. Ideally, local institutions would acquire these skills before governments are forced to give in to international pressures to open their domestic markets, sometime early in the 21st century.

Although government regulations differ by country, they impact the asset management industry in five key areas: how much money will be pooled; which financial institutions can gather money into the pool; which financial institutions can manage the pooled money; where pooled money can be invested geographically; and in which types of instruments pooled money can be invested.

The impact of these regulations generally extends to local and international asset managers in the retail and institutional businesses. Hence, a change in regulation often represents a substantial shift in asset management opportunities. The following are examples of how regulatory changes can impact the first three of these factors, thereby influencing opportunities for private fund managers.

How much money will be pooled?

Government regulations regarding how much money must be pooled in pension plans vary across Asia. Imagine, however, if all Asia moved to pension schemes funded at only 25 percent of Singapore's defined contribution plan. At the end of 1997, public pension programs in Asia totaled US$750 billion (of which US$600 billion was in Japan). If in 1998 all Asian countries outside Japan had developed schemes that were proportionally only a quarter as large as Singapore's (its pension scheme was approximately 52 percent of GDP), the public pension market would have been five times larger than it is. In fact, in 1998 Hong Kong and Japan were in the process of legislating new defined contribution pension schemes in anticipation of future retirement needs. The outcome of such legislation will significantly influence the amount of funds available to institutional asset managers in the decade leading up to 2010.

Which financial institutions can gather money into the pool?

In Asia, regulations on who can sell retail funds have a significant effect on private asset managers. In many countries, such as Malaysia and China, regulations in the late 1990s confined foreign participation in retail fund distribution. In Japan, regulations even limited distribution among local financial institutions. Up until 1998, only Japanese securities houses were allowed to distribute retail mutual funds to the Japanese public. Consequently, from 1990 to 1997, the top four securities houses in Japan (Nomura, Nikko, Daiwa, and Yamaichi) controlled approximately 75 percent of the US$419 billion retail asset management market. At the end of 1998, that exclusive distribution system gave way, and banks were allowed to enter the market. The broader distribution channels through banks — the top ten city banks in Japan own 3,400 branches, compared to the top ten securities houses' 900 offices — will stimulate substantial growth in Japanese retail asset management and create new opportunities for many more competitors.

Which financial institutions can manage the pooled money?

In early 1998, government bodies managed nearly all of the US$150 billion in Asian public pension funds outside Japan. In Singapore, the Government of Singapore Investment Corporation (GIC) and associated government bodies managed 90 percent of the US$51 billion of CPF funds. In Malaysia, the government managed 97 percent of the US$47 billion held by the Malaysian Employee Provident Fund (EPF), while in Korea, the National Pension Corporation managed the entire pension scheme. A move by regulators to place an additional 10 percent of these government-managed funds with private asset managers across Asia would expand the amount of institutional assets available to external managers by US$11 billion. Market size can, and literally will, change overnight in Asia during the first decade of the 21st century.

Events like the stock market and currency turmoil of 1997–1998 naturally put pressure on governments to allow greater geographical (i.e., where pooled money can be invested) and product (i.e., in which instruments pooled money can be invested) diversification. Higher returns from diversification over the long term are essential for governments to be able to provide for their aging societies. As the pressure to diversify grows, governments will have to turn increasingly to private asset managers for regional and international investment expertise. This will be accomplished through regulatory changes, and once again market opportunities will be fundamentally reshaped in a short time frame. Competitors who wish to establish strong retail or institutional asset management platforms in Asia must be able to anticipate and respond to changes in domestic regulations. The tactical advantages that a local presence provides, though, will not be enough. Clear strategic advantages will also have to be created to penetrate emerging retail and institutional asset management opportunities.

Retail Asset Management: Building Pipelines to Customers

The decision to enter Asia's retail asset management market requires a fundamental belief in Asia's long-term growth. At the onset of the 21st century, Asian markets are simply too small, and often too complex, to enable a short-term or opportunistic approach. Competitors looking for substantial profits will have to make important choices in order to embed themselves in chosen markets for the long haul.

Rapid Retail Growth Expected

How developed is Asia's retail asset management market? In 1990, retail assets sourced from Asia totaled US$305 billion — US$285 billion in Japan and US$20 billion in the rest of Asia. By the end of 1996, prior to the onset of the stock market and currency crisis, retail assets under management had grown to US$636 billion. In U.S. dollars terms, in those 6 years the market in Japan grew at an annual rate of 4 percent, while the rest of Asia began to take off, and grow annually at 25 percent. This pace exceeded that of the U.S. market, which grew 17 percent annually in the same period. But Asia is at an early stage of development in virtually all markets.

Retail funds under management through the end of the 1990s consistently represented a small share of individuals' total savings. In Japan, personal wealth (not including mandatory pensions) in 1997 was approximately US$9.3 trillion, the second largest in the world after the U.S., at US$14 trillion. Retail managed funds in Japan represented only 5 percent of total personal savings. In the rest of Asia, outside of Korea and India, mutual fund penetration of personal savings was similarly low (Exhibit 6.1). Korea's high penetration is something of an anomaly. In that country, unit trusts offer guaranteed returns similar to fixed rate deposits, which of course collapsed when the crisis struck. A true mutual fund market, where retail investors hold a direct share of invested securities, will probably replace the defunct unit trust market in the early years of the 21st century.

The emerging nature of Asia's markets becomes apparent when comparing them with established markets in the West. The share of individual savings held in mutual fund products in 1998 was 16 percent in the U.S., 11 percent in the U.K., 19 percent in France, 8 percent in Germany, and 18 percent in Spain. It is fair to argue that most countries in Asia are years away from matching these developed countries' GDP per capita, individual savings, and financial sophistication — which is often a cornerstone for asset management development. It is likewise fair to argue that differences in regulations, tax structure, and even culture may affect the evolution of any one given market, and hence not all markets will end up exactly like those in the U.S. or Europe.

Keep in mind, however, that the U.S., the largest retail asset management market in the world, did not develop in simple correlation to growing national wealth. In 1980, when U.S. GDP per capita was US$12,200, retail mutual funds represented 2.7 percent of total personal savings. By 1990, when U.S. GDP per capita was

Exhibit 6.1

Share of Personal Savings in Mutual Funds: 1997*

US$ billions, percent

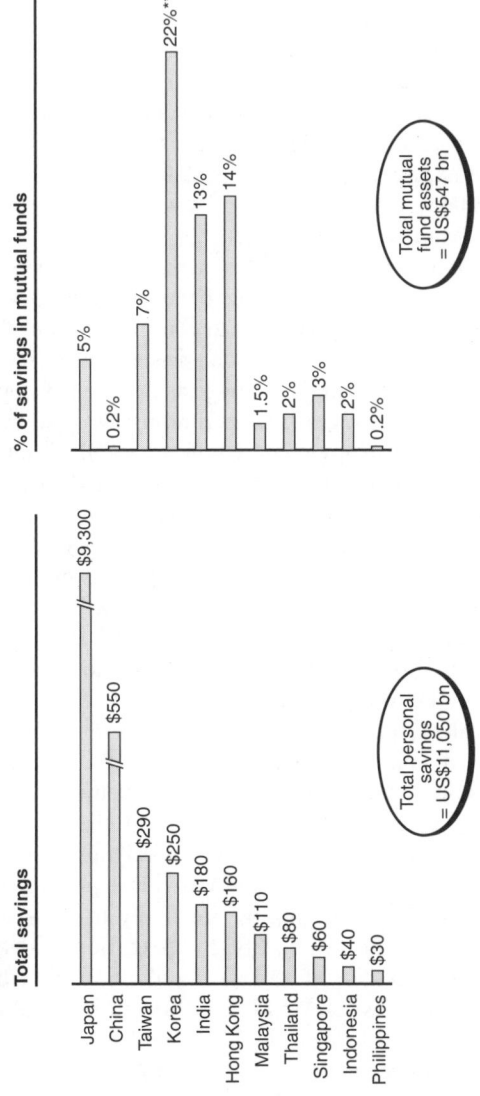

Total savings

Japan $9,300
China $550
Taiwan $290
Korea $250
India $180
Hong Kong $160
Malaysia $110
Thailand $80
Singapore $60
Indonesia $40
Philippines $30

Total personal savings = US$11,050 bn

% of savings in mutual funds

Japan 5%
China 0.2%
Taiwan 7%
Korea 22%**
India 13%
Hong Kong 14%
Malaysia 1.5%
Thailand 2%
Singapore 3%
Indonesia 2%
Philippines 0.2%

Total mutual fund assets = US$547 bn

* Personal savings includes consumer assets held in deposits, insurance, mutual funds, and securities.

** Korea's high figure includes unit trusts, which offer fixed rates of return, much like high-yield deposits.

Source: Micropal; investment fund associations; central bank reports; McKinsey analysis

US$22,980, mutual funds represented 8.5 percent of personal savings. And by 1996, U.S. GDP per capita was US$28,420, and asset management products represented 16 percent of personal savings. In the U.S., it took 8 years for mutual fund penetration of savings to rise from 5 to 10 percent, and 4 years to rise from 10 to 15 percent. It thus took 12 years for the mutual fund share of personal savings to increase threefold to 15 percent, while U.S. GDP per capita grew only twofold in the same period. The key to increased penetration of asset management products is customer education — not simply absolute levels of wealth.

This is borne out by the development of the retail asset management market in Spain. There, it took only 2 years for mutual fund penetration of personal savings to rise from 5 to 10 percent, and one more year to rise from 10 to 15 percent. In the same 3-year period, Spain's GDP per capita grew by 23 percent. In France, mutual fund penetration of personal savings was similarly faster (at lower levels of GDP per capita) than in the U.S. market.

The key to penetrating individual savings is making customers comfortable with new investment concepts. Spain and France benefited from lessons learned in the U.S., namely, how to convey key messages to consumers more effectively in order to develop domestic retail markets faster. The presence in Asia of a large number of competitors from Europe and the U.S. suggests that the development time frame in Asia — tax and investment regulations permitting — could be even faster than in the West. It is likely that many countries in Asia will demonstrate significant increases in their share of individual savings invested in asset management products if competitors effectively market their products.

By 2010, one could reasonably assume that Japan, Hong Kong, and Singapore, which already exceed many European countries in terms of GDP per capita, will have reached between 75 percent and full parity with the developed world's mutual fund penetration levels of personal savings as of 1997 (based on an average of 15 percent for the U.S., the U.K., France, Germany, and Spain in 1997). Taiwan and Korea could reach up to 75 percent of 1997 levels of developed world, while the Philippines, Thailand, and Malaysia could reach up to 50 percent. The less developed countries of Indonesia and China could reach up to 25 percent. We assume in India, where mutual fund or unit trust penetration of personal savings already exceeds the average of the developed world, that penetration levels will remain the same, but assets will grow with the underlying economy. Incorporating the probable growth of the economies and individual savings in Asia, the retail asset management markets in the region are likely to grow to approximately US$2–3 trillion by 2010, of which US$2–2.5 trillion will be in Japan and US$0.5–1 trillion will be in the rest of Asia (Exhibit 6.2). Together, all of Asia is likely to generate approximately US$35 billion in retail asset management revenues in by 2010.

How important will this potential growth make Asia for global competitors? It will make Japan very important. Japan will represent approximately 10 percent of new retail assets accumulated globally by 2010. The rest of Asia, despite rapid growth, is starting from a smaller personal savings base, and consequently will represent less than 5 percent of new retail assets created globally in the years leading to 2010. Higher fees in Asia in the medium term may slightly increase

Exhibit 6.2

Projected Retail Asset Management Assets in Asia: 2010

US$ billions

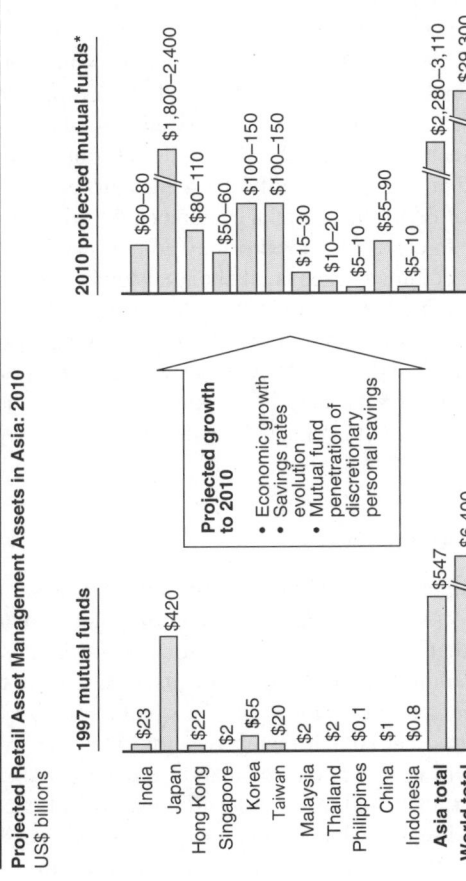

	1997 mutual funds	2010 projected mutual funds*	Projected CAGR 1997–2010
India	$23	$60–80	7–10%
Japan	$420	$1,800–2,400	12–14%
Hong Kong	$22	$80–110	11–13%
Singapore	$2	$50–60	28–31%
Korea	$55	$100–150	14–16%
Taiwan	$20	$100–150	13–17%
Malaysia	$2	$15–30	18–25%
Thailand	$2	$10–20	15–21%
Philippines	$0.1	$5–10	39–46%
China	$1	$55–90	34–39%
Indonesia	$0.8	$5–10	15–20%
Asia total	$547	$2,280–3,110	12–14%
World total	$6,400	$29,300	12%

Projected growth to 2010
- Economic growth
- Savings rates evolution
- Mutual fund penetration of discretionary personal savings

* Includes a projected capital appreciation rate of 11 percent per annum, based on historical bond and equity returns where the assumed portfolio mix is 30 percent bonds and 70 percent equity.

Source: Standard & Poor's DRI; Intersec; International Monetary Fund; Economist Intelligence Unit; investment fund associations; McKinsey analysis

Asia's share of global revenue growth. The reality, however, is that the rest of the world is likely to demonstrate continued retail asset management growth, making the rest of Asia still relatively small on a future global basis. By 2010, Asia ex-Japan retail asset management revenues will be slightly less than those earned in the U.S. in 1997. For retail asset management in Asia ex-Japan, competitors must be prepared to adopt an approach that extends well into the first decade of the 21st century. As competitors shape their strategies, they will have to make three important choices in the next few years that will significantly impact their future success in Asia.

Three Important Choices: Where, How, and with Whom?

Determining a strategy for retail asset management, like that for many of the business lines in Asia, presents a paradox. The markets are small, but the time to enter them is now. As of the late 1990s, local and global competitors had poured into the region, but few had established a strong foothold. Competitors that place a serious stake in the first 5 years of the 21st century can establish a leading brand image, and to a certain extent, define market development and customer expectations to their advantage. In rapidly growing markets with many new entrants and a multitude of first-time potential customers, the winners of 2010 must begin building a pipeline to customers, even if they do not own it. The retail asset management game in the coming decade is all about customer acquisition: forging a path to customers, educating them, getting them to invest, and being positioned to grow with them as underlying economies develop. To forge a cost-effective path, successful competitors will need to: choose where to play and prioritize resources on several local markets; determine how to play — whether to be a distributor, a manufacturer, or both; and decide with whom to play by considering potential partnerships in chosen markets.

Choice 1: Where to Prioritize?

For the majority of competitors wishing to penetrate retail asset management opportunities in Asia, prioritizing markets will be an important element of success. Penetrating a market — that is, acquiring retail customers — requires building on-the-ground capabilities tailored to local environments. The danger for long-term competitors in Asia is attempting to compensate for small markets by entering too many at once. Competitors that stretch themselves too thin take two substantial risks. First, in the medium term, breadth of market coverage may decrease the ability to invest in market depth and result in insufficient critical mass in multiple markets. Second, even if initial business volumes cover costs across markets, the long-term pipelines to customers that are necessary to lock into Asia's future growth may not be adequately developed in each market to withstand future competitive intensity.

Market prioritization can reduce these potential risks. By becoming deeply embedded in chosen markets, competitors will be better positioned to address four key issues in Asian retail asset management: dominance of local products;

importance of customer education; emerging but weak distribution channels; and increasing competitive intensity.

Dominance of local products. Foreign asset managers who rely on their existing portfolio of global fund offerings will be sorely disappointed. As of 1998, in all Asian markets except Hong Kong, over 80 percent of money invested in retail asset management funds were in each country's domestic market. Due to a combination of government regulations and investor knowledge, the local market is typically investors' first choice, followed by other countries in the region, and then, to a much lesser extent, investments in Europe and the U.S. In the decade leading up to 2010, market liberalization will free capital flows in many countries, and international diversification will no doubt dramatically increase. The 1997–1998 currency and stock market crisis, along with greater consumer sophistication, will propel increased interest in international investments. But there is a limit to how much foreign holdings can grow. Even in developed markets, where capital flows are entirely open, foreign holdings in mutual funds rarely exceed 25 percent.

In highly efficient and transparent securities markets, it is increasingly possible to manage equity and bond funds for many countries from a central hub. Fund managers who choose to rely mostly on brokerage reports and the media for information can avoid establishing local operations in a given country. However, in the late 1990s, most of Asia's markets lacked such efficiency and transparency. More often than not, fund managers must be based domestically — and solidly networked within the local community — to develop a comprehensive understanding of the securities markets and the underlying issuers. Fund managers who conduct their own basic research and corporate interviews are likely to find domestic operations essential, particularly when the primary retail investor is local. Since Asian investors often place past performance above all else when considering mutual funds, a fund manager whose domestic performance trails by several percentage points as a result of not having access to local information flows could suffer reduced asset growth.

Importance of customer education. A former head of Standard Chartered retail asset management estimates that it takes about 25 minutes to market a mutual fund to a first-time consumer in Asia. The client must first be familiarized with how a fund works, determine what risks he or she is prepared to take, and then select a fund with attractive historic performance. The salesperson must be knowledgeable to answer questions and build customer confidence. This education process is often the linchpin in developing a successful pipeline to end users. Even with all the right products and attractive performance, low asset growth can result if the correct marketing and customer education process does not occur. To paraphrase those in the industry, mutual funds in Asia are sold, not bought. More often than not, the initial selling process must be conducted face to face so as to convert customer interest into an asset management opportunity. Once a customer is familiar with mutual funds, the next sales effort is, of course, much easier.

Most consumers (more than 95 percent of households) in Asia did not own a mutual fund in the late 1990s. If the institutions selling mutual funds had already perfected the marketing and education process, a fund manager relying on agreements with local distributors could arguably sit thousands of miles away and wait for sales to grow. By the late 1990s, however, local distribution capabilities had fallen far short of perfect.

Emerging but weak distribution channels. In most of Asia, two principal groups market retail asset management products: asset management companies and banks. Several fund management companies, such as Fidelity and Templeton, and several banks, such as Standard Chartered and Citibank, have developed strong distribution capabilities, but most competitors are still battling to put basic marketing capabilities in place. In Japan, securities companies have dominated retail distribution, as banks were not allowed to sell mutual funds up until 1998. The weaknesses Japan's securities companies face have been similar to those experienced by asset management companies in the rest of Asia.

A 1997 Lipper Analytical Services survey illustrated the weakness of asset managers' marketing skills. The survey queried approximately 60 Hong Kong-based asset management companies in order to assess customer sales and service. Over the phone, fund companies were asked to send an application for a specific fund that they offered. It took more than one minute to have a third of these calls referred to the right person. Of the companies that could at least transfer the call, a quarter never replied, while 28 percent took more than a week to respond. Of those that did send information, many either failed to include a subscription form or only included additional promotional material with no indication about how to buy the products. In the same test, fund companies were asked to explain purchasing and selling charges associated with their funds. Again, nearly a third could not explain the fee structure at all or provided answers that were vague or entirely inaccurate. Many asset managers clearly had a gap in their domestic distribution capabilities.

More challenging for asset managers, however, is finding ways to upgrade bank marketing and distribution. In Asia, outside Japan, about two-thirds of retail funds are sold through third-party banks. On the surface, the argument for utilizing banks as an efficient means of tapping individual savings is compelling. In many countries in Asia, the five largest banks own, on average, 50 percent of the branches, and are home to 60 percent of total deposits. The problem, though, is that few people at the branch level understand asset management products any better than the consumers do. Educating tellers to sell is a difficult proposition, as few are accustomed to "pushing" products, much less educating customers on investment decisions. Furthermore, teller turnover is generally high — up to 40 percent annually in Hong Kong branches prior to 1997–1998 — underlining the difficulty of relying on tellers for sales.

A number of banks in the region have tried to get around to using tellers by hiring specialist sales personnel and staffing them in branches. Their success, however, is often tied to getting the support of the branch manager, who is typically in the best position to identify and refer suitable branch customers. Branch managers, however, often feel threatened by sales specialists. Generally, these salespeople are younger, better educated, and more aggressive than almost any staff the manager has previously encountered. On this basis alone, traditional branch managers who have achieved their success by collecting deposits and providing mortgages may discreetly scuttle the entire asset management initiative. Even if there is no personal threat, the branch manager's bonus may be at risk. Every dollar placed in a mutual fund may be seen as a dollar less deposited with the branch. If the branch manager is assessed and rewarded on an annual deposit target, asset management campaigns quickly become stillborn.

The Hongkong and Shanghai Banking Corporation (HSBC) has one of the largest branch networks of all private banks in Asia, but a relatively small share of retail asset management business. HSBC's efforts in the early 1990s to market what was then the Wardley asset management products through its branches met with little apparent success. Lack of shared goals and intra-organizational turf consciousness are cited as the key culprits. Wardley has since been renamed HSBC Asset Management, but at the end of 1997, it was estimated to rank only fifth amongst competitors in terms of total retail funds under management in Hong Kong — the retail banking market it dominates.

Many local banks face the same challenges as HSBC in promoting retail asset management distribution. Banks that are unable to resolve asset management distribution challenges, however, end up losing consumers' deposits in addition to any fees associated with purchasing a mutual fund. In the U.S., where banks were slow to respond to challenges posed by asset management, fund managers in the market circumvented them. In 1990, U.S. banks distributed only 7.5 percent of the US\$150 billion sold to retail consumers. In 1996, after substantial efforts, banks captured 14.5 percent of US\$685 billion in new retail sales. Failing challenges posed by asset management can be a serious threat to retail bank profitability and an irksome problem for the many asset managers who choose to depend on banks to construct a pipeline to consumers.

Whether asset management companies elect to market directly, or utilize third-party banks in Asia, distribution in the region requires significant and continuous efforts to upgrade capabilities. Fund managers who opt to rely on the superior capabilities of a bank, such as Standard Chartered, must understand that their fund will only be one in a pool of approximately 1,000 that the bank markets. Sustainable long-term customer pipelines will not come easily in Asia, particularly as competition grows.

Increasing competitive intensity.   In the late 1990s, the level of competition in any one of Asia's retail asset management markets did not significantly influence a newcomer's potential success. A combination of regulatory restrictions, small local players, and the tentativeness of many foreign players to invest had limited the formation of truly dominant competitors in retail asset management. This is likely to change significantly in the decade leading up to 2010, as competitors who have already set up shop begin to intensify their efforts.

Since 1990, competitors from a broad range of financial institutions have entered the retail asset management market. In Japan in 1990, only securities houses were allowed to sell investment trusts to retail customers. As of 1998, all banks were allowed to sell trusts. In Hong Kong in 1990, Jardine Fleming and a limited number of security and asset management firms sold funds to the public.

By 1998, virtually all the retail banks, a number of insurance companies, and hundreds of local and international asset managers had extended their distribution to the general public. In 1997, Schwab, a U.S. securities house, received approval to sell funds into Hong Kong directly over the Internet, introducing an entirely new form of cross-border competition. In Malaysia in 1990, the mutual fund industry was virtually nonexistent, but by 1998, over 30 banks, securities houses, and asset management firms had joined the fray.

At first glance, the rapid increase in the number of competitors would appear to have overwhelmed the markets. In Hong Kong, fund management companies grew from 33 in 1990 to 84 by 1997, and the number of registered funds offered rose from 452 to 723 during the same period. In Malaysia, growth among competitors was similarly aggressive, with the number of fund companies expanding from nine to 30, and the number of funds from 33 to 77 in the 1990– 1997 time frame. Taiwan was no different, with a fivefold increase in management companies and a fourfold increase in retail funds on offer in the same period. Dividing the amount of retail funds under management in 1997 by the number of funds on offer suggests that the markets were already very fragmented. For example, the average funds under management in Singapore, Malaysia, and Taiwan was US$22 million, US$26 million, and US$115 million respectively. This is small, considering that a retail equity fund in Asia must typically have at least US$100 million just for the fund manager to break even.

The competitive situation across Asia was, however, less advanced than it appeared. In Hong Kong, for example, the high growth in the number of fund management companies in the 1990s was the result of U.S. and European funds establishing a local base in Hong Kong to invest money in Asia sourced from their home markets in the West. Once in Hong Kong, many of these companies simply registered their funds for offering, but did little to actively promote them. In Malaysia and Taiwan, many local concerns set up fund management companies in anticipation of deregulation and future market growth, but few developed extensive operations. The situation in Japan in the late 1990s was similar: banks had access to the retail asset management market for the first time, but they will take years to capitalize on the opportunity before them.

The late 1990s provided aggressive competitors the opportunity to begin building strong customer pipelines. For example, in Hong Kong in 1998, Templeton regularly ran TV advertisements at prime time to develop household brand name awareness and lock in first-time consumers. As we move into the 21st century, the competitors are in place, and intensified rivalry is imminent.

To develop local products, build effective customer distribution, and prepare for real competition, competitors will have to build a significant presence in domestic markets. The complexities of managing local joint venture partners and inexperienced salesforces, or working closely with bank distributors are too great to handle from afar. Competitors with deep pockets may target multiple markets across Asia. The barrier to the number of markets that can be tapped is not the current competitive intensity, but rather the availability of internal talent to manage local infrastructures to build market depth. Which markets should take priority?

Future market size is clearly a filter for prioritization. By 2010, retail asset management markets in Asia (excluding mandatory pension contributions) will probably fall into three distinct sizes. Japan will be in a league of its own, with over US$2 trillion in retail assets under management. China, India, Hong Kong, Korea, Singapore, and Taiwan will make up the second category, with approximately US$50–150 billion in retail assets under management. The third, and smallest group of markets, with assets likely to be less than US$50 billion, will include the Philippines, Indonesia, Malaysia, and Thailand.

Rather than consider size alone, however, competitors must endeavor to prioritize markets where they can quickly acquire market share and build sustainable long-term customer pipelines to lock into Asia's underlying economic growth. With possibly only one 25-minute opportunity to sell to a first-time Asian consumer in the coming decade, distribution pipelines in chosen countries must be fortified by the early years of the 21st century.

Choice 2: How to Play — Distribute, Manufacture, or Both?

A core component of achieving economic success in prioritized markets will be determining where to compete along the retail asset management business chain. This chain consists of four distinct components: distribution, manufacturing, after-service, and administration. Distribution is the process of selling retail funds to customers. Manufacturing is the process of investing pooled customer money. After-service includes working with customers who have bought a fund, by answering questions, arranging for transfers between funds, or liquidating a fund. Administration includes record-keeping for the thousands of transactions executed daily by fund management companies. Administration is typically outsourced to custodial firms, such as State Street, which have the technology to handle large volumes and provide this service economically. After-service is typically conducted by the distributor for the sake of customer convenience. The key decision is thus whether to be a distributor, a manufacturer, or both.

This decision will have a significant impact on how competitors make money. In 1998, retail customers in Asia were typically charged about 5 percent in sales commission when they purchased an equity fund (this varied by country, from emerging no-load funds, i.e., funds sold with no commissions in Thailand, to commissions as high as 9 percent in Malaysia). An additional 1.25 percent or so was deducted from the investment annually as a management fee. Pure retail bond funds commanded half the commissions and annual fees of equity funds. Depending on the specific agreements that parties struck, distributors in the late 1990s usually received a majority stake of the upfront commission, and in some cases, a portion of the annual management fee. A distributor makes money by selling new funds, and a manufacturer profits from amassing a large sum of assets to manage. There is, obviously, no single right answer for all competitors on whether to be a manufacturer, a distributor, or both. Further, what may be the right answer today for a given player, may not apply 5 years from now.

Making the right choice — one that provides the best opportunity for long-term growth and attractive returns — requires competitors to consider three factors:

their starting point; the likely trends in fees and costs; and the potential value of direct communication with the customer, or "customer ownership." Assessing one's starting point or existing strengths helps identify the most natural choices. The extent to which a competitor has access to consumers, possesses investment expertise, or has the resources to acquire critical mass in either, establishes an initial foundation for a competitive position. An understanding of likely trends in fees and costs helps determine the long-term profitability of building distribution, manufacturing, or both. Finally, a strategic perspective on the value of owning the customer relationship — for example, to promote future product cross-selling — highlights the trade-off of being just a distributor or manufacturer. The importance of these three areas is illustrated by three types of retail asset management competitors: Jardine Fleming (a manufacturer and distributor), Standard Chartered (a distributor only), and Schroders (primarily a manufacturer).

The manufacturer and distributor: Jardine Fleming. In 1998, Jardine Fleming employed approximately 3,700 people around the region for its asset management, stock broking, and investment banking activities. Many of its early inroads into the region were built on the back of efforts to serve Western investment flows into Asia. In the late 1980s, as regulations began to relax in Asia, Jardine took advantage of its physical presence and asset management expertise to begin marketing retail funds domestically in such places as Taiwan. Through the mid-1990s it established joint ventures with securities houses and asset management firms — for example, in Thailand, Malaysia, and Indonesia — to secure local distribution channels. In 1987, Jardine Fleming began setting up several specialist investment shops in Hong Kong to market its retail funds directly to consumers. By the end of 1997, Jardine had accumulated approximately US$4 billion in retail assets under management from Asia.

Jardine's retail efforts have had the cost benefit of leveraging pre-existing local infrastructures. Direct control, or a strong influence over distribution channels, have ensured that Jardine's funds were aggressively marketed. By often being both the distributor and the manufacturer, Jardine captured attractive upfront commissions and reasonably steady annual fees. In the future, should Jardine choose to sell other financial services, it is well positioned to identify suitable clients and market directly to them.

Jardine's integrated approach, however, is not without risk. As competition intensifies in the decade to 2010, the hurdle for distribution and investment expertise will rise. Jardine will have to advance its expertise in both to remain competitive overall, though its biggest challenge may be distribution. Indeed, at the beginning of 1998, in the face of the currency and stock market crisis, Jardine decided to shut down its retail ventures in Indonesia and Malaysia to shed costs. In the future, it will face additional challenges. Its relative influence with third-party distributors will probably decline as more manufacturing competition develops, and trying to compensate with increased direct distribution may not be an attractive option. The size of its direct distribution is small, so expanding these channels (to market predominantly one product) is likely to prove very expensive.

Even if Jardine does not pursue expansion, existing distribution could become costly in the longer term if upfront fees diminish substantially — as has been the case in the U.S. Between 1990 and 1998, average sales commissions for all mutual funds sold in the U.S., combining all load and no-load funds, declined from 3 percent to approximately 1.5 percent. The cost versus the benefits of owning distribution channels can clearly evolve in a competitive environment.

The distributor: Standard Chartered. Standard Chartered, together with Citibank, are the success stories in Asia for bank distribution of retail asset management products. Standard Chartered has a large presence in Hong Kong, with approximately 100 branches. It is also fortunate to have small branch networks in the historically protected markets of Singapore and Malaysia. Over the course of 1995 and 1996, after determining it lacked the scale to compete with the global giants, Standard Chartered exited investment banking, institutional stock broking, asset management, and private banking. Instead, Standard Chartered decided to focus on its franchises' strength: strong relationships with retail and corporate banking customers.

In the mid-1990s, Standard Chartered initiated an intensive effort to distribute other manufacturers' funds to its retail customers, and by 1997 it was handling over 1,000 funds. Standard Chartered has succeeded by backing branch-based sales specialists with strong marketing tools. All the funds that Standard Chartered sells are maintained on an on-line sales platform. A customer who is interested in mutual funds fills out a brief questionnaire, the answers are fed into the system, and the customer is slotted into one of four risk categories. The top six performing funds in the customer's risk category are identified and reviewed with the customer. Standard Chartered's approach was so effective that in the first few years, despite its limited branch network in places such as Singapore, it was selling more funds than several of the big four local banks.

Although mutual fund distribution has become one of Standard Chartered's fastest-growing retail businesses, it will nonetheless face significant challenges in the decade leading up to 2010. Other banks, and indeed the fund companies themselves, will probably strengthen their distribution skills. As fund manufacturers develop alternatives, Standard Chartered's ability to command the lion's share of sales commissions will gradually erode. Also, as customers become more familiar with mutual funds, they may seek out on-line providers such as Schwab, which at the end of 1997, offered 140 funds in Hong Kong via the Internet. The presence of lower-cost alternative channels, like Schwab, will eventually pressure sales commissions, which could make Standard Chartered's marketing infrastructure economically unattractive. Standard Chartered would then have to leverage the power of its customer ownership to extract a higher proportion of annual fees from manufacturers.

The manufacturer: Schroders. In Hong Kong alone, Schroders managed approximately US$2 billion of retail investors' funds in 1997. For most of the 1980s and 1990s, it relied on a small direct salesforce and agreements with securities houses to distribute funds to the retail market. In the mid-1990s, however, it expanded distribution through agreements with Citibank, Bank of America, Hang Seng Bank, Hua Chiao Commercial Bank, and a number of leading Singaporean banks. The funds gathered through these agreements leveraged the investment scale that Schroders achieved through its substantial institutional asset management business. Should Schroders, and competitors with a significant asset scale like it, continue to focus internal expertise on manufacturing rather than developing proprietary distribution, it stands to maintain a very attractive cost position. As long as fund performance is strong enough to be distinctive, relying on bank distribution channels will probably provide adequate access to the growing consumer market. And should upfront sales commissions decline rapidly, Schroders, and those similarly positioned, will be sheltered from the monetary drain of owning expensive physical distribution.

The seemingly attractive manufacturing-only option could, however, change over time. By the mid-1990s, index funds began to take hold in the U.S., and by the end of 1997, as much as 10 percent of domestic mutual fund assets were in index funds. These funds simply seek to perform in line with the underlying markets. In relatively efficient capital markets, such as in the U.S., more than 75 percent of fund managers have traditionally underperformed the stock market index. Consumers have realized that better returns can be achieved, with lower fees, by simply buying passive funds composed of a basket of stocks that reflect the market's performance. In a passive investment management environment, it is much harder for fund managers to distinguish themselves. Distribution power and customer ownership become a more important part of channeling investments and capturing fees. While Asian consumers and Asian equity markets are up to a decade away from a predominance of index-based products, there are longer-term risks for players such as Schroders, which have less direct customer ownership.

Choosing whether to be a distributor, a manufacturer, or both is an important, but not an easy, decision. A player must have a clear view of its skills, a perspective of how fees in Asia are likely to evolve, and a long-term view of how critical it is to actually "own the customer." Once the choice is made, directing strategy, prioritizing investments, and optimizing returns become a more straightforward undertaking.

Choice 3: With Whom to Partner?

As distributors or manufacturers, foreign players in many of Asia's local markets will be required by the regulators to partner with local institutions to gain market access. Domestic players will need foreign skills to quickly develop the product and customer education skills crucial to success. Hence, many international and domestic competitors will face the need for cross-border alliances. Historically, however, about three-quarters of all cross-border alliances or partnerships fail. Of those that succeed, one partner usually buys out the other. As local and foreign competitors enter into asset management alliances, they should have a clear vision of the end game. Are they looking to eventually buy or be bought? Is the purpose of the alliance privileged market access, new technology and skills, or someone with whom to share the burden of capital investments? The suitable partner for a local or foreign firm could be very different, depending on the answers to these questions. In retail asset management, given the importance of forming pipelines to customers, all partnerships should probably be considered within the context of a group's long-term manufacturing and distribution strategy.

Within the context of a chosen strategy, individual partnerships may differ significantly. A partnership may provide any one of several missing pieces, for example, regulatory market access, brand name, customer relationships, investment expertise, or operating scale. To fill in these pieces, partnerships may range from simple operating and distribution agreements, to formal joint ventures. The duration may be from several years to perpetuity. Across all possible partnerships, experience suggests both partners' objectives are more likely to be met if there is upfront, mutual agreement in three areas: performance targets, degree of exclusivity, and processes for skill transfer. Finally, the parties of the partnership should set out clear conditions and terms for how the arrangement could eventually dissolve.

Although it is often difficult to establish performance targets within a new partnership, targets are at the core of defining what the partnership seeks to achieve for both parties. In rapidly developing markets such as Asia, performance goals should carry explicit incentives that push both parties to create and capture opportunities. In a partnership between a manufacturer and a distributor, for example, sales commissions should probably be split on a sliding scale, with the distributor receiving a higher proportion for higher volumes or for growing faster than the market. Similarly, the manufacturer should probably receive a larger split of the annual fee if stated investment objectives are achieved. If targets are allowed to become merely incremental, crucial ground in the battle for customer acquisition and market share could be quickly lost.

The second critical area, exclusivity, is all about who a firm will and will not work with for a given period of time. As manufacturers and distributors rush to gain market share in the coming years, important partnerships are more likely to survive if both sides clarify their expectations and competitor sensitivities. Not being frank on this point will lead to tensions, erode performance, and waste resources before agreements are formally broken at a loss to both parties.

Third, skill transfer is often cited as the rationale for forming partnerships in Asia. In asset management, skill transfer is frequently sought to gain cross-border investment expertise. Rather than having good intentions and being vague, partners should commit to specific cross-staffing arrangements. Learning, more often than not, is achieved in the front-line at the person-to-person level, and not in one-off seminars.

Pursuing upfront agreements across these three sensitive areas may prove difficult, but they are clearly preferable to failed partnerships and broken customer pipelines in the early years of the 21st century. A successful retail asset management strategy must comprise equal parts of winning decisions on where to compete, how to compete, and with whom to compete.

Institutional Asset Management: Setting and Meeting New Expectations

Successful partnerships will be a common and critical area in the very different world of institutional asset management. In fact, some of the largest institutional asset managers globally were tying the knot in 1997 and 1998 in Japan. Putnam Investments of the U.S. entered into a venture with the largest insurance company in the world, Nippon Life. The Franklin Templeton Group announced plans to cooperate with Sumitomo Life, and Dresdner Bank and Meiji Life partnered in investment advisory activities. As of 1998, more than half of the top 20 global fund managers have a presence in Japan. Of these, at least five have already created some form of joint effort with Japanese financial institutions, while the remainder have decided to go it alone.

While partnerships will end up being critical to many retail and institutional asset managers, the businesses are distinct; they differ significantly in business economics, investment approaches, and marketing skills. The shared importance of partnerships is where the similarities for success in Asia essentially begin and end for many retail and institutional asset managers.

In Asia, the institutional asset management business will prove challenging for competitors with large aspirations. While the institutional market is likely to demonstrate rapid growth, particularly on the back of changes in Japan, the fees are often razor thin. Breaking into potential institutional investors — or sponsors, as they are often referred to — requires a substantial investment in developing customers. Many of these institutional sponsors are small: the average size of an Asian institutional sponsor outside Japan and Korea (excluding Singapore's CPF and Malaysia's EPF) in 1996 was less than US$3 billion in assets. Yet competition is intense. Despite investor size, global competitors quickly became embedded throughout the region in the 1990s as a result of managing investments in Asia sourced from their home markets. The simple fact that there were fewer than 500 institutional investors in Asia, compared to millions of potential retail consumers, made it relatively easy for global competitors to focus their efforts.

The arrival of this foreign competition, together with increased pressure on institutional sponsors (be they governments or corporations) to improve and diversify investment returns, particularly in the wake of the 1997–1998 turmoil, will lead to institutional sponsors' increasing sophistication. As competition intensifies in the coming decade, local institutional fund managers that do not develop new skills will have the most to lose. While good personal relationships were critical to success in the 1980s and 1990s, they will not be enough to develop opportunities in the future. By 2010, Asian institutional sponsors, and the fund managers competing to serve them, will be almost as sophisticated as their global counterparts.

This is not to say that there will be few winners in institutional asset management in Asia. In Japan, there is scope for a number of fund managers to build large businesses. Outside Japan, there is room for a few big winners as well. Across Asia, smaller institutional fund managers that can develop world-class investment skills and distinguish themselves with unique investment approaches and strong performances are likely to attract adequate assets to carve out niche profits. For all aspirants, big or small, the time to cement relationships with sponsors and develop world-class investment skills is now.

Sources of Strong Growth in Institutional Assets

The modernization of Asia's societies will drive significant growth in Asian institutional sponsors' assets in the first decade of the 21st century. Growing affluence will increase the demand for better health care and for tending to the needs of society's less privileged. As modern nuclear families become the norm in Asia, and family care for the elderly gradually diminishes, a greater need for individuals to plan financially for their own retirement will develop. Of course, with affluence comes the desire to protect it, and individuals and corporations in Asia will increasingly seek ways to minimize and hedge uncertainties. These evolving needs will spawn a growing demand for pension plans, health insurance, life insurance, property insurance, social welfare, and charities.

Until the 1980s, most individuals and corporations outside Japan depended on personal and family savings or retained earnings to meet these needs. In the 1990s, however, institutions began to step in. These institutions vary by country, and include provincial governments, national governments, insurance companies, banks, securities firms, trust companies, and private and public corporations. As of 1996, the top 250 of these emerging institutional sponsors across Asia had gathered an estimated US$6.8 trillion in assets (Exhibit 6.3).

Institutional sponsors' assets across Asia are likely to grow to at least US$22 trillion by 2010, a threefold increase from 1996 levels. Japan will generate 70 percent of this growth, and the rest of Asia will provide the balance. As such, Japan will represent 34 percent of likely institutional asset growth globally, while the rest of Asia will represent a smaller 17 percent. Asia's institutional growth will stem from the modernization trends mentioned previously. The major collection points for newly pooled institutional assets will be threefold: pension plans; insurance companies; and corporations.

Pension plans

The formation of pension savings is likely to be the largest source for institutional asset management growth in Asia. Since the 1970s and 1980s, Singapore, Malaysia, and India have accumulated pension assets under robust schemes to prepare for the aging of their societies. Their mandatory defined contribution pension schemes are likely to provide for over 60 percent of retirees' income needs by 2010. As of the late 1990s, however, these three countries were more the exception than the rule with regards to pension planning. After years of debate, in 1998 Hong Kong passed a legislation instituting a defined contribution scheme under which employees and employers must each contribute 5 percent of annual wages into blocked accounts. While larger corporations had offered private schemes in Hong Kong for some time, they covered less than one-third of the entire workforce. By waiting until the late 1990s to address the issue, Hong Kong's defined contribution scheme will provide for only about 10 percent of retirees' financial needs by year 2010.

Exhibit 6.3

Asian Institutional Assets by Country: 1996*

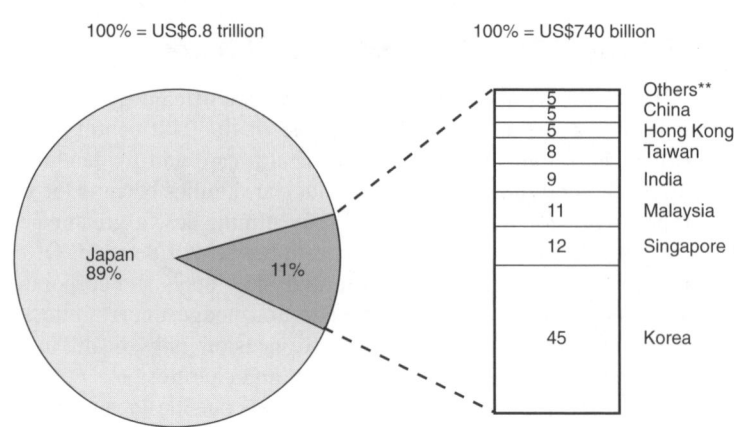

100% = US$6.8 trillion   100% = US$740 billion

* Total assets for each country based on 1996 estimates of major institutional investors in each country. As a result, smaller sponsors may have been omitted. While the 1997 financial crisis will have reduced the size of assets substantially, it is believed that the relative share of assets held has not changed significantly across countries.
** Philippines (2%), Thailand (2%), and Indonesia (1%).

Source: Institutional Investor, McKinsey analysis

Like Hong Kong, other countries around the region are gradually waking up to the pension challenges that lie ahead. Japan faces some of the largest hurdles: in 1990, 12 percent of its population was over 65 years old; by 2020, an estimated 25 percent of its population will be retired. While Japan has the second largest pension savings in the world today at US$1.2 trillion, it still faces substantial gaps in meeting future retiree needs. The annual contribution rate during the 1990s of 16.5 percent of wages simply will not be enough. Industry experts suggest that annual contribution rates will have to rise to as much as 35 percent annually to meet future needs. In the late 1990s, legislative proposals to develop a new and defined contribution scheme were under consideration. While it is impossible to predict what level of contribution will result, one can reasonably assume it will be at least 20 percent of annual wages. If a new 20-percent scheme goes into effect by 2005, Japanese pension assets, net of payments, will rise to approximately US$13 trillion by 2010, enabling mandated savings to meet approximately 18 percent of future retirees' financial needs. The demand for additional private programs will remain great in Japan.

At the end of the 1990s, Korea and the Philippines were at the early stages of wrangling with defined contribution concepts. Korea has committed to formally addressing the issue in 2000, while interest groups in the Philippines are just beginning to lobby for action. The rest of Asia, which has the benefit of far younger populations, currently has limited mandatory schemes. It seems certain, however, that in the wake of the 1997–1998 crisis, the increased presence of global bodies (i.e., the IMF and the World Bank) will gradually raise pension planning to the forefront.

Again, while it is impossible to predict the timing and structure of new schemes, if one conservatively assumes that Korea and the Philippines adopt a minimalist approach, say a cumulative 10 percent annual contribution rate by year 2000, and China, Taiwan, Indonesia, and Thailand do the same by 2005, all of Asia, including Japan, could pool as much as US$18 trillion in assets by 2010 (Exhibit 6.4). This figure does not include the likely evolution of private pension schemes, which could easily expand this conservative estimate by an additional 40 percent. Even then, new schemes in these countries would provide, in many cases, less than 25 percent of retirees' financial needs by 2010 (Exhibit 6.5).

Insurance companies

Along with pension plans, insurance growth will lead to the formation of substantial institutional assets. Both life and nonlife insurance witnessed rapid growth across Asia in the 1980s and 1990s. In Japan, total insurance assets grew 8 percent annually during 1990–1997, to US$1.9 trillion. Japan is home to some of the largest insurance companies in the world. On average, the top ten insurance companies in Japan managed assets of US$280 billion in 1996. In the rest of Asia, emerging market growth rates of 12 percent propelled total insurance assets from US$112 billion to US$224 billion between 1990 and 1997.

Parallel to the trend in other developed countries, growth in life and nonlife insurance premiums in Asia correlates with economic development. As individuals become wealthier and their annual income exceeds US$5,000, their concern and ability to protect themselves increases. By projecting economic growth rates and drawing from experience in more developed countries to assess the relationship between premiums and assets, Asian insurance assets are estimated to reach US$3–4 trillion by 2010. In Japan and Korea, in particular, approximately 50 percent of life insurance assets are actually additional pension savings. Factoring out pension savings from insurance assets (to avoid overlaps with the preceding pension plan figures) suggests that pure insurance assets will grow to approximately US$2.7 trillion by 2010. Japan will be home to 70 percent of these assets, and the remainder will be distributed across Asia.

Corporations

In the U.S., corporations (including banks, securities firms, trust companies, endowments, and charities) represented only 8 percent of total institutional assets in 1997 (specifically, assets belonging to corporations that are separate from pensions). While the U.S. has numerous large corporations and universities and well-developed national charities, in Asia over 90 percent of corporations are entrepreneurial concerns with fewer than 100 employees and little excess cash from retained earnings. While Asian universities and charities are growing, they are likely to remain comparatively small in the first decade of the 21st century. By 2010, corporations in Asia could represent as much as 5–10 percent of total institutional assets, or approximately US$1.5 trillion.

Exhibit 6.4

Projected Public Defined Contribution Plan Assets: 2010
US$ billions

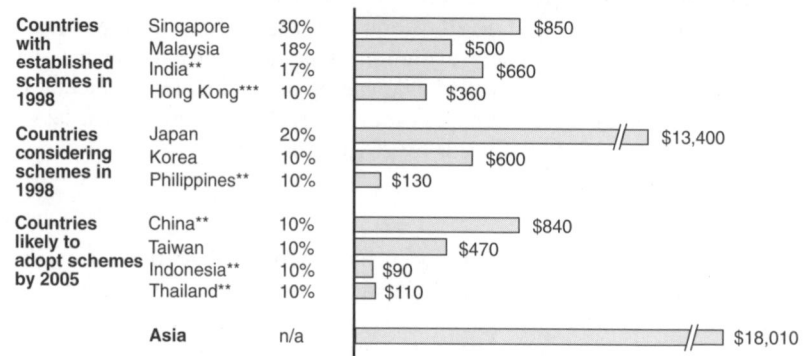

	Projected contribution as % of gross income	Estimated total assets accumulated by 2010*

* Includes assets pooled for those retiring in year 2010 and subsequent years.
** Assumed that scheme would only apply to urban population as implementation in the vast rural sectors is likely to take longer.
*** Established but effective after 2000.

Source: Standard & Poor's DRI; Economist Intelligence Unit; International Monetary Fund; World Bank; government statistics; McKinsey analysis

Who Will the Sponsors Be?

While it is possible to identify and project the needs that will lead to growth in Asia's institutional asset base, it is much more difficult to predict which institutions will become the sponsors for the US$22 trillion in assets. Insurance companies will clearly control insurance assets, but the largest source of new assets, those set aside for pensions, could end up being pooled by governments, insurance companies, local financial institutions, or corporations. If market development is similar to that in the U.S., individual corporations — not governments — will pool money on behalf of their employees and become the principal pension sponsors that decide which fund managers to use. If the pension markets develop under the Singapore model, governments will become the *de facto* clients. The key determinant of which institutions become sponsors for pension assets is, as we discussed at the beginning of this chapter, largely linked to future regulation.

Institutional fund managers will clearly be interested in keeping careful track of regulations, which will determine likely sponsors, for two reasons. First, and simply, the outcome will determine which institutions, whether governments or corporations, are the priorities for long-term relationship development. Second, sponsorship outcomes will probably influence the overall size of the institutional fund management market. If governments become the main pension sponsors, they may be more inclined to manage funds internally rather than utilize external fund

Exhibit 6.5

Estimated Coverage* for Retirement by 2010
Percentage of total financial retirement needs covered by plan

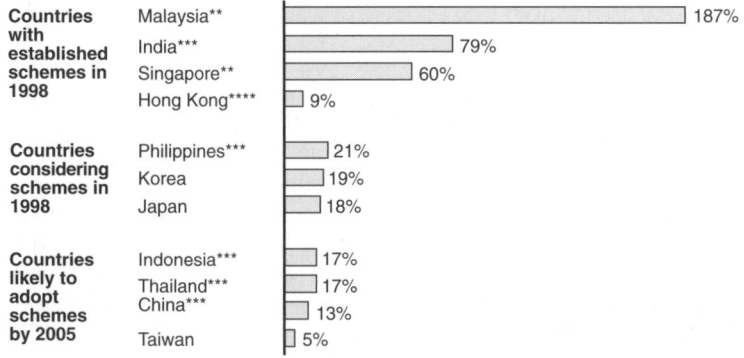

* Level of coverage based on actual contribution rates for Singapore, Malaysia and India, and assumes defined contribution rates equal to average of the establishment schemes of 20% for Japan and at Hong Kong's contribution rate of 10% for remaining countries; for all countries, assume capital appreciation for pooled assets.
** In Singapore and Malaysia, historical investment returns of 3.5% and 7.5% respectively, were used for assumed capital appreciation of pooled assets; no caps on individual contributions were assumed, possibly slightly overstating assets available from the mandatory schemes in Singapore and Malaysia; the apparent "overfunding" in Malaysia may be part of a program to redistribute wealth among ethnic groups.
*** Based on urban population only.
**** Established but effective after year 2000.

Source: Standard & Poor's DRI; World Bank; International Monetary Fund; Economist Intelligence Unit; government statistics; McKinsey analysis

managers. Alternatively, if corporations become the main pension sponsors, they are more likely, due to a lack of scale and internal investment expertise, to turn to external fund managers.

Drawing from examples in the more developed markets, by 2010 the new government-mandated pension schemes are likely to have up to 40 percent of total assets placed with external managers. Insurance companies are likely to outsource only 5 percent of their pooled assets, and corporations are likely to outsource 70 percent of their (nonpension) assets. If these assumptions prove correct, approximately US$8.5 trillion will be available to private asset managers by 2010. If one assumes that fees for institutional asset management will average 25 basis points by 2010, Asia will generate US$20 billion in annual institutional asset management revenues: approximately US$15 billion in Japan, and US$5 billion in the rest of Asia.

Prying Open the Door to Potential Sponsors

Behind these large revenue figures, however, are thin fees, and often very conservative domestically oriented institutional sponsors. In Japan, the typical annual fee for domestically managed assets is 10–15 basis points. If the portfolio is heavily weighted toward equities and invested internationally, Japanese institutions may be willing to pay as much as 25 basis points, but little more. In the rest of Asia, fees are slightly higher, ranging up to 40 basis points for globally invested equity portfolios. In New York and London, large global investors typically pay 10–20 basis points. Global pricing is descending upon Asia.

Larger institutional asset managers must often support a sophisticated marketing team, fund managers, research assistants, a small administrative staff, expensive on-line information services, and costly systems to handle reporting and statements on these fees. The marketing and fund management teams must be large enough to contain product (equity versus debt) and geographical (local, regional, and global) expertise. Clients often expect their key contact, who answers questions and explains results, to be based locally. Across Asia, experience has demonstrated that institutional asset managers must typically manage at least US$300 million to several billion U.S. dollars to break even. In Japan, institutional sponsors are large enough to provide potentially attractive asset volumes, but many of the potential institutions in the rest of Asia are so small that the cost to capture business versus assets gathered often leads to only marginal returns for fund managers handling smaller volumes.

Even when institutional sponsors are large, achieving profits can be difficult. Across Asia, government funds and insurance companies have tended to maintain very conservative domestic portfolios. Often, as much as 85 percent of assets are kept in local time deposits, government bonds, and other local investments, such as real estate. Of course, what is conservative is a matter of definition. Being heavily invested in a single geography or in a single currency, and having assets tied up in illiquid assets such as real estate, is not necessarily the best way to achieve safe, steady conservative returns. However, many of the largest sponsors in the region have historically either been forced by regulation or choose — based on not understanding the alternatives — to invest a majority of their assets in their domestic markets. As of 1996, the ten largest institutional sponsors in Asia ex-Japan had over 85 percent of their assets invested only in their domestic markets. The time spent educating investors to explore new investment instruments in new international markets can be expensive.

The largest Asian institutional sponsor outside Japan, the Singapore Central Provident Fund, and its associated investment arm, GIC, formally request training as a prerequisite to granting mandates to external asset managers. Asset managers winning mandates must commit to formally educating government personnel on financial instruments, how investments are allocated across countries, and how valuations are made in the selection of specific industries and securities. The more than 30 fund managers eager to help Singapore diversify its US$51 billion portfolio internationally have little choice but to comply with training requirements. For many fund management marketing teams, Singapore's approach is preferable to that chosen by many other institutional sponsors — ignoring external asset managers altogether.

Many of the region's institutional sponsors, including governments, insurance companies, corporations, and banks maintain an in-house investment capability and do not work extensively with external asset managers. Up to the end of 1997, only 3 percent of Malaysia's EPF, the largest institutional fund in Malaysia, was invested with external managers. By contrast, in the U.S., public funds and corporations consistently invest a large share of assets with external fund managers. The logic there is that it is more effective from a cost and investment return perspective to source the investment expertise needed across products, industries, and geographies externally, than to build internationally.

Up to now, many institutional sponsors in Asia have had little pressure to consider diversifying investments or using external fund managers. Prior to the 1997–1998 meltdown, rising markets enabled many internal managers to perform well. Senior management at institutions did not request internal managers to justify their performance with an explanation of risks taken. In fact, as long as performance was generally positive, few were held accountable to specific investment targets or even performance versus the underlying market indexes in which they invested.

In the wake of the crisis and mounting losses, sponsors' shareholders will be more likely to push their internal managers for answers. Industry consultants such as Watson Wyatt Worldwide and Frank Russell are becoming more widespread in Asia. Watson Wyatt employed 500 people in Asia in 1997, up from 300 people 5 years earlier. The presence of independent advisors, combined with increased competition from global institutional asset managers, will gradually pry open the doors of local institutional sponsors. As this happens, future winners will need to move quickly to capture share in this thin-fee market.

Global Competition Becoming Embedded

Jardine Fleming's 1995 troubles, mentioned at the outset of this chapter, could not have happened at a more challenging time. Up till the early 1990s, managing sponsors' assets sourced from Asia was a quiet straightforward proposition if the firm was physically present in the region and had regulatory approval. Institutions, such as Jardine Fleming, HSBC, Schroders, Barings, and insurance companies in Japan were positioned as such. Starting in the early 1990s, however, Asia ex-Japan underwent a transformation. Capitalization of the region's markets (ex-Japan) ballooned from US$690 billion in 1992, to US$1.4 trillion in 1993, and to US$1.8 trillion by the end of 1996. Both driving and taking advantage of this growth were the leading institutional fund managers from Europe and the U.S. Their investments in Asia ex-Japan, sourced principally outside Asia, exceeded US$250 billion by 1996. Institutional asset managers followed their money to Asia, and have become a new breed of competitor for local institutions' assets. Jardine's troubles appeared in the midst of a significant increase in locally based foreign competition.

This new breed of competition includes Templeton, Fidelity, Morgan Stanley, Merrill Lynch, Barclays Global Investors, Deutsche Morgan Grenfell (DMG), JP Morgan, and Citibank. Prior to the 1997–1998 turmoil, each managed more than US$9 billion of globally sourced investments in Asia. In the early 1990s, many of these firms were content to manage their investments from the U.S. or Europe. As the scale of their investments increased, however, it made more sense to locate their fund managers and in-house analysts close to the corporations in which they were investing. By 1996, about 50 percent of total funds invested in Asia by foreign institutional investors were managed locally. In 1990, for example, Templeton employed less than 20 people in the region. In 1997, Templeton employed approximately 120 people, with 20 in Singapore to manage its Asia and global emerging markets funds; half focused on investment and research, and the rest on marketing and sales. Templeton also had staff in Hong Kong and Japan that handled trading and other marketing activities.

In 1990, Japan's large pension fund market was mostly the domain of local life insurers. By the end of 1997, the largest pension fund managers, and indeed the largest fund managers overall, were Japan's trust banks. Life insurance companies were somewhat undone by their own poor performance throughout the 1990s. After years of lackluster returns, an April 1996 decision taken in unison by insurance companies to reduce guaranteed returns on pension plans from 4.5 to 2.5 percent, prompted many individuals and corporations to place their pensions elsewhere.

In Japan, "elsewhere" was traditionally limited to Japanese trust banks, and towards the end of the 1990s, to a new line-up of investment advisory firms. These new firms, which had grown from managing approximately 3 percent of pension fund assets in 1996 to almost 13 percent in 1997, implemented a more aggressive, yet well-received, investment approach. In 1997, foreign competitors (the largest of which included Barclays, Schroders, DMG, Merrill Lynch, and Jardine Fleming) represented one-fifth of the assets managed by investment advisory firms, and hence were managing about 3 percent of total Japanese pension funds. But 1997 was in the early days of Japan's efforts to deregulate. While the amounts of money distributed in Japan to new market entrants was still small, the willingness to use new managers was growing quickly. In 1997, 261 Japanese sponsors awarded pension business to foreign managers, up from only 120 the year before. Global players had a foot in the door in Japan and around the region. Local and traditional competitors, such as Jardine Fleming, do have a window of opportunity to strengthen their internal skills and leverage their strong local relationships. That opening will narrow steadily in the decade preceding 2010, however, while the challenges to traditional local players to upgrade skills will be significant.

Institutional Sponsor Sophistication Is on the Rise

On the surface, an obvious split exists concerning how various types of competing fund managers should prepare for the onslaught of increasing competition. Common sense suggests that traditional local fund managers should focus on upgrading their local investment expertise, while foreign competitors should position themselves to benefit from institutional sponsors' increasing foreign investments. Common sense also suggests that local, regional, or global fund managers should prioritize countries — but more importantly, prioritize institutional sponsors — where they are likely to win a significant share of externally managed assets. While all this common sense is useful, it misses a more fundamental challenge confronting all fund managers in Asia: distinguishing themselves from the growing ranks of peers with a clearly stated and executed investment strategy.

With the arrival of a broad range of competitors and investment consultants, and increasing demands for returns, the day for providing world-class portfolio management is not as far off as many would expect. Institutional sponsors, long insistent on managing their own funds, are gradually becoming more sophisticated. In fact, for a number of local institutional sponsors, such as the Hong Kong Jockey Club (HKJC), which has the concession for horse racing in Hong Kong, that day has arrived. For those picturing a betting environment at a race track in Kentucky, try again. The HKJC has to maintain a liquid cash flow nearing US$1 billion during the 10-month season to manage betting at its biweekly races. On the opposite side of the betting till is a serious financial operation that manages three funds: an employee pension scheme for 3,500 employees; a contingency fund; and what the HKJC calls a charity trust capital fund. With approximately US$2 billion in assets at the outset of 1997, it was one of the largest institutional investors in Hong Kong, and among the top 20 private institutional investors in Asia, outside Japan and Korea.

In 1997, a six-man internal investment team oversaw the HKJC's assets. This team focused on managing a small portion of debt securities and working with external consultants and asset managers to identify global asset allocation weightings and the best providers for their range of distinct investment objectives. As of 1997, approximately 30 percent of the HKJC's investments were in debt securities; the remainder were in long-term equities. In 1997, the HKJC used nine institutional managers to invest the distinct risk/reward segments of its portfolio. Among their chosen managers were Fidelity, Jardine Fleming, Credit Suisse Asset Management, Invesco, and Fiduciary Trust.

The HKJC investment team formally reviews the performance of its investment managers at least once every 6 months against benchmarks set at the outset of each review period. These benchmarks may occasionally include underlying market indexes, but more often than not, are based on expected levels of return within specifically defined risk parameters. Under this system, investment managers can be penalized for providing returns that are higher than expected if they achieved them by exceeding stated risk thresholds.

In the aftermath of the 1995 Colin Armstrong scandal at Jardine Fleming, the HKJC put Jardine on immediate review. Despite efforts within Jardine to allay their fears, the HKJC ended up withdrawing a portion of its funds. Since then, the HKJC formally reviews the back office operations of all of its major managers. Operational gaps or potential conflicts are now raised before a relationship commences.

For many international institutional fund managers, the HKJC's criteria are commonplace. But for more local or traditional asset management firms, these criteria represent a big leap from a traditional, largely relationship-oriented approach. Clearly, many local institutional sponsors fall short of the HKJC's degree of sophistication. For foreign firms, however, upgrading investor knowledge is likely to be the key to communicating value and getting through the door. The more clearly distinctive the foreign firm's strategy, the more likely a local investor may perceive the benefits of working together. The fallout from 1997–1998 provides a unique opportunity to present new ideas to the many institutional sponsors that suffered from the massive destruction in wealth.

Local fund managers that adopt more sophisticated approaches, even in a domestic environment, are likely to benefit. How long it will be before most local institutional sponsors follow the HKJC's example is debatable, but there is little disagreement that the Club's approach represents the future. While building new skills and educating sometimes unwilling institutional sponsors is hard going, the alternative is doing nothing, and later being caught out as global competition raises sponsors' expectations.

Big Profits for a Few, Small Profits for Many

In 1995, Goldman Sachs published a report entitled "The Coming Evolution of the Investment Management Industry." It took the view that ultimately the global asset management industry will split into two groups: up to 25 multi-product global players, each managing in excess of US$150 billion; and a greater number of high-performing niche specialists, each typically managing less than US$5 billion. The report asserts that those stuck in the middle will simply get squeezed out. Their suggested day of reckoning — 2001.

In Asia, that day of reckoning may extend to the end of the first decade of the 21st century. In retail asset management, where upfront sales commissions still hover around 5 percent and annual management fees around 1.25 percent, manufacturers and distributors with adequate scale and market penetration should be able to achieve profit margins upward of 30 percent in the medium term. While the threat of no-load funds is real, it will not substantially affect margins in Asia until consumers become knowledgeable enough about mutual funds that a substantial share of sales can flow through low-cost alternative channels. This will happen when customers feel comfortable selecting their own funds without extensive face-to-face discussion. When it occurs, scale and the ability to sell funds, together with a host of other products, will become essential. In the interim, building a pipeline to first-time consumers in chosen markets is the key to survival.

In institutional asset management, Goldman's market assessment strikes a chord in Asia. With regional fees ranging between 10 and 50 basis points, and varying with geography (higher for Asia's emerging markets, lower for established markets such as Japan's) and product (higher for equity, lower for bonds), institutional fund managers have two choices: offer broad geographical and product investment options and cover the large cost base by capturing a consistently large share of sponsors' total assets; or offer a narrow range of investment expertise, but keep costs low to remain profitable with a small asset base. Excellence along either path should allow market leaders to garner returns in excess of 20 percent of revenues over the medium term. As of 1998, at least 50 local, regional, and global fund managers in Asia were at risk of becoming stuck in the middle over the next decade. Whether they grow to scale or develop a niche approach, their core challenge is developing world-class investment skills that make them distinctive to sponsors.

In either case, 2001 is too early for Asia to witness the dramatic split Goldman predicted for global markets. By 2010, we envision Asia's asset management market consisting of three distinct groups of winners: globally integrated providers (up to 15 very large competitors); retail distribution specialists (10–15 moderate to large competitors); and local and regional institutional manufacturing specialists (500-plus small competitors).

Globally Integrated Providers

The 15 or so globally integrated providers will probably dominate retail and institutional asset management across Asia by 2010. Each provider will manage approximately US$400–500 billion in assets sourced from Asian individuals and institutional sponsors, and will generate close to US$2 billion in annual revenues. Each will be able to invest locally gathered assets domestically, regionally, and globally through a broad range of risk/return products. Most of these 15 firms will carry household name recognition as a result of effectively using multiple distribution channels. In the decade leading up to 2010, these firms will initially have to rely on retail distribution agreements and partnering with local asset manufacturers to gain local market access. Over time, however, their market pull and increasing customer sophistication should allow them to bypass initial intermediaries and partners so as to deal directly with a majority of their customers. Part of their evolution towards direct customer access may well involve substantial acquisitions, particularly in Japan.

Retail Distribution Specialists

Across Asia, 10–15 retail distribution specialists will dominate by 2010. These competitors will excel in retail marketing and largely forgo the manufacturing option. They will become specialists at segmenting and educating Asia's emerging financial consumer. Their strength will be in providing products and services that are integrated across traditional and alternative channels. Most will build their business from an existing customer franchise. A number will create distinctive brand names built on reputations for objective advice and high-quality service.

From the turn of the century to 2010, each of the leading distributors will source up to US$55 billion in assets and generate close to US$350 million in annual asset management revenues. To remain profitable in light of inevitably declining fees, however, mutual funds will have to be one of several core financial products the bank or specialist firm sells. A key element of this group's success will be forming product relationships with manufacturers outside of the top 15 globally integrated players, to avoid eventually being displaced by them. Up to two-thirds of these retail distribution specialists are likely to be predominantly single-country players in Japan, India, and China. The remainder will eventually dominate in several countries in North and/or Southeast Asia. Most of these winners are existing financial institutions that are not yet necessarily on the radar screen for asset management products.

Institutional Manufacturers

Institutional manufacturers will demonstrate two strengths: distinctive investment expertise and superior marketing skills. These competitors will serve a broad range of investors, including retail distribution specialists, insurance companies, individual corporates, and government-sponsored funds. They will develop geographical or product-based expertise that will enable them to structure investments to meet clients' specific risk/reward criteria. To communicate their expertise, they will employ professional marketers who can pinpoint how their company's expertise is relevant to specific segments of an investor's portfolio. Investment performance will be the cornerstone of their survival. A number of manufacturers may even tie their fees to performance to demonstrate commitment to clients and enhance their own returns.

There will probably be more than 500 of these small manufacturers concentrated in one or more of the likely major money centers of Tokyo, Hong Kong, Shanghai, Singapore, and potentially Kuala Lumpur and Mumbai. They will need to be in these locations not only to be near customers, but also to be near providers that can handle outsourced administrative functions. Each will manage from as little as several hundred million U.S. dollars to, in some cases, more than US$50 billion. By 2010, the average institutional manufacturer will manage US$7.5 billion in assets and generate US$30 million in annual revenues.

Choosing where and how to compete in Asia's increasingly tough markets will be critical to long-term success. Jardine's late 1998 decision to sell its stake in Jardine Fleming, in exchange for Robert Fleming shares, suggested that Jardine realized that being positioned as a global player was paramount. The question now is whether Robert Fleming can use the former joint venture platform to pursue a globally integrated strategy across Asia as a manufacturer and distributor. Will it be able to compete with significantly larger international players encroaching on Asia? Many asset managers in Asia will reap profits, but how much depends on setting realistic expectations for where they can fit in the highly competitive markets of 2010.

7
PRIVATE BANKING:
A MIRACLE FOR A FEW

Leading private banks in Asia are tapping substantial wealth, but their operations are not without considerable challenges and real risks.

On July 8, 1997, Kevin Wallace — Merrill Lynch's most successful financial consultant in Asia — and his Chinese father-in-law were arrested in Hong Kong and charged with money laundering. Wallace had arrived in Asia in the mid-1970s, and in 1991 joined Merrill Lynch Private Client Group in Singapore. Between 1991 and 1997, Wallace had built a substantial regional base of high-net-worth client relationships. Press estimates put Wallace's client assets at several hundred million U.S. dollars. For his effort, Wallace received more than US$20 million in compensation over his 6 years at Merrill. On May 15, 1997, Wallace was fired following complaints from several clients who reported discrepancies between their financial statements and what he had told them. Following his dismissal, approximately two dozen more clients of Wallace surfaced with shortfalls, and Merrill had to provide over US$45 million in client compensation. Merrill was able to freeze US$15 million of Wallace's personal assets pending the outcome of criminal charges filed against him.

Not As Easy As It Seems

Asia's economic "miracle" is perhaps most evident in the amount of personal wealth created since 1960. Many of the 50,000 new Mercedes Benz purchased across Asia in the late 1990s were bought by people who grew up in families that could not afford a car in the 1940s and 1950s. Immigrants who fled to Hong Kong from China with next to nothing during the communist takeover in the late 1940s and the Cultural Revolution in the mid-1960s played a significant role in determining residential property prices in Toronto, Vancouver, and Sydney in the late 1980s and throughout the 1990s as they established new homes in these places. In 1991, 27 of the world's billionaires listed in *Forbes* were from Asia ex-Japan. By 1996, that number had grown to 82. It is, therefore, not entirely surprising that international and local banks employ some 2,500 private bankers within Asia to serve the wealthy. In 1996, when China conducted missile tests aimed at Taiwan, hundreds of private bankers in Taiwan, Hong Kong, and Singapore were available to help their high-net-worth clients safeguard their assets.

At first glance, Asia's miracle should be a private banker's miracle. Strong wealth creation, laced with occasional economic and political uncertainty, is the ideal recipe for private bankers providing investment advice and a home for flight capital. Up to the late 1990s, for the well-established private banking and financial consulting units of Citibank, Chase Manhattan Bank, Merrill Lynch, Union Bank of Switzerland (UBS), the Hongkong and Shanghai Banking Corporation (HSBC), and a handful of others, it has been that. But for the more than 80 other competitors — both international and local — it is increasingly less so across Asia. The Asian market is not yet as big as many would guess, competition is increasingly intense, and the economics of providing private banking services in Asia are often less attractive than in the West.

In Japan, the second largest country in the world in terms of personal wealth, private banking opportunities have proven especially elusive. Regulations and a national mindset, that until recently tended to shun either international investment or the use of foreign service providers, largely inhibited the development of private banking. Financial products and services commonplace to many of Asia's affluent are unknown to their counterparts in Japan. In the late 1990s, Japan remained one of the smallest established private banking markets in Asia.

In the first decade in the 21st century, as Asia's societies resume prospering and continue aging, and countries relax financial restrictions, the market for private banking will expand. The scandals in Japan and the financial turmoil throughout Asia in 1997–1998 made the affluent reassess how and with whom they invest. For banks that seek only a toehold in this market, growth and crises will probably always create opportunities for small profits. But for those hoping to seriously augment their global profits with private banking — and today, there appears to be many with such aspirations — the challenge is significant, and the winners will be few. Winning private banks in Asia will be those that identify which clients they are best positioned to serve, and then assist them better than anybody else. Ambitious firms aiming to generate at least US$100 million annually in private banking profits by 2010 need to set aspirations, prioritize clients, and align resources now. For those failing to do so in the first years of the 21st century, advancing competitive pressures will ensure that small profit aspirations become the only choice.

Not All Private Banks Are Alike

Private banking in Asia means different things to many people. Some consider private banking as any financial service given to a high-net-worth individual. Others limit the definition to a very exclusive relationship in which high-net-worth individuals are offered traditional bank deposit and lending services. We believe our definition closely reflects the perspective of clients: a private banking relationship is one in which a single designated relationship manager provides integrated banking and/or investment advice to high-net-worth individuals. Thus, a high-net-worth individual who only has accounts sitting unnoticed in a retail branch would be excluded from our definition of private banking, while the high-net-worth client of a full-service broker who uses a relationship management approach would be included.

Under this definition of private banking, there are more than 80 competitors in the region managing approximately US$250–300 billion in assets gathered by Asia-based relationship managers. Outside Asia, for example in Switzerland, New York, and London, relationship managers are estimated to manage up to an additional US$300 billion of assets gathered from Asian clients who have approached them directly offshore. Somewhat surprisingly, in Japan's struggling private banking market, assets managed by locally based relationship managers appeared unlikely to exceed US$15 billion in 1998. Assets include deposits, mutual funds, discretionary funds, and individual securities and derivatives. The competing providers in Asia vary widely, from European private banks with over 200 years of history, to regional private client divisions of global U.S. investment and commercial banks, to units of local banks throughout North and Southeast Asia that are only a few years old.

Private banking in Asia has evolved significantly since its emergence about 30 years ago. The region's rapid changes in economic growth, political stability, and regulation have transformed not only what private banks can offer, but also what high-net-worth individuals demand. The exception is Japan, where the development of private banking has been extremely limited. In the rest of Asia, however, private banks have had to shape their services in line with changes that were the result of three distinct periods. The first was the mid- to late 1960s, a time of significant capital flight. The potentially contagious Cultural Revolution in China, communist insurrections in Southeast Asia, and massacres of ethnic Chinese in Indonesia and on a lesser scale in Malaysia, inspired wealth holders to shuttle their capital abroad. Successful private banks had to provide confidentiality and discretion above all else. Swiss Bank Corporation (SBC), UBS, and Credit Suisse, among other Swiss banks, were at the forefront of meeting these needs.

The 1970s through the mid-1980s were marked by the rapid development of Asian economies. High-net-worth individuals continued to channel money abroad as a hedge, but reinvested much of their capital in their own enterprises at home. During this period, an increasing proportion of clients sought more than a safe parking place for their funds — they wanted to see investment returns.

From the mid-1980s, and prior to the 1997–1998 meltdown, assets rapidly appreciated in Asia. The gradual loosening of capital controls that allowed more money to be invested abroad was balanced by a strong desire to invest in Asia's booming capital markets. Clients not only wanted better returns, they expected their private banks to be able to advise on investments in the West and across Asia. In this demanding environment, private banks that could provide investment performance, investment tips, a wide range of products, lending leverage, and a high level of personal service — a strategy U.S. institutions often used — were among the leaders in satisfying client needs.

The fallout from the Asian crisis is likely to give rise to a new set of customer demands. Clients will increasingly seek carefully thought-out risk diversification and longer-term financial planning. The investment advisory role many private banks in the U.S. and Europe play will strengthen in Asia. Clients will be less likely to believe that they can outperform the markets in the long term by churning their accounts based on their own hunches and insights. Private banking in Asia to 2010 will become more like private banking in the West.

Customers in Japan Are Different

In Japan, high-net-worth individuals have demonstrated a very different set of needs. In the run-up to the economic bubble of the late 1980s, the primary investment vehicle for the affluent was domestic real estate. Of almost equal importance was tax planning. High historic taxes in Japan — up to 70 percent for inheritance tax — made tax avoidance a key investing strategy.

While high-net-worth Japanese have been keen to protect their savings, they have demonstrated little interest in diversifying their investments internationally or in less traditional investment products, where their understanding is limited. A strong preference for secrecy surrounding personal finances has made educating potential clients on the benefits of new products difficult. This secrecy, combined with the fallout from Japan's scandals, has frustrated attempts for much of the 1990s to serve clients with a single relationship manager. Instead, clients have preferred to hedge themselves by spreading their investments across institutions on a product-by-product basis.

A strong preference for local products, an aversion to investing with a single institution, and regulations limiting foreign investment have restricted the advance of private banks in Japan. The few that set up shop in the late 1980s and early 1990s provided a narrow range of products and services. In 1998, growing public awareness of the relatively poor returns offered by real estate and traditional bank deposits, and government efforts to liberalize areas such as foreign investment, spurred the first phase of serious private banking development in Japan. In the decade leading up to 2010, private banking in Japan should finally begin to mirror the rest of Asia, and will be an arena for significant business growth.

The Million-Dollar Question: Who, Where, and How Much?

The primary question for all private banks in Asia, regardless of how developed the market is, who are the rich? Most of Asia's wealthy are established and emerging entrepreneurs, and a lesser number are professionals and senior government officials. Most have amassed their fortunes in the last three decades, although the Philippines and India have a slightly higher proportion of "old money." Throughout Southeast Asia, ethnic Chinese make up the lion's share of the wealthy.

Estimating how many high-net-worth households there are and their total assets is very difficult in Asia. Government and private statistics shed little light on the true distribution of savings. To estimate, one must extrapolate from countries where such data is available, and then adjust for individual countries in Asia based on their relative level of national development, the structure of their corporate economies, and the generally perceived skew in wealth. Estimating with this approach suggests that there are approximately 670,000 high-net-worth families in Asia who possess as much as US$2.9 trillion in assets (Exhibit 7.1). A small change in assumptions significantly alters the estimated market size for the large and most underdeveloped Asian countries, such as China and India.

While one might reasonably argue with the estimates for any given country, we believe that the relative market size among countries is correct. It seems highly improbable, for example, that China, despite its enormous population, would have more millionaires in the 1990s than Hong Kong. What one can safely take away from these simple estimates is that the huge market of Japan, together with Indonesia and three of the Tigers (Korea, Taiwan, and Hong Kong), probably

Exhibit 7.1

Potential Private Banking Assets per Country: 1997

Estimates

Country/ territory	Total number of households	Households with >US$1 million*	Number of households with > US$1 million	Investable assets per household with > US$1 million**	Potential private banking assets
	Millions	Percent	Thousands	US$ millions	US$ billions
Japan	41	0.70	285	5.3	1,509
Indonesia	43	0.15	64	4.0	257
Taiwan	6	1.00	58	4.0	231
Hong Kong	2	3.00	55	4.0	220
Korea	14	0.30	41	3.5	142
Thailand	13	0.25	33	3.5	117
India	185	0.02	37	3.0	111
Philippines	13	0.25	33	3.0	99
China	310	0.01	31	2.5	78
Malaysia	4	0.50	22	3.0	66
Singapore	1	1.00	8	3.5	29
Total	632		667		2,859

* Adjusted for Asian countries based on data from U.S. (3%), Japan (0.7%), Mexico (0.3%), Brazil (0.11%), U.K. (0.09%), and Spain (0.08%).
** Adjusted for Asian countries based on data from Japan (US$5.3 million), U.K. (US$3.5 million), and U.S. (US$3.5 million).

Source: Government statistics; McKinsey analysis

account for more than 80 percent of potential private banking assets in the region at the turn of the 21st century.

What constitutes a high-net-worth client among private banks varies. Some private banks only serve individuals with investable assets of at least US$10 million, while others accept clients with assets of US$250,000. Some banks specialize in traditional products (e.g., time deposits), some in cutting-edge financial engineering, and others in a full range of prepackaged products, such as mutual funds. Given these contrasts, the number of clients that any one relationship manager handles can differ substantially. However, if one assumes that each of the 2,500 relationship managers employed by all competitors serves on average 75–100 high-net-worth accounts (where each account has an average of US$1 million in liquid assets), today's existing market base is somewhere in the range of 180,000–250,000 accounts outside Japan. In Japan, where the private banking concept is just taking hold, fewer than 20,000 accounts existed in 1998. A strong proclivity among Asian high-net-worth clients to distribute their assets among multiple banks suggests that the private banking market catered to approximately 125,000 individuals across all of Asia in the late 1990s.

Spotting potential high-net-worth individuals in Asia is easier than estimating their total number. Many are entrepreneurs. Throughout the region, some 500 million people are employed in non-agricultural sectors. Of these, around 60 percent work in enterprises that employ 100 people or fewer. In Taiwan, for example, 70 percent of the working population is employed by small enterprises that account for 40 percent of gross domestic product. Even in Japan and Korea, which are known for their large conglomerates, about half of the nonagricultural labor force works in companies with fewer than 100 employees. The entrepreneurs at the controls of these small and medium-sized companies have generally fared well in Asia's rapidly expanding economies.

These entrepreneurs have made their money principally in banking, real estate, and trade-related businesses. Take the region's wealthiest 100 people in 1997 as a proxy: a quarter made their fortunes in real estate, a fifth in banking, about a fifth in trading, and the remainder in manufacturing and other services. A similar industry mix exists among the approximately 1,800 private Asian companies that went public in the 1990s: about 25 percent were engaged primarily in manufacturing, 20 percent in technology and engineering, 15 percent in real estate and property development, 15 percent in banking and finance, another 15 percent in trade, and the rest in activities ranging from natural resources to health care.

"80% of Success is Just Showing Up"

Outside these industries, thousands of other individuals throughout the region moved into the high-net-worth category simply by having had family land on the outskirts of Asia's fast-emerging cities. It is not unusual in places like Taiwan or Hong Kong to encounter families whose net worth exceeds US$10 million simply as a result of having owned a plot of land bought before the 1970s, and sold after the mid-1980s. For many, the miracle of Asia's growth is best described by Woody Allen's adage: "80 percent of success is just showing up."

One group that showed up and has consistently been successful is the ethnic Chinese. Instabilities and starvation in mainland China at the turn of the century, and again in the 1940s and 1960s, created large waves of emigration. Today in Asia — outside China, Hong Kong, Taiwan, and Singapore — there are 25 million Asians of Chinese descent. When Chinese emigrants first arrived in Southeast Asia, they were often banned from owning land; they still are often barred from politics. For most ethnic Chinese, local commerce and regional trade were the only options. But Chinese communities have consistently turned adversity into prosperity.

A case in point is the Salim Group, which rose to become one of Indonesia's largest conglomerates in less than 50 years. Liem Sioe Liong, who adopted the Salim name and founded the group, arrived in Indonesia from China in 1938. During Indonesia's 1945–1949 struggle for independence, Salim supplied Suharto, who was a quartermaster at the time, with food, medicine, and military supplies by drawing on his web of Chinese contacts. In 1957, when President Sukarno reclaimed Dutch-owned companies, Salim provided credit and management expertise he had picked up through his business dealings with Chinese merchants in Singapore and Hong Kong. By the time Suharto became president in 1966, Salim had established a substantial business presence, which further prospered as a result of his influential relationship with Suharto. The Salim's business base was nonetheless under threat in 1998 as anti-Chinese sentiment ravished Indonesia and targeted conglomerates that had benefited from close connections with the disposed Suharto family.

While many of the stories of Chinese success in Southeast Asia's economies are not on par with Salim's, the cumulative impact of ethnic Chinese accomplishments are dramatic. In Indonesia, ethnic Chinese comprise 3 percent of the population and control an estimated 75 percent of the wealth; in the Philippines 2 percent controls approximately 55 percent; in Thailand 10 percent controls up to 80 percent; and in Malaysia 30 percent controls an estimated 60 percent.

It is easy to get wrapped up in numbers that measure and dissect Asia's wealth. From a strategic perspective, however, market size and wealth composition is a secondary issue for Asia's private bankers. In a truly mature market, knowing market size and one's market share is essential for setting strategy. They feed directly into setting growth aspirations, pricing, and product development. But in Asia, with over 80 competitors covering up to ten markets — often on a fly-in basis — private banking is not yet a mature market. Also, given that there are approximately 125,000 established private banking customers out of a potential pool of 670,000 high-net-worth customers, the key issue is cost-effectively tailoring services to attract the large variety of wealthy individuals who have not yet signed up for private banking services.

The Million-Dollar Problem

With so much awareness of the growing number of millionaires in Asia, many international private bankers find it difficult to explain their performance to headquarters. Even in the good years preceding the 1997–1998 meltdown, private banking returns in Asia were often not quite what one would have expected. In the

1990s, revenues on assets were either at par or lower than those of Europe or the U.S., and costs were often higher. The resulting margin squeeze means that many private banking operations in Asia must bring in up to three-quarters more assets than would be required in their home markets, to achieve commensurate profits and returns. Since this is often not possible, and so private banking returns in Asia remain frustratingly sub-par.

Private banking economics have four simple components: assets, leverage, fees, and costs. From a bank's perspective, an attractive private banking account has assets that exceed the minimum requirement, grows steadily with limited volatility, and is invested in a number of discretionary investment products that produce recurring annual fees. A very attractive account will actively trade a portion of its assets in equities or other instruments to generate additional commissions. And the truly ideal private banking account will borrow money against existing assets to increase the leverage of its investments, with little risk to the bank. If the client is financially sophisticated and understands the products well, an active portfolio can be effectively managed by a strong relationship manager with reasonably little time devoted to each client. If all goes well, such an account will reward the private banker with referrals to other high-net-worth clients.

Steady assets, consistent revenue streams, a low cost per account, and a flow of new business introductions is a strong combination for private banking profits. These objectives can be delivered while serving the best interests of the client, as long as adequate time is spent upfront to define a client's investment objectives, risk tolerance, and service preferences.

The typical private banking account in Asia, however, is far from ideal. On the asset side, minimums are frequently waived to initiate relationships. As clients distribute their business across multiple banks, assets remain smaller than one would find in the West. Further, assets are often volatile as clients shift funds across private banks in search of the best interest rate on time deposits. The fact that a surprising and significant portion (often exceeding 50 percent) of private banks' assets under management are held in time deposits, where spreads are thin, limits revenues. Strong direct pricing competition further depresses margins. In this environment, lending to clients to leverage their investments can provide the needed revenue boost. Most clients in Asia do seek loans, but not to leverage their investments with private banks. Rather, as entrepreneurs, many seek credit for working capital in their businesses or for financing investments that are not disclosed to the bank. Few private banks in Asia are equipped or mandated to provide these lending facilities.

Revenues in Asia are therefore lower and more volatile, while operating costs are unfortunately higher. The most significant cost is relationship managers. A relationship manager with several years of experience and a small book of client business can easily command an annual package worth US$250,000. Mature and experienced candidates are known to command US$1 million in annual compensation.

This expensive resource, however, is often poorly utilized. Because most foreign private banks in Asia rely on U.S. or European headquarters for decisions and product expertise, relationship managers spend a significant amount of their time shepherding client requests through the system, rather than identifying new business opportunities. Such is the cost of providing "seamless customer service." Moreover, time spent prospecting clients often yields a low hit rate on new business; this is because the typical relationship manager in Asia gets little formal training in identifying client needs, providing investment advice, and communicating distinctive services. High turnover due to aggressive competitor poaching further reduces effectiveness. Each time a new relationship manager is brought in to replace one that has left, there are likely to be lost revenues: either the clients' assets move with the old relationship manager, or it takes time for the new manager to cement relationships and further penetrate accounts.

In operations, the second largest cost category, many international private banks from the mid-1990s incurred the cost of building a new Asian product line to cater to growing client needs for local and regional investment advice. Today, these capabilities are typically housed in the relatively expensive hubs of Singapore and Hong Kong.

The resulting squeeze of lower revenues and higher costs has a different impact on the private banking operations of U.S. investment banks, global commercial banks and emerging local banks. The private client and brokerage units of U.S. investment banks feel the cost pressure in Asia, but are most able to compensate, partially through their product mix and employee compensation plans. U.S. institutions are typically able to generate revenues upwards of 150 basis points on assets under management by providing clients with access to much-sought-after IPOs, encouraging clients to trade actively in their accounts, and offering leveraged and structured products, such as hedge funds, which command higher fees. Because compensation in many of these institutions is directly tied to an account's revenues, management is in a relatively strong position to influence account returns by setting their relationship managers' performance targets. A pay-for-performance approach also limits some cost pressure, as bonuses are tied to business generated.

The private banking units of U.S. and European global commercial banks are less resilient to responding to the profit squeeze. Commercial banks' product mix is made up principally of time deposits and long-term investments in mutual funds or discretionary accounts that generate a steady 75–100 basis points on funds under management. It is difficult to price upward or benefit from increased trading activity in these products. Consequently, many bear the full brunt of the region's rising operating costs. For the less adept private banks, revenues may gravitate closer to 75 basis points, and rising costs may mean that expenditures are closer to 70 percent of revenues than the typical 60 percent benchmark in many home markets. When this occurs, private banking units must gather 75 percent more assets in Asia than at home to reach a given profit target. This is very hard to achieve without, once again, adding costs.

Local private banks are least able to cope with the profit squeeze and thus, are often forced to tolerate losses in their private banking units. New to the business, many local private banks are in the early stages of upgrading their services to high-net-worth clients, and their private banking units frequently lack the investment expertise to market such products as mutual funds or individual securities. Hence many of these banks are principally left marketing time deposits, with occasional lending for investment leverage, or straight lending for high-net-worth client home mortgages. This product mix typically generates 25–50 basis points for funds under management. Local private banks are able to contain costs somewhat by recruiting relationship managers internally from their officer ranks, but at these low revenue levels, any volatility in clients' assets — such as in 1997–1998 — quickly makes these units unprofitable.

The Emerging World of the Haves and Have-Nots

Pressured private banking returns in Asia are the direct result of intensifying competition for people and clients. The rapid build-up by competitors that started in the early 1990s has begun to polarize the private banking industry in Asia ex-Japan. In Japan, the story is, again, quite different.

Today, outside Japan, there are few big players and many small ones. The top ten private banks in Asia control approximately half of the US$250 billion in private banking assets under management sourced from Asia (Exhibit 7.2). This group is composed of formidable leaders in private banking worldwide, including global commercial banks such as Citibank, Chase, HSBC, UBS, Credit Suisse, and BNP, and U.S. investment banks Merrill Lynch, JP Morgan, Morgan Stanley, and Goldman Sachs. Many of the largest players in Asia at the end of the 1990s were from the U.S. (Exhibit 7.3).

The next ten competitors control approximately a quarter of existing private banking assets, and are made up largely of the private banking arms of European commercial banks and several local banks, for example, Bangkok Bank and the Development Bank of Singapore (DBS). The balance quarter of the US$250 billion of existing private banking assets is split among more than 60 competitors, most of whom are either small private banking arms of European commercial banks or the nascent private banking units of local banks.

To put this in dollar terms, the top ten private banks operating in Asia (outside of Japan) share about US$1 billion in revenues and US$200–300 million in profits, while the bottom 60-plus competitors fight over approximately US$500 million in revenues and US$100–150 million in profits. Within this industry structure, small private banks that are content to remain small will probably be able to carve out mediocre profits of up to several million dollars. A small or medium-sized private bank that aspires to become a true leader in Asia must overcome significant internal and external challenges. Already, the gap between market leaders and the rest is quite significant outside Japan.

Citibank's Deep Roots

Citibank, the leading private bank in Asia in terms of assets under management (in excess of US$20 billion in 1998), has been plying the private banking waters in the region for over 30 years. Its private banking hubs in Hong Kong and Singapore have been able to draw on its retail and corporate presence throughout the region, not only to establish a strong brand name, but also to spot the emerging

Exhibit 7.2

Private Banking Assets in Asia by Size of Competitor: 1998   *Estimates*

Assets under management* US$ billions	Number of private banks**	Share of existing private banking assets
>US$15.0	1	10%
5.1–15.0	6	35%
2.6–5.0	10	20%
1.0–2.5	21	20%
<1.0	34	15%
Total	**72**	**100% = approximately US$250 billion***

* Defined here as assets belonging to high-net-worth individuals who are served by dedicated relationship managers.

** Based on information drawn from publicly available sources and McKinsey experience.

*** Based on bottom-up analysis of assets managed by private banks operating in Asia; may be understated by as much as 20 percent.

Source: Literature search; McKinsey interviews

Exhibit 7.3

Private Banking Assets in Asia by National Origin of Competitor: 1998   *Estimates*

Percent

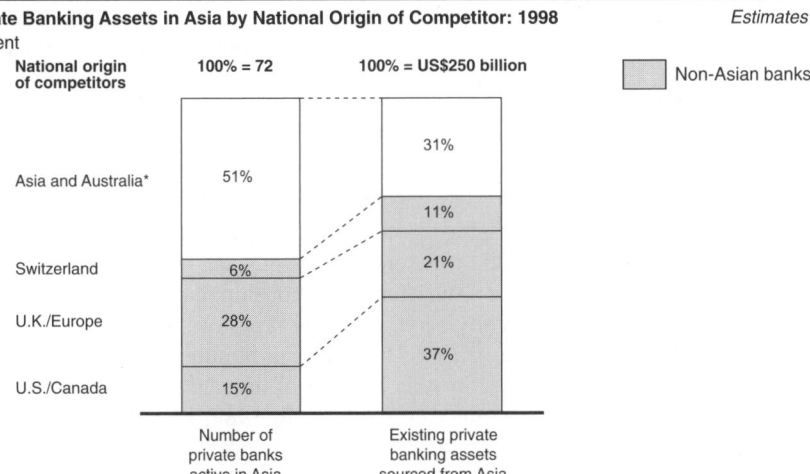

National origin of competitors

100% = 72   100% = US$250 billion   Non-Asian banks

National origin of competitors	Number of private banks active in Asia	Existing private banking assets sourced from Asia
Asia and Australia*	51%	31%
		11%
Switzerland	6%	21%
U.K./Europe	28%	37%
U.S./Canada	15%	

* Includes the Hongkong and Shanghai Banking Corporation, which accounts for about a fifth of Asian and Australian banks' private banking assets in Asia.

Source: Literature search; McKinsey interviews

affluent. Citibank capitalized on its early and strong network in the 1970s by hiring some of the best and the brightest personnel in Asia. Right from the beginning, its commitment to training and developing local professionals had given it broad access to local communities throughout Asia. Citibank's U.S. roots have provided consistent access to the latest in financial concepts and personal investing. The bank's relatively youthful and dynamic image, compared to that of its more conservatively positioned European counterparts, served it well from the late 1980s through most of the 1990s, as an increasing number of educated affluent clients chose performance and service over just confidentiality and safety.

As the 1997 financial crisis extended into 1998, Citibank branches throughout the region saw more new clients and deposits in the unfolding flight to quality. Local and foreign private banking competitors can count on Citibank to take advantage of the nervous customer flows through its doors. It records their names, screens their potential, and systematically deploys its relationship management force to call on new potential high-net-worth clients. Citibank private banking will not be slowing down in 21st Century Asia.

Merrill Lynch: Imported Success Formula

Merrill Lynch Private Client (with private banking assets of approximately US$10 billion in 1998) is a market leader markedly different from Citibank. Its private banking operations are part of a large investment bank that, unlike Citibank, did not have a large Asian branch network to draw upon. Although Merrill Lynch had been in Asia since the 1960s, it did not employ the hundreds of people across Asia that Citibank long had until the early 1990s. In the early 1990s, Merrill Lynch significantly bolstered its regional presence by expanding into the Asian investment banking world. While this investment banking arm was busy establishing corporate relationships and securing its position in the equity and debt-league tables, the Private Client division of Merrill Lynch geared up its services to high-net-worth individuals across Asia. At the outset of the 1990s, Merrill had approximately 70 relationship managers in Hong Kong, Singapore, and a small representative office in Taipei. By 1998, Merrill had close to 200 relationship managers in Asia ex-Japan: 90 in Singapore, 60 in Hong Kong, 40 in Taipei, and a few circulating through a representative office in Bangkok.

Globally, Merrill Lynch employs close to 14,000 relationship managers. In the U.S., they typically serve clients who, on average, have an investable net worth of approximately US$250,000. In Asia, Merrill relationship managers have been able to raise their sights, and typically serve the same types of clients as most private banks, which formally request a US$1 million minimum in investable assets. Merrill's relationship managers in Asia are part of an extensive global operation that is not afraid to take risks in new markets. In 1989, Merrill invested US$8 million in capital to secure a foreign brokerage license in Taiwan so it could market U.S. securities to Taiwan nationals. In 1998, only Merrill had such a license, and its private banking business was growing rapidly. Relationship managers from other private banks in Taiwan were left scurrying in the shadows, trying not to draw too much attention to their unlicensed marketing activities.

Worldwide, Merrill Lynch Private Client is a leader in resolving the systems challenges that must be overcome to provide seamless client service. It has effectively tied together its multiple product groups so that relationship managers can easily market a broad range of products from time deposits to mutual funds and hot IPOs underwritten by its global investment banking team. Merrill has a compensation system that cuts across all these products and directly ties its relationship managers' performance to pay.

In Asia, Merrill Lynch continued to add to these strengths by building new pipelines. The 1995 investment banking acquisition of Smith New Court provided the Merrill operation with strong Asian investment research. This research can be used, in part, to advise high-net-worth clients on their Asian investment strategy, which will remain an important part of portfolios despite the wide-scale wealth destruction in 1997–1998. In 1997, Merrill's acquisition of the failed Yamaichi brokerage network in Japan was the first step towards private banking success in this large but long dormant market. Clearly, Merrill has the investment power and resources to back its aspirations to be a leading private bank throughout Asia.

Stumbling Blocks for Local Banks

Citibank and Merrill Lynch are just two of the top ten. HSBC, Chase, and UBS are three others that have established significant networks, are backed by comprehensive product lines, and aspire to be dominant players in Asian private banking.

In contrast, the private banking units of the local banks in Asia are just getting started, but many of these institutions are sleeping giants. Within their retail customer networks are literally several hundred thousand high-net-worth customers who today have no private banking relationships. Since the late 1980s, local institutions such as Bangkok Bank, Hang Seng Bank, and DBS have woken up to the private banking opportunities at their fingertips. These three are among the roughly 30 local banks around the region that have established private banking units to mine high-net-worth prospects. These 30 or so local competitors manage a total of US$30–40 billion in assets, or about 15 percent of the existing Asia-based market outside Japan. For many, the going is tough. Their good intentions of establishing private banking units often become tangled in a web of strategic and organizational battles that limit their growth potential from the outset.

The first major stumbling blocks for local banks typically appear when a new private banking unit gathers US$1–2 billion in assets. At this point, it has 20 or so employees drawn from around the bank, and has called in most of its favors from branch managers to transfer their high-net-worth clients to the new unit. At about the same time the private banking unit head points out to senior management that it needs to hire experienced private bankers at market prices (which immediately places the unit at the top of the bank's pay scale), someone from accounting starts to question the role of this new private banking cost center. A battle then ensues to justify the private banking unit's existence.

To counter the view that private banking is an unnecessary new overhead, every portion of revenue that can be attached to captured high-net-worth clients is clawed in from around the bank. A helpful soul from one of the central processing units notes that if the unit is intent on managing all high-net-worth client revenues, it should probably be prepared to share some of the centralized costs for IT, MIS, and perhaps the bills department.

When senior management starts to hear all the noise over the new private banking unit, they summon key personnel from Private Banking, Retail, Operations, and perhaps Corporate Banking. If things go well, senior management concludes that if Citibank can do so well with one branch in the country, it should be able to do a lot better with 100; it's just a matter of spending more time at the drawing board. If things do not go so well, senior management concludes that the private banking unit is essentially offering the same services as other units, but at a higher cost. Under the less positive scenario, coffin nails are hammered into the new unit when a retail branch manager notes that the only difference in the private banking unit is that it gives that branch's loyal customers better rates on time deposits, bringing lower returns for the bank. Private banking can quickly become sidelined on the senior management agenda.

The issues facing local banks wishing to get into private banking are numerous and complex. Even if senior management can devote attention to ironing out the organizational issues, significant time and investment is still required to build products and skills, and to implement the systems that provide seamless customer service. This time and investment may be more than some institutions are prepared to tolerate.

Outside Japan, the gap in private banking between an emerging domestic bank and an established global leader is quite evident. Equally clear are the challenges of transforming today's small player — be it local or international — into tomorrow's big player. It can be done, but the window of opportunity is narrowing.

Fledgling Competition in Japan

Competition in Japan, compared to that in the rest of Asia, was virtually nonexistent towards the end of the 1990s. Private banks' penetration of high-net-worth households was at most 5 percent, global competitors were only starting to make their mark. Japan's financial deregulation, which kicked off in earnest in 1998, will facilitate more foreign competition, allow more products to be sold by more institutions, and liberalize capital flows — particularly offshore — in the early 21st century. But deregulation will not immediately change the cautious Japanese investor nor traditional local banks, both of which are just beginning to understand the private banking concept. So growth will be slow. The battle for assets will be between the leading foreign players, which have strong reputations and private banking expertise but little access to clients, and the large local banks, which have deep client relationships from years of business lending but high organizational inertia when it comes to implementing new ideas.

In 1998, the leading foreign players in Japan had less than US$5 billion in private banking assets. All were starting from a small base, but several were gearing up to take a real crack at the Japanese market. The efforts of the most aggressive were perhaps best exemplified by Merrill Lynch and the SBC side of the newly merged UBS. After exiting Japan in the early 1990s, Merrill Lynch Private Client re-entered in 1997 with its purchase of Yamaichi's retail brokerage arm. Merrill's challenge will be to integrate some 2,000 traditional Japanese stockbrokers into its proven system. The acquisition will not immediately move Merrill into the world of private banking, but if it pursues the same strategy in Japan as in the rest of Asia, Merrill will gradually upgrade its business so that high-net-worth individuals become a substantial part of its client ranks in the first decade of the 21st century. Also in 1997, UBS/SBC entered into a partnership with the Long Term Credit Bank of Japan (LTCB) in the expectation of bringing its expertise to its partner's network of personal relationships (although LTCB's financial problems, which became apparent in 1998, resulted in UBS/SBC acquiring the private banking business of the partnership).

The large local Japanese banks are much like their Asian counterparts. They house much of the personal wealth and have the personal relationships, but in the late 1990s were just beginning to grapple with the organizational and skill-building challenges of setting up new private banking operations. Many will try, but only a few are likely to emerge as true leaders in Japan's future private banking landscape.

Four Ingredients for Success

So what do you do if you are the manager of a private bank in Asia? If your institution's aspirations are simply to maintain a small outpost in Asia, then little is required. On the other hand, if you wish to grow and maximize returns, the time to begin is now. While the economics are tough and the competition is daunting, the market is not entirely locked up.

The depth of the 1997–1998 crisis will have motivated many high-net-worth individuals, including those without any private banking relationships, to diversify their investments. Financial deregulation in the years after the crisis will lift capital restrictions that historically prevented many of these individuals from investing internationally. The freedom to diversify will happen as Asia's baby boomers reach their prime saving and investment years. At the end of the 1990s, 15 percent of the region's population was in the key earning and investment years of 40–55. That figure will rise to 18 percent in 2010, and will peak at 20 percent around 2025. In the decade to 2010, most of Asia will recover from the crisis and go on to post strong economic growth. The private banking market will not only grow, but will be augmented by a large influx of currently unserved high-net-worth clients.

Market growth plus a large influx of new customers will not make competition disappear; they will merely give aspirants a little more space in which to maneuver. But success, that is, maximizing returns through profitable growth, will require taking advantage of this extra space in a very disciplined manner. It will mean building on four key elements: customer segmentation; product innovation; cost management; and organizational critical mass.

Private banks seeking to enhance performance can use one or two of these ingredients in isolation, but the impact will be much less dramatic than if they mix all four. Of course, strong credit controls and a clear split between front and back office must be present as well. Otherwise, as the Kevin Wallace story demonstrates, significant achievements and profits could be quickly undermined.

Customer Segmentation

Customer segmentation — the art and science of tailoring and delivering products and services to distinct customer groups — can be a difficult task. But it is built around a reasonably simple principle: know your client. In the private banking world, this means being familiar with two facets of customer needs: the products and services that best meet the customer's investment objectives, and the style of relationship manager that best suits what the client wants from a private bank. The trick with customer segmentation is grouping clients accurately and easily to differentiate service. If you can easily categorize, anticipate, and react to a client's needs by asking him or her a few simple questions, then you have passed the acid test for segmentation.

Institutions often segment customers based on one or more of the following factors: family background, work experience, sex, age, potential profitability of the account, and behavior. Some life insurance companies, for example, use what they call life-cycle segmentation, which combines age and behavior. These companies have determined that the best way to distinguish and predict clients' needs is to assess where they are in their life cycle: going to school, getting married, having children, or retiring. A few simple questions establish a client's life-cycle stage and give a sales agent a reasonable basis for anticipating issues and needs.

There is no right method of segmenting the private banking market in Asia. In the late 1990s, leading competitors organized themselves principally around countries, but as customers become more demanding and competition intensifies, this is unlikely to suffice. A model that combines personal background, age, and behavior will emerge as a more effective means of understanding and penetrating customers. Consider one possible model that segments high-net-worth clients into six categories common across all of Asia: established patrons; passive heirs; established entrepreneurs; emerging entrepreneurs; professionals; and super-high-net-worth individuals.

The logic behind these groupings (see sidebar for detailed descriptions) is that high-net-worth clients choose their investments and display different levels of financial sophistication based on their age and how they obtained their wealth. Matching services and products against the distinct needs of segments such as these is key to growth.

Few institutions can be positioned to serve all segments equally well. Though some institutions may cover every category, few individual relationship managers are able to stretch their expertise across such a broad range of customer needs. This forces private banks to ask a number of strategic questions. How big is each customer segment? How well understood are the needs of each segment? What are the bank's strengths and weaknesses in serving each segment? Which segments are more or less profitable? In which segments is competition more or less developed? And, last but not least, which customer segments are existing staff best suited to serve?

Groups of High-Net-Worth Clients

Established patron. He is likely to be in his 60s or 70s, and no longer involved in day-to-day business. His primary investment objective is capital preservation and smooth distribution of wealth to his heirs. Thus, he wants a private bank that provides conservative investment instruments, tax optimization, and estate planning and handling. His ideal bank will be able serve his family, whether it is in Asia, Europe, Canada, or the U.S. He is interested in working with a mature relationship manager who can sensitively handle the delicate details of family finance, trusts, and wills over the long term. An effective manager will master details of the account and provide responsive, but not intrusive, recommendations and service.

Passive heir. He is typically middle-aged and has inherited money within the past 10 years. He seeks investments that provide steady returns and ensure a certain lifestyle for himself and his family. Most clients in this category look for a private bank that has investment expertise in developed U.S. and European markets, which are perceived as the most secure. The ideal relationship manager has a strong grasp of the overall portfolio and can provide guidance on key decisions, such as financing a home, immigration, or optimizing tax status. This manager will provide convenient and efficient service, and will have the patience to explain products and associated risks.

Established entrepreneur. She is typically a self-made individual in her 40s or 50s, and has created wealth in the last 20–30 years in areas such as manufacturing, trade, or real estate development. She is seeking both capital preservation and capital appreciation. She is looking for a private bank that can provide interesting investment opportunities, be they in local, regional, or global securities. She would like to gain access to products that may not be available to most people, such as primary issues, private placements, or direct investment opportunities. She wants a bank that provides consistent service, new ideas, and takes the time to develop a personal relationship. The relationship manager will have to be adept at determining the client's risk tolerance, and be proactive in identifying suitable opportunities. The relationship manager's reputation and standing in the community will often be important to this type of client.

Emerging entrepreneur. In his 30s or 40s, and in the early stages of wealth creation, he is looking for instruments to both protect and grow his savings. The emerging entrepreneur seeks a private bank that can provide performance and flexibility. For performance, he wants a constant flow of investment ideas that require short- or long-term investment horizons. He tends to test the skills of private bankers before giving them extensive business, and monitors investment advice for some time before acting. But once he has made a decision, he expects the private banker to be available and responsive. Access to 24-hour trading capabilities, for example, is often important to this type of client, who likes to be involved in his investments.

The emerging entrepreneur also expects a degree of flexibility. The line between his businesses and his personal wealth is thin; he will want credit to leverage his investments and to finance his businesses. Private banks that can cater to this demanding client's needs will capture a disproportionate share of his business. Relationship managers need to be street smart, be able to problem-solve, and have a thorough understanding of local and regional investment markets. Relationship managers' knowledge, rather than their reputation, is key.

Professional. She is typically a young to middle-aged executive in a local conglomerate or large multinational corporation. She is well-educated and financially astute, but has little time to handle personal investments. She prefers a private bank that can provide a systematic approach to financial planning. She is looking for a relationship manager who can propose an investment strategy with the right mix of capital preservation and growth. She is likely to be most interested in packaged products that have a clear performance record and transparent pricing, and require little or no input. Relationship managers who prove responsive and find the means to increase this client's assets will be rewarded with the lion's share of her business. Relationship managers will need to understand their products and clients, but need not be as well-versed on individual markets and securities as relationship managers serving the entrepreneurs.

Super-high-net-worth individual. Client needs in the super-high-net-worth category are not necessarily driven by age or background. Possessing often more than US$50 million, this client functions more like a financial institution than an individual. The scale of wealth enables this person to employ in-house financial experts to determine investment needs, set portfolio allocations, and even execute transactions directly on exchanges. As such, private banks are intermediaries used only if they can provide access to specific investment expertise or possibly loans for leveraged investing. In these instances, private bankers serve as contact points to refer specialists or execute transactions. Unlike the other five categories, relationship managers serving the super-high-net-worth client rarely have the opportunity of building personal relationships or advising across the full set of the customer's needs.

Implicitly, customer segmentation forces prioritization. An institution is compelled to evaluate where it can add the most value, and then identify the customers who will appreciate what it has to offer. In a competitive and growing market, effective customer segmentation enables a bank to know who it is going after, and to demonstrate quickly to the chosen clients that it is in a strong position to meet their specific needs. Efforts to build tailored products and services that clients need most, and to educate customers, will result in increasing customer awareness of a given bank's strengths. It is this customer awareness that provides banks with recognition and distinctiveness. And it is this distinctiveness that gives aspirants the ability to stand out from the competition and penetrate the untapped high-net-worth market or capture a deeper share of the existing private banking market. Customer segmentation done well is a key to growth.

Product Innovation

Customer segmentation is also key to maximizing returns through product innovation, the next important ingredient of success. Imagine, for example, a private bank that specializes in serving the fast-growing "emerging entrepreneur" segment. It would perhaps have to develop a strong understanding of small and medium-sized businesses in select Asian markets and industries. With in-depth knowledge of these businesses and their clients, this private bank would be in a solid position to design investment products or offer credit lines that competitors, due to their lack of information and experience, would be unable to match.

Areas of expertise developed by such a bank might include tax optimization strategies for businesses and their owners, or industrial mortgage facilities that enable businesses to unlock and invest the value of their fixed assets. Or more simply, the private bank may establish relationships with a network of real estate agents in the U.K. and Canada to help high-net-worth clients purchase property, if that is their preferred investment vehicle. In doing so, the private bank could be involved in hedging property loans or providing the loans themselves. European private banks with these capabilities report revenues in excess of 300 basis points for a given client relationship. Clearly, a private bank's ability to provide services that few others can, enables premium pricing. Reading distinct customer needs and innovating accordingly is the key to offsetting the likely erosion in core product margins.

Cost Management

Effective customer segmentation also enhances the third ingredient — cost management — in three areas: customers, relationship managers, and back-office functions. A private bank that has a clear vision of which customers it wants to serve can avoid initiating relationships with accounts that they will be unable to serve well, and that are therefore unlikely to be profitable in the long run. Accurate customer selection avoids the high cost of poorly used relationship manager time.

Clearly targeted customer groups also enable management to proactively develop or weed out relationship managers. Today, relationship managers are often given a long time to prove themselves, because management finds it difficult to determine who is competent, who is not, and why. When customer segmentation is clear, management can move much more quickly to identify where relationship managers need to improve, and can quickly replace low performers. If management can focus on developing those with talent, chances are that relationship managers will recognize the training and the impact it has on their compensation, and may be less likely to be poached away — lowering the costs associated with high turnover.

In the back office, a clear understanding of client needs helps management reduce expenditures in areas less important to meeting those needs. When management is comfortable with client strategy and priorities, it is possible to aggressively outsource low-value-added products, services, and infrastructure. Customer segmentation allows management to take a bolder stance on cost reduction, a critical element for improving returns in Asia.

Organizational Critical Mass

Competitors intent on achieving profitable growth in Asia also must ensure that their organizations have the fourth element, critical mass, that is, the right balance of organizational depth and breadth. Organizational depth within Asia enables private banks to identify and respond to opportunities in their chosen customer segments. This depth is measured by the degree of decision-making authority, market information, and customer knowledge within the organization. An operation has sufficient depth in a given market when it knows which industry sectors are doing well, who is generating new wealth, and which clients are approaching investment decisions because, for example, they had a good year, sold their business, or are planning to retire. This type of depth enables private banks to spot opportunities and provide clients with timely, tailored, and innovative ideas.

To ensure depth, organizations must be empowered to act or respond quickly. Many smaller European banks have the information to innovate, but are trapped by having the decision authority housed seven time zones away. When there is sufficient organizational depth, private banks have on-the-ground capabilities to tailor customer solutions, and are able to stay a step ahead of the competition. Without it, operations are more likely to skim the surface of clients' assets by providing only generic lower-margin products.

Organizational breadth provides private banks with flexibility and staying power. Breadth is measured by product range, systems support, and opportunities for personnel development. An operation has adequate breadth when it is big enough to offer a diverse product range, systems tailored to local needs, training for staff, and career advancement for high performers. Breadth enables organizations to survive volatility across products and to invest in capability-building without destroying profits. Breadth also ensures that organizations have enough products and services to capture the lion's share of a client's portfolio.

When there is insufficient breadth, an organization remains unstructured, inefficient, and often unable to sustain growth momentum because relationship managers or clients depart. Simply put: if you are a strong local professional gradually building up a substantial client base, are you going to remain with a private bank that maintains a small outpost, or move to an institution whose solid portfolio enables you to fully capture the potential of your high-net-worth clients?

Many private banks in Asia tend to have some depth or breadth, but rarely both. Many domestic players, however, are weak in both areas. If an operation has depth without breadth, it has difficulty capitalizing on its skills and is likely to experience fitful success. If an operation has breadth without depth, it has a hard time penetrating clients and distinguishing itself in the marketplace. Critical mass requires a mix of both.

This mix can differ from bank to bank, depending on its size and the customer segments it serves. Private bank managers in Asia are often aware of the importance of critical mass, but frequently do not quantify it. Consequently, it is rarely addressed in discussions to set strategy, growth, and performance targets. Competitors who are serious about expanding in Asia need to examine critical mass issues upfront; otherwise, they are proceeding into battle with one arm tied behind their backs.

Private banks that apply the four key ingredients — customer segmentation, product innovation, cost management, and critical mass — in order to grow must always keep one eye on returns. The object is to simultaneously grow assets and profits, such that profits — not revenues — are consistently at least 50–100 basis points of assets under management. A focus on returns ensures execution with the proper balance and timing.

Winning Trust in Japan

In addition to the four key elements, competitors in Japan need to undertake aggressive staff training, build customer confidence, and implement a broad program of customer education.

Competitors in Japan must have a clear vision of which customer segments they want to penetrate. This clarity will provide focus for the massive program of banker and customer training that must occur in Japan. The challenge for all private banks in Japan is to demonstrate to potential clients that they offer something different that clients need. Internal training must give relationship managers the skills to educate potential customers on their institution's and products' strengths.

By the late 1990s, the Japanese were justifiably cynical about financial institutions. A decade earlier, securities firms had manipulated the stock market to favor large institutional clients at retail customers' expense. In the early 1990s, insurance companies guaranteed returns on client investments, only to later cut promised returns by half in the face of mounting losses. During this period, banks provided low rates to depositors to generate cheap corporate funding. This fueled excessive speculation, a bubble, and a recession extending from 1991 through to the end of the decade.

Private banks in Japan, therefore, must demonstrate above all else that their products match clients' interests. Rather than spending time upfront perfecting seamless customer service through relationship management, private banks must probably excel in one or two products to prove to clients that they can enhance returns. Goldman Sachs' investment trust division, for example, launched a series of investment trusts distributed by Nikko and Kokusai Securities that gathered US$5 billion in assets in only 16 months. This was a lot more than either its private banking division or Citibank had accumulated through its relationship management approach in 10 years.

A strong product with a simple value proposition can go a long way. In this regard, guaranteed return products may prove ideal for Japan. By giving up a portion of returns to purchase financial instruments that reduce risks (futures, options), competitors can easily demonstrate an ability to deliver steady and improved performance. The Japanese public has become so accustomed to returns under 5 percent in the 1990s that it would not be difficult to provide a standout product. After building customer trust through such products, banks can then introduce a broader range of offerings, progressively covering new instruments and a wider geographical scope. Over time, it will be possible to graduate from products to relationship management and fuller access to clients' total assets. But the first priority is, clearly, products.

Institutions wishing to excel in Japan must evaluate their ability to carry out wide-scale internal staff education, customer confidence-building, and customer education. The magnitude of the challenges and the complementary capabilities of foreign and local players argue for partnerships. Needless to say, victory in Japan will come to those who demonstrate staying power in the battle to win customer trust.

Victory for a Few

By 2010, private banking operations in Asia (outside Japan) are likely to have in excess of US$1 trillion in assets under management. This assumes that the market continues growing 10 percent a year, and a small proportion of untapped high-net-worth clients begins using private banking services. In Japan, gradual penetration of the market should capture US$300–400 billion in private banking assets. By 2010, US$10–12 billion in revenues will thus be available to competitors serving all of Asia, including Japan.

But the miracle of individual wealth creation, which in all likelihood will resume strongly by 2005 once the medicine of 1997 and 1998 is digested, will be a miracle for only a handful of aggressive private banks. Looking ahead to 2010, the private banking market across the region will probably be composed of three distinct groups: global players, a small number of regional or country specialists, and a long tail of flag carriers.

Global players

About ten global players will consistently achieve annual profits in excess of US$100 million in all of Asia. As a group, they will continue to control about half of total private banking assets under management. Their presence will be deep in multiple markets and in several customer segments. They will be well positioned to serve both the super-high-net-worth clients who function much like financial institutions, and the broader base of high-net-worth clients who possess US$1–5 million in investable assets. To serve multiple segments and align cost with opportunity, these players may well operate under more than one brand name. The global players will be very proficient at both acquiring and growing relationships. They will possess state-of-the-art infrastructure, enabling them to provide on-the-ground service for a global range of products, often more cost effectively than local competitors. Their ability to hire top talent, train and develop relationship managers, delegate authority, and sustain a clear performance culture will be paramount to their continued success.

Regional specialists

Some 10–15 regional specialists will consistently achieve US$30–80 million in annual profits in Asia. As a group, they will control about a fifth of private banking assets under management. They will have a disproportionate share of high-net-worth client business in two or three carefully selected markets, and will focus on one or two customer segments. On average, their ability to understand and meet their chosen customers' needs will be slightly better than that of global players, even though their product range may be narrower. As a group, regional specialists will probably achieve slightly higher returns with their chosen clients than global players, based on their ability to develop more innovative products that fit distinct needs. Their continued success will depend on their ability to become true insiders in the communities or segments they serve. The superior information they gather will be the basis for their competitive advantage.

These organizations will excel at sharing, debating, and acting on discrete pieces of client, market, or industry information. The operating culture within these specialist firms will emphasize and reward strong customer service and new ideas. In this environment, it will be crucial to hire self-assured, independent, motivated personnel. The role of senior management will be to capture and communicate best practices to the entire firm. There were about 30 competitors in operation at the end of the 1990s that could aspire to be in this select group by 2010. A clear majority of the candidates are international, but there are likely to be several with local roots that succeed in the larger markets such as Japan.

Flag carriers

The remaining 50 or more competitors will be flag carriers — or boutiques — for their institutions in Asia. As a group, they will manage up to one-third of private banking assets in Asia, but their individual market share will be small. Competitors in this group will average US$3-10 million annually in profits, although a number might only break even. One of their keys to success will be determining early if they are going to be a flag carrier or if they aspire to be a regional specialist. More banks aim to be regional specialists than space exists. As competition intensifies in the first 5 years of the 21st century, those that have invested in building a specialist business, but are not making it in terms of market and client penetration, stand to suffer some painful losses.

Alternatively, if institutions are content to remain small but profitable, there is clearly business to be done. Optimal returns will be achieved by outsourcing low value-added costs, insourcing superior external products, and ensuring relationship managers' service levels are properly aligned with client potential. A strong manager with a good grasp of operating controls and with entrepreneurial flair will be essential in shepherding seasoned relationship managers, likely as not poached from larger players. A number of local banks could well move into the upper ranks of flag carriers if they can overcome their internal constraints and hold their aspirations to this level.

At the end of World War II, Switzerland had 95 private banks. Today, it is home to fewer than 20. Private banking, in Switzerland and around the world, is well on its way to becoming a competitive global business, where the best-skilled and best-capitalized have the greatest chances of prospering. But private banking is also a business where close personal relationships will remain paramount to success. Despite the intensity of competition in Asia to date, most relationships are not yet fused. Asia's personal wealth miracle will provide substantial profits to the handful of competitors that can cement a significant proportion of these relationships in the years leading up to 2010.

8
RETAIL BANKING:
THE MASSES WILL ENRICH MANY

A visitor to any of Hongkong Bank's 200 branches in Hong Kong is greeted by modern, streamlined décor, glass wall partitions and the bank's trademark color scheme of red, white, and pale gray. There are separate counters for simple and complex transactions. Specialized sales and service desks are available for customers to choose an investment product or take out a loan. A large board advises the public on peak customer traffic hours. ATMs are located both inside the lobby and outside at street level for quick access, and branch telephones link users directly to the customer service department. A deposit or withdrawal at the teller's counter typically takes 2–3 minutes, and the uniformed service representative is courteous and helpful. Most employees in the branch appear to have a customer service function — no back office is visible to the public, and indeed much of the back office is centralized elsewhere, leaving the branch to focus largely on sales and service.

Contrast this with a visit to one of the many state-owned banks from India to Taiwan. The visitor enters a dimly lit lobby, the building is old and damp, and the interior looks like it has not been renovated since the early 1970s. The lobby is bare except for two large tables for filling out forms. People are milling about. Customers cluster in front of the teller counters in not quite orderly queues. Behind the counter, the clerks look bored and surly. Transactions can take up to 10 minutes, especially if you are trying to remit money to another bank. Behind the tellers, other staff are counting money, comparing signatures, manually reconciling balances, and calling other branches on the telephone. The visitor can see large, half-open filing cabinets with customer records, and these are checked frequently, occasionally resulting in files spilling out onto the floor.

The difference between these two types of branches epitomizes the split in Asian retail banking during the 1990s. For the better part of the decade, a handful of financial institutions excelled in understanding customer needs and provided a broad range of services, conveniently and cost-effectively, across their networks. These included Citibank, the Hongkong and Shanghai Banking Corporation (HSBC), Standard Chartered Bank, and a few of the newer domestic banks and finance companies in Japan, Singapore, Malaysia, Taiwan, and Korea. These aggressive retail banks initially posed a mere annoyance to the large government- or family-owned banks that typically had the most branches and controlled a majority of consumer deposits. This dominant latter group tended to view consumers as an inexpensive source of funds to finance their corporate lending activities.

As the 1990s progressed, though, it became clear to some of the larger incumbents that they could no longer afford to be passive with their consumer customer base. A combination of narrowing corporate lending interest rate spreads, growing competition for deposits, and increasing customer sophistication (including a growing willingness to switch institutions) made it clear to most incumbents that a concerted focus on retail banking was not only an opportunity, but an imperative to preserve profits and market position.

The more savvy incumbents came to realize that they were underinvesting in the single largest banking business in Asia. In 1997, before the full brunt of the crisis was felt, Asian retail banking generated about U.S.$150 billion in revenues on the back of US$6.3 trillion in retail deposits and US$4.3 trillion in consumer loans, far surpassing the size of all other banking businesses in the region. As the impact of the crisis unfolded, the importance of retail customers and their deposits became more apparent: a flight to quality drained deposits from the weaker institutions, hastening the failure of some.

Institutions that survive Asia's economic meltdown will no doubt place greater focus on the mass markets that are the backbone of retail banking. It will come as a shock to the 250 or so domestic institutions involved in retail banking as of 1997, however, just how difficult it will be to succeed in the first decade of the 21st century. Senior managers of many domestic banks will find themselves ill-equipped for the fundamental changes that will sweep Asia's retail markets. New customer needs, increasing product complexity, and alternative forms of distribution will be the chief drivers of these changes, and the opening of many of Asia's long-protected consumer banking markets to foreign competitors will accelerate the transformation.

To prepare for and profit from the trends that will shape the first decade of the 21st century, local financial institutions, in particular, will have to revamp their external image, internal operating culture, front-line skills, incentive systems, and processing operations. These far-reaching changes will require substantial investments in people, technology, and marketing. As increased competition raises the hurdle for success, all but the largest institutions will need to develop customer, product, and/or distribution expertise to differentiate themselves in their chosen markets.

At the end of the 1990s, many of Asia's domestic financial institutions lacked the minimum size to make the investments and tackle the challenges that lay ahead. As a result, market consolidation will be a hallmark of retail banking in the first decade of the 21st century. By 2010, retail banking in Asia will probably be dominated by 10–15 global banks or product specialists competing regionally, up to 30 domestic institutions in Japan, and 5–10 domestic competitors in each of the remaining Asian markets. The approximately 100 winners emerging in Asia will dominate projected annual revenues of US$220 billion by 2010. These estimates suggest that retail banking will continue to enrich more competitors than any other banking business in Asia.

The Drivers of Change

A 1998 McKinsey survey, targeted at Asian middle- and upper-income individuals, indicated that 70 percent were satisfied with their current banks, but 60 percent actively shopped around and 41 percent would willingly switch institutions for improved convenience, service, or pricing. This is bad news for intransigent incumbents facing increasing competition in deregulating markets. For innovative providers, incumbent or new, it is the opening required to build a winning retail banking platform. Aggressive domestic and regional retail banks will be able to build upon four drivers of change that will reshape Asian retail banking in the first decade of the 21st century: rapid growth and shifts in core balances; increasing customer sophistication and differentiation; broadening product breadth; and advancement of new distribution channels.

Where the Money Will Be: Rapid Growth and Shifts in Core Retail Balances

Important to identifying future opportunities is understanding the geographic composition of core retail balances in Asia through the first decade of the 21st century. The bulk of retail balances have historically been concentrated in a few markets and, across these markets, concentrated within a minority of total households. The relatively high degree of concentration in the 1990s, however, will gradually dissipate in the years leading up to 2010 as the region develops economically, broadening retail banking opportunities.

In 1997, core retail balances, made up of consumer deposits and loans, totaled US$10.6 trillion. This total was distributed across three distinct subsets of markets (Exhibit 8.1), to which we will refer throughout this chapter. First was Japan, which accounted for only 5 percent of the region's population but 85 percent of core retail balances. Second, the newly industrialized countries (Hong Kong,

Exhibit 8.1

Consumer Deposit and Loan Balances in Asia: 1997
Percent

Asia total

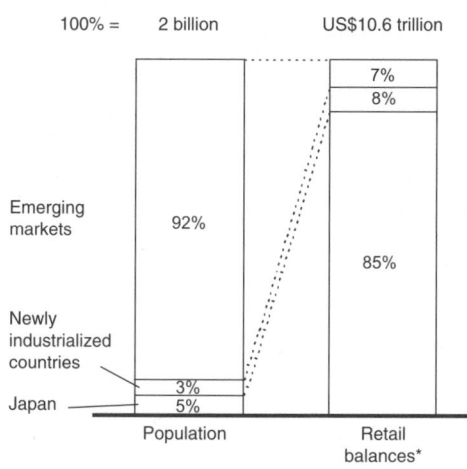

Emerging market breakdown
100% = US$740 billion*

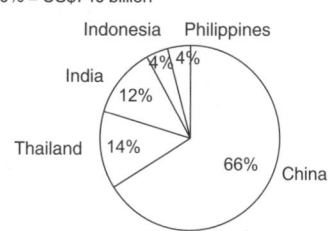

Newly industrialized countries' breakdown
100% = US$850 billion*

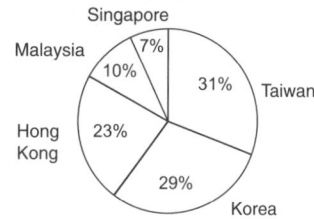

* Total retail deposits and loans.

Source: Central bank reports; International Monetary Fund; McKinsey estimates

Korea, Malaysia, Singapore, and Taiwan) accounted for 3 percent of the population and 8 percent of retail balances. The third subset included the largely populated emerging markets (China, India, Indonesia, the Philippines, and Thailand), which had 92 percent of the population but only 7 percent of retail balances.

Across Asia, retail balances were concentrated in the region's 40 largest cities. By the end of the 1990s, the newly industrialized countries simply housed a majority of their populations in urban and suburban centers. In the emerging economies, it was only the population in and around the cities that had adequate income and savings to warrant a bank account. In economies such as Thailand, China, and India, as much as 60 percent of the population did not have a bank account nor used banking products. In the more remote islands of Indonesia and the Philippines, and in the hinterlands of China and India, several hundred million families stuffed their limited savings away under the proverbial mattress. Excluding the poor account holders with the equivalent of just a few dollars in the bank, a 1998 McKinsey estimate placed the number of middle- and upper-class households that were active users of banks and their products at about 100 million — or about one of every six households in Asia.

The economic growth forecast for Asia in the first decade of the 21st century will substantially broaden the number of "bankable" households and reshape the geographic composition of Asian retail banking revenues. If we look at macroeconomic trends, there is a strong link between the level of economic development — expressed in terms of GDP per capita — and the amount of retail deposits present within an economy. There is similarly a strong correlation between the ratio of retail loans to retail deposits as an economy develops (Exhibit 8.2). These correlations demonstrate that consumer deposits and loans are likely to grow very rapidly as an economy develops from about US$1,000 GDP per capita to US$5,000. Total consumer deposits, for example, are likely to increase from 15–20 percent of GDP at the US$1,000 GDP per capita mark, to about 50–60 percent of GDP as economies approach US$5,000 GDP per capita. What the correlations also demonstrate is from US$5,000 to US$25,000 GDP per capita, total deposits tend to grow in line with the underlying economies and actually begin to decline as a percentage of GDP when economies develop beyond the US$25,000 GDP per capita mark. This is largely because retail depositors in wealthy countries have shifted an increasing share of their deposits into investment products, such as stocks and mutual funds. Consumer lending, by contrast, grows quickly up to the US$5,000 GDP per capita mark, but then continues to grow as a percentage of GDP as countries develop, reflecting a greater use of borrowing to fund major purchases such as houses, cars, and home appliances.

Projecting the likely levels of GDP per capita in Asian countries to 2010 (based on the economic growth projections of Standard & Poor's DRI Group) and crossing these with the correlations identified above, it is possible to estimate Asia's future retail balances. For the region as a whole, core retail deposit and loan balances can be expected to grow from US$10.6 trillion at the end of 1997 to about US$14.9 trillion by 2010. The largest absolute growth will come from the emerging markets, where balances are projected to grow 11 percent annually in the first decade of the 21st century, increasing from US$730 billion to US$3.2

Exhibit 8.2

Relationship Between Retail Banking Balances and Economic Development

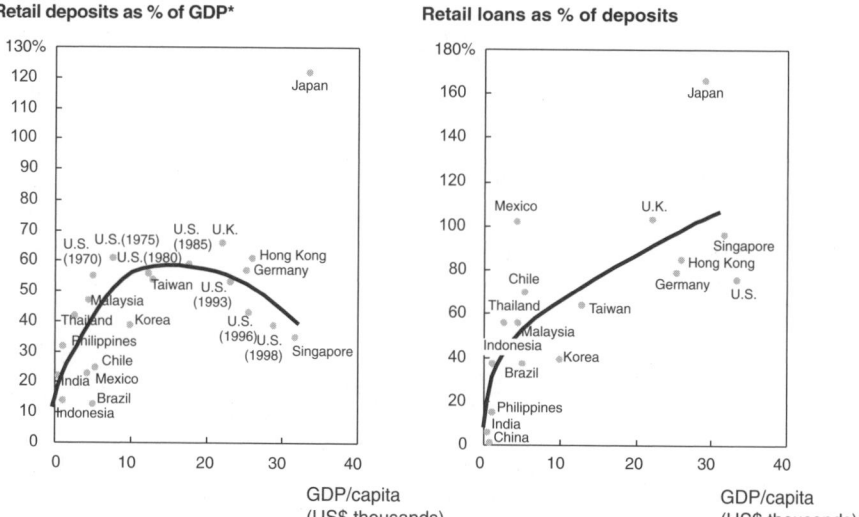

Retail deposits as % of GDP*   Retail loans as % of deposits

GDP/capita   GDP/capita
(US$ thousands)   (US$ thousands)

* 1997 figures unless otherwise indicated.

Source: International Monetary Fund; government statistics; McKinsey analysis

trillion. The newly industrialized countries will follow with growth in balances of 8 percent annually, boosting the total from US$850 billion to US$2.2 trillion.

Japan will present a markedly different picture. Japan's isolated financial markets have created a macroeconomic anomaly. The lack of competition and limited introduction of investment products have led consumers to channel enormous savings into traditional retail banking deposits. By 1997, the ratio of consumer deposits to GDP was around 120 percent, more than double that of most developed countries. Assuming that Japan's "Big Bang," launched in 1996, will adequately liberalize markets so that the allocation of personal savings begins to reflect levels in the rest of the developed world, Japan's net growth in traditional retail banking balances could be small — increasing by less than 1 percent annually and adding less than US$500 billion to the region's core retail balances.

Assuming Asia develops in line with global macroeconomic trends, the geographical mix of core retail banking opportunities should undergo a major shift. Japan's share of the total balances could decline from 85 percent in 1997 to 64 percent by 2010, while that of the newly industrialized countries increases from 8 percent to 15 percent, and that of emerging countries from 7 to 21 percent. This is not to say that Japan will be less attractive, but rather that the breadth of opportunity will spread across the region. In all likelihood, the number of middle- and upper-income banking households could double to 200 million and the number of "un-banked" households could drop to as low as 30 percent, expanding the focus of retail banks beyond Asia's top 40 cities. With traditional retail banking profit margins in some of Asia's markets double that of the developed world in the late 1990s, Asia will provide substantial opportunities for innovative competitors in the early years of the new millennium.

Of course, as the first decade of the 21st century unfolds, traditional retail banking margins across Asia will gradually narrow to global levels. A large driver of the narrowing margins will be increased competition from global retail financial institutions. By 1998, Japan, Hong Kong, Korea, Thailand, Indonesia, the Philippines, and India had all taken steps to ease foreign entry into their retail banking markets. By 2010, with growing WTO pressures, Taiwan, China, and Malaysia will also probably have eased restrictions on foreign entry. Retail banking in the next decade will provide more banks — foreign banks in particular — with greater opportunities to carve out profits than was the case in Asia's fast-growth 1990s.

Customers: New Service Needs, Greater Differentiation

Growth in retail banking will be available only to financial institutions that keep pace with their customers. Across most of Asia, customers' needs are likely to undergo a significant transformation prompted by rising incomes, increasing education and sophistication, new financial realities, and greater choice.

With growing GDP per capita levels comes increasing customer sophistication and demands, spurred by rising educational standards and busier lifestyles. As Asia's emerging markets move progressively toward the US$5,000 GDP per capita level, more people will live in cities, an increasing number will travel abroad, all will have more bills to pay, and many will make large-ticket purchases. Correspondingly, individuals in more demanding jobs will have less time to wait in line, will require more transaction and payment support for travel and bill payments, and will require more loans to fund their new tastes and improving urban lifestyles. One indication of the level of service that customers expect to receive was highlighted in McKinsey's 1998 consumer survey: 66 percent of individuals across Asia indicated a desire for 24-hour service. As of that year, less than 10 percent had access to round-the-clock banking.

In Japan and the newly industrialized countries, two fundamental trends will gradually reshape how the public thinks about their savings. First, in the years leading up to 2010, the number of people over the age of 60 will increase by 50 percent. Second, extended family households, which traditionally cared for the old, show signs of giving way to nuclear families as seen in the West. The combination of these fundamentals will create greater demand for financial self-sufficiency in retirement. If retail banks in the newly industrialized markets wish to keep their middle-aged customers and their assets, they will have to cater to these customers' emerging needs.

The 1997–1998 crisis introduced a new financial reality across Asia, heightening consumers' awareness of their long-term financial needs. The crisis significantly reduced savings in absolute dollar terms and wiped out the economic cushion that many outside Japan had been accustomed to, with rapidly rising stock and property markets throughout the 1990s. The net impact of the crisis was a lot less cash and a realization that rapid economic growth will not consistently support spending and bolster savings. And the significant unemployment created by the crisis underlined the importance of having well-invested savings to cover difficult periods.

For many consumers, the crisis will increase their dependence on financial institutions. With less excess cash in the system, people will have to turn to their banks instead of families to finance major purchases. Recognition of the need to plan effectively for the long term will increase demand for financial advice. Individuals will look to trusted banks to learn how to diversify their holdings and balance risks, in many cases beyond the domestic borders where most of their assets were held in the 1990s. This will be most true in Japan and the newly industrialized countries.

Embedded in consumers' emerging needs are implicit hurdles for financial institutions. Sixty-five percent of consumers across Asia indicated in the 1998 McKinsey survey that they plan to rely primarily on their own savings for retirement, but only 48 percent had any long-term financial plans. Also, a majority could not accurately identify the relative risk/returns of bank deposits, insurance, equities, and mutual funds. In serving the emerging needs of Asia's consumers, banks will have to provide retail clients with the information and education required to make the right choices. In many cases, solutions will have to be sold proactively, as few are likely to walk into branches with a clearly specified list of their needs.

The level of attentive service required to effectively identify and meet customer needs is, of course, a far cry from the model of the dimly lit government bank branch described at the outset of this chapter. But consumers in Asia will not have to wait for the government banks to wake up to their needs. In the first decade of the 21st century, retail customers will enjoy an unprecedented degree of choice. Foreign competitors, entering through greenfield operations or acquisitions, will look to quickly build market share and critical mass by targeting customers' specific needs. This will be a new phenomenon across most of Asia's markets. Even though Thailand and Korea, for example, were at very different levels of economic development in the late 1990s, the crisis uniformly opened their markets to global competitors.

Greater choice will surface latent differences in how customers wish to be served. In the absence of a concerted focus on retail customers by many of the large domestic banks in the 1990s, service tended to be "one size fits all." Yet it is obvious that a customer who has just opened his first bank account is unlikely to have the same needs as a successful retired entrepreneur planning her financial future. The reality is that customers with different backgrounds and incomes, and at different stages of their lives have different financial requirements (see sidebar).

The customer segmentation described in the sidebar is, of course, only one of many ways that competitors can draw on customers' differing needs and preferences to tailor distinct service offerings. The salient point is that as Asia's retail markets grow, and as customers increase in sophistication and take advantage of new choices, financial institutions will not only have to cope with new needs but also differentiate how they serve customers in order to maintain and grow their market share. The days of getting away with uniform service will quickly pass.

Five Distinct Customer Segments Emerging in Asia

McKinsey's 1998 consumer survey targeting middle- and upper-income individuals highlighted the extent to which customer needs vary. A detailed analysis of 3,200 customers' backgrounds, financial status, service preferences, and product usage yielded five distinct customer segments:

Advice seekers (30 percent of all respondents across Asia) are not very well educated as a group and are not demanding in terms of service quality, products, or alternative channels. But, due to their high uncertainty about the future, they desire expert advice or "hand-holding" regarding their investments, and are somewhat willing to switch to foreign institutions to get access to new ideas.

Change seekers (24 percent) tend to be well educated and very open to switching to foreign financial institutions. They demand the convenience of 24-hour ATM and phone banking services, prefer some expert advice on making investments, and are active users of credit.

Personalized service seekers (21 percent) are reasonably well educated, have limited product and service needs, demonstrate a low-risk appetite for investments or use of credit, and in most cases spurn ATMs or phone banking services in favor of prompt face-to-face service.

Status quo seekers (13 percent) are less well educated as a group and tend to be lower-middle income individuals who prefer to be served by their current domestic banks for a limited range of noncredit products. They definitely want to deal face-to-face with their banker and not rely on ATMs or phones, and do not wish to receive advice on investing their savings.

Wealthy independents (12 percent) are well educated as a group, use a broad range of financial products including credit, are active users of ATMs and phone banking, and are very sensitive to service quality. But they are not receptive to receiving financial advice and are unlikely to switch to a foreign financial institution given the opportunity.

Winning banks will need to select which segment(s) they wish to target, and focus their products and distribution approaches accordingly.

Products: New Breadth, New Economics

Economic development, changing customer needs, and deregulation in the financial sector will place significant demands on Asia's retail banks to broaden their product offering. The increasing complexity and cost that comes with product expansion will force most banks in Asia to make a fundamental choice about which customers, or which share of customers' business, they will target. Will a bank try to satisfy all the banking needs of their chosen customers, or act as a specialist that is best positioned, for example, to provide home mortgage loans? How banks structure their product portfolio will affect their economics, market distinctiveness, and ability to extract consistent profits in the first decade of the 21st century.

Continued deregulation across Asia's financial markets will broaden banks' product options. Until the late 1990s, most financial institutions operating in Asia were limited in the retail products they could offer. Regulators were wary that encouraging consumer lending or investment products would reduce deposits available for corporate lending. This was most true in the emerging markets such as China, where funds were needed to support loans to cash-strapped state-owned enterprises. But it was also true in countries as developed as Singapore, where the government viewed banks as an important mechanism in directing consumer funds to strategic growth sectors. In Singapore's case, the government also sought to curtail, for example, credit card borrowing limits — to an equivalent of 2 months' salary — to keep inflation and personal debt in check. In Japan, the government ensured a steady flow of low-cost funds to banks and corporations ailing under recession, by controlling product pricing and enabling only securities firms that possessed comparatively limited distribution to market investment products to consumers.

By 1998, many of these regulatory limits were beginning to disappear. That year, China approved the formation of new asset management companies to market retail mutual funds and began to encourage banks to offer home mortgage loans. Japan enabled banks to begin marketing mutual funds to their customers. Also in 1998, Taiwan regulators approved several alliances between foreign insurance companies and local banks to set up joint ventures that would one day market insurance products through branches. It also allowed banks to take stakes in retail brokerage operations. Across Southeast Asia, in an effort to consolidate their fragmented markets, regulators encouraged integration of stock brokerage firms and finance companies into larger banks. In the first decade of the new millennium, most countries in Asia will tear down the barriers that delineated specific product boundaries for banks, securities firms, asset management companies, and insurers.

The result of these regulatory changes will be the creation of retail banking markets that increasingly reflect models found in the U.S. and Europe, where banks sell just about every financial product. But as banks across Asia consider broadening their product portfolios, it is worth keeping in mind how banks in the U.S., for example, have traditionally made money. A 1997 McKinsey study revealed that while 54 percent of total retail balances were held in nontraditional investment products, 85 percent of retail banking profits were derived from core retail deposits and loans (Exhibit 8.3). The likely lesson for Asia, where traditional consumer deposits and loans accounted for an average 71 percent of retail balances in 1997, is that while offering new investment products to retain customers and generate fee income will be important, the lion's share of profits probably will continue to flow from traditional core banking products.

Building the required capabilities for core products will be a significant challenge for many Asia's banks, particularly in the emerging markets. If the macroeconomic projections described earlier in this chapter prove to be accurate, consumer lending in the emerging markets will grow 22 percent annually from US$60 billion in 1997 to US$770 billion by 2010, representing almost a third of all new consumer lending in the region. This growth will be composed mostly of new home mortgage loans, car loans, and a small amount of personal loans. Making consumer loans in emerging markets, however, is easier said than done. In China, for instance, laws were just taking shape in the late 1990s to give banks the power to enter into lending contracts with individuals and repossess collateral in the event of a borrower defaults. In India, where documentation such as home ownership papers or employment contracts can easily be forged with little threat of legal reprisal, Citibank had to devise on-site inspections of credit card applicants' claimed assets in order to comfortably grant credit lines. Unlike the U.S., where agencies such as TRW provide a wealth of information on individuals' past payment histories to help banks assess credit risk, most of Asia lacks easily accessible data to support lending decisions. To complicate matters, many banks in the emerging markets and in some of the newly industrialized countries were accustomed to making only large corporate loans and so lacked the processes, skills, and automated systems to handle large volume consumer loans.

For many of Asia's banks, there will be equally large challenges in providing traditional deposit and transaction services profitably. Customers' desire for convenient, fast, efficient service will place heavy demands on banks to upgrade their transaction products and processes. Through much of the 1990s, domestic banks captured consumer deposits and transactions by virtue of having a branch located around the corner. But changing customer behavior is likely to erode the traditional advantage of branch-based convenience. Transactions processed through credit cards grew 500 percent in Taiwan, 300 percent in Hong Kong, and 66 percent in Singapore between 1992 and 1997. By 1998, debit cards — which deduct purchases directly from individuals accounts — were becoming commonly used in Taiwan, Hong Kong, and even in parts of China as stores acquired the infrastructure to process noncash transactions. Across Asia, as more people come to work in large corporations, they will no longer receive a monthly paycheck but rather a direct credit to their account through electronic payrolls. By the late 1990s, this was already a common practice in Japan and in the newly industrialized countries, and gradually gaining momentum in the urban centers of emerging markets.

In the more developed markets such as Hong Kong in the early 1990s, the number of people visiting branches at the end of each month swelled by more than 30 percent as individuals came to cash their paychecks and pay their utility bills. By the end of the 1990s, the month-end jump in branch visits eased off as a growing number of people relied on electronic payrolls and programmed direct

Exhibit 8.3

Comparison of Personal Financial Asset Balances and Profitability
US$ billions, percent

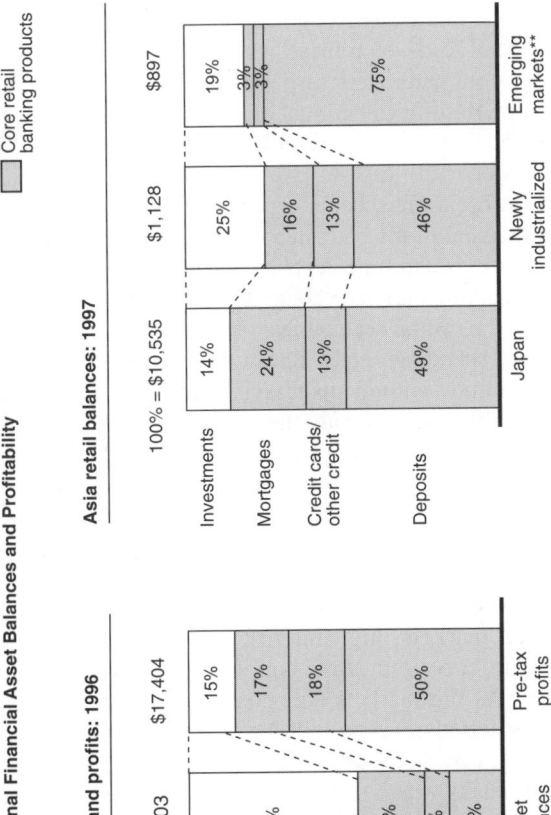

Core retail banking products

U.S. retail balances and profits: 1996

100% = $103 $17,404

	Asset balances	Pre-tax profits
Investments	54%	15%
Mortgages	21%	17%
Credit cards/other credit	8%	18%
Deposits	17%	50%

Asia retail balances: 1997

100% = $10,535 $1,128 $897

	Japan	Newly industrialized countries*	Emerging markets**
Investments	14%	25%	19%
Mortgages	24%	16%	3%
Credit cards/other credit	13%	13%	3%
Deposits	49%	46%	75%

* Hong Kong, Singapore, Taiwan, Korea, and Malaysia.
** China, India, Indonesia, Thailand, and the Philippines.

Source: Federal Reserve Flow of Funds; central bank reports; International Monetary Fund; McKinsey analysis

debit capabilities to automatically pay their monthly bills. The gradual shift in Hong Kong is likely to be played out in other markets across Asia as busier lifestyles and technology come to influence the banking systems. For many banks, this shift will pose a serious challenge. The key to success will be developing processes and systems to handle the growth in electronic transactions. For many of the government and family-owned banks throughout the emerging and newly industrialized countries, this will be hard to achieve. As of the late 1990s, few outside Japan, Singapore, and Hong Kong had the necessary systems in place.

Banks in Asia that fail to develop these systems will see their profits decline. Not only will they miss out on the fees associated with these transaction products, but they will fail to capture sufficient current or checking account deposits. Current account deposits are those that pay no or little interest, and are typically used by customers as a source of ready cash to pay bills and meet their daily spending needs. In Taiwan in 1997, current account deposits made up only 6 percent of total deposits but over 40 percent of the bank deposit income. This was due to the fact that interest-bearing savings and time deposit accounts in Asia yield very narrow margins. For banks to capture current account deposits, they typically have to be a customer's main bank: the central account that receives the paycheck and is tapped for bill payments daily spending needs. Banks that fail to achieve "main bank" status will have to rely almost entirely upon savings and time deposits to fund their lending operations, significantly reducing their profit margins.

Up till the late 1990s, few financial institutions in Asia had achieved main bank status. The average consumer in Asia used three institutions, higher than in the U.S., where the average was 2.3 in 1997 (Exhibit 8.4). The number of products that financial institutions provided to each customer was correspondingly lower, averaging about 1.3 products per customer compared with about 2.5 for high-performing banks in the U.S. and Europe.

In Asia's protected markets, high interest rate spreads enabled domestic financial institutions to carve out attractive profits despite their lack of deep customer penetration. As the markets deregulate and product margins narrow, however, financial institutions in Asia will have to make a fundamental choice. Should they try to meet growing product demands by broadening their offering, or focus on a few key products where they can build distinctive advantages through superior tailoring, risk assessment, or management of costs? Competitors that broaden their product line will have to cross-sell relentlessly — to maximize customer revenues and optimize marketing costs — in order to recover new product investments. Alternatively, financial institutions that specialize in a few products will have to carefully tailor their offering to distinct customer segments in order to build sufficient volume and critical mass. Either approach marks a significant departure from the undifferentiated product set offered in the 1990s by Asia's domestic banks, from India to Japan.

Distribution: Tuning in to New Channels

Changes in retail banking channels will present one of the largest opportunities to new entrants and one of the largest challenges to incumbents. In the years leading

Exhibit 8.4

Number of Financial Institutions Used by Each Customer: 1998

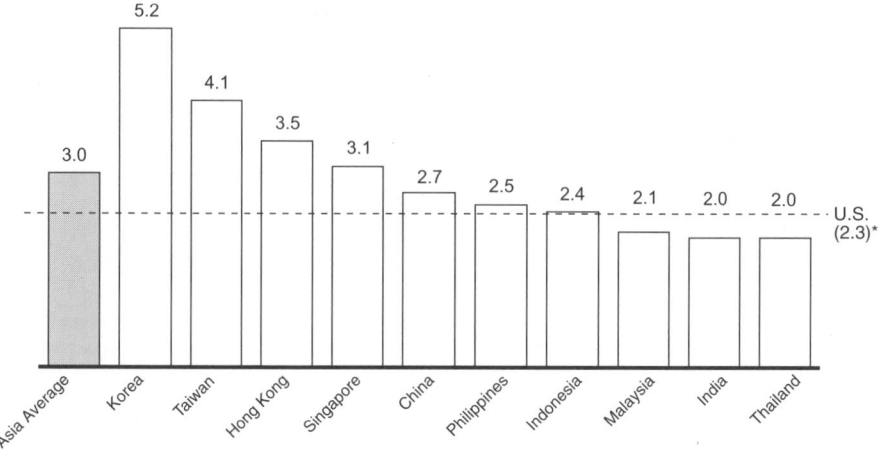

* U.S. figure for 1997.

Source: McKinsey Asia-Pacific Personal Financial Services Survey

up to 2010, the emergence of new channels in Asia will reshape three areas: how competitors build distinctiveness, the cost structure of the retail banking industry, and the role that traditional branches play. Taken together, change in these three areas will strike at the core of banks' ability to maintain and grow market share profitably.

From the 1980s through the 1990s, retail banking strategy in Asia consisted largely of network building. It was almost a business in itself. In Indonesia, in the decade leading up to 1996, 1,560 branches and 2,740 ATMs were brought on-line; in Taiwan 1,200 branches and 7,460 ATMs; and in India 4,470 branches. By 1997, Japan and the newly industrialized countries had achieved comparable — and in some cases exceeded — branch and ATM densities found in the U.S. and Europe (Exhibit 8.5). A stroll down a Taipei major city block in 1998 looked something like this: bank branch, bakery, ATM, 7-Eleven store, bank branch, Tiffany outlet, ATM, real estate agent, coffee house, bank branch. A stroll in Jakarta, Bangkok, or Hong Kong would have revealed similar banking densities. Across Asia, in the absence of significant product or service differentiation, branching was a key component of success. It was the net that banks cast wide to build a brand name and capture deposits.

From the early 1990s, leading regional banks and the newer domestic banks advanced the use of new alternative channels. Phone banking quickly became a mainstay among the more innovative banks. HSBC and Standard Chartered created specialist branches to provide a higher level of service to their most valued retail customers. In 1995, Singapore's United Overseas Bank (UOB) set up specialist "invest shops," a channel focused on marketing new investment products. Newer

Exhibit 8.5

Branches and ATM Densities: 1997

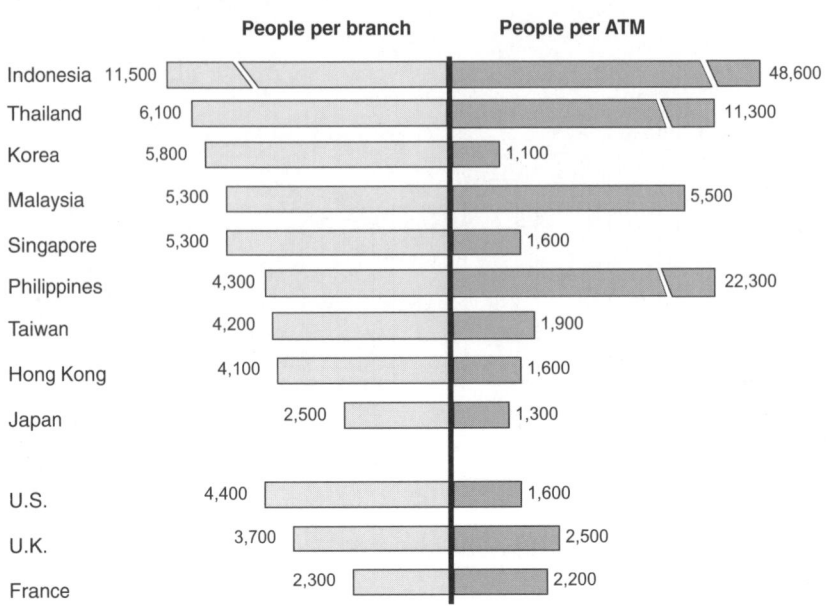

Source: Government statistics; central bank reports

banks in Taiwan, formed in 1991 and facing a limit of five new branches a year, used commission-based sales personnel to develop credit card business outside the branches. Aggressive players, such as Taishin Bank, had more than 400 of these sales agents generating new business by mid-1998. The handful of newer domestic banks across Asia had established PC-based banking and were at the early stages of introducing Internet banking by 1998, although regulations largely limited their offerings to basic account information and prohibited on-line transactions. In a move mirroring the initiatives of leading retail banks in the U.S. (such as Wells Fargo and Citibank), Bank of Asia in Thailand (75-percent-owned by ABN Amro) placed ATMs in McDonald's outlets and Shell gas stations starting in 1998.

By the late 1990s, leading domestic banks had made strides leveraging alternative channels to improve and specialize their services. But none had yet jumped fully into new distribution channels to build a distinctive image and obtain substantial cost advantages. There is no Asian equivalent to the U.K.'s First Direct, a bank established in 1989 with no branches. First Direct succeeded by targeting young professionals with busy lifestyles that valued the convenience of services that were entirely phone-, mail-, ATM-, and PC-based. Innovative marketing campaigns helped First Direct position itself as a modern and fresh-thinking service provider. Part of the money it saved on forgoing branches went into advertising, hiring skilled personnel, and developing systems to provide customers with highly tailored and personalized service.

As of 1998, Asia's more developed retail markets were ripe for innovative banks to increase new channel offerings. Consumer use of ATMs and phone banking in some cases approached or exceeded the levels experienced in the U.S. and Europe. In Hong Kong and Singapore, the 1998 McKinsey survey indicated that 45 percent of middle- and upper-income individuals had used phone banking, compared with 39 percent in the U.S. In China's urban areas, 38 percent of individuals were frequent users of ATM services. Across Asia, survey respondents also indicated a high willingness to try new channels in future. Forty-eight percent of all respondents indicated interest in trying Internet banking when it became available, a figure that jumped to over 60 percent for those aged between 22 and 29. To be sure, banking through new channels will have to be targeted at distinct customer segments in Asia. There appears, however, to be more than enough willing customers to build a viable business. Schwab Securities' rapid growth and the on-line competition that followed its entry into the Hong Kong market in 1997 is an indication of consumers' willingness to adopt new channels.

Schwab Securities: Pioneering New Channels in Hong Kong

In April 1997, U.S. discount broker Charles Schwab established itself as a pioneer in Asian retail financial services with the opening of its Hong Kong office. Schwab's angle in Hong Kong was to offer phone and Internet trading access to U.S. stocks and 140 Hong Kong Securities and Futures Commission-approved mutual funds. By virtue of its product offerings, Schwab was targeting the most sophisticated segment of customers in Hong Kong: the 5 percent or less who were purchasers of mutual funds and the minority who invested directly in U.S. equities. Nonetheless, volume took off faster than expected. Though Schwab would not reveal revenues or assets under management, it did announce that in the first 6 months, new assets grew "10 times faster than expected," making Hong Kong the fastest growing new office it had ever opened, globally. In addition, Schwab estimated that 50 percent of its Hong Kong accounts were on-line, compared with only 20 percent of its U.S. accounts. In June 1998, the company reported that 81 percent of its Hong Kong-based trades were executed through the Internet.

Schwab entered Hong Kong just as acceptance of the Internet was taking off. At the end of 1997, Hong Kong had an estimated 400,000 Internet subscribers and growth was 30 percent a year. A year after Schwab's launch, a local competitor called Boom Securities followed in the marketplace, offering Hong Kong-listed stocks, with execution through third-party brokers. Fortitude Services, originally a hedge fund, followed Boom in 1998, and the on-line brokerage unit of Wall Street's Donaldson Lufkin & Jenrette announced its imminent Hong Kong entry.

For new foreign and nimble domestic competitors looking to quickly build distinctiveness and market share, leveraging consumer readiness for new channels will clearly be a tactical option. Many of the dominant government and family-owned banks will face difficulty responding to new channel offerings. Most lack the processes and systems to convert to an on-line environment, and many are psychologically wed to large branch networks that they typically own rather than lease. The incumbents will provide innovative first movers in new channels with an attractive pricing umbrella. Stuck with the costs of a large network, incumbents will be unable to lower product pricing sufficiently to compete with the convenience offered by new channels. And should they choose to compete on price, the owners of new channels could have a lot more room in which to play.

Innovative providers looking to build substantial retail businesses in Asia will likely develop a multi-channel approach comprising generalist branches, product or customer specialty branches, mini-branches located in retail stores, agency salesforces, phone banking, and Internet services. The level of customer financial sophistication in Asia will require a balance between face-to-face and remote channels. The challenge will be to increase total revenues while managing the costs of multiple channels.

The wave of market deregulation and subsequent acquisition opportunities brought on by the 1997–1998 crisis will provide foreign players, in particular, with the opportunity to establish new market footholds. By acquiring a bank with a small or medium-sized branch network, foreign banks will be able to leverage their skills to roll out new channels gradually. At first, new entrants are likely to target their new channels at existing customers. They will identify those most open to change and introduce them to new phone- or computer-based services, with an eye to moving traditional transaction-based services away from the branches. This will allow them to lower their operating costs and refocus branch resources on sales rather than on processing. The refocused branches will be better positioned to develop product expertise, cross-sell products, and increase revenues per customer. As new foreign entrants succeed in reshaping their channels, they will be in a position to either steal share from others through superior service or acquire new customers through subsequent acquisitions. A strong channel mix will enable buyers to recover acquisition premiums by extracting more revenues per customer, at a lower cost.

Similarly, the acceptance of new channels will facilitate the entry of nonbank financial institutions into Asia's markets. Coupled with product deregulation, insurance companies or consumer finance specialists, such as GE Capital which did not possess extensive branch networks in the late 1990s, will be able to leverage new channels to cost-effectively and rapidly roll out new financial products to a broad range of consumers. As consumers become accustomed to doing their banking outside a branch, there will also be opportunities for retailers — regulations permitting — to provide financial services to customers. In the U.K. in the late 1990s, retailers such as Tesco made substantial inroads into banking by integrating banking services into their stores, fitting conveniently into customers' day-to-day shopping. As new channels become broadly accepted, threats to traditional branch-based banks are considerable.

The introduction and benefits of new channels will not, however, be realized overnight. In emerging markets where basic infrastructure (notably phone lines) is less developed and customer sophistication low, the roll-out of new channels will be slower but crucial to serve low-income, "unbanked" households cost effectively. The banks that own the large dimly lit branches described at the opening of this chapter will either gradually adopt new channels and reposition their branches as sales centers or face a slow demise in the years leading up to 2010. In the U.S., between 1985 and 1993 when new channels were starting to gain wide acceptance, volume through new channels grew from 29 percent of all bank transactions to 57 percent, impacting how banks distinguished themselves, the cost structure of the market, and the role of branches. Assuming a similar trend plays out in Asia in the first decade of the 21st century, first movers leveraging Asian consumer readiness for new channels will capture significant cost advantages and be better positioned to meet customers' emerging needs. Staying tuned to new channels will be critical in differentiating service, building distinctive product expertise, and capturing "main bank" status.

Competitors' Challenges and Choices

The growing geographical breadth of retail business, increasing sophistication and differentiation among consumers, easing product restrictions, and emergence of new channels will provide competitors with more strategic options than they ever had before. At the same time, however, the crisis hastened the opening of new markets and the end of entitlement — the end of protectionist policies that kept foreign competitors at bay, product competition limited, and margins attractive. The net effect of new freedoms and new challenges is a more complex, unforgiving, and fluid market, where winners and losers will be determined by their ability to build skills and organizations that can deliver superior customer service at the right cost. With 41 percent of middle- and upper-income customers across Asia indicating a willingness to switch providers, and large skills gaps handicapping the incumbents, traditional market structures in a number of Asian countries will be turned on their heads in the first decade of the 21st century.

Five Core Skills for Retail Success

By the late 1990s, a number of the government- and family-owned banks that dominated retail banking underwent a makeover. The hallmark brown marble and the multiple clocks telling the time in major world capitals were ripped out of branches and replaced by brightly lit interiors filled with chrome, glass, and digital boards tracking exchange rates across the world. State-of-the-art ATMs offering 24-hour access were installed. At first glance, a visitor to one of these revamped branches would not necessarily appreciate how it differed with HSBC's branch described at the outset of this chapter.

What the banks had done, however, was to change only the hardware. The "software" — the people and their skills — remained largely intact. Unfortunately, such cosmetic makeovers will not be enough to compete effectively in Asia's deregulated markets. Success will require a strategy that delivers distinctive value to customers in terms of convenience, flexibility, pricing, and/or quality of advice. More often than not, retail banks will have to target their strategies to specific customer segments or areas of product expertise to differentiate themselves from other players. And they must support their strategies with five core skills: marketing, sales, risk management, processing, and distribution. The world's leading retail banks excel in at least two or three of these skills, which enable them to provide superior service and generate consistent attractive returns.

Marketing: Eye on the customer

Marketing in domestic Asian banks has typically been a small head office staff function whose principal responsibility was to keep a close eye on products and services that competitors developed. The world's best-performing retail banks, in contrast, see marketing's core job as keeping a very close eye on customers and anticipating their needs. Best-practice marketing organizations relentlessly review customer behavior, by analyzing enormous databases of information on customers' background and transaction history to glean clues on likely product and service needs. For example, an effective marketing database will pinpoint a customer who has moved a large amount of money in or out of her account. If this customer is in his or her early 30s, there is a good chance he or she may be preparing to purchase a home. In this case, the bank would then contact the customer to market its mortgage loan and home insurance products.

Excellent marketing departments also combine customer information with external surveys to help segment the customer base, to identify possible promotions to attract new customers, and to test customer satisfaction. On an ongoing basis, marketing organizations profile customer profitability and take actions to lock in profitable customers or cross-sell to loss-making accounts. Far beyond keeping an eye on competitors, good marketing departments support their banks in shaping and executing strategies that are distinctive to customers. For many domestic banks in Asia that lack the necessary systems support and analytical skills, building effective marketing operations will be a substantial but critical challenge to surmount.

Sales: Breaking away from transaction processing

The world's leading retail banks devote significant management effort to sales. They take care in identifying people who have a real willingness to sell, and introduce the right culture and performance incentives to drive the salesforce and business growth. To get the right people, culture, and incentives in place, leading retail banks often create separate sales organizations. Salespeople may sit in a branch or in a phone banking center but not necessarily report to the branch or phone banking manager. Many U.S. banks, for example, have found that to build sufficient product and customer segment expertise, salespeople must be separately recruited, trained, and coached to ensure their effectiveness.

The need for separate customer- or product-oriented sales organizations stems from the fact that traditional branch managers in the U.S. often lacked consumer sales experience. This was true in Asia up till the late 1990s. As branches in Asia focused largely on processing customer transactions, few had time to sell. If selling was done, it was usually by the branch manager, who concentrated on the largest customers, typically corporates. Hence, few branch managers in Asia had the expertise in the late 1990s to lead a salesforce specializing in, for example, consumer mortgage loans, auto loans, mutual funds, or insurance. Asian banks looking to distinguish themselves through aggressive selling tactics will likely have to draw from the U.S. experience and create separate sales organizations. This will be particularly important for products, such as mutual funds or insurance, which require extensive customer education.

Risk management: Centralizing the science

Risk management for the world's leading retail banks is somewhat of a science. To handle the large volume of lending applications quickly and cost effectively, many automate the approval process. By drawing on the bank's past lending history, they look at borrowers for common characteristics that are likely to predict their ability to repay. Banks have found, for example, that middle-income men and women, married with children, and steadily employed for more than 5 years, are a good risk. Therefore, when customers apply for a loan, they are asked to provide background information that can be matched against the bank's previous lending experience. If the applicant fits a profile that has historically repaid, the loan is granted; if not, the loan request is often denied.

By using a statistical approach, leading retail banks avoid losses incurred due to poor judgment by individual loan officers in remote branches. By developing large pools of credit history, banks are also able to use the information to price consumer loans. Hence, they may lend to a riskier customer if they can charge more for the loan. And they can use the information to target sales efforts at existing deposit customers, for example, that match their profiles for attractive risks. This highly centralized and automated approach enabled Citibank to reduce its U.S. consumer loan losses by more than 50 percent when it was introduced in the late 1970s. Commonly referred to as credit scoring, this approach can be applied to credit cards and the full range of consumer loans, and thus can be critical to retail banking profitability.

For domestic banks in the emerging markets, it will be particularly difficult to develop robust credit-scoring models given the lack of established lending history. But this is all the more reason to begin gathering such information so they can profitably meet demand as it picks up in the years ahead. For banks in Japan and the newly industrialized nations, the challenge will be to develop credit-scoring systems that can be used by front-line salespeople to give customers quick decisions, thereby gaining a competitive service advantage.

Processing: Linchpin to long-term effectiveness

Processing excellence is easy to describe, but for many banks, hard to achieve. The world's leading banks have significantly reduced their operating costs by automating and centralizing much of the paperwork that goes on in retail banking.

Many have removed virtually all back-office processing from branches in order to reduce real estate costs, standardize controls, and gain critical mass in high-volume procedures such as check clearing and remittance handling. To do so, however, they have had to make significant investments in process redesign and information technology, or outsource their processing to third parties.

Up till the late 1990s, many domestic banks across Asia argued against developing processing excellence. Their argument was essentially that human labor is cheap and technology expensive. Indeed, outside Japan, Korea, and Taiwan, many banks in Asia before the crisis were able to operate with highly manual processes and still maintain cost-to-income ratios of less than 45 percent, far below those of U.S. and European leaders. But in the years leading up to 2010, processing excellence will be integral to delivering quality sales and service. Without highly automated transaction systems, banks will be unable to provide fast on-line delivery or capture "main bank" status. And as long as branches retain processing, they are unlikely to make the shift to differentiated sales and service centers. To oversee the difficult and detailed transformation of processing, Asian domestic banks will do well to ensure that their information technology manager is a member of senior management. Often technology managers are excluded, resulting in a failure to align processes with the overall customer and product strategies.

Distribution: Knocking down costs

As discussed in Chapter 5, distribution will undergo rapid change in Asia. The world's leading banks concentrate on preserving a first-mover advantage in new channels. They do so both to lock out the competition and to attract customers through new innovations. As an example, Wells Fargo Bank in the U.S. was quick to realize the potential customer convenience and operational cost savings of in-store branches. It formed exclusive relationships with California's leading supermarkets, locking up more than 60 percent of the state's supermarket outlets by 1996.

As channels proliferate, leading banks carefully track transaction costs per channel to encourage customers to use the most cost-efficient options. In some banks, channel managers are appointed to ensure that new offerings link together in a coherent fashion. This often requires extensive efforts to enable sharing of information across a multitude of supporting systems. Many domestic banks in Asia in the 1990s failed to realize the full potential from new channels. They spent money on ATM and phone banking hardware but failed to launch campaigns in branches to redirect customer service and transaction flows, thus increasing investments without capturing new savings. Proactive management in and across channels should clearly be a priority for senior management in the first decade of the 21st century.

Many CEOs of domestic banks were not well-equipped in the late 1990s to handle the challenges of building new core skills in retail. It is easier for most of Asia's domestic senior bankers to discuss whether or not to grant a substantial loan to a leading corporation than it is to define a new consumer credit process or to redesign the branch network. After all, their expertise and focus for the past several decades was on the former, not the latter. However, with the balance of power shifting to the consumer in the first decade of the 21st century, senior managers will have no choice but to invest significant time in beefing up their retail expertise.

Strategic Choices for Asia's Five Competitor Types

The basis and focus for successfully building new skills in the more challenging retail environment will differ among competitor types. At the end of 1998, there were five principal groups of retail banking competitors in Asia. First were the large government-owned incumbents, which were present in every market except Japan and Hong Kong. In China, India, and Indonesia, the state banks controlled between 50 and 95 percent of the deposits. The government incumbents shared market leadership with the established private (often family-owned) banks that made up the second group. These two groups face the challenge of revamping their core skills to defend market share in the urban centers and to improve network efficiency through emerging channels.

A subset of the privately owned domestic banks — newer and more innovative but smaller (found mostly in Taiwan, Korea, China, the Philippines, and Indonesia) — make up a third group. Their challenges will be similar to those of the fourth group comprising foreign players. The newer domestic banks and foreign players, each of which usually had less than 3–5 percent market share in 1998, will have to quickly build critical mass through alternative channels and/or through acquisitions. The fifth group, which traditionally had a limited market share in Asia, was made up of domestic and foreign product specialists, typically consumer finance and asset management companies. Their strategic challenge will be to sustain distinctiveness and broaden distribution within targeted customer segments as products proliferate and the battle for market share intensifies.

Until 1997, the five competitor groups nudged each other for market share, but market pecking order was largely preserved. That will, of course, change in the first decade of the 21st century. To provide a sense of how far along these groups were in preparing for a more challenging future, here is a snapshot of five representative financial institutions as of 1998.

Government-owned bank:
State Bank of India — A giant awakes

In India's historically restricted market, the State Bank of India (SBI) stood apart from the other 26 public and 34 private banks in 1998 by virtue of its size. With US$40 billion in assets, US$30 billion in deposits, and more than an estimated 20 million accounts, SBI accounted for about a quarter of India's entire banking system. SBI's relative dominance extended to corporate lending, consumer deposits, and to a much lesser extent, consumer lending.

SBI's business mix was a direct reflection of government economic policy. Like all Indian banks, SBI was obliged to direct 40 percent of its lending toward priority sectors, including agriculture and small businesses. Where it was entirely free to lend, SBI directed 50 percent of total loans to India's top corporates and less than 10 percent to consumers. Many of its consumer loans were, in fact, loans granted to the bank's employees. Through much of the 1990s, SBI did little to build a consumer lending business, adhering to an implicit government policy that sought to encourage individual savings, not borrowings.

By contrast, SBI had unparalleled strength in gathering consumer deposits. Its massive network of nearly 9,000 branches extended into virtually every town and village in the country, making the bank a trusted household name. Despite its remarkable franchise, or perhaps because of it, SBI essentially took its depositors for granted for the better part of the 1990s. It offered an extremely limited range of products: a plain-vanilla savings account with checking facilities and a fixed deposit account.

By the late 1990s, however, growing foreign competition forced SBI to abandon its passive stance in retail banking. India had long allowed foreign banks to enter the Indian market but had limited them to a few branches. In 1996, however, the government decided to liberalize the expansion of ATMs. Banks such as Citibank and HSBC were fast to develop networks and were rewarded with rapid business growth. SBI realized that its coveted market share was at risk.

By 1998, SBI had launched definitive steps to strengthen its retail banking operations. It announced plans to create close to 100 specialized personal banking centers throughout the country that could no longer make the mistake of favoring corporates over consumers. It increased its number of ATMs between 1996 and 1998, from zero to 50. To improve overall service and efficiency, SBI began computerizing more than 1,500 targeted branches, which will cover more than 80 percent of its business when completed. It also entered into a joint venture with GE Capital to launch a Visa credit card to its customers.

As the 21st century approaches, SBI is drafting aggressive plans to take further advantage of its extensive distribution network. Among these are plans to become a significant player in India's deregulating insurance market, to develop a comprehensive range of consumer auto, appliance, and home mortgage financing, and to lock up a dominant share of India's transaction and payments markets.

SBI's new retail initiatives demonstrate the bank's ability to break away from decades of bureaucracy and indifference. But before it remain substantial challenges, not least of which will be training its hundreds of thousands of employees for the new tasks, products, and services that lie ahead. SBI, like many of the government-owned banks in Asia, is destined to lose market share in the years leading up to 2010. If it continues to act quickly, however, it should be well positioned to remain a mass-market leader for low- and middle-income consumers' daily banking needs.

Family-owned bank:
Oversea Chinese Banking Corporation —
Instilling cultural change

The rounded rectangular OCBC tower at the edge of the Raffles Place financial district is a familiar landmark to the Singapore business community, and among the first skyscrapers built to house the city-state's big banking institutions. As of 1997, OCBC was Singapore's second largest bank (measured by assets) and one of the Big Four commercial banks that together accounted for about 75 percent of the retail and corporate market. A 65-year-old institution, OCBC had a reputation for conservative practices reinforced under the watchful eye of the Lee family owners. It was a good example of a leading bank in a protected local market, seeking to upgrade its position and skills in anticipation of eventual marketing opening under WTO pressure.

By the late 1990s, OCBC had built a number of advantages that gave the bank a strong starting position for future challenges. Its established branch and ATM network reached well into the island's prosperous middle class. Over the course of the decade, OCBC invested in hardware to support phone banking, Internet banking, and some degree of centralization for branch processes. Through its network, OCBC offered a full range of the traditional bank products, as well as mutual funds, credit cards, and access to retail stockbroking. In an effort to cement relationships with its most attractive customers, OCBC also provided priority and private banking services through distinct channels. In addition, the bank had stakes in companies that could expand its product reach in the future, including an auto leasing company and Singapore's leading insurance provider.

But like many private and family-owned banks in Asia, OCBC faced the challenge of converting its strong starting position into a winning formula for the increasingly competitive markets of the 21st century. Like its counterparts, OCBC had the hardware and products but was still in the process of tying these together to provide truly integrated service and proactive cross-selling. Its challenge is essentially one of cultural change: how to broaden the skills and marketing mindset of traditional branch personnel to sell rather than to just provide transaction services to customers. In the mid-1990s, OCBC launched a major change effort to tackle the organization, skill, management information systems, and compensation issues that are part and parcel of creating a sales environment in branches. OCBC's objective was both offensive and defensive: offensive to increase revenues, defensive to lock in customers with more products prior to market liberalization.

Private bank: Sanwa Bank — Differentiating for the first time

In 1998, Sanwa Bank was one of Japan's five largest banks, holding 2 percent of the consumer deposit market and 6 percent of consumer lending. The bank was part of a privileged group of Japanese city banks, which together set the standard for consumer banking and dominated corporate lending in Tokyo, Osaka, and other large cities. Sanwa had a long and distinguished history since its establishment in Osaka in 1933, and a reputation for catering to small businesses and consumers. Yet behind the bank's public face and well-recognized green and white cloverleaf logo, there was little to differentiate Sanwa from its retail banking competitors. Until Japan's 1996 "Big Bang" deregulation, Sanwa operated in a constrained environment in which products, pricing, and distribution had to meet strict Ministry of Finance guidelines. Consequently, the few ways to optimize performance were through managing volume and cost.

Sanwa, like other Japanese banks, therefore, built advanced retail distribution and payment systems that provided high efficiency but little flexibility. In 1998, Japan had more than twice as many ATMs per capita as the U.S. Its payment systems operated with the lowest error rates in the world. But these systems, and the technology that supported them, were not designed to allow banks to learn much about their customers. Customer information was typically owned by the branches and not accessible by central units, thereby inhibiting bank-wide initiatives that might target offerings to distinct segments. Consequently, up till the late 1990s, most branches operated quite independently, focusing their attention on consumers or corporations as they saw fit. Service to consumers was efficient, but a "one size fits all" approach.

In 1998, as the Big Bang began to take effect, opening the doors to innovation and differentiation for the first time, Sanwa restructured its entire organization into separate business units for retail, corporate, and capital markets. Sanwa also launched major improvements to its retail network, including enhancing phone banking and introducing on-line banking services through the Internet. To get a better grasp of its deep retail customer base, Sanwa initiated the redesign of internal information systems. And, in an effort to be distinctive, Sanwa became the first bank to launch an electronic shopping mall, enabling customers to choose items over the Internet from an array of retailers and debit purchases directly from their bank account.

Thanks to its organizational change and efforts to provide new customer services, Sanwa was widely believed to be one of the likely leaders of retail banking modernization in Japan. Sanwa's challenge, like that of OCBC's, will be to build a retail operating culture that champions sales in addition to service. And as foreign competition gradually makes inroads into Japan, Sanwa will have to differentiate its offerings among customer segments to protect its market share.

Foreign regional bank:
Citibank — Stepping up to Asia's mass markets

Citibank has been described as the only true global consumer bank, with a well-recognized franchise in 98 countries around the world. This was certainly the case in Asia, which accounted for 23 percent of Citibank's global profits in 1996. As of 1998, Citibank had an established presence in 16 Asian countries, and had made an impression far greater than its small number of branches would suggest. Citibank's retail strategy in Asia has been to target the affluent customer segment, to offer a consistent brand based on quality products and services, and to serve its chosen customers through leading-edge technology and marketing. Its aggressive efforts throughout the 1990s put it consistently at the forefront of redefining and raising consumer expectations, and forced many local players to rethink the way they did business.

Citibank's lead product and mainstay in the Asian retail markets was its credit card business. As of 1998, Citibank was the leading issuer across the region, with more than five million cards in circulation. Where allowed, Citibank pioneered multi-currency accounts (which enjoyed significant demand in the wake of the

1997–1998 crisis), consumer loan products, and efficient foreign remittance services. The bank aimed to capitalize on Asia's growing numbers of middle- and upper-middle-class consumers who were relatively young, building wealth, open to technology, willing to utilize credit, and traditionally underserved by domestic banks with undifferentiated offerings.

Citibank succeeded with this strategy despite discriminatory branching restrictions throughout Asia. Fundamental to its strategy was a reliance on ATM, phone banking, and Internet services, where regulation and infrastructure permitted. In Thailand, for example, Citibank was allowed to operate only one branch prior to the crisis. Yet it became one of the largest consumer lenders, with a loan portfolio exceeding US$1 billion, through its effective marketing of credit cards and auto finance products. Citibank Thailand also focused on high-net-worth customers, and was believed to be among the market leaders in serving this segment. In Taiwan, where Citibank established its North Asia consumer banking headquarters, it was allowed only eight branches as of 1997. But, through aggressive promotion and careful customer segmentation, Citibank built a 25 percent market share in credit cards in an intensely competitive environment and began to spearhead unsecured consumer lending. In India, Citibank had only seven branches as of 1996. But once restrictions on ATM expansion were lifted that year, the bank expanded its network to about 25 ATMs in ten cities, enabling it to garner about 1.4 percent of consumer deposits by the end of 1997.

Local banks consistently followed Citibank's lead. For example, Citibank's success helped prompt the awakening of SBI, described earlier. In Japan, Citibank was first to offer 24-hour ATM access in the mid-1990s. Some leading Japanese banks soon followed suit, offering round-the-clock access, cutting fees, and providing their own multi-currency accounts to match their U.S. rival. An official from Sanwa Bank remarked to the press: "Citibank has been an enormous reference for us." HSBC, another of Asia's leading regional players, began a major overhaul of its strategy in 1997, specifically aimed at following Citibank's lead in aggressively marketing credit cards and developing new products to tap the increasingly sophisticated needs of the affluent Asian consumer.

Despite its success, Citibank will still face new challenges in the first decade of the 21st century (over and above those resulting from its merger with Travelers to create Citigroup). Citibank, in many ways, benefited from the tight restrictions that limited foreign player presence, often enabling it to capture first-mover advantages in a number of products and markets. With the markets restructuring and opening at the turn of the millennium, Citibank is likely to face new and stronger competitors that rapidly bolster their positions through acquisitions. In addition, Citibank's global objective to serve one billion customers by 2010 poses a whole new set of issues. To help achieve this target, Citibank Asia will have to extend its horizon beyond the affluent, generating a host of challenges in product design, distribution, branding, people development, and economics. The main question facing Citibank Asia in the 21st century is: can it replicate its success in serving a narrow range of affluent customers in the retail mass markets?

Product specialist: AEON Credit Service — Catering to lifestyle

AEON Credit Service is the Hong Kong subsidiary of Japan's AEON Group, one the leading providers of consumer finance in Japan. The Hong Kong subsidiary was established in 1990 and was listed on the local stock market in 1995. Between 1995 and 1997, AEON Credit Services generated revenue and profit growth in excess of 40 percent.

AEON's success in the Hong Kong financial markets — where leading retail banks HSBC, Hang Seng, and Standard Chartered had more than 450 branches combined — was the result of a strategy carefully built around customer convenience. AEON offered a full range of consumer credit including credit cards, hire-purchase, auto loans, and personal loans. Many of these lending services were integrated through its credit card, which offered distinct benefits to customers. For example, if a customer wished to make a hire-purchase of furniture, he did not have to fill in the usual tedious forms. He simply presented his card, filled in a simplified form, and took delivery of the goods. The same was true for auto loans where again, a simplified form was used, and approval required only two working days. AEON's 20 branches and six convenience stations could issue a new card within 30 minutes. And, its credit card holders could tap more than 170 cash-dispensing machines for immediate cash advances.

In 1998, more than 80 percent of AEON's revenues were derived from its credit card business, which it had grown quickly by taking a segmented approach to the market. AEON's strategy: to a provide a card that is an intimate part of the customer's lifestyle. Among its cards were a *Femme* card targeted at women, and a *Hello Kitty* card targeted at Hong Kong's young female office workers who were fans of the popular Japanese cartoon character. AEON also developed a number of affinity cards linked to stores, foundations, and charities, to appeal to different segments of the population. As of early 1998, AEON had issued more than 400,000 credit cards in Hong Kong and was the territory's fifth largest issuer, by purchasing volume.

AEON's card growth continued at a rate of 30 percent in the first half of 1998 despite the worst recession to strike Hong Kong in decades. Rather than pull back, AEON kept up promotion campaigns. It believed that its lending products were meeting a growing, fundamental need and that, given its many years in the consumer finance business, it could adequately screen risks and control losses. At the end of first-quarter 1998, bad debt credit card provisions stood at 1.4 percent, up about 20 percent from the previous year but representing only 12 percent of revenues, leaving a 30 percent profit margin after costs.

AEON's ability to ramp up market share quickly and profitably in Hong Kong's already competitive market demonstrates the power of a clear value proposition and segmented marketing. In the first decade of the 21st century, an increasing number of product specialists, such as GE Capital, will penetrate Asia's markets, cherry-picking the most attractive product lines and customers. Such product specialists will present a real threat to banks that fail to develop strong marketing capabilities and a clear customer focus.

Victory for the Many Survivors

The impact of the 1997 crisis on the future market structure of retail banking in Asia cannot be underestimated. To cope with the changes that will play out in the first decade of the 21st century, domestic and foreign banks will have to make substantial investments in people, marketing, training, and not least, in information technology. Leading banks in the U.S. and Europe have traditionally spent anywhere from 7 to 10 percent of their annual revenues buying new hardware and developing new applications to support new products, services, and channels. For a bank in Indonesia, where the currency was devalued by more than 80 percent in the wake of the crisis, new technology purchases became prohibitively expensive in U.S. dollar terms. The same was true, though to a lesser extent, throughout Southeast Asia and in Korea.

Investments of this magnitude will require banks to achieve minimum operating scale and maintain strong cash flows. In the 1990s, many banks survived with market shares of 2–3 percent; by 2010, that hurdle will likely top 5 percent. In the wake of the crisis, with many banks facing losses in excess of their equity, the required cash flows will be hard to come by. The crisis, by virtue of opening markets to foreign competition, heightened the need for change and technology, but at the same time — as a result of loan losses and devalued currencies — made it more difficult for domestic banks to finance the necessary investments.

In the early years of the 21st century, these realities will lead to an ongoing consolidation of Asia's banking industry. But mergers alone will not, of course, guarantee success in retail banking. The winners will be those that can consistently provide superior value to customers, but their ascent to market leadership will be gradual. While more than 40 percent of consumers in Asia indicated a willingness to switch banks in 1998, they will not do so immediately.

In the U.S., experience has shown that most consumers are slow to change financial service providers. The process of closing an account and opening a new one, which entails filling out new forms and redirecting billings, is enough of an annoyance that will put many off until advantages of doing so are strikingly apparent. And more often than not, people will open a new account without closing an old one, adding to the time it takes for a new bank to capture the lion's share of a customer's business. However, over time — certainly within a decade — consumers will shift, clearly segregating winners and losers in the market.

As this shift occurs in Asia in the years leading up to 2010, approximately 100 financial institutions are expected to survive and prosper in retail banking across Asia. This is far fewer than the approximately 250 that existed in 1997, but far more than will survive in any other banking business line in Asia. Among the winners garnering projected revenues of US$220 billion by 2010, four competitor groups are likely to emerge: large leading generalists, medium-sized local banks, product-focused banks, and nonbank specialists.

Large Multi-Country Generalists: Locking Up Benefits of Scale

There will likely be 10–15 leading generalists by 2010, each dominating several of Asia's local retail banking markets. These leading generalists will draw their roots from the large family-owned banks of the late 1990s. A few will be the transformed entities of formerly government-owned banks. Up to a third are likely to be foreign-owned, some of which (e.g., HSBC, ABN, Citibank) will operate under the foreign bank's global name. Each of the leading generalists will likely have more than 10 percent market share in their domestic market and generate anywhere from several hundred million to several billion U.S. dollars in annual revenues.

The leading generalists will tend to dominate the urban areas with branches extending into main suburbs of the main cities. They will operate across multiple channels and products, providing their customers with the convenience of integrated service and competitive pricing for their short- and long-term financing needs. Their key competitive advantages will be in having a household brand name, broad distribution, and lower costs derived from superior operating scale. The size and diversity of their organizations will enable them to consistently hire the best talent by virtue of the career paths they will be able to offer. As a number of the leading generalists will dominate several markets, they will need to build a strong corporate culture that nonetheless allows tailoring for local market needs.

Medium-Sized Local Banks: Finding Their Customer Niche

The leading generalists will likely be joined by up to five medium-sized local banks in each of Asia's markets outside Japan. These smaller operations will concentrate on either several customer segments or on a specific geographical area within a given country. Their average market share will likely range between 5 and 10 percent, rising to more than 10–15 percent in their chosen niche. Banks that might end up in this category include Thai Farmers Bank in Thailand, Everbright Bank in China, and Bank of East Asia in Hong Kong.

The medium-sized locals' ability to survive and prosper will hinge on consistently providing service and products that customers perceive to be superior to those of the leading generalists. They may offer more personalized service, more detailed financial advice, greater flexibility in product structures, or simply better pricing. To do so, niche providers will need a detailed understanding of their target customers' risk profile, pricing sensitivity, and financial sophistication. They will constantly look for opportunities where customers are under-served. As such, they will need to develop very strong management information skills and will rely heavily on technology to support their tailored services. Many medium-sized local banks will have to turn to outside product and processing providers to run their businesses cost effectively, as few will have sufficient scale to execute their entire offering in-house. Those that fail to generate superior returns and a high market-to-book value will fall prey to acquisition by the leading generalists.

Product-Focused Banks: Building Distinctive Excellence

Biting into the customer base of generalists and medium-sized locals will likely be two or three product-focused banks in each of Asia's domestic markets ex-Japan. Product-focused banks will evolve from today's small generalist banks, such as Bank Sinopac in Taiwan, and will think of market share, not in terms of customers but rather, in terms of product penetration. Each will likely garner a 5–10 percent share in their target products. To succeed, these banks will focus on only a few products, tailor those to large attractive customer segments. Areas of product expertise may include consumer lending, investments, payments, or transaction processing.

As for medium-sized locals, product-focused banks' survival and prosperity will hinge on their ability to build true distinctiveness. This may be through superior use of innovative channels, or simply faster turnaround times and lower pricing. The key challenge for product specialists will be to find cost-effective means to market and distribute their products. They will have to think broadly about leveraging relationships with other banks, retailers, and community organizations. Those that choose to specialize in consumer lending will have to find market mechanisms to offset their risks, given their potential concentrated exposure to systemic single-market risks.

Nonbank Specialists: Capturing New Competitive Advantages

One or two significant nonbank specialists are likely to emerge in each of Asia's domestic markets, outside Japan, by 2010. These nonbank specialists will include a mix of domestic and foreign competitors. They will be either financial companies, such as insurers, stockbrokers, and consumer finance companies, or nonfinancial entities, such as retailers or utility companies. They may excel in building share by leveraging their existing distribution channels, such as insurance agents or store premises, to market selected banking products to customers. They may build functional expertise, for example, in credit risk management, to cherry-pick attractive customers from banks through superior pricing or lending terms. Or, taking the example of Schwab Securities or Fidelity, nonbank financial institutions may develop new channels or investment products to lure traditional deposits away from banks into diversified assets.

A common feature among the nonbank specialists is they will tend to do a number of simple things very well. Without the baggage of extensive branch networks or bad assets in the wake of the 1997–1998 crisis, they will be able — regulations permitting — to quickly set up new services for existing customers or target new attractive customer segments. They will see the Internet as an opportunity, not a threat. If they choose to focus on nonlending products, they will be able to escape the significant equity requirements linked to asset-based businesses. The nonbank specialists will bring greater choice to consumers and threaten local banks that fail to distinguish their product and service offerings.

Japan: Supporting a Broader Base of Winners

Japan's retail financial markets, the second largest in the world after the U.S., will house all the aforementioned competitor groups. Whereas Asia's smaller markets might support five to ten domestic winners, Japan's enormous and wealthy customer base is likely to support up to 30 domestic victors. As of 1998, in Japan common wisdom dictated that the leading five to ten city banks and top five to ten regional banks were natural candidates for long-term leadership in the country's awakening retail markets. The extensive distribution and operating scale of these institutions provide them with reasonably assured seats in the winners' circle. The remaining 10–20 spots are, however, open to innovative foreign and domestic competitors that succeed in setting and meeting new consumer expectations. Unlike the rest of Asia, where savings growth will broaden the playing field, in Japan, victory will depend upon competing directly for customers' assets held by other institutions.

The likely market structure of retail banking in Asia in 2010 will be very different from that of the 1990s. In 2010, people will no longer talk of retail banking in terms of modern versus dimly lit branches, or local versus foreign competitors. Rather, discussion will focus on the distinctiveness, expertise, and dominance that competitors build across customers, products, or channels. As the retail markets undergo substantial change, however, one aspect will remain constant: retail banking will continue to enrich more financial institutions and other new entrants than any other banking business in Asia.

PART III
WINNING IN KEY COUNTRIES

In this section we review how the new banking world in Asia will develop in the key Asian countries.

The section begins with what are the most developed banking markets at the end of the 20th century, Hong Kong and Singapore. The next most developed, Taiwan and the four big markets of Southeast Asia, are covered in the next two chapters. Then, we turn to two countries, Japan and Korea, which should have developed banking industries but do not. Finally, we discuss the two large opportunities of the 21st century, China and India.

These chapters cover the major business lines in each country, thereby reflecting both the overall differences between the countries and how those differences influence the conduct of specific banking businesses.

CHAPTER 9
HONG KONG AND SINGAPORE:
MANAGED CONSOLIDATION

Social & Economic Indicators (US$)		Hong Kong	Singapore
Overall	– GDP:	$171bn	$98bn
	– Population:	6.6mn	3.1mn
	– GDP per capita:	$26,300	$31,600
	– PPP GDP per capita:	$24,085	$24,610
	– 1985–1997 GDP real growth:	6.9% CAGR	9.3% CAGR
	– Projected 2010 GDP per capita:	$52,400	$79,000
	– Exports (% of GDP):	$187bn (109%)	$127bn (130%)
	– Foreign currency reserves (% of imports):	$98bn (51%)	$74bn (53%)
	– % urbanization:	95%	100%
Corporate	– Top 3 sectors:	Financial Services, Real Estate, Trade	Financial & Business Services, Manufacturing, Commerce
	– Number of corporations with annual sales >$1bn:	28	17
Individual	– Annual savings rate:	35%	51%
	– Average savings per household:	$55,620[1]	$46,280[1]
	– Home ownership:	44%[2]	48%
	– Household car ownership:	12%	30%
	– Telephones /1,000 pop:	515[2]	484[2]
	– Internet subscribers/1,000 pop:	99	23
	– % of 18–22-yr-olds attending university:	21%	22%

All figures as of December 1997 unless otherwise indicated.
[1] McKinsey estimates.
[2] Figures as of December 1996.

Financial Markets & Business Lines (US$)		Hong Kong	Singapore
Overall	– Equity capitalization (% of GDP):	$414bn (242%)	$196bn (200%)
	– Number of listed corporations:	638	294
	– Debt market capitalization[3] (% of GDP):	$43bn (25%)	$17bn (17%)
	– Total domestic loans (% of GDP):	$293bn (171%)	$85bn (87%)
	– Total external debt (% of GDP):	$37bn (22%)	$10bn (10%)
	– Total offshore loans (% of GDP):	$237bn (139%)	$42bn (43%)
	– Number of local banks (>$5bn assets):	10	7
	– Number of foreign banks:	157	140
	– Top 3 banks' market share (deposits):	54%	58%
	– Maximum foreign ownership of a commercial bank:	100%	40%
	– Currency convertibility:	Open	Partially controlled
Corporate	– Domestic corporate loans (% of GDP):	$160bn (94%)	$98bn (100%)
Banking	– Nonperforming domestic loans:	5%[4]	5–10%[4]
Retail	– Total consumer deposits (% of total deposits):	$104bn (30%)	$34bn (40%)
Banking	– Total consumer loans (% of total loans):	$90bn (31%)	$33bn (38%)
	– Persons per branch:	4,100	5,300
	– Persons per ATM:	1,600	1,600
	– Credit cards per capita:	0.8	0.6
Asset	– Retail assets under management:	$22bn	$2.4bn
Management	– Total domestic institutional assets:	$40bn[2]	$88bn[2]
	– Number of asset management firms:	84	17
Trading	– Number of stock brokerage firms:	252[2]	41[2]
	– Average daily equity trading volume:	$1.9bn	$0.3bn
	– Average daily FX trading volume:	$79bn[5]	$139bn[5]
Investment	– Total equity issuance (1994–1997 annual avg):	$11bn	$2.5bn
Banking	– Total debt issuance[3] (1994–1997 annual avg):	$17bn	$5.7bn
	– Number of domestic M&A transactions >$50mn (1992–1997):	172	64
Private	– High-net-worth households (>$1mn investable assets):	55,000[1]	8,378[1]
Banking	– Potential private banking assets:	$220bn[1]	$29bn[1]

All figures as of December 1997 unless otherwise indicated
[1] McKinsey estimates.
[2] Figures as of December 1996.
[3] Maturity greater than 1 year.
[4] Figures as of June 1998.
[5] Figures as of April 1998.

9
HONG KONG AND SINGAPORE:
MANAGED CONSOLIDATION

In 1978, the esteemed U.S. economist Milton Friedman led a discussion of free-market ideas on television while bobbing on the famous Star Ferry in Victoria Harbour, lauding free-market economics as epitomized by Hong Kong. Around that time, many people were less bullish about the prospects for Singapore, Hong Kong's regional rival, which was not as committed to unfettered competition.

Of course, these people were both right and wrong. They were right to notice the philosophical differences between the two economies, but wrong in that both performed strongly in the 1980s and 1990s. On the surface, Singapore and Hong Kong followed similar development paths in the last two decades of the 20th century. GDP in both countries grew strongly from 1980 to 1997. On an annual basis, exports rose by 17 percent in Hong Kong and by 9 percent in Singapore, while foreign exchange reserves increased by 19 percent and 15 percent respectively. Unemployment stayed low, averaging 3.1 percent in Hong Kong and 2.6 percent in Singapore. Both had important and growing stock markets: from the beginning of 1990 to the end of 1997, total market capitalization grew from US$42 billion to US$414 billion in Hong Kong, and from US$49 billion to US$196 billion in Singapore.

But neither market was thoroughly true to its stereotype. Singapore remained one of the world's great free trading ports, and its economy in fact opened up significantly during this period despite its government's well-publicized fondness for controls. Hong Kong, famed for its free port as well as its very low local taxes, carried its noninterventionist philosophy to the point of having no antitrust laws, which led to some very cozy oligopolies.

These two markets competed aggressively to be international financial centers for Asia. To do so, both needed strong domestic financial systems. For this reason, comparing and contrasting their domestic markets — past and future — is valuable. During the 1980s and most of the 1990s, both Hong Kong and Singapore managed their domestic banking systems with some degree of protection. But by the late 1990s, those management philosophies had come under siege. The financial markets in both places were about to truly open, exposing past profit-making approaches to a new era of competitiveness.

Similarities and Differences

From a distance, Hong Kong and Singapore may seem very similar. Both are real or quasi city-states; both survive on being beacons of stability and efficiency to the vast, less stable countries with lower productivity that surround them. Both were founded on immigration from persecution, and of course, both are infused with a strong Chinese work ethic. Finally, both have grown from trading and manufacturing bases into trading and service economies, with GDP per capita levels on par with those of Western developed countries.

But they are also very different. Hong Kong's population is more than twice as large as Singapore's, and it is growing much faster. Hong Kong was a British colony and is now a "Special Administrative Region" of China; Singapore is an independent country. So while Singapore looks to build its own status in the region and act as a sovereign nation, Hong Kong has always had to operate within the context of its broader political and economic ties. Inexorably now, Hong Kong is increasingly turning its attention to the north, while Singapore is far less fixated on any one neighboring country.

These differences will influence the development of the two cities as international financial centers in the first decade of the 21st century. But in this chapter, we focus on Hong Kong and Singapore as domestic banking markets, with corporate, retail, and institutional opportunities like any other market. Even though their combined population is smaller than that of Malaysia alone, their total wealth and financial vibrancy offer vast opportunities by the standards of Asia ex-Japan, and their innovations often point the way for other markets. Relatively open to foreign competition in certain segments, they also are the two places in Asia where foreign banks have made the most inroads into domestic services.

Thus, we will turn first to the economic structures and regulations that will shape these two domestic banking markets. These are different enough to require tailored strategies and organizational approaches from local and foreign competitors.

Vibrant but Different Economies

Hong Kong and Singapore are economies different in many ways.

The most obvious difference is size. In 1997, GDP totaled US$171 billion for Hong Kong and US$98 billion for Singapore. Hong Kong's population was 6.6 million against 3.1 million for Singapore, resulting in 1997 GDP per capita figures of US$26,300 and US$31,600 respectively.

Hong Kong's population is forecast to grow much faster than Singapore's, largely due to increased immigration from China. The planned intake of legal immigrants is set at 150 people per day; illegal immigration will push this figure higher. Between 1997 and 2005, Hong Kong's population is therefore projected to rise from 6.6 million to 7.3 million; Singapore's from 3.1 million to 3.4 million.

Historic economic growth rates, while strong in both cases, have differed too. From 1980 to 1989, Hong Kong recorded overall nominal GDP growth of 255 percent, and Singapore 135 percent. Between 1990 and 1997, their respective growth figures were 139 and 114 percent. These growth rates have translated into GDP per capita increases of 100 percent in Hong Kong and 86 percent in Singapore between 1990 and 1997. In other words, both cities saw enormous increases in personal wealth and buying power during the last 20 years of the century.

Personal income growth was mirrored by extraordinary increases in trading muscle. Always revered as trading powerhouses, in the 1990s both Hong Kong and Singapore achieved robust growth in trade volumes as they benefited from expanding world trade and their unique positions as gateways to fast-growing Asian markets, offering the best port and legal facilities in their respective areas.

So between 1990 and 1997, Hong Kong's overall trade volumes increased from US$165 billion to US$397 billion, and Singapore's from US$114 billion to US$257 billion. In terms of total trade volumes, Hong Kong was the world's eighth largest trading "country" in 1997 (after the U.S., Germany, Japan, the U.K., France, Italy, and Canada) and Singapore was the world's thirteenth largest. Obviously, in both cases these trading volumes were inflated by re-exports of other countries' production to the West or to the rest of Asia. Hong Kong in particular benefited from serving as China's original gateway to the outside world and as an intermediary between China and Taiwan. Nevertheless, the overall figures are startling and represent a huge foundation for wealth creation.

The corporate bases of the two cities evolved rapidly during the 1980s and 1990s, becoming quite different by the end of the century. In terms of size, Hong Kong's corporate base was larger and Singapore's more concentrated. Hong Kong had 13 corporations with revenues exceeding US$2 billion in 1997; Singapore had three. In the next tier (companies with revenues between US$500 million and US$2 billion), Hong Kong had 50 and Singapore 90. Those with revenues between US$100 million and US$500 million numbered 350 in Hong Kong and 290 in Singapore. In the middle market (from US$10 million to US$100 million in sales), Hong Kong had 10,000 firms and Singapore only 1,700. Hong Kong had a much larger small-business base, with 250,000 companies earning revenues less than US$10 million, compared with just 35,000 in Singapore.

An important difference between the two cities' corporate bases is the amount of public ownership of major corporations. In Singapore, many of the largest entities were partially or fully owned by the state. Major firms like Singapore Airlines, Singapore Telecom, and Singapore Technologies were partly privatized but majority state-owned. Indeed in 1997, nine of Singapore's top 20 local companies had direct or indirect government stakes of 15 percent or more (the indirect holdings were through state-controlled investment entities like the Government of Singapore Investment Corporation — GIC). By comparison, none of Hong Kong's top 20 local companies had government stakes of 15 percent or more in 1997 (in August 1998, however, the government's efforts to reduce speculation against the Hong Kong dollar through support of the stock market led to its taking 5–10 percent stakes in some leading companies).

Another key contrast is in the industrial composition of the two economies. By 1997, most of Hong Kong's manufacturing activities had migrated to China or Southeast Asia, and as a result there were few large locally based manufacturers. Singapore, meanwhile, had emerged as a major hub for electronics manufacturing, especially disk drives for personal computers. Electronics provided 17 percent of Singapore's GDP and 71 percent of its non-oil exports by the late 1990s. As a result, of Hong Kong's largest 100 corporations (ranked by revenues), 31 were in wholesale trading, 27 in financial services, ten in real estate and construction, only nine in manufacturing, and 23 in other industries. In Singapore, 43 were in manufacturing, 26 in energy and resources, ten in financial services, seven in transportation, and 14 in other industries.

A final factor in the corporate base of these cities, and a subject of intense rivalry, is the number of Western multinational corporations and banks that based their Asian headquarters in either Hong Kong or Singapore. At the end of 1997, Hong Kong could claim approximately 600 major multinational regional headquarters, including those of Bank of America, British Airways, Goldman Sachs, and Merrill Lynch. Singapore, meanwhile, could claim 120, including Compaq, Hewlett-Packard, and JP Morgan. One of the reasons that both cities attracted so many regional headquarters was that both had legal systems based on Western standards — British in both cases.

As retail financial markets, both Hong Kong and Singapore evolved rapidly during the 1980s and 1990s and in a similar fashion despite their size differential. Population growth between 1980 and 1997 was significant: Hong Kong went from 5.1 million to 6.6 million people, Singapore from 2.1 million to 3.1 million. But far more impressive were the rapid rise in income levels — from US$5,600 to US$26,300 in Hong Kong, US$4,900 to US$31,600 in Singapore — and very high personal savings rates (averaging 34 percent in Hong Kong and 45 percent in Singapore in the 1990s). These combined to pump up personal wealth: the average household in Hong Kong in 1997 had US$56,000 in savings; in Singapore, the comparative figure was US$46,000.

As important as the growth in wealth was the way in which retail segments evolved in both markets. At the top end, for instance, the number of U.S. dollar millionaires and billionaires was extraordinary: as of 1997, Hong Kong had 57,600 millionaires and eight billionaires, while Singapore had 8,400 and three respectively. So, both cities saw intense competition for banking high-net-worth individuals in the 1990s, and each could claim many international banks that based their regional private banking businesses there. However, competition in Singapore was constrained because offshore private banking was not allowed for Singapore citizens; only onshore players could compete.

With these significant increases in wealth, on average and at the higher income levels, came increased customer sophistication and expectations. There were three drivers behind this change. First, of course, wealthier customers naturally expected better service. Second, they had more choice as competition heightened (especially in the higher-net-worth brackets) and as foreign competitors transferred best practices in advertising, product design, pricing, and service. Finally, real education levels rose, most notably in Singapore. From 1980 to 1997, the percentage of the employed population with university degrees increased from 3.5 to 9 percent in Hong Kong, and from 3.1 to 17.7 percent in Singapore.

Two vibrant and evolving city-states, offering attractive corporate and retail banking opportunities that were becoming (on paper at least) more attractive as each year passed. By 1997, Hong Kong had total local currency deposits of US$199 billion, which had grown 16 percent a year since 1990. The comparative figures for Singapore were US$80 billion and 9 percent.

But the overall increases in corporate activity and personal wealth are only part of the banking story in any market. As important are the regulatory approach and the competitive environment it fosters. In both Hong Kong and Singapore, the regulatory environment was attractive to incumbents during the 1990s, but is evolving to a more open framework that will clearly change industry dynamics in the early years of the 21st century.

Firm but Fair Regulation

In both Hong Kong and Singapore, regulators exercised a firm hand. Aspiring to be international financial centers, both cities created (certainly by regional standards) strong legal and banking regulatory environments, where the rule of the law prevailed in commercial disputes, and where the financial health and dynamism of the banking system was seen as a strategic priority. So the two regulators, the Hong Kong Monetary Authority (HKMA) and the Monetary Authority of Singapore (MAS) watched the industry very closely and set tough risk standards, actively intervened to control over-exuberant activity (for instance, in the real estate lending markets), and encouraged domestic banks to build capabilities. Both protected domestic banks, although to differing degrees. The overall strategy in each case was clear. Surrounded by large neighbors that had less transparent or potentially corrupt legal and banking systems, and competing basically on their own wits, both Hong Kong and Singapore put in place regulatory environments that created strong banking industries which could serve as beacons for the whole region, attract foreign capital, and thus support the overall vitality of the two cities.

Both the HKMA and MAS aimed at encouraging strong and vibrant banking systems, and both used three key tools to that end. First, they controlled competition — creating just enough, but not so much that it overwhelmed domestic institutions. Second, they intervened to some degree to control pricing. Third, they imposed firm capital and lending diversification rules or guidelines. To implement these tools, they regularly consulted with individual banks about their activities to ensure they were not straying too far from the agreed direction.

Hong Kong, cherishing its position as the free-market model for the world, had no constraints on new bank licenses. However, all banks formed after 1978 were allowed to have only one branch, thereby limiting them to the wholesale, trading, and private banking businesses. This left retail, middle-market, and small-business banking to established competitors, most notably the Hongkong and Shanghai Banking Corporation (HSBC), Standard Chartered Bank, the 13 banks owned by the Bank of China Group, Hang Seng Bank, Bank of East Asia, Citibank, Dao Heng Bank, Wing Lung Bank, Shanghai Commercial Bank, and Overseas Trust Bank. (Exhibit 9.1 provides an overview of Hong Kong's major local banks in 1997.) The logic behind this branch limit was that there were already enough banks to provide a competitive environment; the regulators wanted to avoid excess competition, which would drive profits down so low as to threaten industry stability.

In addition, Hong Kong imposed a series of rules on deposit interest rates that for a time limited the banks' cost of funds. Until 1994, interest rates paid on savings deposits, deposits of less than HK$0.5 million with more than 3 months' maturity, and fixed-term deposits with less than 15 months' maturity had to be uniform. Only Bank of China and other local Chinese banks were allowed to offer marginally higher rates. In 1994, the HKMA began relaxing these rules, but after some instability in the money markets (and hot debate by the consumer lobby, which was pressing for the complete removal of deposit-rate controls) it decided

Exhibit 9.1

Hong Kong's Leading Banks: 1997

	Total assets US$ billions	Net profits US$ millions	Number of branches
Hongkong & Shanghai Bank	189	2,538	220
Hang Seng Bank	50	1,200	147
Bank of East Asia	17	267	98
Dao Heng Bank	16	270	48
Standard Chartered*	n/a	n/a	100
Citibank*	n/a	n/a	17

* Financial information for Hong Kong subsidiaries not available.

Source: Companies annual reports; McKinsey interviews

to retain controls on current, savings, and time deposits with maturity or call periods of less than 7 days. This meant, however, that after 1995, 95 percent of retail deposits were subject to full competition.

However, the market was still not fully free. This was because the Hong Kong Association of Banks (comprising HSBC, Bank of East Asia, Bank of China, Standard Chartered Bank, ABN Amro, BNP, Bank of Tokyo-Mitsubishi, Hang Seng Bank, Chase Manhattan Bank, Morgan Guaranty Trust, Nanyang Commercial Bank, and Wing Lung Bank) would meet every week to set the maximum rates on fixed-term deposits with less than 7 days' maturity, and thereby set overall market spreads. So, the HKMA and the banking industry managed competition and pricing.

The HKMA also specified lending guidelines. Real estate was both the driver of bank profits and the potential weak spot on bank balance sheets. Therefore, the HKMA set a cap on mortgage loans, fixing it at 70 percent of the property's value from the mid-1990s onwards. It also asked banks to try to keep their total real estate loans at less than 40 percent of all loans, although the industry average was near 44 percent and for some of the smaller local banks at around 50 percent. (In mid-1998, the HKMA recognized reality and relaxed this rule.) As a group, Hong Kong consumers were somewhat more leveraged than those in Singapore, having on average total debt of US$49,300 per household, compared with US$38,800 in Singapore. So, in sum, the HKMA managed the industry to maintain margins and capital strength, while allowing as much competition as possible to ensure the industry gave consumers and corporations reasonable service and prices.

In **Singapore**, the regulator was more active. The MAS stopped issuing full banking licenses in 1973, so competition for retail, middle-market, and small business opportunities was effectively controlled by the Big Four: the Development Bank of Singapore (DBS), Oversea-Chinese Banking Corporation (OCBC), United Overseas Bank (UOB), and Overseas Union Bank (OUB). In addition, the Post Office Savings Bank (POSB), Tat Lee Bank, Keppel Bank, HSBC, Standard Chartered Bank, Citibank, and some small banks and finance companies (many of which were affiliates of the big four) competed in the domestic market. (Exhibit 9.2 lists Singapore's major banks as of 1997.)

Like its counterpart in Hong Kong, the MAS wanted to restrain competition to maintain margins. However, the MAS went further in its quest for industry stability. Not content with the 8 percent capital adequacy requirement set by the Bank for International Settlements, the MAS required Singapore banks to hold capital equivalent to 12 percent of their risk-weighted assets. MAS policies also reflected certain moral and political attitudes of the Singaporean elite. This group revered savings and frowned on credit, or at least the "excessive credit" they perceived in the U.S. economy. So, the MAS did not allow banks to issue credit cards to people under 21 years of age (except to students studying abroad), and would regularly interact with the banks to control their credit card lending, usually capping it at a certain number of months of income. Interaction was not subtle; banks were told in private meetings to toe the line, or presumably they would face a very tough time at the hands of the MAS when regulatory reviews came up.

Perhaps the best example of the historical difference between the MAS and the HKMA came in the early days of the 1997–1998 crisis. The HKMA managed

Exhibit 9.2

Singapore's Leading Banks: 1997

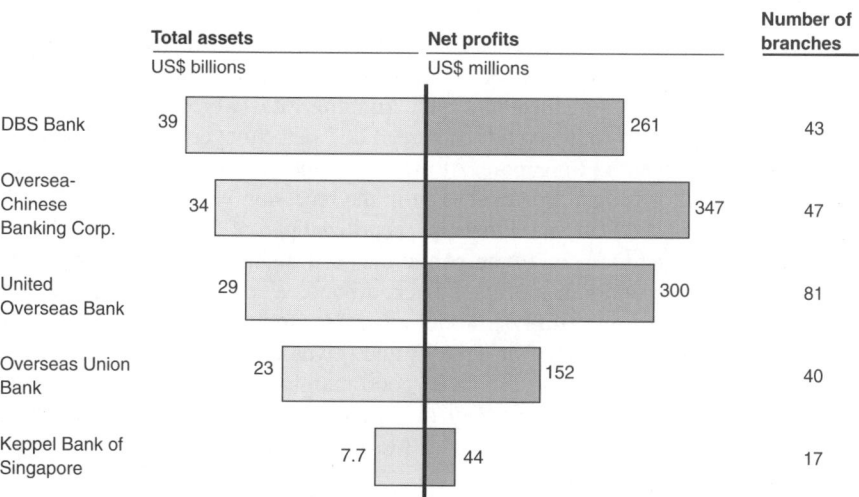

	Total assets US$ billions	Net profits US$ millions	Number of branches
DBS Bank	39	261	43
Oversea-Chinese Banking Corp.	34	347	47
United Overseas Bank	29	300	81
Overseas Union Bank	23	152	40
Keppel Bank of Singapore	7.7	44	17

Source: Companies annual reports; McKinsey interviews

interest rates as the Hong Kong dollar came under pressure, and worked diligently with the banks to ensure sufficient liquidity and smooth handling of the few major bankruptcies that took place (most notably Peregrine). These were the normal activities of any central bank in times of a liquidity squeeze/currency crisis. In Singapore, the new MAS chairman announced to Parliament the composite 1997 results for the Big Four as well as the details of their exposure to crisis countries in Asia — before any of these banks had reported their results! This went far beyond what most regulators considered normal. The MAS seemed to regard the niceties of corporate independence and corporate prerogatives as secondary to its need to reassure the market in detail.

So these were wealthy, high-growth markets, regulated to constrain competition — a banker's paradise. Indeed, up to the mid-1990s, fortunes were made in banking in both Hong Kong and Singapore.

Attractive Banking Opportunities to Date

Where did these profits come from? As in most markets, the answer lies in the economics of each customer segment, but in both cities retail profits were very important.

Good Returns from Retail Banking

In the retail market, as in most countries, profits came from the higher-income segments, with a special contribution from private banking. But across all income segments there were some interesting product emphases. Both cities placed great importance on owning real estate, and so the mortgage business drove profits in many banks, especially in Hong Kong. In Singapore, the mortgage opportunity was important, but many borrowers could borrow against the value of their mandatory Central Provident Fund accounts (CPF), so opportunities for banks were more limited.

Spreads on mortgages in both markets were generous, and collateral values held up well even in times of crisis. In 1997, average spreads on the predominantly floating-rate mortgages against interbank funding rates were 1.5 percent over prime in Hong Kong (producing a total spread of 2 percent over interbank funding costs), and 3.4 percent in Singapore. At the same time, default rates on mortgages were very low, at less than 2 percent even in the recession year of 1998. In 1997, Bank of East Asia and Dah Sing Financial securitized part of their mortgage books. In doing so they had to reveal to the public the performance of their mortgages in the past to give investors in mortgage-backed bonds a sense of potential default rates. They revealed amazingly low default rates, suggesting that across their portfolios they had only seen four defaults and (given collateral) no actual losses.

Other lending products also produced good margins. As of 1997, credit cards were producing returns of 17 percent against interbank funding costs in Hong Kong and 11 percent in Singapore, with losses running in both cities at normal Western levels of 3–4 percent or less.

On the other hand, deposit spreads were more cyclical. Retail deposits provided spreads against interbank funding of about 1 percent in some periods, but in others (for instance, 1995 in Singapore) they fell into negative territory as they were bid up despite falling interbank rates.

The combination, however, of rich credit spreads dominated by mortgages (and associated credit card and mortgage fees), and reasonable if somewhat volatile deposit spreads, meant that retail banking in both cities offered good returns to those that could build volume and thereby reduce unit operating expenses. The regulatory controls on competition ensured that, for most established banks, it was possible to garner enough volume to spread operating expenses and sustain good margins.

Beyond traditional banking products, returns in retail stockbroking were also potentially attractive. The Chinese population's fondness for betting on stocks gave rise to significant volumes, and regulations again sustained pricing. So in Singapore, retail broking commissions were 1 percent, the highest in any developed economy, and in Hong Kong they were 25–50 basis points.

Hong Kong's retail broking market was very fragmented. Although the market as a whole produced good profits in many years, no single firm had more than 4 percent of the total. So, even in the 1996 bull-market year, none of the players pulled in profits exceeding US$30 million. In contrast, Singapore's market was more concentrated, with the top five brokerage firms controlling about 36 percent of retail volumes. The result was that a firm like Vickers Ballas, which focused on the retail market first in Singapore, then in a few other countries, could produce US$34.4 million in profits in 1996, and US$29.7 million in 1997, from basically just three million people in Singapore. Part of these profits came from commissions, but margin lending and custodial services provided additional opportunities for profits, although they would create risks for many brokers in a downturn when collateral values declined and some of their customers defaulted.

The mutual fund markets were less attractive in the 1990s. Hong Kong's market was far more advanced than Singapore's, but both were still tiny compared with developed Western countries. In 1997, Hong Kong funds represented just US$20 billion, and Singapore's US$2 billion, compared with an asset base of exceeding US$2.5 trillion in the U.S. and US$136 billion in the U.K. Although pricing was rich (nearly all funds carried a front-end load of 4-5 percent and management fees topping 1 percent), the small size of many funds limited overall profit potential. Distribution of these funds offered opportunities for some players, however. In 1998, for example, Standard Chartered offered 800 of the 1,400 mutual funds available in the Hong Kong market, earning a percentage of the load upfront for doing so, without incurring any of the fund management challenges or costs.

Corporate Banking: Large and Segmented

As in all markets, corporate banking in Hong Kong and Singapore provided the bulk of lending by asset volume but was highly segmented. At one extreme were large corporations — for example, Cheung Kong, Great Eagle, Hongkong Telecom, and Swire Group in Hong Kong, and City Developments, Cycle & Carriage, Singapore Airlines, and Singapore Telecom in Singapore — which could demand the same level of pricing and service as the western multinationals. Also in this category were the major quasi-public projects that needed large amounts of funding; Hong Kong's new Chek Lap Kok airport and the surrounding bridges, tunnels, and railways connecting the airport to Hong Kong Island and Kowloon was a huge project in the 1990s. At the other extreme were the small retailers, importers, and service businesses that could be charged attractive spreads on loans and often left deposits in branches requiring relatively low interest rates. But serving these customers required a costly branch network, and they were subject to significant losses when the economy, or parts of it, slowed. In the middle were the growth companies, subject to both spectacular rises and falls, with good spreads available.

Another interesting segment of the corporate market were the principal investing firms — professional firms that raised institutional investor money to buy significant stakes in small to medium-sized businesses (usually) in Asia. These firms needed credit to leverage the capital they were investing, as well as a range of investment banking and commercial banking services as they pursued transactions and then tried to improve the performance of the businesses in which they invested. Finally, both cities had a significant stockbroking community whose activities needed to be financed, both to fund their margin lending activities and to fund their general balance sheets.

As in all corporate markets around the region, the size of the profit pools and the profit margins varied between these different segments. Large corporations represented large asset opportunities at low spreads. Meanwhile, small businesses offered better margins on loans and deposits as well as interesting trade finance opportunities, but it was more difficult to build volumes and scale with each of the many customers that needed to be won and served.

Institutional Less Exciting Than It Appears

Both Hong Kong and Singapore appeared to offer institutional investment management opportunities, although these proved less exciting than expected during the 1990s. The sources of such institutional funds would normally be threefold: investment funds of insurance companies and some local commercial banks; corporations' long-term pension and on-balance sheet funds; and large quasi-governmental funds.

Unfortunately, these opportunities were not consistently attractive during much of the 1990s. Local insurance companies in both markets tended to manage their funds largely in-house. Corporate pension fund opportunities were not as large as the corporate base might suggest. Hong Kong's weak pension requirements did little to encourage companies to set up funds, and state-mandated pension schemes in Singapore limited the scope for private corporate funds during the 1980s and much of the 1990s.

The corollary of limited corporate pension opportunities in Singapore was that government-controlled funds (such as the GIC and CPF) were very large indeed, as was the quasi-state Temasek Holdings investment fund. As of end-1997, the CPF represented US$51 billion in investable assets. Coupled with official foreign reserves of US$70 billion, this meant that in theory there was at least US$120 billion of quasi-governmental investment opportunities in Singapore. In practice, however, little of this money was available to private-sector fund managers: in 1997, only 5 percent of the US$120 billion, or US$6 billion. Still, this represented a big improvement since the early 1990s, and as of July 1998, the government was considering placing another US$15 billion with private fund managers by year 2000. Similarly, internal fund managers largely controlled the GIC and Temasek investment funds. Such constraints obviously stifled full development of the fund management opportunity in Singapore.

In Hong Kong the situation was even less attractive. Although the combination of foreign exchange reserves (US$98.1 billion in 1997) and government funds (US$8.5 billion in 1997) suggested significant opportunities, Hong Kong's funds were largely managed in-house or by a select few local banks. The exception was bond fund management across currencies for the largest bond houses. Looking ahead, Hong Kong's new Mandatory Provident Fund (MPF), which will require all companies to provide pensions to their employees, will create greater opportunities for fund managers to garner funds rather than just use the city as a base for managing Western money directed toward Asia. By 2010, the MPF is expected to have total assets of US$350 billion.

As discussed earlier, regulators were critical to profits in both cities. However, they required strong capital bases from the banks and controlled excessive lending practices. As a result, while attractive return on assets were available, strong returns on equity was harder to achieve. In fact, published returns were further depressed in the 1980s and 1990s as regulators in both places allowed banks to sequester some of their profits in hidden reserves so that year-on-year earnings could be smoothed. In 1995, Hong Kong moved to reveal hidden reserves and stop the transfers, so that declared profits were comparable to those in the U.S. and U.K. at least. Singapore was due to move to more transparent accounts by 2000. The result of all these forces was that banks in Hong Kong averaged returns on equity of 17.1 percent from 1990 to 1997; banks in Singapore, due to hidden reserves and higher capital requirements, averaged 10.9 percent in the same period. Add back hidden reserves in some of the earlier years (and the unaccounted value of some old real estate assets of certain banks), and these were still attractive returns.

In essence, the key to domestic profits in Hong Kong and Singapore during the 1980s and 1990s was to be allowed to compete at all, that is, to have a full license with branching rights. With these rights, good margins were pretty well assured for banks that stuck to the basics. Those that avoided outrageous credits or lending to bank insiders and held costs down could expect reasonable returns. Low costs were important contributors to returns: compared with U.S. banks, which in 1995 averaged cost-to-income ratios of 62 percent, Hong Kong banks had cost-to-income ratios of 41 percent and Singapore banks, 40 percent. Good returns were available to those that built up disproportionate market shares in each city, and introduced enough new products and services to fend off incursions of foreign banks or local finance companies. In addition, the second-tier banks had to recognize that in the large corporate market, the large banks and international investment banks had significant competitive advantages. Thus, the smaller banks needed to avoid excessive lending in this segment since it would only depress overall returns on capital.

Beyond these pressures, however, banking in Hong Kong and Singapore in the 1980s and 1990s were relatively attractive businesses. Change came, but given the controlled competition, local banks had the time to experiment and build up more advanced products, services, and distribution systems. In fact, the major management worry of the mid-1990s was finding enough qualified managers to pursue all the opportunities in front of the banks. But the severe management gaps in both cities were really a warning for the future. Too many of the local banks did not have what it took to keep up with a steadily changing world in the 1990s. They would be the ones shocked into rapid change after the 1997–1998 crisis.

The Challenges of the 21st Century

Despite the inevitable ups and downs, much of the 1990s were good years for bankers serving the domestic Hong Kong and Singapore markets. At the same time, many aspects of the business were changing.

As we have seen, regulation underpinned the profitability of both markets. Yet the combination of WTO pressure to open up financial markets and the two governments' evolving views on what would be needed to sustain their respective positions as a global financial center, meant that bankers could not rely indefinitely upon those regulations remaining in place. Hong Kong had signaled through its introduction of transparent reporting and the gradual lifting of deposit controls that old protections were under threat. While Singapore had moved less quickly, the fact that the city aspired to compete with Hong Kong meant that safety blankets for domestic banks could not last forever. Changes at the MAS in 1997 suggested that Singapore was about to change its approach dramatically.

The likelihood of reform increased with the mid-1990s trend toward large mergers in the global banking industry, a trend that produced giants such as Bank of Tokyo-Mitsubishi in Japan and NationsBank (and subsequently BankAmerica) in the U.S. The emergence of these enormous banks created concern among regulators in both cities that (apart from HSBC) none of the domestic banks could thrive in a more complex and scale-dependent environment. So regulators started to worry about the architecture of the local banking market in the context of global change.

The need for scale was also prompted by changes in market needs. Trading markets became more complex (and certainly more volatile in Asia in the late 1990s). Corporations became more demanding, expecting their bankers to make major investments in IT and staff training to serve them. And the whole retail banking environment grew more capital intensive as, again, IT led to a proliferation of channel options and costs for banks.

All these trends threatened the cozy status quo that had enabled many medium-sized banks in both cities to earn attractive returns (Exhibit 9.3).

Hong Kong: Consolidation

By the end of the 1990s, there were clear signs that the old oligopoly in Hong Kong would have to change, and that the umbrella of good margins shielding the

Exhibit 9.3
_____

Performance of Large and Medium-sized Banks
Return on equity; percent

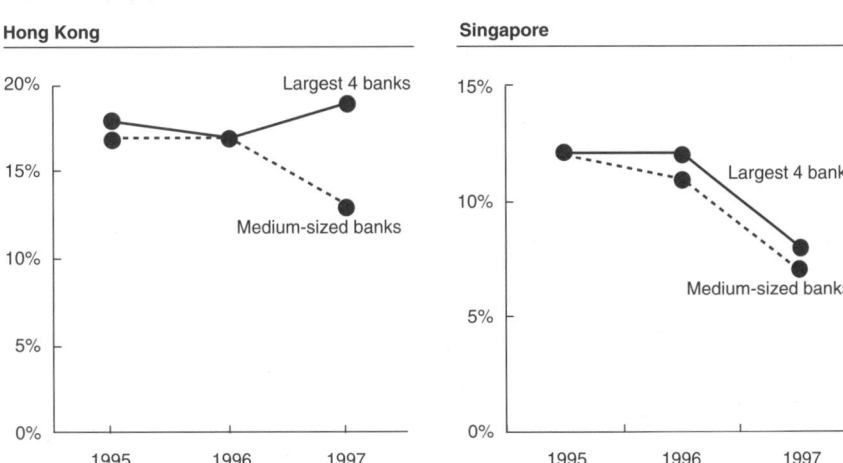

Source: Datastream; McKinsey analysis

smaller banks would start to wither. When the 1997–1998 financial crisis hit, Hong Kong had no deposit insurance in place. The flights to quality that occurred at that time, combined with the rise in Hong Kong Interbank Offered Rate (HIBOR) and local deposit rates required to protect the Hong Kong dollar peg to the U.S. dollar, put all banks — especially the smaller local banks — into a funding squeeze. Moreover, the government's August 1998 intervention in the stock market raised questions about the regulatory posture of the authorities and added a new degree of uncertainty to the environment.

In 1997, the Hong Kong deposit market was split among a variety of banks. HSBC, the dominant player by far, controlled 38 percent of deposits; Hang Seng Bank (64-percent-owned by HSBC) had 12 percent, 13 small Chinese banks owned by the Bank of China had 10–15 percent, Standard Chartered had about 7 percent, Bank of East Asia had 4 percent, and Citibank had 3–5 percent. The remaining 20–30 percent was split among a host of smaller players.

But the ways in which some of the smaller banks were making money in the late 1990s came under pressure. WTO and local consumer pressure would no doubt eventually lead to removal of the last vestiges of controls on retail deposit pricing and to the market's opening to more foreign entrants. Already, during the mid-1990s both ABN Amro and GE Capital had entered the mortgage market in Hong Kong to cherry-pick the fat margins in that area. And at the end of 1998, Singapore's DBS purchased Kwong On Bank. Other competitive actions could be expected to undermine the local industry's traditional profit streams.

At the same time, however, local banks could tap into exciting new opportunities. After the handover of Hong Kong from the British to China in July

1997, immigration from the mainland was expected to drive the population over 7 million by the early years of the 21st century. While a number of these immigrants would be at the low end of the retail market, they point to good growth in the future. At the high end, further expansion of the high-net-worth private banking market could be expected once the economy recovered. Finally, the year 2000 MPF introduction creates new investment management opportunities. So although competition could be expected to increase, so would the size and range of opportunities for banks.

Taking advantage of these opportunities while grappling with a more uncertain and competitive world is likely to prove difficult for many of Hong Kong's smaller banks. Thus, the first decade of the 21st is likely to be marked by consolidation of domestic competitors. Signaling the likely changes in store, in early 1998 the HKMA launched a formal review of the outlook and desired profile of the banking industry. Most people in the local banking community saw this as a first step in a process of industry consolidation in preparation for these new challenges and opportunities.

Singapore: Opening Up

Regulatory controls and steady economic growth enabled the Big Four Singaporean banks, along with Citibank, Standard Chartered Bank, HSBC, and the two smaller banks, Keppel and Tat Lee, to prosper from the local Singapore market in the 1990s. The local finance companies also fared well, funding high-rate assets with high-rate deposits.

Another important local player, the Post Office Savings Bank (POSB), grew enormously during the 1990s. POSB was a unusual breed of competitor, and the evolution of its strategy and actions offers insights into the changing dynamics of the Singapore market. Founded in 1972, and operating under a government mandate as a statutory board, POSB was effectively the nation's savings bank. POSB deposits were tax-exempt and government-guaranteed. At the same time, use of these deposits was controlled: 10 percent of deposits were placed in government securities, 33 percent in other government entities or companies, 40 percent in other local commercial banks, and the rest in POSB mortgages and credit card assets.

POSB was a very important deposit gatherer, having 130 branches and 670 ATMs (huge in comparison with the 43 branches and 246 ATMs of DBS, the largest commercial bank). Under its motto, "Tomorrow is worth saving for," POSB used its market advantages and reach to build up a base of US$15 billion in customer deposits (17 percent of the market) by 1997, from five million savings accounts and 600,000 current or checking accounts. Given such an extensive base, many of the accounts were inevitably unprofitable; probably 75 percent were too small to make money from. But the bank's whole philosophy was aimed at small savers: if you deposited over S$100,000, you received one-quarter percent less (not more) interest, and those on a simple save-as-you-earn scheme received 20 percent more interest. As a result of all these steps, practically all adults in Singapore had a deposit at POSB.

But by the mid-1990s, POSB was becoming more aggressive in the face of a changing environment and increased competition. While it retained its unique tax advantages, the April 1994 introduction of the GST sales tax and the raising of tax thresholds and lowering of rates meant that about 70 percent of Singapore's residents no longer paid income tax, thus reducing the advantage of POSB's products. So POSB had to compete aggressively for savings. The bank introduced POSBline, its own phone banking service. It launched an aggressive strategy to attract child depositors, both as a public service (to encourage the savings culture the government admired) but also to establish early loyalty to POSB. As part of this initiative, the bank introduced school education programs, complete with magicians to tell the story in a fun way. An Internet product, with the endearing name Smiley Scramble, came next, complete with word games to keep children interested. In December 1997, POSB started to sell third-party mutual funds through its ATM network, and in 1998, it joined the market introduction of debit cards, based on the Plus/Interlink systems.

POSB's actions were representative of an increasingly saturated retail banking market. By 1997, Singapore had 5,300 persons per branch and 1,600 persons per ATM, compared to 4,100 and 1,600 in Hong Kong, and 3,200 and 3,000 in the U.S. Given these ratios and the increasing need to find Singapore dollar funding for the great lending opportunities, competitive moves quickened during the late 1990s. Singapore's local banks invested in telephone banking, Internet experiments, and continued to strengthen the capabilities of their ATM offerings. The Big Four banks developed NETS (Network for Electronic Transfers) to link their ATM networks together. Then they added ESA (Electronic Share Application), EPS (Electronic Payment for Shares), UTA (Unit Trust Applications), and IPO (Initial Public Offerings), all ways to make unit trust or share transactions through ATMs. It was possible to inquire about the results of an application for shares through an ATM, and to make transactions on a CPF personal retirement fund account through an ATM. Banks were also investigating new smart-card applications.

So during the late 1990s, Singapore became a unique market where the government protected local banks but also encouraged investment in expensive technological developments and constrained growth of certain credit products (such as credit cards for young people). But by 1997, this model was under stress. Increased internal competition, combined with credit losses both in Singapore and overseas, put some banks under pressure. At the same time, the government wanted to create new service and finance jobs, and so had to find ways to attract more foreign financial services companies. All this could only mean more competition for the domestic banks. The old ways of the MAS could not last.

In late 1997, the government faced up to this by appointing a more aggressive MAS chairman, B.G. Lee Hsien Loong, who formed a taskforce to review the future of Singapore's financial market. B.G. Lee sparked a revolution in attitudes at the MAS. Quickly it became clear that long-standing protections would disappear; for instance, more CPF funds would be made available for professional fund managers, and the old stockbroking commission price controls would be removed. Just as in Hong Kong, the old system would have to change, and so the old ways of making profits would have to change too.

Symbolic of this change was the appointment in mid-1998 of a Western banker from JP Morgan, John Olds, as chief executive of DBS. The government of the mostly Chinese Singapore was prepared to look to the West to modernize and grow this big state bank. The changes came quickly; just before Olds took up his formal appointment as CEO on August 1, 1998, DBS announced it was merging with POSB to create a bank large enough to dominate the local market and to step out into the region aggressively. Almost immediately, OCBC, another of the big four banks, brought in an outsider, Alex Au (formerly of Hang Seng Bank in Hong Kong, and then, very briefly, Standard Chartered) as CEO. Singapore banks were preparing for a new era.

Elements of the New Profit Recipe

The changing competitive environments in both Hong Kong and Singapore mean that banks will need to try harder in every arena. Many will find that they cannot be all things to all people, that they must make choices and be prepared to cede some sectors to local or foreign banks that are simply stronger competitors for particular types of business. The small universal bank is unlikely to be successful.

In the corporate banking arena, competitors will need to understand clearly the margins they are able to generate from different segments and the real costs of serving those segments, in terms of operating costs, risk exposure, and use of capital. In many cases, the attractive profits will be in businesses that only a few banks with access to the international capital markets can pursue. But the need to analyze the corporate business with great care will apply to local and multinational banks alike, and to the many second-tier investment banks that will build up costs and risk exposure only to be disappointed by the revenues.

We have seen how the retail area has been very profitable for some banks. However, in the first decade of the 21st century the costs of competing for these revenues will increase. Not all banks will be able to afford the technology and staff training required to remain credible with customers and to garner enough market share. As smart-card instruments such as Mondex expand, and as channels to the customer — through the Internet, ATMs, phone banking, branches and kiosks — proliferate, the costs of leadership will increase. To pay for all these services and convenience, a few banks will start to gain market share and will improve cross-selling success. A few new competitors may be able to follow the route of firms like Virgin Direct of the U.K., by offering direct banking services coupled with innovative product packaging, and attack the entrenched revenues of the market leaders, which will be unable to respond because of fears of profit cannibalization. At the same time, many of the smaller banks will find that in this heady atmosphere they cannot sustain deposit market share, and will be tempted to sell their business to one of the market leaders.

While retail banking will no doubt become a tougher business, retail stockbroking is likely to become very different in both cities. The changes will come as commissions deregulate and as new on-line competitors like Boom, Yahoo, Schwab, and E-Trade enter the markets. Already, in 1998 in Hong Kong, Boom was the leading on-line trader of local stocks and Schwab offered 140 mutual funds that could be purchased on-line. If patterns from other markets hold in Hong Kong and Singapore, then the existing retail brokers will survive only if they start offering asset accumulation and portfolio advice, and find ways to ensure their customers retain a good share of their wealth with them. Trading alone is likely to become a tough business for a full-service retail broker to survive on.

Alternatively, some banks will secure their futures by pursuing niche opportunities. Some will flourish in private banking in the two cities, others will move into the trading markets aggressively. Neither of these two types, however, will be able to survive on business from Hong Kong and Singapore alone, but instead will depend on broader Asia strategies.

All banks will have to manage their balance sheets more aggressively than they had to in the 1980s and 1990s, recognizing declining spreads and thus the need to increase asset turns. So institutions like the Hong Kong Mortgage Corporation, which by 1998 was helping local banks securitize mortgages, and other securitization options will be important. In addition, instruments that restructure balance sheets, such as credit derivatives and interest-rate and currency swaps, will be used more and more.

Just as banks must recognize that nearly all segments of the Hong Kong and Singapore markets will change, they must also recognize that both the HKMA and the MAS will want strong and stable banking systems. Winners, therefore, will focus on the quality of their risk management and lending policies. Those that consistently pursue sound policies can expect to win opportunities and favor from regulators as the markets evolve.

Likely Winners

The structure of the banking markets in Hong Kong and Singapore will change as the markets themselves evolve. Around the turn of the century, there will likely be more mergers than in all of the previous decade, and more forays by international competitors into the heart of the local markets. What will emerge is probably fairly predictable. Consolidation will result in a few dominant local banks in each market plus a few specialist firms. Easier market entry will strengthen some multinational banks, but the strengthened position of the enlarged domestic banks will actually limit the scope for new multinational entrants to fresh approaches like direct on-line banking.

Both markets will definitely see fewer local banks than existed at the end of the 1990s. Already in 1998, Singapore's Keppel Bank and Tat Lee Bank, and DBS and POSB, announced they would merge, essentially reducing the banking market to five local commercial banks and the three active international players: Citibank, HSBC, and Standard Chartered. Similarly, some of the smaller Hong Kong banks will merge or more likely be taken over by their larger brethren. Government permitting, they might even be purchased by international entrants in the local middle-market and retail businesses (such as DBS's entry in 1998).

In retail stockbroking and mutual funds, both markets will see similar trends, as the tougher competitive environment leads to broker mergers, linkages with banks for distribution, and larger mutual fund companies. In both markets, competitors that can build strong distribution and business flows will squeeze out weaker players.

After rushing into both cities in the 1990s, some of the multinational banks are likely to withdraw. Only those dedicated to building large local Asian businesses will have the skills and commitment to succeed in building significant domestic businesses in Hong Kong and Singapore. As of late 1998, Citibank, HSBC, Standard Chartered, and perhaps ABN Amro were well placed to win, and they already enjoy major advantages over any potential new entrants into the truly local opportunities. Besides new-game competitors that try to cream off profits in certain segments, very few banks or brokers will be able to make the investment in multiple channels to challenge the local banks and the three leading international competitors in both cities.

So just as the regulatory barriers in both cities start to decline, and the local banks lose the easy profits they gained in the 1980s and the 1990s, so a new set of barriers will emerge, the barriers of intense competition. Faced with the realities of even larger, more entrenched local leaders, like DBS in Singapore and HSBC in Hong Kong, and the determination of firms such as Citibank to maintain and expand their franchises, many competitors will continue to see Hong Kong and Singapore as a base for regional business, but not many will have significant domestic businesses there.

CHAPTER 10
TAIWAN: FOCUSING FOR VICTORY

• Taipei

•Kaohsiung

Social & Economic Indicators (US$)

Overall	– GDP: $227bn – Population: 22mn – GDP per capita: $12,800 – PPP GDP per capita: $15,370 – 1985–1997 GDP real growth: 7.5% CAGR – Projected 2010 GDP per capita: $37,700 – Exports (% of GDP): $122bn (46%) – Foreign currency reserves (% of imports): $84bn (65%) – % urbanization: 67%
Corporate	– Top 3 sectors: Electronics, IT, Steel – Number of corporations with annual sales >$1bn: 47[2]
Individual	– Annual savings rate: 25% – Average savings per household: $28,000[1] – Home ownership: 76% – Household car ownership: 51%[2] – Telephones /1000 pop: 460[2] – Internet subscribers/1000 pop: 40 – % of 18–22-yr-olds attending university: 45%

Financial Markets & Business Lines (US$)

Overall	– Equity capitalization (% of GDP): $326bn (118%) – Number of listed corporations: 404 – Debt market capitalization[3] (% of GDP): $40bn (14%) – Total domestic loans (% of GDP): $388bn (140%) – Total external debt (% of GDP): $30bn (11%) – Total offshore loans (% of GDP): $20bn (7%) – Number of local banks (>$5bn assets): 25 – Number of foreign banks: 45 – Top 3 banks' market share (deposits): 31% – Maximum foreign ownership of a commercial bank: 30% – Currency convertibility: Partially controlled
Corporate Banking	– Domestic corporate loans (% of GDP): $323bn (117%) – Nonperforming domestic loans: 7%[4]
Retail Banking	– Total consumer deposits (% of total deposits): $161bn (49%) – Total consumer loans (% of total loans): $104bn (27%) – Persons per branch: 4,200 – Persons per ATM: 1,900 – Credit cards per capita: 0.4
Asset Management	– Retail assets under management: $20bn – Total domestic institutional assets: $59bn[2] – Number of asset management firms: 21
Trading	– Number of stock brokerage firms: 236[2] – Average daily equity trading volume: $4.6bn – Average daily FX trading volume: $48bn[5]
Investment Banking	– Total equity issuance (1994–1997 annual avg): $9.1bn – Total debt issuance[3] (1994–1997 annual avg): $9.3bn – Number of domestic M&A transactions >$50mn (1992–1997): 18
Private Banking	– High-net-worth households (>$1mn investable assets): 58,000[1] – Potential private banking assets: $231bn[1]

All figures as of December 1997 unless otherwise indicated.
[1] McKinsey estimates.
[2] Figures as of December 1996.
[3] Maturity greater than 1 year.
[4] Figures as of June 1998.
[5] Figures as of April 1998.

10
TAIWAN:
FOCUSING FOR VICTORY

Between 1992 and 1997, Taiwan's leading conglomerates destroyed US$2.2 billion in shareholder value through their foray into banking. How could corporations with strong track records in their respective industries manage to destroy value of this magnitude? In 1991, banking in Taiwan was generally perceived as a license to print money. Although large, ponderous, and bureaucratically structured, the government-owned banks that dominated the financial sector nonetheless generated an average return on equity (ROE) exceeding 20 percent. When the Ministry of Finance opened up the market to new competitors in 1991, conglomerates felt this was too good an opportunity to miss. Expecting the ministry to grant only a few licenses, these firms scrambled to line up the required US$400 million in capital to apply. Excitement spawned an active underground gray market for applicants' shares in anticipation of which ones would win the right to play.

The Ministry of Finance surprised everybody. By awarding 16 new licenses, the number of competitors increased by more than 50 percent in the course of 1991 and 1992. In 1992 alone, the banking industry's ROE plunged by 10 percentage points. Incumbent government banks, constrained by salary and headcount ceilings, could only stand by and watch as the new competitors poached experienced staff for their fledgling operations. With US$400 million in paid-in capital to leverage through loans, the new banks had little choice but to pursue aggressive growth. The ensuing price competition and salary war rapidly redefined banking industry economics. The initial excitement was replaced by a battle for survival that will continue into the 21st century. Taiwan's leading conglomerates, far from having been granted a privilege, now struggle to find new ways of carving out profits in an intensely competitive and rapidly evolving environment.

Focus or Perish

Banking in Taiwan is challenging, but market share is by no means locked up. Faced with an unprecedented degree of choice, corporations and retail consumers are becoming increasingly sophisticated and demanding. Banks, regardless of their size, are under significant pressure to differentiate themselves through pricing, products, and services. They must do so in a market that is becoming deregulated and made increasingly complex by the convergence of competition across product lines. Traditional boundaries between deposit-taking, lending, stock broking, investment banking, and foreign and local players are being whittled away by market liberalization. Generalist banks that lack a particular product, industry, or customer expertise stand to suffer most. Customer loyalty is gone, and market share is up for grabs in Taiwan.

By the late 1990s, most domestic banks had responded to the changing environment by pursuing aggressive growth across various products and customers. The logic had been that superior scale and bigger revenue streams would generate profits. Instead, intense competition has reduced margins and fragmented individual customer revenue. Banks in Taiwan with traditional organizational structures — where the link between branches and central units is often weak and the coordination across products low — have had difficulty coordinating efforts to lock in customers and profits. More often than not, growth has been achieved through market and product breadth, rather than customer penetration and market depth.

To increase future market share, banks in Taiwan will have to innovate. Competitors will need to use rising customer expectations and the increased complexity of eroding product boundaries to their advantage. Product innovation and integrated services for select customers will be the means of capturing the lion's share of their business. Bank management will have to develop a consensus on where to focus resources, and invest extensive effort to build matching products, operating skills, and organizational structures. The demands on management's time alone will force virtually all banks to sharpen their strategic focus and hone their investments to fit specific product and customer segments.

Continued market liberalization, an emerging split between high- and low-performing banks, and a limited shareholder tolerance for value destruction will lead to consolidation in Taiwan's financial sector — probably by 2005, but certainly by 2010. Financial institutions in Taiwan that do not focus and generate higher returns early in the 21st century, face the prospect of perishing through acquisition or by outright business failure.

Where to Focus?

The critical issue for domestic and international banks in Taiwan is therefore establishing customer and product focus. To arrive at a viable strategy, each bank will have to factor in its existing customer base, relative competitive position, and investment appetite. Banks must also consider Taiwan's economic structure and how it will impact potential risks and profits in financial markets. Successful institutions will weigh all these factors to determine whether to focus on corporate, retail, or institutional customers and products.

Dynamic Economy and Sizable Financial Markets

Taiwan is the 15th largest economy in the world, and the fourth largest in Asia. The four principal cities of Taipei, Kaohsiung, Taichung, and Tainan are home to 59 percent of its population of 22 million, and about 70 percent of its economic activity. Gross domestic product (GDP) per capita rose to US$12,800 by 1997, up from US$7,920 in 1990, and US$2,360 in 1980. Taiwan's economic growth rate of 11 percent through the 1980s slowed to a still-aggressive 7 percent in the 1990s, and is expected to average 6–8 percent from 1998 to 2010. Taiwan's growth has traditionally been export-led, with international, trade-related businesses generating over 40 percent of GDP. As of 1997, Taiwan was the world's largest semi-conductor manufacturer, and maintained over a 50 percent global market share of a broad range of electronic components, including sound cards, display monitors, keyboards, scanners, and motherboards. In many ways, Taiwan is at the heart of the world's international and high-growth technology markets. As such, bankers in Taiwan are compelled to stay abreast of trends in the global marketplace.

Taiwan's large and prosperous economy fared relatively well in the 1997–1998 financial turmoil, in part because it had no foreign currency government debt, and had the fourth largest foreign currency reserves in the world — US$84 billion. When the crisis struck, Taiwan — unlike much of Southeast Asia — was not sitting on an asset bubble; the island's speculative excesses had largely occurred in the late 1980s. Taiwan had paid for its excesses with its own crisis in 1990, when the stock market index plummeted from 12,000 to 2,500 in 9 months. The crash highlighted growing domestic concern over Taiwan's cost competitiveness, and spurred a wave of foreign direct investment by manufacturers throughout the region. Between 1990 and 1997, Taiwan's corporations invested approximately US$84 billion across Asia, making it one of the top three investors in China and much of Southeast Asia. Steps to deregulate its domestic markets spurred greater competitiveness across many domestic industries. Consequently, Taiwan was fundamentally in better shape when the crisis began sweeping Asia in 1997. Further, the economy as a whole was less exposed to the systemic market and banking risks that surfaced in Korea and Southeast Asia during the early part of the crisis.

Historically, Taiwan has maintained growth through difficult periods by remaining flexible in what it produced and with whom it traded. From the early 1980s, and progressively through much of the 1990s, Taiwan shifted its economy from lower-end manufacturing to higher-end products and services. Faced with mounting trade pressures from the U.S., and quick to take advantage of growth opportunities in the rest of Asia, Taiwan was able to diversify its exports away from a relatively high U.S. concentration in the early 1980s. Part of the shift in trade reflects Taiwan's having relocated its manufacturing base to China and Southeast Asia.

The dynamism of the economy has been fostered not only by changes in global market opportunities, but also because corporations are allowed to fail. From 1986–1991, 31 percent of corporations in Taiwan either went bankrupt or changed businesses — a phenomena that continued through the 1990s. This contrasts significantly with Korea, Malaysia, and Thailand, where governments historically played a more active role in supporting what they deemed national interests, or have favored politically connected business owners through "policy loans." The banking market in Taiwan is thus closer to that of global markets, where each counter-party is judged on the merits of its relative business strengths.

Taiwan's dynamic, high-growth economy has spawned one of the largest financial markets in the region. In 1996, capitalization of Taiwan's equity market reached US$274 billion, the fourth largest in Asia. In the midst of the Asia crisis, in early 1998, Taiwan's market leaped to third place behind Japan and Hong Kong as Kuala Lumpur declined. From 1994 to 1997, Taiwan's equity market turnover represented 35 percent of the region's total (ex-Japan). Despite the island's small size and competitive environment, total corporate and retail commercial banking profits of US$3.8 billion (based on Asia's top 500 banks) were the fourth highest in the region in 1996, after Japan, China, and Hong Kong. Medium-sized corporations and retail consumers have traditionally generated the bulk of Taiwan's financial institutions' profits.

Entrepreneurial Corporate Sector

The significant role of small and medium-sized businesses has been largely responsible for Taiwan's dynamism and nimbleness. In 1997, of its one million corporations, 95 percent had sales under US$4 million and 70 percent of the workforce was employed in companies with fewer than 100 employees. In 1997, small and medium-sized corporations (with less than US$2 million in paid-in capital) accounted for approximately 50 percent of total exports, and 36 percent of total manufacturing sales value. Taiwan housed a number of large corporations: approximately 400 exceed US$100 million in annual sales, but only 14 of these were as large as U.S. *Fortune 500* companies in revenue terms. The small and medium-sized corporations are spread throughout the island's principal cities, while the large corporations typically maintain their headquarters in Taipei.

Not surprisingly, a large share of Taiwan's corporate banking profits are from small and medium-sized corporations. Industry participants estimate that these corporations account for over half of total corporate loans. As in other markets, interest spreads for smaller corporations are on average significantly higher — above 150 basis points. Compared to large corporates' 50–75 basis points, smaller and medium-sized corporations are more profitable for banks. Trade financing fees often boost the profitability of small and medium-sized corporations. Historically, however, regulatory limitations on swaps and other derivatives have made it difficult to enhance returns for large corporate customers. Deregulation in the late 1990s facilitated marketing higher-margin risk management products, but banks have had to contend with the limited number of large corporations.

The relative scarcity of large corporations has to some extent capped Taiwan's participation in international investment banking markets. In international cross-border capital markets, Taiwan ranked ninth out of Asia's 11 major countries for total debt and equity issuance volume between 1994 and 1997. In international equity markets, Taiwanese corporations raised US$8.9 billion during this 4-year period, and represented 10 percent of Asia's total cross-border equity volume. Taiwan's participation in international debt markets, however, was much less significant — accounting for only one percent of the US$127 billion of cross-border debt issuance between 1994 and 1997.

By contrast, domestic investment banking markets have been far more active. Between 1994 and 1997, Taiwan's corporations raised US$27.6 billion domestically, making it the second largest local equity-underwriting market in Asia in terms of volume. But thin underwriting fees in Taiwan, averaging only 75 basis points for domestic stock issuance, have made it a medium-sized domestic investment banking market in the region in terms of revenues.

Looking ahead in investment banking, government efforts to privatize 51 state-owned enterprises, which will release at least US$40 billion worth of shares to the public, will create spikes in domestic and cross-border underwriting volumes through 2005. Compared, however, to the likely future underwriting volumes in Japan, China, Korea, and Southeast Asia, underwriting flows emanating from Taiwan will remain only medium-sized through the first decade of the 21st century.

Active Retail Sector

The success of small and medium-sized businesses has placed a large proportion of corporate profits in the hands of individuals. Individuals account for approximately 60 percent of total financial institution revenues, and a higher proportion of profits in Taiwan (Exhibit 10.1). The national savings rate hovered around 25 percent for much of the 1990s. Individual bank deposits totaling US$161 billion in 1997 — an average of US$28,000 per household — made Taiwan the fourth highest savings-per-capita country in Asia after Japan, Singapore, and Hong Kong. Private bankers operating in Taiwan have placed the number of households with more than US$500,000 in investable assets at 50,000–80,000. In the late 1990s, Taiwan was the largest market for Mercedes and the third largest market for Visa in Asia (outside Japan). About one-third of the island's population travels abroad annually. In 1997, homes in Taipei cost an average of US$450,000. By almost all measures of consumer wealth — that is, savings or consumption, in absolute or per capita terms — Taiwan ranks as one of Asia's wealthiest retail markets.

Individual wealth has fostered an active retail financial sector. Consumer and mortgage loans represented 30 percent of total banking loans in 1997, having grown 145 percent between 1992 and 1997. Similarly, credit card issuance expanded 505 percent between 1992 and 1997, making Taiwan third in Asia in terms of cards per capita. Average interest rate spreads on consumer loans and credit card outstanding balances were attractive at approximately 200 and 700 basis points respectively.

The Taiwanese are active traders and investors. Individuals have accounted for over 90 percent of the turnover in the equity market, and have traditionally made up the lion's share of investors in the emerging commercial paper market — which had a turnover of US$739 billion in 1997. Retail domination of Taiwan's trading businesses is unique among countries at similar levels of economic development. In asset management, retail investors are similarly the dominant investment body. In 1997, individual investors owned approximately US$20 billion in unit trusts, making Taiwan the fourth largest retail asset management market in Asia. Given the significant role entrepreneurs play in the economy, it is not surprising that Taiwan is also an attractive base for private banking. Approximately 300 private banking relationship managers — over 10 percent of the total relationship managers based in the region — serve 20,000–30,000 domestic clients from the potential of 50,000 to 80,000 households.

Taiwan is among the three most profitable markets in Asia for Citibank's retail operations, Merrill Lynch's private banking operations, and Fidelity's retail asset management arm. The relative wealth and sophistication of Taiwan's average consumer, which will increase with the economy, makes Taiwan a core retail market in Asia. In terms of absolute size, Taiwan's retail market will retain its

Exhibit 10.1

Sources of Revenue in Taiwan's Domestic Financial Markets: 1997
US$ millions

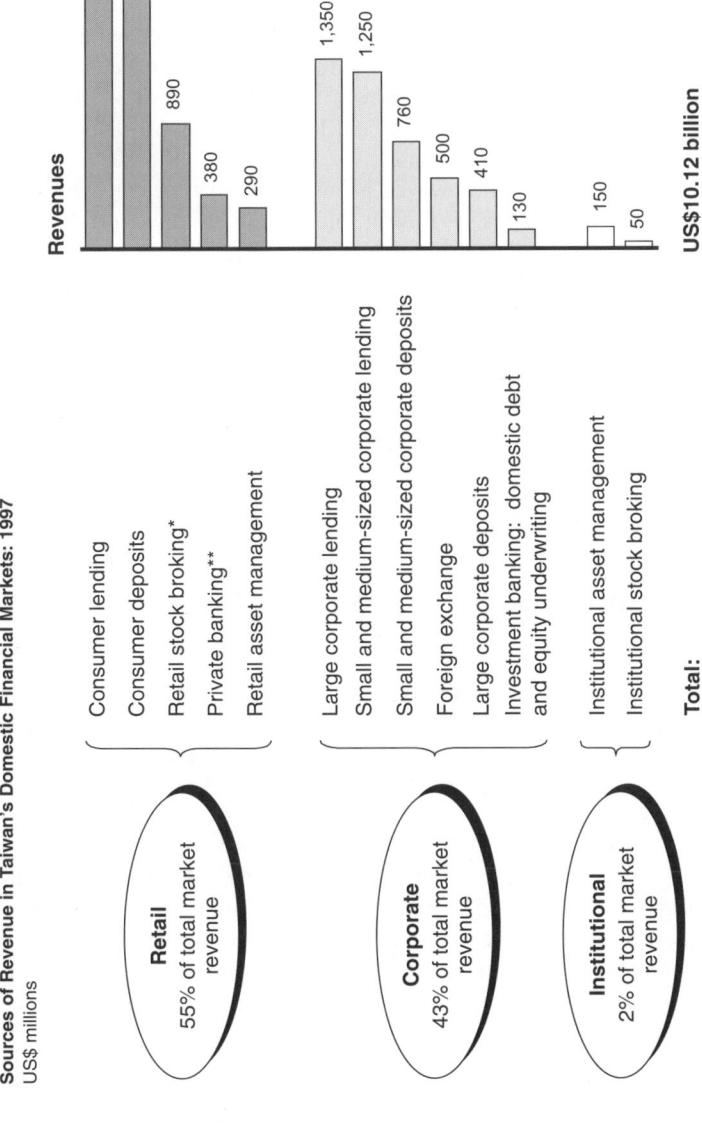

Revenues

Retail
55% of total market revenue

- Consumer lending — 2,170
- Consumer deposits — 1,790
- Retail stock broking* — 890
- Private banking** — 380
- Retail asset management — 290

Corporate
43% of total market revenue

- Large corporate lending — 1,350
- Small and medium-sized corporate lending — 1,250
- Small and medium-sized corporate deposits — 760
- Foreign exchange — 500
- Large corporate deposits — 410
- Investment banking: domestic debt and equity underwriting — 130

Institutional
2% of total market revenue

- Institutional asset management — 150
- Institutional stock broking — 50

Total: **US$10.12 billion**

* Average of 1995 and 1996 because 1997 was an exceptional year: 1997 stock broking revenue = US$2.9 billion.
** Assumes 300 private bankers, each serving 100 clients with an average of US$1 million in assets generating 1% in annual fees/spreads from assets.

Source: Taiwan's Ministry of Finance; Datastream; China Economic Information Company; McKinsey analysis

relative importance in the region for most of the first decade of the 21st century — until some of the region's larger developing markets displace it in terms of absolute size.

Large but Inactive Institutional Sector

The institutional investor base — the sixth largest in the region — is composed principally of insurance companies, and public and private pension schemes. Institutions controlled more than US$60 billion in assets in 1998, but as of the late 1990s, little of that money had been distributed to external financial institutions for management. By 2010, the likely growth in pension schemes, and a greater willingness among insurance companies and the government to appoint outside fund managers, will create a moderately sized institutional asset management market. The institutional sector, however, is only likely to represent a core market for a few financial institutions in Taiwan, most probably those offering global trading and asset management capabilities.

By 2010, a majority of Taiwan's financial market revenues and profits are likely to be derived from retail consumers in banking, stock broking, and asset management. Private banking and small and medium-sized corporate banking will provide attractive opportunities for bankers. Large corporate and institutional investment banking, trading, and asset management will grow, but probably will not eclipse retail opportunities in total profits prior to 2010. While it is clear where most banks in Taiwan should focus customer and product development, it is equally important that they be able to respond to the emerging forces that are reshaping the ingredients for success.

Deregulation: Changes, Opportunities, and Challenges

The forces of change unleashed initially by banking deregulation in 1991 continue to the present. On the one hand, deregulation offers banks greater flexibility for developing new products and services. The erosion of product boundaries gives competitors in Taiwan the opportunity to capture a greater share of targeted customers' business.

On the other hand, deregulation has produced a host of new challenges: domestic banks will increasingly compete head to head with global competitors; increased domestic and foreign competition will continue to erode margins in traditional products; and greater customer sophistication, thanks to wider choices, raises the hurdle for banks' breadth of products, variety of service outlets, quality of service, and, in many cases, level of pricing. Even new products that can generate additional sources of revenue can also create risks that may require new skills and information technology to manage.

As banking deregulation is part of Taiwan's bid to protect its access to the global economy, the current forces driving change are unlikely to dissipate early into the 21st century. Before moving on to the impact of deregulation, it is worthwhile understanding its impetus and objectives.

Objectives of Deregulation

The Ministry of Finance's aggressive banking deregulation program launched in the early 1990s had two objectives: to increase local bank competitiveness in anticipation of greater foreign competition; and to bring the large underground financial market (perhaps as much as 30 percent of the total market in the early 1990s) into the regulatory fold to help protect consumers and manage economic growth.

With these objectives in mind, the government issued 16 new bank licenses in 1991 and subsequently allowed seven trust companies and credit cooperatives to attain full banking licenses. Prior to deregulation, Taiwan's banking market was dominated by government-owned banks. Operating in a protected market with high returns, and staffed by government employees (whose mindset was often closer to a civil servant's than to that of a profited-oriented businessperson), these banks were perceived as lumbering giants that were difficult to change. The growing prevalence of the underground financial market and the realization that small and medium-sized businesses required greater funding than was being provided, was a key impetus for government deregulation.

The decision to act was further spurred by Taiwan's desire to become a member of the World Trade Organization (WTO). Keenly aware of its isolated political status — enforced by mainland China — and conscious of the need to protect its access to global trading markets, Taiwan viewed compliance with WTO market-opening requirements as essential. Like many of the governments in Southeast Asia, Taiwan foresaw that unless it first reformed its financial markets internally, market opening and foreign competition could decimate local competitors.

In the early 1990s, Taiwan positioned its banking deregulation process as part of a loftier objective: to become one of Asia's fully liberalized regional financial centers by 2000. While the type of financial center was not clear, the government systematically attempted to strengthen local financial institutions so they could meet new challenges. As of 1998, 47 domestic banks were fully licensed as commercial banks. While many of these banks are small, they are still larger than the 69 credit cooperatives and 311 agricultural and fishing cooperatives operating in local communities. Government plans called for upgrading these cooperatives to fully licensed banks or merging them into the existing 47 commercial banks. The aim has been fewer, but larger and stronger, competitors.

Government initiatives have further sought to strengthen commercial banks by enabling them to acquire new capabilities. In 1998, domestic banks were granted permission to conduct stock broking, trading, and investment banking activities through subsidiaries. In the past, stock broking and investment banking had largely been the domain of Taiwan's 206 local stock broking firms. By allowing competition across product lines to converge, and enabling domestic competitors to form alliances with global leaders in the late 1990s, the government hoped to spawn a new breed of fortified universal banks that would meet Taiwan's needs in the first decade of the 21st century.

More Competition and Customer Sophistication Results in Value Destruction

Market deregulation such as that initiated in Taiwan typically prompts a battle for customers and profits that plays out in three distinct stages: initial competitor build-up; gradual separation of winners and losers; and market consolidation led by the winners. By 1998, the Taiwan banking market was rapidly making the transition from the first to the second stage.

Stage 1: Competitor build-up

The first stage started in 1991, with the arrival of new banks. In a battle for market share, competitors rapidly strengthened distribution channels. Between 1991 and 1997, ATMs increased fourfold and branches, partially capped by government regulation, increased from approximately 3,800 to 5,000. On a per capita basis, there were at least as many ATMs and branches in Taiwan as in the U.S. or the U.K. New banks have typically led new distribution channels, but the incumbents have quickly followed. By 1998, more than two-thirds of all domestic banks offered basic phone-banking and web-based services — although regulation limited functionality.

The competitive build-up in the early 1990s provided corporate and retail customers with an unprecedented degree of choice. In response to corporate demands for better pricing, average interest rate spreads declined by half from 1992 to 1997. Foreign banks that dealt with the top 400 corporations in Taiwan saw U.S. dollar spreads for short-term financing and syndicated lending decline lower than those commanded by corporations in Hong Kong, New York, and Europe. One foreign banker complained: "Interests rates were uniform before the new banks entered, but now there is no pricing benchmark in Taiwan…it's crazy."

Despite the increased competition among banks, many of Taiwan's largest corporations remained dissatisfied with service. In cash management, for example, corporations expressed frustration over banks' lack of IT infrastructure: "We would like to receive bank statements that show payee data and other information, not just dates and amounts. Also, we would like to give the bank a disk, and the bank can make all the payments via checks and wire." Complaints regarding foreign exchange support have been similar: "Yes, our bank offers 'on-line' prices. But they are one day old! I still have to make phone calls to get the real prices." Many corporations found their domestic banks were unable to provide adequate risk management advice and services.

The largest corporations, accustomed to global banking services, often understand more complex, nontraditional products better than the domestic banks. In 1998, a number of domestic banks were scrambling to learn about capital markets, into which large corporations were tapping for more than a quarter of their total financing needs. The head of a leading privately owned bank with a substantial corporate customer base and direct access to many CEOs and CFOs, noted that it could do little to meet long-standing customers' emerging needs. Without investment banking and trading capabilities, many of Taiwan's traditional commercial banks simply cannot compete for large corporate business.

Competitor build-up equally impacted the retail market. Consumers polled in a mid-1990s McKinsey survey claimed they would switch banks for either better financial terms, improved service, or greater convenience (Exhibit 10.2). By the late 1990s, the average consumer had become increasingly sophisticated: many used multiple banks to secure the most attractive terms on a product-by-product basis, and more than 50 percent were using a secondary bank for credit cards, car loans, and mortgages. Loyalty to a particular bank had all but disappeared: less than 5 percent of customers indicated they would choose a bank based on a personal or long-standing business relationship.

The net effect was that retail banks had become stuck with all the costs of operating a full branch network, but were capturing a declining share of their customers' business. In other developed markets, the key to profitable consumer banking is cross-selling. By capturing several key products of a given customer, such as deposits, mortgage, insurance, credit card, and mutual fund business, banks can generate sufficient revenues to cover personnel, information technology, and real estate costs, and still earn a respectable profit. In banks where cross-selling is successful, 30–40 percent of the customers generate more than 100 percent of the profits, and effectively subsidize the majority of bank customers that are unlikely to ever become profitable. But many banks in Taiwan lacked data on their customer base to assess profitability and target cross-selling initiatives.

Often, commercial banks have been reluctant to jump into new products that could broaden retail cross-selling opportunities. No sooner do they identify a product they would consider, then margins become unattractive for all but the largest players. Take the credit card market for example. In 1995, leading credit

Exhibit 10.2

Switching Factors for Main Banking Relationships
Percentage of respondents considering factor among top three reasons for switching

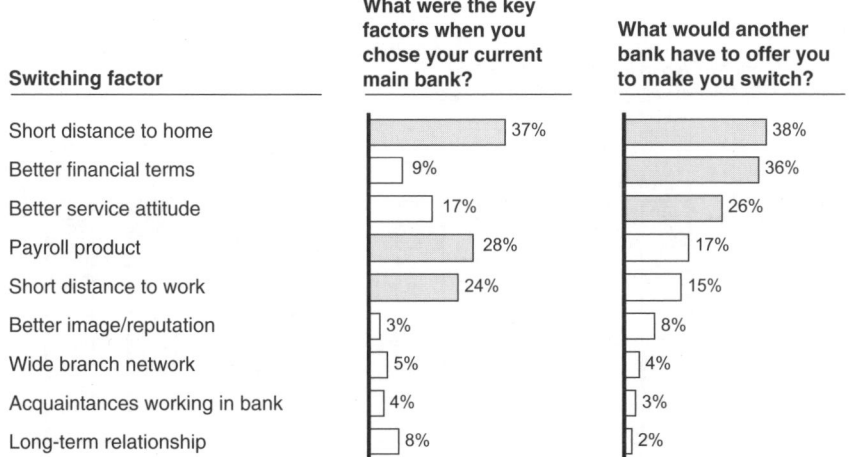

Switching factor	What were the key factors when you chose your current main bank?	What would another bank have to offer you to make you switch?
Short distance to home	37%	38%
Better financial terms	9%	36%
Better service attitude	17%	26%
Payroll product	28%	17%
Short distance to work	24%	15%
Better image/reputation	3%	8%
Wide branch network	5%	4%
Acquaintances working in bank	4%	3%
Long-term relationship	8%	2%

Source: McKinsey Retail Survey

card competitors in Taiwan estimated that a minimum circulation of 200,000 cards was required for a profitable operation, but by 1997 only eight of the 56 domestic credit card competitors had achieved that scale. By 1998, the leading competitors were moving to a no-annual-fee policy to promote market share growth — which effectively raised the break-even point for smaller competitors. Deregulation had opened the door to new cross-selling opportunities in Taiwan, but only aggressive first movers stood to profit.

Stage 2: Separation of winners and losers

In the late 1990s, faced with growing customer sophistication, narrowing returns, and customer relationships that could be as easily lost as won, banks were moving into the second stage of a post-deregulation environment — the separation of winners and losers. Each of the five types of contenders for market share in Taiwan will face a distinct set of challenges as the 21st century unfolds.

The first, and largest group of contenders, with about 60 percent market share in 1997, are the 13 *government banks* (Exhibit 10.3). Their assets ranged from US$3 billion to US$55 billion, with an average of US$25 billion. Despite their size, these banks were struggling to sustain their market leadership. Until they are privatized — and as of 1998 only four had been — these contenders are subject to government micromanagement of their day-to-day operations. At a time when market responsiveness has become critical, these institutions have their hands tied by hiring freezes, limits on the number of senior management, restrictive pay and bonus stipulations, and the inability to fire poor performers. Decisions on branching and management information systems (MIS) expenditure, for example, traditionally required approval from the provincial assembly. This often-lengthy annual process has put these banks at a disadvantage to their new, more nimble counterparts. Although when privatized the banks gain more freedom, they are often years behind newer competitors.

Exhibit 10.3

Market Share by Type of Institution: 1991–1997
Percent; US$ billions; year-end outstanding

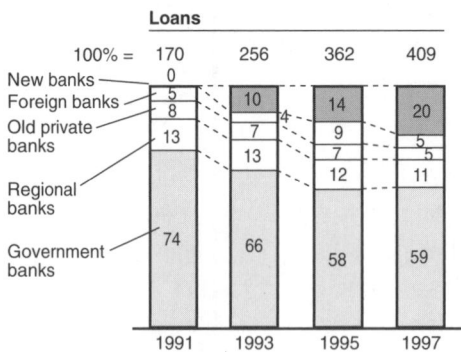
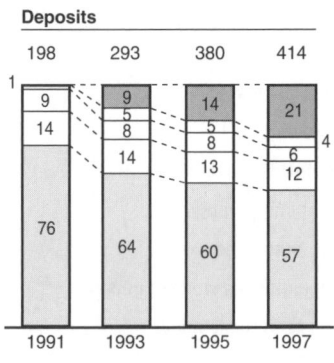

Source: Bank annual reports; Taiwan's Ministry of Finance

The 16 *new banks* — the second largest group — with 19 percent market share in 1997, built their operations from scratch in the early 1990s. Although they started with the advantage of a clean slate, these new banks have had to compete tirelessly for talented staff to propel growth. Relying on branch managers drawn largely from the incumbent government banks, the new banks had to standardize operating procedures, pricing, and credit risk evaluation. In the first several years, a number of the new banks had to curb eager branch managers' decision-making to avoid deep pricing discounts and loan losses.

Efforts to grow by instilling new organizational practices, such as placing several small branches under one manager, encountered regulatory resistance. As of the late 1990s, regulators viewed each branch as a miniature bank, and insisted each one have a general manager with at least 10 years' banking experience. By definition, at one time such bankers had to have worked in an incumbent bank. However, few self-respecting senior bankers, steeped in an incumbents' hierarchy, were willing to be assigned to a small branch. Operational and cultural difficulties, bred by the pre-deregulation environment, were often at the center of new banks' challenges. Such difficulties impeded centralizing expertise to optimize decision-making and minimize costs. With an average of US$5 billion in assets and one percent market share, new banks remained under significant pressure to find ways to achieve critical mass and secure a sustainable market position.

The nine incumbent *regional banks* and three *private banks*, the third and fourth largest groups of contenders respectively, together had a 16 percent market share in 1997. In terms of size, these banks, which average US$5 billion in assets, were closer in market position to the new banks than to their fellow government incumbents. Although they benefit from long-established customer relationships and the freedom to act, these banks continue to face the challenge of defining themselves in a rapidly evolving market. The temptation to do a little bit of everything as products proliferate could stretch them beyond their means. Many regional banks, which historically have been limited to serving customers within their allocated province, were given the freedom through deregulation to expand island-wide by the early 1990s. Their challenge is to identify their competitive advantages and invest accordingly, before joining the island-wide fight for market share.

Despite their number, Taiwan's 45 *foreign banks* had achieved only a 5 percent share of the domestic market by 1997 — the result of branching restrictions that limited access to local deposits. The lack of an efficient New Taiwan dollar interbank market has traditionally made participation in the local markets extremely difficult. Consequently, foreign banks had generally focused on offshore U.S. dollar lending and trade finance. The exception was Citibank, whose domestic assets exceed US$8 billion. In 1997, Citibank generated over US$100 million in annual profits, four times those of similarly sized new banks. Its biggest challenge has been preventing its well-trained staff from being poached by the aggressive new banks. With the domestic market gradually opening up to foreign players, the challenge for other foreign banks, such as ABN Amro — which chose to spearhead its entry into regional retail banking from Taiwan — is to take advantage of unfolding deregulation to invest and become a locally embedded competitor.

Deregulation has gradually allowed all the contenders to address their challenges and gain a more equal footing in the domestic markets. As of the late 1990s, however, the impact of deregulation has been a steady decline in industry performance. Increased competitive pressures between 1992 and 1997 far outweighed the 13 percent annual loan and deposit market growth. Pre-tax ROE fell from 21.1 percent in 1991, prior to deregulation, to just 12.0 percent by 1997. Consequently, all domestic banks created only about US$1 billion in shareholder value from 1992 to 1997. The incumbents created approximately US$3.3 billion in value, while the new banks cumulatively destroyed US$2.2 billion. In other words, shareholders of new banks could have earned US$2.2 billion more if they had simply invested their equity in the Taiwan stock market (Exhibit 10.4).

More telling for the future are the historical trends in value creation and destruction. The industry converged on a 12 percent ROE by 1997 — the cost of capital for banks in Taiwan. In the same year, as much as one-fifth of the profits were derived from strong proprietary investment performance in the Taiwan stock and debt markets. As competition continues to intensify in the 21st century, and proprietary returns vary from year to year, Taiwan's banking industry is poised to fall into net value destruction.

This industry perspective, however, masks an emerging separation of winners and losers. While the incumbent banks, as a group, systematically created value through 1997, an increasing number was beginning to witness returns below 12 percent ROE. Similarly, while new banks cumulatively destroyed value from 1992 to 1997, four new banks surpassed 12 percent ROE in 1997 — the first time in their operating histories. Competitive pressures drove down industry returns and provoked an increasing divergence of individual bank performance (Exhibit 10.5).

Exhibit 10.4

Value Creation/Destruction in Taiwan Banking Industry: 1993–1997
Cumulative

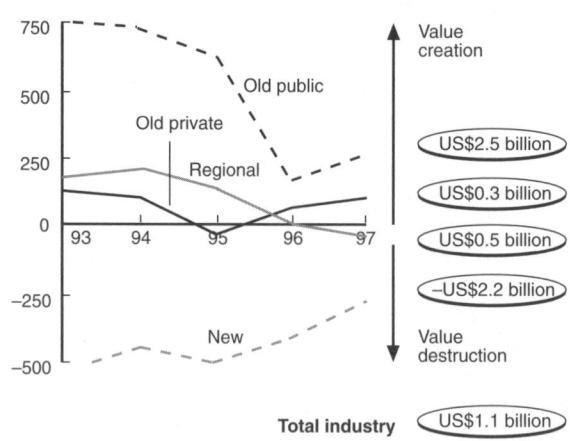

Source: Banks annual reports; Bloomberg; McKinsey analysis

Exhibit 10.5

Divergence of Winners and Losers in Taiwan
Return on equity; percent

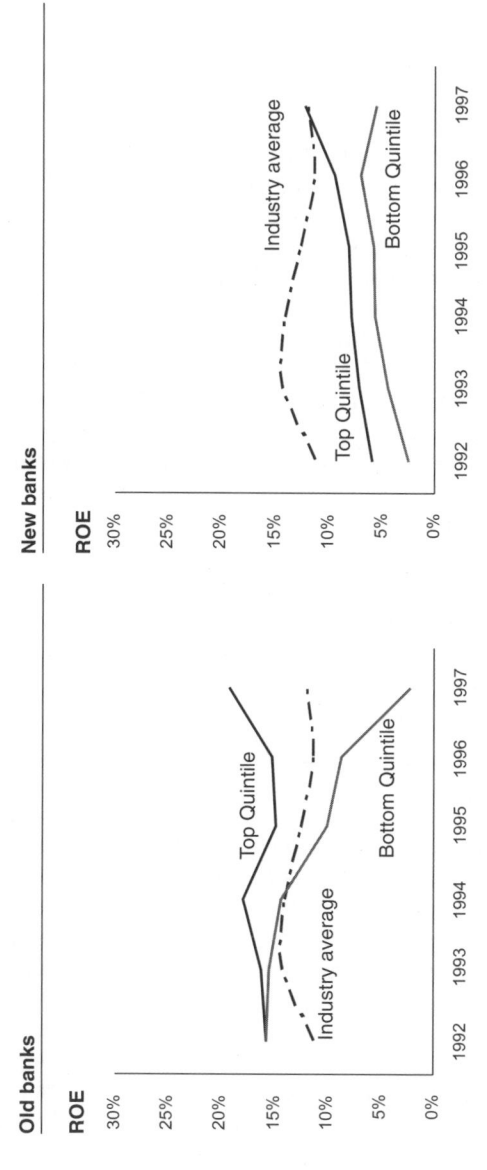

Old banks

New banks

Source: Taiwan's Ministry of Finance; banks annual reports; McKinsey analysis

This resulted essentially from the stronger players upgrading their skills and stealing market share from the weaker contenders. In developed markets, prolonged periods of shareholder value destruction at the industry level typically lead to the stronger banks beginning to acquire the weaker ones to improve scale and operating efficiency, thereby launching industry restructuring through consolidation.

Stage 3: Consolidation

The Taiwan banking market will probably enter the third stage of a post-deregulation environment — consolidation — by 2005. Indeed, in September 1998, legislators began to call for the merger of the country's three largest recently privatized banks to create a single institution possessing scale by global measures. As consolidation unfolds, the survivors are likely to be those institutions that achieve either significant scale and/or above-average market profits. In other words, institutions with a high book value and/or a high market-to-book value are more likely to remain independent (Exhibit 10.6). Smaller competitors with a high market-to-book ratio typically have access to capital, and through their superior skills are able to improve the performance of small, poorly performing banks. Large banks — even those with low market-to-book ratios — have sufficient profits through scale to acquire small, weaker performers. Given that many banks in Taiwan were in the bottom left-hand corner of Exhibit 10.6 — that is, lacking both large book value and high market-to-book ratio — industry consolidation through acquisition appears imminent. Banks that pursue unfocused growth will continue to generate poor returns, and face perishing altogether by 2010 through consolidation or outright business failure.

How to Focus: Innovative Products, Integrated Services

How must banks in Taiwan operate to improve performance? What does focusing on select customers entail? Essentially, banks must rebuild around distinct customer needs in the 21st century. Rather than taking the traditional view of their organizations as a collection of independent branches, processing units, and product lines, banks must reshape around distinct customer groups, such as large corporations, medium-sized entrepreneurs, and retail consumers. As customer sophistication grows, each group will require increasingly differentiated products, skills, and services. Banks that offer integrated services, understand special customer needs, and design pertinent, innovative products, stand to capture the lion's share of their target customers' business. Superior returns will come from consolidating marketing costs across product lines, gaining a more thorough understanding of customer risk, obtaining more business from fewer customers, and facilitating new business growth as a result of a distinctive reputation for proactive and quality service.

Exhibit 10.6

Strategic Control Map of Taiwanese Banks

Book value as of fiscal year-end 1997; market value as of March 3, 1998

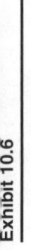

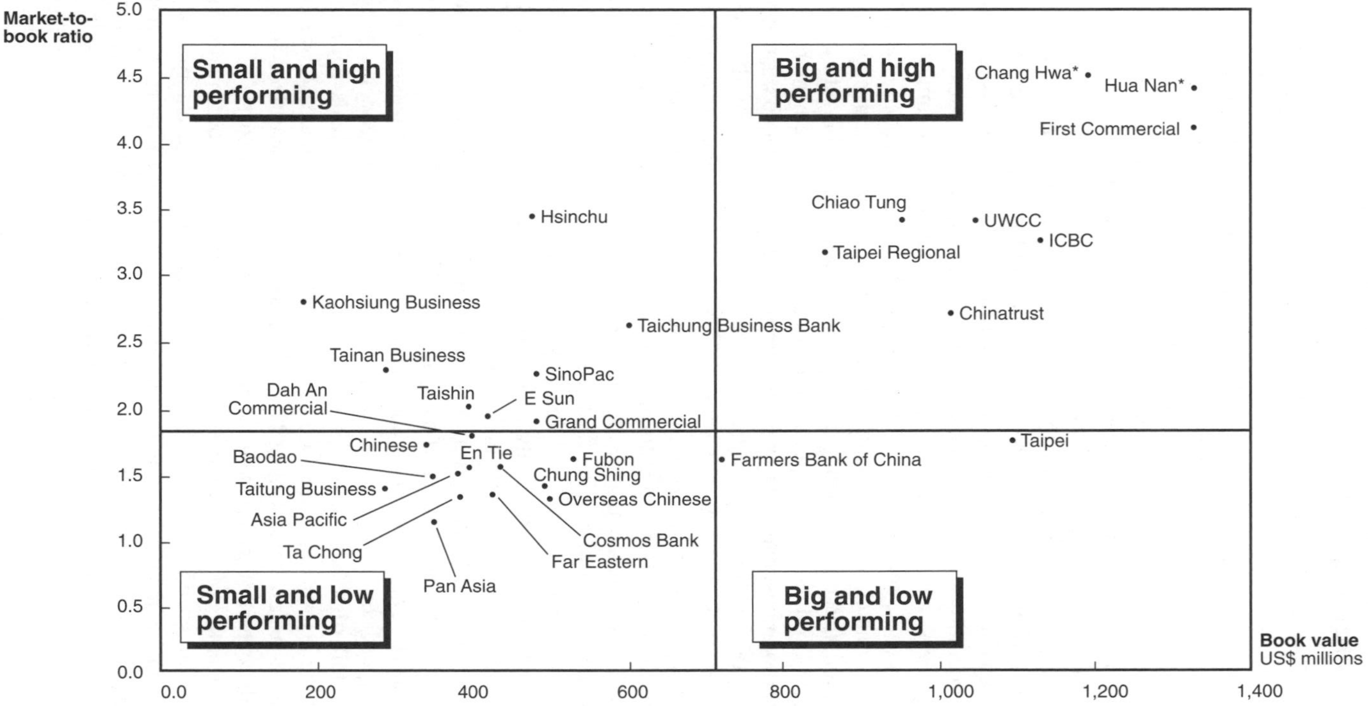

Market-to-book ratio

Small and high performing

Big and high performing

Small and low performing

Big and low performing

- Chang Hwa*
- Hua Nan*
- First Commercial
- Chiao Tung
- UWCC
- ICBC
- Taipei Regional
- Chinatrust
- Hsinchu
- Taichung Business Bank
- Kaohsiung Business
- SinoPac
- Tainan Business
- E Sun
- Taishin
- Grand Commercial
- Dah An Commercial
- En Tie
- Fubon
- Chung Shing
- Overseas Chinese
- Cosmos Bank
- Chinese
- Far Eastern
- Baodao
- Taitung Business
- Asia Pacific
- Pan Asia
- Ta Chong
- Farmers Bank of China
- Taipei

Book value
US$ millions

0.0   200   400   600   800   1,000   1,200   1,400

0.0 0.5 1.0 1.5 2.0 2.5 3.0 3.5 4.0 4.5 5.0

Note: Not listed or traded in OTC market; data unavailable: Bank of Kaohsiung, Bank of Taiwan, The Central Trust of China, Chinfon, Export-Import Bank, Hualien Business Bank, Kaohsiung Business Bank, Land Bank, Lucky, Makoto, Panhsin, Shanghai Commercial & Savings Bank, Sunny, Taiwan Cooperative Bank.

* Market-to-book ratio may be slightly overstated due to historic valuation of investment assets and largely owned branch network.

Source: Taiwan's Ministry of Finance; Bloomberg

Corporate Focus: Build Separate Marketing Teams with Centralized Expertise

The power of focusing is derived from developing organizations, products, and operating skills tailored to Taiwan's core customer segments within the corporate and retail sectors. Up until the mid-1990s, many banks served corporations — regardless of size — at the local branch level. The branch manager and his officers handled marketing: after making an initial credit assessment, they would pass loan documentation to head office for final transaction approval. Larger corporations were easier to target because head office would be familiar with them and they would reward the branch manager's time with higher volumes than could a small or medium-sized corporate. But the one-size-fits-all approach is no longer sufficient in Taiwan. In order to penetrate opportunities and maximize returns, banking specialists — with different skills and product expertise — are required for large corporations, medium-sized enterprises, and small businesses.

The large corporations in Taiwan pose enormous challenges for domestic banks. Due to thin spreads, core lending products are unlikely to ever generate attractive returns. Banks that choose to serve large corporates must develop an entirely new range of capital markets and trading products to generate acceptable returns. Many of these new products *will* require sophisticated risk management tools. To penetrate corporations, banks will have to initiate a new relationship management function capable of providing large corporates with integrated multi-product solutions for a single transaction. To empower relationship managers and monitor the risk a bank takes with a single customer across transactions and across multiple bank departments, significant investments in information technology are necessary. To attract and retain the talent necessary for new products, compensation schemes will have to be revamped, moving from a seniority-based to a performance-based structure. The demands for skill building, organizational restructuring, and cultural change are so far-reaching that only a few domestic banks will ever be likely to serve the large corporate segment in Taiwan profitably.

Government-owned banks privatized in the late 1990s are among the natural candidates for establishing universal banking capabilities to serve large corporates. Thanks to their hefty balance sheets, they have developed strong relationships with Taiwan's largest corporates. These banks' extensive branch networks provide access to retail distribution, which is essential since individuals compose a majority of the investment base of Taiwan's capital markets. A glance, however, at Taiwan's sixth-largest bank, Chang Hwa Commercial Bank, privatized in 1998, highlights the extent of the challenges these banks face (see sidebar).

The complexities of serving large corporates in Taiwan will force many banks to target medium-sized enterprises. Like larger corporates, these enterprises will require specialist account managers and credit officers to integrate product offerings and penetrate opportunities with adequate risk controls. The key to success in this corporate segment is innovating to become an industry insider.

Medium-sized enterprises in Taiwan, as in many countries in Asia, typically maintain three accounting ledgers: one for the bank, one for the tax man, and one for the entrepreneur. The role of account officers in this customer segment often

Chang Hwa Broaches Universal Banking

In early 1998, Chang Hwa Commercial Bank, one of Taiwan's largest banks, established securities and asset management operations to build equity expertise and bring it one step closer to investment banking. It had taken Chang Hwa until 1995 to consider setting up a central unit in its headquarters to coordinate corporate relationships within the branch network. A centralized unit is, of course, only the first step. The challenge is coordinating the central unit and the new securities functions. In leading banks around the world, getting commercial bankers, investment bankers, and securities brokers to work together is a substantial challenge. Differences in age, educational backgrounds, and compensation can bring a bank's best intentions of integrating product capabilities to a grinding halt.

Assuming Chang Hwa succeeds at building new product and marketing capabilities, it will still face significant risk management challenges. In 1997, Chang Hwa's nonperforming loans were 8 percent, twice the industry average. The credit department will not only have to upgrade its approval and monitoring processes for traditional lending, but develop entirely new skills as well. Any advance into securities underwriting requires an ability to value and price corporate cash flows. Subsequent efforts to provide related market-making and securities trading services mean developing a risk management function within credit to track and predict the impact of potential market volatility. It has taken leading international banks years to build methodologies and systems to manage these risks. Banks such as Chang Hwa will either have to partner with a leading global bank or face competing against them for large corporate business in the first years of the 21st century. Alone, its chances of succeeding are marginal — at best.

spans marketing and part of the credit function. Account officers must dig deep enough into medium-sized corporations' operations to assess their true creditworthiness. The last ledger account officers in Taiwan want to rely on is the one for the banks. Successful account officers build effective information networks within select industries. Since they need to call on enterprises' suppliers and customers to validate alleged performance, they should be based in principal cities close to their customers. In developed markets, for example, the U.S., institutions such as Dun & Bradstreet provide indicators of medium-sized corporate performance: revenue growth, earnings trends, credit use, and repayment history.

Banks use this information to augment internal decisions. Although Dun & Bradstreet operates in Taiwan, the lack of accounting transparency stymies its efforts to build a comparable and reliable service.

The burden therefore falls on banks to use their local account officers to provide key input into centralized proprietary databases. These officers must work closely with internal credit specialists (preferably industry-focused), to score less tangible aspects of medium-sized corporations' creditworthiness. They must examine, for example, management talent, market position, sensitivity to raw material costs, and the impact of foreign exchange movements. Credit units serving medium-sized corporations need to maintain a dynamic perspective of industry profitability, competitiveness, and potential threats. As of the late 1990s, few banks in Taiwan had developed rigorous, innovative processes that ensure long-term profitability in this otherwise potentially attractive segment. Building these skills requires the focus of a specialized centralized operation capable of integrating account officers based around the island.

Profitable penetration of the island's 950,000 small businesses requires yet another tack. Traditionally, these businesses have either been handled expensively by dedicated corporate account officers, or underserved as common retail consumers, but neither approach has fully realized this segment's potential profitability. Largely standard products, marketing campaigns, and semi-automated credit processes to handle the thousands of potential customers are essential. Success also depends on centralized marketing and credit units working closely with locally based branch managers to identify and evaluate small business customers.

Retail Banking Priorities: Couple Product Pioneering with Systematic Cross-Selling

For much of the late 1990s, the emphasis in Taiwan retail was on developing innovative products to attract new customers and grow market share. Competitors built product-based sales and credit expertise to capture customers in this increasingly challenging environment. To ensure long-term profitability, leading retail banks must couple enhanced marketing with systematic cross selling. Cross-selling will: help improve individual customer returns as traditional loan and deposit product margins inevitably decline; and strengthen banks' ability to lock in market share by providing broader, one-stop customer services.

A handful of banks in Taiwan are well positioned to augment their product and credit skills with integrated service. Among them, two stand out: Taishin Bank and Bank SinoPac. Within each are vestiges of Citibank's pioneering success in Taiwan: seven of Taishin's senior business unit managers were drawn from Taiwan First Investment and Trust Company, a former Citibank affiliate; and since its start-up, Bank SinoPac has hired over 100 former Citibank employees.

Taishin Bank (1,165 employees, 23 branches in 1997) is owned by the Shin Kong family group, which also owns one of the largest insurance concerns in Taiwan and the island's tenth largest stock broker. Thanks to its relatively small size, Taishin Bank has the organizational flexibility and access to products to cross-sell a broad range of integrated personal financial services. Taishin was the most profitable of the 16 new banks (in terms of ROE) in 1997. From the outset in 1992, it made consumer banking its core business. In 1997, almost half of its assets outstanding were to individuals. Its superior performance has been based on focused products and service innovation. Three high-growth consumer products stand out: *credit cards, car loans,* and *second mortgages.*

Taishin entered the fast-growing *credit card* business in 1993. To distinguish itself, the bank segmented the market and launched the "Rose" card, which targeted women. In tandem with the card, it published a women's magazine to advertise and build brand image. Twenty percent of Rose card holders subscribed to it. Following that success, Taishin initiated the "Apollo" card, which targeted men.

Priming its growth in credit cards was a direct salesforce of 400 people. To stay ahead of the pack, Taishin was the first to provide a 24-hour hotline, and among the first to adopt a no-annual-fee policy for credit cards. By mid-1998, Taishin's card circulation exceeded 500,000, making it the third largest player in Taiwan. In 1997, Taishin's credit card profits exceeded US$10 million on the back of approximately US$200 million in revolving credit. Taishin's profit per card in 1996, prior to adopting the no-fee policy, was approximately US$30 — triple the average profitability per card in the U.S.!

Taishin was similarly aggressive in entering the *car loan* market in 1992, which few banks had targeted for business development. By 1995 it had become the market leader amongst banks, having garnered a 20 percent market share and US$4 million in profits.

Also in 1995, Taishin launched a *second mortgage* loan product, and by 1997 the bank had become an industry leader in the field. The focus in 1998 was expanding its specialist mortgage salesforce from 25 to 50 personnel. Taishin had been able to move aggressively into new forms of lending because it maintained a central credit unit that evaluated risks taken versus returns to be earned. The bank's credit-scoring system evaluated customer loans on a noncollateral basis.

Taishin was building centralized expertise in products and markets where competitors, which had traditionally relied on the generalist expertise of their individual branch managers, had feared to tread. In the case of second mortgage loans, Taishin earned interest rates of 18–20 percent in a market where the main competition was the community loan shark, who charged up to 30 percent. Despite aggressively growing its businesses, Taishin's bad debt ratio as of 1997 was only 1.9 percent — half the industry level.

Focusing has enabled Taishin to develop distinct competitive advantages. By identifying new areas of need, fielding specialist salesforces, using new forms of advertising, and developing centralized credit expertise to evaluate and price risk, Taishin is positioned to achieve an average ROE above 12 percent into the first years of the 21st century.

Bank SinoPac (1,050 employees, 25 branches in 1997) was Taiwan's fifth most profitable new bank in 1997. Like Taishin, SinoPac made a conscious decision from the outset in 1992 to derive a significant share of its profits from the consumer market. With its ranks of credit-sophisticated ex-Citibankers, SinoPac's strategy was to grow with a carefully managed book of risks. By maintaining a clear, focused vision, SinoPac was well positioned to monitor market trends and proactively manage the exposure inherent in its various marketing initiatives. This approach stands out in the domestic market, where historically, detailed breakdowns of asset exposure and problem loans have been anything but transparent to senior management and shareholders.

In the marketing arena, SinoPac has been a leader in designing information systems that enable the front-line to effectively identify and evaluate market opportunities. These systems allow the bank to monitor profitability by product, department, and account. In mature markets, these tools are essential for directing areas for future investment, as well as for developing proprietary knowledge about customers to target cross-selling products and services.

Such management information systems are also the basis for moving to a much more performance-oriented environment. Updated customer information can be used to set targets and evaluate individual account managers' performance — a key for maximizing personnel productivity. In other words, management information is the bridge between the hardware (branches and ATMs) and the software (skills and behaviors). Armed with facts, senior management can build a strong sales culture, the linchpin for success in highly competitive markets such as Taiwan's.

In addition to its strong information position, SinoPac has been a leader in generating innovative products. In 1997, the bank purchased California-based Far East National Bank (FENB) for approximately US$95 million. In early 1998, SinoPac integrated FENB's capabilities to offer distinctive products in Taiwan, labeling them "Continental Financial Services." These new products enabled consumers to borrow U.S. dollars based on the value of their Taiwan property. Additionally, customers will be allowed — on condition of regulatory approval — to make U.S. dollar deposits in FDIC-insured (Federal Deposit Insurance Corporation) accounts in SinoPac's U.S. branch. This was an attractive proposition when banks and currencies were collapsing around the region — and not one that competitors could easily duplicate. To ensure the success of product launch, SinoPac primed 30 account officers to market the new capability to clients. SinoPac excelled by being focused in its marketing and innovative in meeting emerging customer needs.

Taishin and SinoPac are two of a handful of competitors that have focused their efforts and innovated their products and services accordingly. Citibank, Chinatrust, and Fubon Bank are investigating new products, skills, and organizational approaches to better meet customer needs and extract higher returns. Honing new approaches in the corporate and retail sectors is essential to optimize returns and capitalize on industry consolidation.

Competitors Must Focus to Win

The first years of the 21st century will be an important period for domestic and foreign competitors to focus their efforts in Taiwan. The hundreds of banks and nonbank financial institutions (including credit cooperatives and securities firms) operating in Taiwan at the end of the 1990s will probably shrink to fewer than 50 by 2010. Only those that have innovative products and that can selectively build customer-focused organizations are likely to achieve deep customer penetration and survive the three stages of a post-deregulation environment: build-up, separation of winners and losers, and consolidation.

Local winners will spend the first years of the 21st century penetrating and locking in customer relationships by effectively segmenting their customer base and cross-selling an integrated range of deposit, loan, and investment services to best meet customers' financing and investment needs. Armed with superior market knowledge and skills, these local institutions will acquire weaker domestic competitors to achieve a sustainable market position. By 2010, up to ten local contenders (a mix of today's banks and securities firms) and three to five global institutions (that already possess key skills and are willing to invest — possibly through acquisition — to build a substantial platform) will dominate the significant retail, small, and medium-sized corporate banking opportunities in Taiwan.

These same domestic and foreign competitors will probably also dominate retail asset management and stock broking. They will use their superior marketing skills and well-managed distribution channels to match clients and products. An additional three to five local and foreign investment specialist firms will build market share by cooperating with the leaders and by developing specialist sales channels to distribute mutual funds and equities.

By 2010, a subset of the above domestic leaders in retail banking, asset management, and stock broking may have established successful private banking operations. By drawing on customer relationships, product expertise, and marketing skills, a maximum of only five domestic institutions may be able to provide an Asia-focused private banking service. As few domestic institutions are positioned to offer integrated services and global products to high-net-worth individuals today, and given the strength of foreign competition, the private banking market in Taiwan is likely to remain the domain of the world's top 10–20 private banking leaders.

Outside Taiwan, investment banking and institutional trading, through the 1990s, became dominated by fewer than ten global investment banks. With superior risk management skills and extensive global product and distribution capabilities, leading global competitors are often best positioned to provide domestic corporations with the most flexible and least expensive sources of financing. Similarly, 10–20 global fund managers have become clear leaders in capturing institutional asset management business. Having said that, a number of local niche investment banks and asset managers in the U.S. and Europe have developed sufficient expertise to also carve out attractive profits. In Taiwan, perhaps up to three domestic financial institutions will be able to leverage existing corporate and institutional relationships to build sustainable domestic investment banking and institutional asset management businesses. A majority of Taiwan's market share for these businesses, however, will probably be captured by the dominant global leaders.

In the first decade of the 21st century, Taiwan's domestic markets — which are considerably larger than the more internationalized markets of Singapore and Hong Kong — will become an important testing ground for the evolution of banking in Asia. After emerging from years of protected regulation, Taiwan's efforts to fully liberalize will provide important lessons in banking for China and Southeast Asia. Taiwan's experience will shed light on how domestic banks must focus and innovate to survive in a globally competitive marketplace, as well as offer insight to global competitors looking for a niche in one of Asia's dynamic domestic markets.

CHAPTER 11
SOUTHEAST ASIA'S BIG FOUR:
REINVENTING FOR THE 21ST CENTURY

Social & Economic Indicators (US$)		Indonesia	Malaysia	Philippines	Thailand
Overall	– GDP:	$209bn	$95bn	$82bn	$159bn
	– Population:	202mn	22mn	73mn	62mn
	– GDP per capita:	$1,100^2	$4,600^2	$1,200^2	$3,100^2
	– PPP GDP per capita:	$4,140	$9,835	$3,020	$8,165
	– 1985–1997 GDP real growth:	6.6% CAGR	7.6% CAGR	3.8% CAGR	8.5% CAGR
	– Projected 2010 GDP per capita:	$1,500	$7,200	$2,000	$5,900
	– Exports (% GDP):	$54bn (26%)	$79bn (83%)	$25bn (31%)	$59bn (37%)
	– Foreign currency reserves (% of imports):	$16bn (30%)	$20bn (23%)	$8.6bn (24%)	$26bn (29%)
	– % urbanization:	34%	54%	53%	36%
Corporate	– Top 3 sectors:	Manufacturing, Agriculture, Trading	Electronics, Machinery, Chemical	Manufacturing, Agriculture, Trade	Manufacturing, Wholesale & Retail Trade, Public Administration
	– Number of corporations with annual sales >$1bn:	8	24	9	13
Individual	– Annual savings rate:	37%	41%	16%	36%
	– Average savings per household:	$950[1]	$25,000[1]	$2,500[1]	$6,000[1]
	– Home ownership:	67%	60%	70%	25%
	– Household car ownership:	23%[2]	72%	19%	12%
	– Telephones/1000 pop:	14[2]	174[2]	30[2]	77[2]
	– Internet subscribers/1000 pop:	0.4	11	1	2
	– % of 18–22-yr-olds attending university:	10%	12%	26%	19%

All figures as of December 1997 unless otherwise indicated.
[1] McKinsey estimates.
[2] Figures as of December 1996.
[3] Maturity greater than 1 year.
[4] Figures as of June 1998.
[5] Figures as of April 1998.

Financial Markets & Business Lines (US$)		Indonesia	Malaysia	Philippines	Thailand
Overall	– Equity capitalization (% of GDP):	$54bn (26%)	$97bn (102%)	$31bn (38%)	$36bn (22%)
	– Number of listed corporations:	281	703	221	431
	– Debt market capitalization[3]				
	(% of GDP):	$13bn (6%)	$39bn (41%)	$30bn (37%)	$16bn (10%)
	– Total domestic loans (% of GDP):	$128bn (62%)	$122bn (128%)	$57bn (69%)	$185bn (116%)
	– Total external debt (% of GDP):	$136bn (65%)	$43bn (45%)	$45bn (55%)	$92bn (58%)
	– Total offshore loans (% of GDP):	$7bn (3%)	$7bn (7%)	$0 (0%)	$8bn (5%)
	– Number of local banks (>$5bn assets):	8	8	3	8
	– Number of foreign banks:	10	13	14	21
	– Top 3 banks' market share (deposits):	28%	34%	29%	54%
	– Maximum foreign ownership of				
	a commercial bank:	100%	30%	60%	100%
	– Currency convertibility:	Open	Controlled	Partially controlled	Open
Corporate Banking	– Domestic corporate loans (% of GDP):	$124bn (59%)	$102bn (107%)	$35bn (43%)	$167bn (105%)
	– Nonperforming domestic loans:	50–70%[4]	20–25%[4]	15–20%[4]	35%[4]
Retail Banking	– Total consumer deposits (% of total deposits):	$22bn (50%)	$49bn (46%)	$26bn (70%)	$67bn (70%)
	– Total consumer loans (% of total loans):	$9bn (11%)	$28bn (29%)	$4bn (18%)	$35bn (19%)
	– Persons per branch:	11,500	5,300	4,300	6,100
	– Persons per ATM:	48,600	5,500	22,300	11,300
	– Credit cards per capita:	0.01	0.2	0.02	0.04
Asset Management	– Retail assets under management:	$0.8bn	$1.8bn	$0.1bn	$2.1bn
	– Total domestic institutional assets:	$6.4bn[2]	$82bn[2]	$19bn[2]	$15bn[2]
	– Number of asset management firms:	64	30	185	12
Trading	– Number of stock brokerage firms:	142[2]	57[2]	185[2]	46[2]
	– Average daily equity trading volume:	$0.2bn	$0.6bn	$0.1bn	$0.1bn
	– Average daily FX trading volume:	$1.5bn[5]	$1.1bn[5]	$0.8bn[5]	$3.0bn[5]
Investment Banking	– Total equity issuance (1994–1997 annual avg):	$7.3bn	$4.4bn	$3.2bn	$4.2bn
	– Total debt issuance[3] (1994–1997 annual avg):	$7.9bn	$12.7bn	$8.9bn	$12.7bn
	– Number of domestic M&A transactions >$50mn (1992–1997):	47	141	32	22
Private Banking	– High-net-worth households (>$1mn investable assets):	64,000[1]	22,000[1]	33,000[1]	33,000[1]
	– Potential private banking assets:	$257bn[1]	$66bn[1]	$99bn[1]	$117bn[1]

All figures as of December 1997 unless otherwise indicated.
[1] McKinsey estimates.
[2] Figures as of December 1996.
[3] Maturity greater than 1 year.
[4] Figures as of June 1998.
[5] Figures as of April 1998.

11
SOUTHEAST ASIA'S BIG FOUR:
REINVENTING FOR THE 21ST CENTURY

Many of Southeast Asia's family business empires have at some point had a major stake in banking. The Tejapaibul family of Thailand is one example. Starting in the liquor and pawnshop businesses in the early 1900s, the Tejapaibuls became a dominant player in Thailand's distillery industry by the 1950s. Udane Tejapaibul, the eldest of 11 children, led the family businesses from the 1940s well into the late 1990s, and moved the family into banking in 1950 with the establishment of Bangkok Metropolitan Bank (BMB). Up until the late 1980s, when domestic and global capital markets became a viable means for Southeast Asia's leading families to fund expansion, owning a bank was the best way to ensure access to capital. In the course of the 1970s and 1980s, the Tejapaibuls extended their banking interests by acquiring controlling stakes in Thailand's First Bangkok City Bank and Bank of Asia.

However, family squabbles in the early 1980s slowed the family's momentum. In 1981, Udane sold the family stake in Bank of Asia to one of Thailand's leading liquor families. A near-collapse of First Bangkok City Bank in 1986 drove Udane's brother, who headed the bank, into hiding and led to a forced sale of the family's equity to a Thai whisky magnate. In the early 1990s, Thailand's central bank became increasingly concerned about how BMB was managed, believing that up to 60 percent of the bank's loans flowed to related Tejapaibul companies. As a result, in 1993, the central bank took greater control of BMB by inserting a managing director, a board member, and a personal advisor to the bank's family president. BMB's troubles continued into 1996 when it made U.S. headlines for being the only foreign bank in U.S. history, other than Daiwa Bank, to ever have its U.S. operations shut down by the federal government. American regulators charged BMB with irregular banking practices and falsifying records.

The Tejapaibuls' involvement in banking came to an unceremonious end in early 1998. Faced with nonperforming loans in excess of 40 percent in the wake of the crisis, the family turned to Taiwan in search of friendly investors. But banks there balked at the family's asking price and unwillingness to relinquish management control. In January 1998, left with little choice, 84-year-old Udane stepped down as chairman as the Thai government recapitalized BMB, exchanging the family's implicit debt from the recapitalization for equity. In the process, the government deeply discounted the value of BMB shares, forcing the Tejapaibuls to realize a loss of close to US$100 million. The price of trying to retain management control was high indeed.

The End of an Era

As the Tejapaibuls witnessed their final moments in banking, they perhaps derived some comfort in knowing that they were not alone. Indeed, as the Thai government took over BMB, banks that the Tejapaibuls had previously invested in were experiencing a similar fate. Within the same few weeks, First Bangkok City Bank came into government hands after failed merger talks with Citibank, and Bank of Asia announced that ABN Amro would acquire a 75 percent stake.

The 1997–1998 crisis marked the end of a banking era across Southeast Asia. In Thailand, Malaysia, Indonesia, and to a lesser extent the Philippines, the shortcomings of informal relationship-based lending in an environment of excessive enthusiasm and weak controls were ruthlessly exposed. While it is essential to understand what caused the crisis, it is ultimately more important to understand the new forces unleashed onto the region's banking markets. Chief among these are massive financial industry consolidation, increasing foreign competition, a gradual but inevitable change in key decision-makers in banks, corporations, and governments, and the rise of new customer needs. In the first decade of the 21st century, these forces will shape a new era of opportunity in Southeast Asia in which banking practices and successful strategies will rapidly approach those of the developed world.

To capture the opportunities, financial institutions will have to reinvent themselves. Doing so will require many to secure new lifelines. Long-held notions of ownership and control will have to be sacrificed in exchange for capital. Moreover, the need for rapid aggressive strategic restructuring will require institutions to alter sacred assumptions about who should lead, what products to pursue, which customers to keep or discard, and, for many, which long-standing employees to retain.

Restructuring done well will result in lean, highly motivated, and focused organizations. Done badly, institutions will emerge from a difficult process demoralized and fragmented, ultimately with insufficient direction to pursue distinctive market leadership in the region's recovering markets. To secure leadership and garner sustainable profits, long-term winners in Southeast Asia will have to build world-class skills that demand unprecedented and continuous investments in technology and people. These investments will pay off only if institutions learn how to develop and delegate responsibility to strong managers throughout the organization.

A well-managed transformation will enable Southeast Asia's most dynamic competitors to reinvent themselves for the 21st century. The process will be as much about changing operating culture and expectations as about introducing new technical skills. Fewer than 100 of the more than 500 financial institutions (including banks, finance, and securities companies) in Southeast Asia at the end of 1997 are apt to be able to implement the dramatic changes required to endure through 2010. Joining the domestic survivors will likely be 10–15 global competitors that will take advantage of the post-crisis turmoil to embed themselves in Southeast Asia's domestic markets. By 2010, observers are likely to look back on the 1997–1998 crisis as the period that ushered in true global capabilities and competitiveness in Southeast Asian banking.

An Era of Rapid Development and Opportunity

In the decade preceding the 1997–1998 crisis, the financial markets of Thailand, Malaysia, Indonesia, and the Philippines (Southeast Asia's "Big Four") grew rapidly. While these four markets are clearly very different in terms of absolute economic and social evolution (refer to country data pages), their financial markets witnessed similar growth patterns, product development, regulatory change, and competitive dynamics. These similarities make it possible to describe the four markets in parallel.

Unprecedented economic growth

The decade leading up to the crisis was characterized by exceptional growth. Thanks to the relatively low cost of raw material and labor, Southeast Asia expanded rapidly on the back of growing export markets. Between 1986 and 1996, exports grew threefold across Southeast Asia, and represented, on average, 39 percent of each country's GDP by 1996. These exports helped fund the region's industrialization. For most of the decade, agricultural workers poured in from the countryside to take jobs in expanding manufacturing and service industries. By 1996, Kuala Lumpur, Bangkok, Manila, and Jakarta housed, on average, 9 percent of their country's populations and were the source of, on average, 30 percent of national income. The wealth created in and around these cities fueled rapid rises in national incomes. Between 1986 and 1996, GDP per capita grew from US$1,700 to US$4,600 in Malaysia, from US$820 to US$3,100 in Thailand, from US$530 to US$1,200 in the Philippines, and from US$480 to US$1,100 in Indonesia.

Industrialization and the concentration of income in urban centers spawned an emerging middle class in all four countries. By 1996, approximately 5.9 million out of a total 69 million households in Southeast Asia earned more than US$10,000 a year. These households were avid purchasers of large-ticket consumer items. From the early to mid-1990s, 2.8 million cars, 4.9 million refrigerators, and 4.9 million washing machines were sold across Southeast Asia's Big Four. For those in the middle class and the millions of others living in and on the edge of Asia's megacities, amenities of the modern industrialized world were either at hand or appeared tantalizingly close to those who could not yet afford them. Thus, the opportunity to improve quality of life was a very real driver of Southeast Asia's rapid economic development.

Financial boom

Financial institutions benefited substantially from the region's growing industrial base and rising national wealth. Despite the absolute increases in consumer spending, national savings rates rose steadily throughout the decade leading up to the crisis: rising from 32 to 42 percent of national income in Malaysia, from 26 to 36 percent in Thailand, from 27 to 34 percent in Indonesia. The Philippines was the outlier with savings rates hovering at 18 percent. These high rates swelled financial institutions' deposits. Between 1986 and 1996, domestic deposits grew, on average, 22 percent annually across Southeast Asia's Big Four, reaching

US$490 billion by 1996. This represented 20 percent of total consumer deposits in Asia outside Japan. That same year, consumer deposits per household reached US$18,200 in Malaysia, US$9,100 in Thailand, US$2,500 in the Philippines, and US$1,300 in Indonesia.

Strong economic growth, increasing capital investments in industry, and high domestic savings rates fostered a financing boom. Local lending in these countries expanded sixfold between 1986 and 1996. The average leverage of these economies, expressed in terms of total loans to GDP, at the end of the boom decade were 110 percent for Indonesia and the Philippines, and 150 percent for Malaysia and Thailand. The ratio of total Southeast Asian loans to GDP was one-and-a-half to three times proportionally greater than that of the U.S. by the late 1990s. The demand for new capital was ravenous.

Southeast Asia's capital markets boomed on the back of this demand. Between 1990 and 1996, equity market capitalization increased by between 320 percent and 1,300 percent. Following closely were Southeast Asia's domestic debt markets, which saw capitalization expand six times in this same period. In keeping with the new capital market age, corporations and governments in Southeast Asia's Big Four extended beyond their home markets and actively tapped global equity and debt markets. Each country tapped between US$12 billion and US$24 billion from the international capital markets between 1994 and 1997 (Exhibit 11.1).

In the decade preceding the crisis, foreign capital played an important role in the growth of Southeast Asia's financial markets. Enthusiastic global investors owned roughly US$200 billion of Southeast Asian equities, an average of 33 percent of domestic-market capitalization by the end of 1996. Creditors, primarily Japanese and Western banks, extended more than US$300 billion in credit to

Exhibit 11.1

Cross-Border Debt and Equity Issuance: 1994–1997
US$ billions

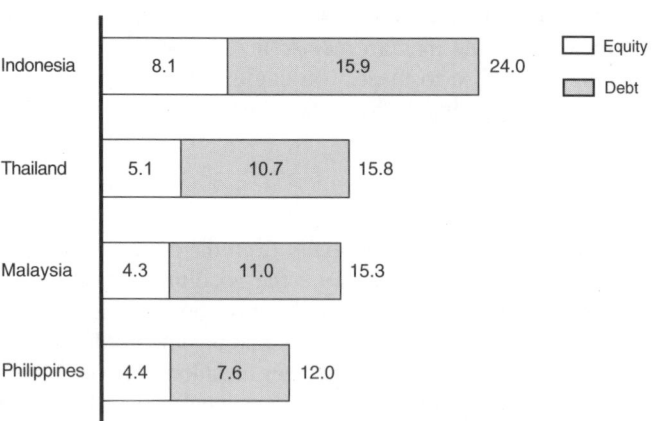

Source: Bondware

Southeast Asia by the end of 1996: US$40 billion to Malaysia, US$40 billion to the Philippines, US$90 billion to Thailand, and US$130 billion to Indonesia. Altogether, foreign credit represented 39 percent of Southeast Asia's total loans.

Protected but deregulating markets

At the center of the deposit, lending, and capital market boom were the protected domestic financial institutions. Domestic institutions intermediated not only local funding, but also much of the foreign lending and investment in local enterprises. Foreign investments often had to pass through local securities firms, while foreign lending was frequently channeled through domestic banks that borrowed in dollars and lent in local currencies. Domestic institutions profited from Asia's boom with little immediate threat of direct foreign competition. Outside Indonesia, where foreign banks could own up to 85 percent of joint ventures, foreign competitors had limited market access. In Malaysia, foreign banks held 16 of the 37 full banking licenses granted before the licensing freeze in the early 1980s. But foreign banks were prohibited from opening new branches and limited to employing a maximum of two expatriates. As the Malaysian market grew in the 1990s, foreign bank market share was quickly diluted. Twenty-one and 14 foreign banks operated in Thailand and the Philippines respectively, but until 1997 they were restricted to a handful of branches.

Up to the 1997–1998 crisis, foreign players were forced to play at the margin of Southeast Asia's rapidly expanding local financial markets. Global investment banks could handle cross-border underwriting but were largely barred from participating in the bigger local underwriting markets. International corporate and retail banks, with few branches and limited access to local funding, could participate actively in the foreign exchange markets yet were limited to niche positions. Only the private banks, which kept a low profile from offshore centers in Singapore and Hong Kong, had reasonably unfettered access to their targeted high-net-worth clientele in Southeast Asia.

Incumbent local financial institutions in Southeast Asia, however, did not stand entirely unchallenged in their home markets during this high-growth era. Governments, aware of strong WTO pressure to open markets, adopted policies to increase local competition and strengthen domestic institutions. The most dramatic opening was in Indonesia, where the number of fully licensed banks grew from 20 to 240 between 1988 and 1996. In Thailand (which had 15 local banks in 1997), Malaysia (20), and the Philippines (30), banking licenses remained tightly restricted between 1986 and 1996.

Though they kept a tight lid on the number of banks, Thailand and Malaysia allowed domestic finance companies to burgeon. In Thailand, the lending market share captured by the finance companies grew from 13 to 25 percent between 1986 to 1996, while in Malaysia finance companies' market share increased from 18 to 33 percent in the same period.

The erosion of product boundaries provided a further boost to domestic competition. By 1989 and 1991, select banks in Indonesia and the Philippines respectively, could apply for universal banking licenses, greatly increasing competition between traditional banks and the newer securities firms. In Thailand and Malaysia, universal banking licenses were not issued, but many banks were able to participate in all but name by becoming important shareholders in new security companies. On the consumer front, banks across the Big Four were increasingly permitted to market new products such as mutual funds and insurance, marking a clear trend in the convergence of competitor types.

Along with changes allowing new competition and products, regulators in Southeast Asia relaxed controls on interest rates. Indonesia did so as early as 1983, the Philippines in 1986, Malaysia in 1987, and Thailand as late as 1990. Pricing deregulation allowed local financial institutions to compete openly for customer business for the first time. Interest rate deregulation was crucial to growth of the newer and smaller finance companies, which needed to offer higher interest rates to attract consumer deposits. As a result of interest rate deregulation, lending spreads declined from an average of 580 basis points in 1986 to 310 basis points by 1996 across the Big Four. Of course, Southeast Asia's largest corporations were commanding spreads as little as 25 basis points for short-term lending up to the eve of the crisis.

Rashid Hussain: Riding the Rising Wave

In the decade preceding the 1997–1998 crisis, aggressive institutions prospered in Southeast Asia's fast-growing and still largely protected domestic financial markets. It remains to be seen, however, whether these institutions can parlay their past successes into solid 21st century market leadership.

The rapid rise and uncertain future of Malaysia's Rashid Hussain is one such tale. Rashid, educated in the U.K., initially worked with the old-line brokerage firm of Strauss Turnbull in London from 1971 to 1975. In 1976, he joined Malaysia's Bumiputra Merchant Bank, where he stayed for the next 7 years. During this time he was seconded to Rothschild in London, Salomon Brothers on Wall Street, and Daiwa in Tokyo. By the time he set up his own brokerage operation in 1983, he had seen how some of the world's best did business. By 1988, his firm became the first securities house to list on Malaysia's stock exchange. Flush with cash from his public offering and growing profits, in 1990, he was able to acquire 20 percent of a local bank and rebrand it the Rashid Hussain Bank.

Between 1992 and 1997, Rashid Hussain's group profits grew eight times to US$149 million. The group's success was the result of being an aggressive first mover. It was the first to introduce Islamic broking, telebroking, unit trusts, and stock lending, as well as the first Malaysian brokerage house to try to disintermediate foreign brokers by establishing direct links with foreign investors through offices opened in 1995 in New

York and London. Having developed a strong brokerage base at home, Hussain broadened his reach regionally by acquiring stakes in brokerages in Singapore, Indonesia, and the Philippines. But more central to profits was the Hussain group's dominance in the domestic investment banking markets. The group led underwriting for a third of all IPOs in Malaysia between 1993 and 1996. In the same period, it was the largest underwriter for long-term debt, ranked second for all equity rights and short-term debt issues, and third in syndicated lending.

By interweaving the underwriting, brokerage, and commercial banking worlds, Rashid Hussain was able to simultaneously serve a broad range of corporations' financing needs and capture significant profits in the largest retail and institutional equity broking markets in pre-crisis Asia, outside Japan. Acquisitions of Malaysia's Kwong Yik Bank in 1996 and the failed Sime Bank in early 1998 (in total worth close to US$1 billion) secured the group's position as the second largest bank in Malaysia.

The financial crisis, however, took its toll on Hussain's ambitious plans, and the group suffered a loss of US$246 million in its 1997 fiscal year. In November 1998, Hussain's control of his empire came to an abrupt end with the government's announcement of a US$870 million rescue plan. This bailout effectively gave the government nearly 30 percent controlling stake in the group, while reducing Hussain's holding from 29.6 to 17.5 percent. Only time will tell whether Hussain can draw on past experience to hammer out a new path to success in the first decade of the 21st century.

Significant changes in market structure

Regulatory changes affecting everything from pricing to the number of competitors resulted in significant changes in market leadership. Measured in terms of loan assets, only half of Southeast Asia's top 20 banks in 1986 were still in the top 20 in 1997. The banks that stayed on top grew their loan assets an average of seven times between 1986 and 1996 and dominated smaller banks and new finance companies (Exhibit 11.2). In all places except Indonesia, where the largest banks remained state-owned and were long plagued by nonperforming loans, larger competitors generally performed as well and often better than smaller ones, achieving an average return on equity of 18 percent between 1986 and 1996. This fast growth resulted in a growing gap between market leaders and new smaller players, though all competitors fought head-to-head for market share.

On the eve of the crisis, Southeast Asia's financial markets were exponentially larger, more diverse, sophisticated, and competitive than when they began their rapid expansion a decade earlier. But there was a darker side to the boom decade.

Exhibit 11.2

Estimated Market Share of Top Five Banks: 1997
Percent

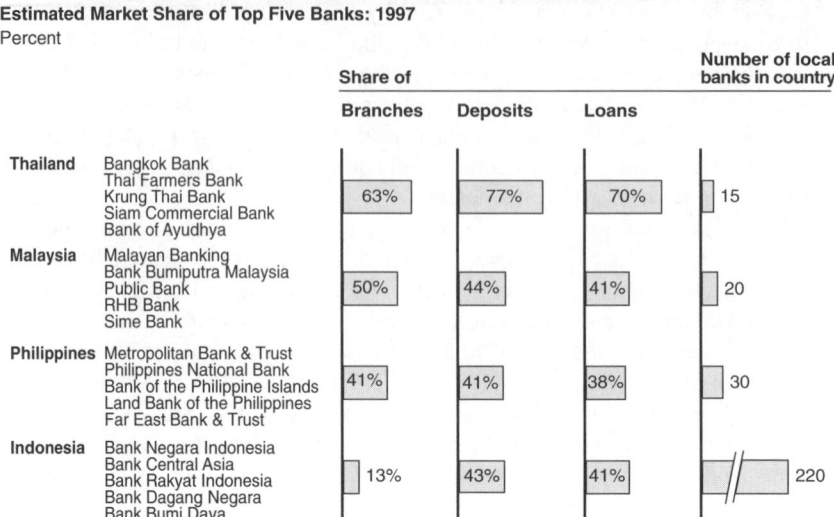

		Share of			Number of local banks in country
		Branches	Deposits	Loans	
Thailand	Bangkok Bank Thai Farmers Bank Krung Thai Bank Siam Commercial Bank Bank of Ayudhya	63%	77%	70%	15
Malaysia	Malayan Banking Bank Bumiputra Malaysia Public Bank RHB Bank Sime Bank	50%	44%	41%	20
Philippines	Metropolitan Bank & Trust Philippines National Bank Bank of the Philippine Islands Land Bank of the Philippines Far East Bank & Trust	41%	41%	38%	30
Indonesia	Bank Negara Indonesia Bank Central Asia Bank Rakyat Indonesia Bank Dagang Negara Bank Bumi Daya	13%	43%	41%	220

Source: Asiaweek Financial 500; central bank reports; McKinsey analysis

An Era Riddled with Structural Weaknesses

In late 1997 and early 1998, most people involved in the financial industry, from Udane Tejapaibul of Thailand to Prime Minister Mahathir of Malaysia, to bankers and analysts globally, could only watch numbly as Southeast Asia's financial institutions and economies unraveled. Initially, faced with nonperforming loans ranging between 20 percent and 50 percent of total loans and widespread economic recession, players and observers began to search frantically for the cause. How could seemingly healthy economies suddenly collapse? How could domestic and foreign bankers, and the global capital markets so involved in Southeast Asia's rapid development have missed the warning signs?

One school of thought is that Southeast Asia was a victim of widespread panic ignited by a currency collapse in Thailand that, with the help of "unscrupulous" speculators, created contagious fear, resulting in creditors and investors withdrawing funds from the fundamentally different economies of Malaysia, Indonesia, and the Philippines. Under this scenario, bankers and analysts were forgiven for not predicting events that were not supposed to occur. Another school points to excessive optimism, insufficient transparency, government corruption, weak regulators and bankers, and misguided capital allocation as fundamental causes of the crisis. Using this reasoning, bankers and analysts were blamed for getting caught up in the optimism, but partially forgiven because they often lacked the facts to make sound judgments.

In reality, both schools are right. Panic and contagion did exacerbate real problems in all Southeast Asian financial sectors. In an ideal world, stricter regulatory oversight, and greater transparency earlier could have avoided a full meltdown. While there may be some merit in limiting the potential for future speculative excesses in emerging markets, the real work of the early 21st century must focus on repairing the fundamental problems in the region's financial sector that allowed widespread panic. Until these problems are addressed, the confidence and capital needed to jump-start Southeast Asia's growth engine are unlikely to return.

Understanding three major financial sector weaknesses — informal bank decision processes, lack of reporting transparency, and insufficient regulatory enforcement and independence — is therefore critical to fully understanding the evolution of Southeast Asia's financial markets and the challenges that will confront financial institutions seeking to reinvent themselves. The similarities among the Big Four, here too, make it possible to view the four countries in parallel.

The informal relationship bankers

Perched atop almost every Southeast Asian economy in the decade leading up to 1997 was a tightly knit business elite. Some reigned from wealthy families that had retained their privileged position for several generations; many were self-made millionaires and billionaires who culled their fortunes from the region's rapid development. Many owed their success to being able to act quickly in an often Darwinian environment where commercial law offered little protection and few facts were available to analyze business risks and opportunities. More often than not, their success was reliant on strong business instincts and trust-based relationships with others in the business community. Ultimately, the strength accorded to business leaders did not come from a strong balance sheet but rather from their personal reputations afforded by a track record of personal integrity and past business successes.

This business elite owned many of Southeast Asia's leading banks (Exhibit 11.3). They were often entrepreneurs first, bankers second. The banks they

Exhibit 11.3

Banks in Southeast Asia by Type of Ownership*: 1997, Pre-crisis
Percent

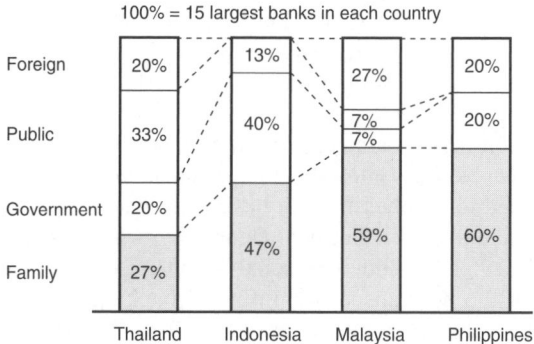

100% = 15 largest banks in each country

	Thailand	Indonesia	Malaysia	Philippines
Foreign	20%	13%	27%	20%
Public	33%	40%	7% / 7%	20%
Government	20%		59%	60%
Family	27%	47%		

* Based on the largest shareholder.

Source: EXTEL; Tara Siam Business Information; Bank Watch

formed generally served as funding tools to advance their own businesses and strengthen ties with their key business counterparts. As such, loans were often granted within an informal framework that did not necessarily measure the specific risks associated with the intended use of funds. What was often more important to banker-entrepreneurs, such as Udane Tejapaibul of Thailand, was how they could use their banks to advance or preserve their influence within the business community.

In much of Southeast Asia there was a fine line between where the business community ended and the government began. Frequently, the two overlapped and domestic bankers had to contend with political considerations when allocating their capital. Take, for example, the Suharto government's 1990 decision to build an Indonesian national car. The objective was to develop a low-cost model that would compete locally against primarily Japanese imports. As Indonesia had no experience in car manufacturing, the government decided to subsidize the effort until competitiveness was achieved.

Foreign car manufactures called foul, and local opinion surveys indicated little public interest in buying a national car. Indeed, many argued that with Jakarta's already horrendous traffic in the mid-1990s, the last thing Indonesia needed was a bigger car market. But the government persevered; its strategy was that a best defense is a strong offense. One of President Suharto's sons, Bambang, spearheaded the project with Kia Motors, the Korean auto manufacturer laboring under heavy debt, both its own and that guaranteed for Kia affiliates. In 1996, domestic banks, fearing the long-term implications of not supporting the project, provided an additional US$690 million as new national cars rolled off the assembly line and gathered, unsold, in large parking lots: a clear example of good money being forced upon bad ideas.

In Malaysia, domestic bankers often faced similar pressures to support government initiatives. The country's vision of achieving developed-country status by 2020 involved constructing symbolic landmarks including a new airport, a multi-media industrial park, the world's tallest twin-tower building, and the world's longest building, "KL Linear City," measuring a half a kilometer. The airport opened in June 1998, but as of late that year the twin Petronas Towers remained 30 percent unoccupied and construction of the other two projects was delayed. In the absence of formal supply, demand, and risk analysis, many of Malaysia's banks that had supported the hallmark projects were stuck with deteriorating loan portfolios.

Informal decision-making among bankers was not limited to banking families advancing their own business interests or government initiatives. Much of the debt and equity extended to Southeast Asian businesses was sealed with a handshake between banks and corporate chairmen. George Ty, who founded Metro Bank in the Philippines in 1962 and built a personal fortune of roughly US$2.5 billion by 1997, excelled in the nontransparent, informal banking world of the overseas Chinese. Rather than concentrate on cash flows or commission detailed assessments of a company's strategy and projects — which would in all likelihood have alienated his secretive clients — Ty maintained a strong personal network within the Chinese community to keep abreast of who was doing well and who was not. He remained involved in all the bank's significant credit decisions. Between 1990 and 1997, Metro Bank's profits grew more than 20 times to US$197 million, on loan assets that mushroomed from US$2 billion to $10 billion, making Metro Bank one of the Philippines' largest banks.

George Ty, though not free from systemic risks in times of widespread crisis, at least had the benefit of being a true insider. Many institutions that relied on relationships and informal credit decisions in the high-growth era were often running blind by comparison. This was perhaps most true for the newer banks in Indonesia and the burgeoning finance companies throughout Southeast Asia, many of which were started by businesspeople from outside the elite. Without superior relationships and inside information, they were often left with cast-off, riskier projects or simply betting on second-tier corporations and entrepreneurs. Moreover, the newer banks and finance companies typically recruited less experienced staff, which further impeded their ability to improve on the informal banking model. With a limited name in competitive markets, newer and smaller players were frequently left to compete primarily on price for both loans and deposits. Like the failed U.S. savings and loan institutions, many newcomers were inadvertently forced into higher-margin, higher-risk businesses, such as real estate lending, to carve out profits.

In high-growth markets, optimism can be infectious. While for years foreign bankers scoffed at the informal and risky lending practices of their local brethren, even they were seduced by the region's success story. In fact, Western banks, armed with aggressive aspirations and growth targets for Asia, often came to accept — and imitate — the Asian relationship-based lending approach.

A corporate lending relationship manager, working for a leading U.S. bank in Indonesia in the 1980s, recounted how they would fill in loan applications for their Indonesian clients to secure loan approvals. If the loan was, for example, for a new palm oil processing plant, the bank's relationship managers would conduct a study of the industry's dynamics and develop a pro-forma P&L of the plant's projected revenues and profits. They would show this to the Indonesian client, who would treat it as interesting mental exercise and sign off on it to obtain funding.

Limited typically to a handful of branches in the national capital, often led by a foreign manager who rotated every several years, foreign banks were often aware of the difficulty of either gathering hard facts or becoming a true insider in the Southeast Asian markets. While many stuck to short-term trade-related finance to maintain a clear understanding of how funds were being used, more aggressive players placed their bets with members of the business elite. A businessman indirectly related to the Thai royal family remembers foreign bankers offering him credit lines nearing US$100 million in the 1990s, simply because they believed that his connections would ensure the success of any venture he pursued. A number of foreign banks, although a step removed from the tight inner circle of the business elite, had, in their optimism, become practitioners of informal banking.

Management without numbers

The lack of transparency and financial reporting before the crisis amplified the risks of informal banking. Insufficient information within banks made it very difficult for bank managers to maintain a consolidated view of their funding and lending portfolios. More often than not, each informal credit decision was taken in isolation. As institutions grew rapidly, they were increasingly unaware of the concentrations of risk they were acquiring within a given industry, customer, or currency. So while independent decisions may have been taken with confidence, bankers were unaware of the impact on the overall health of their portfolios. For example, they may not know that 40 percent of their loan portfolio was either invested in, or backed by, real estate. They may not have known that by lending to many subsidiaries of a single conglomerate, that 20 percent of their entire equity was exposed to a single counterparty. Nor might they have known what a 10 percent movement in a short-term interest rate or a currency exchange rate would do to net interest margins or the ability of their debtors to repay.

As most managers were not using consolidated figures internally, it was of course, unlikely for bankers to report the allocation of their portfolios to the market. Hence, no one in the market, bar perhaps some regulators, knew the concentration of risks that were being taken by the financial industry as a whole within certain economic sectors, customers, or currencies. Without this information it was impossible for managers to know the risks of their informal and independent decisions.

The absence of a consolidated view of customers and markets, combined with limited disclosure requirements for corporations and individuals, made it possible for less-scrupulous customers to abuse the system. Some borrowed from one bank to repay another. In fact, the lack of strong management information systems even enabled customers to borrow more money from a bank to repay previous obligations to that same bank. As long as Southeast Asia's economies grew, excesses, abuses, and shortfalls remained hidden.

The absence of clear or enforced reporting of financial institutions' bad loans, reserves, and real profits also made distinguishing between good and poor financial intermediaries impossible for regulators, depositors, and investors. An outsider could not know the relative strength of George Ty's decisions at Metro Bank versus those of a newly established finance company taking substantially greater risks, for example, in speculative real estate projects. As a result, good money was unknowingly invested after bad. Over time, the lack of reporting allowed both excesses and real losses to accumulate invisibly within the financial system while investors gladly provided more capital.

Weak compromised regulators

One could reasonably ask what the regulators were doing while all this went on. To be fair, they exercised some control. While not perfect, the regulators in Malaysia and the Philippines kept tolerably apace with the rapidly growing and increasingly complex financial markets. The scorecard is less impressive, however, in Indonesia and Thailand.

Indonesian and Thai regulators often played second fiddle to politicians and the business elite. From the early 1990s, their independence and ability to enforce key decisions was compromised on a regular basis. A poignant example in Indonesia is the case of PT Bank Summa, run by the son of a tycoon who was close to

President Suharto. In 1992, after years of clear problem signs, the regulators finally shut the bank down. But by 1998, the bank had never been liquidated, and apparently nothing was done to recover the US$180 loans extended by the central bank. In 1998, in the wake of the crisis, the IMF looked on in wonder as Suharto fired the central bank's president for carrying out IMF demands to close 16 failing banks. Only further surprise could be expressed when two of the 16 — each owned by one of Suharto's sons — brazenly remained open despite the local regulator's decree. In Indonesia, the powers of the banking regulatory body were significant and sound — on paper. In reality, however, survival often had more to do with political connections than financial soundness.

In keeping with the understated Thai style of doing business, regulatory influence was often quietly compromised behind closed doors. It was standard practice for the elite to migrate among regulatory, political, and banking positions. Consequently, it was not unusual for senior regulatory officials to base decisions on how those decisions would impact their stature in the banking or political community. Rather than force an important industry contact to expose loan losses, regulatory authorities hid the problem while quietly trying to fix it. In addition to being sensitive, Thailand's regulatory authorities frequently were overstretched by the market's rapid development. In trying to keep up with growth, the authorities were left to focus only on the largest institutions, allowing the newer and smaller finance companies a longer leash.

The sensitivity and restricted focus of Thai regulatory authorities proved to be a lethal combination. When the economy slowed in 1996 and 1997, the finance companies — with their higher-risk portfolios — were the first to show signs of distress. Without informing the markets, the regulatory authorities quietly propped them up with around US$15 billion in foreign currency reserves. When it was disclosed in June 1997 that the government had spent more than 90 percent of its reserves defending the currency and bailing out the finance companies, the baht went into free-fall, and the Asian financial crisis entered the history books.

In retrospect, the financial era in Southeast Asia preceding the crisis comprised two stories: one of unprecedented domestic growth and opportunity, backed by real economic advancements; and the other of financial institutions, practices, and regulators outgrown by their own success. Panic played a role in initiating and deepening the crisis, but the problems had structural roots in all of Southeast Asia's Big Four, albeit to varying degrees. Competitors hoping to reinvent themselves and garner significant profits in the first decade of the 21st century must keep one eye on resolving the structural weaknesses that felled good and bad financial institutions alike.

Crisis Unleashes New Forces, Challenges, and Opportunities

If the crisis had not occurred, Southeast Asia, under the umbrella of its protected domestic financial markets, would have adopted new banking practices in its own time. With some government prodding, the larger and best-connected domestic financial institutions would have absorbed smaller players as competition increased, and they would have dominated the markets by 2010. Foreign players, backed by the WTO, would have entered as governments were forced to tear down investment barriers, and several of them might have carved out medium-sized businesses.

But the crisis, and the very real economic recession that followed, will transform Southeast Asia's financial markets by 2010. Rather than gradual evolution, wrenching changes will redefine who will win and what it will take to win. Massive loan losses will lead to wide-scale industry consolidation. The need for large capital injections within the financial system will usher in increased foreign ownership and competition. Crisis-induced bankruptcies, mergers, and political reshuffling will produce a new generation of decision-makers in financial institutions, corporations, and regulatory bodies.

Intensive efforts to recapitalize financial institutions, corporations, and governments will create broader demand for capital market products, reducing to some extent the role commercial bankers have played in intermediating risk and capital. Slower economic growth and the low likelihood of rapidly rebounding domestic real estate and capital markets will force individuals to seek longer-term borrowing and investment strategies. Finally, the widespread realization of the risks associated with investing within a single economy will prompt individuals and institutions to pursue greater cross-border investment diversification.

In sum, the crisis has amplified three fundamental trends, which in turn will shape both the challenges and opportunities for competitors in Southeast Asia's Big Four financial markets. First, industry consolidation and the growing clout of global competitors point to greater opportunities, but for fewer players. Second, the rise of professional stakeholders will bring new money for those institutions that can meet these stakeholders' tougher demands. Third, the modernization of corporate, institutional, and retail customer needs spells opportunities for innovative institutions.

Industry Consolidation and Stronger Global Competitors Point to Greater Opportunities for Fewer Players

Leading up to the crisis, governments in all four Southeast Asian countries tried to persuade domestic financial institutions to merge. But moral suasion and attempts to raise minimum capital requirements were often insufficient, particularly when it came to convincing family owners to give up control. Unfriendly takeovers were then next to impossible, as family members and key business partners held equity closely. The crisis, however, made all past resistance and family preferences moot. Enormous losses among banks and consumer finance companies — ranging from one to five times paid-in capital — gave regulators power to act.

And in late 1997 and early 1998 they did. Thailand closed 58 of its 91 finance companies, and gained control of four of the country's 15 banks, with the plan to either merge among the four or sell them individually to foreign buyers. Malaysia forced 38 finance companies to merge with their parent banks or into the six leading finance companies, and shepherded the country's weaker banks towards merging with stronger ones. Indonesia initially mandated that the country's 220 banks be merged to form 20 banks by the end of 1998. As the crisis continued to unravel into late 1998, the Indonesian government was compelled to change tack. Fifty of the country's weakest institutions, which represented more than 35 percent of outstanding domestic loans, were placed under a newly formed restructuring agency. Four of the larger government-owned banks were merged to form the country's largest new bank, Bank Mandiri. The central bank forced the 160-plus remaining banks to undertake a business review that was expected to result in a government-directed consolidation process, leaving fewer than 50 banks by early in the 21st century. The Philippines, affected less dramatically by the crisis, continued to pressure smaller institutions to find larger parents.

These 1997–1998 closures and mergers marked only the beginning of a medium-term industry consolidation. Through to 2010, Southeast Asia will probably see its financial institutions contract sharply, from approximately 500 banks, securities, and finance companies pre-crisis to fewer than 100.

While closures and mergers help focus government clean-up efforts, they do not solve all the problems. By late 1998, more than US$70 billion, equivalent to about 25 percent of each of the Big Four's annual GDP, was required to recapitalize Southeast Asia's beleaguered financial systems. The widespread destruction of national wealth will place the burden of recapitalization largely on the West. Part of that capital will come from IMF loans, part from foreign institutional investors, and a significant portion from foreign competitors taking direct controlling stakes in local financial institutions. In response to the crisis, Thailand and Indonesia relaxed long-standing restrictions on foreign ownership to facilitate capital injections, while the Philippines lifted its cap to 60 percent. Malaysia begrudgingly began considering increased (but still minority) foreign stakes in its leading institutions but then backpedaled when it issued capital controls in late 1998.

Meanwhile, many foreign competitors that would have grabbed ownership opportunities before the crisis remained on standby, awaiting the right buying opportunity. Lack of transparency, and political instability in Indonesia's case, quelled a buying rush. The first to take the plunge into majority ownership was ABN Amro, which acquired a 75 percent stake of Thailand's 11th largest bank, the Bank of Asia, in early 1998. ABN Amro moved quickly because it was impressed by the bank's professional management, and because it reached agreement on a formula that based the price of a portion of its equity stake on the bank's future performance. The markets viewed ABN Amro's pricing mechanism as an important precedent for structuring acquisitions in periods of extreme uncertainty. But, perhaps most importantly, the ABN Amro transaction made it clear that Thailand was serious about opening its markets to foreign competitors.

By 2010, there may well be 10–15 global players with significant stakes in one or several Southeast Asian countries. Even Malaysia, which hopes to muddle through the crisis largely under its own steam, will eventually confront WTO pressures and have to liberalize market access in the early years of the 21st century. By 2010, intense competition in each market will revolve around the 10–20 domestic competitors that survive restructuring plus the 5–10 global players that take advantage of new access and become locally embedded across all banking business lines.

Rise of Professional Stakeholders Will Bring New Money for Those that Can Meet New Demands

The years leading up to 2010 will bring a significant shift in the people who have traditionally overseen and influenced financial institutions in Southeast Asia. Declining in influence will be the family owners and managers of banks, politically appointed regulators, and domestic retail investors.

Professional managers drawn from domestic and foreign banks will take the place of family members, many of whom are ready for retirement. These new professional managers, many educated abroad in the 1980s, will bring modern finance and management skills, the tools to restructure Southeast Asia's informal banking systems.

Also on the rise will be independent technocrats within the regulatory bodies. While in 1998 much of the regulatory old guard was still entrenched, their influence was often tied to aging political leaders. Nowhere was this truer than in Indonesia and Malaysia. President Suharto, who dominated Indonesia's political and economic landscape for 32 years, was deposed amid the crisis-induced turmoil when he was in his 70s. With his departure, scores of regulatory officials lost their patron, and their personal influence declined rapidly. Prime Minister Mahathir Mohammad, who ruled Malaysia with a tight grip from 1981, was also in his 70s when the crisis struck. The removal or retirement of long-time leaders will mark a turning point in the management of regulatory bodies. In all countries except Malaysia, the IMF will probably be present and insist that the new guard be chosen based on their skills, and be granted adequate autonomy to expose and correct structural weaknesses in the financial system.

Armed with the power of much-needed capital, global institutional investors are likely to become much bigger and more demanding stakeholders. With the historical shackles on foreign ownership reduced or removed altogether, institutional investors will be able to acquire influential stakes in local players. And Southeast Asian banks will have little choice but to court these global funds in the absence of strong buying power among local institutional and retail investors. Such was the case with Thailand's two largest banks — Bangkok Bank and Thai Farmers Bank — in early 1998. They launched the two biggest cross-border equity transactions in Thailand's history to recapitalize their balance sheets. By seeking US$1.5 billion and US$834 million respectively, Bangkok Bank and Thai Farmers Bank increased their foreign equity ownership to 48 and 49 percent from levels previously below 25 percent.

For these two and the many other banks likely to take this route, institutional ownership will present new challenges. Ask U.S. CEOs who are their most critical stakeholders, and many will answer: fund managers. They demand complete transparency of strategy, earnings, reserves, performance shortfalls, and even senior management compensation. Any material changes in strategic direction, management composition, or risk exposures must be fully and carefully explained to analysts. Companies and financial institutions that consistently meet projected profits by undertaking stated risks are rewarded with a steady supply of funding. Those that fail to deliver, or avoid full disclosure, are often spurned.

Southeast Asian financial institutions — be they family- or government-owned — will have to relinquish control to professional managers to meet new demands of tougher regulators and institutional investors. As the influence of these professional stakeholders increases, the exclusive relationships between Southeast Asia's business and political elite will be further eroded, making the markets more open to skill-based competition.

New Customer Needs Spell Opportunities for Innovators

The 1997–1998 turmoil was, of course, more than just financial. Corporations, institutions, and individuals were also deeply affected by the meltdown of Southeast Asia's domestic economies. As currencies and stock markets fell more than 70 percent in Indonesia, 40 percent in Thailand, 30 percent in Malaysia, and 30 percent in the Philippines, customers of all types experienced substantial losses. More troubling, though, is that the economies and financial systems, starved of liquidity, are unlikely to bounce back quickly to their former heights. There is unlikely to be a rush of traditional bank funding to recapitalize the region's ailing conglomerates. Governments will be less able to tap shrinking national reserves to bolster infrastructure and stimulate growth. And individuals can no longer count on sustained domestic bull markets to help finance major purchases or augment their long-term savings.

In the absence of a rapid rebound in traditional funding and investment channels, corporations, institutions, and individuals must find new ways to meet their financial needs. Lacking short-term "easy money," customers will have to turn to longer-term financing and investment solutions. Over the next decade, this is likely to spawn demand for a new range of financial products and services, many of which already are common in today's developed world. Financial institutions that can develop these products and skills to serve emerging customers needs will advance — and prosper — from Southeast Asia's gradual recovery.

Corporations

Southeast Asia's private corporations and state-owned enterprises (SOEs) face a host of new needs. Most immediate among these is the repackaging of existing corporate debt. Private corporations, SOEs, and governments in Southeast Asia had in 1998 more than US$700 billion in outstanding debts, extended by a multitude of banks. In Indonesia, that multitude meant as many as 60–70 institutions. Corporations and governments will require financial advisory support to renegotiate and stage repayment schedules across their creditors to reduce short- and medium-term obligations. Where rescheduling is not possible, bankers can help companies initiate debt-for-equity swaps to lessen the load of near-term interest payments.

Relieving immediate cash-flow burdens is only the first step. Corporations and SOEs, like their fellow bankers, need to pare their business portfolios and focus on areas where they are truly competitive. Bankers can provide support on two fronts: splitting apart nontransparent and inefficient conglomerates to provide markets with a clear understanding of the various businesses' cash flows; and selling off noncore assets to help recapitalize key business areas. While Southeast Asian private and state-owned corporations were largely unwilling to pay for corporate-finance advisory services in the past, the daunting prospect of all-out business failure should make them more amenable to fees that typically range between 1 and 2 percent of the transaction value.

With recession, the first 5 years of the 21st century will probably be filled with unprecedented restructuring and merger work for domestic and global financial institutions. The historic parallel is the US$1 trillion of restructuring activity (through mergers, acquisitions, and leveraged buy-outs) that occurred in the U.S. between 1985 and 1990, when corporate America refocused its business portfolios to arrest declining performance. In those 5 years, U.S. restructuring resulted in transfers of capital equal to 4 percent of GDP. An equivalent level of restructuring in Southeast Asia would mobilize US$130 billion in capital and generate up to US$2 billion in financial institution revenues between 2000 and 2005. Roughly 30 percent of this activity is likely to be in Thailand, 30 percent in Indonesia, 20 percent in Malaysia, and 20 percent in the Philippines.

As this restructuring proceeds, companies will also need to recapitalize their operations to resume growth. Despite the economic slowdown, Southeast Asia still has a tremendous need to upgrade its roads, ports, telecommunications, and power supplies, and this will create opportunities for many of the largest corporations. In the next decade, infrastructure projects in the Big Four will require more than US$300 billion in new investment. As traditional commercial banks and governments are unlikely to possess sufficient liquidity to meet the funding needs of all corporations and projects, larger companies in particular will increasingly have to tap the domestic and global capital markets.

It is difficult to predict domestic and global investor appetite for Asian issuers in the first decade of the 21st century. But if debt and equity issuance volumes recover and expand with the underlying economies, it is possible to project ballpark issuance volumes through 2010. Assuming that Southeast Asia's economies recover to their pre-crisis levels by 2005, and that the pre-crisis relationship between capital needs and economic growth remains, local corporations could issue up to US$80 billion in new debt and equity a year by 2010. This would spawn approximately US$1.4 billion in annual underwriting revenues and represent a doubling of the yearly average revenue in the three years before the crisis.

Government efforts to privatize state-owned enterprises will be a key driver of increased capital market activity. Privatization, long seen as an important part of improving industrial competitiveness in Southeast Asia, has historically faced resistance from entrenched public-sector employees. But governments desperate for funds may show a much stronger will to overcome this resistance. In early 1998, Indonesia and Thailand announced plans to speed up the privatization process. Both have substantial SOE assets: by the end of 1997, the book value of SOEs totaled US$73 billion in Indonesia and US$27 billion in Thailand. If only a quarter of their SOEs are privatized from 2001 to 2005 and only 60 percent of shares are publicly placed, Indonesia and Thailand will respectively experience threefold and fivefold increases in privatization activity compared with 1992–1996.

The increased advisory and capital market activity likely handled by investment banks in the early 21st century will certainly not make traditional corporate banks redundant. Large corporations will continue to require credit for day-to-day working capital. Many infrastructure projects will require traditional bridge loans, guarantees, and lending syndications to fund the earlier stages of investment. Corporations, severely burned by unhedged foreign currency loans, will be looking for increased support in the foreign currency and derivative products. In a liquidity-short environment, corporations will look to their banks to help optimize cash management, trade finance, and repayment schedules; they will also seek new ways to mortgage the value of locked-up capital investments. So there will be more, not less, demand for corporate banking support. This will be all the more true for small and mid-sized businesses that have to restructure and recapitalize their operations, many without the aid of capital markets. By 2010, traditional corporate banking activities (lending, deposits, forex, and derivatives) should be at least 50 percent larger in U.S. dollar terms than before the crisis.

More restructuring, capital market, and traditional corporate activities will provide substantial opportunities for corporate and investment banks that survive in the new millennium. Financial institutions that can resolve corporations' problems in a time of great need will be able to penetrate customers once dominated by other institutions solely on the basis of superior personal relationships. The corporate market in Southeast Asia is open to being substantially redefined by innovative competitors.

Institutions

Outside Malaysia, Southeast Asia's institutional investors are at an early stage of development. Assets held by public and private pension funds, insurance companies, and private enterprises (such as corporations and financial institutions) totaled approximately US$120 billion by the end of 1996. As a result of its robust mandatory contribution pension scheme and higher insurance penetration, Malaysia held 67 percent of Southeast Asia's institutional assets. The Philippines accounted for 16 percent of the total, Thailand 13 percent, and Indonesia 4 percent. While limited today, institutional assets are poised for rapid growth as economies recover.

Wealth destruction and unemployment created by the crisis are likely to increase public awareness of the need for long-term savings and protection planning. If the Thai, Indonesian, and Philippine governments implement pension schemes by 2005 and the insurance industry develops in line with recovering GDP-per-capita levels, institutional assets will rise to almost US$850 billion by 2010. The investment strategies pursued by the institutions that manage these funds are likely to be markedly different from those of the past decade. Historically, Southeast Asia's institutional assets have largely been invested in domestic markets and often in illiquid holdings, such as real estate. Governments, insurance companies, and private enterprises have typically relied on internal staff to make investment decisions. The crisis is likely to step up risk diversification and investment in tradable securities. As such, by 2010, institutional investors will probably invest more abroad in more liquid securities, often soliciting the help of professional fund managers to guide their decisions.

The pressure to develop and protect long-term savings plans was already mounting in early 1998. In the wake of the crisis, the Malaysian government faced controversy in an attempt to use public pension funds to bail out failing financial institutions. With the increased risk of social instability, governments will have to work quickly to develop new pension and investment schemes and protect old ones. Financial institutions that are able to help in this regard could benefit from an increase of up to sixfold in Southeast Asian institutional assets by 2010. By then, institutional asset management in the Big Four could generate as much as US$2 billion in annual fees.

Individuals

The turmoil struck consumer banking markets at a critical point in Southeast Asia's economic development. By 1997, people in the region had become accustomed to almost a decade of steadily improving lifestyles and increasing purchasing power matched by an explosion in available consumer goods. With 92 percent of households owning a TV in Malaysia, 90 percent in Thailand, 57 percent in the Philippines, and 31 percent in Indonesia, some 180 million people in Southeast Asia were exposed to new lifestyle expectations. In the decade to 1997, advertising spend rose an average of ninefold across Southeast Asia as domestic and foreign companies, from soft drink to car manufacturers, vied for a share of growing household spending.

Despite the boom in consumer wealth and spending, for the better part of the decade before the crisis, few banks in Southeast Asia targeted individuals for anything but traditional deposit gathering. Rather, these customers were viewed primarily as a core source of funding for corporate lending. To illustrate, in 1997 there was one branch for every 4,300 people in the Philippines, 5,300 in Malaysia, 6,100 in Thailand, and 11,500 in Indonesia. This is in stark contrast to the U.S., which has one branch for every 3,200 people. More importantly, family-owned and managed banks, such as the Tejapaibuls' BMB, did little to equip branches to handle individuals' borrowing and investment needs. Marketing dollars and personnel were directed mainly to corporate interests. Banks saw their retail network as a necessary cost of gathering deposits, and net interest income was credited almost entirely to corporate activities.

In the late 1980s, foreign competitors with a significant regional presence — such as Citibank, Standard Chartered Bank, and Hongkong and Shanghai Banking Corporation (HSBC) — recognized the potential of Southeast Asia's untapped retail markets and began to cater to individual needs. In the early 1990s, domestic banks and finance companies also started to market loans and investment products to individuals. But by 1997, business generated from individuals still represented a small part of overall banking activity: consumer and mortgage loans accounted for only 29 percent of total domestic loans in Malaysia, 19 percent in Thailand, 11 percent in Indonesia, and 8 percent in the Philippines. Assuming that all personal lending was concentrated on Southeast Asia's middle and upper classes, then loans to these households averaged less than US$45,000 in 1997, representing a loan-to-income ratio averaging 0.8. This compares with a ratio of 1.4 in the developed world, leaving ample room for future growth.

Southeast Asia's rising incomes, high savings rates, and booming property and stock markets created enough liquidity in the respective economies that consumers could get by without extensive financing from financial institutions. Extended families were able to pool enough savings to purchase homes, cars, and other desired amenities. However, the 1997–1998 crash dried up most excess domestic liquidity. The crisis struck at a critical juncture in the development of Southeast Asia's consumer banking markets: by the late 1990s, people had already developed a strong taste for the consumer society. The crisis significantly reduced individual earning and spending power in global terms, but it did not change people's lifestyle aspirations. Slower economic growth will, however, force individuals to seek longer-term financing for most major purchases, significantly boosting mortgage and consumer finance revenues in the early 21st century.

Moreover, the realization that investments can be as quickly lost as gained will lead consumers to adopt longer-term, more diversified investment strategies, and to turn increasingly to professional financial intermediaries. Before the crisis, consumers accounted for about 40 percent of the US$240 billion average annual turnover in the Southeast Asia's equity markets. In 1997, retail mutual funds totaled only US$4.4 billion in assets across Southeast Asia, and accounted for less than 2 percent of total personal savings. Mutual funds should become a more common means for consumers to access professionally managed investments in the first decade of the 21st century. By 2010, if Malaysia, Thailand, and the Philippines place, proportionally, only half as much — and Indonesia a quarter as much — of total personal savings in mutual funds as does the developed world, retail assets under management in Southeast Asia could grow to approximately US$70 billion. Under this scenario, revenues from retail asset management would increase 14-fold to US$860 million annually — a significant increase over pre-crisis levels.

As much as the lack of liquidity will force consumers to rely more on financial institutions, it will also force those institutions to focus more on retail customers. Thus, the crisis may well mark a watershed in the development of retail banking in Southeast Asia. In the absence of active interbank markets, local financial institutions will have to battle increasingly for consumer deposits to fund their lending activities. The meltdown resulted in a substantial flight of deposits to what were perceived to be safer financial institutions, domestic and foreign alike. Many banks will have to work hard to win back public confidence and deposits. Those efforts should result in improved customer service and a greater willingness among financial institutions to meet individuals' borrowing and investment needs. Indeed, a number of surviving Southeast Asian financial institutions may find it easier and more profitable to refocus their extensive branch networks around the needs of customers, rather than fight for a share of corporate business in Southeast Asia's increasingly complex, consolidated, and globally competitive markets.

For financial institutions operating in Southeast Asia, the next decade will clearly pose substantial challenges. Domestic financial institutions, in particular, will have to cope with growing global competition, more demanding stakeholders, and increasingly diverse and sophisticated customer needs. On balance, however, the challenges unleashed by the crisis should also spawn a new era of opportunity, as corporations, institutions, and individuals broaden their use of financial products and services. The opportunities, far from being confined to the business and political elite, will flow to competitors that best execute against market demands. Institutions that respond well to the challenges and survive into the 21st century should find themselves in less-fragmented markets, well positioned to drive — and profit from — Southeast Asia's gradual economic recovery.

Different Priorities Among the Big Four

Development trends and the nature of future challenges and opportunities in Southeast Asia are similar, but banking priorities within the Big Four will differ. These differences stem from the relative impact of the 1997–1998 crisis, variations in national economic structures and development, and specific domestic regulations. They will affect how domestic institutions reinvent themselves, and how quickly global competitors should invest to serve corporations, individuals, and institutions in each country. Below we focus in turn on Thailand, Malaysia, the Philippines, and Indonesia, which is the order in which we expect these countries to recover from the crisis

Thailand: Early to Fall, Early to Rise

In 1998, Bangkok's skyline presented an eerie picture of economic excess. Motionless cranes atop partially finished skyscrapers dotted the horizon. If completed, they would only worsen the 25 percent vacancy rates that permeated Bangkok's commercial property sector. The stock market was in the doldrums, with market capitalization having collapsed from US$142 billion in 1995 (the sixth-largest in Asia ex-Japan) to US$22 billion by mid-1998 (sinking to ninth place, ahead only of Indonesia). The cranes and markets stood largely inactive, but Thailand's government bodies were beginning to move.

While the first 6 months of the crisis were filled with finger-pointing, by early 1998 Thailand was addressing the structural challenges of economic and financial reform. The government moved quickly to close or take over the weakest financial institutions. It shored up bankruptcy laws and tightened nonperforming loan definitions. Limits on foreign ownership were lifted, and global investors were invited to participate in the auction of failed institutions' assets. Formal public inquiries were launched to expose and correct the wrongdoings and shortfalls within leading regulatory bodies. Working with the IMF, the government trimmed planned spending and reprioritized key infrastructure projects. By late 1998, Thailand was systematically addressing banking reform, passing legislation to increase reporting transparency and shore up risk management systems. If Thailand can maintain this early restructuring momentum, its economy and financial system should recover to pre-crisis levels within the first 4 years of the 21st century.

As the economy recovers, competitors should concentrate on serving traditional corporate and retail needs, while monitoring developments within the institutional client base. In 1996, traditional corporate banking activities dominated the financial sector, with businesses accounting for 51 percent of the estimated US$10 billion in total industry revenues. Of corporate revenues, about 9 percent were generated by multinational corporations, 54 percent by Thailand's 200 largest corporations (annual sales exceeding US$100 million), 23 percent by 700 mid-sized companies with US$5-100 million in sales, and the remaining 14 percent by 300,000 small businesses with less than US$5 million in sales. While Thailand ranked seventh in Asia ex-Japan for total domestic and cross-border underwriting (publicly listed debt and equity), and raised US$67 billion between 1994 and 1997, investment banking accounted for only 6 percent of revenues generated from corporations. Stepped-up restructuring and privatization, however, should lead to a significant increase in domestic and cross-border investment banking opportunities.

Retail customers are likely to displace corporations as the largest source of financial institution profits by 2010. In 1996, individuals accounted for about 40 percent, or US$4 billion, of financial sector revenues. Consumer loans generated 50 percent of these retail revenues, deposits 26 percent, cross-border private banking activities about 12 percent, domestic retail stockbroking 8 percent, and domestic retail asset management 4 percent. As GDP per capita recovers from US$2,600 in 1997 to a projected US$5,900 by year 2010, the pool of individuals that have enough income to support a deposit or loan account will increase substantially, greatly expanding retail volume. As of the late 1990s, about half of Thailand's 16 million households were "unbanked."

The concentration of wealth in Thailand makes it possible for savvy competitors to capture significant retail market share with an efficient distribution network. Approximately two million Thai households earned more than US$10,000 in 1996. While the crisis cut the absolute income of the middle class and affluent, these households still represent 20 percent of the population, and approximately 50 percent of the nation's entire income, with 85 percent of that income concentrated in Bangkok. Put another way, the wealthiest one million households in Bangkok account for at least 40 percent of retail banking revenues and a significantly higher proportion of retail banking profits. Competitors that target this market, however, will have to be both innovative and aggressive. In a late 1990s survey, less than 20 percent of Bangkok's consumers indicated that they were willing to switch banks. The key will be meeting emerging demands for longer-term financing and investment options. The rewards could be significant, and provide market leaders with more than US$100 million in potential retail banking profits by 2010.

As one would expect in an economy with a skew in wealth, Thailand will continue to provide attractive opportunities for private bankers. Before the crisis, an estimated 33,000 households had investable assets exceeding US$1 million. As a group, these households held up to US$117 billion, the sixth largest potential private banking market in Asia. Leading competitors that can provide discreet and comprehensive services for the rich will continue to be rewarded well.

Thailand's institutional sector, by contrast, will probably provide opportunities for only a few players. Insurance assets, which totaled US$4 billion at the end of

1997, will grow in line with economic development but are likely to remain internally managed. The large unknown is how quickly Thailand will introduce more comprehensive pension programs. In 1997, mandatory pension assets were drawn from less than half the population, and approached only US$2.2 billion. Should Thailand institute a comprehensive defined contribution system — say by 2005 — that requires 10 percent of all employees' income to be put aside, pension assets would reach approximately US$110 billion by 2010. Financial companies targeting this sector would have to share approximately US$150 million in revenues, making this sector a low priority compared with corporate and retail banking.

Malaysia: Muddling Through on Its Own Terms

For years, Malaysia managed its development with a carefully controlled economic and political agenda. Industries flourished and wealth was created and redistributed within the society under Prime Minister Mahathir's watchful eye. More than any other Southeast Asian country, Malaysia moved forward with a plan that was to steer it into developed-country status by the third decade of the 21st century. And more than the other Southeast Asian countries, Malaysia avoided turning to outside capital to achieve its objectives. It is perhaps because Malaysia followed its own path that its leaders were so angered by a crisis that they viewed entirely as an externally prompted event. Senior political officials, including Mahathir, reacted like bitter victims of a disease that was knowingly spread by selfish outsiders, including Western banks, traders, and governments.

Malaysia's anger did not, of course, protect it from the widespread meltdown. The country's equity market capitalization, topping US$320 billion at the end of 1996 — the second largest in Asia ex-Japan — was reduced to US$67 billion (sixth place) by mid-1998. Characteristically, Kuala Lumpur refused outside help from the IMF and other international bodies, choosing instead to muddle through on its own (similar to Japan's approach from the early 1990s). This isolationist approach is likely to delay recovery until well into the first decade of the 21st century and slow the emergence of significant opportunities for bankers. The imposition of capital and currency controls in September 1998 mean that foreign investment is unlikely to speed the country's convalescence, which must instead rely on internally driven consolidation and restructuring of the financial sector.

Despite its small population of 22 million, Malaysia is by many measures the largest and most developed financial market of Southeast Asia's Big Four. Malaysia's approximately 600 large corporations, with more than US$100 million in sales (pre-crisis), outnumber the rest of Southeast Asia's large corporations combined. In 1996, the market capitalization of Malaysia's 16 largest conglomerates (approximately US$100 billion) exceeded the individual market capitalizations of Indonesia, Thailand, and the Philippines. Between 1994 and 1997, Malaysia's government and large corporations, together with a subset of 3,000 medium-sized corporates, raised US$54 billion in local equity and debt markets, representing Asia's seventh largest domestic investment banking market. Comparatively less active in the cross-border capital markets, Malaysia raised only

US$14 billion between 1994 and 1997, and it ranked seventh in total cross-border issuance in Asia for this period.

The mainstay banking revenues generated by corporations in Malaysia, like the rest of Southeast Asia, have been traditional corporate lending, forex, and cash management. In 1996, commercial banks' corporate loans to Malaysia's 360,000 companies (including small businesses) topped US$100 billion. The government has expressed its desire to consolidate the banking market to about six domestic universal banks, which will allow the surviving institutions to share in excess of US$2 billion in annual corporate banking revenues by early in the 21st century. Corporate banks that target segments well can expect profits topping US$100 million, once bad loans work their way out of the system, probably by 2002. Up to 20 percent of profits are likely to be derived from investment banking activities, given the sizable base of large corporations.

Malaysia's retail financial market will offer the most attractive opportunities of Southeast Asia's Big Four. In 1996, personal savings neared US$200 billion — 50 percent more than in Thailand, three times more than in the Philippines, and nearly eight times more than in Indonesia. With 300,000-plus households generating more than US$20,000 in income before the crisis, Malaysia had Southeast Asia's largest emerging middle class. Retail investors have participated very actively in the domestic stock market and accounted for 50 percent of average daily turnover and 80 percent of IPO purchases in the 1990s. Market protection resulted in retail stockbroking commissions of 1 percent, yielding annual revenues of more than US$3 billion in the years preceding the crisis.

While Malaysian consumers showed broad acceptance of new financial products, the market was still largely underpenetrated in the late 1990s. A 1998 survey that focused on the emerging middle class in Malaysia's biggest cities revealed that only 51 percent of those polled carried a mortgage, 51 percent had a car loan, and only 25 percent owned mutual funds. The 1998 consolidation of banks and finance companies will give surviving institutions the opportunity to develop sizable retail businesses. By 2010, profits from the retail sector could exceed those earned from corporations.

Unlike the rest of Southeast Asia's Big Four, Malaysia's institutional customer segment will provide substantial opportunities for financial institutions in the first decade of the 21st century. Standing at US$82 billion at the end of 1996, Malaysia's institutional assets were the third largest in Asia ex-Japan, after Korea and Singapore. Institutional assets comprise the Employment Provident Fund (EPF), other government savings plans, and insurance company assets. Unlike in other Asian markets, the presence of sizable domestic institutional investors has created a significant domestic institutional stockbroking business in Malaysia. Local institutions represented as much as 30 percent of domestic equity market turnover in the middle and late 1990s. The key question, of course, is when will these assets become available to external asset managers. As of 1998, only 3 percent of EPF assets were outsourced to fund managers. By 2010, Malaysia's institutional assets should approach US$500 billion. If 40 percent of the government-sponsored funds are outsourced, Malaysia's institutional asset management market will generate in excess of US$500 million in annual revenues.

For even established global players, this institutional market will represent an attractive and well-concentrated opportunity.

Malaysia, more than any other Southeast Asian country, will offer considerable corporate, retail, and institutional opportunities. The only business segment that is likely to be surprisingly small — owing to a careful redistribution of wealth — will be private banking, where Malaysia represented Asia's second smallest market before the crisis. While Malaysia's independent spirit will probably keep its financial markets largely protected up to 2005, changes in government leadership and WTO pressures will gradually tear down the economic fences and open the markets to global competitors.

The Philippines: Rebounding by the Book

The Philippines was the latecomer to Southeast Asia's growth bonanza. It was not until the early 1990s that the country truly began to recover from the Marcos era's corruption, economic mismanagement, and financial-industry nationalization. With only US$12 billion in national reserves in mid-1997, the Philippines was an easy target for speculators anticipating regional fallout from the crisis. However, the country's financial fundamentals were not as shaky as those of its Southeast Asian cousins. The system did contain excesses, but they were largely concentrated in the greater Manila area. Even so, growth had been managed by clear economic policies that had long incorporated IMF support and was carefully monitored by a strong independent central bank. While nonperforming loans, which reached 20 percent in 1998, spelled real problems for the financial sector, the strong constructive relationship between the government and the IMF should enable the country to stage a recovery "by the book" in the early years of the 21st century.

The financial markets and key customer groups in the Philippines are not uniformly developed, as they are in Malaysia. As in Indonesia and India, only a portion of assets in the Philippines have found their way into the formal financial system. As such, generating profits in this country will require focusing on clear geographical and customer priorities.

Compared with the rest of the Big Four, the Philippines' corporate banking market was small and concentrated in the late 1990s. Total corporate loans reached US$35 billion in 1996. As a percentage of GDP, corporate loans were Asia's lowest outside India. Much of the corporate lending base revolved around 60–70 large domestic companies (with sales exceeding US$100 million) and up to 1,000 mid-sized corporates, which generated more than US$10 million in sales. The ownership and management of these companies was concentrated among 15–20 Philippine families and several hundred trade-driven entities owned by entrenched Chinese entrepreneurs. Only a limited portion of the country's 740,000 small businesses was served by commercial banks in the late 1990s.

This small base of larger corporations has historically supported a small-to-medium-sized investment banking market. The Philippines' equity market capitalization sank to US$30 billion as of mid-1998 from its 1996 high of more than US$80 billion. Nonetheless, between 1994 and 1997, it supported US$8 billion in domestic equity issues, topping both China and Singapore. Strong domestic accounting practices — among Asia's most developed — made it easier for Philippine companies to tap the global capital markets. In the same years, the Philippines sourced US$12 billion from the global equity and debt markets, exceeding the cross-border issuance volumes of Taiwan, India, and Singapore, and trailing Thailand and Malaysia, whose economies were more than double the size. Financial institutions that are able to penetrate Manila's clubby and relationship-oriented corporate markets will be able to develop a medium-sized Asian corporate and investment banking business.

The Philippines' mass consumer market will probably provide limited opportunities for all but the few largest competitors. Despite government efforts to promote savings, the national savings rate persisted at around 18 percent throughout the 1990s. Consumer savings and investments held in the nation's banks and brokerages totaled only US$50 billion at the end of 1996, the second lowest in Asia, after Indonesia. While several billion dollars more of mass-market liquid assets certainly sit outside the financial system, they are widely dispersed across an archipelago comprising more than 7,000 islands. Only 14 percent of the country's 73 million people reside in and around the major cities, which are themselves scattered across several major islands. As in India and Indonesia, the challenge for financial institutions focusing on the mass consumer market lies in providing cost-efficient banking services across vast areas to predominantly low-income households.

The opportunities in the high-end consumer banking market will, however, be substantially greater. Perched atop Filipino society is a small group of super-wealthy, composed of leading local families and Chinese entrepreneurs. While many of the wealthy lost a lot of money in the crisis, previously their assets were reportedly close to US$100 billion. As such, the Philippines' private banking market, made up of approximately 30,000 households, is believed to be larger than the private banking markets in China, Singapore, and Malaysia. For financial institutions that can provide a substantial range of offshore products, the Philippines will be reasonably easy to tap, given the prevalence of English and a long history of investing overseas.

The Philippines' institutional investor market is unique in its predominantly private structure. Unlike much of Southeast Asia, where institutional assets, apart from those held by insurance companies, are mostly government sponsored, the Philippines has a medium-sized private pension market. Drawn from employees in the larger companies, private pension assets were estimated to be as high as US$20 billion before the crisis. The Philippines has also developed guaranteed-return investment products that cater to lower-income households. Called "pre-need" products, they pay out lump sums for education, retirement, and funerals. Sixty to 70 relatively unregulated investment firms managed an estimated US$10 billion in assets placed in these products by 1997. There is clearly latent demand for broadening long-term pension and savings programs. If lobbyists pressing for new pension regulation in the late 1990s are successful, the Philippines could accumulate as much as US$130 billion in pension assets by 2010, generating a small institutional asset management market.

The forces that will reshape Southeast Asia's banking markets will undoubtedly impact the Philippines. Most competitors will find, however, that real opportunities will probably be confined to the large corporate and high-end consumer segments in the years leading up to 2010.

Indonesia: Will Chinese Investors Stay?

Will Indonesia follow the path of the Philippines in the early 1970s? In the late 1960s, the Philippines was commonly viewed as the country in Asia with the greatest development potential. At that time, South Korea was still largely decimated by its war with the North. Taiwan was tied to an umbilical cord of U.S. dollar funding to ensure no one would develop a communist agenda for its future. Hong Kong was still perceived as a high-risk British enclave, plagued by street riots, and flooded with waves of refugees from China's Cultural Revolution. Looking around the region at that time, the Philippines was comparatively stable. Benefiting from both U.S. financial aid and a U.S.-influenced legal structure, it was — in the view of the Western world — the best bet in Asia. But then, of course, came the Marcos years, which removed the country from Asia's fast development track. Will the same happen to Indonesia in the first decade of the 21st century? Will the events of 1997–1998 remove Indonesia from the bankers' map of the world?

Some believe Indonesia shot itself in the foot by failing to contain the post-crisis social turmoil. Though ethnic Chinese make up only 3 percent of the population, they have long dominated Indonesia's business and financial worlds. In the late 1990s, they owned 80 percent of the country's equity market capitalization and were believed to hold a similarly disproportionate share of national wealth. When looters took to the streets in May 1998, it was more often than not Chinese businesses and homes that they targeted. Chinese attempting to flee were stopped on the way to the airport, dragged from their cars, and beaten. Indonesia's recovery is largely pinned on these same Chinese returning, with their skills and capital, to help rebuild the ruined economy. If a large proportion ultimately decide not to reinvest, then Indonesia could mirror the Philippines of the early 1970s and spend most of the first decade of the 21st century trying to regain its pre-crisis economic status.

If the wealthy Chinese reinvest in Indonesia, there are substantial global banks and institutional investors whose interests will be best served by helping them mend their businesses and the economy. Foreign banks and institutional investors had placed close to US$200 billion in Indonesia through loans and holdings in domestic equities and bonds before the crisis. Indonesia's recovery is, of course, their best option to recoup a portion of that capital. Bankers participating in any recovery will have to muster a clean-slate mentality; the financial markets have to be completely rebuilt. Optimistically, there could be attractive banking opportunities in Indonesia should the Chinese return.

The core opportunity during recovery would be serving corporations. Indonesia, like the Philippines, built its economy around several hundred large corporations. Before the crisis, 70–80 of Indonesia's largest companies accounted for about half of GDP. Two million small and medium-sized businesses, together with a sizable agricultural sector, accounted for the rest. Several hundred leading companies accounted for most of Indonesia's US$124 billion domestic corporate lending market. They were also the source of US$21 billion in domestic equity issues during 1994–1997, making Indonesia the fourth largest domestic equity underwriting market in Asia excluding Japan. These same corporations issued US$24 billion in debt and equity in the same period on the global markets, making Indonesia the fourth largest market for cross-border investment banking in Asia ex-Japan, after Korea, Hong Kong, and China.

The crisis, of course, significantly reduced the potential business to be garnered from Indonesia's large private- and state-owned corporations: up to half of the corporate loan market defaulted; devaluation of the rupiah reduced the value of remaining good loans to less than US$30 billion; and underwriting virtually halted. But if Indonesia recovers, it will probably be these same corporations that will require the loan rescheduling, recapitalizing, and medium-term business portfolio restructuring. It will be the top 70–80 companies, many Chinese-owned, that will need extensive banking services for loans, cash management, and risk management to foster their businesses and lead the economy into recovery. Domestic and foreign financial institutions that provide these services to corporations could split US$2–4 billion in annual corporate and investment banking revenues by 2010, if Indonesia regains economic momentum.

Indonesia's mass consumer banking markets, like those in the Philippines, will probably provide significant opportunities to only the largest competitors. The crisis reduced the stock of personal savings for Indonesia's 200 million population from about US$80 billion to $20 billion. While a majority of these assets are held on Java, the island that includes Jakarta, the rest is dispersed across approximately 16 million households, many of them in small, rural towns. With the planned massive consolidation of the Indonesian banking market, a few institutions will achieve the scale to profitably tap this sector in the coming decade. And while the demand for consumer credit and investment products is likely to increase over what it was in the decade before the crisis, volumes will remain small relative to the rest of Asia, making retail banking in Indonesia a comparatively low priority.

In contrast, Indonesia's high-end consumer market, composed of 60,000 households (principally in Jakarta), will continue to support one of Asia's most important private-banking markets. Pre-crisis, Indonesia's high concentration of wealth had placed up to US$250 billion in the hands of roughly the top one-quarter of 1 percent of Indonesia's population, making it Asia's second largest potential private banking market after Japan. The key question is whether this market will be attractive only in the medium term. If wealthy Chinese gradually leave Indonesia, the transfer of their wealth will create a burst of global private banking activity that may ebb by the early years of the 21st century. If they remain, increased diversification of their holdings will probably provide private banking competitors with more than US$1 billion in annual revenues from Indonesia by 2010. One challenge private bankers may face in coming years is an attempt by the government to recall assets siphoned off by Suharto and others in the years preceding the crisis. Such assets could easily run to tens of billions of dollars.

The enormous skew in wealth and increased social pressure to address economic inequities is likely to prompt Jakarta to address long-term savings issues. As of 1997, before the worst of the crisis had hit, insurance companies and the state pension system held less than US$10 billion in domestic institutional assets. If Indonesia is able to institute a far-reaching pension scheme by 2005 that draws 10 percent of employees' wages into a defined contribution plan annually, institutional assets could balloon to as much as US$100 billion by 2010. While this would represent significant growth in institutional assets, annual asset management revenues would likely approach only several hundred million U.S. dollars — still small by global standards.

If Indonesia succeeds in guiding its economy out of meltdown, the principal customer priorities in the first decade of the 21st century will be similar to those in the Philippines: large corporations and wealthy individuals. If there is prolonged unrest, the departure of ethnic Chinese and their capital could take Indonesia out of the picture for bankers for quite some time.

Reinventing from Within

Southeast Asia's Big Four markets will clearly provide opportunities for winners, but how should local banks in particular manage the many challenges when their very survival is in question? The crisis, and its vast wealth destruction, was wrenching and dispiriting, but rebuilding and meeting new investor and customer needs could prove even more daunting for long-sheltered, traditional organizations.

Two Fundamental Risks

Senior management teams in Southeast Asia face two fundamental risks as they move into the 21st century: falling into denial or becoming overwhelmed by the choices they have to make. Of the two, denial is the greater danger. It is easy to spot financial institutions whose senior management teams are in denial. They speak of the crisis in terms of a temporary and unfair aberration in the markets that has robbed them of medium-term profits. They cannot foresee and plan for the sweeping changes in competitive structure and customer needs that lie ahead. No matter how large, institutions that wait stubbornly for the return of the pre-crisis status quo, believing that their past successes somehow entitles them to a future role, are in for a rude awakening.

For those financial institutions that do not fall into denial, the risk of being overwhelmed by the challenges — which range from recapitalizing for survival to developing customer-focused strategies and world-class skills — is substantial. Addressing these issues requires uniting under strong leadership, charting a clear direction, and prioritizing among the many tasks that must be done. Confusion, insufficient coordination, frustration, and early failures in change efforts may exhaust the will of even the most committed employees, and undermine the ability of institutions to reinvent themselves in time to win in the newly competitive and global environment.

The Reinvention Process

So what does reinvention require, and where does one start? For Southeast Asia's hundreds of banks and finance companies, securing a lifeline is the first critical step, and that requires changing long-held assumptions about ownership and control. To obtain capital from governments, Western institutional investors, or new foreign partners, bankers throughout Asia will have to dilute their holdings. In most cases new money will come with strings attached.

Branches with less potential will have to be closed, employees cut, and organizational structures altered to accommodate investors' demands. For many family-owned financial institutions, relinquishing the leadership reins will be painful. Relatives of the long-standing owner-patriarchs will no longer have easy access to banking positions that have traditionally carried significant prestige. More broadly, organizations that have rewarded loyalty with job security will have to redefine their employee propositions. While some may balk at these tough moves, their hunger for capital will give them little choice but to comply.

Once survival is assured, bank managers will need to look deeply at their organizations and markets to rewrite their strategies, giving serious thought as to where and how they can compete. Which clients can they keep and which will they have to give up? Which product lines can they defend and grow, and which ought to be abandoned? Which capabilities should be maintained in-house and which can be outsourced? Can they compete for the concentrated wealth and sophisticated customers in major urban centers, or must they retreat and build new businesses in the relatively under-banked townships and rural areas? Will they continue to rely on branch-based distribution or experiment with new technologies such as ATMs and phone banking centers? Will their distinctiveness be based on excellent service, product expertise, superior pricing, and/or simple but exceptional convenience? How will their choices make them stack up against the competition?

The answers to all these questions will form the blueprint for reinvention. Yet it is in the process of searching for answers that many institutions will become overwhelmed and falter. Rigorous analysis, open debate, and "out of the box" thinking drawn from across the organization are all critical to thoughtful strategic restructuring. The loyalty-laden hierarchies of many of Southeast Asia's institutions will need to embrace these approaches, however alien they may seem.

It is difficult, but it can be done. Corporate America up to the early 1980s was deeply change-resistant and not very open to involving a broad range of employees in targeting improvements and setting strategy. But increasing competition gradually led to greater employee participation and greater use of cross-functional teams to identify and solve problems. Southeast Asian institutions will have to get comfortable with new collaborative forms of strategy definition in a very short period of time. Senior management teams will have to depart from their traditional hierarchies and draw on the ideas of younger, front-line employees to better understand evolving customer needs and competitors' strategies. This will require enormous will, as the resistance from middle management could be substantial.

Seeking broad participation and views in defining new strategies will help financial institutions overcome the biggest hump: implementation. The more people that get involved, and the more transparent the rationale for change, the easier it will be to implement new approaches. Employees who are empowered by facts and involved in determining their own fate will be more willing and able to undertake the difficult and far-reaching changes required of financial institutions in Southeast Asia. Organizations that are able to develop a structured and participatory approach to strategic restructuring stand the greatest chance of not becoming overwhelmed. And those that emerge from the hard work of restructuring with a clear vision and empowered employees will be best positioned to institute world-class skills.

Financial institutions, despite their intrinsic complexities, often succeed or fail depending on their ability to do a few simple things very well. Most customers, after all, do not spend a great deal of time deliberating over which bank to use. What customers care about is whether a bank will give them what they need quickly and clearly, without hassles or errors, at a good price. Financial institutions in Southeast Asia will need to look closely at their new customer and product strategies to determine the few things that they must do really well in the first decade of the 21st century. Success or failure will then largely become a matter of execution.

In the face of increasing competition from global competitors, the standards to beat — in marketing, distribution, credit processing, whatever — will likely be those set by foreign institutions. Southeast Asian banks will have to be as good as, if not better than, foreign players to attract customers, retain market share, and generate attractive profits. Having world-class skills means nothing more than executing at or above the level of the world's best — a simple concept but no simple task. To succeed, most domestic banks will have to revamp their information management systems, incentives, training programs, and delegation and decision-making processes. They also must instill performance-driven cultures that thrive on continuous improvement.

For many financial institutions in Southeast Asia, the complexity, changes in culture, and investment in man-hours and money that constitute reinvention may seem daunting. However, those that aspire to compete in Southeast Asia's new era have little choice. Few will be able to manage the process of reinvention without a highly structured approach. The demands of major change, coupled with economic recession in the immediate post-crisis years, heightened foreign competition, and new customer needs, are likely to whittle down the number of domestic competitors significantly. From approximately 500 at the beginning of the crisis, the number of financial institutions in Southeast Asia's Big Four will probably shrink to fewer than 100 by 2010.

The Winners' Camp

Southeast Asia's winners will be those that successfully reinvent their organizations, having learned from their pre-crisis errors and from global best practice. In 2010, it may be difficult to describe the leading competitors as simply domestic or foreign. Mergers with foreign partners and increased foreign equity ownership in locally licensed financial institutions will blur the distinction.

Southeast Asian financial markets, customers, and competitors will probably look and operate much as they do in developed countries today. Thailand, Malaysia, the Philippines, and Indonesia will still be classified as emerging markets in terms of their relative economic development, but their banking structures, the availability of financial products and services, and customer demands will be increasingly shaped by global trends.

In each of Southeast Asia's Big Four, around 20–30 institutions will prevail. Three or four large universal banks will lead in overall market share and revenues in each country. They will be very domestic in their business orientation but may be partly or wholly owned by international players and investors. These banks will probably serve most customer segments, across most products, and derive their competitive advantages from economies of scale and broad national branch distribution networks. Many of these universal banks will build their leading positions through acquisition of smaller, weaker institutions.

Competing directly with the universal banks will be six to eight leading commercial banks. These players will most likely develop strong business platforms in the traditional corporate and retail customer and product segments. Through superior products and services, they stand a good chance of dominating targeted geographies within a given country, or developing leading market shares with customer sub-segments, such as the emerging middle class in retail or mid-sized companies in corporate. For their chosen segments, their product and service offering will be quite comprehensive. In retail sub-segments, for example, these commercial banks will provide loans, broking, asset management, and insurance services carefully tailored to meet customer needs. Three or four of these commercial banks could be international players that establish a dominant domestic position through acquisition early in the 21st century. The remaining three or four will probably be banks with domestic roots that have successfully restructured their operations, perhaps with the help of foreign alliances. This latter group of banks may establish a stronghold by penetrating many of Southeast Asia's currently "unbankable" retail and small business customers.

Both the universal and commercial banks will face stiff competition in the large corporate segment from the leading five to ten international investment banks. Superior deal structuring and distribution networks will enable top global players to solidify their relationships with the biggest conglomerates as they help them recapitalize and/or privatize in the years to 2003. These global players' role in large mergers, equity, and bond offerings will probably be unsurpassed by any of the domestically focused banks. They also are likely to dominate services to local institutional investors in trading and asset management.

In each country, however, no more than three or four local investment banks — focused entirely on local mergers, underwriting, and broking — may generate moderately sized businesses with niche strategies. They will probably target medium-sized companies in the corporate segment for underwriting and corporate finance services, and lower- and middle-income households to provide basic retail asset management and broking services.

Up to ten other institutions will build small to medium-sized specialist businesses in consumer finance, retail asset management, institutional asset management, and private banking. The competitive advantages of these specialists will be founded on providing highly tailored, innovative products and services to their carefully chosen customers. They will probably lure key staff away from global competitors. In their chosen businesses, however, the market share of these specialists will be small next to the universal, commercial, and investment banks. Private banking, in particular, will largely remain the domain of the leading international competitors that can provide a full range of offshore services.

The race to win for the 20–30 institutions in each of Southeast Asia's Big Four will, of course, differ. Winners in Malaysia, Thailand, and the Philippines will tend to emerge through the carefully managed consolidation of several players. In Indonesia, winners will have to integrate operations from as many as 20–30 banks left in ruins by the crisis, or start from an entirely clean slate. While reinventing for the 21st century will be difficult, many winners in Southeast Asia — domestic and foreign — may look back on the crisis as the period that launched some of their greatest opportunities.

CHAPTER 12
JAPAN: MODERNIZING THE SYSTEM, MOBILIZING THE WEALTH

Tokyo

Osaka

Financial Markets & Business Lines (US$)

Overall	– Equity capitalization (% of GDP): $2,085bn (50%) – Number of listed corporations: 3,139 – Debt market capitalization[3] (% of GDP): $3,600bn (86%) – Total domestic loans (% of GDP): $5,587bn (133%) – Total external debt (% of GDP): $1,783bn (43%) – Total offshore loans (% of GDP): $357bn (9%) – Number of local banks (>$5bn assets): 123 – Number of foreign banks: 101 – Top 3 banks' market share (deposits): 20% – Maximum foreign ownership of a commercial bank: 100% – Currency convertibility: Open
Corporate Banking	– Domestic corporate loans (% of GDP): $3,216 bn (77%) – Nonperforming domestic loans: 15%[4]
Retail Banking	– Total consumer deposits (% of total deposits): $5,122bn (59%) – Total consumer loans (% of total loans): $721 bn (13%) – Persons per branch: 2,500 – Persons per ATM: 1,300 – Credit cards per capita: 1.9
Asset Management	– Retail assets under management: $419bn – Total domestic institutional assets: $6,010bn[2] – Number of asset management firms: 145
Trading	– Number of stock brokerage firms: 225[2] – Average daily equity trading volume: $4.6bn – Average daily FX trading volume: $149bn[5]
Investment Banking	– Total equity issuance (1994–97 annual avg): $29bn – Total debt issuance[3] (1994–97 annual avg): $358bn – Number of domestic M&A transactions >$50mn (1992–97): 54
Private Banking	– High-net-worth households (>$1mn investable assets): 285,000[1] – Potential private banking assets: $1,509bn[1]

Social & Economic Indicators (US$)

Overall	– GDP: $4,194bn – Population: 126mn – GDP per capita: $33,200 – PPP GDP per capita: $23,440 – 1985–1997 GDP real growth: 2.9% CAGR – Projected 2010 GDP per capita: $55,500 – Exports (% of GDP): $411bn (10%) – Foreign currency reserves (% of imports): $220bn (48%) – % urbanization: 78%
Corporate	– Top 3 sectors: Real Estate, Wholesale/Retail, Construction – Number of corporations with annual sales >$1bn: 967
Individual	– Annual savings rate: 31% – Average savings per household: $230,000[1] – Home ownership: 60% – Household car ownership: 80%[2] – Telephones /1000 pop: 485[2] – Internet subscribers/1000 pop: 47 – % of 18–22-yr-olds attending university: 30%

All figures as of December 1997 unless otherwise indicated.
[1] McKinsey estimates.
[2] Figures as of December 1996.
[3] Maturity greater than 1 year.
[4] Figures as of June 1998.
[5] Figures as of April 1998.

12
JAPAN:
MODERNIZING THE SYSTEM, MOBILIZING THE WEALTH

Bankruptcies of major financial institutions were not supposed to happen in Japan, yet on December 17, 1997, Yamaichi Securities declared it was shutting down. What was once Japan's leading securities company could not be saved by Fuji Bank, its huge lead bank, or by the powerful Ministry of Finance (MOF).

Yamaichi's demise made two things clear. First, the old rules no longer applied. The "Big Bang" financial deregulation launched in late 1996 was undercutting the ability of the MOF and a small group of leading financial institutions to orchestrate events. Market forces could determine outcomes like never before. Second, one player's miseries meant opportunities for others. Merrill Lynch moved quickly to hire Yamaichi's core retail broker force and take over most of its domestic branch network. Societe Generale acquired Yamaichi's institutional asset management unit, and Sanwa Bank acquired its retail mutual fund subsidiary.

What happened to Yamaichi is bound to happen to other Japanese financial institutions as the full impact of the "Big Bang" takes hold. At the same time, however, many more players — both domestic and foreign — stand to profit from the unprecedented opportunities that will arise as Japan's enormous wealth becomes mobilized more efficiently to the benefit of all. By 2010, Japan will finally have a modern banking system that is worthy of the world's second richest economy.

Mobilizing Wealth Is Key to Growth and Modernization

By the end of 1996, Japan's economy was in its sixth straight year of stagnation. The bursting of the stock market and real estate bubbles in the early 1990s had left the financial industry with huge and largely undisclosed bad debts. Despite government efforts to bolster the industry through aggressive interest rate reductions, the banks continued to fester. Worse yet, the banks' problems exerted an insidious, crippling effect on the Japanese economy. Repeated attempts to stimulate the economy through fiscal spending had little impact, with growth edging up from 1% in 1993 to 2.8% by 1996 but then back down to 0.3% in 1997. It became clear that without more fundamental action, Japan would continue to drift slowly toward recession.

The problem at the core of the Japanese economy was a mountain of bad debt. The 1980s bubble economy had created a one-time US$1.5 trillion surge in bank debt, linked mainly to the overheated real estate market. By 1997, total debt in Japan still equaled 175 percent of GDP, compared with less than 90 percent in the U.S. and the U.K. Approximately US$1 trillion, or 13 percent, of this total debt was bad. Relative to the size of the economy, Japan's bad-debt burden was at least five times larger than the U.S. savings and loan crisis of the 1980s.

Japan, however, was not at risk of melting down as many of its Asian neighbors did in 1997–1998. The Japanese economy and banking system were huge by any standards, boasting a 1998 GDP higher than US$4.2 trillion, 141 of the world's top 500 corporations, six of the world's top ten banks in terms of assets, and per-capita personal wealth of more than US$80,000. Unlike many other Asian nations, Japan had a vast reserve of wealth locked up in low-productivity deposits and postal savings accounts — wealth that could be leveraged to work off the bad debt.

Also, Japan's bad-debt problem was fundamentally a domestic issue, and one unlikely to have serious direct ramifications for its trading partners. Japan's economy is more domestic than is often realized; exports during the 1990s ranged from roughly 8 percent to 10 percent of GDP, versus more than 30 percent for Korea and nearly 50 percent for Taiwan. Even if half of all Japanese loans to Asian countries in 1998 were completely unrecoverable, losses incurred owing to the Asian economic crisis would only increase Japanese bad debt by 15 percent, leaving the nation a very comfortable distance from bankruptcy.

Still, the question in the closing years of the 20th century remained: Would Japan make the tough decisions needed to mobilize its immense wealth, get its economy back on track, and develop a modern financial system worthy of the world's second largest economy?

A "Guided" Country's Financial System

Despite its size, Japan's financial system at the launch of the "Big Bang" deregulation in late 1996 was still structured to drive the growth of a rapidly developing post-war economy. Although many of the world's largest financial institutions were Japanese, their names rarely came up in discussions of the innovations that swept the global financial markets since the early 1970s. The collapse of the Bretton Woods fixed exchange rate framework exposed financial institutions around the world to substantially higher interest rate and foreign exchange volatility, launching a long process of restructuring and innovation. Japanese institutions, however, remained cocooned in a highly structured and protected financial system that was designed to collect personal savings through low-cost deposits and to funnel capital to favored corporate sectors.

Exhibit 12.1 provides an overview of the key domestic banking players in Japan as of 1997. Nine city banks dominated the system in terms of assets (40 percent of the nearly US$9 trillion total) and overall clout. Ranked by asset size, they were Bank of Tokyo-Mitsubishi, Sumitomo, Dai-Ichi Kangyo, Sanwa, Fuji, Sakura, Tokai, Asahi, and Daiwa. The 129 regional banks ranked second in both assets (25 percent) and branches (32 percent). Within the public sector was the huge Japanese post office system, the world's largest retail financial institution, with US$1.7 trillion in deposits. Post offices represented nearly 60 percent of all deposit-taking branches in Japan and competed directly with the banks. Rounding out the domestic players were ten specialist institutions — seven trust banks and three long-term credit banks. In addition, more than 90 foreign banks had invested in Japan by 1997. Of these, however, Citibank was the only foreign player with a meaningful retail presence — at least in Tokyo, where it had 20 branches.

Exhibit 12.1

Key Domestic Bank Players in Japan: 1997
Percent

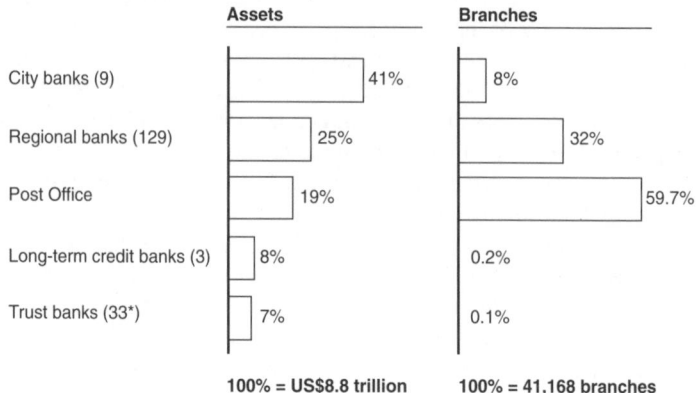

100% = US$8.8 trillion   100% = 41,168 branches

* 7 domestic banks, 17 subsidiaries of securities companies, and 9 foreign subsidiaries.

Source: Federation of Bankers Associations of Japan

Japan's banking system had its origins in the massive restructuring of the economy that began after World War II. In the 1950s, the powerful MOF and Ministry of International Trade and Industry (MITI) began laying the foundations for some of the largest and most profitable Japanese corporations, a significant number of which ranked at the top of their industries globally by the 1980s. Immediately after the war, the government nurtured the development of infrastructure industries, such as steel and power generation, to rebuild the devastated economy. By the late 1950s, however, MITI deliberately shifted the focus to capital- and technology-intensive industries such as transportation, electronics, and heavy equipment. The MOF, through a highly regulated banking system, channeled cheap debt capital to these designated sectors.

This coordination of industrial development policy and financial policy paid off handsomely in economic terms, as evidenced by Japan's stunning post-World War II advances. Yet, while the economy grew at a dizzying speed after the 1950s, modernization of banking system processes lagged behind. Even though Japan had sufficient capital for several decades and there was no longer a need to target specific corporate sectors for lending, banks continued to intermediate the flow of a tremendous proportion of the nation's savings into low-productivity debt. In many ways, Japan's financial system in the late 1990s was still guided by the MOF than it was shaped by the forces of open competition.

First, Japanese financial institutions were much more protected than their counterparts in other countries. Strict MOF guidelines prevented competition on product, price, or channel, resulting in a "big is beautiful" culture in which banks vied to maximize assets and volume as a means of influencing the market.

Second, Japanese financial institutions pursued just enough profitability to sustain growth; generating high returns on equity was of secondary concern. Their ownership was dominated by cross-shareholdings with sister companies in their *keiretsu* — the industrial groups that control much of Japan's economy — and independent shareholders had little influence. As a result, strong capital levels and ROE were given lower priority than the size of loan portfolios and overall balance sheets.

In exchange for accepting MOF restrictions and "administrative guidance," the banks received an implicit guarantee of their financial health and long-term survival. The MOF provided behind-the-scenes support for those in trouble, sometimes going as far as to orchestrate mergers. When deemed expedient for broader purposes, the MOF also manipulated or supported markets, for example, by directing institutional investors and government-controlled agencies to purchase corporate shares to support the stock market.

This approach worked until the bubble economy excesses of the late 1980s began draining profitability from the financial system. The stock market bubble burst in 1990 and the real estate market followed suit in 1991, putting pressure on collateral and banks' loan portfolios. As profits deteriorated, financial institutions responded by competing harder to boost lending, which further reduced spreads and led to the booking of lower-quality assets.

When U.S. banks were similarly faced with huge bad debts in the 1980s, Washington simultaneously lowered interest rates and established the Resolution Trust Corporation as a clearinghouse to deal with the debt problem. Tokyo, however, was hesitant to take the debt bull by the horns and go beyond lowering interest rates to make banks more profitable. Not until late 1998 — confronted by a rapidly deteriorating yen, the worst recession in 40 years, and strong international pressure — did the government move to recapitalize the banking sector and absorb the bad debt of insolvent institutions. In mid-September 1998, Prime Minister Keizo Obuchi bowed to opposition demands and agreed to nationalize the ailing Long Term Credit Bank, one of the country's largest banks. He also curtailed the MOF's supervisory powers by creating a new independent commission to oversee the banking clean-up. In early October, at least US$500 billion in taxpayer funds was earmarked for injection into a troubled banking system that had outlived its usefulness.

Japan hung onto its "guided" banking system for several reasons. One explanation lay in the consensual nature of Japanese society, which is reflected in the political system in particular. Banking reform was discussed at various times, but until the late 1990s there was never enough pressure for change and/or political will to force reform on industry interest groups. Furthermore, the general economic climate in both good and bad times gave the government good excuses to put reform on the back burner. The growing wealth of the 1960s and 1970s obscured the need for change, while the oil crisis in the mid-1970s diverted attention elsewhere. Reform was again discussed — but tabled as potentially disruptive — during the boom years of the bubble economy. When that bubble burst in 1990–1991, the government was too distracted by the resulting situation and afraid that deregulation would sink the very institutions it was trying to save.

After 6 years of painful stagnation, the government realized it had little choice but to deregulate the financial industry. In December 1996, it launched the "Big

Bang" (see sidebar), with the hope that unleashing competitive forces would reinvigorate the financial industry and, in turn, put the economy back on a growth trajectory.

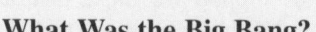

What Was the Big Bang?

Japan's Big Bang was designed to overhaul the financial markets in just 4 years — much more quickly than reform efforts in other countries. By comparison, the U.S. took more than 20 years to deregulate its financial markets. The impact of reform was also expected to be greater than elsewhere, given Japan's starting point of higher protection and segregation of financial activities.

Underpinning the Big Bang was a vision of transformation — away from a financial system focused on banks, bank debt, and corporate customers, and towards one that will disintermediate banks and unlock retail investors' wealth to reinvigorate the financial sector and the economy overall. To that end, the government relaxed the rules on product and price competition, market entry, and distribution channels.

Increased product and price competition

Previously, the MOF controlled new products and their pricing in excruciating detail. The Big Bang allowed complete freedom in many instances, and in others switched from a strict case-by-case approval process to a notification and review process. In some areas (e.g., insurance), the MOF is no longer directly in charge of product and pricing approval. Approval of new life and nonlife insurance companies with new products was shifted to the Financial Supervisory Agency, an independent agency reporting to the Prime Minister's office, not the MOF.

Easier market entry

The Big Bang opened the door to foreign and domestic new entrants in many financial activities. Foreign exchange, which was previously the exclusive domain of banks, was opened to all types of players — from stockbrokers to convenience stores — in April 1998, that is, since 1993, life insurers have been able to set up nonlife insurance subsidiaries, and vice-versa. By 2001, banks too will be allowed to participate in the insurance business. Entry into mutual fund or securities businesses was also eased: competitors simply had to register with the MOF, whereas previously applicants were subjected to a lengthy and complicated licensing process.

More distribution channels

The Big Bang eased channel constraints in many ways. It dramatically reduced restrictions on banks' branch placement and hours, and opened up new channels, such as electronic banking. Bank employees were permitted to sell retail investment trusts (mutual funds) for the first time. In addition, direct marketing was allowed in several sectors, including investment trusts and insurance.

Bumpy Road to Modernization

The road toward full financial deregulation and modernization is bound to be a bumpy one. Though challenges to reform will no doubt arise in the early years of the 21st century, these will slow but not derail the deregulation process. Even if the government were to halt the Big Bang before its planned 2001 completion, Japan's financial services industry would be transformed: many significant changes were already working their way through the financial system and markets by the end of the 1990s, and competitors were beginning to behave differently.

Bumps in the road are inevitable as Japan, a society that prizes stability and order, begins to grapple with the realities of a deregulated financial system — more bank failures, consolidations, write-offs, and layoffs. Such events will provide fuel for those who fear that change is happening too fast after five decades of tight control.

Another obstacle to a smooth transformation is that neither the elected government nor the MOF have articulated a clear vision of the desired end game — that is, the ideal post-deregulation financial system. Issues left unaddressed as of late 1998 include new roles for institutions, the resulting industry structure, market operating rules, and solvency requirements. In addition, policymakers have not set clear objectives for consumer benefits. And, importantly, the role of MOF itself in the post-deregulation environment has yet to be defined. Thus, the MOF's ability to overcome bottlenecks in the reform process and instill confidence in the outcome remains uncertain.

Despite these hiccups, by 2010 Japan should finally have a financial system that matches its economic clout. The nature of the opportunities available in the interim will evolve markedly, and so will the factors that separate the winners from the losers.

Deregulation Breeds Opportunities

The forces of deregulation, along with the growing frustration and sophistication of both retail and corporate customers, will significantly alter the opportunities in Japanese banking. Until the late 1990s, most major domestic financial institutions defined their customer domains in the same way. They all maintained significant businesses targeting large corporations, middle-market corporates, small businesses, and retail customers, for both their domestic and international banking needs. In the early 21st century, all but a handful of banks will abandon this "serve everyone everywhere" approach, and a range of more differentiated players will emerge.

In 1997, the top 20 Japanese banks suffered an aggregate net loss for the second year in a row due to a collective US$25 billion in write-offs. These write-offs, however, masked healthy operating profits in traditional corporate and retail businesses, where the spreads were attractive, thanks to extremely low interest rates. In the late 1990s, corporate banking products — mainly loans and deposits — accounted for more than 70 percent of total bank revenues and pre-write-off operating profits. Traditional retail products, such as deposits and mortgages, accounted for about 20 percent, with the balance consisting mainly of capital market and proprietary trading profits.

Corporate banking will struggle through at least the first few years of the 21st century to get past its bad debt problem and regain its position as a net profit generator. Its overall contribution to banking revenues and profits is likely to shrink, however, as disintermediation and aggressive competition for the lending business that remains take their toll. The retail sector will pick up much of this slack and become a more important source of profits as consumers turn to banks for a broader array of financial products and services. Pre-write-off operating profits from retail banking and other personal financial services are likely to increase from 20 percent of total bank profits in 1997 to roughly a third by 2010. New savings and investment products, such as investment trusts and capital-protected investments, are likely to drive revenue and profit growth as individuals continue to accumulate personal financial assets and as banks introduce higher-value services.

Serving Retail Customers:
Profitable but Increasingly Competitive

Traditionally, retail banking was a steady and profitable business line that most Japanese banks took for granted. Even though retail banking businesses earned about US$30 billion a year in pre-write-off operating profits through the 1990s, banks viewed individual customers as little more than a low-cost source of funding. Product selection was poor, and the Japanese public was given little choice but to save rather than invest. In the late 1990s, retail customers were frustrated with existing products and channels. According to the extensively used Nikkei Needs personal financial services survey, only 22 percent of individuals were satisfied with the services and products of their main financial institution. Many said they were willing to switch to new service providers if better offerings were made available. This willingness to move for a better service offering was evident in the case of consumer finance companies — one of the few examples of a redesigned retail financial service business. Poor treatment of mass-market customers seeking unsecured credit drove ten million individuals to turn to innovative consumer finance companies that offered products and ATM networks designed to make borrowers feel like important customers (see sidebar).

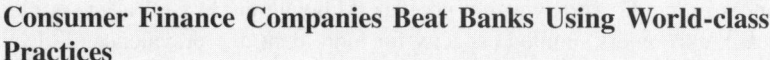

Consumer Finance Companies Beat Banks Using World-class Practices

In the late 1990s, Japan's most profitable retail financial services businesses were not banks but consumer finance companies. The top five unsecured consumer finance companies — Takefuji, Acom, Promise, Aifle, and Lake (which was acquired by GE Capital in June 1998) — generated pretax profits of 20 percent and after-tax ROEs of 15 percent in 1997. According to *The Consumer Credit Monthly,* these five commanded an aggregate 70 percent of revenues in this US$15 billion market. Far from their origins as loan sharks, providing credit to those who could not get it from banks or others, they fundamentally transformed consumer lending in Japan.

Unsecured consumer finance was perhaps the only retail financial business in Japan that attained world-class standards before the Big Bang. Each of the leading players built nationwide branch and ATM networks that relied on state-of-the-art technology. By the late 1990s, they were using sophisticated, behavior-based credit-scoring models that assessed more than 100 variables. Understanding that Japanese consumers are embarrassed about applying for credit, these companies located their shops discreetly, in second- and third-floor offices. Upon entering a shop, a customer was greeted by an unmanned ATM kiosk (not a person), which accepted the credit application. A video link was used to collect the "face-to-face" data needed for credit scoring, such as the type of clothing and accessories worn by the applicant. Customers could complete a credit application, finalize a loan agreement, and receive and pay cash all through the ATM. They could also conveniently repay loans via electronic transfers from regular bank accounts.

Despite interest rates averaging 28 percent in 1998, ten million consumers had taken out unsecured consumer finance loans at least once. This was 25 percent of the 20-to-45-year age bracket, which made such loans mass-market products, not the sub-standard products they still were perceived to be. Taking out a loan is convenient, easy, and discreet. And customers feel like customers, instead of second-class citizens, which is the way they are treated at banks.

In the late 1990s, Japanese consumers on average had the same amount of debt as in other developed markets, such as the U.S. However, the mix in Japan was skewed toward real estate debt and mortgages, leaving the average Japanese with less capacity for credit-card and other forms of debt. Running up large revolving balances on credit cards was not popular. Although credit card usage is likely to increase, consumers' limited capacity for more debt, the prevalence of electronic transfer payments, and the aging population's resistance to changing money management practices will keep Japan's credit-card debt lower than that of other developed countries.

The retail mortgage market is likely to evolve only slowly. In the late 1990s, this market remained the territory of major domestic banks, regional credit unions, and the government, which together held more than 95 percent of all residential mortgage debt. Securitizing the market and making it more liquid would require structural changes, such as the creation of standard rating agencies (like the Freddie Mac and Fannie Mae in the U.S.) and the development of a secondary market for mortgage securities. But these are unlikely to be seen as priorities before 2002, by which time Japan should have cleared its more pressing deregulation hurdles.

Serving High-Net-Worth Individuals: A Large Latent Market that Will Grow over Time

Japan's retail financial services providers can tap into an enormous amount of wealth — private financial assets neared US$11 trillion in 1997. Including real estate, personal assets that year swelled to over US$25 trillion, making more than 4.5 million Japanese households millionaires. This wealth was concentrated geographically around three cities — Tokyo, Osaka, and Nagoya — which were home to 47 percent of Japan's affluent households.

Restrictive regulations, limited product offerings, and conservative investment attitudes have stifled this potentially attractive private banking market. In addition, Japanese investors have been averse to concentrating their assets in a single financial institution because of security and privacy concerns. More liberal foreign investment and financial service distribution regulations in the 21st century should lead to a much broader array of service offerings. These changes, along with increased frustration with the relatively poor returns offered by real estate and traditional bank deposits, are likely to spur private banking development — but only gradually.

In the 1990s, most Japanese high-net-worth individuals relied on tax advisors and commercial bankers to manage their assets, usually a mix of real estate and commercial assets. Reducing income and inheritance tax liabilities was the top priority for many, as inheritance taxes could reach 70 percent. The major banks were all too happy to accommodate these wealthy customers until a late 1980s attempt to capture tax advantages through real estate holdings backfired. Under this scheme, an investor could earn both real estate and inheritance tax breaks, for example, by constructing an apartment building on an open piece of land and taking out a large bank loan. The real estate market bubble drove seemingly ever-increasing property values, and the banks provided loans based on the market value of the property, not on cash flows from the apartments. This scheme became unviable after real estate prices started falling in 1991. The result was losses for many clients and a pile of bad debt on the banks' balance sheets. Consequently, by 1993, city banks, such as Fuji Bank, Bank of Tokyo-Mitsubishi, and Sumitomo Bank, as well as leading brokers, such as Nomura Securities, had eliminated or significantly cut their private banking services.

In the late 1990s, Fuji Bank, Bank of Tokyo-Mitsubishi, Sumitomo Bank, and Nomura Securities began to re-energize their private banking services, this time focused more on investment advice. Clients were given private bankers who served in private offices away from the main floors of the mass-market branches. New products and value-added services were still missing, however, and the effectiveness of these services was unproven.

By 1998, several leading foreign institutions also offered private banking services, but their volume was minimal. Players such as Citibank and UBS typically provided international investment products and advisory services, while the investment banks focused on restructuring privately held companies to diversify assets into a broader set of investment products or to transfer wealth to future generations. Goldman Sachs and JP Morgan, for example, each had a small private banking operation that was linked to their main investment banking and asset management businesses. These two banks each served no more than a few hundred core private banking clients.

Serving Large Corporations: A Sputtering Profit Engine

Despite the steadily deteriorating spreads and massive loan write-offs that created net losses during the 1990s, corporate banking is expected to regain its position as a profit generator for Japan's banks in the early 21st century. According to the Bank of Japan, 80 percent of the total US$6.5 trillion in debt held by Japanese banks in 1997 was in corporate loans, which generated an estimated US$40 billion in pre-write-off operating profits. To turn these gross cash flows from corporate banking into net profits, however, Japanese banks must overcome two significant challenges.

First, banks will need to bring credit loss levels in line with those of other developed economies. This will require a complete reworking of bank loan underwriting processes and risk management controls. Achieving this would turn losses into net profits, but given the very low spreads on corporate banking, it would still only generate returns on equity of 5–7 percent — well below international standards.

The banks' second challenge, therefore, is to increase returns on assets from their corporate customer portfolios. This will occur gradually as new products are introduced and assets are deployed more carefully. But the process will be painful, with many weaker banks forced to exit or to reduce their corporate lending significantly. The need to boost returns will also require banks to replace traditional lending and deposit products with off-balance-sheet credit and asset management products — mirroring the evolution of the North American and European markets during the 1990s. According to the Bank of Japan, 1995 marked the first year in which large corporates raised more *new* funds directly from the securities markets than they did through bank borrowing — although outstanding bank loans were still the largest single source of capital for corporates.

Over the first decade of the 21st century, sheer size will keep corporate banking as the major — though shrinking — revenue generator for most Japanese banks. Banks with large multinational-company portfolios will see lending volumes contract as their top-tier customers, some with better credit ratings than the banks, increasingly access direct debt and equity capital markets. The battle for this new securities issuance business will become intense as big corporations continue disaggregating their use of financial institutions based on market expertise and capability, rather than on past relationships. As is true in every major market around the world, the real threat to the large corporate banking franchise is sophisticated securities houses and investment banks. Exhibit 12.2 shows the striking contrast between Japanese and U.S. corporations' reliance on loans versus other sources of corporate funding.

In the late 1990s, Japanese banks were not prepared to shift from lending to issuing securities. A growing share of the issuance volume was in international markets, where foreign and Japanese securities firms — not banks — had skill and placement advantages. Realistically, only the top few Japanese banks stand a chance of picking up more than a token share of this global business on their own. By 1998, this realization had already led to several major alliances between banks and securities firms — for instance, Industrial Bank of Japan and Nomura Securities, and Sumitomo Bank and Daiwa Securities.

The domestic debt market story was somewhat brighter. By 1997, after only 5 years in the business, Japanese banks had captured a 40 percent share of debt underwriting for major corporates. (Equity underwriting by banks or their subsidiaries was not yet allowed.) While long-term relationships worked in the banks' favor, their success was largely thanks to aggressive pricing against

Exhibit 12.2

Comparison of Corporate Funding in Japan and U.S.: 1995
Percent, US$ trillions

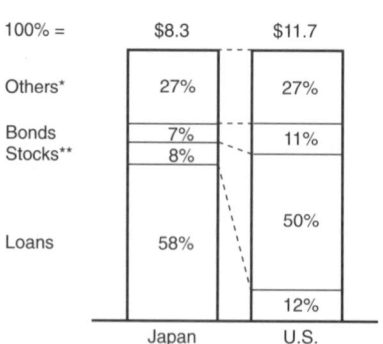

* Trade credits and other current liabilities.
** Book values.

Source: Bank of Japan

incumbents too wounded to respond. In the second half of the 1990s, the leading domestic securities brokers were plagued by extended market losses and a series of internal scandals.

In an attempt to broaden their large corporate franchises and stave off the securities firms, Japanese banks began building more sophisticated capital market capabilities, for example, in derivatives. By 1997, major banks dominated the fixed-income and foreign-exchange derivatives markets, which generated annual revenues of about US$8 billion. Most of the other banks, however, were ill prepared to do battle in sophisticated capital market services requiring leading-edge skills and efficient global networks. Among the few that could emerge as strong long-term players are the giant Bank of Tokyo-Mitsubishi and the Industrial Bank of Japan-Nomura Securities alliance. Foreign players that possessed the necessary skills and experience had a strong advantage in this area, and several tried to strengthen their access to Japanese corporations through alliances in the late 1990s. One example was the Travelers-Salomon tie-up with Nikko Securities, in which Nikko sold a 25 percent equity stake to its U.S. partner.

Serving Small and Medium-Sized Businesses: Things Will Get Worse Before They Get Better

In the late 1990s, nearly 99 percent of Japan's 2.45 million companies fell in the small to medium-sized bracket, defined as having less than US$1 million in paid-up book capital. Lending to these companies made up 56 percent of all Japanese bank lending in 1998, though they account for only half of total sales and a third of operating profits (Exhibit 12.3). Small and medium-sized business customers

---

Exhibit 12.3

Mix of Businesses in Japan by Size: 1997   *ESTIMATES*

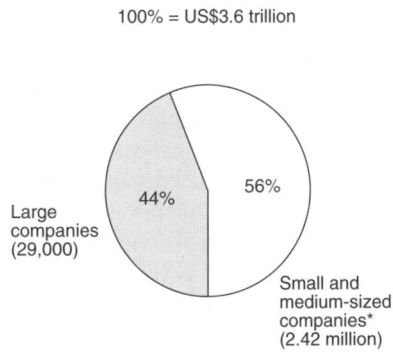

Composition of bank lending
Percent

100% = US$3.6 trillion

Large companies (29,000): 44%

Small and medium-sized companies* (2.42 million): 56%

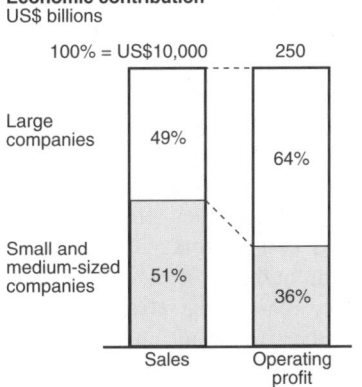

Economic contribution
US$ billions

100% = US$10,000   250

	Sales	Operating profit
Large companies	49%	64%
Small and medium-sized companies	51%	36%

* Less than US$1 million in paid-up capital.

Source: Ministry of Finance; McKinsey analysis

need and value broad-based relationships with their bankers. Indeed, the average Japanese middle-market company borrows slightly more than 80 percent of its capital from banks, with most of the rest in equity held by its customers, suppliers, and perhaps the founder's family. These companies are likely to remain an important banking segment over the medium term, although the winners and losers among this group will change. The late 1990s credit crunch, for example, reinforced the ties between the highest quality companies and their banks, and squeezed many others that had no viable alternatives.

Small and medium-sized companies will remain under strong profit pressure at least through 2001. Their profitability will eventually rebound, but the market for banking services to these companies is likely to contract before expanding again. In the meantime, significant inefficiencies need to be driven out of below-scale manufacturers, overlapping distribution layers, and unsophisticated service operations. The surge in unemployment that began in 1997 offered a sign that this restructuring was under way; after years of hovering around 2 percent, the unemployment rate reached 4.3 percent by fourth-quarter 1998. The Nikko Research Center estimated that, without higher economic growth, Japanese companies would have to cut 2.55 million jobs to restore pre-recession profitability levels. This would drive unemployment to 7.9 percent.

Pharmaceutical distribution offers a dramatic example of an industry undergoing restructuring. Until the mid-1990s, a fragmented collection of regional players prospered under regulated — and extremely high — drug pricing. Then the Ministry of Health and Welfare began reducing prices gradually. In the first half of 1998, this triggered a massive consolidation wave that saw seven of the top ten drug distributors enter into mergers to cut costs and create greater scale economies.

On the other hand, the late 1990s also saw an explosion of small and medium-sized players in the software, networking, and systems integration industries, including companies like Softbank, IIJ, and SAP Japan. As major manufacturers, banks, and telecommunication companies struggled to move from mainframe-dominated to more distributed systems architectures, spending on packaged software and systems consulting skyrocketed. This drove industry growth rates over 10 percent annually during a period when the overall economy was contracting.

A new "checkerboard" landscape thus will emerge in Japan for middle-market and small businesses, and by extension for banking services to these customers. Businesses creating new value-added products and services will have growing demand for banking services and will want increasingly sophisticated products, such as structured finance, private placements, and international cash management services. Meanwhile, other sectors facing significant cost pressure and/or new types of competitors will have to "shrink to grow." Consolidation and cost reduction in these sectors will reduce their need for banking services at least until the early years of the 21st century, when economic growth is likely to pick up.

Another important change in this market is the move toward management buyouts and spin-offs. In 1998, many of Japan's leading corporate and financial conglomerates began selling or spinning off divisions that were losing money or not deemed to be part of their core strategy. Although the numbers were still small, this trend was beginning to create a new set of middle-market bank customers.

Examples include Hitachi's spin-off of two appliance manufacturing plants as independent entities, retailing giant Daiei's sale of its credit division to GE Capital, and Nissan Motor's spin-off of its transmission division.

Major changes in Japan usually take a very long time to initiate — much longer than in most other societies — but once accepted, transformations can proceed with surprising speed. Once industry leaders begin to manage their total business portfolios based on profitability and unload businesses that do not fit with overall corporate objectives, restructuring could proceed quickly. The expected unbundling of major conglomerates such as Hitachi, Toshiba, Mitsubishi Electric, and Nissan Motors should lead to a marked increase in the number of medium-sized companies. Although the banking profit pool would likely be small until at least 2005, serving these new companies could represent an attractive opportunity.

Serving Private Investors:
A Large but Unsophisticated Market

Japan's retail asset management market is one of the areas in which the "Big Bang" will have its greatest impact. Given per capita liquid financial assets of US$80,000 and a stockpile of wealth that continues to grow as the aging population reaches its peak savings years, asset management clearly represents an enormous opportunity for those with high-quality and attractive products. Traditionally, this market has been tightly regulated, and opportunities for new entrants are limited. Deregulation, however, will result in significant restructuring among the players and the emergence of new product offerings.

Retail asset management

Japan remains an extremely affluent country despite the economic problems experienced during much of the 1990s. In 1997, a remarkable 30 percent of all Japanese households — 12 million — had more than US$100,000 in savings and investments, while less than one percent of households had more than US$1 million. The US$11 trillion pool of liquid financial assets held by individuals in 1997 will increase by roughly US$500 billion annually through 2002, creating the largest growth opportunity in Japan's financial markets.

The challenge for retail asset managers in the 21st century will be to transform a nation of savers into a nation of investors. In the late 1990s, Japanese individuals still kept most of their money in low-risk, low-return investments, though they were beginning to dabble in the new higher-return products that emerged after deregulation. As of 1998, about 60 percent of all personal financial assets in Japan were invested in very safe, low-return retail bank or post office accounts, or similar deposit-like products. A further 22 percent went into savings-type life insurance products, and the remaining 18 percent was in higher-risk securities and mutual funds. Yet moderate-risk investment products, most of them offered by Western asset managers, were starting to draw considerable interest. In 1997, for example, Goldman Sachs launched a family of limited-risk, international fixed-income mutual funds (known as investment trusts in Japan) that attracted an amazing US$7 billion in assets in less than 18 months. This success was echoed in large gains by Alliance Capital, Merrill Lynch Mercury Asset Management, and others.

Until 1998, sales of retail mutual funds were the exclusive preserve of Japanese securities houses and investment trust companies. Consequently, the top four securities houses — Nomura, Nikko, Daiwa, and Yamaichi (before its closure) — controlled about 75 percent of the US$419 billion in retail assets under management. Retail investors had no choice but to deal with these providers, and they were very frustrated with the limited products and channels available to them. A 1997 Nikkei Needs survey of more than 3,000 affluent individuals revealed that, on average, only 22 percent of retail investors were satisfied with the service and offerings of their primary financial institution. Customers of securities brokers felt especially abused after having their accounts turned over 100 percent per year, or more, year in and year out. Only 16 percent of securities customers gave their brokers satisfactory ratings, and they eagerly awaited the emergence of banks and other — including foreign — providers of investment products.

The 1998 entry of banks and insurers into the retail mutual fund market provided some relief for frustrated investors by triggering an explosion of new products and new outlets. By December of that year, every major domestic bank had lined up an impressive series of offerings to compete with the brokers and each other. And leading global asset managers, such as Fidelity, UBS, Deutsche Bank, Putnam, and Mellon-Dreyfus, scrambled to enter or expand their positions, often by pairing up with leading banks that could provide distribution.

Institutional asset management

Most bankers in Japan have their eye on pension and other institutional asset management services. This business was reserved for domestic life insurers and trust banks until the mid-1990s, at which point commercial banks, securities companies, and foreign financial institutions received the right to set up institutional asset management subsidiaries. With the entry of these new competitors, some of the market shifted to investment management companies and foreign funds. However, despite the terrible returns on funds managed by life insurers and trust banks, these incumbents still controlled more than 80 percent of the total institutional asset management market in 1998.

The Japanese institutional money market is a "good news/bad news" market for new entrants. The good news is that during the 1990s it was one of Japan's fastest-growing financial services markets: assets under management in pension funds grew at more than 10 percent a year as the population aged. The bad news is that the fees and profits from this business were very poor. Fees in the late 1990s were typically half those of other developed markets, averaging only 25–30 basis points. Skilled, especially Western, competitors were able to accumulate funds several times faster than the market's underlying growth rate. But, given the meager fees, many foreign players that had built up US$5–10 billion in assets under management still had not reached break-even in the late 1990s.

Institutional asset management in Japan has traditionally been a relationship-based business. In the late 1990s, however, there was some indication that customers were beginning to choose asset managers based on performance and underlying product quality. Major pension funds began shifting assets away from very-low-return life insurers toward asset managers that had better performance records. In the fiscal year that ended in March 1997, life insurers on average lost almost 20 percent of their pension funds under management. More encouraging was that some foreign managers appeared to be commanding higher fees for better-performing funds. However, this was an early trend and the market still needs to change structurally and to move from balanced mandates — where one manager is given funds to invest in a broad range of asset classes — to asset-class-specific mandates.

One hope for more profitable growth is the introduction of defined-contribution pension plans, which is expected by year 2000. This may provide an opportunity for foreign players and domestic banks to make further inroads into the life insurers' and trust banks' stronghold. This opportunity was being targeted by several new alliances, including domestic tie-ups (e.g., Nomura Securities with Industrial Bank of Japan, the Mitsubishi Group financial companies with Fuji Bank, Dai-Ichi Kangyo Bank with Yasuda Trust) and Japanese/Western ventures (e.g., Putnam with Nippon Life, and Prudential of the U.S. with Mitsui Trust).

What It Will Take to Win: Basics with a Twist

As deregulation strips away the comforts of protected markets and profitability shifts from corporate banking to new areas, Japanese financial institutions will have to contend with the same competitive challenges that shook markets around the world in the 1980s and 1990s. Those that survive this shakeout will have the will and initiative to make fast, bold restructuring moves. But these moves must be grounded in the sound application of basic banking rules and a strategy that differentiates the institution from its competitors.

Applying Basic Banking Rules

For the Japanese financial system to regain its vitality, many domestic financial institutions will have to dramatically transform their management practices, getting "back to the basics" of what it takes to be a successful player. As performance refused to improve in the late 1990s, some institutions began to recognize the difficult changes required to ensure their survival. A key first step — and one that required a radically different mindset — was to place higher priority on cash flow and profitability than on undifferentiated growth. Leading banks, such as Bank of Tokyo-Mitsubishi, responded to the new reality by setting ROE targets for the first time.

This new focus on cash flow and profits will force changes across the entire banking system. In particular, banks will need to strengthen their skills in functions such as credit rating, pricing, product distribution, and marketing. Japanese banks are still aggregations of their branches — each of which is essentially a mini-bank with a complete mix of corporate and retail products and its own balance sheet. In this structure, a cadre of talented generalists carries out all functions close to the front-line, and the vast majority of the bank's human resources remain under the tight control of powerful but traditional branch managers. This hinders the development of centralized, professional functions and business units that would offer higher quality and efficiency.

Loan underwriting decisions are made in decentralized branches with only minimal benefit from the statistical techniques and honed industry expertise so heavily relied upon by Western banks. Loan pricing is negotiated with the customer by a relationship manager whose main incentive is to increase lending volume — not to maximize profits over the life of a loan. Branch managers control product distribution decisions yet lack the tools, resources, and training to optimize distribution among tellers, salespeople, telephones, direct mail and the Internet. Selecting the right product to market to the right customer at the right time through the most cost effective media is not possible without empowering central product managers with flexible databases, rich with the behavioral history of the 3–8 million customers of the average city bank. In all of these basic areas, Japanese banks lag 5–10 years behind their Western counterparts. Though many bank executives understand these issues and skill requirements, the practical challenge of transforming their conservative, change-resistant institutions is enormous.

Putting profitable growth ahead of growth at any cost will require tough organizational changes, including headcount reductions and compensation and incentive adjustments. The late 1990s brought the first large-scale layoffs, unheard of in the past, among more troubled institutions such as the long-term credit banks, securities houses, and some of the second-tier banks. Early restructuring of compensation programs also was occurring. For example, in 1998, Daiwa Bank announced a 10 percent compensation reduction across-the-board for all employees. Executive bonuses were cut, and stock option plans introduced. By the end of 1998, most of the 19 largest banks had announced similar restructuring actions — spurred on at least in part by the government's requiring profit improvement plans from banks seeking public capital infusions.

Becoming a Differentiated Player

Beyond building a new organization with sound fundamentals, successful banks in Japan will realize that the old rules of strategic behavior are slowly beginning to change. As mentioned earlier, it will no longer be possible or desirable to "serve everyone everywhere." And, it will no longer be enough to copy every move of one's top competitors. For example, all the major city banks had traditionally extended loans to all segments of the corporate sector. In 1998, however, Daiwa Bank bucked tradition by announcing that it would reduce its lending to the big corporations and focus on smaller companies.

By the end of 1998, all but a couple of the leading banks, such as Bank of Tokyo-Mitsubishi and the Industrial Bank of Japan, had decided to shrink their international branch networks to no more than a few offices in key financial centers like New York, London, and Singapore. Outside the top ten, most banks decided to close their international branches entirely or replace them with representative offices to reduce capital requirements and focus resources on the Japanese domestic market. Daiwa was among this group.

While these are steps in the right direction, many banks will need to fundamentally rethink the scope of their businesses and choose where to compete in the deregulated markets of the 21st century. Some customer segments should be cut, products added, and certain functions, like transaction processing or international mutual fund manufacturing, completely outsourced. The leading banks also must think carefully about whether they should maintain an international focus — with strong capital market operations like IBJ or Bank of Tokyo-Mitsubishi, or with commercial banking networks across Asia like Sanwa — or become superior domestic players to better serve their clients at home.

Examples of clearly differentiated players among the domestic institutions have yet to emerge. Among foreign competitors, Citibank broke the status quo in 1994 when it defeated the MOF and the banking industry and obtained approval for operating 24-hour ATMs. Citibank is the only international bank in the 50-plus years since World War II that has been determined to build a retail business in Japan, and it has shown great perseverance and willingness to challenge the MOF. Because Citibank had no large installed base of business that had to be protected in negotiations with the government, the MOF did not have the same degree of leverage that it does over domestic banks. Major Japanese banks were also reluctant to cry foul against such a strong U.S. bank when Citibank was not targeting their core corporate franchise.

Bold, Innovative Players Will Win

Deregulation and market forces will unleash major changes in Japan's banking industry structure during the first decade of the 21st century. Fewer than a dozen of the 19 largest banks in 1997 will likely survive as independent entities by 2010; the rest will have been acquired, merged, or closed.

Major alliances will also alter the competitive landscape as banks reach out to others that have the skills they need to succeed. Alliances will be particularly important for players that want to serve the large corporate market, which was already moving away from traditional relationship banking and dependence on bank loans by the closing years of the 20th century. We are sure to see more alliances — both purely domestic tie-ups across financial sectors as well as cross-border links — among competitors looking to build new capital market and credit-product capabilities and to gain better access to Japanese corporates.

City Banks: Overcoming Complacency Is Key

Overcoming the deeply entrenched belief that their position and power are unconquerable will be key to the success or failure of the nine city banks at the core of Japan's financial system. Although deregulation will require enormous change for these banks, they still have many potentially winning cards to play.

To understand their mindset, we need to cross the tracks from Otemachi, Tokyo's modern financial district, to Hitamachi, the old downtown area that was the birthplace of many of Japan's top financial institutions. Here, time has stood still in many ways. Within a one-kilometer radius, six of the top city banks continue to conduct business on the original sites of their founding branches and to operate and compete in much the same way for the past 80 years. Very tight relationships with corporate customers are the hallmark of these banks.

The Hitamachi Kobunacho branch of Fuji Bank, for example, has traditionally been the heart of the bank's industrial group. Seventy percent of this branch's corporate accounts are those where Fuji Bank has the main banking relationship with the company. This contrasts with the 18 percent average for most of Fuji's other branches across the country, where competition for new core banking relationships is intense. This branch houses several million dollars worth of artwork and it used to have a private bathhouse and a personal barber for bank managers — all signs of the highly respected position that it holds within the branch network hierarchy.

Another characteristic of the Hitamachi bank branches is their complete lack of competition. As little new business comes into the area, there is no need to compete for new customers. Furthermore, the banks maintain a gentleman's agreement not to approach each other's customers. In other words, positions and relative size are the same as they always have been and, as far as the banks are concerned, they will remain the same in the future.

This mindset, so clear in the microcosm of Hitamachi, dominates the way that the city banks think about their relative positions and the way they compete in general. Their view of themselves as the infallible brokers of power — both within the banking system and in the economy overall — prevents them from seeing their inevitable decline in power and, thus, from taking appropriate action.

Though their relative power will wane, the city banks as a group are still in the best position to win in Japan's post-deregulation financial system. They still have vast resources and employ some of the nation's brightest people. Moreover, they remain at the center of their industrial groups and retain a certain degree of both direct and indirect management influence over many of the corporations and even some of the smaller banks and nonbank financial institutions within their groups. All of these factors will continue to work in the city banks' favor, but not all of the nine will necessarily make the cut. Only those city banks that have the will to restructure quickly and behave in new ways will make the transition to the faster-moving competitive world of the 21st century.

Regional Banks: Consolidation Will Lead to Strong Competitive Positions

If the city banks have ruled the banking system and economy from their strongholds in the cities, the regional banks have been the lords of the Japanese countryside. Historically, these second-tier commercial banks have provided an extended distribution network throughout the small metropolitan and rural areas. As of 1997, the 129 regional banks controlled more than US$2.2 trillion in assets through 13,000-plus branches. Many of these banks have been quite solid financially, in addition to having both product and management links to some of the major city banks.

Leading regional banks often have the largest market share within their geography, usually beating out the local offices of the city banks. Their customer bases naturally tend to consist of more small and medium-sized businesses and fewer large corporates than the city banks. Given this customer mix and the fact that competition in rural areas has not been quite as intense as in the cities, average regional bank margins on lending products have not been as thin as those of city banks.

Deregulation and the economic problems of the late 1990s, however, created significant pressure for change among the regional banks. Several regional economies — such as Hokkaido and the Tohoku region in northern Japan — began contracting several years before the nationwide recession officially began in 1998. This was a major reason behind the collapse of Hokkaido-Takushoku Bank, the smallest of the city banks, in late 1997. Also, the regional banks lack the product and marketing skills that will be increasingly necessary to compete as deregulation works its way into the countryside and increases the pace of change.

Those regional banks that manage to improve their cost efficiency and achieve sufficient competitive scale are destined to become long-term winners in the 21st century. Some consolidation among the smaller and weaker banks is inevitable, but we believe that as many as half of the regional players could survive to 2010.

The restructuring drive will be two-pronged. First, most of the regional banks will need to root out the cost inefficiencies embedded in their functionally integrated structures. Moves to slash costs will likely include outsourcing those functions in which the banks lack critical scale, for example, in information processing and asset management product manufacturing. Second, we will see a push for geographic scale. This likely will result in the emergence of super-regional banks with more cost-efficient, large-scale operations covering natural markets such as the areas surrounding Japan's three or four largest urban centers.

Some of these will be brand-focused super-regional banks whose purpose in gaining scale and concentration is to compete with the large city banks rather than to suppress costs. Such banks could form either across broad rural areas or around urban centers. For example, three banks that serve the area surrounding metropolitan Tokyo — Asahi Bank, a smaller city bank with strength, in Saitama Prefecture to the north, Chiba Bank in Chiba Prefecture to the east, and Yokohama Bank in Kanagawa Prefecture to the south — could form a doughnut around Tokyo. This would give them a distribution network strong enough to compete with the city banks in the retail market and corporate middle market.

Specialist Banks: Total Transformation Critical

Japan's banking system after World War II included specialist banks with very strictly defined niches. These unique institutions had no direct counterparts in other major banking markets. They grew quickly, and by the mid-1990s, the country's three long-term credit banks and seven trust banks were quite substantial financial institutions.

Deregulation and changes in the economy pulled the carpet from under the feet of these institutions. In the late 1990s, they had no base on which to build their futures and, as a result, no choice but to completely transform themselves. The chairman of the Nippon Credit Bank, Hiroshi Kubota, made the gravity of this situation poignantly clear at the 1997 announcement of his bank's alliance with Bankers Trust (subsequently acquired by Deutsche Bank in late 1998). Kubota told of having learned that the price of not transforming an institution quickly enough to keep pace with changes in the marketplace is almost certain extinction.

Long-term credit banks

The mission of Japan's three long-term credit banks — Nippon Credit Bank, the Industrial Bank of Japan (IBJ), and the Long Term Credit Bank (LTCB) of Japan — was to extend long-term capital to help drive the development of the Japanese economy. They were almost semi-public institutions and heavily influenced by the economic development plans of the MOF and MITI. To carry out their role effectively, the government granted these institutions preferential status; for example, they were allowed to float bank and secured debentures, which gave them a reasonably low-cost source of capital to fund their lending needs.

By the 1980s, Japan had little need for specialized long-term credit banks; there was much less demand for major capital investment and dependence on bank debt for funding. In 1997, the government removed the banks' regulatory niche by announcing that other banks could also issue debentures. One strength they retained nonetheless was a pool of some of the most talented people in Japanese financial services, recruited from the nation's top universities.

As the "Big Bang" got under way in 1997 and 1998, all three long-term credit banks struggled to reposition themselves in order to survive. The strongest of the three, IBJ, aimed to transform itself into a global wholesale, securities, and investment banking organization. While there is no doubt that the bank possessed the raw talent to do this, it lacked the specific skills. The immediate challenge was thus to sharpen its capital market, securities, and asset management capabilities and become a leading player in at least some areas. IBJ targeted asset management and securities transaction services and investment banking advisory businesses, such as corporate finance. To increase its chances of success, IBJ forged an alliance with Nomura Securities in 1998. Both institutions were hoping to strengthen their investment banking and asset management businesses, both in Japan and globally.

The experience of LTCB demonstrates the difficulty of this repositioning process. Despite various attempts at restructuring and recapitalizing itself — by forming three joint ventures with UBS, then selling equity to UBS, and potentially merging with Sumitomo Trust Bank — LTCB, in the end, was nationalized in September 1998. LTCB's fatal flaw lies in not dealing with the rot in its lending portfolio soon enough. Based on the scanty public numbers available at the time of its nationalization, at least 20 percent of LTCB's loans were unrecoverable. This problem extended to troubled affiliated institutions such as Nippon Leasing, to which LTCB had lent at least US$2 billion. Instead of aggressively working out its loan portfolio in the mid-1990s when it might have had a chance to survive,

LTCB instead focused on strengthening its capabilities for future businesses. In the meantime, the economic downturn was exacerbating LTCB's bad-debt problem to the point that the total debts needing to be written off exceeded the bank's capital. LTCB was bankrupt, and the government felt it had no choice but to nationalize it to prevent a broader banking system panic — perhaps extending beyond the borders of Japan.

Nippon Credit Bank (NCB), in contrast, was the first of the three long-term credit banks to announce its intention to restructure its credit portfolio. Always the smallest of the three and burdened with a particularly bad loan portfolio, it aligned with Bankers Trust in 1997 — which subsequently was itself acquired by Deutsche Bank — in an attempt to build the credit workout skills needed to restructure its bad debt and overall balance sheet. With this "shrink to grow" strategy, NCB hoped to buy enough time to build a new platform to compete probably in corporate banking.

But this plan fell apart as NCB's financial predicament worsened amid the economic deterioration of 1997–1998. With the announcement of the government's bank restructuring plan in October 1998 and the nationalization of LTCB, NCB's future became very unclear. It almost certainly did not have enough resources to survive on its own, and its corporate customer relationships and product skills were not unique enough to make it an especially attractive partner for a stronger institution. In mid-December, the government forcibly nationalized NCB and said it would write off the bad loans and sell what was left to another bank.

Trust banks

Japan's seven domestic trust banks are a very different set of institutions, whose privileged role was to provide trust-based investment services under the trust legal structure. Capitalizing on this position, they were to create interesting products for the pension market, which they split with the life insurance companies. The other major role of the trust banks was to provide trust and custody services for various types of investment funds. As the law required that these funds be managed through a trust, trust banks found themselves in a unique position and with a significant source of funds. The trust banks also operated as normal commercial banks, with 60 percent or more of their revenues coming from corporate lending products.

The trust banks were wrestling with two big issues at the end of the 1990s. First, the deregulation process was opening their institutional asset management niche up to other players. Second, as a group they had bad-debt problems in their balance sheets from the bubble period, when they made loans very aggressively. Given these issues, the trust banks faced the question of how to transform themselves.

One option was to become a specialized custodial and securities processing business like State Street Bank and Bank of New York. However, some of the trust banks (including Sumitomo Trust) sold their position in processing to other players. Another option was to make a play in the higher end of the retail market (like Republic National Bank in the U.S.), perhaps in private banking. A third possibility was to lead fund management innovations as the market moved toward defined contribution plans. This could involve partnering leading-edge Western players; for example, Mitsui Trust allied with Prudential and Mitsubishi Trust with AIG. A trust bank could also combine its asset management business with a life insurance company to try to create a truly global asset management operation.

A final possibility was to merge with each other or with their city bank brethren to capture efficiencies in the commercial banking and retail operations that make up the majority of a trust bank's business. In January 1999, three trust banks announced major alliances: Yasuda Trust was to become a controlled subsidiary of Fuji Bank; Mitsui Trust was merging with Chuo Trust; and Toyo Trust was creating a broad asset management alliance with Sanwa Bank.

Assuming that they successfully overcome their near-term debt problems, trust banks have some interesting assets and resources to bring to bear if they follow these new paths. These include huge asset pools, bolstered by the banks' relatively solid asset management capabilities, and a concentrated higher-net-worth customer base, supported by a surprisingly strong, if somewhat small, branch network. Furthermore, trust banks come in a close second to city banks in terms of reputation and customer respect.

Foreign Players: Unprecedented Opportunities for Those Willing to Commit

In the first decade of the 21st century, Japan's banking markets will remain 70–80 percent under the control of domestic institutions. Yet the handful of foreign players willing to make the commitment to build towards large positions in Japan will have unprecedented opportunities to do so. Japanese bankruptcies, business exits, alliances, and general turmoil in the financial markets are creating once-in-a-lifetime chances for foreign players to acquire platforms from which they can launch significant domestic businesses. Success will require extensive investments of capital and skills, but the door is open to those that want to try. Foreign entrants have two options: they can try either to become insiders in Japan's highly relationship-driven market, or to differentiate themselves from the domestic banks by offering niche products and services.

The insider route

Only a handful of foreign institutions, most notably Citibank and AIG, have managed to establish an early and enduring presence and stay focused consistently on the Japanese market. They also have put regular pressure on the system to change. As described earlier, Citibank pressed the MOF to allow it to provide a more complete set of innovative retail banking services. AIG, meanwhile, persuaded the government through trade talks to further open up the insurance sector to foreign players and helped maintain foreign privileges in the so-called third arena of insurance products, which include profitable niche personal injury and medical products such as cancer insurance.

Such persistence paid off handsomely: by the late 1990s, these two players were considered the most innovative leaders in the market. Their appeal as stable yet bold insiders was clearly demonstrated by Citibank's picking up 40 percent growth in new accounts during the confidence crisis in late 1997 and early 1998.

The unlocking of the market in the late 1990s attracted a new wave of foreign players that aimed to build significant insider positions. Notable examples include Merrill Lynch's acquisition of Yamaichi Securities to create a new retail securities company (see sidebar), GE Capital's string of acquisitions in consumer finance and life insurance, and Fidelity Investment's investment in a leading-edge call center to distribute mutual funds.

Merrill Lynch: Bid to Become a True Insider

Since entering Japan in 1972, Merrill Lynch has built one of the leading foreign brokerages. Its main focus during the late 1990s was to build an excellent capital markets and investment banking business. At the end of 1997, Merrill Lynch was ranked as the top trader on the Tokyo Stock Exchange, surpassing the major Japanese firms, which were struggling with internal scandals. Outside Japan, Merrill Lynch was one of the leading underwriters of Japanese corporate bonds. These successes were the result of aggressive organic growth led by Hisashi Moriya, who had headed Nomura Securities' U.S. operations in the 1980s.

Merrill Lynch's big move came in February 1998, when it took over the core of the domestic salesforce and 33 of 50 branch locations of the failed Yamaichi Securities, which was at one time Japan's leading broker. This was a bold entry into the distribution of financial products and services to the retail market, and significantly strengthened Merrill Lynch's hand in competing for other markets, such as corporate underwriting.

With this move, Merrill Lynch crossed an important hurdle to becoming an insider in Japan, where commitment and relationships are still valued even by the largest corporates. As proof, in June 1998 just 5 months after the Yamaichi announcement, Merrill Lynch underwrote a US$282 million yen-denominated bond for Japan Finance Corporation to Municipal Enterprises, thus becoming the first foreign securities company to lead underwrite a major domestic bond issue. Its new distribution clout also enabled Merrill to join the underwriting syndicates for corporate bonds offered by Kyushu Electric Power and Hokkaido Electric Power in November of that year.

Since the mid-1990s, GE Capital has been building a significant insider position through targeted acquisitions. Its parent company, General Electric, had been in Japan for many years but had not made any move into financial services until 1994. That year, GE Capital bought a small consumer credit operation from Minebea, a medium-sized manufacturer. Over the next 4 years, GE Capital completed six more consumer-credit-related acquisitions, culminating in the July 1998 takeover of Lake, a consumer finance company with US$1.5 billion in revenue.

In addition to these consumer-credit deals, GE Capital engineered the first takeover of a major life insurer in Japan since World War II. In early 1998, it effectively acquired the operations of Toho Life, a struggling second-tier player with about 3 percent share of the huge domestic life insurance market. GE Capital used a creative deal structure to overcome the mutual ownership structure of Toho Life and leave the existing damaged balance sheet and policy book in the parent company. All ongoing operations and new business were folded into a new joint venture, which GE Capital controls with 90 percent of the voting rights. Taking its deals in aggregate, GE Capital was placing the biggest bets on entering the Japanese financial markets than any foreign player in decades.

Fidelity Investments took a different tack, but it too was committed to becoming an insider in Japan. Up until 1997, Fidelity had not had much impact on the Japanese mutual fund market. Despite having been in the market for several years, it had achieved limited success selling through the traditional securities brokers. Deregulation allowing the direct marketing of mutual funds and then sales of mutual funds through banks, beginning in 1998, spurred Fidelity to change its strategy. In early 1998, it began constructing a major call center on the outskirts of Tokyo and linking up with major banks to distribute its funds. As of November of that year, it had agreements with 27 banks to supply branded mutual funds. Some observers felt that the direct marketing investment was being made ahead of demand, given that Japanese retail investors rarely buy financial products from direct marketers, and that Fidelity might have to absorb years of losses. On the other hand, this could be a small price to pay if Fidelity eventually picks up a few percentage points of Japan's US$11 trillion retail financial asset pool.

Other foreign firms contemplating an insider position should not expect to find business or distribution systems readily available for purchase that would enable them to quickly bring their value proposition into the market. Rather, new players probably will need to buy or partner with a Japanese player and then transform the business as necessary, especially on the distribution side. Another possibility is to make a significant investment to build an independent distribution network, as Fidelity is doing.

The niche player route

The majority of foreign players entering the Japanese financial services sector have opted for the second attractive option, leveraging their global capabilities to build a niche business in Japan. These companies chose a limited market niche (e.g., foreign investment funds or specialized insurance products), tried to gain distribution and market access through someone else's retail network or their own limited institutional network, and made a play based on leading-edge skills or world-class products. Niche businesses can be attractive both in their own right and as the Japanese component of a truly global business.

In asset management, for example, some foreign players with strong products linked up with local or other foreign players that had distribution capabilities. Many good examples exist. In 1997, Putnam allied with Nippon Life Insurance to both manage institutional funds and develop mutual funds for the insurer's retail customer base. In 1998, JP Morgan, which had investment banking and trust bank businesses in Japan, announced a 50:50 equity joint venture with Dai-Ichi Kangyo Bank to offer mutual funds and other retail investment products to the bank's eight million retail customers.

One of the most dramatic examples was Goldman Sach's previously mentioned 1997 success in attracting US$7 billion in assets into a family of retail mutual funds, all distributed through major Japanese securities brokers. Although Goldman clearly came up with the right product for the market at that time, a multi-currency, high-quality, fixed-income fund with currency risk protection, much of its success was due to working well with the Japanese brokers. Goldman invested significant time and resources educating front-line brokers about the value of the product for retail investors. To build a longer-term brand franchise, Goldman also invested heavily in mass-media advertising.

The niche or product-focused strategy can add value in two ways. First, it can capture incremental profit in Japan for players with global fund management capabilities. On the institutional side, this could be accomplished by playing a sub-advisory role. On the retail side, it could be accomplished either by selling products developed overseas in Japan or by tailoring products to the local market and pumping them through others' distribution channels. Another way to create value would be through complimentary relationships, whereby the foreign niche player would supply a product to the Japanese partner in return for a better-quality Japanese product that the foreign player makes available to its global customers.

Niche markets are likely to be very attractive into the first decade of the 21st century. Japanese players lack world-class skills and products in many areas (e.g., equity and credit derivatives, securitization, and investment banking advisory services, such as M&A), and they are relatively open to alliances that provide access to these capabilities. At the same time, these profit pools may have limited duration. Profitability decreases as a niche commoditizes, and the joint venture loses its necessity as the local partner learns the core skills. Japanese institutions will have much less need for these relationships once they strengthen their own capabilities. This means foreign investors must take care to think through the end game of any new relationship and to evolve the partnership through the introduction of fresh products or skills.

In the closing years of the 20th century, Japanese banking was not a pretty business. The economy was in recession, banks were unprofitable, and the bad-debt problem still looked like an iceberg whose full extent was hidden below the surface. There was, however, a brighter side, in that the magnitude of the problem was forcing real change. By the end of 1998, the government had created a plan to restructure and recapitalize the banking system and had funded it to the tune of US$500 billion. Japan's immense wealth in the form of retail savings and deposits would prevent a complete meltdown. Finally, Japanese financial institutions were more open to alliances, equity investments, and even, in extreme cases, sellouts to foreign players. This created a window of opportunity for market entry and expansion that was larger than at any time since World War II.

Looking ahead to 2010, the opportunities in Japan are attractive. In terms of revenues or volume, almost every financial services market will be among the two or three largest in the world. Many of these markets are likely to reap healthy profits once the financial system restructures and returns on invested capital are forced to reflect the inherent risks of the businesses. The challenge is bridging through the difficult restructuring period. If banks and other participants spend enough time understanding the changing competitive requirements for success, their returns over the long run will be high enough to justify their investments.

CHAPTER 13
KOREA:
A NEW ORDER IN THE MAKING

•Seoul

SOUTH
KOREA

Pusan•

Financial Markets & Business Lines (US$)

Overall	– Equity capitalization (% of GDP): $55bn (12%)
	– Number of listed corporations: 776
	– Debt market capitalization[3] (% of GDP): $174bn (38%)
	– Total domestic loans (% of GDP): $391bn (72%)
	– Total external debt (% of GDP): $151bn (33%)
	– Total offshore loans (% of GDP): $34bn (7%)
	– Number of local banks (>$5bn assets): 25
	– Number of foreign banks: 53
	– Top 3 banks' market share (deposits): 28%
	– Maximum foreign ownership of a commercial bank: 100%
	– Currency convertibility: Partially controlled
Corporate Banking	– Domestic corporate loans (% of GDP): $349bn (77%)
	– Nonperforming domestic loans: 25-30%[4]
Retail Banking	– Total consumer deposits (% of total deposits): $177bn (75%)
	– Total consumer loans (% of total loans): $69bn (18%)
	– Persons per branch: 5,800
	– Persons per ATM: 1,100
	– Credit cards per capita: 1.0
Asset Management	– Retail assets under management: $60bn
	– Total domestic institutional assets: $339bn[2]
	– Number of asset management firms: 49
Trading	– Number of stock brokerage firms: 38[2]
	– Average daily equity trading volume: $0.6bn
	– Average daily FX trading volume: $35bn[5]
Investment Banking	– Total equity issuance (1994–1997 annual avg): $8.3bn
	– Total debt issuance[3] (1994–1997 annual avg): $71bn
	– Number of domestic M&A transactions >$50mn (1992–1997): 23
Private Banking	– High-net-worth households (>$1mn investable assets): 41,000[1]
	– Potential private banking assets: $142bn[1]

Social & Economic Indicators (US$)

Overall	– GDP: $455bn
	– Population: 46mn
	– GDP per capita: $9,900
	– PPP GDP per capita: $12,390
	– 1985–1997 GDP real growth: 7.6% CAGR
	– Projected 2010 GDP per capita: $12,200
	– Exports (% of GDP): $140bn (33%)
	– Foreign currency reserves (% of imports): $8.9bn (6%)
	– % urbanization: 81%
Corporate	– Top 3 sectors: Trading, Construction, Life Insurance
	– Number of corporations with annual sales >$1bn: 94
Individual	– Annual savings rate: 37%
	– Average savings per household: $18,000[1]
	– Home ownership: 52%
	– Household car ownership: 70%
	– Telephones /1,000 pop: 425[2]
	– Internet subscribers/1,000 pop: 7
	– % of 18–22-yr-olds attending university: 48%

All figures as of December 1997 unless otherwise indicated.
[1] McKinsey estimates.
[2] Figures as of December 1996.
[3] Maturity greater than 1 year.
[4] Figures as of June 1998.
[5] Figures as of April 1998.

13
KOREA:
A NEW ORDER IN THE MAKING

Between the 1960s and the 1990s, South Korea went from being a poor agricultural country to an industrial powerhouse. Critical to this transformation was the government-controlled banking system, which channeled consumer savings into a capital base for a relatively small number of *chaebol* or industrial groups. Korea Exchange Bank (KEB) was among those at the forefront of the nation's remarkable rise. Founded in 1967 with US$8 million equity, by 1997 KEB was the biggest of Korea's Big Four commercial banks. Boasting assets of US$45 billion and more than 400 branches and subsidiaries within Korea (plus another 42 in key overseas locations), KEB was an extremely strong institution with strong links to "Korea Inc."

By early 1998, however, KEB — like most Korean financial institutions — was struggling for its very survival under the strain of large and growing nonperforming loans and collapsed investment portfolios. Like most of Korea's 26 banks, KEB failed to meet the 8 percent capital adequacy requirement set by the Bank for International Settlements (BIS). Roughly 25 percent of KEB's loan portfolio could be considered nonperforming — not surprising, given that Korean corporate bankruptcies averaged 500 a month during the first half of 1998. And the meltdown of Southeast Asia's economies dealt a further blow to KEB as well as other Korean banks that had significant overseas investment exposures.

Under orders from the Financial Supervisory Commission (FSC) to clean up their act, KEB and the other three big banks (Cho Hung Bank, Hanil Bank, and Commercial Bank of Korea) were scrambling to slash costs by closing branches, cutting staff, and selling off real estate. They also were forced to shop around for foreign investors. By July 1998, only KEB had managed to attract a suitor. Germany's Commerzbank agreed to inject US$250 million in equity capital in exchange for two seats on the board and management oversight. Commerzbank now owns about 30 percent of KEB, among the largest foreign stakes in any Korean financial institution.

The tie-up with Commerzbank appears very promising and may well give KEB a second lease on life. But foreign capital alone offers KEB no guarantee of success in the 21st century. As Korea emerges from the crisis of 1997–1998, few, if any, of its financial institutions will escape far-reaching change. Indeed, between July and September 1998, all Korean banks underwent rigorous FSC-mandated management, governance, and performance reviews. These reviews culminated with the announcement of eight bank mergers — three voluntary and five forced by the government.

To survive in the new world of Korean banking, these institutions will need to develop a management focus on shareholder value creation (rather than volume or revenue growth), sharpen their business strategies, and demonstrate excellence in banking fundamentals such as risk management and asset-liability management. In short, Korean banks will have to cram 10–15 years of the U.S. or U.K. banking evolution into just 2 or 3 years — at most — and do so in a change-resistant environment with historically strong unions.

From Economic Miracle to Muddle

Korea's economic transformation in the three decades leading up to the late 1990s was phenomenal by any standards. In 1962, Korea was a farming economy with average per capita income of US$200, on par with the Congo. By 1996, it was the world's 11th largest economy and Asia's third largest after Japan and China. Manufacturing drew more than 90 percent of the country's invested capital and represented 61 percent of GDP, while the agricultural sector shrank to less than 6 percent. Total GDP peaked in 1996 at US$484 billion and averaged over US$10,000 on a per capita basis, a fiftyfold real increase since 1962. In 1997, Korea became a full member of the OECD, a milestone most Koreans consider formal acknowledgment as a "developed" country. That same year, luxury retailer Chanel's Seoul operation boasted one of the highest revenues per square meter of any of its outlets worldwide, and Prada opened its largest Asian store in Seoul, on a street nicknamed Rodeo Drive for its row of fashion boutiques rivaling that of Beverly Hills.

Understanding the formula for Korea's extraordinary growth — often referred to as the "Miracle on the Han River," for the large river running through Seoul — requires understanding the complex web of relationships linking the government, the banks, and the big business groups that have dominated the economy since the early 1960s. Essentially, this "miracle formula" was based on government-directed investments in about 30 large family-owned conglomerates (the chaebol) and another 30-odd state-owned giants (mostly monopolies), using funds generated by high consumer savings rates.

Until as recently as the early 1990s, these favored companies were given specific investment and export goals in key sectors the government sought to promote (e.g., chemicals, steel, automotive, semiconductors, and consumer electronics). In exchange for meeting these goals, they received preferential treatment, including access to business licenses, protection from foreign investors and imports, and cheap financing funneled through largely government-controlled banks. The banks played the important middlemen in this process. The Korean government not only regulated interest rates, it also restricted the sectors and companies to which the banks could lend — much like the Japanese system — while promoting consumer savings through nationwide campaigns.

This growth formula worked well enough on the surface and remained a defining characteristic of the Korean economy up to the crisis of 1997–1998. However, as the capital base grew, so did the expansionist demands of the chaebol owners, and the underlying weaknesses of the web became increasingly exposed.

Ironically, for a country with relatively few large players and a heavily government-directed growth model, competition was extremely intense. For example, by 1997, Korea had four well-established automakers, five fully integrated chemical companies, and four semiconductor manufacturers. Getting bigger and faster than anyone else, was the name of the game. The chaebol focused on achieving dominant market share and on top-line revenue growth, with little or no regard for profit growth or return on invested capital. For most of the leading groups, return on sales measured less than one percent and return on capital was less than the cost of debt throughout much of the 1990s.

By 1996, Korea essentially had become an input-driven economy, again much like the Japanese system. More specifically, Korea invested 98 percent of U.S. capital levels — on a per capita basis — but achieved only 51 percent of U.S. productivity levels. Except for the steel industry, which is a leader in the world, all major Korean sectors (e.g., automotive, chemicals, electronics, food processing) were substantially less productive than those of leading countries.[1]

Over the years, the chaebol relied largely on debt financing (and hence bank financing). Most of the groups had average debt-to-equity ratios well above 5:1 just before the crisis broke in 1997. What little equity they had typically was largely family-controlled, with scant accountability to outside shareholders. Thus, the equity capital markets were very much a sideshow in terms of funding and discipline. And ongoing revenue growth to cover increasing bank funding and ever-higher interest payments was critical to the groups' survival.

The price to be paid for this reliance on debt became clear by July 1997, when the Kia Group — Korea's eighth largest conglomerate, with interests in autos, trucks, steel, parts, and electronic components — defaulted on loans worth US$6.8 billion. Kia's bankruptcy was soon followed by the collapse of the Jinro Group (distillery, retail) in September, and that of the Halla Group (construction, paper, heavy machinery) in December. Three chaebol failures in the space of 6 months shattered both foreign and domestic confidence in the Korean economy.

In November 1997, the bubble finally burst in the Korean financial system — a system in which assets had grown by more than 25 percent a year from 1991 to 1997, in an economy that had racked up 8 percent real growth annually during the same period. Over the course of 1997, the Korea Stock Price Index (KOSPI) plunged by more than 50 percent, while interest rates doubled from 12 to 25 percent. Three factors contributed to this evaporation of confidence in Korea: the government's early stumbling on much-needed financial system reforms, its clumsy response to the Kia and other chaebol collapses, and, finally, its ill-fated effort to prop up the failing merchant banks.

On January 3, 1997, President Kim Young-Sam kicked off his last year in office by announcing his intent to launch sweeping financial reforms. He established the Financial Reform Committee and gave it the mandate to develop proposals for overhauling Korea's weak financial supervisory system within 3 months. One of the committee's key recommendations was to strip the Bank of Korea (the central bank) and the mighty Ministry of Finance and Economy of their regulatory powers and to consolidate all supervision of banks, securities firms, and insurance companies within one large entity. The committee also recommended reducing the barriers separating players in the banking, insurance, and securities businesses. By June, however, greatly weakened by a bribery scandal involving his son, Kim was unable to push these changes through Parliament. It was not until November 1997 — and only in the aftermath of the market collapse — that most of these reforms were passed.

---

[1] "Productivity-Led Growth for Korea," McKinsey & Company Seoul Office, McKinsey Global Institute, March 1998.

The government's handling of the chaebol bankruptcies caused even greater concern than its delay on financial reform. Although it was apparent to all industry watchers that Kia was unsustainable and should be sold at auction or broken up, the government forced all financial institutions to keep the company's credit lines open — in other words, forcing the banks to throw a further US$500 million of good money after the US$6.8 billion that Kia already could not pay back. More broadly, from July until November 1997, financial institutions (including nonbanks) were compelled to freeze up to US$18 billion in loans to ten large insolvent corporations.

Finally, the merchant banks brought the system down. In 1997, about 19 percent of Korea's total financial services assets were held by "investment institution," primarily merchant banks, investment trusts, and securities companies. The merchant banks funded themselves through commercial paper issuance and in the wholesale overnight deposit markets. They also borrowed in U.S. dollars. Without a stable supply of cheaper retail deposits, the merchant banks' cost of funds was relatively high. Seeking a hefty yield on their assets, they invested in Indonesian and Thai corporate bonds or in riskier domestic loans. As Southeast Asian economies went into a tailspin in mid-1997, the merchant banks faced huge losses on their bond portfolios. At the same time, they incurred losses on some of their Korean corporate loans. Depositors panicked, especially those holding U.S. dollar funds. They pulled their deposits or terminated loan rollovers, forcing the merchant banks to swap won for U.S. dollars.

At that time, the central bank made the ill-fated decision to defend the won at the exchange rate of W800:US$1 — a decision that cost it nearly its entire reserves of US$30 billion over the next 3 months. The continuous selling pressure by the merchant banks was soon exacerbated by that of other investors exiting Korea, which appeared to be imploding. By the end of October 1997, the game was over. As the central bank acknowledged defeat, the won fell from W850:US$1 within 6 weeks to the unheard-of level of W1,700:US$1.

On November 23, the government turned to the IMF and received a funds confirmation totaling US$55 billion, US$10 billion of which had to be injected before Christmas 1997 to stanch the bleeding. At this point some observers commented that it might well take another miracle for Korea to rebuild its shattered economy and financial system.

A Financial System Managed for Weakness

Three decades of strong economic growth propelled Korea's financial market into Asia's second largest by the mid-1990s. Financial assets totaled about US$1.4 trillion in 1997, up from US$243 billion a decade earlier. These assets were equivalent to 260 percent of GDP, a ratio similar to those of Canada and Sweden. In domestic banking assets, institutional assets, and cross-border debt, Korea ranked second after Japan; in domestic debt, it trailed only China. Banks accounted for more than 60 percent of the country's total financial assets, or about US$862 billion as of 1997; the rest was split among investment institutions, savings institutions, and insurance companies (Exhibit 13.1).

Exhibit 13.1

Share of Financial Assets in Korea: 1997
Percent

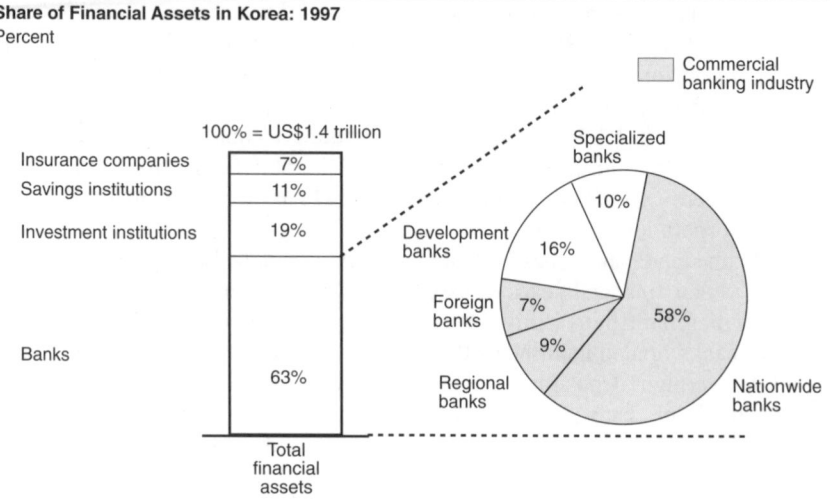

Source: Bank of Korea

Korea's banking industry was designed very much along the lines of the Japanese model. The players included specialized banks focused on particular segments of the economy (e.g., the Industrial Bank of Korea, Housing & Commercial Bank, and several national cooperatives), development institutions (Korea Development Bank, Export-Import Bank of Korea, and Korea Long-Term Credit Bank), and nationwide and regional commercial banks.

Dominating the scene prior to 1997–1998 were eight so-called traditional nationwide banks, which served the chaebol as well as mass-market retail customers. In 1997, these eight controlled more than 70 percent of commercial banking assets and loans (Exhibit 13.2). Also operating on a nationwide basis, but with far less clout, were four relative newcomers: Shinhan Bank (established in 1982), KorAm Bank, a 1983 joint venture between Bank of America and Daewoo Group, and Hana Bank and Boram Bank (both formed in 1991). These four concentrated primarily on high-end retail customers, though they also served corporates. Fourteen others, including ten regional and local banks focused on specific geographical areas, likewise pursued both retail and corporate business.

Except for the four newcomers, all banks in Korea were under considerable government influence, both directly — through complete or partial ownership status — and indirectly — through approval of key executive appointments and lending "recommendations." The combination of significant "noninterfering" shareholders (including foreign shareholders for KorAm and Hana) and the challenge of entering a market with dominant nationwide players forced the newcomers to differentiate themselves, and deserves at least partial credit for their relatively healthy position in the late 1990s. In fact, these four (plus Kookmin Bank and Housing & Commercial Bank) were endorsed as "leading banks" by the FSC in late 1998.

Exhibit 13.2

Dominance of Traditional Nationwide Commercial Banks: 1997
Percent, US$ billions

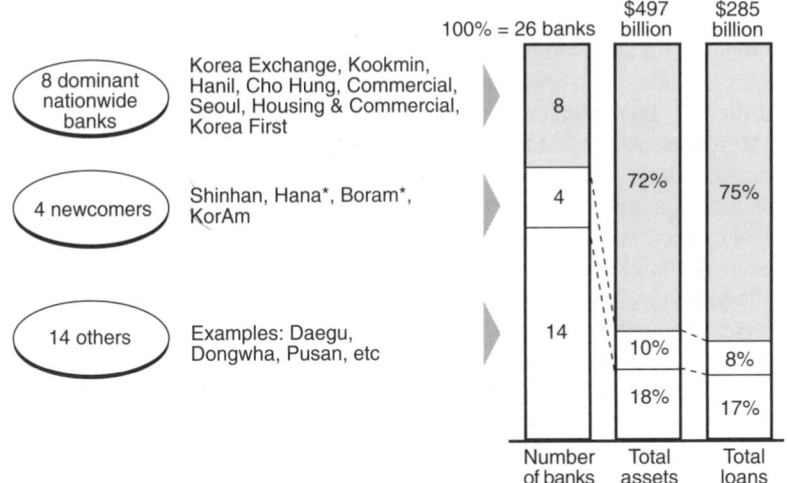

* Hana and Boram agreed to merge in late 1998.

Source: Bank of Korea

The new banks tended to have a better understanding of customers and the economics of the business; they focused more on serving affluent customers with specialized channels and services. They also tended to be more innovative and disciplined in their activities. Boram Bank, for example, introduced VIP services and branches for high-value retail and corporate customers in 1995 (including personal bankers for retail customers and relationship managers for corporate customers) and hired the first CFO in the banking industry in 1996. KorAm Bank, under Bank of America's leadership, introduced a rigorous risk management system that has ensured it a strong capital base and loan portfolio.

Prior to 1998, foreign participation in the banking system was severely limited, with foreign-held assets accounting for just 7 percent of total bank assets. In addition to the KorAm Bank joint venture, Korea had 52 foreign bank branches as of that year. Except for Citibank, which focused largely on retail customers through its 11 branches, most of the foreign banks concentrated on wholesale banking activities, particularly corporate lending, foreign exchange transactions, capital markets, and trade finance businesses.

Despite its size and scope, Korea's banking industry was an industry "managed" to be weak. The symptoms of this "managed weakness" were fivefold: poor profit orientation and performance; inadequate regulation and supervision; excessive industry fragmentation, which resulted in sub-scale players; insufficient credit risk assessment and management skills; and limited product and service innovation.

Poor Profit Orientation and Performance

Prisoners of the country's supply-driven economic strategy, most of Korea's banks were run neither to serve retail customers' needs nor to return profits to shareholders. Rather, their primary purpose was to channel consumer savings into cheap funding for strategic industries and companies. To that end, the government directed the banks to issue so-called policy loans at discounted interest rates and forced them to buy monetary stabilization bonds at substantially below-market rates. Moreover, it rewarded the banks on the basis of their lending volume, not their profitability.

This lack of autonomy and profit focus (along with other weaknesses described later in this section) contributed, inevitably, to laggard bank performance. Total profits in the banking system (excluding foreign players' results) peaked at US$1.06 billion in 1996 before plunging to a negative US$2.8 billion in 1997. That same year, Citibank Korea made a profit of US$207 million, that is, more money than all the profitable domestic banks combined.

Kookmin Bank, Korea's best-performing bank from 1991 to 1997, earned a return on assets of just 0.36 percent in 1997. The three-year ROA average for *all* domestic banks in 1995–1997 was a mere 0.16 percent, less than one-tenth the earnings of world-class banks. Returns on equity were equally dismal.

Inadequate Regulation and Supervision

Until the crisis of 1997–1998 prompted the government to act, Korea's approach to bank regulation and supervision left much to be desired. Measured against international standards such as those outlined by Morris Goldstein of the Institute for International Economics,[2] Korea fell short in eight areas: public disclosure, the accounting and legal framework, internal controls (including asset classification systems and loan portfolio concentration limits), government involvement, connected lending, capital adequacy requirements, incentive-compatible safety nets, and consolidated supervision.

For example, in contrast to Hong Kong and Singapore's relatively well-capitalized banks, Korea's banks were significantly undercapitalized, with an average official BIS ratio of 6.75 percent in 1997. Moreover, throughout the 1990s, this ratio was consistently overstated as embedded losses were not recognized. By 1998, most analysts believed the entire banking system was in a net negative equity position.

Gaps and overlaps among the various government bodies overseeing the financial system exacerbated the regulatory shortcomings. For instance, bank deposit accounts came under the auspices of the Bank of Korea (BOK), whereas commercial bank trust accounts plus the entire insurance sector and all nonbank financial institutions were overseen by the Ministry of Finance and Economy

---

[2] "The Case for an International Banking Standard," Morris Goldstein, Institute for International Economics, April 1997.

(MOFE). Many smaller financial institutions such as credit unions were not supervised at all. The MOFE had the authority to issue new banking licenses, close institutions, or indeed change any of the rules. It even had a major influence on the selection and approval of most commercial bank presidents. The BOK focused on supervision and examination of the banking sector. However, very little money and effort went into the training and career development of examiners.

A related problem was the unfortunate mismatch between the Korean regulators' appetite for supervising financial institutions and their aptitude for doing so. The supervisory style of the MOFE and BOK was perceived to be ad hoc and at times discriminatory by players in the industry. Political interests figured heavily in the process, and some financial institutions were perceived to be subject to unfair audits and seemingly vindictive penalties. Moreover, poor communication between the MOFE and BOK led to bank-examiner findings and issues often being left unnoticed and/or unresolved. For example, unhedged foreign exchange positions and chaebol debt exposure across financial institutions were not reviewed or dealt with systematically.

Fragmented Industry with Sub-scale Players

One of the striking characteristics of the Korean financial system prior to the 1997–1998 financial crisis was its significant fragmentation. In 1997, there were more than 30 securities companies and 350-plus nonbank financial institutions, including 50 insurance companies and other community-based saving institutions.

This fragmentation was due to the strict separation of business lines (e.g., between securities and banking), the existence of specialized lending institutions (e.g., Housing & Commercial Bank, which handled all mortgage lending), and the chaebol practice of each having "its own" financial institution to ensure funding for growth. (These were informal or *de facto* ties based on long-standing relationships, not equity.) Mergers and acquisitions involving financial institutions were practically nonexistent: until the late 1990s, there was only one domestic deal (in 1976, between Seoul Bank and Korea Trust Bank) and that was regarded as a failure due to strong cultural clashes.

Consequently, Korea had few truly large banks. Kookmin Bank, Korea's largest in terms of market capitalization (US$1.2 billion), ranked 61st in Asia as of April 1998. In other words, many of the global or even Asian financial institutions looking for growth opportunities could easily swallow the largest Korean banks without so much as a footnote in their annual accounts.

Relatively high fixed costs were a by-product of excessive industry fragmentation. Average cost-to-income ratios reached 78 percent in 1997, much higher than those in more developed countries. This was due primarily to over-branching and relatively low labor productivity. For example, few banks had centralized retail loan-processing units and strong labor unions limited options to reduce bank staff through greater use of technology.

Insufficient Credit Skills

Among the dangerous legacies of the government-directed lending model was a banking system with fundamentally bad credit risk assessment and management skills. During the high-growth 1990s, most banks lent money based on the "name" of the corporation (some of which were believed to be too big to fail) and the asset value of the collateral backing the loan. Very few institutions used any sort of cash-flow or credit-scoring models, the exceptions being those with significant foreign ownership (e.g., KorAm Bank) and some of the new banks (e.g., Hana and Shinhan).

Limited disclosure and transparency of corporate information hampered even those few institutions that purported to have such decision tools. Also typically lacking were other key elements of an effective risk management organization: for example, bank-wide measures such as risk-adjusted returns on assets and concentration ratios, disciplined enforcement of procedures among all loan officers, early warning systems to catch nonperforming loans, and separation of bad assets into workout units. Moreover, most banks rewarded loan officers only for volume growth, thereby downplaying any incentive to demonstrate prudent risk management.

The pricing of products and services to ensure a reasonable return was another area in which skills were scarce. For example, some institutions priced 5- to 10-year mortgages based on current short-term deposit rates. There was limited differentiation of interest rate charges in line with customer risk profiles. And fees for banking services — standard practice in more developed markets — were relatively rare in both the retail and corporate sectors. As of 1998, no bank charged teller transaction fees for demand deposits, all ATM transactions during "working hours" (9:30 a.m.–4:30 p.m.) were free, and banks charged minimal transaction fees (less then 25 cents) for withdrawing money from competitors' ATMs. Minimum balances for money market certificate-type products were only recently introduced.

Given these skills gaps, it should have come as no surprise when the ratio of nonperforming to total loans topped 20 percent in 1998. Even before the crisis, loan losses averaged about 4.2 percent of assets against an average of one percent for U.S. banks. Warburg Dillon Read forecast in late 1998 that the bailout of Korean banks would cost US$100 billion. The recapitalization of all Korean financial institutions could run as high as US$130 billion.

Limited Product and Service Innovation

Because the banking industry was used primarily as a funding vehicle for the industrial sector, and because the government did not encourage the development of domestic capital markets or allow foreign competitors in, there was little product innovation in either the wholesale or retail markets. Indeed, compared with the offerings in other Asian financial markets, the range of products and services available to Korean borrowers and investors was quite meager.

In the wholesale markets, the primary challenge was the lack of a real yield curve. The MOFE controlled interest rates, and the won was essentially only quoted at the call and 3-year rates. This made it very difficult to create a domestic yield curve and a diversified set of domestic debt instruments. At the same time, regulation of capital flows meant that it was hard to hedge in U.S. dollars — but this did not stop many borrowers from "going naked" on U.S. dollar borrowing for Korean assets. Asset securitization, largely used in developed markets, was not possible until 1998, when the government enthusiastically supported legal changes.

Barriers to mergers and acquisitions — such as cultural apprehension, limited legal and financial transaction skills, and limits on foreign shareholdings — meant that the advisory component of wholesale financial services was also severely constrained. This too changed in 1998, with M&A activity picking up in all sectors of the economy. In the wake of the crisis, many foreign banks, including Banque Nationale de Paris, Salomon Smith Barney, Goldman Sachs, and Warburg Dillon Read, stepped up their Korean M&A resources.

Therefore, lending represented nearly the only wholesale financial services opportunity for domestic banks — and, as discussed above, it was not a very profitable one. The retail sector, in contrast, served as the cash cow for Korean financial institutions, especially banks, during much of the 1990s. Yet, while retail accounted for the bulk of bank profits in 1997, with some estimates as high as 75 percent, the banks largely neglected this side of the business. Rather, their large branch networks served as a conduit for collecting consumer deposits and channeling these savings into funding for corporate growth. As of 1997, Korean banks had a branch for every 5,800 people, approaching the developed-market benchmark of roughly 3,000–4,000 customers per branch. If the branches of savings institutions were included, there was a branch for every 2,200 people.

As elsewhere in Asia, the retail banking boom in Korea was largely thanks to tremendous advances in consumer wealth. The population grew from 37 million to 46 million between 1980 and 1997. Average annual household income increased even faster, from US$4,632 to US$32,100 just prior to the crisis, and personal savings were among the highest in Asia, averaging 35 percent throughout the 1990s. Income distribution in the late 1990s was relatively balanced: the middle class comprised more than 87 percent of households, with annual household incomes averaging US$28,440 prior to the crisis. There was a small yet growing poor population (5 percent of households, with average annual incomes below US$13,140) and relatively few wealthy households (8 percent, with average pre-crisis annual incomes of US$60,840).

Total retail deposits with financial institutions amounted to around US$200 billion in 1996. Some 100,000 households held more than US$400,000 in bank deposits that year, while another 1.7 million households had average deposits of US$80,000. Indeed, Korean consumers put well over half of their savings into bank deposits, similar to the situation in Japan but in stark contrast to the U.S., where bank deposits account for only 23 percent of savings. Insurance products (15 percent of total savings) and stocks (8 percent) made up the bulk of nondeposit savings.

This high proportion of bank savings deposits was at least partly due to the lack of asset management alternatives. To ensure deposits were available for corporate loans, the government restricted the development of retail asset management products during the 1980s and 1990s. Total retail assets under management in 1997 reached approximately US$60 billion, equivalent to one-third of bank deposits. Although the penetration of managed assets seems high in comparison to other Asian countries, most of these assets were in unit trusts which offered fixed rates of return much like high-yield deposits.

Retail banking development was further suppressed by regulations capping deposit rates and by limited consumer loan options. Certain products and services were available only on a limited basis (e.g., auto loans and other secured lending) or were tightly regulated (e.g., mortgages), while others were not available at all (e.g., revolving credit cards). As a result of these controls, in 1996, Korea's personal consumer finance market was equivalent to just 14 percent of its GDP, versus 70 and 73 percent, respectively, for the U.S. and the U.K. Consumer loans in 1996 totaled US$71 billion, or 20 percent of all commercial bank loans in Korea. Based on 1997 data, mortgage financing per household averaged only US$11,000, versus US$135,000 in the U.S. Not only were housing loans the monopoly of the Korea Housing & Commercial Bank, but extremely restrictive mortgage guidelines prevailed through the late 1990s. For example, consumers could borrow only up to 30 percent of the underlying collateral value of real estate, up to a maximum of US$50,000 per person for a first mortgage.

Rebuilding Korean Banking

There is no question that these weaknesses in the financial system contributed to the 1997–1998 crisis. The good news, however, is that the crisis brought this flawed system to the point of no return, unleashing fundamental changes in government regulation, in competitive priorities, and in consumer behavior. The result will be a banking industry essentially rebuilt from scratch. This section describes the key forces that are shaping the rebuilding process.

Regulatory Change

Some of the most dramatic changes will occur on the regulatory front. President Kim Dae-Jung's government, which took office on February 25, 1998, has set its sights on moving to a regulatory system modeled on those of advanced Western economies, which rely heavily on market incentives and disciplines. Thus, the coming decade will see an end to the cozy relationship between the government and a few large corporations in favor of a more transparent system in which economic value drives business decisions. By 2005, as the domestic capital markets approach critical mass and Korean corporations become more dependent on international funding sources, government management of financial flows will simply no longer be possible.

Major moves in this direction were under way in December 1997, as Korea launched its own version of a "Big Bang." First came a barrage of deregulation announcements, the most important of which scrapped limits on the foreign ownership of shares (except those in state-owned firms) and liberalized product pricing and brokerage commissions. In March 1998, the new government established the FSC as a separate ministry reporting directly to the President. The FSC focused on revitalizing and restructuring the financial sector and the corporate sector in Korea. Under chairman Hun-Jae Lee, it launched a series of initiatives with World Bank support, including financial regulatory reforms and bank restructuring.

In April 1998, the government consolidated all four financial supervisory bodies into one integrated and independent unit, the Financial Supervisory Service. This effectively removed the supervisory power of the BOK and MOFE over financial institutions. In setting up this unified body, the government opted for one of the most advanced functional structures, recently adopted by the U.K. in the aftermath of the Barings scandal. The new functional structure represented a shift from the traditional industry-based approach (i.e., with separate oversight of banking, insurance, and securities) to one built around core supervisory functions (e.g., grouping examination activities for all financial institutions into one organizational unit). The aim was to recognize and enable convergence across the financial sector and to engineer significant change in the supervisory groups.

Next, in June 1998, the FSC launched a far-reaching banking industry restructuring program that encouraged the exit of poor-performing and under-skilled management teams, and forced bank mergers and acquisitions, including hostile takeovers. As part of this restructuring effort, it pressed financial institutions to meet international standards for capital adequacy, asset classification, corporate governance, and disclosure.

Foreign Competition

Faced with these changes, troubled local banks must shape up quickly or risk liquidation or takeover. Indeed, aggressive foreign players have already begun taking advantage of the market opening by buying out their former joint ventures and acquiring majority stakes in failing institutions. The Commerzbank purchase of nearly 30 percent of Korea Exchange Bank (mentioned at the start of this chapter) is only one example. Another is the December 1998 memorandum of understanding for 51 percent equity stake in Korea First Bank; the foreign buyers were Newbridge and GE Capital.

In late 1998, a bevy of foreign investors — ranging from foreign banks with strategic interests to principal investors and fund managers — were pursuing all five of the leading banks (Housing & Commercial, Hana, Shinhan, KorAm, and Kookmin). The International Finance Corporation increased its equity stake in Hana Bank from 0.5 to 14.5 percent (including convertible bonds), Hana and Boram agreed to merge under the Hana name, and three strategic investors were courting the combined entity for an alliance. The Housing & Commercial Bank also had several foreign suitors interested in taking anywhere between 10 and 51 percent of its equity. In addition, the government was encouraging foreign financial institutions to buy Seoul Bank, one of the remaining troubled state-owned banks. And, a number of foreign players and domestic investment groups were actively considering greenfield entry.

In the absence of government protection, domestic banks that hope to survive as independent entities in the face of increasing global competition will have no choice but to instill a performance-driven culture underpinned by a clear business strategy. At the same time, they must build world-class skills in risk management, customer segmentation, pricing, and cost management. Moreover, as the barriers to foreign competition come down, Korean banks must cope with the global forces revolutionizing the banking industry. Significant technology innovations — such as low-cost, high-speed global communications, the development of secure and efficient electronic channels, and sophisticated database marketing tools — will up the ante for local players.

More Demanding Consumers

Another major push for change will come from Korean consumers, for whom the 1997–1998 crisis triggered a new wariness toward the government and domestic financial institutions. People are painfully aware of how their funds were mismanaged, particularly by the investment trusts and merchant banks. And, to add insult to injury, they now must foot most of the bill for recapitalizing and restructuring the banking system.

As deposit guarantees are lightened and more banks fail, consumers are thinking hard about which institutions they can entrust with their savings and, thus, are demanding more transparent information on financial players' competitiveness and soundness. Moreover, they are beginning to look beyond domestic options to reputable foreign companies. In response, many domestic banks are exploring joint ventures with foreign asset managers that might burnish their brand names.

This frustration and mistrust of anything having to do with the old system will lead to significant opportunities for the few relatively strong domestic banks, for foreign entrants offering innovative products and services, and for greenfield start-ups that are quick to fill the gaps in the financial marketplace. Clearly, the days of consumers funding the Korean growth miracle while having few options for maximizing their own financial assets are over.

Opportunities in the New Order

The forces of change will bring about a new financial order in Korea, an order characterized by greater competitiveness, diversity, and specialization. For many financial institutions, the issue will be where to play — where can they build the greatest competitive advantage to achieve scale and generate profits? Unlike some countries in Asia, where only selected market areas are likely to provide a large base for potential profits, Korea in the first decade of the 21st century will offer significant opportunities across the retail, corporate, and institutional customer segments.

Modernizing Retail Banking

We have seen how the retail sector was traditionally a neglected but profitable segment for many banks. This segment will grow significantly in the first decade of the 21st century, as lending restrictions are removed and as wealth levels increase. At the same time, however, competition will intensify much further, making this an attractive market only for those that have the scale to make the necessary technology investments and the marketing skills to effectively target and cross-sell to customers.

Foreign players such as globalizing credit-card issuers, mortgage companies, and consumer finance companies will find the Korean retail market very attractive. Greenfield technology-driven retail firms using telephone and computers to access and serve customers will also likely become significant players. In the late 1990s, Korean consumers were open to new ways to manage their financial transactions: between 1996 and 1997, telephone transactions quadrupled and home banking business tripled. On-line stock trading accounted for 4 percent of total transactions as of October 1998 and was expected to reach 10 percent within a year. Domestic retail banks will have to improve their game on all fronts as consumers look for the best offer with little or no regard for the seller's country of origin.

Major business opportunities will arise as Korea builds the infrastructure for a sound and profitable banking system. For example, a prime opportunity area will be transaction-processing technology and services such as those provided by Fiserv and FDR, which reduce processing costs and extract more consumer data. Information provision — including credit ratings, asset management fund performance, and industry data on corporate loan pricing and deal structuring — will be another growth area, creating openings for companies like TRW, Equifax, Morningstar, and the Loan Pricing Corporation.

Korea's retail payments system could, like that of the U.S., undergo substantial change in the years leading up to 2010. As of 1996, only about 30 percent of Korean transactions were electronic and more than 30 percent were cash, against 88 and 4 percent respectively, for the Netherlands (Exhibit 13.3). From 1997, some forms of debit cards (e.g., for public transportation and telephones) were introduced; however, those accounted for a mere one percent of transactions. Efforts were under way to move to a more advanced electronic system by adding debit and smart cards and more electronic distribution channels such as ATMs, phone banking, and personal computer banking.

Shifting Focus in Corporate Banking

The corporate banking business in Korea will undergo sweeping changes in the first decade of the 21st century. Specifically, we will see a reduction in the significance of loans as the dominant revenue and profit source, and a corresponding increase in corporate advisory, and debt and equity underwriting businesses. We will also see a shift in focus from the top 30 chaebol toward the relatively underserved middle-market and small-business sectors. And, as discussed earlier, we will see a change in the industry structure, as a result of much more foreign participation (both directly and through alliances with local players) and some mergers between domestic banks and local brokerage firms.

Loans have been by far the single most important product for Korean corporate bankers over the past 20 years. Revenue from corporate loans accounted for more

Exhibit 13.3

Comparison of Retail Banking Payments: 1994
Number of transactions in millions; percent

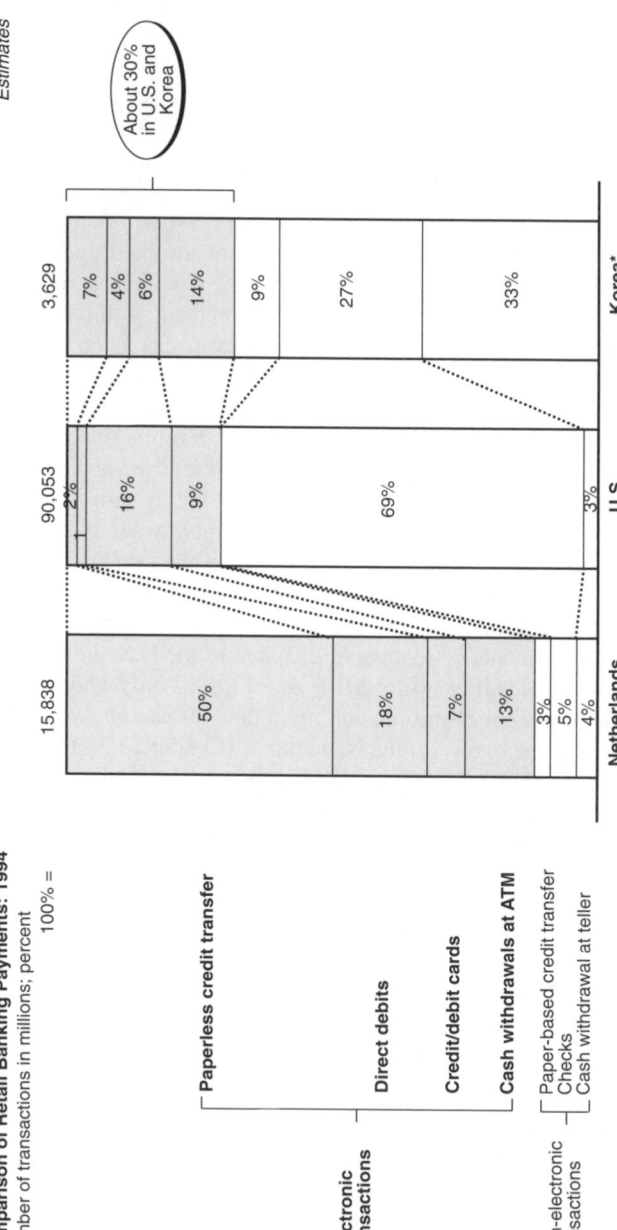

Estimates

Source: McKinsey estimates; Bank for International Settlements; Bank of Korea; National Statistics Office of Korea; industry interviews

* 1995 data.

than 60 percent of total bank revenues in 1997. Driven by the government's mandate to reduce debt-to-equity ratios from an average of 5:1 to 2:1 by the year 2000, the chaebol will increasingly need to turn to the capital markets, and particularly the equity market, to raise more than US$35 billion in funds. Corporate advisory services in M&A and divestitures, as well as underwriting skills, especially structuring and distribution capability, will be in high demand. Foreign banks such as BNP and Warburg Dillon Read, along with domestic players like Korea Exchange Bank, are already staffing up in these areas. The "quality" large corporates will also increasingly go to the international capital markets for financing where they may be able to obtain lower prices and will require financial institutions with good distribution, and swap and hedging capabilities to serve them.

Given these trends, by 2010, Korea is likely to have developed well-functioning equity and debt capital markets with a market-driven yield curve (prompted in part by increasing government bond issuance across a broader range of maturities). In the late 1990s, however, the wholesale debt and equity capital markets remained small and relatively illiquid. For example, in 1996, Korea's total equity market capitalization was equivalent to 30 percent of its GDP, compared with 112 percent for the U.S. Similarly, its corporate bond market capitalization was at 45 percent of GDP, compared with 126 percent for the U.S.

As large conglomerates reduce their reliance on loans, the banks will need to look to other corporate customers. The medium-sized corporate sector, which has been fairly concentrated to date, will likely change significantly over the next 10 years. In 1997, Korea had roughly 4,800 companies with average sales of US$85 million. Many of these companies will disappear as their chaebol customers are rationalized and as industries are consolidated. For example, the number of auto parts suppliers will shrink markedly as Korea's auto industry consolidates from five to three or fewer players. New companies in the retail, service, and technology sectors and the survivors from the existing batch of medium-sized players will represent attractive opportunities for banks that can provide tailored one-stop shopping (including, for example, cash management, corporate lending, foreign exchange, and trade finance).

Korea's large and relatively ignored small-business segment, with over 2.8 million companies in 1997, will also go through a significant shakeout amid the economic struggles around the turn of the century. However, we believe that this segment will become an important source of customers for the banking industry, as it has in developed markets like the U.S., Canada, and the U.K. Recognizing that small businesses employ nearly half of the Korean workforce and offer tremendous potential as a growth engine for the economy, the government will likely provide stimulus and support, perhaps via tax incentives and other financial perks. To make money from small businesses, banks will need more transparent financial information, which has long been suspect, and the ability to serve the personal banking needs of their owners. As of 1998, the Korea Federation of Small Business was reviewing measures to make serving its constituency more attractive to financial institutions.

Given the differing needs of large, medium-sized, and small customers, Korean banks will need to pursue tailored approaches and, in most cases, confront tough choices as to whether they will be able to serve all three segments profitably. In most developed countries, the small business segment is traditionally considered part of a bank's retail business because the product and service requirements are similar.

Changes in banking industry structure and skills will be most apparent among banks serving large corporates, as these customers require broader and more sophisticated products and services, and they look beyond Korea for the best providers of financial advice and financing. In line with the globalization of wholesale financial services, familiar global providers, such as Goldman Sachs, Citigroup, Morgan Stanley Dean Witter, and Hongkong and Shanghai Bank, will be major players in this segment in Korea. Domestic banks will have little choice but to pursue a combination of alliances and joint ventures with global names, or to merge with some of the more skilled domestic securities firms to supplement their corporate finance, advisory, and underwriting skills. This has happened in other markets like Canada, where the major banks bought most of the securities companies in the late 1980s. Signs that this will happen in Korea are already in evidence, with joint bidding by banks and securities houses on government privatization contracts occurring in late 1998.

Whether they go it alone or team up, banks that wish to serve large and medium-sized corporations effectively will need to attain global standards and skills in credit risk management, capital allocation, pricing, and client service approaches (e.g., industry expertise, cross-selling, total customer profitability hurdles). For example, loan-underwriting skills that ensure sufficient returns on capital and the ability to break down and sell off risk will be core to the business.

Emerging Opportunities in the Institutional Sector

Korea's institutional investor base is one of Asia's largest after Japan. In 1998, assets under management totaled about US$100 billion, including some US$30 billion in pensions and US$70 billion in funds managed by investment trust companies. According to the Korea Life Insurance Association, pension funds are expected to grow to around US$45 billion by 2002. Three of the six existing investment trust companies, Korea, Daehan, and Citizen, had a combined market share of 90 percent. However, these companies face huge structural problems caused by a combination of mismanagement and inappropriate government policies. In addition to the investment trust companies, the other local institutional players were 50 insurance companies, a limited public pension scheme (the National Pension Program), and 20 newly set up investment trust management companies. These new companies are allowed only to manage trust funds; they must use other distribution channels and are limited in their range of investment tools.

Two major forces will drive substantial change in the institutional business segment: government measures to create a larger safety net for employees, and regulatory changes in the management of pension assets. The government is pushing the private sector to establish pension plans for all employees, particularly where they do not currently exist, and it is increasing the mandatory contribution set aside for pensions. For example, in 1998, the government planned to boost the defined contribution from 6 percent (4 percent from employer, 2 percent from the employee) to 8 percent of monthly standard compensation.

More regulatory reforms are in store. Historically, pension assets have not been clearly separated from corporate assets, which has enabled some companies to misuse pension funds, for example, as loan collateral. In 1998, the FSC required financial institutions to guarantee pension participants' principal (i.e., defined benefits). This will protect employees but will also encourage fund managers to invest conservatively and primarily in government or blue-chip corporate bonds. We believe that the government is likely to move away from guaranteed principal/ defined benefits toward defined contribution plans with more professional asset management, and to take further steps to separate and protect pension assets within corporations.

Almost none of these assets were outsourced to external asset managers in 1998. However, this will probably change as Korean interest rates drop and as consumers get more comparative information on fund management performance. Some estimates project that as much as 20 percent of assets will be outsourced to external asset managers by 2005. Overseas outsourcing of asset management may present an attractive alternative to resolving duration mismatches between pension plan assets and liabilities, particularly when domestic interest rates are falling.

These institutional assets will play an important role in driving the development of the debt and equity markets as government restrictions are lifted. Improving transparency in the domestic equity market and removing the guaranteed principal requirements will allow these funds to move from debt to the equity markets. Institutional investors will also drive the development of the longer-term bond market (e.g., beyond 10 years) to help them resolve their duration mismatch problems.

Although small in the late 1990s, the institutional client base will become increasingly important for financial institutions over the next 10 years. Two factors will fuel this growth: improving research and analytical capabilities of institutional investors and increasing consumer demand for more diversified investment portfolios that yield higher returns.

Likely Winners

In the first few years of the 21st century, Korea's banking system will undergo significant consolidation, leading to domination by fewer but larger players and many more foreign participants, operating either independently or in alliance with domestic partners. Several product- and customer-segment-focused retail players, including some new foreign entrants and nontraditional players such as retailers and technology-driven companies (e.g., Hewlett-Packard and FDR), will also likely play a key role in the market.

Restructuring and consolidation will affect the securities and insurance industries as well as banking. Accordingly, of the 26 local and nationwide commercial banks, 50 life and nonlife insurance companies, and 30 securities companies in existence in late 1997, only a select few will remain as winners. We foresee the emergence of four to six broad-line retail and commercial financial services companies plus five or six additional product-oriented players such as asset management companies and consumer finance companies. The likely new winners will include, for example, large asset or wealth management institutions built from combining securities, life insurance, investment trust, and high-net-worth customer-oriented retail banks. As in many other advanced markets, there will probably be room for community-based banks serving local needs very well, but the number will be dramatically reduced from the 300 or so that existed in 1997.

The potential victors, which will likely include some of the five FSC-designated "leading banks," are actively pursuing multi-pronged change programs in the late 1990s. These banks are determining what businesses they should and should not be in, restructuring their organizations around distinct business units, and developing technology strategies that will bring them up to par with modern standards. They also are building core capabilities in areas such as risk management and customer segmentation, as well as in M&A and post-merger management capabilities. In some cases, they are bringing in experienced people with key skills, such as retired U.S. mortgage bankers or credit risk management executives. And some banks are looking for foreign partners in select business lines or parts of their business system like processing or technology.

For example, in late 1998, the new CEO of Housing & Commercial Bank, Kim Jung-Tae — one of *Business Week*'s top 50 leaders in Asia — launched a far-reaching change program revolving around shareholder value creation and world-class transparency to all stakeholders. Similarly, Hana Bank president Seungyu Kim was in the midst of a broad strategy review for his rapidly growing and profitable institution. Leadership changes at many of the underperforming banks will likely occur.

Foreign players will gain a more important presence on the Korean financial scene. Names such as Citibank, Prudential, Merrill Lynch, and the Zurich Group, among others, will become familiar logos down Chongno 1-Ka to 3-Ka — Korea's business center — and around Apkuchong Dong — Seoul's Fifth Avenue.

Much of the large corporate and investment banking business that has been globalized in the 1990s (e.g., corporate bond and equity underwriting and distribution, and foreign exchange trading) will become the domain of the multinational players such as Merrill Lynch, Morgan Stanley, JP Morgan, Goldman Sachs, and Warburg Dillon Read. There is no reason to doubt that this will happen in Korea, much like it has happened in investment banking in Japan and the U.K.

The traditional retail stock brokerage business will also change dramatically. Consolidation, foreign domination, and discount offers will be key trends in the industry. We expect consolidation from more 30 to far fewer larger players; the top five could well account for more than 50 percent of the business. Foreign players, such as Merrill Lynch, Morgan Stanley, and Goldman Sachs, will likely dominate this industry in the institutional sector, as they already do in Japan. Local players will have to form alliances with foreign players or focus solely on the retail brokerage business, much as the U.K. brokerages did after the 1986 "Big Bang". We believe that some leading domestic banks will buy securities firms, and some of the stronger securities firms will themselves buy banks or portions of banks as a move to broaden asset management strategies takes hold.

So, by 2010, we will likely see a banking system comprising less than one-third the number of players in existence in 1996, but with several Korean players that are significant by global standards in terms of scale and performance. Foreign participation will increase dramatically — from less than 1 percent of assets in 1996 to over 40 percent — as existing foreign players grow and new ones enter, particularly in the wholesale business. Korea will have a much more advanced technology infrastructure and many more information providers (e.g., rating agencies), which are critical to transparent and well-functioning markets. Regulation and supervision will have moved closer to international standards, and the market will provide much of the discipline and incentives for banks, corporations, and consumers.

The required restructuring of Korea's financial system will be vast by any measure, and tinkering is not an option. Human capital, more than anything else, will be the essential ingredient in the rebuilding of Korea Inc. Risk management, product development, marketing, and information technology management skills will all be in strong demand. Korea's strong labor unions will also have to be managed carefully, or they could slow reforms dramatically. Although many of the "hard" system changes can be swiftly implemented, the "soft" behavioral changes will not be as easy, given the long-standing emphasis on volume-driven growth over profitability. To survive, management will have to shift their reward systems to more of a team or even individual performance-focused model rather than the time-honored seniority model that is deeply rooted in the Korean culture.

The good news is that fundamental changes in government regulation, management focus, and consumer behavior were well under way in the late 1990s. With 46 million relatively well-educated people in a relatively well-industrialized economy with an intense work ethic, South Korea is destined to become an attractive financial services market before long.

What will happen with North Korea is a large open question, and one that could alter the story dramatically over the coming decades. Given the lack of economic development in North Korea and the wide disparity in incomes, education, and skills, reunification would impose significant economic costs for at least 5–10 years, especially if the unification experience of West and East Germany is any indication. However, there is no doubt a unified Korea of more than 80 million people would offer a much larger platform for financial services over the very long term.

CHAPTER 14
CHINA:
SUSTAINING A CAREFUL BALANCE

Beijing
Tianjin
Shanghai
Wuhan

Financial Markets & Business Lines (US$)

Overall
- Equity capitalization (% of GDP): $206bn (22%)
- Number of listed corporations: 720
- Debt market capitalization[3] (% of GDP): $77bn (8%)
- Total domestic loans (% of GDP): $931bn (101%)
- Total external debt (% of GDP): $147bn (16%)
- Total offshore loans (% of GDP): $63bn (7%)
- Number of local banks (>$5bn assets): 16[2]
- Number of foreign banks: 13
- Top 3 banks' market share (deposits): 68%
- Maximum foreign ownership of a commercial bank: 5%
- Currency convertibility: Restricted

Corporate Banking
- Domestic corporate loans (% of GDP): $669bn (72%)
- Nonperforming domestic loans: 15–40%[4]

Retail Banking
- Total consumer deposits (% of total deposits): $470bn (60%)
- Total consumer loans (% of total loans): $2bn (0.2%)
- Persons per branch: 4,500
- Persons per ATM: 88,600
- Credit cards per capita: 0.02

Asset Management
- Retail assets under management: $1.2bn
- Total domestic institutional assets: $30bn[2]
- Number of asset management firms: 3[4]

Trading
- Number of stock brokerage firms: 135[2]
- Average daily equity trading volume: $2.4bn
- Average daily FX trading volume: $0.2bn[5]

Investment Banking
- Total equity issuance (1994–1997 annual avg): $3.5bn
- Total debt issuance[3] (1994–1997 annual avg): $27bn
- Number of domestic M&A transactions >$50mn (1992–1997): 43

Private Banking
- High-net-worth households (>$1mn investable assets): 31,000[1]
- Potential private banking assets: $78bn[1]

Social & Economic Indicators (US$)

Overall
- GDP: $924bn
- Population: 1,330mn
- GDP per capita: $750
- PPP GDP per capita: $3,240
- 1985–1997 GDP real growth: 8.1% CAGR
- Projected 2010 GDP per capita: $2,800
- Exports (% GDP): $183bn (20%)
- Foreign currency reserves (% of imports): $141bn (92%)
- % urbanization: 30 %

Corporate
- Top 3 sectors: Manufacturing, Agriculture, Trade
- Number of corporations with annual sales >$1bn: 79

Individual
- Annual savings rate: 40%
- Average savings per household: $1,800[1]
- Home ownership: 33%
- Household car ownership: 3%
- Telephones /1,000 pop: 41[2]
- Internet subscribers/1,000 pop: 0.3
- % of 18–22-yr-olds attending university: 6%

All figures as of December 1997 unless otherwise indicated.
[1] McKinsey estimates.
[2] Figures as of December 1996.
[3] Maturity greater than 1 year.
[4] Figures as of June 1998.
[5] Figures as of April 1998.

14
CHINA:
SUSTAINING A CAREFUL BALANCE

For both foreign and domestic bankers, China's banking scene presents two starkly different landscapes. On one hand, there appears to be boundless growth and opportunity, fueled by the tremendous vitality of the economy's market-driven sectors. On the other is potentially catastrophic turmoil, perhaps even a complete financial meltdown. This meltdown could be sparked by the deteriorating performance and the resulting bad debts of state-owned enterprises (SOEs) unable to compete in an increasingly open and market-driven economy and/or by the collapse of poorly controlled investment trusts. During most of the 1990s, the government and financial institutions carefully maintained a rough balance between these two extremes.

The ability of banks and other financial services firms to prosper in China will hinge on the landscape that emerges in the decade leading up to 2010. Banks have already benefited from China's wealth explosion, both individual and corporate. With few investment options, Chinese consumers and corporations had nearly US$976 billion in deposits in Chinese banks in 1997, a number that grew at 27 percent per year from 1987 to 1997. Chinese corporations had few alternatives to bank borrowing, which fueled spectacular loan growth. In the same period, bank loans grew by 22 percent per year.

With China's fixed interest rate regime, the revenues from these traditional banking activities were substantial, around US$20 billion for 1997 before credit losses were accounted for. But the large and fixed margin between deposits and loans came with significant credit risks associated with lending to SOEs, risks that Chinese banks, financial institutions, and regulators were ill-prepared to manage.

Will the Chinese financial system be able to sustain this balance? How will reforms play out? Will a set of globally competitive firms emerge in China? If the past is a reliable guide, several outcomes are likely. First, although growth is likely to slow relative to the torrid pace set during the 1980s and 1990s, China will continue to enjoy above-average growth rates relative to the developed world. Second, continued growth will give the government room to implement gradual, incremental reforms that balance social and economic goals. And third, reforms will not affect all players uniformly. Deregulation and the continued globalization of the Chinese economy will spur the development of a relatively modern and competitive group of banks and securities firms. Essential for China's continued growth and encouraged by the government, these firms will, by 2010, drive China's financial system. During the process, this new group of banks and securities firms will also substantially change the competitive landscape and industry structure. Left behind in the transformation process will be the banks and institutions unable to compete in the market economy and still dependent on the state for support.

To understand how successful China's strategy of gradual economic reform has been, and why China will likely continue this approach, consider its economic situation in 1978. China was then among the world's poorest countries with a rapidly expanding population. Incentives to create wealth and growth were largely absent, suppressed by years of political upheaval. Since 1978, the Chinese have made a remarkable transition. Why would the leadership change a winning strategy?

China's Economy in Transition

When, in 1978, Deng Xiaoping decided to begin reforming China, his guiding principle was simple and to the point: "To get rich is glorious!" Over the next 20 years, buoyed by a strong and globalizing world economy eager to support Chinese economic expansion, China delivered economic growth rates remarkable for a country of its size. During this period, China's economy grew at an average rate of 9 percent a year, rivaling the earlier stellar performances of Japan and the Four Tigers (Hong Kong, Korea, Singapore, and Taiwan). Exports grew from US$2 billion in 1970 to US$183 billion in 1997. Combine this rate of growth with a population of 1 billion, and the amount of wealth created during Deng's rule was unprecedented globally.

The two decades of reform can be separated roughly into three phases. From 1978 to the mid-1980s, Deng focused his attention on the agricultural sector and the countryside, where more than 80 percent of the population lived and worked. In the second phase, from the mid-1980s to the early 1990s, the reforms turned to macroeconomic and industrial policies. During the next phase, which began in the mid-1990s, the government focused on further reducing its involvement in businesses and the economy, and grappling with China's integration into the world economy.

Phase 1: Opening to Market Forces (1978–1985)

The first phase of reforms, which took place in the agricultural sector, were experiments to retreat from a centrally planned economic policy and let market forces operate. From the late 1970s, peasants were allowed to lease land, subject to a minimum quota of state-controlled agricultural production. Any surplus production could be sold in a relatively open market. Prices for the surplus were subject to market forces, although the government was careful to prevent large fluctuations in prices for key staples: wheat and rice.

Deng also began to open China to the outside world during this period. The Open Door policy announced in 1979 selectively invited, for the first time in 40 years, foreigners to invest in China. Four special economic zones were established with the explicit goal of attracting investment through offer of relaxed regulations, tax incentives and special foreign exchange provisions. The frontier town of Shenzhen, just over the border from Hong Kong, was the most successful and (in)famous of the zones. The combination of no-holds barred capitalism with Hong Kong's know-how and capital transformed Shenzhen from a small village to a sprawling city of more than 1 million people in just 18 years. In the process, Shenzhen broke the record for growth from zero to one million people held by another frontier start-up, Chicago.

Deng's agricultural reforms were a big success. Between 1980 and 1985 agricultural productivity soared and average rural incomes rose by about

75 percent, allowing China to feed itself for the first time in decades. Overall economic growth was strong: from 1980 to 1985, the Chinese economy grew at 9 percent annually. However, early reforms did not address the industrial or financial sectors, which dominated urban China and remained almost completely under state control. But Deng's early reforms allowed him to mobilize widespread support for further reforms by improving the lot of China's poorest and most-numerous classes, scoring a major victory for the incremental approach.

Phase 2: Reforms of Economic Structure and Industrial Policies (1985–1993)

From the mid-1980s, the reform effort focused on the complicated task of transforming the state-owned enterprises (SOEs). Located primarily in the urban and suburban areas of China, the SOEs dominated China's industrial sectors. Emerging from the planned economy and still grossly inefficient, most SOEs produced expensive and outdated products. Managers were trained to meet budget and output objectives with no regard for profits or capital efficiency, and bank loans were always available to mask cash-flow problems. The high household-savings rate provided banks with the liquidity to support the SOEs.

Reforming SOEs was highly politically sensitive. Most SOEs functioned not only as business entities, but also as social service providers to their employees. SOEs typically provided housing, health care, and education for workers and their families. Making SOEs more efficient would inevitably translate into massive layoffs, which in turn could cause serious social unrest in urban areas. Unlike governments in the U.S. or Europe, the Chinese government did not provide a comprehensive range of social services to the poor and unemployed. The large SOEs were the social services providers of last resort in China.

Faced with this difficult and delicate task, the government took an incremental (and safe) approach. It tried to increase accountability and incentives for SOE management through the Contract Responsibility System. Instead of production and social obligation targets, SOEs were required to meet financial performance targets, and management was given greater authority to redesign products and change working procedures.

In addition, the government began to slowly reduce the influence of SOEs on the economy by encouraging the growth of township and village enterprises (TVEs). TVEs were small companies collectively owned by a small number of towns, villages, and private investors. They specialized in light industries due to a lack of capital. They were not subject to any contracted quotas from the government and were allowed to keep all after-tax profits. As a result, they were flexible and efficient. In the mid-1980s, the government also allowed the establishment of small private enterprises. Together, the TVEs and small entrepreneurial businesses significantly reduced the SOEs' share of the country's output. SOE output as a percentage of China's total fell from more than 80 percent before 1978 to 26 percent in 1997.

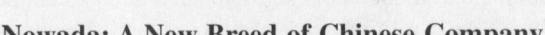

Nowada: A New Breed of Chinese Company

Nowada, a leading local beverage producer, illustrates how a well-run TVE can compete successfully in China. Nowada was started in 1989 by the deputy general manager of a pharmaceutical company located in Zhongshang, Guangdong province. The manager, He Baoqian, saw a need in the children's market for a healthy drink that kids would actually enjoy. Looking around in other Asian markets such as Hong Kong, Japan and Taiwan, he found a yogurt-based milk that could fill this need. After successfully convincing the management of his pharmaceutical company of the product's potential, he assembled a small team of four, obtained US$200,000 financing from the company, and started what would later become Nowada.

Among the many management qualities demonstrated by Nowada, its marketing skills probably contributed most to the company's success. The management recognized the importance of brand from the very beginning. In 1991, a competition was launched in the Beijing University for the name of the company, and "Nowada" was born. The somewhat foreign-sounding "Nowada," along with the name of its flagship products, "Robust," helped in part to convey the message of innovation and credibility. After the success of its initial products, Nowada leveraged the "Robust" brand into various other products. From a small initial capital base of US$200,000 in 1989, the company reached US$162 million in sales in 1997, and employed 4,300 people.

During Phase 2, China continued to grow rapidly at 8.9 percent annually as the Nowada story (see sidebar) was played out thousands of times. Urban and industrial incomes also grew quickly, closing the income growth gap with farmers. Deng's success continued, but the twin problems of an inefficient SOE sector and a weak financial system were only masked by China's high savings rate and the success of the TVEs and the export sectors. In an economic downturn, these two weaknesses would be exposed and China's new leaders would be challenged to continue Deng's legacy.

Phase 3: Restructuring the SOEs and the Financial System (1993 Onwards)

Although the development of the nonstate sectors carried China through a period of stellar economic growth, by the mid-1990s the problems at the SOEs had yet to be solved. The SOEs were still highly inefficient, and more importantly, they represented a significant drain on the country's resources. In 1993, fiscal subsidies to the SOEs were estimated to be 3.5 percent of China's GDP. If low-cost policy loans to these SOEs for financing short-term working capital were also included, the total subsidies would be over 10 percent of GDP. The country's banks were loaded with nonperforming loans to the SOEs, and yet the banks were continuously directed to funnel cash to the SOEs, increasing the cost of capital for more productive sectors of the economy. For Chinese policymakers, the 1997–1998 Korean crisis further highlighted the risks of politically driven, noneconomic lending to government-preferred enterprises. It was clear that something drastic had to be done with the SOEs. In the third phase of the reform, which could last well into the next decade, the focus will be on transforming the SOEs and reviving the country's financial system.

By 1998, the Chinese central, provincial, and municipal governments had controlling interests in more than 300,000 companies. These state-owned enterprises participated in nearly all sectors of the economy and came in all shapes and sizes. The largest of the SOEs, about 100,000 of them, operated in the heavy industrial sector. Of the 100,000 largest SOEs in 1998, about 46 percent were expected to lose money. The SOE sector consumed more than 80 percent of China's new loans, but contributed less than 30 percent to the nation's total output.

The Chinese bicycle industry illustrates how life changed for the SOEs. In 1980, four large SOEs made almost 90 percent of the bikes in China. By the end of the 1990s, these same four companies had a 35 percent market share, and one of them was virtually gone. So who rode these bike giants down? Small domestic TVEs and foreign joint ventures controlled more than 50 percent of the market. In contrast to the heavy, black old-fashioned, and expensive SOE bikes, these smaller players introduced a wider range of colorful and sophisticated bikes at lower prices. Unburdened by redundant employees and high social costs, these companies easily beat the SOEs with cheaper and more innovative bikes.

The magnitude of SOE bad debts created significant and immediate problems for China's largest commercial banks. Estimates of these bad debts in early 1998 ranged from around US$25 billion to nearly US$400 billion. The most generally accepted number was around US$250 billion or about 30 percent of the total loans in the Chinese banking system. As shown in Exhibit 14.1, these bad debts were concentrated in China's four large state banks. At these equity levels, assuming a favorable recovery rate of 20 cents for every dollar of nonperforming loans, three of the four were insolvent by Western accounting standards. Their continued existence depended on the confidence of their depositors, the presumed state guarantee of safety and currency stability, and the absence of any widely available savings alternatives, for example, mutual funds, that would compete for deposits.

The first major steps to deregulate the banking system were taken in 1993 when China began to move away from a credit quota system. Under the quota system, in place since the early 1950s, the People's Bank of China (PBOC — the central bank), and the state set specific loan targets for individual banks down to the branch level. Beginning in 1993, banks were allowed greater discretion and the

Exhibit 14.1

China's Nonperforming Loans — Early 1998 Estimates
US$ billions

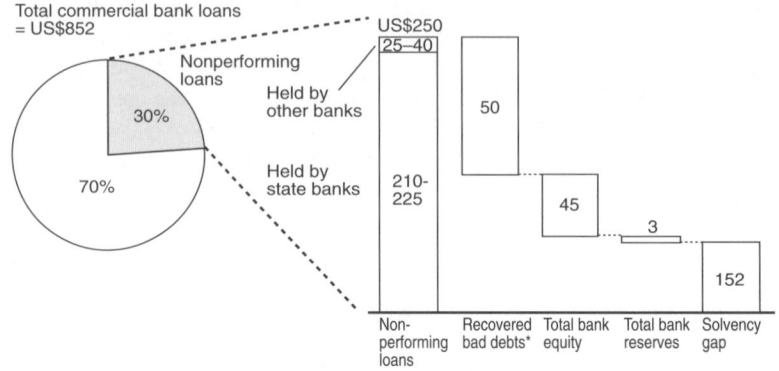

* Assuming a favorable 20% recovery rate.

Source: Standard & Poor's DRI; company reports; McKinsey estimates

quota was not so rigorously applied, although in the 1990s the PBOC still met with banks to "hand out files and make loan suggestions." In 1998, the quota system was completely abolished. Or at least until the Asian crisis began to bite into China's growth targets.

By mid-1998, the government was again pushing banks to lend money in support of an elusive 8 percent growth target. Bank lending, low interest rates, and massive state spending on infrastructure would insulate China from the worst of the Asian crisis. What appeared to be an important policy shift seemed to be delayed. Significantly, however, the renewed lending pressure was not falling equally on all players. Some of the newer and more independent banks were not subjected to the same pressures. Essentially, the government was driving the creation of a two-part banking system — one subject to direct political control and the other more market oriented.

Overview of China's Financial System

In the late 1990s, China's financial system was heavily regulated by the PBOC and other Chinese government bodies. As shown in Exhibit 14.2, the PBOC sat atop a large infrastructure of state banks, credit cooperatives, development banks, securities companies, and assorted smaller institutions. The PBOC cooperated with several other bodies, including the Ministry of Finance (MOF) and the China Securities Regulation Commission to set a wide range of rules and regulations that generally far exceeded the scope and reach of Western banking and securities regulations.

For example, at the end of the 1990s, the PBOC still set all loan rates in China and carefully managed the value of the PRC currency, the renminbi (Rmb). The PBOC and MOF had substantial input into senior-level staff decisions in the

Exhibit 14.2

Structure of China Banking System

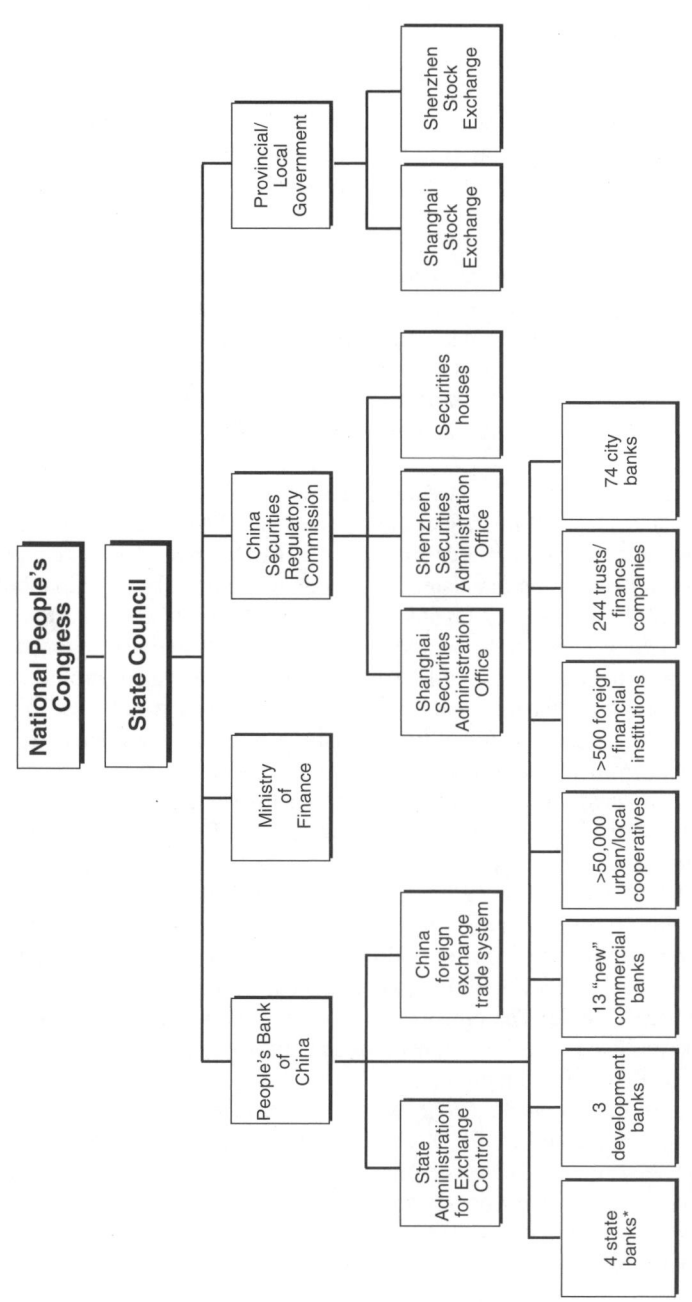

* One state bank, Bank of China, reports directly to the State Council.

Source: China's Financial Outlook 1998; Almanac of China's Finance and Banking 1997; literature search; interviews

banking system and exerted considerable control over banking policies and procedures. For example, branch manager appointments, the key jobs on the front-line of Chinese banking, were still subject to some degree of formal and informal control by both the PBOC and Communist Party's personnel processes. The PBOC also strictly regulated the terms and conditions of credit card lending and all other consumer loans. While this level of intervention may seem excessive by Western standards, the regulatory approach in the late 1990s already represented a significant liberalization of the Chinese financial system.

The PBOC and other government authorities were fully aware of the challenges facing the financial system and understood the benefits of careful deregulation and the corresponding introduction of market forces. At the same time, Asia's 1997–1998 financial crisis reinforced China's desire to control the renminbi tightly and restrict the role of foreign banks, particularly in local currency activities. Thus, China's financial reform effort that began in the mid-1990s had two thrusts: a relatively aggressive effort to improve domestic performance, and a more modest effort to increase foreign participation where there would be clear skill transfers to domestic players.

Domestically, the PBOC focused on three areas. First, it sought to improve the soundness and safety of the Chinese banking system by closing weak players and mandating modern practices. For example, the PBOC introduced a five-part debt rating system that will be mandated for all commercial banks in China, but at the end of the 1990s was still in pilot phase. The system required the banks to conduct a debt rating review every half year and classify their debts in five categories ranging from "normal" to "loss." During the 1990s, the government also curtailed the free-wheeling activities of the trust and investment corporations, which were initially set up to fund long-term investment using trust deposits and bank loans. It reduced their number from 750 in 1988 to 240 in 1998. The 1998 closures of one of the largest, the Guangdong International Trust and Investment Corporation (GITIC), and the Hainan Development Bank marked the PBOC's first Western-style interventions and liquidations, but also signaled the severity of the credit crisis.

Second, the PBOC allowed banks to introduce new products as basic control skills developed, for example, uniform accounting and data processing processes, and stronger credit procedures. For instance, the PBOC encouraged the development of the residential mortgage market and set aggressive industry growth goals for loan volume. The aim was to stimulate domestic spending and reduce state housing subsidies. Similar relaxation and experimentation was occurring in a wide range of consumer credit areas.

Third, the PBOC worked to reduce the influence of local and provincial governments on the banks. In 1998 the Central Party Finance Working Committee was established to coordinate personnel decisions in the large banks and reduce the influence of local party bosses seen as likely to put inappropriate pressure on local bankers. In November 1998, the PBOC eliminated the oversight functions of its provincial branches and consolidated authority into nine regional branches directly supervised by Beijing. The move was aimed to further reduce the widespread local-level interference that had forced state bank loans to flow into economically unviable companies.

All of these trends will continue and are likely to accelerate as the PBOC itself develops more skills and gains confidence in its ability to control the system. Up until the late 1990s, the PBOC did not allow banks to offer a wider range of products (e.g., foreign exchange hedging products or consumer loans) partly because of its own inability to monitor the banks and its concern that unskilled bankers could make large errors. These concerns appeared justified — as of 1997, the PBOC had roughly 300 bank examiners, against approximately 1,200 in the U.S. Federal Reserve System.

With regard to foreign financial institutions and the renminbi, quite simply, regulators did not feel the need for large-scale foreign participation or investment in the financial sector. So, except in select areas where technical know-how is severely lacking, such as derivative products and corporate finance, foreign bankers should not expect a dramatic change in PBOC policy.

Big Four State Banks

From the early 1980s, the PBOC began moving to a central bank model and away from its previous role as China's sole bank, responsible for holding all deposits and making all loans. As part of this process, the PBOC spun off several major departments, creating the Big Four state banks that dominated China's financial system. In 1979, the divisions responsible for agricultural lending and foreign trade became the Agricultural Bank of China (ABC) and the Bank of China (BOC) respectively, and the project finance and construction lending divisions were spun off into the People's Construction Bank of China, which subsequently changed its name to the Construction Bank of China (CCB). In 1984, the PBOC's commercial banking business was moved to the new Industrial and Commercial Bank of China (ICBC). By the end of the 1990s, the four state banks were truly enormous institutions (Exhibit 14.3) in terms of number of branches and employees. Each was virtually a state within itself, providing medical care, training and education, housing, and social activities to millions of employees and dependents.

In terms of service quality and product offerings, the four state banks were on par. Their products and performance set the *de facto* market standard, particularly in the consumer-banking arena. Walking into a branch of these banks was like going back in time. The branch was enormous with vast open space in front of an imposing row of about 30 teller windows. The floor was polished marble and the colors were uniformly brown and gray. The most striking aspect was the number of employees; at a branch in Beijing there would be more than 50 employees in the main area alone. Most would be busy working behind small desks on operational tasks. Customer service was not their job. Product promotion, in the form of brochures and signs, was modest by Western standards.

As former divisions of the PBOC, the four state banks had little experience with market-driven banking practices. For example, as of the end of the 1990s, the banks were only just beginning to calculate meaningful profitability numbers, and most could not separate deposit and loan earnings. The banks were struggling to create a standard credit policy used throughout the system and to reduce the ability

Exhibit 14.3

China's State-Owned Commercial Banks: 1997

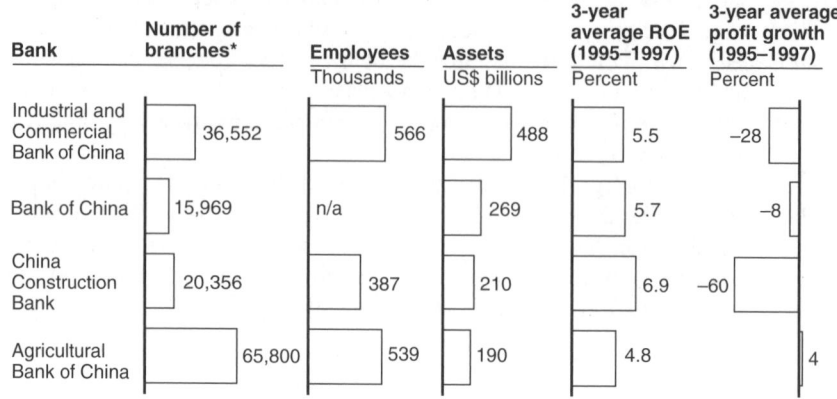

Bank	Number of branches*	Employees Thousands	Assets US$ billions	3-year average ROE (1995–1997) Percent	3-year average profit growth (1995–1997) Percent
Industrial and Commercial Bank of China	36,552	566	488	5.5	−28
Bank of China	15,969	n/a	269	5.7	−8
China Construction Bank	20,356	387	210	6.9	−60
Agricultural Bank of China	65,800	539	190	4.8	4

* Includes legal branches and other business locations.

Source: Almanac of China's Finance and Banking

of local managers to approve loans without some form of head office control. All were installing new IT systems and expanding ATM networks.

Because of their size and importance to the economy, the state banks were under pressure to improve performance and continue to support rapid economic growth. For the state banks, the growth imperative meant finding more deposits and making more loans. At the same time, the state banks were striving to improve their asset quality and clean up the nonperforming loan problem caused by years of state-directed SOE lending. Financial performance had deteriorated sharply at each of the banks in the 5 years from 1992 to 1997, with reported ROEs hovering around 5 percent by 1997, as the state banks were forced to write off loans and support a bloated payroll. At the same time they were spending enormous amounts on modernizing their operations.

As a result of increased performance pressure, the four large state banks were each moving beyond their original customer base, the legacy of their PBOC origins. For example, all four were active in the consumer debit/ATM card market. The most successful, the Agricultural Bank of China, had almost seven million cards in circulation. The Bank of China, the old international department of the PBOC, created a large banking business in China and Hong Kong.

Besides finding new customers, the four state banks were asked to improve their internal operating skills. The PBOC issued a range of directives aimed at requiring the state banks to adopt more transparent accounting standards, better internal control systems, tougher credit standards, and information technology capable of supporting nationwide operations in their far-flung geographic network. At the end of 1998, each was moving to create a dedicated workout function to manage the large amount of bad credits in its portfolio.

Development Banks

From the 1990s, the PBOC recognized that the four state banks could not simultaneously build sound banking skills and continue to fund SOE and state-sponsored projects. In addition, experience from other countries suggested that isolating bad bank debt by forming "bad banks" would improve the overall recovery rate on nonperforming loans and free up state-bank resources to support healthy enterprises. In 1994, the Chinese government established three development banks — the Agriculture Development Bank (ADB), the State Development Bank (SDB), and the Export-Import Bank (EIB) — to assume responsibility for SOE and state project lending. Funding for the development banks came from bond sales to the commercial banks, which had to purchase a mandatory quota based on their deposit volume.

In 1997, total assets of the development banks were close to US$150 billion. The ADB was by far the largest, with about US$100 billion in assets and 35 branches in China. While the ADB focused on agricultural project funding, the SDB's mandate was to support large infrastructure projects, such as the Three Gorges Dam. The SDB had US$45 billion in assets and just five branches. The smallest development bank, the EIB, provided trade-finance support and had assets of about US$4 billion and six branches.

By the end of the 1990s, the development banks had had a modest impact on the banking system. Their main activity had been to provide funding for large-scale projects, always working with a Chinese commercial bank that managed the customer relationship — including disbursement and collection. Given the difficulties of valuing and transferring bad debts and the government actions to directly recapitalize the state banks, the development banks are unlikely to become the "bad banks" of China. Instead, each of the banks will need to carve out a market-driven role, based on achieving some level of economic return. Given their weak positions relative to the commercial banks, a feasible approach for the development banks may be to improve their corporate finance and project valuation skills to become China's merchant banks. In late 1998, the SDB took a step in this direction by purchasing China Investment Bank and its branch network.

New Commercial Banks

By the mid-1980s, the weaknesses in the Chinese economy were already apparent. The SOEs were growing slowly or not at all, but were absorbing enormous quantities of cash in the form of bank loans. The banking system was unable to meet the credit needs of small businesses, responsible for virtually all of China's growth. Corruption in the financial system was rampant since these same small business and individual borrowers sometimes bribed bank managers to procure loans, even at interest rates twice the legal limit.

To address these concerns the government adopted an approach similar to the TVE-led growth strategy — reduce the importance of the state banks, and increase the availability of credit by creating new and independent commercial banks free from the controls of the planned economy. Like most of China's reforms, the government moved cautiously at first, restricting the number and scope of the new banks. Over time, restrictions were lifted and by the end of the 1990s, the new banks competed on an equal footing with the state-owned giants. By 1998, there were 13 new commercial banks in China.

The new banks had a variety of ownership structures, as shown in Exhibit 14.4, although all of them had a significant component of state ownership. As a result, all new banks were still subject to some degree of state influence. All new bank presidents were party members, and senior bank appointments (including the critical branch manger jobs), were still subject to approval from the central party, PBOC, and the owning state entity, for example, CITIC Group in the case of the CITIC Industrial Bank.

The new banks' true independence was difficult to measure, as it varied by bank. In any case, their independence did increase over time. President Dou Jianzhong of CITIC Industrial Bank said in 1998: "We rarely get pressure from local officials to fund projects. They are becoming increasingly knowledgeable about finance and are not putting the kind of pressure they used to on small banks like ours. They know that would be against the spirit of the market economy."

President Dou's comments were supported by the comparatively stronger asset quality reported by the new banks. Despite loan growth of 20 percent annually, the new banks were estimated to have nonperforming-loan-to-total-loan ratios of around 5–10 percent in 1998. By comparison, estimates for the Big Four state banks were around 30 percent. However, for both the new banks and the state banks, these figures masked considerable problems. Many "new loans" were simply rolled-over old bad debts. The definition of nonperforming loan was also problematic, as the traditional debt classification system made no differentiation

Exhibit 14.4

Shareholders in Select "New" Commercial Banks: 1997

Bank	Exchange traded shares (Y/N)	Primary government shareholder (% ownership)	Primary private shareholder (% ownership)
Bank of Communication	N	Ministry of Finance (57%)	–
China Everbright Bank	N	China Everbright Group* (100%)	–
China Investment Bank	N	China Construction Bank (100%)**	–
China Merchants Bank	N	China Merchant Agency (28%)	China Ocean Shipping Group Company (26%)
CITIC Industrial Bank	N	CITIC Group* (100%)	–
Shanghai Pudong Development Bank	N	Shanghai Provincial Government (15%)	–
Shenzhen Development Bank	Y	Shenzhen Investment Administration Co. (10%)	–

*   Wholly owned by the State Council.
** The State Development Bank purchased China Investment Bank at the end of 1998.

Source: Company reports

between loans past due for 1 day or 2 years. Adjusting for those two factors by adopting Western accounting standards might result in a much grimmer picture for the new banks. While the new banks were considerably better off than the state banks, they still had serious asset quality problems.

The SOE debt problem and the difficulties of the four large state banks were both a blessing and a curse for the new banks. On the positive side, many of the new banks were able to avoid the worst SOE lending and focus on specific customer segments, typically the private corporate segment, tailoring their branch systems and operations accordingly. On the downside, the regulatory stalemate created by the SOE debt problem reduced the scope of business that new banks could pursue. To support the Big Four banks and prevent the new banks from stealing an even larger chunk of deposits, the PBOC maintained relatively strict controls on consumer lending, channel growth (e.g., ATMs and phone banking), and product pricing. The PBOC also moved slowly to permit nonbank investment alternatives that meet basic savings requirements, such as money-market funds. As a result, the new banks and other financial service providers were not able to fully capitalize on their advantaged position.

Despite these constraints, the private banks grew rapidly since their formation in the early 1980s. Total private bank assets mushroomed from zero to US$132 billion in 1997, a 50 percent annual growth rate and well above the state banks' average of 23 percent. That same year, private banks accounted for 12 percent of all loans and 11 percent of all deposits in the Chinese banking system. Profitability was respectable by Chinese banking standards: in 1996, the average reported ROE for the group was 22 percent compared with the reported 5 percent average ROE of the state banks. Performance would have been worse for both the private and state banks if bad debts were taken into account, and the resulting gap in performance even larger. Although the private banks as a group fared relatively well, performance varied widely among the banks, reflecting the challenges faced by individual private banks (Exhibit 14.5).

Foreign Commercial Banks

Foreign commercial banks had a long history in China, yet only a very limited presence in the market at the end of the 20th century. This situation was unlikely to change quickly: the PBOC made it clear that substantial foreign participation in the banking system was many years away. For most Rmb-denominated products and services, the government believed that domestic banks were doing just fine and, therefore, restricted foreign players mainly to hard-currency lending to joint ventures, trade finance and some investment banking activities.

These limitations are likely to remain in place until the SOE loan problem is at least partially cleaned up, except for specific areas where the Chinese desperately need foreign financial know-how. The slow pace of SOE consolidation and bad-debt transfers to the development banks, in part, reflected the inability of the financial system to cope with issues related to asset valuation, and merger and acquisition financing. The financial system was simply too inflexible to allow for complex internal transactions. By requiring foreign firms to partner with local

Exhibit 14.5

China's Select "New" Commercial Banks*

Bank	Headquarters location	Number of branches**	Employees	Assets (US$ billions)	3-year average ROE (1995–1997) (Percent)	3-year average profit growth (1995–1997) (Percent)
Bank of Communications	Beijing	2,416	43,000	54.0	17.0	−13
CITIC Industrial Bank	Beijing	179	4,265	15.0	18.7	42
Shanghai Pudong Development Bank	Shanghai	140	2,620	12.0	51.4	68
Guangdong Development Bank	Guangdong	250	n/a	10.0	8.7	−36
China Investment Bank	Beijing	129	n/a	9.0	10.5	77
China Everbright Bank	Beijing	99	2,432	7.3	13.7	90
Hua Xia Bank	Beijing	34	1,874	4.8	14.6	33
Shenzhen Development Bank	Shenzhen	107	2,958	3.9	28.5	41
China Minsheng Bank	Beijing	27	n/a	2.4	n/a	n/a

* Year-end 1997 data unless otherwise noted.
** Includes legal branches and other business locations.

Source: Almanac of China's Finance and Banking

players, the government hoped to encourage local skill development. Likely areas for future foreign collaboration and participation include loan workout and balance sheet restructuring, derivatives and hedging activity, and project financing.

As shown in Exhibit 14.6, foreign banks in China in 1998 fell into three groups. The first group of banks had branch offices and had received permission to conduct limited Rmb business, primarily deposit and lending activities for foreign-owned companies and joint ventures. The second group of banks operated branches without Rmb capabilities. And the third group of banks operated representative offices and carried out a very limited set of advisory activities for their multinational clients and related joint ventures.

The move by the PBOC to grant 19 Rmb licenses (nine in December 1996 and ten additional ones in September 1998) created excitement and controversy within the Chinese international banking community. Chase's senior country officer, Christian Murck, labeled the move as "inconsequential and immaterial in the context of China's needs." Tight regulation of foreign banks' Rmb deposit-taking business had certainly controlled the growth of foreign banks' Rmb lending operations. At the end of March 1998, total Rmb deposits of the Rmb-licensed banks stood at US$68 million and loans were US$71 million, or about 0.2 percent of foreign banks' total assets in China. For bankers the primary challenge in the Rmb business has been to collect the deposits to loan out. As of late 1998, foreign banks were restricted to deposit business only with Shanghai- and Shenzhen-based expatriates and joint ventures or wholly foreign-owned companies. Despite these restrictions, local Rmb business was still profitable and growing. In 1997, the first

Exhibit 14.6

Foreign Commercial Banks* in China: 1998

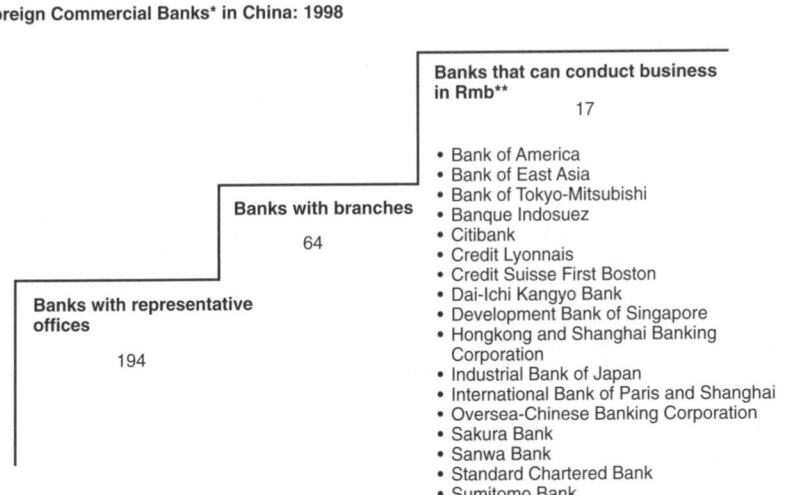

Banks that can conduct business in Rmb**
17

- Bank of America
- Bank of East Asia
- Bank of Tokyo-Mitsubishi
- Banque Indosuez
- Citibank
- Credit Lyonnais
- Credit Suisse First Boston
- Dai-Ichi Kangyo Bank
- Development Bank of Singapore
- Hongkong and Shanghai Banking Corporation
- Industrial Bank of Japan
- International Bank of Paris and Shanghai
- Oversea-Chinese Banking Corporation
- Sakura Bank
- Sanwa Bank
- Standard Chartered Bank
- Sumitomo Bank

Banks with branches
64

Banks with representative offices
194

* Includes Sino-foreign joint ventures.

** PBOC announced that 19 licenses were available, but as of November 1998, only 17 banks had obtained the licenses.

Source: China Financial Outlook 1998; literature search

nine Rmb-licensed banks reported 100 percent asset growth and a 28 percent increase in profits, not surprising given a guaranteed 297-basis-point spread on Rmb loans and the low level of reported nonperforming assets.

Foreign banks were also building small, but profitable, businesses in foreign exchange and credit risk protection. Foreign banks worked with local banks to identify Chinese companies that would be hurt by changes in the Rmb's relative value, for example, against the Japanese yen. The foreign banks provided dollar-yen protection and the local bank repackaged the protection for the local client. As long as the dollar-Rmb rate held, the client had some measure of protection against falling yen. Foreign banks were also starting to work with local banks to better manage credit risk by offering standby letters of credit to support loans.

In total, foreign banks accounted for only US$38 billion in assets in China or less than 3 percent of total Chinese banking assets in 1997. This made China, by far, the world's least-open major economy in terms of relative foreign bank participation. However, the role of the foreign banks was much greater than their loan portfolios would suggest. For example, more than 50 percent of China's export earnings came from joint ventures, and foreign banks provided most of their hard-currency funding. Like the new domestic banks, the foreign banks seemed to be playing a critical and highly leveraged role in the Chinese economy.

Was China profitable for foreign banks? With the exception of the banks with Rmb licenses, Hong Kong banks with strong China linkages, and banks with capital market skills, probably not. For foreign banks lending in hard currencies to Chinese corporations and joint ventures, spreads have generally been inadequate to cover credit losses and high operating costs. The late 1998 GITIC bankruptcy highlighted the danger of lending to Chinese companies based on perceived government connections. While the losses for Hong Kong and foreign banks were relatively small, they were large enough to wipe out years of China earnings for some. Most banks will be slow to lend again, and some will opt out altogether.

Domestic and foreign investment banks

At the end of the 1990s, China's fledgling capital markets were still small and evolving. The equity markets were divided into two separate markets: a closed domestic market available for only domestic issuers and investors, the "A-share" market, and a smaller and less dynamic "B-share" market, open to foreign investors and foreign investment bankers. China's debt markets consisted mainly of government debt sold to banks and individuals based on a mandatory purchase quota. And blue-chip Chinese companies could also access foreign capital markets, for example, in Hong Kong or New York, with the government's approval.

While still small compared to the Chinese economy, the capital markets grew rapidly and were beginning to exert a real influence on capital allocation and economic performance. Just the thought of a potential IPO encouraged the management of small Chinese companies to perform and innovate, and larger firms recognized the need for stable and long-term funding sources. Overall equity market capitalization in China soared from US$44 billion in 1994 to US$206 billion in 1997. Like many Asian markets, equity issuance dominated the corporate fund raising and domestic A-shares dominated the Chinese markets.

About 80 percent of the underwriting and trading volume of domestic equities was controlled by 20 or so large local securities firms, all created in the 1980s and all pursuing rapid expansion across China. They focused nearly exclusively on corporate underwriting, retail distribution, and proprietary trading. Lacking clear product or service differentiation, the underwriting spreads were thin and competition for wealthy investors was intense. Profit pressures on the proprietary trading business led several large firms to commit spectacular violations of China's confusing securities laws.

J&A Securities: The Case of Uncontrolled Growth

J&A Securities benefited enormously from the expansion of the capital markets in China. J&A was founded in 1992 by Zhang Guo Qing, a former regulator and employee at PBOC, with an initial focus on stockbroking. Over the next 5 years, the company recognized the increasing need to access the capital markets among Chinese corporations, as well as the growing interest among local investors in securities investment. J&A quickly established itself as a full-service securities house, providing underwriting and advisory services in addition to stockbroking.

J&A also rapidly expanded throughout China in a bid to capture market share and to provide nationwide services to its clients. By 1997, the company had more than 80 branches across the nation, and employed over 5,000 workers. Its aggressiveness and innovative services paid off — the company was consistently on the top of the underwriting league tables, and often led the market in trading volume.

Despite increasing market shares and expanding operations, the company experienced frequent scandals and trading irregularities. The latest scandal, which surfaced in mid-1998, was linked to chairman Zhang and J&A's largest shareholder, which was controlled by the People's Liberation Army. While official information on the alleged scandal was scarce, improper use of client funds and overseas capital transfers was said to be rampant, and the PLA's support for the company enabled the company to sidestep the regular government investigations. In July 1998, the company was ordered to merge with another large brokerage firm, Guotai Securities, which was generally viewed to have strong internal compliance management.

The debt market in China at the end of the 1990s was dominated by quota-driven government issues. There was essentially no market-based pricing mechanism and very limited secondary market liquidity. Only domestic banks and foreign banks with an Rmb license were authorized to deal in government debt.

Faced with a growing demand for foreign currency financing and lacking a sophisticated domestic investment banking business, Chinese firms and the government turned to foreign investment banks to raise capital and structure complex transactions. In 1997, Chinese companies and the government raised over US$13 billion from foreign investors, excluding direct bank lending and project financing. The typical Chinese international equity issue was highly complex, with tranches offered in Hong Kong, London, and New York and perhaps denominated in several currencies. Due to poor accounting and disclosure rules in China, the deals were carefully explained to potential investors and the investment banks had to stand by the offering.

As a result of these tough investor requirements, several global firms dominated the "international Chinese league tables." The top five firms for the 3 years 1994 to 1997 as measured by lead-managed mandates were Goldman Sachs, Peregrine (bankrupt in 1997), Merrill Lynch, Morgan Stanley, and Bear Stearns. Together they controlled more than 40 percent of the equity underwriting market. They were betting on the future. Although underwriting spreads in China were a healthy 3–4 percent, banks incurred substantial costs in bringing Chinese firms to foreign markets. For example, Chinese financial statements had to be translated and recast to meet Western accounting standards, business forecasts and strategic plans developed, and legal ownership claims documented. In addition to high costs, Chinese deals often required an unusual level of after market support. For example Morgan Stanley agreed to hold a small stake in Beijing Enterprises after the 1997 IPO — a practice very unusual in developed markets. Other lucrative investment banking opportunities were still in the very early stages in China. Advisory services in support of mergers and acquisitions and restructurings had only just started to develop. In 1996, Chinese M&A transactions amounted to less than US$1 billion.

Broad Market Opportunity

How the different groups of banks will fare in the future largely depends on the evolution of China's financial markets. Assuming its leaders can sustain the balance between reforms and growth, China's financial industry will likely generate close to US$60 billion in annual revenues by 2010, up from US$20 billion at the end of the 1990s. Partly because of the enormous capital needs of China's corporations and partly because of the government's intention to channel the nation's assets into the corporate sector, serving corporate customers will remain the focus of the banks in the first decade of the 21st century. Retail revenues will grow quickly, but mainly from deposit margins. The asset management business is the wild card. On both the retail and institutional levels, government regulations will be the single largest determinant of how fast asset management will grow.

Banking on Corporations Becomes More Professional

By 1997, there were about 31 million businesses registered in China, ranging from the giant Sinochem with annual sales of US$18 billion to millions of small village cooperatives. From a financial services perspective, most of these were too small to bank. However, there were still over 20,000 firms in China with annual sales greater than $500,000. These firms fall into four segments.

Pillar companies are large firms in "strategically critical" industries, such as coal, steel, oil, and electricity generation. At the end of the 1990s, around 200–300 firms with sales greater than US$100 million were in this group. Seventy of these companies had annual sales in excess of US$1 billion. These firms have long been the darlings of the state planners and have enjoy preferential access to funds from the big four state banks and the development banks. Pillar companies seek a wide range of financial services and are able to push down prices and spreads to low levels.

Troubled giants are the rotten core of the financial system. Troubled giants are found in most industries and regions in China, making the situation more difficult to resolve. They need restructuring and redesign but have been generally unable to pull it off. For most banks and securities companies in China, banking the troubled giants is considered an unfortunate responsibility.

Market leaders are China's emerging corporate elite. Although most are technically SOEs, the 500 or so companies in this group operate in a more market-oriented manner. Some of China's leading companies are in this group, including the electrical appliances producer Haier, the Chrysler JV Beijing Jeep, and the Kunming and Changsha Cigar Company. All of these companies have more than US$50 million in annual sales and are pursued actively by banks and securities firms in China. They generate substantial deposits and are driving the banks to develop better operating and capital market products.

Private players are privately owned enterprises without any government support. Most of the 19,000 private companies do not have access to reliable bank funding. In 1996, these companies generated 10–15 percent of total GDP while receiving only 3–5 percent of new loans. A 1998 survey of 200 private companies in Hangzhou found that more than 80 percent of them said that obtaining bank financing was their biggest problem. One manufacturer of wooden combs in Chongqinq resorted to newspaper advertising to attract the attention of local bankers. The company needed credit and would bank anywhere to get it.

As has happened in other Asian markets, the best banks in China will realize the need to segment the corporate market and to develop nontraditional, fee-based, corporate banking products to serve the different segments. The private banks will take the lead in these efforts as they seek and fight for corporate customers that are within their capabilities to serve. Wary of the bad-debt problems and overexposure to a few companies, the private banks will try to avoid traditional lending to the largest corporations. Instead, they will actively pursue the market leaders and, to some extent, the private players. At the same time, they will seek opportunities to serve the largest companies through specialized noncredit services such as cash management.

The largest companies will still depend on the big four banks for loan volume. Although more companies will accessg the capital markets directly for funds, the relatively shallow domestic markets and the lack of international recognition of Chinese companies will force thems to rely mainly on bank financing for growth.

Cash management

Chinese corporates need a comprehensive, efficient, and safe cash management system that allows them to receive and make payments throughout China and invest their excess cash effectively. At the end of the 1990s, all corporations in China still processed physical cash through the inefficient branch systems of China's banks. The average time delay between receiving funds in a remote location and availability of funds at the companies' central location was about 3 days. Payments were equally cumbersome. As a result, the aggregate float in the system, not paying interest to either transaction party, was about US$41 billion. For banks, the value of the total float, assuming it was invested in the interbank market at the 1997 rate of 8.2 percent, was US$3.4 billion in annual pre-tax earnings.

Recognizing an opportunity to leverage their national branch networks, the state banks introduced more sophisticated cash management services for their large corporate customers. The BOC and the ICBC offered nationwide cash management services that included overnight balance reporting and transaction tracking. Most large corporate customers still depended on the state banks, but the situation may change in the future. As one Chinese CFO said: "We need to open accounts with multiple banks (state-owned and new commercial banks), to facilitate payments among offices and to see who is better. But we are not likely to reduce our business too much with the ICBC, as our relationship with them is very important to us."

According to Chinese CFOs, the new commercial banks offered better services at the branch level. The same CFO said: "[The new commercial banks] approach us very aggressively and offer us real benefits such as check delivery and lower interest rates. We are treated better, with a professional service attitude. We hope their networks will build up soon."

While true cash management products will grow rapidly in terms of balances, the net effect on banking profits will be negative. By more efficiently completing customer transactions, banks will reduce the profitable float in the system. Individual banks that grow market share may gain, but for the banking industry, better cash management will mean higher expenses and reduced profits. The real winners will be customers that enjoy much more efficient use of their funds.

Traditional lending

Faced with relatively immature domestic capital markets and ever-growing financing demand, Chinese companies had few choices beyond traditional bank loans. In most of the 1990s, about 70–80 percent of total corporate financing was provided by bank loans. Even China's largest 30 companies, which presumably had some ability to tap capital markets, were still heavily dependent on bank loans, with about 60 percent of their funding coming from banks. For banks, the continued reliance of the corporate sector on loans and the continuing growth of small and middle-market customers assured strong loan demand. Not including loan losses, revenue available from corporate lending was around US$6 billion in 1997. The size of the corporate lending market will at least triple by 2010, making China one of the largest traditional lending markets in the world. At the same time, however, banks will be challenged to improve net pricing, develop stronger credit skills, and avoid large losses.

Through the 1990s, deposit and lending rates in China were regulated by the PBOC. The monthly guidelines on rates issued by the PBOC did not clearly allow for pricing adjustments based on credit risk, and banks were permitted to price products within 20 basis points above and 10 basis points below the guideline rates. In 1997, the one-year deposit rate in China was 5.67 percent, and the one-year loan rate was 8.64 percent, producing a spread of 297 basis points. The fixed interest rates created a higher-risk segment that was not served by the banks. High-risk customers would pay higher rates if they could; instead, they pursued two options, both harmful to the system. First, they illegally tried to obtain credit, paying higher rates by conspiring with bank insiders. The insiders pocketed the excess interest. And second, companies intentionally misled the banks concerning their true credit status. Thus, winning in the corporate lending business required strong credit and internal controls. There were few reliable external data providers along the lines of Dun & Bradstreet in the U.S., so banks needed to get real accounting data from customers and tap into other public and private sources of financial information. Consistent credit policies, proper incentives, and effective compliance mechanisms were equally critical.

On average, traditional lending to corporate customers did not appear to be profitable. After loan losses and operating costs, the 297-basis-point spread virtually vanished. At the end of the 1990s, Chinese banks were only just starting to search for more attractive segments, a process under way throughout Asia. The search for more attractive segments was hindered by PBOC's restrictions on loan pricing, which prevented banks from enticing lower-risk customers with relatively low interest rates, or from charging more to higher-risk companies. Until banks are given greater pricing latitude, traditional lending will be a marginal source of real value for most banks.

Investment banking

In the late 1990s, all banking products in China were growing fast, but capital markets products were poised to explode, albeit from a small base. Several factors will drive the rapid growth of all aspects of capital markets products.

The first factor driving growth is the continued increase in the number of companies able to issue securities. From 1990 to 1997, the number of companies listed on China's domestic stock exchanges ballooned from 10 to 720. The next two factors driving capital markets' growth will be the deepening of the domestic capital markets, and Chinese corporations' increased access to international markets as global institutional investors, lured by high returns, became confident in some of the pillar companies and market leaders. Taking into accounts these factors and the growth of the underlying economy, by 2010 corporates' annual debt and equity issuance will potentially reach US$30–35 billion domestically and US$100–110 billion internationally (including companies that will issue through Hong Kong), about eight to nine times the underwriting volume of 1996.

This rapid growth will create lucrative business opportunities across the spectrum of investment banking and asset management activities. With equity origination fees of 200–300 basis points and bond origination fees of 40–75 basis points, underwriting revenue will approach US$4 billion per year by 2010, or about 15–20 percent of the total revenues from corporate customers, including gross revenues from lending and cash management.

Retail Market Set to Take Off

As the Chinese economy transitioned from an essentially agricultural economy to an industrial economy, the differences in income, living conditions, and access to technology among consumers increased. Approximately 1.3 million households, representing 0.5 percent of China's population, were breaking away from the rest of the population. These "high flyers" had average incomes of over US$50,000 annually. Nearly all had access to a telephone and fax, and they were rapidly buying computers, high-performance TVs, DVD players, and other high-tech products. Most of the high flyers were concentrated in the coastal cities and Beijing, where they were the targets of intense marketing battles in many industries, including banking.

A second group of consumers, about five million households, were also enjoying rapid income growth. This group, the "successful middle," earned between US$20,000 and US$50,000 per year. A typical household in the successful middle owned a TV and a telephone. They collectively were driving demand for basic household goods such as refrigerators, furniture, and clothing. While concentrated in coastal provinces, they were much more dispersed than the high flyers. The successful middle segment represented only 2 percent of the population but generated about a quarter of the retail deposits in the Chinese banking system.

The largest consumer group in China, the "mass market," had basic banking needs — savings and transaction products. Individual savings were low, about US$3,000 per household. Collectively this group accounted for 21 percent of the population and more than 35 percent of retail banking deposits.

The final and largest group was the rural market. This group saw relatively high income growth, but from a very small base. Most of the economic activity came from trading and bartering. Their banking needs were small and were met by state-owned institutions with large national networks.

In 1997, China's retail market was the largest in Asia ex-Japan, with retail balances (deposits and loans) amounting to US$475 billion. Government regulations limiting savings options and consumer credit availability ensured that most of the available retail deposits would ultimately be channeled to corporations. As a result, 82 percent of personal savings were held in deposits, compared with 40 percent in Korea and 48 percent in Singapore. Consumer loans were also virtually nonexistent, representing only one percent of the total retail balance, compared with an average of 11 percent in India, Indonesia, and Philippines, and 43 percent in Hong Kong, Singapore, and Taiwan.

In the first decade of the 21st century, the retail banking market will still be a game of fighting for market share in deposits, and the consumer credit market will still be relatively undeveloped. The liquidity crunch, caused by the 1997–1998 financial crisis and the high-profile closures of some state-controlled enterprises, will further delay the development in the consumer credit business as the PBOC channels liquidity to the corporate sector. In the decade to 2010, however, the consumer credit market will start to take shape. By 2010, revenues for retail deposits and loans will approach US$12–15 billion and US$7–10 billion respectively, creating a retail banking industry that is double the size of that at the end of the 1990s.

The fight for deposits

Given that most of the potential in the retail banking business lies in deposits, the fight for deposits will likely occur at two levels. At a broad level, the government will continue attempts to increase deposits in the banking system by developing a more efficient payment infrastructure to capture the cash holdings. At an industry level, banks themselves will begin to look at retail customers with a new perspective, providing better-quality services to increase their market share of deposits and other retail products.

By 1998, China had no checking system and no national system to clear retail payments and ATM transactions. In the first decade of the 21st century, banks and other network providers will create large value by simply enabling easy and efficient transactions. China was heavily dependent on cash at the end of the 1990s. Nearly 70 percent of all transactions were settled in cash, and for the average consumer the figure was closer to 100 percent. For Chinese businesses and consumers, completing basic transactions was a major headache and there was a large and unmet demand for a more efficient payment system.

In response to this demand, and in order to improve financial efficiency and reduce fraud, the government sponsored a series of projects to create a nationwide payments system based on smartcard and ATM technology — the so-called "Golden Card" projects. These efforts focused on creating multi-bank ATM networks in major cities built around a common electronic clearing and settlement network. The government discouraged the development of paper-based check systems due to their perceived inefficiency and poor security. Personal identification, essential for a check-based system, was particularly difficult in China, and a major benefit of the smartcard system was the on-chip identification and security features built into the system.

Banks responded enthusiastically by offering combined ATM and debit cards linked to deposit accounts and by significantly expanding and integrating ATM networks. From a base of zero in the early 1990s, 40 million cards were in circulation by 1997. Of these, about 50 percent had some, generally small, credit line attached to the account, and for many Chinese it was their only source of consumer credit. The focus of payments-system development will be on expanding these networks to include multiple banks. The largest multi-bank networks were located in Guangzhou and Shanghai and each included about 10,000 ATMs and 9,000 merchants. Despite the lack of a nationwide ATM systems, these cards had become an important part of the payments system. In 1996, approximately US$130 billion worth of transactions were completed on bankcards in China, making China by far the largest card market in Asia outside Japan as measured by transaction volume. Nearly 90 percent of these transactions were either withdrawals or fund transfers between accounts, the latter being an important payment mechanism for small businesses.

For domestic banks, transaction accounts were highly profitable. Banks that were able to create broad, accessible ATM networks captured and retained high margin deposits. In 1997, Chinese consumers and corporations held nearly US$13 billion in deposits linked to cards. Including fees, float earnings, and overdraft interest, the average annual revenue per card account was about US$45. After deducting US$17–20 in variable costs and about US$0.3 in credit losses per account (losses were low due to tight restrictions on card borrowings), the average card account generated US$25–30 annually, or more than US$1 billion in total, before accounting for the retail system's fixed costs.

Besides using ATM and debit cards to increase deposits market share, banks also started focusing on customer service and product offerings to lure deposits, even though in both of these categories the Chinese banks had a long way to go relative to their counterparts in developed markets. Even the state banks seemed to be reacting to the challenges posed by the new banks. The BOC, for example, added four new deposit products in 1997. The ICBC broadened its already large network in order to line up to its slogan: "A bank within your reach."

Consumer credit

One of the most striking aspects of the Chinese financial services landscape was the near absence of consumer credit products, such as residential mortgages, auto loans, and revolving-balance credit cards. As mentioned earlier, China had about 1.3 million households earning more than US$50,000 annually, which were excellent potential customers for consumer credit products. Yet the government blocked the development of these products to focus bank lending and China's financial resources on industrial and commercial growth.

The card business revealed how consumer credit was discouraged. The PBOC set strict limits on borrowing at US$1,200 and US$600 respectively for gold and standard credit cards. The maximum time overdraft balances could be outstanding was 60 days, and the interest rate rose sharply after day 15. For a full 60-day balance, the effective annual interest rate was approximately 30 percent. Despite these onerous restrictions, consumers still borrowed small amounts frequently to manage their daily spending. The average overdraft card in China had about US$10 outstanding, creating about US$400 million in consumer assets for the banking system.

The PBOC allowed the card overdraft product to grow because it was tightly tied to a specific account and bank. The amount of borrowing could be closely controlled and fraud problems were minimal. The same was not true of real credit cards, and as a result the PBOC restricted credit cards to consumers with demonstrable international spending needs, for example, businesspeople and government officials. There were probably fewer than 100,000 true domestic credit cards in China at the end of the 1990s. While almost all cards in China carried the Visa or Mastercard logo, the cards were not compatible with the Visa or Mastercard networks, and Visa and Mastercard received no fees or royalties from most issuers. Visa and Mastercard were giving away the logo to build a brand in China, hoping that some day they would be able to work with Chinese banks to issue true credit cards.

The home mortgage program, in contrast, was encouraged by the government. As part of the effort to restructure the SOEs, the government tried to reduce SOE liabilities by encouraging private home ownership. The CCB started mortgage lending in 1992, and mortgage terms were adjusted several times in favor of borrowers between 1992 and 1998. At the end of 1998, the maximum loan amount was increased to 70 percent of the property value, and the maturity was extended to a maximum of 20 years. Furthermore, all local commercial banks were permitted to offer mortgages. As a result of the policy changes, mortgage loans became by far the largest category of personal financial assets in the banks, representing more than 85 percent of total retail loans at the end of 1997. Competition for mortgage businesses was also fierce. All the banks attempted to simplify application and monthly payment processes. The CCB and ICBC began advertising on TV for their mortgage businesses.

The development of the retail lending market in the immediate years after the 1997–1998 financial crisis will be considerably slower, as the liquidity crunch will discourage the government from further deregulating the market. However, during the decade leading up to 2010, rapidly growing income will significantly increase the demand for consumer credit. Although the actual evolution of this market still largely depends on government regulation, it is not unreasonable to assume that retail loan assets will grow at an average annual rate exceeding 30 percent per year until 2010.

Asset Management: Uncertain Development of a Large Opportunity

Similar to the consumer credit business, retail and institutional asset management was embryonic at the end of 1990s, but may represent a large opportunity during the first decade of the 21st century. However, how attractive the asset management industry will be to private asset managers is largely still an unknown, as government regulation will be the single largest determinant of market evolution.

The retail market

With very few securities available and tight regulation, the mutual fund and asset management industry in China was nascent at the end of the 1990s. By mid-1998, there were only US$1.2 billion in mutual fund assets in China, representing about

0.4 percent of total personal savings, compared with 15–20 percent in the developed economies and 2–13 percent in the rest of Asia. But concerns about speculation and a lack of professional approach in the equity markets encouraged the government to begin experimenting with mutual fund products that will provide diversification and professional advice to investors. Assuming that, by 2010, China would have reached up to 25 percent of the developed world's mutual fund penetration levels, total mutual fund assets in China will range between US$55 billion and US$90 billion.

The government's main concern regarding the development of this market is how mutual funds will affect the flow of deposits to banks and ultimately to corporations. While mutual funds can more efficiently channel the nation's savings directly into the capital markets, they will also take away deposits from the banks, over which the government has more direct control. Even if the government decides to let the market develop freely, many obstacles remain. Distribution, despite large existing bank networks, will prove difficult because of conflicts with the banks' desire to collect deposits and the lack of trained personnel to educate customers about mutual fund products. Partly to get around the problem of distribution, most of the mutual funds in China by the end of 1990s were closed-end funds traded on stock exchanges, a product relatively uncommon in the developed markets.

The institutional market

The institutional asset market is where many private asset managers are paying close attention, as China's large and aging population promises to generate a large sum of institutional assets. China lags behind its Asian neighbors in developing a pension scheme. Assuming that it will adopt a scheme by 2005 at a contribution of 10 percent of gross income, China's pension assets will reach US$840 billion by 2010, making it Asia's third-largest market after Japan and Singapore.

How much of these pension assets will actually be available to private asset managers depends on how government regulation evolves. The government will need to decide who will manage the nation's savings, as well as how assets will be allocated. If the government emulates its Asian neighbors, private managers will have no role: at the end of the 1990s, government bodies managed nearly all public pension funds across Asia outside Japan. In addition, the government will likely restrict where assets may be invested. By 1998, both pension funds and insurance premiums could only be invested in bank deposits and government bonds. The only relief to these strict regulations will come from the government's realization of the need to diversify pension assets, reduce risks, and enhance overall returns.

Likely Winners

The size and long-term growth rate of the Chinese economy guarantee that, absent a total breakdown, many foreign and domestic institutions will eventually be successful in China. Some will win with broad-based strategies and serve millions of customers; others will adopt more focused strategies and serve only a few high-value customers with distinctive products. By 2010, although the state banks will continue to control more than half of the total banking assets, their dominance will wane, releasing large opportunities for other players. In this picture, foreign banks' participation, however, will probably still remain limited.

The Big Four State Banks: Too Big to Change?

It is easy to underestimate the long-term potential of the four state banks. Despite their poor past performance, they still possess some very important assets. As of 1996, the big four collectively controlled nearly 75 percent of branches and financial assets. Their branch networks will be an important advantage in serving China's vast and geographically dispersed customer base. Their large asset base and lending capability also make them more capable of serving the large corporations relative to smaller private banks. Finally, despite their relatively poor service quality, they had built formidable brand awareness and customer relationships. In a 1998 McKinsey survey on personal financial services, 66 percent of Chinese retail customers indicated they were "very loyal" to their current banks.

Against these strengths are two equally formidable obstacles. To succeed in the new century, each of the state banks must first stabilize and then reduce its nonperforming loans and recapitalize its balance sheet. Solving the bad-debt issue had proven to be very difficult. The total solvency gap, around US$180 billion, is large relative to China's economy, and much larger than the relative size of the U.S. savings and loan bailout. Assuming the bad debts issues were solved, the state banks still face the difficult challenge of refocusing themselves on market-based performance objectives. While part of the problem lies in the lack of skills in credit assessment, marketing, and operations, the greatest challenge is to transform the culture of these organizations. How does one go about, as in the case of ICBC, moving 566,000 employees in 37,000 branches in a radically new direction? Restructuring a state-owned bank will prove as difficult as restructuring any SOE.

In the late 1990s, some banks demonstrated willingness to change in response to the oncoming competition. Some broadened their product offerings and developed more personalized services. For example, ICBC began a wage-payment service for enterprises. Some attempted fairly aggressive organization redesign. The BOC, for instance, in 1996 ran ten pilot projects on separating the loan origination and credit approval functions.

Based on its relatively clean balance sheet and better skills, the BOC will probably emerge as the most successful and most focused of the group. In China, it can be more selective about offering new products and services to both consumers and corporations. The bank will probably make a major move into investment banking and is better positioned to import know-how thanks to its strong presence in Hong Kong.

The other three banks face stiffer challenges. A potentially feasible approach in transforming these banks is to split them into smaller pieces according to business activities, and to consolidate these specialized pieces into new, more rational entities. Thus, for example, the project finance and construction lending divisions of the banks could be spun off and consolidated into one or two banks. This would make organizational changes easier as these new entities would be only a fraction of the original organizations in terms of size and scope.

In summary, the state banks will look very different by 2010, both in terms of their organizational forms and their corporate cultures. While the state banks' influence in China's banking industry will remain enormous, it will be significantly reduced, and in the process generate large opportunities for the private banks.

Private Banks: Room to Grow

The poor pricing and service standards set by the state banks during the 1990s create attractive growth opportunities for private banks. By targeting specific customer segments, the private banks can deliver better services and more attractive pricing while still achieving attractive returns. Unburdened by bad debts from SOEs, and blessed with much smaller networks and staffs, private banks can respond much more rapidly to customer needs. These operating advantages were reflected in better financial performance relative to the large banks. The private banks were much more efficient, with expense-to-revenue ratios generally in the 50 percent range compared with 80–90 percent for the state banks.

What will these banks need to do to win? At least two winning models appear likely. The corporate-focused banks will continue the winning formula used in the 1990s, and focus on serving mid-to-large Chinese corporates with better services on a range of traditional products. For example, the China Minsheng Bank was penetrating some of the most profitable corporations by offering quicker decision on loan applications — a week to 10 days at Minsheng versus potentially months at state banks. The corporate-focused banks may develop strong corporate finance skills and could be candidates for investment banking partnerships with foreign players. The major challenge for the corporate-focused banks will be to develop better credit skills and the capability to act on better information, for example, to learn how to reprice or restructure loans or improve recovery rates.

Another winning private-bank model likely to emerge is the high-end retail bank. Unfortunately for the private banks, the highly regulated retail market provides little room for product differentiation. Instead, these banks will primarily differentiate themselves from state banks on customer service and brands. Leading retail banks will also develop strong alternative distribution capabilities to offset their branch network size disadvantage relative to the state banks. Many banks will tighten their geographic focus and build retail strength in a few metropolitan areas. Finally, consumer-focused private banks will learn to make, buy, and sell a range of investment and insurance products. Given the lack of good information concerning financial services in China, and the trusted role the banks can play, several private banks could develop strong franchises across a broad range of personal financial services and advisory products.

Although private banks will enjoy large growth opportunities, examination of these banks' performance during the 1990s suggests that not all private banks will succeed. Aside from building the capabilities to provide differentiated products and services cost-effectively, the private banks must successfully overcome two other critical challenges to capture the large opportunities.

Most private banks at the end of the 1990s were very small. The sixth-largest private bank of the 13, China Investment Bank, had assets of US$9 billion by 1997. This was equivalent to about 5 percent of the assets held by the Agricultural Bank of China, the smallest of the state banks. Insufficient size will prevent the small banks from achieving the necessary economies of scale and diversification levels. Investment in technology, staff, and distribution networks will be limited. Thus, one of the critical success factors for the smaller banks is the quality growth of the balance sheet, through expanded lending supported by equity injection or earnings.

The new banks also need to be prepared to fend off government pressure to lend to SOEs on a noneconomical basis. This can be very difficult, as demonstrated by the Hainan Development Bank (see sidebar), but failure to do so can prove to be extremely costly.

Hainan Development Bank:
The Early Death of a New Private Bank

The Hainan Development Bank (HDB), established in August 1995, was one of the new private banks created to capture the large and growing opportunities in China's banking industry. In June 1998, it also became the first bank to be closed since Communist China was founded in 1949.

The bank was established to finance the development of Hainan, a special economic zone located on the southern coast of China. Its shareholders included the Hainan government and some of China's largest corporations. In its initial years, the future of the bank looked promising. It made pretax profits of US$15 million after one year in operation, and collected US$500 million in deposits. By 1998, it had 300 branches, six of which were in cities outside of Hainan, and employed 3,000 people.

Although questions on the quality of HDB's assets were starting to surface, the bank's ultimate demise began in May 1997 as the financial state of Hainan's 33 credit unions deteriorated. After then-vice-premier Zhu Rongji sent inspection teams to look at the credit unions' books, he found that most of these financial institutions, caught up in the property craze in Hainan in the early 1990s, were technically bankrupt.

Zhu initially suggested the closure of these credit unions, but the provincial government balked at the decision. Instead, the Hainan government proposed that HDB take over most of the credit unions. Before the takeover, HDB had assets of US$1.3 billion. The credit unions that HDB acquired had combined assets of US$1.7 billion. After the takeover, HDB found that of the US$1.7 billion in assets, about two-thirds were nonperforming loans. Despite the government's last-gasp US$500 million injection, HDB was bankrupt.

Multinational Banks: Waiting on the Sidelines

Judging from the trends in government policy toward foreign banks' participation during the 1990s, multinational banks will play an increasing role in China's large financial markets. However, their participation will still be restricted until at least 2002, especially in the core traditional markets of deposits and loans.

In the commercial banking sector, despite the issuance of more Rmb licenses in 1998, the government will likely maintain strict Rmb deposit regulations on foreign banks. With limited and restrictive borrowing capability from the interbank market, foreign banks' scope of business will be restricted due to a shortage of Rmb deposits. They will largely engage in foreign exchange services, trade financing, syndicated loans, and financial advisory services. In effect, what the foreign banks will be waiting for is successful restructuring of the state banks. Only when the government becomes confident that the state banks can compete effectively without the bad-debt burden will the banking environment open to foreign commercial banks.

For the multinational investment banks, the story is slightly different. Even though, for the most part, they will be barred from the domestic securities business, foreign investment banks will be relied upon more heavily for international financing and restructuring expertise. While the international underwriting business is much more competitive, issuance volume will also be two to three times larger than domestic volume by 2010. Including revenues from advisory services, total investment banking revenue available for foreign players by 2010 can potentially be eight to ten times larger than in 1997.

For both foreign commercial and investment banks, long-term success in China will depend on relationship management in the first decade of the 21st century. Relationship management is required with both potential customers and local players. At the customer level, foreign banks will be building up brand awareness as well as an understanding of retail and corporate clients. About two-thirds of retail customers surveyed by McKinsey indicated that dealing with a local financial institution was important to them. Multinational banks need to be perceived as local in order to compete with the formidable relationships the state banks have built up with their customers. To serve corporate customers, it is also important to build relationships with their key stakeholders, usually central and local government departments.

Building relationships with local players will benefit foreign players in the short term in developing leads into the corporate sector. But more importantly, should China eventually allow foreign investment into local financial institutions, as Korea and Thailand did in 1997–1998, an intimate knowledge of and relationships with local players will enable foreign banks to quickly enter into the market through acquisitions.

A business case based on relationship management for an extended period is hard to swallow, as the costs are real but the returns are not quantifiable. A case in point is Merrill Lynch's arrangement of China's Yankee bond in 1994. The day before launch, U.S. interest rates spiked up and the issue was a disaster. Merrill, however, earned loyalty points with government officials by buying a large number of the bonds back, suffering heavy losses in the secondary market. While losses can be observed immediately, how much the loyalty points were worth is debatable. The challenge for multinational banks investing in China is thus to establish performance objectives not based on immediate returns, but rather the quality of the established relationships, and to sustain the effort over the long term.

China's financial markets by 2010 will be the largest in Asia ex-Japan. At the same time, building a profitable business will require extraordinary creativity and drive in the face of unique obstacles. For the most part, China's banking industry will still be a regulator's world, and if China's economic reforms during the 1980s and 1990s are a guide, future financial industry deregulation will take an incremental approach. Yet, during this period of incremental deregulation, the competitive balance will change significantly. The banks that will ultimately become major players in China will be those that understand where the long-term potential of this market lies, build strong risk controls, and develop superior organizations capable of winning the most profitable businesses. By 2010, the eventual long-term winners will be clear, so the serious competitors in China will be making their moves in the first few years of the next century.

CHAPTER 15
INDIA:
STRUGGLING FOR FREEDOM

Delhi •

Calcutta •

• Mumbai

• Chennai

Social & Economic Indicators (US$)

Overall	– GDP: $370bn
	– Population: 963mn
	– GDP per capita: $380
	– PPP GDP per capita: $1,500
	– 1985–1997 GDP real growth: 6.6% CAGR
	– Projected 2010 GDP per capita: $870
	– Exports (%GDP): $36bn (10%)
	– Foreign currency reserves (% of imports): $24.7bn (60%)
	– % urbanization: 27%
Corporate	– Top 3 sectors: Manufacturing, Agriculture, Transport
	– Number of corporations with annual sales >$1bn: 25
Individual	– Annual savings rate: 28%
	– Average savings per household: $1,000[1]
	– Home ownership: 87%
	– Household car ownership: 5%
	– Telephones /1000 pop: 14[2]
	– Internet subscribers/1,000 pop: 2
	– % of 18–22-yr-olds attending university: 7%

All figures as of December 1997 unless otherwise indicated.
[1] McKinsey estimates.
[2] Figures as of December 1996.
[3] Maturity greater than 1 year.
[4] Figures as of June 1998.

Financial Markets & Business Lines (US$)

Overall	– Equity capitalization (% of GDP): $109bn (29%)
	– Number of listed corporations: 9,000
	– Debt market capitalization[3] (% of GDP): $99bn (27%)
	– Total domestic loans (% of GDP): $86bn (23%)
	– Total external debt (% of GDP): $88bn (24%)
	– Total offshore loans (% of GDP): $21bn (6%)
	– Number of local banks (>$5bn assets): 7
	– Number of foreign banks: 39
	– Top 3 banks' market share (deposits): 33%
	– Maximum foreign ownership of a commercial bank: 100%
	– Currency convertibility: Restricted
Corporate Banking	– Domestic corporate loans (% of GDP): $62bn (17%)
	– Nonperforming domestic loans: 17%
Retail Banking	– Total consumer deposits (% of total deposits): $85bn (65%)
	– Total consumer loans (% of total loans): $6.3bn (7%)
	– Persons per branch: 19,300
	– Persons per ATM: 1.8 mn
	– Credit cards per capita: 0.003
Asset Management	– Retail assets under management: $23bn
	– Total domestic institutional assets: $64bn[2]
	– Number of asset management firms: 35
Trading	– Number of stock brokerage firms: 7,000[2]
	– Average daily equity trading volume: $0.7bn
	– Average daily FX trading volume: $2.4bn[4]
Investment Banking	– Total equity issuance (1994–1997 annual avg): $7.9bn
	– Total debt issuance[3] (1994–1997 annual avg): $25bn
	– Number of domestic M&A transactions >$50mn (1992–1997): 15
Private Banking	– High-net-worth households (>$1mn investable assets): 36,000[1]
	– Potential private banking assets: $111bn[1]

15
INDIA:
STRUGGLING FOR FREEDOM

In 1997, the State Bank of India (SBI), India's largest commercial bank, decided to combine its domestic and foreign exchange treasuries, to leverage its large local and foreign exchange dealing volume more effectively. This seemingly innocuous decision was in fact a bold one, as the foreign exchange treasury happened to be located in Calcutta, while the domestic treasury was in Mumbai. SBI's unions strongly opposed the move, as did foreign exchange brokerage firms in Calcutta. The state government also launched a campaign against the merger, and tried to persuade the bank to keep its dealing functions in Calcutta. SBI's objective of making treasury management more efficient was lost in the public outcry against its alleged lack of social responsibility. It was more than 18 months before the bank could finally enter into its first interbank foreign exchange trade from the Mumbai dealing room.

Often torn between such conflicting demands, Indian banks walk a tightrope between strengthening their businesses and not treading on stakeholders' toes. For decades, the banks' development was driven by the dictates of India's command-economy model. One of the unfortunate legacies of planned development is a relatively unsophisticated and slow-moving financial system dominated by state-owned banks and development finance agencies, and often stifled by regulatory control, trade unionism, and political interference. In such an environment, the banks find it difficult to shed their traditional "lumbering elephant" image and evolve into leaner, nimbler competitors.

In the 1990s, however, regulators, policymakers, and the banks themselves took initiatives to strengthen and liberate India's financial system. In line with increasing economic liberalization, Indian banks moved through three distinct eras, from rapid, unbridled expansion to tighter regulation and then greater competition. Consolidation and market-driven asset restructuring will mark the next phase of banking evolution. In this environment of new opportunities, but also new and more stringent demands, Indian banks will need to sharply define their product/market focus, shore up their credit and distribution skills, and improve operating efficiency. Banks that respond and adapt to these challenges will survive and win in the long term.

Controlled Economy Giving Way to Liberalization

The evolution and growth of India's banking system must be understood in the context of the nation's economic structure and development. In the 1990s, India made the transition from a long period of planned economic development to a more liberal market-oriented economy. During the same period, the Indian financial system underwent a similar evolution.

Economy Unshackled

After colonial rule ended in 1947, the government pursued the dual national objectives of attaining self-sufficiency in grain production and manufactured goods and promoting social equity. It adopted a command economy model, with planned agricultural initiatives and a public sector-driven industrial policy. In the late 1990s, agriculture remained the dominant economic sector, though its share had fallen from 56 percent in 1951 to 30 percent in 1996. Meanwhile, manufacturing's share nearly doubled, from 15 to 28 percent. The early development of the manufacturing sector focused on basic industries, particularly ferrous metals, paper, cement, chemicals, and fertilizers. Notably, India did not adopt a strategy of export-led growth, as did most Asian economies. In 1998, exports accounted for only about 9 percent of GDP, although this ratio had doubled from the mid-1980s. The public sector dominated the economy, and most business decisions — even those of privately owned companies — required government approvals.

The planned model of economic development, with its stress on self-reliance and protectionism rather than competitive advantage, resulted in average real GDP growth of 5.6 percent per annum in the 1980s — slow by Asian standards — dipping to a low of 0.8 percent in 1992. Thereafter came a first phase of economic liberalization, which sparked new optimism in the business community. The 1992 liberalization package included a progressive reduction of tariffs and direct taxes, the de-licensing of most sectors, a more conducive environment for foreign technology and foreign ownership of local enterprises, and a freeing of capital issue pricing, which gave the equity markets a boost. Real GDP growth averaged 6.5 percent p.a. during 1993–1998, in a relatively stable monetary and exchange environment.

Financial System Reflects Both
State-Directed and Market Forces

The structure of the Indian financial system in the late 1990s resembles the same story of planned development giving way to tentative liberalization. Many of India's commercial banks and insurance companies date back to the colonial period. The financial infrastructure created after India's independence from Britain in 1947 reflected the post-colonial government's emphasis on industrial and rural development. In 1948, the government began setting up the industrial credit infrastructure, including long-term financing institutions (the all-India development banks) and a large number of smaller state-owned industrial financing agencies. In 1964, it established the state-owned Unit Trust of India to help channel small savings to industrial projects. To promote rural development, the government created a network of regional rural banks in 1975.

In the last quarter-century, reflecting the growing demand for specialized financial products and the government's increasingly market-friendly stance, the number of privately owned financial sector players grew rapidly. These include stock brokerages, housing finance companies, nonbank finance companies (NBFCs), mutual fund companies, foreign portfolio investors and investment banks, and private commercial banks. The Indian financial system is thus a unique blend of state and private ownership. Though the bulk of assets are controlled by largely state-owned enterprises, private entities play an important role in shaping and defining product, pricing, and customer service standards.

The top regulator is the Reserve Bank of India (RBI), which supervises commercial banks, NBFCs, and industrial and agricultural finance agencies. The RBI also oversees monetary policy and exchange control. The other major financial regulator is the Securities and Exchange Board of India, which regulates capital markets, including the mutual fund companies, stock brokerages, foreign portfolio investors, and investment banks. Both regulators have traditionally worked closely in tandem with the Ministry of Finance. Exhibit 15.1 shows the major groups of players in the Indian financial sector and their relative assets.

Four Phases of Banking System Evolution

The evolution of India's banking system has reflected the government's changing priorities. The planned conscious growth and development of the banking sector commenced in 1969. Since then, the sector has evolved through three distinct phases. The first phase, spanning all of the 1970s and 1980s, was characterized by unbridled branch expansion and asset growth. The second phase, in the early 1990s, brought initial reforms aimed at building a sound banking foundation. The third, from 1995 onward, involved further reforms, mostly geared to enhancing competition. As the 1990s drew to a close, Indian banks were on the verge of entering a fourth phase, one likely to be marked by consolidation.

Unbridled Expansion (1969–1991)

The banking sector was identified as the key instrument of economic development in 1969. The government nationalized 14 banks that year and another eight in 1980. (By 1997, public sector banks accounted for 80 percent of all banking assets.) In addition, policymakers imposed a strict credit-rationing approach, prescribing formula-based lending norms and high directed credit obligations to ensure that banks channeled funds to strategic sectors.

During this period, Indian banks pursued branch network expansion and asset growth almost to the exclusion of any other aim. The result was widespread network reach and enviable distribution capability. The geographical scope of India's banking system, illustrated in Exhibit 15.2, is probably unparalleled globally. The number of bank branches grew from about 8,300 in 1969 to about 60,000 in 1991. Banking density improved from 64,000 people per bank branch in 1969 to just 14,000 people per branch in 1991. Thanks to this explosion of branches, India's gross domestic savings rate rose from 15.7 percent in 1970 to 24.2 percent in 1991, and banking deposits grew at a rapid 19 percent compound annual growth rate (CAGR).

But the results were all not rosy. With interest rates climbing throughout the 1980s, most banks carried large hidden losses in their portfolios of long-dated fixed-income securities. By 1990, over one-quarter of bank loans were nonperforming, and many banks were massively overstaffed and heavily

Exhibit 15.1

Structure of the Indian Financial System
Assets in 1997, US$ billions

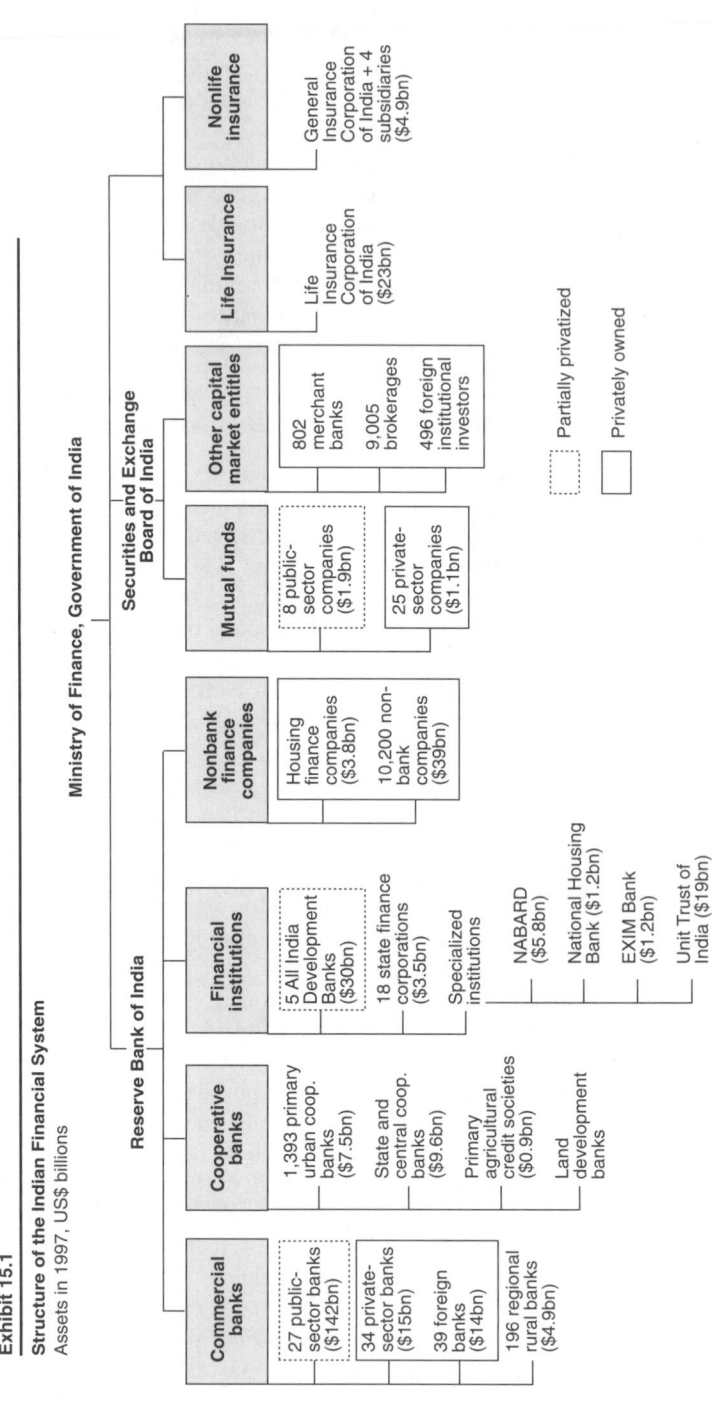

Source: Reserve Bank of India

Exhibit 15.2

Spread of Indian Banks' Branch Network
Total branches: 63,513 in 1997

Jammu & Kashmir: 797

Delhi

Delhi, Punjab, Haryana, Himachal Pradesh: 5,932

Rajasthan: 3,247   Uttar Pradesh: 8,719

North Eastern states: 1,944

Bihar: 4,948

West Bengal: 4,328

Gujarat: 3,533   Madhya Pradesh: 4,411

Orissa: 2,153

Mumbai

Calcutta

Maharashtra & Goa: 6,253

Andhra Pradesh: 4,902

Karnataka: 4,499

Chennai

Andaman & Nicobar Islands: 40

Kerala: 3,116

Tamil Nadu: 4,691

Source: Reserve Bank of India

unionized. These fundamental weaknesses went virtually unnoticed as the relentless focus on asset growth made Indian banks pay little attention to profitability and financial performance.

Early Reforms (1992–1995)

In an attempt to align the Indian financial system more closely with the international order, the RBI launched its first wave of financial reforms in 1992. These initial reforms focused on cleaning up bank balance sheets and forcing greater disclosure and transparency in accounting. Specifically, the RBI introduced unambiguous policies for asset classification, income recognition, and loan loss provisioning, coupled with mandatory compliance with BIS capital-adequacy standards and more stringent norms for investment valuation.

From a regional perspective, these reforms put India up near the head of the regulatory class. For some of its Southeast Asian neighbors, it took the 1997–1998 crisis to precipitate the tougher application of loan accounting and provisioning policies that India put in place 5 years earlier.

But these early reforms caused much pain for Indian banks. Indeed, 12 of the 27 public sector banks reported losses in 1993. The government stanched the bleeding with repeated equity infusions, totaling US$4.2 billion over 1992–1997, and in 1993, it forced the merger of the large, profitable state-owned Punjab National Bank with the chronically ill New Bank of India. By 1995, most of the accumulated losses of the past 30-odd years had surfaced at last, and the bleeding had waned. As a group, the public sector banks moved from a net loss position of 0.99 percent of total assets in fiscal year 1993 (India's fiscal year runs from April 1 to March 31) to a net profit position of 0.25 percent of total assets in 1995. Two public sector banks, SBI and the Oriental Bank of Commerce, issued maiden IPOs, marking the first dilution of government bank ownership.

Competition (1995–1999)

In this third phase, financial reform continued, although the changes were less dramatic. The focus of reform shifted to promoting competition and market pricing mechanisms. While the first wave of reforms had a one-time impact on banks' balance sheets, the latter wave will have a more fundamental effect on their business strategies. For instance, the RBI allowed banks to compete freely for loan customers, doing away with the archaic consortium system that forced borrowers to parcel out business among their existing set of bankers. The central bank also freed interest rates across virtually the entire maturity spectrum, with rates now only influenced, rather than determined, by the RBI's market signals. Nine new private banks were permitted to commence operations in this period. Windows to foreign capital were opened, and Indian banks thus faced a whole new range of competitors. The result was a sharp decline in margins in most traditional product/market segments by 1997.

Despite this, banks managed to post higher profits than in the past due to volume expansion and fewer incremental problem loans. Of the eight public sector banks that reported net losses in 1995, only three remained in the red by 1997. As a group, the public sector banks more than doubled their net profit ratio, from 0.25 percent of total assets in 1995 to 0.56 percent in 1997. Most of the recapitalized banks managed to turn the corner, and some even repaid the government its equity. Four more public sector banks made their first public stock offerings in this period, furthering lessening the sector's dependence on government capital.

As before, India's next phase of reforms is likely to follow a road map charted by specially constituted committees, quasi-think tanks for the government. In 1991, the first such committee, comprising eminent leaders of banking and industry and chaired by M. Narasimham, identified the required direction and pace of change. Events from 1992 to 1998 proceeded, for the most part, along that road map. In 1998, the government once more appointed a committee under Narasimham to sketch the structural reforms required to take the financial sector forward. This committee strongly emphasized the need for consolidation, a move toward universal banking, greater autonomy for bank management, and a reduction in the level of nonperforming assets. It proposed higher private shareholding in state-owned banks, the merger of strong banks, the closure of unviable ones, and a drastic reduction in directed credit obligations (see sidebar for details). The Narasimham Committee and other government-appointed think tanks act as public opinion builders, and are likely to provide India's leaders with the ammunition needed to implement the next phase of financial sector deregulation and reform.

Recommendations of the Committee on Banking Sector Reforms, April 1998

Capital Adequacy

- Capital adequacy ratio to be raised from 8% to 10% by 2002
- 100% of fixed income portfolio marked to market by 2001 (up from 70%)
- 5% market risk weight for fixed income securities and open foreign exchange position limits (no market risk weights previously)
- Commercial risk weight (100%) to government-guaranteed advances (previously treated as risk-free)

Asset Quality

- Banks should aim to reduce gross nonperforming assets to 3% and net NPAs to 0% by 2002
- 90-day overdue norm to be applied for cash-based income recognition (down from 180 days)
- Government-guaranteed irregular accounts to be classified as NPAs and provided for
- Asset Reconstruction Company to take on NPAs of weak banks against issue of risk-free bonds
- Directed credit obligations to be reduced from 40% to 10%
- Mandatory general provisions of 1% of standard assets and specific provisions to be made tax-deductible

Systems and Methods

- Banks to start recruitment of skilled, specialized manpower from the market

- Overstaffing to be dealt with by redeployment and right-sizing via voluntary retirement schemes
- Public sector banks to be given flexibility in remuneration structure
- Rapid introduction of computerization and technology

Industry Structure

- Only two categories of financial sector players to emerge: banks and nonbank finance companies; DFIs to convert to banks or remain nonbank companies
- Mergers to be driven by market and business considerations, not imposed by regulators
- Weak banks to convert to "narrow banks,"[*] restructure, or close down if proven unviable
- Emergence of 3–4 international banks, 8–10 national banks; rest to play regional/local roles.
- Entry of new private sector banks and foreign banks to continue
- Banks to be given greater functional autonomy, and minimum government shareholding to be reduced to 33% from 55% for State Bank of India and 51% for other public sector banks

Regulation and Supervision

- Banking regulation and supervision to be progressively de-linked from monetary policy
- Board for Financial Regulation and Supervision to be constituted with statutory powers; board members should be professionals
- Greater emphasis on public disclosure as opposed to disclosure to regulators

Legal Amendments

- Broad range of legal reforms to facilitate recovery of problem loans
- Introduction of laws governing electronic funds transfer
- Amendments in the Banking Regulation Act, Nationalization Acts, and State Bank of India Act to allow greater autonomy, higher private sector shareholding, etc.

---

[*] By focusing on retail deposit mobilization and reducing their credit intermediation role substantially.

Consolidation (2000–2010)

Indian banks face tough times in the first decade of the 21st century. Assuming the government can muster sufficient political will, the reform process will continue, forcing banks to achieve higher standards of disclosure and transparency, apply tighter loan loss-provisioning norms, and attain higher capital-to-risk asset ratios. Indeed, the RBI announced in its 1998 credit policy that banks would have to increase their capital ratios from 8 to 9 percent and adopt tighter provisioning norms for nonperforming assets in the year 2000.

Meanwhile, the financial system faces a bad debt predicament, but one of moderate intensity by Asian standards. The disclosed ratio of nonperforming assets to total loans was about 16 percent in 1998, but market estimates based on the strictest international accounting norms place the ratio at 20–21 percent. The crisis is likely to be overcome through a gradual process of tighter reform, legal overhaul, and industry restructuring and consolidation. The pace of change will be slow, as long as the problem appears controllable. In the less probable event that it intensifies into a full-blown crisis, the government will likely respond with sharply accelerated reforms forcing the financial system to modernize.

Sheer asset growth alone is unlikely to save banks in future. State-sponsored mechanisms such as an asset reconstruction fund to buy out problem loans in exchange for government-guaranteed bonds would serve a limited purpose, as have the various state-sponsored credit-guarantee schemes. These mechanisms might give weak banks some breathing space, but are unlikely to provide long-term solutions to the problems caused by India's arcane legal framework, its high degree of political intervention, and banks' poor credit skills and information systems. Improving the lending environment will require substantial legal overhaul and the evolution of market mechanisms, including securitization of loan receivables, development of a deep and liquid secondary market for loans, and growth in tradable credit-derivative instruments such as guarantees, liquidity supports, and risk participation certificates.

Creating a viable industry structure will demand vision and bold action on the part of the government. It will need to modernize and strengthen regulation, for the RBI is as much in need of reform as most banks. As the financial system becomes market-oriented, it will inevitably trigger a consolidation of India's banking industry. Some banks will manage to survive, but many others of sub-optimal scale will be merged, acquired, or shut down. Though India had 296 banks as of 1997, 100 commercial banks held 97 percent of all assets (Exhibit 15.3). The six biggest banking groups — the SBI and its associate banks, along with the five large public sector banks (Bank of Baroda, Punjab National Bank, Bank of India, Canara Bank, and the Central Bank of India) — accounted for more than half of 1997 assets. From a global perspective, however, these "big six" are quite small; SBI, India's largest commercial bank, had assets of only US$40 billion in 1997. The new private sector banks, which started up in 1994, grew fast over their first 4 years but remain dwarfed by their much older public sector competitors. And the 39 foreign commercial banks operating in India controlled a tiny 8 percent of total banking assets in 1997.

Exhibit 15.3

Share of Banking Assets in India: 1997
Percent

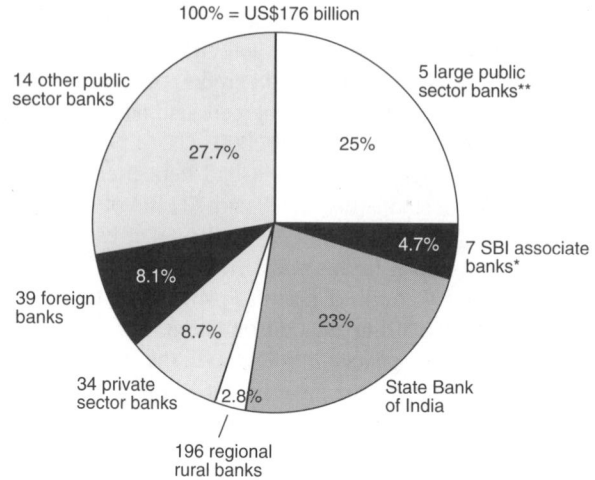

100% = US$176 billion

14 other public sector banks — 27.7%

5 large public sector banks** — 25%

7 SBI associate banks* — 4.7%

8.1%

39 foreign banks

8.7%

34 private sector banks

2.8%

23% — State Bank of India

196 regional rural banks

* State Bank of Hyderabad, State Bank of Travancore, State Bank of Bikaner and Jaipur, State Bank of Mysore, State Bank of Saurashtra, State Bank of Indore, State Bank of Patiala.

** Bank of Baroda, Punjab National Bank, Bank of India, Canara Bank, Central Bank of India.

Source: Reserve Bank of India

Given the government's high stake in the banking system, consolidation is unlikely to be a completely market-driven process. Government consensus on the need for and benefits of consolidation will be needed, as will the political will to take the process forward. Regulators are likely to move towards building such a consensus, though the pace of change will hinge on the political leadership's priorities.

Opportunities Increasing Across the Banking Spectrum

Despite its many banks and the rapid growth in branches and assets through the 1970s and 1980s, at the end of the 1990s India remained an under-banked economy. Indian households kept more than a quarter of their savings in nonfinancial assets, mainly real estate and gold, indicating the high scope for growth as these savings entered the banking system. As of 1997, bank loans were equivalent to just 26 percent of GDP, significantly lower than in Southeast Asian countries, where loans reached 120 percent of GDP. But the trend is clearly toward increasing financial intermediation, making India a fast-growing market for banking products. For instance, gross household financial savings rose from 6.3 percent of GDP in 1980 to 10.6 percent in 1997. In the decade from 1987 to 1997, total bank deposits grew at a rapid 17.7 percent CAGR.

Further economic development and reforms in the first decade of the 21st century will give rise to attractive opportunities all along the banking spectrum. On the retail side, steady increases in per capita income will lead to higher consumer aspirations and growing demand for personal financial products. In the late 1990s, Indian retail customers had limited access to bank credit products, faced an unexciting range of savings products, and suffered indifferent service. This will change.

Meanwhile, massive investments in basic infrastructure, including telecommunications, power, roads, ports, and water supply, will create equally massive demand for wholesale financial services. Annual investments required for infrastructure are projected to grow to US$50 billion by 2006, up from US$17 billion in 1996. Mustering the funds for investments of this order will likely require the government to unshackle the insurance sector, liberalize pension and provident funds, and further open the economy to foreign capital. The anticipated rise in domestic contractual savings and overseas capital flows, coupled with the demand for long-term capital from the infrastructure segment, is expected to boost investment banking and capital markets activities.

The following sections highlight the opportunities for banks in India across three broad customer segments: large corporations, middle-market companies, and retail customers.

Large Corporations: Still the Bread and Butter

Large industrial companies in India are typically family-owned business houses, state-owned entities operating in core sectors, or multinational corporations. This group of companies, with annual sales in excess of US$50 million, accounted for 88 percent of market capitalization of the Bombay Stock Exchange in 1997. It includes both very large corporations as well as those that would be considered middle-market companies elsewhere. Traditionally, commercial banks prospered by serving these customers through a range of working-capital product lines: secured overdraft accounts, trade bill discounting facilities, letters of credit and guarantees, foreign exchange covers, and payment products. Despite lower credit risk, banks were able to charge high interest rates and fees, to earn net margins of as much as 600-800 basis points from this segment. The 100 largest customers for each bank would typically account for a third of the bank's commercial credit exposure, and more than half of its profits.

Large Indian corporations flourished in the old controlled economy, when production licenses were scarce. Post-liberalization, they faced stiff competition from new domestic and foreign players and from imports. The tougher corporate environment made bankers, with their newfound preoccupation with nonperforming assets and capital adequacy, wary of extending illiquid loans. Around the same time, the RBI liberalized banks' investments in tradable instruments (bonds, commercial paper, and equity), freed interest rates, and eased norms for foreign capital mobilization. In response, large corporate entities increasingly raised capital by selling bonds locally to banks, financial institutions, mutual funds, and insurance companies in India, and by issuing foreign currency debt and equity. While this led to lower interest rates and margins for banks in traditional lending, it gave rise to new opportunities in investment banking.

India opened its investment banking business to foreign participation during the second wave of financial reforms, in the mid-1990s. A large number of international players responded enthusiastically, entering the markets for portfolio investment, asset management, institutional brokerage, and management of overseas debt and equity issues. These players judged the market's growth potential to be high, fueled by Indian companies' easier access to external commercial borrowings and global depository receipts (GDRs), the government's privatization program, and relaxed regulations on foreign ownership of domestic companies.

India's local currency capital markets, too, were vibrant, offering attractive opportunities for investment banking. Local companies raised rupees via public equity flotation totaling US$37 billion between 1991 and 1997. Annual equity flotation grew at a CAGR of 20 percent in rupee terms and 12 percent p.a. in U.S. dollar terms over 1991–1997, while the number of companies listed on the Bombay Stock Exchange grew at 15 percent p.a. over the same period. Meanwhile, public debt issuance by Indian corporations added up to US$28 billion over 1991–1997, and grew at 14 percent CAGR in rupee terms but only 6 percent p.a. in U.S. dollar terms (Exhibit 15.4).

As competition heightened during the late 1990s, margins shrank. Still, local equity issue gross fees at 150–200 basis points represented a revenue pool of about US$60 million p.a. as of 1997. Issue management fees on corporate debt were lower, at about 30 basis points, but still suggested a revenue pool of about US$25 million a year as of 1997. Looking to the early 21st century, rupee-denominated equity and debt issues are likely to grow at a sustainable average annual rate of at least 15 percent, in line with nominal economic growth. Even discounting for

Exhibit 15.4

Capital Issues by Indian Corporations
US$ billion

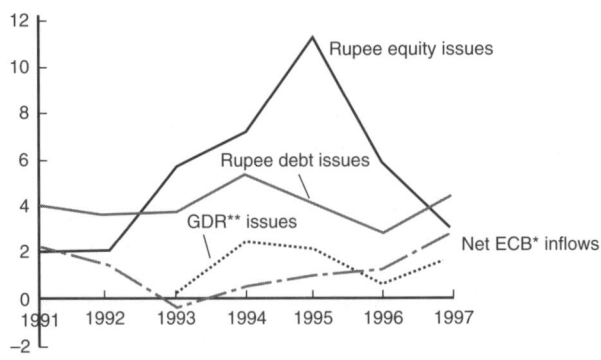

* External commercial borrowings.
** Global Depository Receipts.

Source: Center for Monitoring the Indian Economy

falling margins in the placement business, this represents a large opportunity for efficient players in Indian investment banking.

Issuance of foreign-currency-denominated equity instruments was liberalized only in 1993. Between 1993 and 1997, Indian corporations cumulatively raised about US$7.3 billion in GDRs and Euro-convertible bonds, with issuance growing at 65 percent a year, before plummeting to US$291 million in 1998. Net external commercial borrowings totaled US$9.1 billion over the same period (Exhibit 15.4). Issue management fees for the GDR/Euro-convertible segment dropped to about 2 percent in 1997, representing an annual revenue pool of about US$35 million. Debt syndication fees that year varied based on the tenure and credit quality of the paper, but generally averaged about 0.3 percent, representing revenues of US$20 million p.a.

Despite calls for full capital account convertibility, the government is unlikely to relax constraints on overseas borrowing radically in light of the 1997–1998 Asian economic crisis and its link with high short-term foreign currency borrowings. Though India was relatively unaffected by the Asian crisis, local politics created turmoil of a different kind. Nuclear blasts in 1998 and subsequent U.S. trade sanctions cast a damper on corporate plans to raise foreign currency debt, and raised doubts about the country's fiscal and exchange stability. In response, international credit rating agencies downgraded their sovereign ratings of India. But even so, primary issues of foreign currency-denominated instruments could grow at over 20 percent p.a. in the early part of the 21st century, provided the political environment remains benevolent to foreign investors.

Morgan Stanley: Repositioning for the Long Haul

The mid-1990s investment banking boom in India was marked by a degree of over-optimism among foreign players. In anticipation of huge deal flows, most of the new entrants built high-cost personnel and infrastructure bases that were out of line with their ability to generate revenues. Realization of this folly coincided with the global consolidation of the investment banking industry and reconsideration of Asia strategies. The inevitable shakeout reached India in 1997, and at least six foreign investment banks exited the country. But the scenario is brighter for those that remain, particularly in view of the anticipated takeoff in big-ticket infrastructure financing. Morgan Stanley is among those committed for the long haul, and one that has adapted its approach to reflect market realities.

Morgan Stanley made its first foray into India by launching a mutual fund in January 1994. The fund mobilized a record amount from retail investors, making the Indian market appear simple for foreign firms to understand and conquer. However, the timing was poor, and the fund's performance fell short of expectations. This coincided with a prolonged bear phase in the equity markets, leaving retail investors reluctant to touch equity offerings.

In 1996, Morgan Stanley shifted its focus to institutional brokerage, managing foreign capital inflows into the Indian secondary markets, and mobilizing foreign equity and debt capital for top-end public and private sector clients in India. It achieved a fair degree of success with this approach, garnering an estimated 15 percent market share as of 1997.

In late 1997, Morgan Stanley surprised the financial markets by announcing an alliance with JM Financial, one of India's top-tier players, selected by *Asiamoney* as "Domestic Investment Bank of the Year" in 1997. The two firms agreed to merge their businesses in investment banking and institutional sales and trading into two joint ventures, thus bringing together a winning combination of foreign and domestic skills and resources. Underpinning the deal was Morgan Stanley's recognition that the limited deal flow from the overseas business of top-end Indian clients would be insufficient to sustain a high-cost operation, and that it needed a local partner to build domestic capital deal flows. Morgan Stanley will benefit by gaining access to JM's mid-cap clientele and retail distribution network. Likewise, the alliance gives JM access to Morgan Stanley's international capital mobilization, sales, and trading capabilities, so it can offer clients a full range of corporate finance and capital market services.

Morgan Stanley was not the first foreign player to seek an Indian partner; Merrill Lynch and Goldman Sachs had already done so. However, this was the first partnership cemented after the Asian crisis and India's slowing growth. The Morgan Stanley alliance suggests that, despite near-term setbacks, some foreign banks still wanted to retain an option on India, and recognized the combination of global capital and expertise and local skills and relationships that are required to win in this environment.

Middle Market: A Newly Attractive Segment

India's mid-cap manufacturing companies, trading, and services companies represent a large market for banking services. Of the more than 5,000 publicly listed corporations, 87 percent had annual sales of less than US$50 million in 1997. That same year, these companies accounted for 31 percent of exports and 18 percent of sales of all listed companies. Mid-cap companies need the full spectrum of traditional banking products, ranging from term loans for capital equipment finance to working-capital finance. The RBI, in an effort to promote small industry, requires banks to earmark 12 percent of total advances to small-scale industrial companies, defined as companies with fixed assets of less than US$750,000. Yet, there is a fast-growing and profitable segment of companies that does not qualify for directed credit, and has traditionally been squeezed for finance.

For example, companies in trading and services have suffered from inadequate institutional funding — even though these sectors are among India's fastest growing. Trade, hotels, transport, and communications grew at a CAGR of 20 percent between 1981 and 1997, rising from 16.7 to 22.3 percent of GDP over that period. Meanwhile, bank finance to the trading sector amounted to less than 5 percent of total bank credit in 1997. This anomaly was largely due to the collateral-based lending models that shaped the RBI's prescribed policies for credit appraisal and loan approval. For decades, the public sector banks developed credit policies in line with RBI guidelines, which provided an inadequate framework to assess nonmanufacturing entities.

Trading and service companies turned to the unorganized sector and NBFCs for finance, and some of the latter earned attractive profits from such lending. For example, Sundaram Finance, India's leading financier of transport operators, had assets of US$50 million and a 4.5 percent ROA in 1997. However, lenders like Sundaram are themselves under pressure from a dwindling resource base and tighter regulation. And, with a sluggish primary market, the ability of small and medium-sized companies to raise equity capital through IPOs is even more dismal. Under this scenario, players with a greater risk appetite may find exciting opportunities in venture capital financing for India's emerging breed of innovative and growth-oriented mid-cap companies.

Making Selective Bets in Indian Venture Capital

Though venture capital in India had been around since 1975, it got its real impetus only in the 1990s, when the government freed capital issue pricing and brought venture capital under the ambit of the Securities and Exchange Board. The two pioneering Indian venture capital firms were Risk Credit Technology Corporation (RCTC), and TDICI (formerly the Technology Development and Investment Corporation of India), both domestic development financial institutions. From 1995, the industry slowly shifted gear with the entry of foreign venture capital and private equity funds. Private equity firms in India had estimated investable funds of US$1 billion in 1997, and active foreign players included Alliance-DLJ, AIG, HSBC, Indocean Chase, ING Barings, GE Capital, Schroders, and Draper International. While the industry was small by global standards, most players were optimistic, expecting 25–35 percent annual returns in U.S. dollar terms.

In the late 1990s, these funds were making small, selective investments. From greenhorn entrepreneurs and untested technologies, their focus was turning to projects that had reached critical mass, in knowledge-based, growth-oriented sectors, such as information technology, biotechnology, retailing, and telecommunications. For instance, Baring India Investment (BII), of the ING Group, earmarked about US$250 million to invest in Asian IT companies, of which a large portion was expected to go to India. In 1998, BII concluded deals to acquire large equity stakes in two medium-sized software firms, and similar deals were struck by Indocean Chase Capital Advisors' client funds. The Tamil Nadu Industrial Development Corporation, along with the Small Industries Development Bank of India and IL&FS Venture Corporation, launched a fund to invest exclusively in software companies. Meanwhile, IL&FS Venture Corporation established the India Auto Ancillary Fund, with a targeted capital of US$30 million, to invest in small and medium-sized domestic auto component producers. In an even more ambitious move, TDICI planned to launch India's first fund, with a corpus of over US$25 million, to invest in loss-making companies with turnaround potential.

The critical obstacle in the flow of capital to small but growth-oriented Indian companies is the absence of an efficient exit mechanism. The thicket of regulations and an illiquid capital market with few active institutional players mean that funds have not been able to provide for a smooth exit at an attractive price. Most venture capital deals include a provision for repurchase by the entrepreneur. But this is not a solution, since most Indian entrepreneurs are unable to muster the funds themselves to buy back equity at fair valuations. Only an efficient and vibrant equity market, with a large number of institutional investors with varying risk appetites, can provide a sustainable exit route in the long term. Once such a market develops, there will be little to hold back the venture capital industry in India.

Retail Banking: Tomorrow's New Frontier

Retail banking has traditionally been a neglected segment in India, despite representing a potential market of about 50 million households. The public sector banks have viewed households as a captive source of funding, and have competed primarily on network and reach rather than on product innovation and service. While foreign banks have acknowledged the need for high-quality service and a larger range of retail products, high minimum account balances and high fees have made their services attractive only to high-net-worth customers. Thus, middle-class households had little choice but to suffer indifferent service at their neighborhood bank branches.

The market for savings products is easily the largest, though not necessarily the most lucrative. In 1996, 63 percent of SBI's domestic deposit base came from personal banking and agricultural small savings accounts. Across the whole banking system, an estimated 65 percent of deposits came from retail sources; these deposits totaled US$85 billion in 1997. They were either in savings accounts (earning average interest of about 4 percent p.a.) or in term deposits with average maturity of about 2 years. In the late 1990s, banks earned about US$1 billion a year in profits from these deposits — a large pie, of which the public sector banks had the dominant slice.

With the continued decline in interest rates on government and corporate debt, banks turned their attention to retail credit products, including mortgage loans, auto financing, and credit cards. Despite low penetration levels, these retail credit markets were already characterized by stiff competition.

The housing finance market grew 25 percent a year from 1992 to 1997, and home loans outstanding amounted to about US$2.6 billion in 1997. The market represented an annual profit pool of about US$60 million — most of which went to the dominant player, the Housing Development and Finance Corporation (HDFC), which has a 56 percent market share. HDFC demonstrated that an efficient player could make a net ROA of about 3 percent in the housing finance business.

Over the coming decade, this segment is likely to grow at a 30 percent annual rate, driven by higher financing penetration, loan to value ratios, and home ownership. In the late 1990s, only about 20 percent of housing purchases were financed through institutional sources, and average loan-to-value ratios were less than 50 percent, reflecting Indian consumers' conservative attitude toward mortgages and the difficult environment for foreclosure. Though a large proportion of Indians already own their own homes, there is likely to be a surge in new home acquisition as people trade old dwellings for superior ones and as the nuclear family norm spreads.

Foreign banks, as well as some NBFCs in collaboration with foreign auto manufacturers, have found India's passenger car finance segment very attractive. Car ownership density at the end of the 1990s was low — about four cars per 1,000 people — and so was penetration: only about 60 percent of passenger car purchases were financed, versus 90 percent in the commercial vehicle segment. Auto finance disbursements grew at about 50 percent p.a. from 1993 to 1995. Notwithstanding a disappointing slowdown in 1997, the industry conservatively estimates growth in passenger car sales of 20 percent a year, leading to sales of roughly 635,000 cars by 2000. With penetration levels likely to rise to 90 percent, the passenger car finance market could grow at 40 percent p.a. and represent annual financing opportunities of US$4.5 billion by 2000.

In the late 1990s, the auto financing market was fragmented among more than 150 NBFCs, auto dealers, and banks. The five largest players together commanded about 43 percent of the total market. A shakeout was already under way, but those that survive will profit from this business.

Big Opportunities in Auto Financing for the Big Boys

The passenger car segment of the vehicle finance market in India was dull up to 1985, reflecting the limited options for consumers. The advent of Maruti Udyog Limited (MUL), the Indian government's joint venture company with Suzuki of Japan, revolutionized the auto finance market. MUL was the first company in India to manufacture and market an affordable four-wheel passenger vehicle incorporating anything near international quality standards. The result was a boom in demand for cars that far exceeded the supply.

The first few years saw long queues of potential buyers waiting to purchase MUL's cars, paying large advances to book vehicles in short supply. Indian car dealers, NBFCs, and a few foreign banks rushed to tap the new market for auto finance, with Citibank quickly emerging as the leader. Many Indian finance companies made money in this early boom. But several continued holding large positions in order bookings, whose value eroded as supply finally caught up with demand. Subsequently, credit quality suffered, repossession rates climbed, and the secondary market value of cars declined. The advent of big players triggered price wars, and smaller finance companies saw spreads fall dramatically as lending rates plummeted from 28 percent to as low as 18–20 percent. A few large companies managed to upgrade service standards, maintain a favorable liability profile, and keep recovery rates high enough to protect margins.

The inevitable shakeout in auto finance came in tandem with the liberalization of the auto sector. Several multinational automakers entered India in both the small-car and luxury ranges, and multinationals launched auto finance businesses. For instance, MUL tied up with the GE Capital-HDFC Indian subsidiary, Countrywide Consumer Financial Services Limited in October 1995. Ford Motor Credit Company partnered with Mahindra & Mahindra, a leading auto manufacturer, and Kotak Mahindra Finance, an NBFC. General Motors entered India through its auto finance subsidiary, GMAC Financial Services, which subsequently linked up with Indian NBFC 20th Century Finance Corporation Limited.

These firms had access to capital at competitive rates, which enabled them to beat down prices. They were successful in putting in place networks and systems that enabled them to offer superior customer service. The woes of the smaller Indian NBFCs further multiplied by 1996–1997, when they started facing a funding crunch — institutional finance was in short supply, and their share of retail term deposits slipped away to the commercial banks. Amid more fierce competition from multinationals and rising disintermediation, poorly capitalized companies without stable funding are unlikely to survive.

Entering the 21st century, the Indian auto finance market represents a big opportunity for well-capitalized firms and banks that have access to cheap funds. Indicative of this potential, in 1998, MUL explored setting up another auto finance subsidiary, this time in collaboration with Citibank. This signified MUL's belief that the market can accommodate more large players, but also its recognition that a large capital base, the ability to mobilize funds at competitive rates, and broad distribution capability are all vital to success in this business.

India had a credit card member base of 2.7 million in 1997, representing a penetration level of only 0.55 percent. Citibank dominated the card market, with a 38 percent share. The growth of India's credit card market has been hampered by the widespread use of (undeclared) cash income, the low availability of electronic communication infrastructure, and debt-averse attitudes of Indian consumers. Average credit utilization was estimated at only about 30 percent of sanctioned credit limits. Yet total card spend grew by a whopping CAGR of 80 percent from 1991 to 1997, reaching US$1.5 billion in 1997. It is expected to shoot up at an annual 50 percent rate over 1998–2003, driven by 25–30 percent annual growth in both cardholders and per-card spending.

Such rapid growth is likely to give India a card member base of six million by the turn of the century. SBI, a new entrant in this segment in collaboration with GE Capital, expects to issue two million of these additional cards. With high capital investments required to set up processing technology and distribution networks, card issuers do not expect to break even over their first 5 years. For those taking a long-term view, however, the card market in India will offer an exciting opportunity.

What It Will Take to Win

Winning banks in India will be those that clearly focus on key customer segments, build strong distribution and credit capabilities, and improve operating efficiency. Faced with declining market share and eroding margins on plain-vanilla lending products, wholesale banking players will need to develop new product design and marketing skills, so as to offer capital market, trading, and risk-management offerings tailored to the needs of each customer segment. Meanwhile, in retail banking, successful competitors must identify and reach out to consumers in a cost-effective manner, leveraging technology to provide convenient, low-cost and value-added services. In addition, Indian banks face the challenge of building the asset book and protecting asset quality in a relatively difficult credit environment.

Segmentation

Most Indian banks have used a "one-size-fits-all" principle in customer sales and service. But as consumers get more discerning, successful players are beginning to segment the market, identifying target customers and shaping products and services for each segment. Banks are reorganizing themselves to focus better on individual market segments. These trends are apparent in both wholesale and retail banking.

For instance, in 1998, ICICI decided to organize its functions — and those of its subsidiaries — under three strategic groups: major clients, growth clients, and personal financial services. This reorganization was aimed at ensuring better, more focused client coverage. The major client group will handle the business of ICICI's 150–200 largest clients through dedicated relationship management teams. These relationship managers will concentrate exclusively on clients within their portfolio and will cross-sell products from ICICI and its commercial and investment banking subsidiaries. The growth-client group will focus on medium-sized and smaller growth-oriented companies, and will provide these clients with the full spectrum of commercial banking services. The personal financial services group will focus on building a strong distribution franchise to sell deposit, loan, payment, and capital markets products to urban Indian consumers.

Similarly, in retail banking, Citibank in India uses behavioral and attitudinal data to segment its high-net-worth customers, and to identify and cater to their product and service needs more effectively. Going forward, such a clear organizational focus on segmentation will be a critical differentiator between winners and losers.

Distribution

India's geographical spread and diversity make distribution enormously complex. As of 1997, only 27 percent of India's population resided in urban areas, and the 23 largest cities held a mere 8 percent of the total. In contrast, many Asian countries, with the exception of China, had upward of 10–15 percent of their populations residing in one huge metropolis. Likewise, bank deposits are much less concentrated in India than in the rest of the region. In 1997, the top 20 cities in India accounted for about 40 percent of the nation's bank deposits, while the single largest city in several Southeast Asian countries typically attracted 60–70 percent of total bank deposits. Just 27 million of India's 936 million people are employed in private corporate enterprises in the organized sector, and less than a third of its 157 million households have annual incomes of more than US$1,500. Thus, identifying and serving affluent and middle-class Indian consumers represents a unique, often frustrating, challenge.

Thanks to their vast distribution infrastructure, the public sector banks enjoy a formidable advantage over private and particularly foreign commercial banks. Their single-minded focus on growth during the 1969–1991 era resulted in more than 60,000 branches, about half of which are located in small semi-urban centers and rural areas. In comparison, the 34 local private banks had an estimated 250 branches in total by 1998, mainly in large cities. Many foreign banks, meanwhile, operated with less than a dozen branches, versus the 500-odd branches of state-owned banks of similar size. (In the late 1990s, the government still limited expansion by foreign banks to a total of 15 new branches every year, although that may change when India aligns itself completely with the WTO.)

Looking forward, the state-owned banks have the opportunity to leverage their distribution clout, for example, by selling third-party products through their many branches. For the private local and foreign banks, advancements in communications technology and customer acceptance of electronic channels probably hold the best keys to bridging the gap. Winning for these players will require not only low-cost distribution alternatives but also defying the conventional mindset about product pricing. Citibank is leading the way on this front (see sidebar).

Credit Skills

Given the high rate of non-performing assets in the late 1990s, credit skills will be another key to success in Indian banking. Indian banks managed to reduce gross nonperforming assets from 23 percent in 1994 to 17 percent (and 9 percent after provisions) in 1997, but these figures are still high by Western, if not Asian, standards. Credit quality is particularly poor in certain lending segments; for example, an estimated one-third of priority-sector agricultural and small industrial advances were nonperforming in 1997. With increasingly stringent provisioning norms in the pipeline, strong credit skills will be a prerequisite for success in both wholesale and retail.

Corporate credit risk management

At the end of the 1990s, the Indian banking system was ahead of the Asian class in terms of corporate credit risk appraisal and monitoring systems. Over the years, the RBI devoted much time and energy to developing credit underwriting guidelines and norms to monitor credit quality on an ongoing basis. Traditionally, Indian banks were required to classify advances into eight health codes, later replaced by the international loan classification basis of standard, substandard, doubtful, and loss assets. Documentation required from borrowers was elaborate and comprehensive.

However, as banks discovered in the early stages of reform, these credit management skills were inadequate to protect them from severe loan losses. The poor credit quality of Indian banks stemmed from a combination of factors, many beyond the control of the banks themselves. These included political interference in lending decisions, high levels of directed credit to weak sectors, a slow judicial system (which delayed legal action on defaults), and the strong overhang of socialism (which made it virtually impossible to liquidate companies and recover debts). These problems were exacerbated by banks' poor use of technology. Most Indian banks could not analyze portfolio credit quality on a consolidated and real-time basis, due to lack of automated and networked accounting systems across their many branches.

In future, winners in Indian banking will be those that strengthen credit risk management skills and technology to achieve superior credit quality, even in this difficult operating environment.

India Is the Global Testing Ground for Citibank's Retail Banking Strategy

Citibank has had considerable success in retail banking in India, but it has traditionally been perceived as a bank for the affluent. In 1997, the bank had a retail depositor base of only about 300,000 customers, compared with SBI's 15 million-plus. In a radical departure from its past approach, in 1998 Citibank began spearheading a mass-market strategy, dubbed the New Millennium Bank. It chose India as the global test site for this new concept, under which it aims to offer affordable products to the middle class, using sophisticated electronic product delivery and data warehousing to attain mass volumes.

For its initial launch, Citibank selected Bangalore, where it test-marketed a product package branded "Suvidha," or "Convenience." The package provides direct electronic access to the account, by means of an ATM-cum-debit card, Internet connectivity, and telebanking facilities. Amazingly, this is available for an account balance of a mere US$25, compared with the previous minimum balance of US$7,600. Virtually all services come free with this account. And this is just the beginning — Citibank intends to offer uniquely designed banking products for customers at each stage of the lifecycle — from 18-year-old students to pensioners.

With the Bangalore test, Citibank demonstrated its belief that traditional brick-and-mortar branches are not the most effective way to penetrate the Indian retail banking market. Citibank's hypothesis is that middle-class Indian consumers are ready to embrace remote, electronic banking. The bank aims to install 80 ATMs in Bangalore, as well as point-of-sale (POS) equipment at more than 2,000 retail establishments. Since home computer ownership is still low among the middle class, Citibank is also linking its computer facilities with those of large corporations, giving customers access from their place of employment. This technological leapfrogging could well place Citibank at the forefront of banks riding the retail banking wave in India. The early customer response, however, has been slower than expected, so Citibank will need to further refine its model before using it to penetrate retail markets in other large emerging economies, such as Brazil, Russia, and China.

Retail credit scoring

The Indian retail credit market is characterized by more primitive risk management systems. In the absence of reliable data on household income, expenditure and asset, most retail financiers perform rudimentary, often subjective, credit evaluation. These players typically depend on strong, sometimes unorthodox, collection mechanisms to protect credit quality.

However, a few leading companies are ahead of the pack in terms of credit risk management skills. For instance, major credit card issuers use proprietary databases culled from their loan portfolios to develop credit scoring models, and a few foreign banks have credit decision support systems for their card businesses. HDFC, with over one million retail borrowers, has computerized its operations and loan-tracking systems, and undertakes portfolio analyses regularly to provide inputs to the sales and recovery functions.

In the late 1990s, there was growing recognition of the need for better risk assessment — and particularly better credit-scoring systems — to prepare for the impending retail credit boom. In 1998, multinational business solution firms Experian and Equifax held discussions with leading Indian finance companies and banks to set up consumer credit bureaus. Experian was hoping to establish a joint venture credit bureau, with 49 percent of the equity held by five or more Indian companies. Equifax, meanwhile, aimed to enter into a joint venture with HDFC. And several leading banks were in talks to set up a shared credit information pool for retail lending.

Operating efficiency

Across all segments of the financial services industry in India, a critical distinguishing factor between winners and losers will be their ability to improve efficiency. Doing so will require a two-pronged approach: banks must tackle their low productivity and high cost structures on the one hand, and improve their technological capability on the other.

Improve productivity

India's public sector banks suffer from low manpower efficiency, and most are grossly overstaffed. For instance, in 1997 the Indian public sector banks had a cost to income ratio of 64 percent, compared with less than 50 percent for the top local players in Southeast Asia. The loss-making banks are overstaffed to the tune of 30–35 percent, even when compared to their profitable, though still inefficient, public sector peers. The unions have a stranglehold on the banks; as of the late 1990s, no public sector bank had been able to successfully implement a voluntary retirement scheme, and it was virtually impossible to dismiss employees even on strong grounds of breach of discipline, unprofessional behavior, or fraud.

Wage costs have escalated, with base salaries being negotiated upwards every 3–4 years. Among the public sector banks, strong employee unions collectively bargain for wage hikes with the industry representative, the Indian Banks Association. Moreover, the highly unionized staff works at sub-optimal levels and implementation of new technology is difficult and slow. For several banks, these problems are compounded by a workforce that is under-skilled and probably too old to learn new tricks.

Towards the end of the 1990s, there was growing awareness that a rigid and high cost structure was not sustainable amid intensifying competition. The RBI empowered banks to negotiate special allowances, other than basic pay and cost-of-living adjustments, independently with their respective unions, and several progressive banks were considering this. Many banks implemented a virtual recruitment freeze, except in specialized areas where they had notable skill gaps.

Normal attrition and retirement should lead to a natural contraction in headcount from 2002 onwards (given that the first major recruitment wave occurred in 1969, following the nationalization of large banks). But this will be a slow process. In the meantime, the more nimble foreign and private banks are likely to steal a march over their public sector counterparts.

Upgrade technology base

Even the more efficient public sector banks have shockingly low automation levels. By 1996, for instance, SBI had automated less than 10 percent of its 8,835 branches; these branches handled less than 50 percent of the bank's assets. At the best public sector banks, no more than 70 percent of business is brought in through computerized branches. A negligible proportion of these branches is networked on a real-time basis. Most Indian banks have poor management information, confined largely to statutory requirements. They are unable to accurately measure and monitor basic risk indicators, such as portfolio credit quality and interest rate mismatch.

The spread of electronic retail banking channels and services has been equally slow. For every one million people, India has only half an ATM, compared with 88 in Thailand and 909 in Korea. India's first in-branch ATM was installed in 1985 by HSBC, and its first off-site ATM was launched, again by HSBC, as recently as 1995. The key players in the ATM market are the foreign banks and the new private sector banks, both constrained by their tiny branch networks.

Handicapped by their poor technology base, the public sector banks have been slow to launch new products and have lost out on emerging opportunities. SBI, for example, managed to launch its electronic funds transfer product only in 1997, while Citibank, with a handful of branches, created and proceeded to dominate the EFT market in India over a decade earlier.

The first decade of the 21st century will see the rapid spread of electronic banking in India — of which Citibank's New Millennium Bank strategy is a precursor. There will be growing demand for electronic delivery of banking products from both retail and corporate segments. Foreign banks are likely to win this game by redefining the delivery channel, thereby exponentially increasing their reach and eroding the edge enjoyed by the public sector banks.

Who Will Win?

Winners will need to do three things in India: build and preserve capital as the financial system rides out the bad-debt storm; strengthen operating capabilities as described earlier; and find a way to grow profitably. Growth will be vital for a multitude of reasons. None of the Indian players will be able to compete globally unless they ramp up their size. With radical cost restructuring politically difficult in the medium term, business growth on a static cost platform is the only quick way to improve operating efficiency. Credit concentration has reached alarming proportions in some sectors, and growth with diversification seems the only feasible way to improve asset quality. Thus, identifying how well banks will manage growth is key to differentiating tomorrow's winners from the losers. Indian banks can choose among three routes to growth: extending geographical coverage, expanding product/market coverage, and merging with or acquiring others. Successful players will likely pursue a combination of these three.

Growth Through Geographical Extension

Successful Indian banks will be those that explore and conquer new geographical territories going forward. A few of the stronger and more efficient banks have begun establishing overseas branch networks. SBI and Bank of Baroda, for instance, each derived about 12 percent of their loans from offshore branches as of 1997, while the Bank of India issued 20 percent of its loans from overseas branches. In the past, however, Indian banks have burned their fingers on offshore business: they focused on ethnic Indian trading communities, a high-risk client profile, and were unable to compete on price because of their high funding costs. The challenge for these banks in future will be to grow to a significant scale overseas and to capture a better quality of clientele, perhaps by allying with globally competitive partners.

Within India, the winners among regional banks will be those that grow into a national role. For example, Corporation Bank is a relatively small bank with a dominant presence in southern India. Until 1996, over 70 percent of its 507 branches were located in four southern Indian states. As a result of an aggressive network expansion program, the bank aimed to reach more than 700 branches by 1999; virtually all of these new branches were in the northern, eastern, and western parts of the country. As of 1997, Corporation Bank had a presence in 77 of India's 100 largest centers for banking business. It plans to cover all 100 centers by year 2000. The bank's growth strategy has already reaped dividends: between 1993 and 1998, deposits rose by 23.7 percent each year, outstripping the 15.7 percent industry average. This rapid growth is expected to continue.

Growth Through Product/Market Expansion

Going forward, specialization will diminish as Indian players move towards universal banking. In the late 1990s, wholesale banks already have begun building retail businesses. For instance, ICICI embarked on an ambitious retail diversification drive. It acquired a nonbank finance company with a retail depositor franchise, as well as substantial shareholdings in two regional commercial banks. ICICI also established a commercial bank with a mid-cap and retail business focus, and was attempting to develop a retail consumer credit business through a subsidiary company. Similarly, commercial banks such as SBI were building long-term credit (project and infrastructure finance) portfolios rapidly, and several (e.g., Corporation Bank, Vysya Bank) launched housing finance businesses. Diversification was occurring within the retail banking spectrum too. HDFC set up joint venture companies for auto loans and consumer credit, as well as a commercial bank.

Regulators and policymakers are broadly in favor of financial institutions diversifying their business mix. However, they need to make fundamental policy changes before institutions can evolve into truly universal banks. For instance, commercial banks have high reserve requirements and directed credit obligations. These need to be removed or extended to all players to achieve a level playing field. Such enabling regulations are likely to be put into place sooner rather than later, as the government faces increasing pressure from all kinds of players to facilitate diversification.

Growth Through Acquisition

The obvious growth strategy for the large national players will be through acquisition — and India's fragmented banking sector contains many attractive targets. The country's remarkable geographical diversity has led to the emergence of regional banks with strong local franchises. Several of these banks have small capital bases and low price-earnings multiples, making them noteworthy takeover candidates for larger national banks seeking to grow. The rising private shareholding of state-owned banks will orient their growth strategies towards increasing shareholder value. As a corollary, market-driven acquisitions of small regional banks are more likely than state-directed mergers of large profitable state-owned banks with smaller loss-making ones.

For instance, many of the older private banks, which escaped nationalization in 1969 and 1980 because they were too small, are based in regions with thriving trade, services, and small industry and affluent pools of nonresident Indian savings. These assets will make them attractive to potential acquirers. In the early part of the 21st century, some of these regional banks will choose to merge or ally with larger banks. Those that attempt to grow on their own may face hostile takeovers and/or rapid erosion in their franchises, as competitors ally with larger players. Already, in 1998, the industry witnessed signs of market-driven M&A. Chase Manhattan Bank kicked off plans to ally with HDFC Bank, a fast-growing and well-managed private sector bank. Several other, albeit weaker, banks were reportedly up for grabs, and ICICI executed acquisitions of two weak NBFCs in 1997–1998.

Consolidation Will Distinguish Winners from Losers

All signals indicate that the first decade of the 21st century will be a phase of consolidation in the Indian financial sector. The RBI's likely tough stance on prudential norms for credit and market risk will force marginal and weak players to merge with stronger ones or perish. This will lead to fewer but larger and healthier banking institutions. We are likely to see the emergence of two or three globally competitive Indian banks whose primary business focus will be the subcontinent and allied markets. These banks will be true universal banks, significant players in several market segments along the wholesale-retail spectrum. To achieve the best standards in product design and delivery, risk management, and technology, they are likely to forge alliances with overseas partners. This top tier of banks could well control about 30–50 percent of the market in India by 2010. Banks such as SBI, ICICI, IDBI, and Bank of Baroda will aspire to this leadership role. Nonbank financial players such as the HDFC, Life Insurance Corporation of India, and Unit Trust of India could also evolve into global/Asian financial intermediaries.

The next tier of banks would be those that have attained a nationally significant scale of operation, each with, say, a 5–7 percent share of banking system assets. Banks in this group will likely compete among themselves for local business from medium-sized companies and retail customers. There is likely to be room for no more than five or six national banking institutions, and many regional banks and finance companies will get merged into these. Players such as Corporation Bank and a few of the large public sector banks will be among this category.

Regional diversity and the sheer size of India's economy will ensure some place in the sun for smaller regional banks and large NBFCs. These players will not be able to compete on scale. The challenge for them will be to identify niches and customer needs that are not being effectively serviced by large players. They will, in effect, be arbitrage players, which exploit temporarily unsatisfied customer needs in localized markets through product and service innovation. Such companies will need a high degree of organizational flexibility and entrepreneurial spirit in order to shift from one business segment to another, staying just ahead of the larger players that muscle their way in behind them.

The outlook for foreign banks depends largely on the Indian government's willingness to open the financial system to outsiders. The direction of reform is clearly towards allowing greater competition from foreign players. However, the pace of change will likely be slow. Unless a crisis provokes their radical unshackling, foreign banks as a group will not evolve into India's Main Street banks. They will, however, be the most efficient and profitable class of niche players in the Indian financial system. They will continue to define industry standards in product, service, and technology, and cater to a dedicated, though small, segment of customers. Citibank plus a few others that leverage technology aggressively to overcome growth barriers are likely to remain leading players in retail banking.

Going forward, India will remain a unique challenging piece in the Asian jigsaw puzzle. Solutions that appear simple defy application in the Indian context, with its fluid political environment, strongly entrenched interest groups, and perpetual tightrope walk between command- and market-economy models. Yet, the language of economic rationalism is being more widely spoken and understood in India. "Survival of the fittest" is an outcome that is increasingly being accepted by all stakeholders alike. Financial policymakers have proved remarkably progressive in driving change forward, and bank management is demonstrating an ability to respond innovatively.

This is an ongoing process. The Indian financial sector will evolve slowly towards greater competition, and the winners will be those that identify attractive market segments in which they can build a sustainable and controllable business. For such players, the underlying size and growth of India's national and regional markets will offer attractive returns.

PART IV
CONCLUSION

16
BUILDING WINNERS IN THE NEW ASIAN MARKETS

In 1990, the four largest banks in Argentina and the four in Venezuela were either privately owned by locals or owned by their respective governments. Foreign banks controlled less than 5 percent of assets in each country. During that decade, both countries experienced enormous economic dislocations and suffered periods of recession and bank crises because of nonperforming loans — and recovered to grow again. Over time, the governments of both countries realized that a sound banking system was a prerequisite for sustained economic growth. Recovery involved redesigning the banking systems and opening them to more intense foreign competition to upgrade skills and improve risk management. Foreign investment in local financial institutions was allowed. By 1997, foreigners were the largest shareholders of two of the four largest banks in both Brazil and Venezuela, and foreign-controlled banks held 40 and 45 percent of total banking assets in each country respectively.

Banks and investment banks in Asia face similar — or greater — changes after the 1997–1998 financial crisis. Local institutions must respond to immediate financial traumas, and then grapple with a more demanding customer base and more open markets. International institutions, too, will have to weather reduced Asian revenues toward the turn of the century, but will also have unprecedented opportunities. Foreign firms need to establish a coherent set of strategies to avoid frittering away capital and talent in unstructured, random, and high-risk activities.

What, then, are the key challenges for each group of competitors? How should boards and management teams approach building winners in the new Asian markets? First, we will describe the specific transition program that will help many key local private- and state-owned commercial banks to survive. Then we will turn to the need to be global, and yet local, needs that global commercial banks operating in Asia will face. Finally, we will describe how global, regional, and local investment banks should manage their capital and people in a globalizing Asian securities world.

Local Commercial Banks Must Reform

Across Asia, privately and state-owned local banks will face vastly changed markets in the 21st century, compared to those of the 1980s and much of the 1990s. Customers will be more demanding, competition more intense, and accounting much more transparent. Going forward, these institutions must fundamentally reform to succeed.

Tinkering at the Edges Will Not Work

To meet the needs of a new era, local financial institutions in Asia cannot tinker at the edges. They need to pursue clearly stated, systematically implemented programs — often called change programs — to improve performance.

What are change programs? They are management processes that guide whole organizations through a series of discrete tasks that, added together, meet broad performance improvement objectives. These programs are carried out by the most talented people in an organization, regardless of seniority. On a full- or part-time basis, they work within appointed teams to reshape strategy, redesign key processes, develop new systems, draft new human resource policies, or integrate new acquisitions. The teams typically work within and across formal organization structures to provide senior management with unbiased facts with which they can quickly make decisions to drive changes forward. To be successful, change program teams must have direct access to senior management, be held accountable for their work, and be protected from reprisals within the organization when their facts and recommendations inevitably threaten the status quo.

Effective change programs are needed in local Asian banks because they provide senior management with a real opportunity to reshape the way their organizations work — quickly. By forming a change program, senior management essentially develops access to dedicated "SWAT teams" that can plow through traditional middle-management bureaucracy and bring perspectives directly from customers and the front- line into the boardroom. In an organization of several thousand people, change programs will often eventually involve as many as 100–200 people. With this level of involvement, the entire organization senses the momentum for change, and many people take an interest in its direction. There will always be those who resist change — particularly in the once-comfortable and protected markets of Asia — but few will challenge broad momentum, particularly if it is backed by transparent logic and clear facts. Once a change program is initiated, senior management must tirelessly monitor it to remove bottlenecks, spur progress, communicate successes, demand results, manage sensitivities, and reprioritize initiatives as challenges and opportunities emerge.

There is, of course, no one program that can meet the needs of all local financial institutions fighting for survival in Asia. Each institution will have to tailor its approach and pace in accordance with its challenges, skills, and aspirations. Having said that, we believe that most change programs required in Asia will confront a similar set of issues through the first 5 years of the 21st century. We also believe that the likely sequence for addressing the many issues will occur in three common stages.

The first stage will be *securing a lifeline*, when local Asian financial institutions will need to recapitalize and restore public confidence in the immediate aftermath of the 1997–1998 crisis. The second stage, *refocusing,* will need to proceed nearly in parallel, or follow immediately on the heels of Stage 1. It will probably take 2–3 years to complete, and will involve refocusing the institutions' businesses to areas where they can build the greatest competitive advantages. The third stage, *raising skills levels*, may occur in parallel with Stage 2. In this stage, financial institutions should attempt to implement world-class skills in such areas as leadership, human resources, and risk management to achieve global standards of competitiveness. The strongest local financial institutions in Asia could complete all three stages successfully by 2005. As managing change of this magnitude in this relatively short time is not entirely intuitive, each stage requires some elaboration.

Stage 1: Securing a lifeline

By the second half of 1998, the equity of at least two-thirds of the financial institutions in Korea, China, and Southeast Asia was technically negative or far below regulatory guidelines. The very survival of many of these institutions depended upon recapitalizing and quickly restoring public confidence to bring back fleeing depositors. In the context of a change program, the first step for senior management is to lay out a recovery strategy. Members of senior management from across the institution need to convene and draft a plan that broadly describes future business strategy (i.e., which businesses will be emphasized or exited), estimates future income, prioritizes cost-cutting efforts, categorizes loan losses, determines the organization's ability to implement the plan, and specifies the amount of financing required to recapitalize the institution in the medium term.

Once the recovery plan has been drafted, a subset of the board and major shareholders would form a team to identify capital-raising options, for example, raising equity in the global markets, merging with a domestic or foreign player, or opting for nationalization. Once a no-doubt difficult consensus is achieved, this senior team would systematically market the recovery plan, along with the financing options, to potential partners and investment banks.

Concurrently with seeking financing, senior management would market the recovery strategy to employees and customers to assure them that action was being taken. To provide an immediate sense of momentum, senior management would also probably choose to launch a number of internal teams focusing on, for example, cost-cutting plans, loan workouts, reporting transparency, and debt securitization. To help retain the best employees in these uncertain times, senior management should attempt to place the highest performers at the head of the teams. This would communicate to the organization that performance, and not necessarily seniority, would be valued most going forward.

In a period of crisis, as most institutions fight for survival, competitors outdo their peers to increase the chances of securing a lifeline. By demonstrating real efforts to tackle problems head on, banks can both distinguish themselves with potential investors, and potentially buy time with creditors.

Stage 2: Refocusing

Unfortunately, recapitalizing is only the first step on a difficult path. To prosper in the long term, most local banks in Asia will have to reassess in which businesses they can develop and sustain a truly competitive position. The days of trying to be all things to all customers are gone for all but the largest players. As clients become more sophisticated, and their needs more distinctive, most Asian financial institutions will increasingly have to specialize. Banks will have to rebuild their organizations and skills around select products, customers, and distribution channels. For many, determining a new business focus and restructuring around it will be the most challenging stage of transformation.

Thai Farmers' Battle

Thai Farmers Bank, Thailand's second largest bank, was fast off the block in 1998 to ensure its survival. The extent of the crisis overwhelmed its initial strategy, however, forcing a rapid second attempt to secure its lifeline. By championing a strategy that was already well articulated prior to the crisis, the organization was able to raise US$834 million in equity in the global markets in March 1998, at a price of 88 baht per share. In doing so, the controlling Lamsam family diluted its holdings to less than 10 percent as foreign institutional investors acquired a 49 percent stake. To shore up short-term cash flow, it announced a hiring freeze and began prioritizing other areas for cost cutting. To attack potentially crippling bad loans, it established eight specialist teams with a total of 150 staff to focus on loan collections. Thai Farmers was quick to recognize that the business of collecting bad loans is quite different from lending money, and often requires an independent force — less attached to the customer relationship — to solicit repayment.

Yet, due to the continuing deterioration of the credit situation, even these initiatives were not enough. In June 1998, the bank announced that it was buying the 51 percent of Phatra Thanakit it did not already own. This finance company was experiencing funding problems, as depositors feared the worst about its asset quality. Thai Farmers shares fell to 40 baht. In July, seven Thai banks announced surprisingly poor results due to provisions, and Thai Farmers share price fell to 35.5 baht. In mid-August, Thai Farmers forecast that its nonperforming loans would peak at 38 percent of total credit in mid-1999, and 50 percent of these nonperforming loans would need to be written off. Its share price at this point was around 20 baht. It was clear that the initial US$834 million raised in the global markets was insufficient: this capital infusion had been swallowed up by growing loan-loss reserves. At the end of August, Thai Farmers announced that it needed to raise a further US$3 billion through a mix of preferred shares, capital securities, and debentures. The timing of this plan depended on market conditions. Shares of Thai Farmers closed at 18.5 baht after the announcement.

Thai Farmers initially attempted to secure its lifeline by confronting its problems proactively and demonstrating an ability to mobilize its resources creatively to tackle new challenges. But the realities of the size of the credit problems overwhelmed this first recapitalization effort, and the bank had to seek a second infusion. In early 1999, the bank announced a 1998 loss of US$1.1 billion, heightening the need to pursue a new fundraising approach.

Why will refocusing be so difficult in Asia? First, few local institutions have experience in carrying out comprehensive, fact-based strategic analysis. Accustomed to high-growth protected environments, few have needed to understand underlying market sizes, the industry's profitability for different types of customers and products, and their institutions' relative strengths and weaknesses from a client's perspective. Second, even the more advanced organizations that would like to adopt a more fact-based approach to developing their business often lack the internal information systems to analyze which customers, products, and departments are truly profitable. These institutions have historically lacked the facts to make important trade-offs in allocating resources. Third, the operating culture in many of Asia's financial institutions has not promoted open debate between senior managers and front-line staff to identify how to better serve customers and improve performance. Directives from senior personnel, regardless of their virtue, was typically not challenged or questioned. Traditionally, little room is left for the thorough and open discussions needed to develop and refine winning strategies.

These barriers will have to be overcome to create a strong, transparent, and logical foundation for change. Without clear facts, a compelling vision, and broad consensus, it will be particularly difficult for institutions to make the tough decisions, which will probably include exiting entire categories of long-standing customer relationships, closing down unattractive departments and products, making significant new investments in technology and skills, and fundamentally altering employees' roles, responsibilities, and positions through organizational restructuring. Many decisions will appear threatening to staff whose careers have been based on skills and customer relationships that may play only a minor role in a revamped strategy. If staff understand the rationale for change, they are more likely to embrace it. If they do not, chances are infighting or silent dissension will lead to inertia and apathy, and undermine implementing a new strategy.

It is therefore critical that the second stage of any bank's change program build a clear, fact-based understanding of the future challenges and opportunities that will be the basis for refocusing. Senior management would probably establish teams to review each of the major customer segments: mass-market retail, private banking clients, small businesses, middle-market corporates, large corporates, and institutions. Such teams would be charged with shaping a broad-based understanding of each segment's current size, future growth, profitability, and changing product needs, and pinpointing gaps the institution may have in trying to serve each segment well. The teams would probably discover different segments within each customer group they review. That is, the retail team might discern different groups within the retail market, and develop different approaches for each group. Once senior management had drawn on all the teams' analyses to determine its priorities, it would expand membership in the teams to systematically implement a new strategy. The expanded teams would work with the relevant business unit managers to develop and implement, for example, new products, new systems, training programs, job descriptions, and explanations of the new strategy for customers and staff.

Senior management groups in Asia that can build a strong fact base and excitement for change will reposition their organizations to prosper as economies recover. Those that fail to create a compelling vision for a new focus, or stumble in their will to implement it, will be at serious risk of disappearing through acquisition or outright business failure in the early years of the 21st century.

Stage 3: Raising skills levels

Domestic institutions that can successfully build distinct competitive advantages by refocusing their resources on customers and products will have won 70 percent of the battle for long-term survival in their markets. However, to overcome the threat of growing global competition, winning domestic institutions will have to raise their skills to world-class levels. Successful banks will be able to compete head-to-head with the global financial leaders that will have established formidable domestic market positions in many Asian markets by 2005.

Instituting world-class skills touches upon both the daily transactions of a bank and its overall operating culture. It requires focusing on six key areas: leadership; human resources; risk management; marketing; distribution; and processing. The world's best-performing financial institutions typically demonstrate a number of common characteristics in each area.

The *leadership* of the best financial institutions is typically driven by clear, measurable performance targets that senior management is deeply committed to meeting. These targets may include growth, profitability, and customer satisfaction, all geared to enhancing shareholder value. To ensure employee commitment to these targets, they are often broadcast openly within the organization. Also at the core of many top banks is their ability to attract and retain some of the best talent in the market. As such, *human resource* capabilities for developing performance-based compensation, actively managing individuals' career tracks, and providing training that broadens individuals' skills are very well developed. More often than not, human resource management is at the top of the agenda for most senior and business unit managers. Developing clear operating targets and performance-based compensation requires a substantial shift in operating culture for many institutions in Asia to greater internal transparency and a move away from seniority-based organizational hierarchies.

World-class leaders invest heavily in developing *risk management* skills. They spend millions of dollars in technology every year to improve measuring and reporting the various risks to which the institution is exposed. Capital is deployed to business units annually based on their ability to provide returns that are commensurate with the risks they take. Risk managers have clearly specified authority in all major business decisions, and are granted a strong independent voice among senior management. For institutions in Asia, upgrading risk management will require an infusion of new technical capabilities, and often a substantial change in the organizational power granted to risk management functions.

Marketing and *distribution* within the world's leading financial institutions are characterized by a high degree of customer-driven segmentation. Top financial companies are able to tailor products, services, pricing, and channels to the differentiated needs of groups of retail, corporate, or institutional customers. By creating specialized business units with clearly delegated authority, and yet fostering close communication across units through teamwork, leading institutions can be responsive to individual customer needs. At the same time, by sharing common resources in such areas as product development and operations, they can remain cost-effective. In order to garner the benefits of a highly segmented approach, local financial institutions in Asia will have to foster close cooperation across a number of specialized business units. This will be difficult for large departments that were accustomed to building dedicated (and often duplicate) infrastructures prior to 1997–1998.

Excellence in *processing* is often the linchpin in global leaders' ability to capture economies of scale and serve the increasingly complex needs of their customers and organizations. Top-performing financial institutions systematically redesign key processes to consistently improve turnaround times and lower costs. They do this by religiously automating, relocating (to a lower-cost environment), and outsourcing much of their back-office work. In many banks in Asia where large capital investments in technology were avoided to minimize costs, processes have remained highly manual and consequently prone to human error. In the years leading up to 2010, leading Asian institutions will have to transform their perception of processing, see it as an important area for creating competitive advantage — and invest accordingly.

Instituting world-class skills in these six areas requires a continuous effort that should be initiated at the outset of a change program. For instance, in order to execute the second phase of change, refocusing, many banks need to address their human resources/compensation and risk-management approaches simultaneously with selecting product and market priorities. Senior management should not underestimate the challenges in this third stage of reinvention. Implementing rigorous performance targets, new human resource policies, and greater use of shared resources strikes at the heart of an organization's culture and power structure.

Some aspects of an aggressive change program — its complexity and the investment in man-hours — may be daunting to many financial institutions in Asia. The reality is that the three-stage change program described here *is* hard work. But domestic institutions that aspire to compete in Asia's new era can afford to do little less, and few will be able to manage the magnitude of reinvention without a highly structured approach.

The performance improvement programs described here are relevant for both state-owned and privately owned banks in Asia. However, each group faces its own unique challenges.

Start Again at the State Banks

The major state-owned banks dominated many banking markets in Asia during much of the 1990s. In China, Taiwan, Indonesia, and Malaysia for example, state-controlled banks held significant shares of the market in 1997 (Exhibit 16.1). In some cases, the state was involved in banking as a critical element of a supply-driven economic strategy, where funneling funds to priority industrial sectors was part of a centrally controlled economic policy. To ensure that this strategy was

Exhibit 16.1

State-Controlled Banks' Estimated Share of Deposits: 1997
Percent

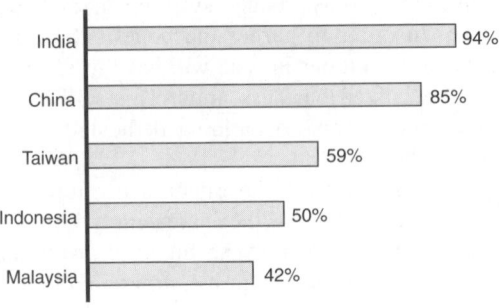

Source: Asiaweek Financial 500; McKinsey analysis

properly implemented, governments felt compelled to control a significant share of banking activity. Through combined Ministry of Finance and Central Bank guidance to all banks, and firm control of state banks, the governments hoped to manage the flow of funds to key sectors. In other cases, state ownership of banks was part of a corrupt or crony government style that delivered profits to the family that effectively controlled the government.

In both cases, state banks were not designed for maximum performance in any familiar dimension. They were not governed to ensure objective credit decisions, that were independent of short-term political or insider needs. They were not managed internally to promote skill development and excellence among staff. They were certainly not guided by any normal measures of economic return, that is, return on assets or return on equity.

While state banks' internal functioning presents considerable barriers to change, they do possess certain important assets. In many cases, they have extensive branch networks and relationships with all types of customers: large corporations; middle-market companies; and consumers. Further, they are very well known in the local market. If harnessed, their franchises could be very valuable.

In the first decade of the 21st century, state-controlled banks will, therefore, be in urgent need of change if they are to take advantage of their franchises in the new Asian markets. However, the challenges for some may be overwhelming. They may achieve the first stage of a change program — recapitalization — more easily than local institutions, through government bail-outs. But this very ease of recapitalization may hold the seeds of their long-term demise. Because they can feed so easily at the government's coffers, these banks face overwhelming moral hazards that extend beyond their lending practices. Why should they reform at all as long as the government can save them? Further, which governments are prepared to give up using these institutions for "policy lending", especially after recapitalizing them? Still, without this crucial change, these organizations cannot even start to be truly commercial entities. Reforming many of these state-owned banks is really a task of turning a bureaucracy into a market-oriented, profit-making entity. This is a major challenge at the best of times — and a potentially overwhelming one during a financial crisis, when state banks may be the crucial sources of liquidity for the economy.

Singapore's state-controlled bank, DBS, faced this challenge. In August 1998, the Singapore government turned to a Westerner, John Olds, from JP Morgan, to run the bank and set it on a new path. This included merging with another effectively state-controlled bank, POSB, to create a strong platform for regional expansion.

DBS basically operates in one city-state with just 4,000 staff, all of whom speak English fluently. Few other governments will face such a simple situation, will be so bold, or will be able to attract strong reform-oriented managers. How would the Chinese government attract an experienced group of managers committed to reforming one of the Big Four state-controlled banks? In 1997, the largest of these employed over 600,000 staff, operated across every province in the country, and functioned only in Mandarin and other Chinese dialects. Similar challenges face those trying to reform state banks in Indonesia or India.

State banks can choose to move down the reform path. In 1998, Taiwan launched its government-controlled banks (Chang Hwa Commercial Bank, First Commercial Bank, and Hua Nan Commercial Bank) towards reform. First Commercial Bank branches quickly put up splashy banners to herald the new name, "First Bank." But real change would be long in coming: the bureaucratically run branches behind the banners had not changed. At least in Taiwan a tradition of market-oriented management and privately owned banks gives these formerly government-controlled banks a chance of success. In other markets, however, it will be very difficult to undertake all the necessary changes. The management of these banks may decide to adopt a change program, but no one should have any illusions about the scale of the challenge they are taking on.

Given the degree of change state banks must undergo to become real profit-oriented, fully fledged commercial entities, rather than arms of state funding, many might be best advised not to attempt the full transformation. Instead, banks could be broken up into areas specializing in particular activities, and ally themselves with other entities to extract the value of their customer relationships and networks without trying to overcome the enormous cultural challenges involved in a full change program. Many state banks are deeply involved in infrastructure lending, so splitting this part of the institution away to become a project financing enterprise might make sense. Allying this focused entity with a means of raising money from the capital markets, with all the discipline that entails, could be a way of transforming a relatively focused entity. Similarly, the large corporate lending business could be hived off to become part of a specialized investment or wholesale bank (although the existing loan book might have to be scrubbed clean by the government before any private institution would accept it). If these two large wholesale businesses could be moved into stand-alone specialized units, then basically only the retail and small business activities, mostly contained in the large branch networks, would be left. While these networks are overwhelmingly inefficient, and distant provinces or regions in some countries are subject to local political influence, the networks could be very valuable to a local or foreign entity wanting to make a major push into the market. Through alliance, merger, or even outright sale, the government could release the power of this franchise to energize the local economies under a more market-oriented management.

Local Private Banks Must Change or Withdraw

Since the challenges for many state banks will be overwhelming, some are best advised not to attempt the complete change program, but instead break into constituent parts. Private local banks face a similar set of stark choices. On the one hand, local banks can aggressively adopt a change program to build the capital, products, organizations, and skills required in a more competitive environment. While less change-resistant than state banks, reinvention for these local banks will not be easy. These institutions must also deal with customers' expectations and competitors' growing capabilities.

As local market product regulations and demarcations are eased, these organizations will have to resist the immediate temptation to be true universal banks. They cannot be all things to all people. Instead, they will have to define their market niche. Which customers can they serve with what range of products to generate attractive, risk-adjusted returns? How can they attract quality staff as global banks expand in their markets? As local institutions focus, they will need to invest in their chosen businesses and build risk management capabilities.

Beyond these strategic challenges, local banks will need to resolve organizational issues. Many were family-owned at the end of the 1990s, and as they face up to more intense competition, the role of the family in management must be reviewed. These banks will need the best managers they can find, and whether family members qualify for senior roles will need to be judged with complete objectivity. Also, as these banks expand, their capital needs will increase. The family will have to be prepared to meet their share of capital requirements, or reduce their ownership in the institution. As most family-owned banks in the West have experienced, the dual issues of management skill and capital needs will slowly squeeze many families out of dominant roles in "their" banks. This pressure will raise real issues of pride, or "face", for these families: through the 1990s in many Asian countries, owning a bank was a prerequisite for being a leading business family.

The other option for private local banks is deciding, in the early years of the 21st century, that the markets have so changed that a fundamental shift in corporate strategy is required. Exhibit 16.2 shows the strategic control map we used in the Taiwan chapter, but here it is applied across all of Asia. It highlights the average value of the top three private banks in all Asian markets relative to the average value of the leading U.S. and European banks, as of June 30, 1998. Apart from those in Japan, all the banks were relatively small by international standards. Small size is not the only corporate strategic challenge for these banks: they are also relatively undiversified within Asia. Due to past regulatory constraints, the top three banks in each market have the overwhelming majority of their assets in their home country. The combination of the relative size of the leading Asian private

Exhibit 16.2

Strategic Control Map of Listed Banks
Average of 3 largest listed banks in each country/region*; book value as of fiscal year end 1997; market value as of September 30, 1998

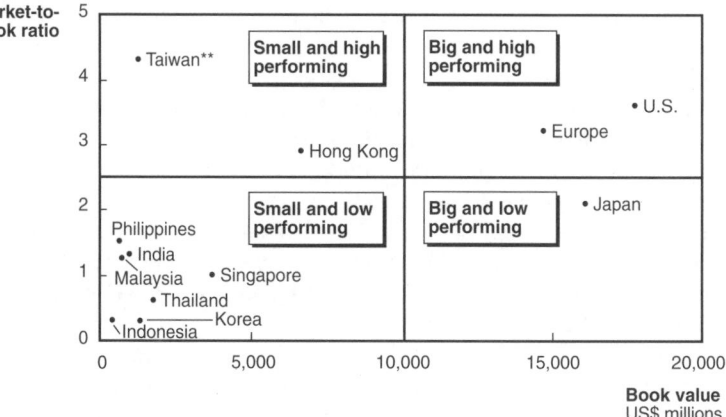

* China is excluded as there is only one bank listed.
** Market-to-book ratio is high due to under-stated book values for top three banks.

Source: Datastream; *Asiaweek* Financial 500

banks and their lack of international diversification makes them very vulnerable. Those below the top three in each market are even more challenged. They will struggle to fund the necessary upgrades in products, technology, and skills necessary to compete, and in a world of declining margins they will be subject to continued geographical concentration of credit risk without the appropriate reward.

The corporate strategy for these banks must include resolving these challenges. The scale of the financial problems resulting from the 1997–1998 financial turmoil will force some banks to sell or ally themselves with foreign institutions in order to grow their capital base and acquire the necessary skills to compete. For instance, in 1998, Bank of Asia in Thailand sold 75 percent of its equity to ABN Amro. Other banks, however, could pursue inter-regional mergers to create regional banks of scale with greater geographic diversification. Why should the only broadly based pan-regional competitors be the Hongkong and Shanghai Banking Corporation (HSBC), Standard Chartered, Citibank, and ABN Amro? For most banks, acting alone will be tough going, and will only lead to a narrow niche role or eventual sale from weakness.

Expanding Multinational Banks

The 1997–1998 meltdown brought new opportunities to the major multinational lending banks active or interested in the region (e.g., ABN Amro, BankAmerica, BNP, Chase Manhattan, Citibank, Credit Suisse, Deutsche Bank, HSBC, ING,

Indosuez, Paribas, Standard Chartered, and UBS). Certainly, some of them suffered large credit or trading losses in Asia in this period, but compared to the impact on local banks, they emerged relatively unscathed. Booming profits in the U.S. and Europe covered the losses in Asia.

The turmoil generated two important changes in the Asian markets. First, many local competitors were mortally wounded, which created opportunity for the multinationals. For instance, when the crisis hit, HSBC and Standard Chartered were flooded with deposits as panicked consumers and corporations withdrew their savings and corporate cash from local banks. Second, long-term opportunities stemmed from the new regulatory attitude adopted in many markets. Prior to 1997–1998, local regulators had barred the expansion of foreign banks in key countries in the region. After the crisis, Korea, Thailand, and Japan were added to Hong Kong, Indonesia, and the Philippines as markets where foreign banks could enter aggressively and relatively easily. Even longer term, WTO pressures would open up other markets.

Before the shakeout, regulations limited strategic options available to multinational banks in the region. The grandfathered institutions — HSBC, Standard Chartered, and to some extent, Citibank — had broad business lines in Hong Kong, Malaysia, and Singapore. Beyond that, they were in the same regulatory situation as other multinational banks, such as ABN Amro, Bank of America, and Chase Manhattan. First, these entities were effectively barred from activity in Japan. The CEO of a major Western bank could agree that Japan was a huge market, but take refuge in the regulations, which denied his institution access to the market. Japan, therefore, was not a strategic issue for the bank. However, the "Big Bang" in Japan and the consequent need for capital and Western technology and skills at many institutions suddenly made Japan a potential opportunity for many Western banks. Strategic options were richer, but the puzzle had become more challenging. Second, in the rest of the region, banks had little access to retail or medium-sized corporate customers. As a result, they had to concentrate on large corporate lending, trade finance, private banking, and securities and foreign exchange trading. A few tried to build cross-country credit card businesses.

Some of the largest multinational banks were generating about US$10 billion in annual profits by the end of the 1990s. For the capital exposure and management time involved in Asia to make sense for these banks, they need to earn at least US$1 billion a year from the region. Institutions with limited wholesale banking activities at the end of the 1990s that aspire to Asian earnings face complex issues. They must be wary of "flag-planting," that is, setting up a series of sub-scale businesses across the region. Instead, they need to focus on growing large pan-Asian businesses (for instance, wholesale lending and credit cards), or building scale in a few countries. Because of Japan's size, these banks must consider whether and how to enter and build businesses there. Even if they adopt a pan-Asian product strategy, these institutions need to determine their priority geographical markets. For many, it will be North Asia, simply because of its relative size compared to that of Southeast Asia.

Many multinational banks will want to grow by acquisition. They must ascertain how they can implement their global standards of risk management and branding, and assure world-class skills in their acquired banks — yet retain the local contacts, staff, and knowledge they are buying. Their stability relative to that of local institutions, and their aggressive, expansionary approach, will be an advantage for attracting the best staff, but they will need to avoid creating a "glass ceiling" for local hires.

These banks will also want to grow their lending and trading businesses in the region, and move deeper into the higher-risk middle-market and small-business segments with their higher spreads. This will require centralizing risk management standards and leveraging central product design and other costs over the region.

The more complex strategic options for multinational banks in Asia break down into three sets of choices: building from their existing large corporate, foreign exchange trading, and potentially, private banking bases, they can play it safe, build a dominant product position, or become true insiders in a few countries.

Playing it safe

Some global banks will decide that the risk-reward equation in Asia is simply not attractive, and that the political, social, and financial pitfalls exhibited during the 1997–1998 crisis make the markets low priorities. But as a result of the crisis, even these banks will have opportunities to expand because of the weaknesses of local competitors. They can build on their few existing branches and subsidiaries in the Asian markets, and hire more qualified local staff disillusioned with local banks. They can also take advantage of the relaxed regulatory situation to make small acquisitions in a few countries, for instance buying weak finance companies to expand their branch networks. But their goal will be to gradually build the Asian business and expand further into the retail and middle market, but not to make a major sweep into a country, or in a product, to become a dominant player.

Dominating a product

Increasingly demanding Asian customers will be attracted by a bank that can provide the best in a single product. Just as in the U.S. and Europe, specialized mortgage, credit card, mutual fund, and auto loan providers will have opportunities in Asia to build large businesses. Multinational competitors that do not want to build broad in-country banks can instead choose in Asia to focus on just a few products across a number of key countries. The challenge with this approach will be to differentiate the products from those that local banks offer, and to develop a strong brand and a low cost position.

Becoming true insiders

The most dramatic move for a multinational bank will be to build an insider position in one or more countries in Asian. For HSBC or Standard Chartered, this means trying to replicate their positions in Hong Kong, Malaysia, and Singapore. For other institutions, it could mean focusing on one or two countries. For all the banks, becoming a true insider is likely to involve full or majority acquisition of an existing local bank. By taking on the branches, staff, and franchise of a local player, these banks can leapfrog into an insider position with a full range of large corporate, middle-market, small-business, and retail customers. They can then attempt to marry this franchise with their more sophisticated product range, and introduce more rigorous management practices.

GE Capital: Buying into Asia

The financial services arm of General Electric of the USA, GE Capital, was the world's largest consumer finance company in the late 1990s, with assets of around US$230 billion. The firm sought ways to build its consumer finance and related personal financial services businesses in Asia through an aggressive acquisition program.

In March 1998, the chairman of GE, Jack Welch, in a letter to shareholders and employees, declared that the company is "determined and poised" to invest in Asia, and that "the path to greatness in Asia is irreversible, and GE will be there." GE had a long tradition of building through acquisitions, and was not afraid to move swiftly as local firms became available.

Between December 1997 and July 1998, GE Capital made three major moves in Japan, acquiring Koei Credit and Lake Company, two consumer finance companies. More spectacularly, the firm paid close to US$1 billion in February 1998 to purchase the distribution and product capabilities of the beleaguered Toho Mutual Life (without absorbing any of the under water historic book of business), thus gaining access to the huge life insurance market in Japan.

GE Capital was also active in Thailand, again making two investments in the consumer finance field in February and then March 1998, including providing private-label credit card services to one joint venture partner. In May 1998, GE Capital continued its life insurance theme by acquiring Philippine Asia Life Assurance Corporation, a medium-sized insurance company owned by the Knights of Columbus Fraternal Association of the Philippines. In August, the firm acted in Korea, purchasing 51 percent of Shindo-GE Finance.

All these moves reflected a view that building scale in Asia was most easily done through acquisition, and that the financial crisis presented a unique opportunity that the firm had to take advantage of, and had the risk management skills to handle. Of course, this route was not painless, and GE Capital had to deal with both the immediate problems of reduced demand following the crisis and the longer-term issues of retaining customers and integrating processes as a result of an acquisition.

The greatest challenge facing all competitors, whichever of the three strategies they choose, is deciding what to do about Japan. A serious step forward there involves much higher levels of capital than in any other country, a long-term commitment to building a winning business, and, for multinational banks, a good number of managers with Japanese language skills. Japan is the biggest prize for those financial institutions that can make it work, but it may well be the toughest challenge with the largest risks.

Winning Investment Banks

The investment banking markets in Asia in the 1990s involved three basic types of competitors: large, global firms like Goldman Sachs, Merrill Lynch, J P Morgan, and Morgan Stanley from the U.S.; regional firms, such as Jardine Fleming and Indosuez/W.I. Carr; and firms predominantly focused on their home country, such as Arab-Malaysian Merchant Bank in Malaysia.

Over the course of the 1980s and 1990s, the capital markets of the world became dominated by the largest investment banks, particularly the leading U.S. firms. The major British merchant banks lost relative position, and were either bought by expanding continental European banks (e.g., Deutsche Bank's purchase of Morgan Grenfell, Swiss Bank Corporation's purchase of S.G. Warburg, ING's purchase of Baring Brothers) or largely withered away, like Hambros.

The same trends were visible in Asia in the 1990s, and the crisis of 1997–1998 quickened the pace of decline of locally based banks. The most visible events were the collapse of Peregrine Securities of Hong Kong and Yamaichi Securities of Japan. Other locally based firms also suffered: W.I. Carr in Hong Kong cut back staff, Jardine decided to sell its stake in Jardine Fleming to Robert Fleming (in exchange for Robert Fleming shares), and in Thailand, Phatra Securities was taken over by Merrill Lynch. Across the region, banks that survived only on local underwriting, trading, and advisory business suffered, while globally based firms were able to take market share and attract the best staff.

Into the 21st century, the markets will be divided between the three groups. The leading global firms will dominate the business with the largest corporations, undertake the most attractive privatization work and capital-raising for governments, and be able to transact the largest and most complex securities trades. Second-tier firms, which possess valuable franchises in the region (such as equity brokerage businesses) but do not have as large a capital base or an all-important U.S. trading and placement base, will try to carve out sustainable product or geographical niches. Finally, the local firms, which compete in protected local markets, will be able to generate attractive profits from local underwriting and trading, and from regulated co-underwriting positions on global issues for local companies. Markets such as China, India, and Taiwan will continue to offer these protected market opportunities.

All three groups face the challenge of surviving the collapse in trading and underwriting revenues of 1997 and 1998, and the consequent pressure through the turn of the century. Some firms will not survive, or will elect to scale back in Asia so much that they are no longer serious competitors. After this very difficult period, the three different groups of investment banks will face different challenges.

Global investment banks will need to build their local knowledge and contacts further in order to lock in corporate and institutional opportunities and gain the best sources of information for their trading businesses. Around the world, the leading investment banks often generate close to 50 percent of their profits from trading businesses, and will want to do so in Asia, too. The challenge will be to work out how to do so in markets that are notoriously fickle and illiquid, and where short-selling is often impossible — making long positions the only realistic option. They will also need to decide whether to operate from just two or three centers in Asia (Hong Kong, Singapore, Tokyo) or if they can be more local than that. Given the collapse in liquidity in many of the local markets in 1997–1998, many will choose, for control and cost reasons, to centralize in a few locations. As well as solving these problems and building capabilities, the leading firms will need to consider opportunities to acquire local firms or teams that can be successfully integrated into the global whole. These opportunities will be judged on their attractiveness versus building the business internally, and may be more interesting simply because there will not be enough trained, local-language-proficient staff within the global firm.

Second-tier firms will need to consolidate the advantages that have underpinned their success to date. As global firms' local knowledge and contacts grow, second-tier firms will try to stay one step ahead in their quality of local research and staff. Nevertheless, the challenges of increasing information technology costs, larger capital needs for trading activity, and the incursion of global firms into their core client base will place second-tier firms under enormous pressure. Just as European firms collapsed or merged with larger commercial banks, so in Asia, second-tier firms will have to examine merging as a means of generating the scale that will retain customers and staff and fund necessary investments.

Locally protected investment banks, like the commercial banks in many Asian markets in the 1990s, will struggle to balance taking advantage of short-term opportunities and preparing for when protection will cease. The challenge will be to manage these firms as if they are not in a protected market in order to build the skills and work ethic required for success when the markets do deregulate. Importantly, they must grow their relationships with local investors as a sustainable placement advantage when their markets are opened. What happened when the big four Japanese firms were presented with a tougher environment in the 1990s suggests this overall change will be a difficult task. Only those that manage to segregate the comfort of today's profits from the way the firm's culture develops will be able to build long-term profit sustainability in what will be a niche position when viewed globally.

All three groups of investment banks will grapple with important organizational issues, including moving resources (people, systems, and capital) between rapidly changing product and market opportunities, and creating firms that can attract, motivate, and retain the best talent in Asia. Global firms will have immense advantages here, due to the range of career options and the compensation they can offer, backed by the relative security of their size and geographical diversification.

Their ability, too, to invest in leading-edge technology will attract the best staff in trading and asset management. These personnel, in turn, will be crucial to the success of the corporate finance business. However, if staff are cut back too far in times of crisis, it will dissipate this recruiting advantage. Second-tier and locally protected firms' most serious long-term challenge will be their relative weakness in drawing talent. They will need to find ways (perhaps through equity participation and management opportunities) to attract staff in Asia. Otherwise, the march of the global firms will continue.

Commercial and investment banking in Asia during the 1980s and 1990s saw periods of great wealth creation and destruction. Those cycles will probably be repeated in the first decade of the 21st century, but what must be different for the winners of that decade is how they strive for profits. In an environment across nearly all businesses and geographies of more transparent information, more sophisticated customers, and more open competition, it will be necessary to manage all elements of every financial business with far more discipline than in the 1990s. At the same time, as this new environment exposes the weaknesses of some competitors, the eventual winners will need to be ready to make major acquisitions to secure their leadership positions. From the cozy world of protected markets, good margins, and few mergers or acquisitions in the 1980s and much of the 1990s, banking in Asia will become a competitive arena of narrower margins and consolidation in the first decade of the 21st century. The new era will be one which marks the end of entitlement for all competitors in Asia.

Data Sources for Country Profile Pages

Below are sources for the data pages that precede each of the country chapters. Unless otherwise indicated on the chapter cover pages, 1997 data is used from these sources.

Social & Economic Indicators

Asian Development Bank
Asiaweek
Economist Intelligence Unit
Far Eastern Economic Review
Government statistics (all Asian countries)
International Data Corporation
World Bank
Worldscope

Financial Markets and Business Lines

Asian Business
Asia-Pacific Securities Handbook
Asiaweek
Asiaweek Financial 500
Bankscope
Bank for International Settlements
Central banks (all Asian countries)
Datamonitor
Datastream
Economist Intelligence Unit
Federation Internationale des Bourses de Valeurs
Federation of Bankers' Association of Japan
Government statistics (all Asian countries)
Institutional Investor
Japan Consumer Credit Industry Association
Japan Securities Investment Advisers Association
Micropal
Stock exchanges (all Asian countries)
World Bank

Index